FIA

FMA

ACCA

PAPER F2

MANAGEMENT ACCOUNTING

INTERACTIVE TEXT

BPP Learning Media is the sole **ACCA Platinum Approved Learning Partner –
content** for the FIA and ACCA qualifications. In this, **the only FMA/F2 study text to
be reviewed by the examiner:**

- We **highlight** the **most important elements** in the syllabus and the key skills
  you will need

- We **signpost** how each chapter links to the syllabus and the study guide

- We **provide** lots of **exam focus points** demonstrating what the examiner will
  want you to do

- We **emphasise key points** in regular **fast forward summaries**

- We **test your knowledge** of what you've studied in **quick quizzes**

- We **examine your understanding** in our **exam question bank**

- We **reference all the important topics** in our full index

BPP's **Practice & Revision Kit** and **i-Pass** products also support this paper.

Note
FIA *FMA* and ACCA *Paper F2* are examined under the same syllabus and study guide.

FOR EXAMS FROM FEBRUARY 2013 TO JANUARY 2014

BPP LEARNING MEDIA

First edition March 2011
Second edition September 2012

ISBN 9781 4453 9967 6
Previous ISBN 9781 4453 7306 5
eISBN 9781 4453 9243 1

British Library Cataloguing-in-Publication Data
A catalogue record for this book is available from
the British Library

Published by

BPP Learning Media Ltd
BPP House, Aldine Place
142-144 Uxbridge Road
London W12 8AA

www.bpp.com/learningmedia

Printed in the United Kingdom by

Polestar Wheatons
Hennock Road
Marsh Barton
Exeter EX2 8RP

Your learning materials, published by BPP
Learning Media Ltd, are printed on paper
obtained from traceable sustainable sources.

We are grateful to the Association of Chartered
Certified Accountants for permission to reproduce
past examination questions. The suggested
solutions in the exam answer bank have been
prepared by BPP Learning Media Ltd.

Contents

Helping you to pass – the ONLY FMA/F2 study text reviewed by the examiner!

BPP Learning Media – the sole Platinum Approved Learning Partner - content

As ACCA's **sole Platinum Approved Learning Partner – content**, BPP Learning Media gives you the **unique opportunity** to use **examiner-reviewed** study materials for exams from February 2013 to January 2014. By incorporating the examiner's comments and suggestions regarding the depth and breadth of syllabus coverage, the BPP Learning Media Interactive Text provides excellent, **ACCA-approved** support for your studies.

The PER alert!

To become a Certified Accounting Technician or qualify as an ACCA member, you not only have to pass all your exams but also fulfil a **practical experience requirement** (PER). To help you to recognise areas of the syllabus that you might be able to apply in the workplace to achieve different performance objectives, we have introduced the '**PER alert**' feature. You will find this feature throughout the Interactive Text to remind you that what you are **learning in order to pass** your FIA and ACCA exams is **equally useful to the fulfilment of the PER requirement**.

Your achievement of the PER should be recorded in your online *My Experience* record.

Tackling studying

Studying can be a daunting prospect, particularly when you have lots of other commitments. The **different features** of the Text, the **purposes** of which are explained fully on the **Chapter features** page, will help you whilst studying and improve your chances of **exam success**.

Developing exam awareness

Our Texts are completely **focused** on helping you pass your exam.

Our advice on **Studying FMA/F2** outlines the **content** of the paper and the **recommended approach to studying**.

Exam focus points are included within the chapters to highlight when and how specific topics might be examined.

Using the Syllabus and Study Guide

You can find the Syllabus and Study Guide on page ix of this Interactive Text.

Testing what you can do

Testing yourself helps you develop the skills you need to pass the exam and also confirms that you can recall what you have learnt.

We include **Questions** – lots of them – both within chapters and in the **Exam Question Bank**, as well as **Quick Quizzes** at the end of each chapter to test your knowledge of the chapter content.

BPP LEARNING MEDIA

Chapter features

Each chapter contains a number of helpful features to guide you through each topic.

Topic list	Tells you what you will be studying in this chapter and the relevant section numbers, together with the ACCA syllabus references.
Introduction	Puts the chapter content in the context of the syllabus as a whole.
Study Guide	Links the chapter content with ACCA guidance.
Fast Forward	Summarises the content of main chapter headings, allowing you to preview and review each section easily.
Key Term	Definitions of important concepts that can often earn you easy marks in exams.
Exam Focus Point	Tell you how specific topics may be examined.
Formula	Formulae which have to be learnt.
PER Alert	This feature gives you a useful indication of syllabus areas that closely relate to performance objectives in your Practical Experience Requirement (PER).
Question	Gives you essential practice of techniques covered in the chapter.
Chapter Roundup	A full list of the Fast Forwards included in the chapter, providing an easy source of review.
Quick Quiz	A quick test of your knowledge of the main topics in the chapter.
Exam Question Bank	Found at the back of the Interactive Text with more exam-style chapter questions. Cross referenced for easy navigation.

Studying FMA/F2

How to Use this Interactive Text

Aim of this Interactive Text

> To provide the knowledge and practice to help you succeed in the examination for Paper FMA/F2 *Management Accounting*.

To pass the examination you need a thorough understanding in all areas covered by the syllabus and teaching guide.

Recommended approach

(a) To pass you need to be able to answer questions on **everything** specified by the syllabus and teaching guide. Read the Text very carefully and do not skip any of it.

(b) Learning is an **active** process. Do **all** the questions as you work through the Text so you can be sure you really understand what you have read.

(c) After you have covered the material in the Interactive Text, work through the **Exam Question Bank**, checking your answers carefully against the **Exam Answer Bank**.

(d) Before you take the exam, check that you still remember the material using the following quick revision plan.

    (i) Read through the **chapter topic list** at the beginning of each chapter. Are there any gaps in your knowledge? If so, study the section again.

    (ii) Read and learn the **key terms**.

    (iii) Look at the **exam focus points**. These show the ways in which topics might be examined.

    (iv) Read the **chapter roundups**, which are a summary of the **fast forwards** in each chapter.

    (v) Do the **quick quizzes** again. If you know what you're doing, they shouldn't take long.

This approach is only a suggestion. You or your college may well adapt it to suit your needs. Remember this is a **practical** course.

(a) Try to relate the material to your experience in the workplace or any other work experience you may have had.

(b) Try to make as many links as you can to other papers at the Introductory and Intermediate levels.

> For practice and revision use BPP Learning Media's Practice and Revision Kit, iPass and Passcards.

What FMA/F2 is about

The aim of this syllabus is to develop a knowledge and understanding of the principles and techniques used in recording, analysing and reporting costs and revenues for internal management purposes. It covers management information, cost recording, costing techniques, budgeting and performance measurement.

Approach to examining the syllabus

Paper FMA/F2 is a two-hour paper. It can be taken as a written paper or a computer based examination. The questions in the computer based examination are objective test questions – multiple choice, number entry and multiple response. (See page xvi for frequently asked questions about computer based examinations.)

The written examination is structured as follows:

	Number of marks
50 compulsory multiple choice questions of two marks each	100

The December 2011 examiner's report (found on the ACCA website) advised students to

- Study the whole syllabus

- Practise as many questions as possible in preparing for the examination

- Read questions very carefully in the examination

- Attempt all questions in the examination (there are no negative marks for incorrect answers)

- Try to attempt the 'easy' examination questions first

- Not spend too much time on apparently 'difficult' questions

- Read previous Examiner's Reports

Syllabus and Study guide

DETAILED SYLLABUS

A   The nature, source and purpose of management information

1. Accounting for management

2. Sources of data

3   Cost classification

4   Presenting information

B   Cost accounting techniques.

1. Accounting for material, labour and overheads

2. Absorption and marginal costing

3. Cost accounting methods

4. Alternative cost accounting principles

C   Budgeting

1. Nature and purpose of budgeting

2. Statistical techniques

3. Budget preparation

4. Flexible budgets

5   Capital budgeting and discounted cash flow

6   Budgetary control and reporting

7. Behavioural aspects of budgeting

D   Standard costing

1   Standard costing system

2   Variance calculations and analysis

3   Reconciliation of budgeted and actual profit

E   Performance measurement

1. Performance measurement - overview

2   Performance measurement - application

3   Cost reductions and value enhancement

4. Monitoring performance and reporting

APPROACH TO EXAMINING THE SYLLABUS

The syllabus is assessed by a two hour paper-based or computer-based examination. The examination will consist of 50 two mark questions. ACCA will introduce longer style questions in the future and as such approved learning content materials will contain some of these longer style questions. ACCA will provide sufficient notice on when the longer style questions will be introduced.

Study Guide

A THE NATURE, SOURCE AND PURPOSE OF MANAGEMENT INFORMATION

1. Accounting for management

a) Describe the purpose and role of cost and management accounting within an organisation.[k]

b) Compare and contrast financial accounting with cost and management accounting.[k]

c) Outline the managerial processes of planning, decision making and control.[k]

d) Explain the difference between strategic, tactical and operational planning.[k]

e) Distinguish between data and information.[k]

f) Identify and explain the attributes of good information.[k]

g) Explain the limitations of management information in providing guidance for managerial decision-making.[k]

2. Sources of data

a) Describe sources of information from within and outside the organisation (including government statistics, financial press, professional or trade associations, quotations and price list.[k]

b) Explain the uses and limitations of published information/data (including information from the internet) .[k]

c) Describe the impact of general economic environment on costs/revenue.[k]

d) Explain sampling techniques (random, systematic, stratified, multistage, cluster and quota) .[k]

e) choose an appropriate sampling method in a specific situation.[s]

(Note: Derivation of random samples will not be examined)

3. Cost classification

a) Explain and illustrate production and non-production costs.[k]

b) Describe the different elements of non production costs- administrative, selling, distribution and finance.[k]

c) Describe the different elements of production cost- materials, labour and overheads.[k]

d) Explain the importance of the distinction between production and non production costs when valuing output and inventories.[k]

e) Explain and illustrate with examples classifications used in the analysis of the product/service costs including by function, direct and indirect. fixed and variable, stepped fixed and semi variable costs.[s].

f) Explain and illustrate the use of codes in categorising transaction.[k]

g) Describe and illustrate, graphically, different types of cost behaviour.[s]

h) Use high/low analysis to separate the fixed and variable elements of total costs including situations involving semi variable and stepped fixed costs and changes in the variable cost per unit.[s]

i) Explain the structure of linear functions and equations.[s]

j) Explain and illustrate the concept of cost objects, cost units and cost centres.[s].

k) Distinguish between cost, profit, investment and revenue centres.[k].

l) Describe the differing needs for information of cost, profit, investment and revenue centre managers.[k]

4. **Presenting information**

a) Prepare written reports representing management information in suitable formats according to purpose.[s]

b) Present information using tables, charts and graphs (bar charts, line graphs, pie charts and scatter graphs) .[s].

c) Interpret information (including the above tables, charts and graphs) presented in management reports.[s]

B **COST ACCOUNTING TECHNIQUES**

1. **Accounting for material, labour and overheads**

a) Accounting for materials
   (i) Describe the different procedures and documents necessary for the ordering, receiving and issuing of materials from inventory.[k]
   (ii) Describe the control procedures used to monitor physical and 'book' inventory and to minimise discrepancies and losses.[k].
   (iii) Interpret the entries and balances in the material inventory account.[s].
   (iv) Identify, explain and calculate the costs of ordering and holding inventory (including buffer inventory)[s]
   (v) Calculate and interpret optimal reorder quantities.[s]
   (vi) Calculate and interpret optimal reorder quantities when discounts apply.[s].
   (vii) Produce calculations to minimise inventory costs when inventory is gradually replenished.[s].
   (viii) Describe and apply appropriate methods for establishing reorder levels where demand in the lead time is constant.[s]
   (ix) Calculate the value of closing inventory and material issues using LIFO, FIFO and average methods.[s]

b) Accounting for labour
   (i) Calculate direct and indirect costs of labour.[s]
   (ii) Explain the methods used to relate input labour costs to work done.[k]
   (iii) Prepare the journal and ledger entries to record labour cost inputs and outputs.[s]

(iv) Describe different remuneration methods: time-based systems, piecework systems and individual and group incentive schemes.[k]
(v) Calculate the level, and analyse the costs and causes of labour turnover.[s]
(vi) Explain and calculate labour efficiency, capacity and production volume ratios.[s]
(vii) Interpret the entries in the labour account.[s]

c) Accounting for overheads
   (i) Explain the different treatment of direct and indirect expenses.[k]
   (ii) Describe the procedures involved in determining production overhead absorption rates.[k]
   (iii) Allocate and apportion production overheads to cost centres using an appropriate basis.[s]
   (iv) Reapportion service cost centre costs to production cost centres (using the reciprocal method where service cost centres work for each other)[s]
   (v) Select, apply and discuss appropriate bases for absorption rates.[s]
   (vi) Prepare journal and ledger entries for manufacturing overheads incurred and absorbed.[s]
   (vii) Calculate and explain the under and over absorption of overheads.[s]

2. **Absorption and marginal costing**

a) Explain the importance of, and apply, the concept of contribution.[s]

b) Demonstrate and discuss the effect of absorption and marginal costing on inventory valuation and profit determination.[s]

c) Calculate profit or loss under absorption and marginal costing.[s]

d) Reconcile the profits or losses calculated under absorption and marginal costing.[s]

e) Describe the advantages and disadvantages of absorption and marginal costing.[k]

3. **Cost accounting methods**

a) Job and batch costing:

(i) Describe the characteristics of job and batch costing.[k]

(ii) Describe the situations where the use of job or batch costing would be appropriate.[k]

(iii) Prepare cost records and accounts in job and batch costing situations. [s]

(iv) Establish job and batch costs from given information.[s]

b) Process costing

(i) Describe the characteristics of process costing.[k]

(ii) Describe the situations where the use of process costing would be appropriate.[s]

(iii) Explain the concepts of normal and abnormal losses and abnormal gains.[k]

(iv) Calculate the cost per unit of process outputs.[s]

(v) Prepare process accounts involving normal and abnormal losses and abnormal gains.[s]

(vi) Calculate and explain the concept of equivalent units.[s]

(vii) Apportion process costs between work remaining in process and transfers out of a process using the weighted average and FIFO methods.[s]

(viii) Prepare process accounts in situations where work remains incomplete.[s]

(ix) Prepare process accounts where losses and gains are identified at different stages of the process.[s]

(x) Distinguish between by-products and joint products.[k]

(xi) Value by-products and joint products at the point of separation.[s]

(xii) Prepare process accounts in situations where by-products and/or joint products occur. [s]

(Situations involving work-in-process and losses in the same process are excluded).

c) Service/operation costing

(i) Identify situations where the use of service/operation costing is appropriate.[k]

(ii) Illustrate suitable unit cost measures that may be used in different service/operation situations.[s]

(iii) Carry out service cost analysis in simple service industry situations.[s]

4 Alternative cost accounting

a) Explain activity based costing (ABC), target costing, life cycle costing and total quality management (TQM) as alternative cost management techniques.[k]

b) Differentiate ABC, Target costing and life cycle costing from the traditional costing techniques (note: calculations are not required) .[k]

C BUDGETING

1. Nature and purpose of budgeting

a) Explain why organisations use budgeting.[k]

b) Describe the planning and control cycle in an organisation.[k]

c) Explain the administrative procedures used in the budgeting process.[k]

d) Describe the stages in the budgeting process (including sources of relevant data, planning and agreeing draft budgets and purpose of forecasts and how they link to budgeting).[k]

2. Statistical techniques

a) Explain the advantages and disadvantages of using high low method to estimate the fixed and variable element of costing.[k].

b) Construct scatter diagrams and lines of best fit.[s]

c) Analysis of cost data.

(i) Explain the concept of correlation coefficient and coefficient of determination.[k]

(ii) Calculate and interpret correlation coefficient and coefficient of determination.[s]

(iii) Establish a linear function using regression analysis and interpret the results.[s]

d) Use linear regression coefficients to make forecasts of costs and revenues.[s]

e) Adjust historical and forecast data for price movements.[s]

f) Explain the advantages and disadvantages of linear regression analysis.[k]

g) Describe the product life cycle and explain its importance in forecasting.[k]

h) Explain the principles of time series analysis (cyclical, trend, seasonal variation and random elements) .[k]

i) Calculate moving averages.[s]

j) calculation of trend, including the use of regression coefficients .[s]

k) Use trend and seasonal variation (additive and multiplicative) to make budget forecasts.[s]

l) Explain the advantages and disadvantages of time series analysis[k]

m) Explain the purpose of index numbers [k]

n) Calculate simple index numbers for one or more variables.[s]

o) Explain the role and features of a computer spreadsheet system.[k]

p) Identify applications for computer spreadsheets and their use in cost and management accounting.[s]

3. Budget preparation

a) Explain the importance of principal budget factor in constructing the budget'.[k]

b) Prepare sales budgets[s]

c) Prepare functional budgets (production, raw materials usage and purchases, labour, variable and fixed overheads) [s]

d) Prepare cash budgets[s]

e) Prepare master budgets (Income statement and statement of financial position) [s]

f) Explain and illustrate 'what if' analysis and scenario planning [s]

4. Flexible budgets

a) Explain the importance of flexible budgets in control[k]

b) Explain the disadvantages of fixed budgets in control[k]

c) Identify situations where fixed or flexible budgetary control would be appropriate[s]

d) Flex a budget to a given level of volume[s]

5. Capital budgeting and discounted cash flows

a) Discuss the importance of capital investment planning and control[k]

b) Define and distinguish between capital and revenue expenditure[k]

c) Outline the issues to consider and the steps involved in the preparation of a capital expenditure budget[k]

d) Explain and illustrate the difference between simple and compound interest, and between nominal and effective interest rates[s]

e) Explain and illustrate compounding and discounting[s]

f) Explain the distinction between cash flow and profit and the relevance of cash flow to capital investment appraisal[k]

g) Identify and evaluate relevant cash flows for individual investment decisions. [s]

h) Explain and illustrate the net present value (NPV) and internal rate of return (IRR) methods of discounted cash flow[s]

i) Calculate present value using annuity and perpetuity formulae[s]

j) Calculate NPV, IRR and payback (discounted and non-discounted) [s]

k) Interpret the results of NPV, IRR and payback calculations of investment viability[s]

6. **Budgetary control and reporting**

a) Calculate simple variances between flexed budget, fixed budget and actual sales, costs and profits[s]

b) Discuss the relative significance of variances[k]

c) Explain potential action to eliminate variances[k]

d) Define the concept of responsibility accounting and its significance in control[k]

e) Explain the concept of controllable and uncontrollable costs[k]

f) Prepare control reports suitable for presentation to management. (to include recommendation of appropriate control action [s]

7. **Behavioural aspects of budgeting**

a) Explain the importance of motivation in performance management[k]

b) Identify factors in a budgetary planning and control system that influence motivation[s]

c) Explain the impact of targets upon motivation[k]

d) Discuss managerial incentive schemes[k]

e) Discuss the advantages and disadvantages of a participative approach to budgeting[k]

f) Explain top down, bottom up approaches to budgeting[k]

D **STANDARD COSTING**

1. **Standard costing systems**

a) Explain the purpose and principles of standard costing. [k]

b) Explain and illustrate the difference between standard, marginal and absorption costing[k]

c) Establish the standard cost per unit under absorption and marginal costing[s]

2 **Variance calculations and analysis**

a) Calculate sales price and volume variance.[s]

b) Calculate materials total, price and usage variance.[s]

c) Calculate labour total, rate and efficiency variance.[s]

d) Calculate variable overhead total, expenditure and efficiency variance[s]

e) Calculate fixed overhead total, expenditure and, where appropriate, volume, capacity and efficiency variance.[s]

f) Interpret the variances.[s]

g) Explain factors to consider before investigating variances, explain possible causes of the variances and recommend control action.[s]

h) Explain the interrelationships between the variances .[k]

i) Calculate actual or standard figures where the variances are given.[k]

3 **Reconciliation of budgeted and actual profit**

a) Reconcile budgeted profit with actual profit under standard absorption costing.[s]

b) Reconcile budgeted profit or contribution with actual profit or contribution under standard marginal costing.[s]

E **PERFORMANCE MEASUREMENT**

1. **Performance measurement overview**

a) Discuss the purpose of mission statements and their role in performance measurement[k]

b) Discuss the purpose of strategic and operational and tactical objectives and their role in performance measurement[k]

c) Discuss the impact of economic and market conditions on performance measurement[k]

d) Explain the impact of government regulation on performance measurement[k]

2 Performance measurement - application

a) Discuss and calculate measures of financial performance (profitability, liquidity, activity and gearing) and non financial measures[s]

b) Perspectives of the balanced scorecard
   (i) discuss the advantages and limitations of the balanced scorecard[k]
   (ii) describe performance indicators for financial success, customer satisfaction, process efficiency and growth[k]
   (iii) discuss critical success factors and key performance indicators and their link to objectives and mission statements[k]
   (iv) establish critical success factors and key performance indicators in a specific situation[s]

c) Economy, efficiency and effectiveness
   (i) explain the concepts of economy, efficiency and effectiveness[k]
   (ii) describe performance indicators for economy, efficiency and effectiveness[k]
   (iii) establish performance indicators for economy, efficiency and effectiveness in a specific situation[s]
   (iv) discuss the meaning of each of the efficiency, capacity and activity ratios[k]
   (v) calculate the efficiency, capacity and activity ratios in a specific situation[s]

d) Unit costs
   (i) describe performance measures which would be suitable in contract and process costing environments[k]

e) Resource utilisation
   (i) describe measures of performance utilisation in service and manufacturing environments[k]
   (ii) establish measures of resource utilisation in a specific situation[s]

f) Profitability
   (i) calculate return on investment and residual income[s]

(ii) explain the advantages and limitations of return on investment and residual income[k]

g) Quality of service
   (i) distinguish performance measurement issues in service and manufacturing industries[k]
   (ii) describe performance measures appropriate for service industries[k]

3. Cost reductions and value enhancement

a) Compare cost control and cost reduction[k]

b) Describe and evaluate cost reduction methods[s]

c) Describe and evaluate value analysis[s]

4 Monitoring performance and reporting

a) Discuss the importance of non-financial performance measures[k]

b) Discuss the relationship between short-term and long-term performance[k]

c) Discuss the measurement of performance in service industry situations[k]

d) Discuss the measurement of performance in non-profit seeking and public sector organisations[k]

e) Discuss measures that may be used to assess managerial performance and the practical problems involved[k]

f) Discuss the role of benchmarking in performance measurement[k]

g) Produce reports highlighting key areas for management attention and recommendations for improvement[s]

The Computer Based Examination

Computer based examinations (CBEs) are available for the first seven FIA papers (not papers FAU, FTX or FFM) and ACCA papers F1, F2, and F3, in addition to the conventional paper based examination.

Computer based examinations must be taken at an ACCA CBE Licensed Centre.

How does CBE work?

* Questions are displayed on a monitor

* Candidates enter their answer directly onto the computer

* Candidates have two hours to complete the examination

* When the candidate has completed their examination, the final percentage score is calculated and displayed on screen

* Candidates are provided with a Provisional Result Notification showing their results before leaving the examination room

* The CBE Licensed Centre uploads the results to the ACCA (as proof of the candidate's performance) within 72 hours

* Candidates can check their exam status on the ACCA website by logging into myACCA

Benefits

* **Flexibility** as a CBE can be sat at any time

* **Resits** can also be taken at any time and there is no restriction on the number of times a candidate can sit a CBE

* **Instant feedback** as the computer displays the results at the end of the CBE

* Results are notified to ACCA within 72 hours

CBE question types

* Multiple choice – choose one answer from four options

* Multiple response – select more than one response by clicking the appropriate tick boxes

* Multiple response matching – select a response to a number of related statements by choosing one option from a number of drop down menus

* Number entry – key in a numerical response to a question

The January 2012 issue of ACCA *Student Accountant* magazine contains an article on CBEs. Ensure that you are familiar with this article.

http://www.accaglobal.com/content/dam/acca/global/PDF-students/2012s/sa_jan12_cbe.pdf

For more information on computer-based exams, visit the ACCA website.
http://www.accaglobal.com/en/student/Exams/Computer-based-exams.html

Tackling Multiple Choice Questions

MCQ's are part of all FIA exams and ACCA papers F1, F2 and F3. They form the paper-based exams and may appear in the CBE.

The MCQs in your exam contain four possible answers. You have to **choose the option that best answers the question**. The three incorrect options are called distracters. There is a skill in answering MCQs quickly and correctly. By practising MCQs you can develop this skill, giving you a better chance of passing the exam.

You may wish to follow the approach outlined below, or you may prefer to adapt it.

Step 1	Skim read all the MCQs and identify what appear to be the easier questions.
Step 2	Attempt each question – **starting with the easier questions** identified in Step 1. Read the question **thoroughly**. You may prefer to work out the answer before looking at the options, or you may prefer to look at the options at the beginning. Adopt the method that works best for you.
Step 3	Read the four options and see if one matches your own answer. Be careful with numerical questions as the distracters are designed to match answers that incorporate common errors. Check that your calculation is correct. Have you followed the requirement exactly? Have you included every stage of the calculation?
Step 4	You may find that none of the options matches your answer. • Re-read the question to ensure that you understand it and are answering the requirement • Eliminate any obviously wrong answers • Consider which of the remaining answers is the most likely to be correct and select the option
Step 5	If you are still unsure make a note and continue to the next question
Step 6	Revisit unanswered questions. When you come back to a question after a break you often find you are able to answer it correctly straight away. If you are still unsure have a guess. You are not penalised for incorrect answers, so **never leave a question unanswered!**

After extensive practice and revision of MCQs, you may find that you recognise a question when you sit the exam. Be aware that the detail and/or requirement may be different. If the question seems familiar read the requirement and options carefully – do not assume that it is identical.

The January 2012 issue of ACCA *Student Accountant* magazine contains an article on how to answer MCQs. Ensure that you are familiar with this article.

http://www.accaglobal.com/content/dam/acca/global/PDF-students/2012s/sa_jan12_mcq.pdf

part

A

The nature, source and purpose of management information

This chapter provides an introduction to **Management Accounting**. We look at **data** and **information** and introduce you to **cost accounting** and the differences between **financial accounting** and **management accounting**. We also outline the managerial processes of planning, control and decision-making. The sources of data are covered in the next chapter. Chapters 3 and 4 provide basic information on how costs are classified and how they behave.

Accounting for management

Study Guide	Intellectual level
A **The nature, source and purpose of management information**	
1 **Accounting for management**	
(a) Describe the purpose and role of cost and management accounting within an organisation	K
(b) Compare and contrast financial accounting with cost and management accounting	K
(c) Outline the managerial processes of planning, decision making and control	K
(d) Explain the difference between strategic, tactical and operational planning	K
(e) Distinguish between 'data' and 'information'	K
(f) Identify and explain the attributes of good information	K
(g) Explain the limitations of management information in providing guidance for managerial decision-making	K

EXAM FOCUS POINT

Although this chapter is an introductory chapter it is still highly examinable. You should expect questions on every study session including this one.

1   Information

1.1 Data and information

> **Data** is the raw material for data processing. Data relate to facts, events and transactions and so forth.
>
> **Information** is data that has been processed in such a way as to be **meaningful** to the person who receives it. **Information** is anything that is communicated.

Information is sometimes referred to as **processed data**. The terms 'information' and 'data' are often used interchangeably. It is important to understand the difference between these two terms.

Researchers who conduct market research surveys might ask members of the public to complete questionnaires about a product or a service. These completed questionnaires are **data**; they are processed and analysed in order to prepare a report on the survey. This resulting report is **information** and may be used by management for decision-making purposes.

1.2 Qualities of good information

> Good information should be **relevant**, **complete**, **accurate**, **clear**, it should **inspire confidence**, it should be **appropriately communicated**, its **volume** should be manageable, it should be **timely** and its **cost** should be less than the benefits it provides.

Let us look at those qualities in more detail.

(a)   **Relevance**. Information must be relevant to the purpose for which a manager wants to use it. In practice, far too many reports fail to 'keep to the point' and contain irrelevant paragraphs which only annoy the managers reading them.

(b) **Completeness**. An information user should have all the information he or she needs to do their job properly. If he or she does not have a complete picture of the situation, they might well make bad decisions.

(c) **Accuracy**. Information should obviously be accurate because using incorrect information could have serious and damaging consequences. However, information should only be accurate enough for its purpose and there is no need to go into unnecessary detail for pointless accuracy.

(d) **Clarity**. Information must be clear to the user. If the user does not understand it properly they cannot use it properly. Lack of clarity is one of the causes of a breakdown in communication. It is therefore important to choose the most appropriate presentation medium or channel of communication.

(e) **Confidence**. Information must be trusted by the managers who are expected to use it. However not all information is certain. Some information has to be certain, especially operating information, for example, related to a production process. Strategic information, especially relating to the environment, is uncertain. However, if the assumptions underlying it are clearly stated, this might enhance the confidence with which the information is perceived.

(f) **Communication**. Within any organisation, individuals are given the authority to do certain tasks, and they must be given the information they need to do them. An office manager might be made responsible for controlling expenditures in the office, and given a budget expenditure limit for the year. As the year progresses, the manager might try to keep expenditure in check but unless they are told throughout the year what is the current total expenditure to date, they will find it difficult to judge whether they are keeping within budget or not.

(g) **Volume**. There are physical and mental limitations to what a person can read, absorb and understand properly before taking action. An enormous mountain of information, even if it is all relevant, cannot be handled. Reports to management must therefore be **clear** and **concise** and in many systems, control action works basically on the 'exception' principle.

(h) **Timing**. Information which is not available until after a decision is made will be useful only for comparisons and longer-term control, and may serve no purpose even then. Information prepared too frequently can be a serious disadvantage. If, for example, a decision is taken at a monthly meeting about a certain aspect of a company's operations, information to make the decision is only required once a month, and weekly reports would be a time-consuming waste of effort.

(i) **Channel of communication**. There are occasions when using one particular method of communication will be better than others. For example, job vacancies should be announced in a medium where they will be brought to the attention of the people most likely to be interested. The channel of communication might be the company's in-house journal, a national or local newspaper, a professional magazine, a job centre or school careers office. Some internal memoranda may be better sent by 'electronic mail'. Some information is best communicated informally by telephone or word-of-mouth, whereas other information ought to be formally communicated in writing or figures.

(j) **Cost**. Information should have some value, otherwise it would not be worth the cost of collecting and filing it. The benefits obtainable from the information must also exceed the costs of acquiring it, and whenever management is trying to decide whether or not to produce information for a particular purpose (for example whether to computerise an operation or to build a financial planning model) a cost/benefit study ought to be made.

You may find this graph helpful. The point is that perfect information probably isn't worth paying for.

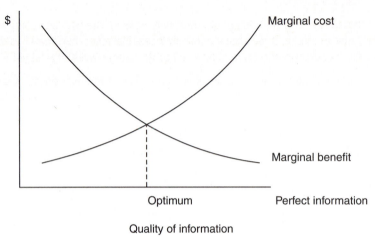

 QUESTION   *Value of information*

The value of information lies in the action taken as a result of receiving it. What questions might you ask in order to make an assessment of the value of information?

ANSWER

(a)   What information is provided?
(b)   What is it used for?
(c)   Who uses it?
(d)   How often is it used?
(e)   Does the frequency with which it is used coincide with the frequency with which it is provided?
(f)   What is achieved by using it?
(g)   What other relevant information is available which could be used instead?

An assessment of the value of information can be derived in this way, and the cost of obtaining it should then be compared against this value. On the basis of this comparison, it can be decided whether certain items of information are worth having. It should be remembered that there may also be intangible benefits which may be harder to quantify.

1.3 Why is information important?

Consider the following problems and what management needs to solve these problems.

(a)   A company wishes to launch a new product. The company's pricing policy is to charge cost plus 20%. What should the price of the product be?

(b)   An organisation's widget-making machine has a fault. The organisation has to decide whether to repair the machine, buy a new machine or hire a machine. What does the organisation do if its aim is to control costs?

(c)   A firm is considering offering a discount of 2% to those customers who pay an invoice within seven days of the invoice date and a discount of 1% to those customers who pay an invoice within eight to fourteen days of the invoice date. How much will this discount offer cost the firm?

In solving these and a wide variety of other problems, **management need information**.

(a)   In problem (a) above, management would need information about the **cost of the new product**.

(b)   Faced with problem (b), management would need information on the **cost of repairing, buying and hiring the machine**.

(c)   To calculate the cost of the discount offer described in (c), information would be required about **current sales settlement patterns** and **expected changes to the pattern** if discounts were offered.

The successful management of *any* organisation depends on information: non-profit seeking organisations such as charities, clubs and local authorities need information for decision making and for reporting the results of their activities just as multi-nationals do. For example a tennis club needs to know the cost of undertaking its various activities so that it can determine the amount of annual subscription it should charge its members.

1.4 What type of information is needed?

Most organisations require the following types of information.

- Financial
- Non-financial
- A combination of financial and non-financial information

1.4.1 Example: Financial and non-financial information

Suppose that the management of ABC Co have decided to provide a canteen for their employees.

(a)   The **financial information** required by management might include canteen staff costs, costs of subsidising meals, capital costs, costs of heat and light and so on.

(b)   The **non-financial information** might include management comment on the effect on employee morale of the provision of canteen facilities, details of the number of meals served each day, meter readings for gas and electricity and attendance records for canteen employees.

ABC Co could now **combine financial and non-financial information** to calculate the **average cost** to the company of each meal served, thereby enabling them to predict total costs depending on the number of employees in the work force.

1.4.2 Non-financial information

Most people probably consider that management accounting is only concerned with financial information and that people do not matter. This is, nowadays, a long way from the truth. For example, managers of business organisations need to know whether employee morale has increased due to introducing a canteen, whether the bread from particular suppliers is fresh and the reason why the canteen staff are demanding a new dishwasher. This type of non-financial information will play its part in **planning, controlling** and **decision making** and is therefore just as important to management as financial information is.

Non-financial information must therefore be **monitored** as carefully, **recorded** as accurately and **taken into account** as fully as financial information. There is little point in a careful and accurate recording of total canteen costs if the recording of the information on the number of meals eaten in the canteen is uncontrolled and therefore produces inaccurate information.

While management accounting is mainly concerned with the provision of **financial information** to aid planning, control and decision making, the management accountant cannot ignore **non-financial influences** and should qualify the information provided with non-financial matters as appropriate.

2 Planning, control and decision-making

2.1 Planning

> Information for management is likely to be used for **planning**, **control**, and **decision making**.

An organisation should never be surprised by developments which occur gradually over an extended period of time because the organisation should have **implemented a planning process**. Planning involves the following.

- Establishing objectives
- Selecting appropriate strategies to achieve those objectives

Planning therefore forces management to think ahead systematically in both the **short term** and the **long term**.

2.2 Objectives of organisations

An **objective** is the aim or **goal** of an organisation (or an individual). Note that in practice, the terms objective, goal and aim are often used interchangeably. A **strategy** is a possible course of action that might enable an organisation (or an individual) to achieve its objectives.

The two main types of organisation that you are likely to come across in practice are as follows.

- Profit making
- Non-profit seeking

The main objective of profit making organisations is to **maximise profits**. A secondary objective of profit making organisations might be to increase output of its goods/services.

The main objective of non-profit seeking organisations is usually to **provide goods and services**. A secondary objective of non-profit seeking organisations might be to minimise the costs involved in providing the goods/services.

In conclusion, the objectives of an organisation might include one or more of the following.

- Maximise profits
- Maximise shareholder value
- Minimise costs
- Maximise revenue
- Increase market share

Remember that the type of organisation concerned will have an impact on its objectives.

2.3 Strategy and organisational structure

There are two schools of thought on the link between strategy and organisational structure.

- Structure follows strategy
- Strategy follows structure

Let's consider the first idea that **structure follows strategy**. What this means is that organisations develop strategies in order that they can cope with changes in the structure of an organisation. Or do they?

The second school of thought suggests that **strategy follows structure**. This side of the argument suggests that the strategy of an organisation is determined or influenced by the structure of the organisation. The structure of the organisation therefore limits the number of strategies available.

We could explore these ideas in much more detail, but for the purposes of your **Management Accounting** studies, you really just need to be aware that there is a link between **strategy** and the **structure** of an organisation.

2.4 Long-term strategic planning

Long-term strategic planning also known as corporate planning, involves selecting appropriate strategies so as to prepare a long-term plan to attain the objectives.

The time span covered by a long-term plan depends on the **organisation**, the **industry** in which it operates and the particular **environment** involved. Typical periods are 2, 5, 7 or 10 years although longer periods are frequently encountered.

Long-term strategic planning is a **detailed, lengthy process**, essentially incorporating three stages and ending with a **corporate plan**. The diagram on the next page provides an overview of the process and shows the link between short-term and long-term planning.

2.5 Short-term tactical planning

The **long-term corporate plan** serves as the **long-term framework** for the organisation as a whole but for operational purposes it is necessary to convert the corporate plan into a series of **short-term plans**,

usually covering **one year**, which relate to **sections**, **functions** or **departments**. The annual process of short-term planning should be seen as stages in the progressive fulfilment of the corporate plan as each short-term plan steers the organisation towards its long-term objectives. It is therefore vital that, to obtain the maximum advantage from short-term planning, some sort of long-term plan exists.

The planning process

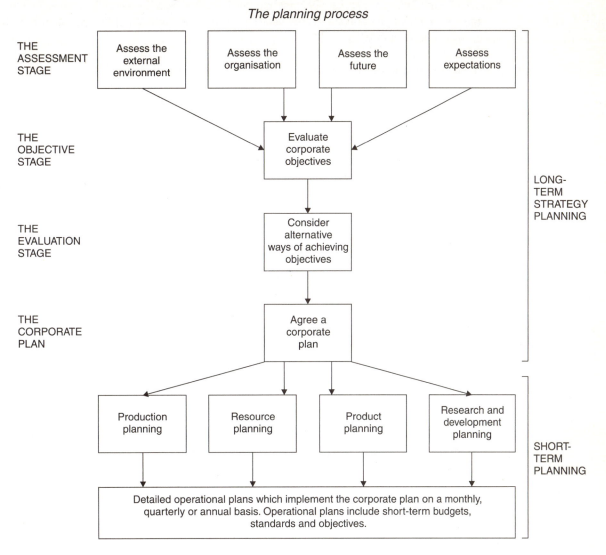

2.6 Control

Remember that we said that information for management is likely to be used for planning, control and decision making. We have just looked at planning. Now we'll look at control. There are two stages in the **control process**.

(a)   The **performance of the organisation** as set out in the detailed operational plans is compared with the actual performance of the organisation on a regular and continuous basis. Any deviations from the plans can then be identified and corrective action taken.

(b)   **The corporate plan** is reviewed in the light of the comparisons made and any changes in the parameters on which the plan was based (such as new competitors, government instructions and so on) to assess whether the objectives of the plan can be achieved. The plan is modified as necessary before any serious damage to the organisation's future success occurs.

   Effective control is therefore not practical without planning, and planning without control is pointless.

An established organisation should have a system of management reporting that produces control information in a specified format at regular intervals.

Smaller organisations may rely on informal information flows or ad hoc reports produced as required.

2.7 Decision-making

Management is decision-taking. Managers of all levels within an organisation take decisions. Decision making always involves a **choice between alternatives** and it is the role of the management accountant to provide information so that management can reach an informed decision. It is therefore vital that the management accountant understands the decision-making process so that he/she can supply the appropriate type of information.

2.7.1 Decision-making process

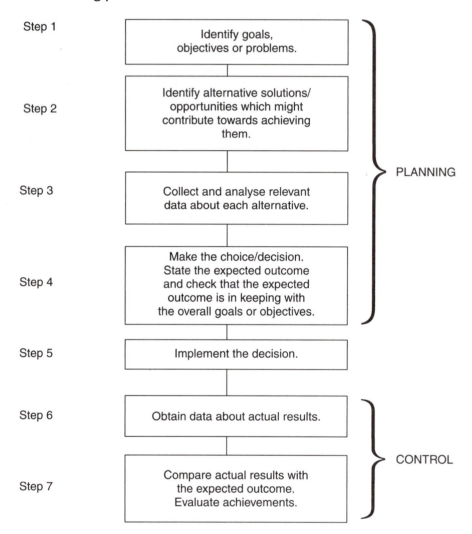

Step 1 — Identify goals, objectives or problems.

Step 2 — Identify alternative solutions/ opportunities which might contribute towards achieving them.

Step 3 — Collect and analyse relevant data about each alternative.

Step 4 — Make the choice/decision. State the expected outcome and check that the expected outcome is in keeping with the overall goals or objectives.

PLANNING (Steps 1-4)

Step 5 — Implement the decision.

Step 6 — Obtain data about actual results.

Step 7 — Compare actual results with the expected outcome. Evaluate achievements.

CONTROL (Steps 6-7)

2.8 Anthony's view of management activity

Anthony divides management activities into strategic planning, management control and operational control.

R N Anthony, a leading writer on organisational control, has suggested that the activities of **planning, control and decision making should not be separated** since all managers make planning and control decisions. He has identified three types of management activity.

(a)   **Strategic planning:** 'the process of deciding on objectives of the organisation, on changes in these objectives, on the resources used to attain these objectives, and on the policies that are to govern the acquisition, use and disposition of these resources'.

(b)   **Tactical (or management) control:** 'the process by which managers assure that resources are obtained and used effectively and efficiently in the accomplishment of the organisation's objectives'.

(c)   **Operational control:** 'the process of assuring that specific tasks are carried out effectively and efficiently'.

2.8.1 Strategic planning

Strategic plans are those which **set or change the objectives**, or **strategic targets** of an organisation. They would include such matters as the selection of products and markets, the required levels of company profitability, the purchase and disposal of subsidiary companies or major non-current assets and so on.

2.8.2 Tactical/Management control

Whilst strategic planning is concerned with setting objectives and strategic targets, **management control** is concerned with **decisions about the efficient and effective use of an organisation's resources** to achieve these objectives or targets.

(a)   **Resources**, often referred to as the **'4 Ms'** (men, materials, machines and money).

(b)   **Efficiency** in the use of resources means that optimum **output** is achieved from the **input** resources used. It relates to the combinations of men, land and capital (for example how much production work should be automated) and to the productivity of labour, or material usage.

(c)   **Effectiveness** in the use of resources means that the **outputs** obtained are in line with the intended **objectives** or targets.

2.8.3 Operational control

The third, and lowest tier, in Anthony's hierarchy of decision making, consists of **operational control decisions**. As we have seen, operational control is the task of ensuring that **specific tasks** are carried out effectively and efficiently. Just as 'management control' plans are set within the guidelines of strategic plans, so too are 'operational control' plans set within the guidelines of both strategic planning and management control. Consider the following.

(a)   Senior management may decide that the company should increase sales by 5% per annum for at least five years – **a strategic plan**.

(b)   The sales director and senior sales managers will make plans to increase sales by 5% in the next year, with some provisional planning for future years. This involves planning direct sales resources, advertising, sales promotion and so on. Sales quotas are assigned to each sales territory – **a tactical plan** (management control).

(c)   The manager of a sales territory specifies the weekly sales targets for each sales representative. This is **operational planning**: individuals are given tasks which they are expected to achieve.

Although we have used an example of selling tasks to describe operational control, it is important to remember that this level of planning occurs in all aspects of an organisation's activities, even when the activities cannot be scheduled nor properly estimated because they are non-standard activities (such as repair work, answering customer complaints).

The scheduling of unexpected or 'ad hoc' work must be done at short notice, which is a feature of much **operational planning**. In the repairs department, for example, routine preventive maintenance can be scheduled, but breakdowns occur unexpectedly and repair work must be scheduled and controlled 'on the spot' by a repairs department supervisor.

2.9 Management control systems

A **management control system** is a system which measures and corrects the performance of activities of subordinates in order to make sure that the objectives of an organisation are being met and the plans devised to attain them are being carried out.

The management function of control is the measurement and correction of the activities of subordinates in order to make sure that the goals of the organisation, or planning targets are achieved.

The basic elements of a management control system are as follows.

- **Planning:** deciding what to do and identifying the desired results
- **Recording** the plan which should incorporate standards of efficiency or targets
- **Carrying out** the plan and measuring actual results achieved
- **Comparing** actual results against the plans
- **Evaluating** the comparison, and deciding whether further action is necessary
- Where **corrective action** is necessary, this should be implemented

2.10 Types of information

Information within an organisation can be analysed into the three levels assumed in Anthony's hierarchy: **strategic**; **tactical**; and **operational**.

2.10.1 Strategic information

Strategic information is used by senior managers to plan the objectives of their organisation, and to assess whether the objectives are being met in practice. Such information includes **overall** profitability, the profitability of different segments of the business, capital equipment needs and so on.

Strategic information therefore has the following features.

- It is derived from both **internal** and **external** sources.
- It is summarised at a **high level**.
- It is relevant to the **long term**.
- It deals with the **whole organisation** (although it might go into some detail).
- It is often prepared on an **'ad hoc'** basis.
- It is both **quantitative** and **qualitative**.
- It cannot provide complete certainty, given that the future cannot be predicted.

2.10.2 Tactical information

Tactical information is used by middle management to decide how the resources of the business should be employed, and to monitor how they are being and have been employed. Such information includes **productivity measurements** (output per man hour or per machine hour), **budgetary control** or **variance analysis reports**, and **cash flow forecasts** and so on.

Tactical information therefore has the following features.

- It is primarily generated internally.
- It is summarised at a lower level.
- It is relevant to the short and medium term.
- It describes or analyses activities or departments.
- It is prepared routinely and regularly.
- It is based on quantitative measures.

2.10.3 Operational information

Operational information is used by 'front-line' managers such as foremen or head clerks to ensure that specific tasks are planned and carried out properly within a factory or office and so on. In the payroll office, for example, information at this level will relate to day-rate labour and will include the hours worked each week by each employee, the rate of pay per hour, details of the deductions, and for the purpose of wages analysis, details of the time each person spent on individual jobs during the week. In this example, the information is required weekly, but more urgent operational information, such as the amount of raw materials being input to a production process, may be required daily, hourly, or in the case of automated production, second by second.

Operational information has the following features.

- It is derived almost entirely from internal sources.
- It is highly detailed, being the processing of raw data.
- It relates to the immediate term, and is prepared constantly, or very frequently.
- It is task-specific and largely quantitative.

3 Financial accounting and cost and management accounting

3.1 Financial accounts and management accounts

> **Financial accounting systems** ensure that the assets and liabilities of a business are properly accounted for, and provide information about profits and so on to shareholders and to other interested parties. **Management accounting systems** provide information specifically for the use of managers within an organisation.

Management information provides a common source from which information is drawn for two groups of people.

(a) **Financial accounts** are prepared for individuals **external** to an organisation: shareholders, customers, suppliers, tax authorities, employees.

(b) **Management accounts** are prepared for **internal** managers of an organisation.

The data used to prepare financial accounts and management accounts are the same. The differences between the financial accounts and the management accounts arise because the data is analysed differently.

3.2 Financial accounts versus management accounts

Financial accounts	Management accounts
Financial accounts detail the performance of an organisation over a defined period and the state of affairs at the end of that period.	Management accounts are used to aid management record, plan and control the organisation's activities and to help the decision-making process.
Limited liability companies must, by law, prepare financial accounts.	There is no legal requirement to prepare management accounts.
The format of published financial accounts is determined by local law, by International Accounting Standards and International Financial Reporting Standards. In principle the accounts of different organisations can therefore be easily compared.	The format of management accounts is entirely at management discretion: no strict rules govern the way they are prepared or presented. Each organisation can devise its own management accounting system and format of reports.
Financial accounts concentrate on the business as a whole, aggregating revenues and costs from different operations, and are an end in themselves.	Management accounts can focus on specific areas of an organisation's activities. Information may be produced to aid a decision rather than to be an end product of a decision.
Most financial accounting information is of a monetary nature.	Management accounts incorporate non-monetary measures. Management may need to know, for example, tons of aluminium produced, monthly machine hours, or miles travelled by sales people.
Financial accounts present an essentially historic picture of past operations.	Management accounts are both an historical record and a future planning tool.

QUESTION

Management accounts

Which of the following statements about management accounts is/are true?

(i)   There is a legal requirement to prepare management accounts.
(ii)   The format of management accounts is largely determined by law.
(iii)   They serve as a future planning tool and are not used as a historical record.

A   (i) and (ii)
B   (ii) and (iii)
C   (iii) only
D   None of the statements are correct.

ANSWER

D

Statement (i) is incorrect. Limited liability companies must, by law, prepare **financial** accounts.

The format of published financial accounts is determined by law. Statement (ii) is therefore incorrect.

Management accounts do serve as a future planning tool but they are also useful as a historical record of performance. Therefore all three statements are incorrect and D is the correct answer.

3.3 Cost accounts

Cost accounting and management accounting are terms which are often used interchangeably. It is *not* correct to do so. **Cost accounting is part of management accounting. Cost accounting provides a bank of data for the management accountant to use.**

Cost accounting is concerned with the following.

- Preparing statements (eg budgets, costing)
- Cost data collection
- Applying costs to inventory, products and services

Cost accounting is the 'gathering of cost information and its attachment to cost objects, the establishment of budgets, standard costs and actual costs of operations, processes, activities or products; and the analysis of variances, profitability or the social use of funds.'

CIMA *Official Terminology*

Management accounting is concerned with the following.

- Using financial data and communicating it as information to users

Management accounting is the 'application of the principles of accounting and financial management to create, protect, preserve and increase value for the shareholders of for-profit and not-for-profit enterprises in the public and private sectors.'

CIMA *Official Terminology*

3.3.1 Aims of cost accounts

(a)   The **cost** of goods produced or services provided.

(b)   The **cost** of a department or work section.

(c)   What **revenues** have been.

(d)   The **profitability** of a product, a service, a department, or the organisation in total.

(e)   **Selling prices** with some regard for the costs of sale.

BPP
LEARNING MEDIA

(f) The **value of inventories of goods** (raw materials, work in progress, finished goods) that are still held in store at the end of a period, thereby aiding the preparation of a statement of financial position of the company's assets and liabilities.

(g) **Future costs** of goods and services (costing is an integral part of budgeting (planning) for the future).

(h) **How actual costs compare with budgeted costs.** (If an organisation plans for its revenues and costs to be a certain amount, but they actually turn out differently, the differences can be measured and reported. Management can use these reports as a guide to whether corrective action (or 'control' action) is needed to sort out a problem revealed by these differences between budgeted and actual results. This system of control is often referred to as budgetary control.

(i) **What information management needs** in order to make sensible decisions about profits and costs.

It would be wrong to suppose that cost accounting systems are restricted to manufacturing operations, although they are probably more fully developed in this area of work. **Service industries**, **government departments** and **welfare activities** can all make use of cost accounting information. Within a manufacturing organisation, the cost accounting system should be applied not only to **manufacturing** but also to **administration**, **selling and distribution**, **research and development** and all other departments.

4 Cost accounting information and decision making

Cost accounting information is, in general, unsuitable for decision making.

The **information required for decision making is different from the information provided by conventional cost accounts. Decision-making information should be relevant**. However, absorption costing (a widely-used method of costing products and services which we will be looking at later) provides information that in many situations is misleading and irrelevant.

All decision making is concerned with the future and so there will **always be some degree of uncertainty** surrounding the possible outcomes of a decision. **Information for decision making should therefore incorporate uncertainty** in some way. The methods of incorporating uncertainty are outside the scope of this syllabus, but you should realise that if cost accounting information does not take account of uncertainty it is unsuitable for decision making. If an attempt to incorporate uncertainty is made the information should be more suitable for decision making but can **never be risk free**.

QUESTION
Uncertainty

Can you think of any factors which contribute to the uncertainty an organisation might face?

ANSWER

Here are a few suggestions. You probably thought of others.

The actions of competitors
Inflation
Interest rate changes
New government legislation
Possible shortages of material or labour
Possible industrial disputes

CHAPTER ROUNDUP

↳ **Data** is the raw material for data processing. Data relate to facts, events and transactions and so forth.

Information is data that has been processed in such a way as to be **meaningful** to the person who receives it. **Information** is anything that is communicated.

↳ Good information should be **relevant, complete, accurate, clear**, it should **inspire confidence**, it should be **appropriately communicated**, its **volume** should be manageable, it should be **timely** and its **cost** should be less than the benefits it provides.

↳ Information for management is likely to be used for **planning, control** and **decision making**.

↳ An **objective** is the aim or **goal** of an organisation (or an individual). Note that in practice, the terms objective, goal and aim are often used interchangeably. A **strategy** is a possible course of action that might enable an organisation (or an individual) to achieve its objectives.

↳ Anthony divides management activities into **strategic planning, management control** and **operational control**.

↳ A **management control system** is a system which measures and corrects the performance of activities of subordinates in order to make sure that the objectives of an organisation are being met and the plans devised to attain them are being carried out.

↳ Information within an organisation can be analysed into the three levels assumed in Anthony's hierarchy: **strategic; tactical**; and **operational**.

↳ **Financial accounting systems** ensure that the assets and liabilities of a business are properly accounted for, and provide information about profits and so on to shareholders and to other interested parties. **Management accounting systems** provide information specifically for the use of managers within the organisation.

↳ Cost accounting and management accounting are terms which are often used interchangeably. It is not correct to do so. **Cost accounting is part of management accounting. Cost accounting provides a bank of data for the management accountant to use**.

↳ **Cost accounting information** is, in general, unsuitable for decision making.

QUICK QUIZ

1 Define the terms **data** and **information**.

2 The four main qualities of good information are:

- .... • ....
- .... • ....

3 In terms of management accounting, information is most likely to be used for:

(1) ....
(2) ....
(3) ....

4 A strategy is the aim or goal of an organisation.

True ☐

False ☐

5 State the main objective of the following organisations:

A Profit making
B Non-profit seeking

6 What are the three types of management activity identified by R N Anthony?

(1) ....
(2) ....
(3) ....

7 A management control system is

A A possible course of action that might enable an organisation to achieve its objectives

B A collective term for the hardware and software used to drive a database system

C A set up that measures and corrects the performance of activities of subordinates in order to make sure that the objectives of an organisation are being met and their associated plans are being carried out

D A system that controls and maximises the profits of an organisation

8 List six differences between financial accounts and management accounts.

9 Information provided by conventional cost accounts is ideal for decision making. True or false?

ANSWERS TO QUICK QUIZ

1   **Data** is the raw material for data processing. **Information** is data that has been processed in such a way as to be meaningful to the person who receives it. **Information** is anything that is communicated.

2   • Relevance   • Accuracy
    • Completeness   • Clarity

3   (1) Planning
    (2) Control
    (3) Decision making

4   False. This is the definition of an **objective**. A strategy is a possible course of action that might enable an organisation to **achieve** its objectives.

5   A   Profit making = maximise profits
    B   Non-profit seeking = provide goods and services

6   (1) Strategic planning
    (2) Management control
    (3) Operational control

7   C

8   See Paragraph 3.2

9   False

Now try ...

Attempt the questions below from the **Exam Question Bank** (at the back of this book)

Number

Q1 – Q4

BPP LEARNING MEDIA

02

Sources of data

In this chapter we will look at types of data and sources of information from within and outside the organisation. Data can be primary or secondary and discrete or continuous. Data can come from various sources other than from the organisation itself. Examples include government, professional associations, financial press, quotations and price lists. We will finish the chapter by looking at various sampling techniques.

Study Guide	Intellectual level
A **The nature, source and purpose of management information**	
2 **Sources of data**	
(a) Describe sources of information from within and outside the organisation (including government statistics, financial press, professional or trade associations, quotations and price list)	K
(b) Explain the uses and limitations of published information/data (including information from the internet)	K
(c) Describe the impact of general economic environment on costs/revenues	K
(d) Explain sampling techniques (random, systematic, stratified, multistage, cluster and quota)	K
(e) Choose an appropriate sampling method in a specific situation	S

1 Types of data

Data may be **primary** (collected specifically for the purpose of a survey) or **secondary** (collected for some other purpose).

Discrete data/variables can only take on a countable number of values. **Continuous** data/ variables can take on any value.

Data may be classified as follows.

(a) Primary and secondary data
(b) Discrete and continuous data
(c) Sample and population data

Primary and secondary data

(a) **Primary data** are data collected especially for a specific purpose. Raw data are primary data which have not been processed at all, and which are still just a list of numbers.

(b) **Secondary data** are data which have already been collected elsewhere, for some other purpose, but which can be used or adapted for the survey being conducted.

1.1 Discrete and continuous data

Quantitative (measurable) data may be classified as being **discrete** or **continuous.**

(a) **Discrete data** are data which can only taken on a finite or countable number of values within a given range.

(b) **Continuous data** are data which can take on any value. They are measured rather than counted.

An example of discrete data is the number of goals scored by Arsenal against Chelsea in the FA Cup Final: Arsenal could score 0, 1, 2, 3 or even 4 goals (**discrete variables** =0, 1, 2, 3, 4), but they cannot score 1½ or 2½ goals.

Continuous data include the heights of all the members of your family, as these can take on any value: 1.542m, 1.639m and 1.492m for example. **Continuous variables** = 1.542, 1.639, 1.492.

1.2 Sample and population data

(a) **Sample data** are data arising as a result of investigating a sample. A sample is a selection from the population.

(b) **Population data** are data arising as a result of investigating the population. A population is the group of people or objects of interest to the data collector.

The diagram below should help you to remember the ways in which data may be classified.

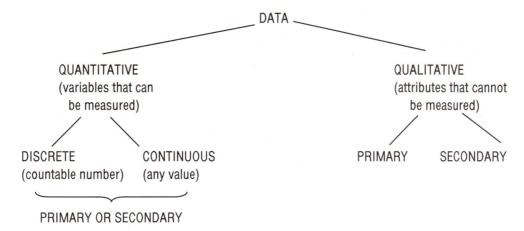

Now we know what sorts of data we may come across, and how it is classified, we can take a look at the different **sources of data.**

2 Sources of data

Data may be obtained from an **internal** source or an **external** source.

2.1 Internal sources of data

2.1.1 The accounting records

There is no need for us to give a detailed description of the constituents of the accounting records. You are by now very familiar with the idea of a system of sales ledgers and purchase ledgers, general ledgers and cost ledgers. These records provide a history of an organisation's business. Some of this data is of great value outside the accounts department, for example sales data for the marketing function. Other data, like cheque numbers or employees' PAYE codes, is of purely administrative value within the accounts department.

You will also be aware that to maintain the **integrity of its accounting records**, an organisation of any size will have systems for and controls over transactions. These also give rise to valuable data. An inventory control system is the classic example. Besides actually recording the monetary value of purchases and inventory in hand for external financial reporting purposes, the system will include purchase orders, goods received notes, goods returned notes and so on, and these can be analysed to provide management information about speed of delivery, say, or the quality of supplies.

2.1.2 Other internal sources

Much of the data that are not strictly part of the financial accounting records are in fact closely tied in to the accounting system.

(a) **Data relating to personnel** will be linked to the payroll system. Additional data may be obtained from this source if, say, a project is being costed and it is necessary to ascertain the availability and rate of pay of different levels of staff, or the need for and cost of recruiting staff from outside the organisation.

(b) **Much data will be produced by a production department** about machine capacity, fuel consumption, movement of people, materials, and work in progress, set up times, maintenance requirements and so on. A large part of the traditional work of cost accounting involves ascribing costs to the physical information produced by this source.

(c) **Many service businesses** – notably accountants and solicitors – need to keep detailed records of the time spent on various activities, both to justify fees to clients and to assess the efficiency of operations.

2.2 External sources of data

We hardly need say that an organisation's files are also full of invoices, letters, advertisements and so on received from customers and suppliers. These documents provide data from an external source. There are many occasions when an active search outside the organisation is necessary.

(a) A **primary source** of data is, as the term implies, as close as you can get to the origin of an item of data: the eyewitness to an event, the place in question, the document under scrutiny.

(b) A **secondary source**, again logically enough, provides 'second-hand' data: books, articles, verbal or written reports by someone else.

You will remember that **primary data** are data collected especially for a specific purpose. The **advantage** of such data is that the investigator knows where the data came from and is aware of any inadequacies or limitations in the data. Its **disadvantage** is that it can be very expensive to collect primary data.

Management accountants often collect primary data when they carry out investigations. A good example would be the establishment of the direct cost of a product. This might be carried out by analysing materials invoices and wages costs over a representative period.

3 Secondary data

The main sources of **secondary data** are: Governments; banks; newspapers; trade journals; information bureaux; consultancies; libraries and information services.

Secondary data are data which have already been collected elsewhere, for some other purpose, but which can be used or adapted for the survey being conducted.

Advantage of secondary data	Disadvantage of secondary data
They are cheaply available	Since the investigator did not collect the data, he/she is therefore unaware of any inadequacies or limitations of the data.

Secondary data sources may be satisfactory in certain situations, or they may be the only convenient means of obtaining an item of data. It is essential that there is good reason to believe that the secondary data used is **accurate** and **reliable**.

External sources of data may have been obtained for many different reasons, and care should be taken to ensure that it is used properly. This is because the data will have been collected for a specific purpose, and then used as secondary data.

Despite the limitations of secondary data, they can be very valuable in many situations. The main secondary data sources are as follows.

(a) Governments
(b) Banks
(c) Newspapers
(d) Trade journals

3.1 Governments

Official statistics are supplied by many Governments. In Great Britain, official statistics are supplied by the Office for National Statistics (ONS), and include the following.

Title	Detail
The *Annual Abstract of Statistics*	This is a general reference book for the United Kingdom which includes data on climate, population, social services, justice and crime, education, defence, manufacturing and agricultural production.
The *Monthly Digest*	An abbreviated version of the *Annual Abstract of Statistics.*
Financial Statistics	A monthly compilation of financial data. It includes statistics on Government income, expenditure and borrowing, financial institutions, companies, the overseas sector, the money supply, exchange rates, interest rates and share prices.
The United Kingdom National Accounts (The Blue Book)	A source of data on the gross national product, the gross national income and the gross national expenditure. It gives a clear indication of how the nation makes and spends its money.
The United Kingdom Balance of Payments (The Pink Book)	This annual publication gives data on the inflows and outflows of private capital in the United Kingdom.
Social trends	This annual publication provides data on the population, income, householders, families and many other aspects of British life and work.

Monthly statistics are also published by many Government departments. For example, the Department of Employment in Britain publishes *The Department of Employment Gazette* which gives details of retail prices, employment, unemployment, unfilled job vacancies and other statistics relating to employment.

Population data is published by many Governments around the world, and includes population numbers, births, deaths, marriages and so on. In Britain the Government carries out a full census of the whole population every ten years.

3.2 Banks

The Bank of England issues a quarterly magazine which includes data on banks in the UK, the money supply and Government borrowing and financial transactions.

3.3 Financial newspapers

Financial newspapers contain detailed business data and information. Financial newspapers include the *Financial Times,* the *Wall Street Journal,* the *Singapore Business Times* and the *Nikkei Weekly.* Such newspapers provide data on foreign exchange rates, interest rates, gilts and other share prices.

3.4 Trade journals

Most industries are served by one or more trade journals. Journals contain data on new developments in the industry, articles about competitors' products, details of industry costs and prices and so on.

3.5 Other sources

(a) **Advice or information bureaux.** Provide information in the form of advice, information leaflets or fact sheets.

(b) **Consultancies.** These include general market research organisations such as MORI and Gallup. There are also specialist market research companies which provide data on specific industries.

(c) **Specific reference works.** Different businesses will have different reference works or so called 'bibles' which are always used as a point of reference.

(d) **Libraries and information services.** Most countries have free public library systems. Educational institutes and business organisations may also provide library services which are available to their members.

(e)   **Electronic sources** such as local and national radio and TV, teletext and the **Internet**. The **Internet is becoming more important** as a data source. Many of the sources described in this section can be accessed through their **Website** on the Internet.

3.6 The Internet

The **Internet** is a global network connecting millions of computers. The Internet allows any computer with a telecommunications link to **send and receive information** to and from any other suitably equipped computer.

A **website** is a collection of images and text that **provide information** which may be viewed on the World Wide Web. Most organisations now have a website and many are able to **process transactions** (known as electronic commerce or **e-commerce**).

Connection to the Internet is made via an **Internet Service Provider** (ISP). ISPs, such as AOL and Virgin provide their **own information services** in addition to Internet access and e-mail capability.

Users access the Internet through interface programs called **browsers**. The most popular and best known is **Microsoft Internet Explorer**.

Browser software packages provide a facility to **store Internet addresses** so that users can access frequently-visited sites without having to go through a long search process. So in business use, if you **regularly need up-to-date information**, say, on inventory market movements, new government legislation, or the activities of a competitor, you can simply click on the appropriate entry in a personal 'favourites' directory and be taken straight to the relevant site.

Searching the Net is done using a **search engine** such as Yahoo!, Google or AltaVista. These guide users to destinations throughout the web: the user simply types in a word or phrase to find related sites and documents.

All search engines work in a similar way. The illustrations that follow show the opening ('home') page of Google.co.uk. To perform a search, you simply click in an empty box (if the cursor isn't flashing there already), type in a word or words and click on Search or, for Google, on Google Search.

In the following example, the user is using the Google.co.uk search engine to find web pages from the UK containing information regarding share prices.

BPP
LEARNING MEDIA

The results of the search are shown below

Google found hundreds of websites or documents relating to share information. To view a document, you simply click on the highlighted document title.

Remember, when you are looking at information on the Internet it is **not necessarily good information**, just because it is 'published'. **Anybody** can put information on the Internet. The **reliability** and **reputation** of the **provider is important**. For example, The Financial Times site, FT.com, is a respected source of financial information. On the other hand, a site such as 'Fred's Financial Advice' may contain unreliable information.

QUESTION

External data sources

Which of the following are secondary external sources of data.

I   *Economic Trends* (published by the Office for National Statistics in the United Kingdom).

II   The *Singapore Business Times.*

III   Data collected for a survey which was commissioned in order to determine whether Donald Co should launch a new product.

IV   Historical records of expenditure on canteen costs in a hospital in order to prepare current forecasts.

A   I and II only
B   I, II and III only
C   I, II and IV only
D   I, II, III and IV

ANSWER

The correct answer is C.

Economic Trends and the *Singapore Business Times* are both sources of secondary external data. Historic expenditure data of canteen costs were not collected specifically for the preparation of forecasts, and are therefore also secondary data. Data collected through personal interview for a particular project are primary data.

3.7 The economic environment

The **economic** environment affects firms at national and international level, both in the general level of economic activity and in particular variables, such as exchange rates, interest rates and inflation.

The economic environment is an important influence at **local and national level**.

Factor	Impact
Overall growth or fall in gross domestic product	Increased/decreased demand for goods (eg dishwashers) and services (eg holidays).
Local economic trends	Type of industry in the area. Office/factory rents. Labour rates. House prices.
Inflation	Low in most countries; distorts business decisions; wage inflation compensates for price inflation.
Interest rates	How much it costs to borrow money affects cash flow. Some businesses carry a high level of debt. How much customers can afford to spend is also affected as rises in interest rates affect people's mortgage payments.
Tax levels	Corporation tax affects how much firms can invest or return to shareholders. Income tax and sales tax (eg VAT) affect how much consumers have to spend, hence demand.
Government spending	Suppliers to the government (eg construction firms) are affected by spending.
The business cycle	Economic activity is always punctuated by periods of growth followed by decline, simply because of the nature of trade. The UK economy has been characterised by periods of boom and bust. Government policy can cause, exacerbate or mitigate such trends, but cannot abolish the business cycle. (Industries which prosper when others are declining are called counter-cyclical industries.)

The **forecast state of the economy** will influence the planning process for organisations which operate within it. In times of boom and increased demand and consumption, the overall planning problem will be to **identify** the demand. Conversely, in times of recession, the emphasis will be on cost-effectiveness, continuing profitability, survival and competition.

4 Sampling

Data are often collected from a **sample** rather than from a population. If the whole population is examined, the survey is called a **census**.

In many situations, it will not be practical to carry out a survey which considers every item of the **population**. For example, if a poll is taken to try to predict the results of an election, it would not be possible to ask all eligible voters how they are going to vote. To ask the whole population would take far too long and cost too much money.

In such situations where it is not possible to survey the whole population, a **sample** is selected. The results obtained from the sample are used to estimate the results of the whole population.

In situations where the whole population is examined, the survey is called a **census.** This situation is quite rare, which means that the investigator must choose a **sample.**

Disadvantages of a census

(a)   The high cost of a census may exceed the value of the results obtained.

(b)   It might be out of date by the time you complete it.

Advantages of a sample

(a)   It can be shown mathematically that once a certain sample size has been reached, very little accuracy is gained by examining more items. The larger the size of the sample, however, the more accurate the results.

(b)   It is possible to ask more questions with a sample.

4.1 The choice of a sample

One of the most important requirements of sample data is that they should be **complete.** That is, the data should **cover all areas** of the population to be examined. If this requirement is not met, then the sample will be **biased**.

5 Sampling methods

A **probability sampling method** is a sampling method in which there is a known chance of each member of the population appearing in the sample.

Probability sampling methods

–   Random
–   Stratified random
–   Systematic
–   Multistage
–   Cluster

Random sampling requires the construction of a **sampling frame**. A sampling frame is a numbered list of all items in a population.

A **non-probability sampling method** is a sampling method in which the chance of each member of the population appearing in the sample is not known, for example, **quota sampling**.

You must be aware of the characteristics and advantages and disadvantages of the sampling methods covered in this chapter.

Once data have been collected they need to be **presented** and **analysed.** It is important to remember that if data have not been collected properly, no amount of careful presentation or analysis can remedy this defect.

5.1 Probability sampling methods

A **probability sampling method** is a sampling method in which there is a known chance of each member of the population appearing in the sample.

(a)   Random sampling
(b)   Stratified random sampling
(c)   Systematic sampling
(d)   Multistage sampling
(e)   Cluster sampling

5.2 Random sampling

A **simple random sample** is a sample selected in such a way that every item in the population has an equal chance of being included.

If a sample is selected using random sampling, it will be free from bias (since every item will have an equal chance of being selected). Once the sample has been selected, valid inferences about the population being sampled can be made.

For example, if you wanted to take a random sample of library books, it would not be good enough to pick them off the shelves, even if you picked them at random. This is because the books which were out on loan would stand no chance of being chosen. You would either have to make sure that all the books were on the shelves before taking your sample, or find some other way of sampling (for example, using the library index cards).

A random sample is not necessarily a perfect sample. For example, you might pick what you believe to be a completely random selection of library books, and find that every one of them is a detective thriller. It is a remote possibility, but it could happen. The only way to eliminate the possibility altogether is to take **100% survey (a census)** of the books, which, unless it is a tiny library, is impractical.

5.3 Sampling frames

If random sampling is used then it is necessary to construct a **sampling frame**

A **sampling frame** is a numbered list of all items in a population.

Once a numbered list of all items in the population has been made, it is easy to select a random sample, simply by generating a list of random numbers.

For instance, if you wanted to select a random sample of children from a school, it would be useful to have a list of names:

0	J Absolam
1	R Brown
2	S Brown
…	

Now the numbers 0, 1, 2 and so on can be used to select the random sample. It is normal to start the numbering at 0, so that when 0 appears in a list of random numbers it can be used.

Sometimes it is not possible to draw up a sampling frame. For example, if you wanted to take a random sample of Americans, it would take too long to list all Americans.

A sampling frame should have the following characteristics.

(a) **Completeness**. Are all members of the population included on the list?
(b) **Accuracy**. Is the information correct?
(c) **Adequacy**. Does it cover the entire population?
(d) **Up to dateness**. Is the list up to date?
(e) **Convenience**. Is the sampling frame readily accessible?
(f) **Non-duplication**. Does each member of the population appear on the list only once?

Two **readily available sampling frames** for the human population of Great Britain are the **council tax register** (list of dwellings) and the **electoral register** (list of individuals).

5.4 Drawbacks of random sampling

(a) Selected items are subject to the full range of variation inherent in the population.
(b) An unrepresentative sample may result.
(c) An adequate sampling frame might not exist.
(d) The numbering of the population might be laborious.
(e) It might be difficult to obtain the data if the selected items cover a wide area.
(f) It might be costly to obtain the data if the selected items cover a wide area.

5.5 Stratified random sampling

A variation on the random sampling method is **stratified random sampling**.

Stratified random sampling is a method of sampling which involves dividing the population into strata or categories. Random samples are then taken from each stratum or category.

In many situations, stratified sampling is the best method of choosing a sample. Stratified sampling is best demonstrated by means of an example.

5.6 Example: stratified sampling

The number of cost and management accountants in each type of work in a particular country are as follows.

Partnerships	500
Public companies	500
Private companies	700
Public practice	800
	2,500

If a sample of 20 was required the sample would be made up as follows.

		Sample
Partnerships	$\dfrac{500}{2,500} \times 20$	4
Public companies	$\dfrac{500}{2,500} \times 20$	4
Private companies	$\dfrac{700}{2,500} \times 20$	6
Public practice	$\dfrac{800}{2,500} \times 20$	6
		20

Advantages and disadvantages of stratification are as follows.

Advantages	Disadvantages
The sample selected will be representative since it guarantees that every important category will have elements in the final sample.	The main **disadvantage** of stratification is that it requires **prior knowledge of each item in the population**; sampling frames do not always contain such information.
The structure of the sample will reflect that of the population if the same proportion of individuals is chosen from each stratum.	
Each stratum is represented by a randomly chosen sample and therefore **inferences can be made about each stratum.**	
Precision is increased. Sampling takes place within strata and, because the range of variation is less in each stratum than in the population as a whole and variation between strata does not enter as a chance effect, higher precision is obtainable.	

5.7 Systematic sampling

Systematic sampling a sampling method which works by selecting every nth item after a random start.

If it were decided to select a sample of 20 from a population of 800, then every 40th (800 ÷ 20) item after a random start in the first 40 should be selected. The starting point could be found using the lottery method or random number tables. If (say) 23 was chosen, then the sample would include the 23rd, 63rd, 103rd, 143rd ... 783rd items. The gap of 40 is known as the **sampling interval**.

Advantages and disadvantages of systematic sampling

Advantages	Disadvantages
It is easy to use	It is possible that a biased sample might be chosen if there is a regular pattern to the population which coincides with the sampling method.
It is cheap	It is not completely random since some items have a zero chance of being selected.

5.8 Multistage sampling

Multistage sampling is a probability sampling method which involves dividing the population into a number of sub-populations and then selecting a small sample of these sub-populations at random.

Each sub-population is then divided further, and then a small sample is again selected at random. This process is repeated as many times as is necessary.

Multistage sampling is best demonstrated by means of an example.

5.9 Example: multistage sampling

A survey of spending habits is being planned to cover the whole of Britain. It is obviously **impractical to draw up a sampling frame**, so **random sampling is not possible**. Multistage sampling is to be used instead.

The country is divided into a number of areas and a small sample of these is selected at random. Each of the areas selected is subdivided into smaller units and again, a smaller number of these is selected at random. This process is repeated as many times as necessary and finally, a random sample of the relevant people living in each of the smallest units is taken. A fair approximation to a random sample can be obtained.

Thus, we might choose a random sample of eight areas, and from each of these areas, select a random sample of five towns. From each town, a random sample of 200 people might be selected so that the total sample size is 8 × 5 × 200 = 8,000 people.

Advantages and disadvantages of multistage sampling

Advantages	Disadvantages
Fewer investigators are needed	There is the **possibility of bias** if, for example, only a small number of regions are selected.
It is not so costly to obtain a sample	The method is **not truly random** as once the final sampling areas have been selected the rest of the population cannot be in the sample. If the population is heterogeneous, the areas chosen should reflect the **full range of the diversity**. Otherwise, choosing some areas and excluding others (even if it is done randomly) will result in a biased sample.

5.10 Cluster sampling

Cluster sampling is a non-random sampling method that involves selecting one definable subsection of the population as the sample, that subsection taken to be representative of the population in question.

For example, the pupils of one school might be taken as a cluster sample of all children at school in one county.

Advantages and disadvantages of cluster sampling

Advantages	Disadvantages
It is a good alternative to multistage sampling if a satisfactory sampling frame does not exist.	There is potential for considerable bias.
It is inexpensive to operate.	

QUESTION
Systematic sampling

Which of the following are disadvantages of systematic sampling? Tick as appropriate.

	The sample chosen might be biased
	Some samples have a zero chance of being selected so sampling method is not completely random
	Prior knowledge of each item in the population is required

ANSWER

✓	The sample chosen might be biased
✓	Some samples have a zero chance of being selected so sampling method is not completely random
	Prior knowledge of each item in the population is required

Non-probability sampling methods

A **non-probability sampling method** is a sampling method in which the chance of each member of the population appearing in the sample is not known.

The only non-probability sampling method that you need to know about is **quota sampling.**

5.11 Quota sampling

In **quota sampling**, randomness is forfeited in the interests of cheapness and administrative simplicity. Investigators are told to interview all the people they meet up to a certain quota.

5.12 Example: quota sampling

Consider the figures in Paragraph 5.6, but with the following additional information relating to the sex of the cost and management accountants.

	Male	Female
Partnerships	300	200
Public companies	400	100
Private companies	300	400
Public practice	300	500

An investigator's quotas might be as follows.

	Male	Female	Total
Partnerships	30	20	50
Public companies	40	10	50
Private companies	30	40	70
Public practice	30	50	80
			250

Using quota sampling, the investigator would interview the first 30 male cost and management accountants in partnerships that they met, the first 20 female cost and management accountants in partnerships that they met and so on.

Advantages and disadvantages of quota sampling

Advantages	Disadvantages
It is **cheap** and **administratively easy**.	The method can result in certain **biases**. For example, an interviewer in a shopping centre may fill the quota by only meeting people who can go shopping during the week.
A much larger sample can be studied, and hence more information can be gained at a faster speed for a given outlay than when compared with a fully randomised sampling method.	The non-random nature of the method rules out any valid estimate of the **sampling error** in estimates derived from the sample.
Although a fairly detailed knowledge of the characteristics of a population is required, **no sampling frame is necessary** because the interviewer questions every person they meet up to the quota.	
It may be the **only possible approach** in certain situations, such as television audience research.	
Given suitable, trained and properly briefed field workers, quota sampling **yields enough accurate information** for many forms of commercial market research.	

The diagram below summaries the various sampling methods.

EXAM FOCUS POINT

Make sure that you understand how each sampling method works so that you can choose an appropriate method in a specific situation.

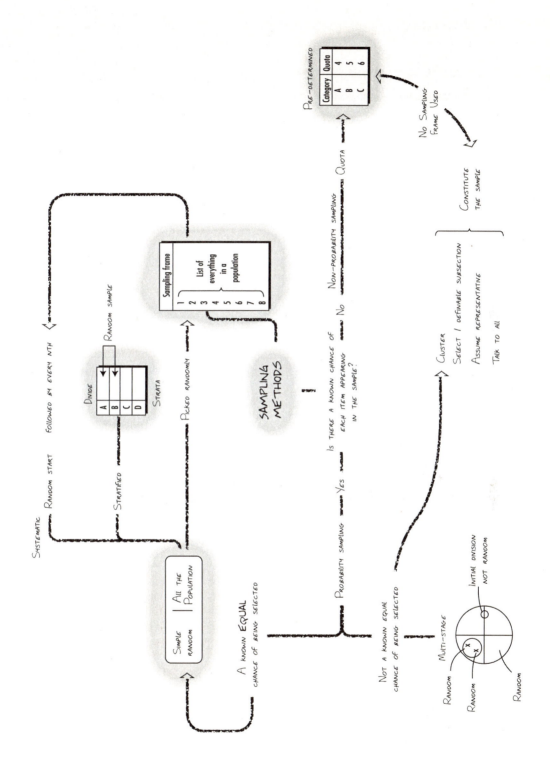

CHAPTER ROUNDUP

↳ Data may be **primary** (collected specifically for the purpose of a survey) or **secondary** (collected for some other purpose).

↳ **Discrete** data/variables can only take on a countable number of values. **Continuous** data/variables can take on any value.

↳ Data may be obtained from an **internal** source or an **external** source.

↳ The main sources of **secondary data** are: Governments; banks; newspapers; trade journals; information bureaux; consultancies; libraries and information services.

↳ The **economic** environment affects firms at national and international level, both in the general level of economic activity and in particular variables, such as exchange rates, interest rates and inflation

↳ Data are often collected from a **sample** rather than from a population. If the whole population is examined, the survey is called a **census**.

↳ A **probability sampling method** is a sampling method in which there is a known chance of each member of the population appearing in the sample.

Probability sampling methods

– Random
– Stratified random
– Systematic
– Multistage
– Cluster

↳ Random sampling requires the construction of a **sampling frame**. A sampling frame is a numbered list of all items in a population.

↳ A **non-probability sampling method** is a sampling method in which the chance of each member of the population appearing in the sample is not known, for example, **quota sampling**.

↳ You must be aware of the characteristics and advantages and disadvantages of the sampling methods covered in this chapter.

↳ Once data have been collected they need to be **presented** and **analysed** It is important to remember that if data have not been collected properly, no amount of careful presentation or analysis can remedy this defect.

QUICK QUIZ

1   List four main secondary data sources.

2   What is the main advantage of using primary data over secondary data?

3   Identify the following as either primary or secondary data.

	Primary data	Secondary data
Annual Abstract of Statistics		
Wall Street Journal		
Investigator's survey		
Survey questionnaire		
Management Accounting		
BPP's website		

4   Fill in the blanks in the boxes below using the words in the box.

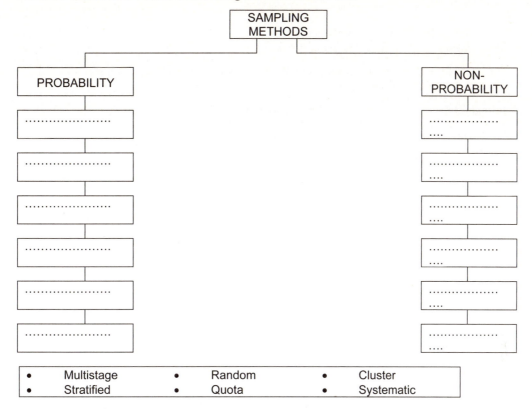

•	Multistage	•	Random	•	Cluster
•	Stratified	•	Quota	•	Systematic

5   A simple random sample is a sample selected in such a way that every item in the population has an equal chance of being included.

True   ☐

False   ☐

6   I   If a sample is selected using random sampling, it will be free from bias

     II   A sampling frame is a numbered list of all items in a sample

     III   Cluster sampling is a non-probability sampling method

     IV   In quota sampling, investigators are told to interview all the people they meet up to a certain quota

     Which of the above statements are true?

     A   I, II, III and IV
     B   I, II and IV only
     C   I and II only
     D   I and IV only

7   The essence of systematic sampling is that

     A   Each element of the population has an equal chance of being chosen
     B   Members of various strata are selected by the interviewers up to predetermined limits
     C   Every nth item of the population is selected
     D   Every element of one definable sub-section of the population is selected

ANSWERS TO QUICK QUIZ

1   (a)   Governments   (c)   Newspapers
    (b)   Banks   (d)   Trade journals

2   The user of the information knows where it came from, the circumstances under which it was collected and any limitations or inadequacies in it.

3   **Primary data**   **Secondary data**

    Investigator's survey   Wall Street Journal

    Survey questionnaire   *Annual Abstract of Statistics*

                                        Management Accounting

                                        BPP's website

4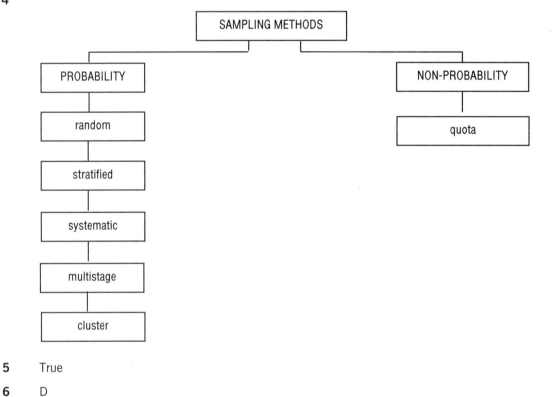

5   True

6   D

7   C

Now try ...

Attempt the questions below from the **Exam Question Bank**

Number

Q5 – Q9

BPP
LEARNING MEDIA

Cost classification

The **classification of costs** as either **direct** or **indirect**, for example, is essential in the costing method used by an organisation to determine the cost of a unit of product or service.

The **fixed** and **variable cost classifications**, on the other hand, are important in **absorption** and **marginal costing**, **cost behaviour** and **cost-volume-profit analysis**. You will meet all of these topics as we progress through the Study Text.

This chapter therefore acts as a foundation stone for a number of other chapters in the text and hence an understanding of the concepts covered in it is vital before you move on.

Study Guide	Intellectual level
A **The nature, source and purpose of management information**	
3 **Cost classification**	
(a) Explain and illustrate production and non-production costs	K
(b) Describe the different elements of non-production costs – administrative, selling, distribution and finance	K
(c) Describe the different elements of production cost – material, labour and overheads	K
(d) Explain the importance of the distinction between production and non-production costs when valuing output and inventories	K
(e) Explain and illustrate with examples classifications used in the analysis of the product/service costs including by function, direct and indirect, fixed and variable, stepped fixed and semi-variable costs	S
(f) Explain and illustrate the use of codes in categorising transaction	K
(j) Explain and illustrate the concept of cost objects, cost units and cost centres	S
(k) Distinguish between cost, profit, investment and revenue centres	K
(l) Describe the differing needs for information of cost, profit, investment and revenue centre managers	K

EXAM FOCUS POINT

Cost classification is one of the key areas of the syllabus and you can therefore expect to see it in the exam that you will be facing.

1 Total product/service costs

The total cost of making a product or providing a service consists of the following.

(a) Cost of **materials**

(b) Cost of the **wages** and **salaries** (labour costs)

(c) Cost of **other expenses**

    (i) Rent and rates

    (ii) Electricity and gas bills

    (iii) Depreciation

2 Direct costs and indirect costs

Technical competences 9 and 10 require you to demonstrate you are competent in recording and analysing data relating to direct and indirect costs. The knowledge you gain in this chapter will help you demonstrate your competence in this area.

2.1 Materials, labour and expenses

A **direct cost** is a cost that can be traced in full to the product, service, or department that is being costed. An **indirect cost** (or **overhead**) is a cost that is incurred in the course of making a product, providing a service or running a department, but which cannot be traced directly and in full to the product, service or department.

Materials, labour costs and other expenses can be classified as either **direct costs** or **indirect costs**.

(a)   **Direct material costs** are the costs of materials that are known to have been used in making and selling a product (or even providing a service).

(b)   **Direct labour costs** are the specific costs of the workforce used to make a product or provide a service. Direct labour costs are established by measuring the time taken for a job, or the time taken in 'direct production work'.

(c)   **Other direct expenses** are those expenses that have been incurred in full as a direct consequence of making a product, or providing a service, or running a department.

Examples of indirect costs include supervisors' wages, cleaning materials and buildings insurance.

2.2 Analysis of total cost

Materials	=	Direct materials	+	Indirect materials
+		+		+
Labour	=	Direct labour	+	Indirect labour
+		+		+
Expenses	=	Direct expenses	+	Indirect expenses
Total cost	=	Direct cost	+	Overhead

2.3 Direct material

Direct material is all material becoming part of the product (unless used in negligible amounts and/or having negligible cost).

Direct material costs are charged to the product as part of the **prime cost**. Examples of direct material are as follows.

(a)   **Component parts**, specially purchased for a particular job, order or process.

(b)   **Part-finished work** which is transferred from department 1 to department 2 becomes finished work of department 1 and a direct material cost in department 2.

(c)   **Primary packing materials** like cartons and boxes.

2.4 Direct labour

Direct wages are all wages paid for labour (either as basic hours or as overtime) expended on work on the product itself.

Direct wages costs are charged to the product as part of the **prime cost**.

Examples of groups of labour receiving payment as direct wages are as follows.

(a)   Workers engaged in **altering** the condition or composition of the product.

(b)   Inspectors, analysts and testers **specifically required** for such production.

(c)   Foremen, shop clerks and anyone else whose wages are **specifically identified.**

Two **trends** may be identified in **direct labour costs.**

- The ratio of direct labour costs to total product cost is falling as the use of machinery increases, and hence depreciation charges increase.

- Skilled labour costs and sub-contractors' costs are increasing as direct labour costs decrease.

QUESTION   Labour costs

Classify the following labour costs as either direct or indirect.

(a)   The basic pay of direct workers (cash paid, tax and other deductions)

(b)   The basic pay of indirect workers

(c)   Overtime premium

(d)   Bonus payments

(e)   Social insurance contributions

(f)   Idle time of direct workers

(g)   Work on installation of equipment

ANSWER

(a)   The basic pay of direct workers is a direct cost to the unit, job or process.

(b)   The basic pay of indirect workers is an indirect cost, unless a customer asks for an order to be carried out which involves the dedicated use of indirect workers' time, when the cost of this time would be a direct labour cost of the order.

(c)   Overtime premium paid to both direct and indirect workers is an indirect cost, except in two particular circumstances.

    (i)   If overtime is worked at the specific request of a customer to get his order completed, the overtime premium paid is a direct cost of the order.

    (ii)   If overtime is worked regularly by a production department in the normal course of operations, the overtime premium paid to direct workers could be incorporated into the (average) direct labour hourly rate.

(d)   Bonus payments are generally an indirect cost.

(e)   Employer's National Insurance contributions (which are added to employees' total pay as a wages cost) are normally treated as an indirect labour cost.

(f)   Idle time is an overhead cost, that is an indirect labour cost.

(g)   The cost of work on capital equipment is incorporated into the capital cost of the equipment.

2.5 Direct expenses

Direct expenses are any expenses which are incurred on a specific product other than direct material cost and direct wages

Direct expenses are charged to the product as part of the **prime** cost. Examples of direct expenses are as follows.

- The **hire of tools** or equipment for a particular job
- **Maintenance costs** of tools, fixtures and so on

Direct expenses are also referred to as **chargeable expenses.**

2.6 Production overhead

Production includes all indirect material costs, indirect wages and indirect expenses incurred in the factory from receipt of the order until its completion.

Production overhead includes the following.

(a) **Indirect materials** which cannot be traced in the finished product.

Consumable stores, eg material used in negligible amounts

(b) **Indirect wages**, meaning all wages not charged directly to a product.

Wages of non-productive personnel in the production department, eg foremen

(c) **Indirect expenses** (other than material and labour) not charged directly to production.

(i) Rent, rates and insurance of a factory
(ii) Depreciation, fuel, power, maintenance of plant, machinery and buildings

2.7 Administration overhead

Administration overhead is all indirect material costs, wages and expenses incurred in the direction, control and administration of an undertaking.

Examples of administration overhead are as follows.

- **Depreciation** of office buildings and equipment.
- **Office salaries**, including salaries of directors, secretaries and accountants.
- Rent, rates, insurance, lighting, cleaning, telephone charges and so on.

2.8 Selling overhead

Selling overhead is all indirect materials costs, wages and expenses incurred in promoting sales and retaining customers.

Examples of selling overhead are as follows.

- **Printing** and **stationery**, such as catalogues and price lists.
- **Salaries** and **commission** of salesmen, representatives and sales department staff.
- **Advertising** and **sales promotion**, market research.
- Rent, rates and insurance of sales offices and showrooms, bad debts and so on.

2.9 Distribution overhead

Distribution overhead is all indirect material costs, wages and expenses incurred in making the packed product ready for despatch and delivering it to the customer.

Examples of distribution overhead are as follows.

- Cost of packing cases.
- Wages of packers, drivers and despatch clerks.
- Insurance charges, rent, rates, depreciation of warehouses and so on.

QUESTION   Direct labour cost

A direct labour employee's wage in week 5 consists of the following.

		$
(a)	Basic pay for normal hours worked, 36 hours at $4 per hour =	144
(b)	Pay at the basic rate for overtime, 6 hours at $4 per hour =	24
(c)	Overtime shift premium, with overtime paid at time-and-a-quarter $\frac{1}{4} \times 6$ hours $\times$ $4 per hour =	6
(d)	A bonus payment under a group bonus (or 'incentive') scheme – bonus for the month =	30
	Total gross wages in week 5 for 42 hours of work	204

What is the direct labour cost for this employee in week 5?

A $144   B $168   C $198   D $204

ANSWER

Let's start by considering a general approach to answering multiple choice questions (MCQs). In a numerical question like this, the best way to begin is to ignore the available options and work out your own answer from the available data. If your solution corresponds to one of the four options then mark this as your chosen answer and move on. Don't waste time working out whether any of the other options might be correct. If your answer does not appear among the available options then check your workings. If it still does not correspond to any of the options then you need to take a calculated guess.

Do not make the common error of simply selecting the answer which is closest to yours. The best thing to do is to first eliminate any answers which you know or suspect are incorrect. For example you could eliminate C and D because you know that group bonus schemes are usually indirect costs. You are then left with a choice between A and B, and at least you have now improved your chances if you really are guessing.

The correct answer is B because the basic rate for overtime is a part of direct wages cost. It is only the overtime premium that is usually regarded as an overhead or indirect cost.

3 Functional costs

3.1 Classification by function

> **Classification by function** involves classifying costs as production/manufacturing costs, administration costs or marketing/selling and distribution costs.

In a 'traditional' costing system for a manufacturing organisation, costs are classified as follows.

(a) **Production** or **manufacturing costs.** These are costs associated with the factory.

(b) **Administration costs.** These are costs associated with general office departments.

(c) **Marketing**, or **selling** and **distribution costs.** These are costs associated with sales, marketing, warehousing and transport departments.

Classification in this way is known as **classification by function**. Expenses that do not fall fully into one of these classifications might be categorised as **general overheads** or even listed as a classification on their own (for example research and development costs).

3.2 Full cost of sales

In costing a small product made by a manufacturing organisation, direct costs are usually restricted to some of the production costs. A commonly found build-up of costs is therefore as follows.

	$
Production costs	
Direct materials	A
Direct wages	B
Direct expenses	C
Prime cost	A+B+C
Production overheads	D
Full factory cost	A+B+C+D
Administration costs	E
Selling and distribution costs	F
Full cost of sales	A+B+C+D+E+F

3.3 Functional costs

(a) **Production costs** are the costs which are incurred by the sequence of operations beginning with the supply of raw materials, and ending with the completion of the product ready for warehousing as a finished goods item. Packaging costs are production costs where they relate to 'primary' packing (boxes, wrappers and so on).

(b) **Administration costs** are the costs of managing an organisation, that is, planning and controlling its operations, but only insofar as such administration costs are not related to the production, sales, distribution or research and development functions.

(c) **Selling costs**, sometimes known as marketing costs, are the costs of creating demand for products and securing firm orders from customers.

(d) **Distribution costs** are the costs of the sequence of operations with the receipt of finished goods from the production department and making them ready for despatch and ending with the reconditioning for reuse of empty containers.

(e) **Research costs** are the costs of searching for new or improved products, whereas **development costs** are the costs incurred between the decision to produce a new or improved product and the commencement of full manufacture of the product.

(f) **Financing costs** are costs incurred to finance the business such as loan interest.

QUESTION

Cost classification

Within the costing system of a manufacturing company the following types of expense are incurred.

Reference number

1	Cost of oils used to lubricate production machinery
2	Motor vehicle licences for lorries
3	Depreciation of factory plant and equipment
4	Cost of chemicals used in the laboratory
5	Commission paid to sales representatives
6	Salary of the secretary to the finance director
7	Trade discount given to customers
8	Holiday pay of machine operatives
9	Salary of security guard in raw material warehouse
10	Fees to advertising agency
11	Rent of finished goods warehouse
12	Salary of scientist in laboratory
13	Insurance of the company's premises
14	Salary of supervisor working in the factory
15	Cost of typewriter ribbons in the general office
16	Protective clothing for machine operatives

Required

Complete the following table by placing each expense in the correct cost classification.

Cost classification	Reference number					
Production costs						
Selling and distribution costs						
Administration costs						
Research and development costs						

Each type of expense should appear only once in your answer. You may use the reference numbers in your answer.

ANSWER

Cost classification	Reference number					
Production costs	1	3	8	9	14	16
Selling and distribution costs	2	5	7	10	11	
Administration costs	6	13	15			
Research and development costs	4	12				

4 Fixed costs and variable costs

A different way of analysing and classifying costs is into **fixed costs** and **variable costs.** Many items of expenditure are part-fixed and part-variable and hence are termed **semi-fixed** or **semi-variable costs.**

A **fixed cost** is a cost which is incurred for a particular period of time and which, within certain activity levels, is unaffected by changes in the level of activity.

A **variable cost** is a cost which tends to vary with the level of activity.

4.1 Examples of fixed and variable costs

(a)   Direct material costs are **variable costs** because they rise as more units of a product are manufactured.

(b)   Sales commission is often a fixed percentage of sales turnover, and so is a **variable cost** that varies with the level of sales.

(c)   Telephone call charges are likely to increase if the volume of business expands, but there is also a fixed element of line rental, and so they are a **semi-fixed** or **semi-variable overhead cost.**

(d)   The rental cost of business premises is a constant amount, at least within a stated time period, and so it is a **fixed cost.**

5 Production and non-production costs

For the preparation of financial statements, costs are often classified as **production costs** and **non-production costs**. Production costs are costs identified with goods produced or purchased for resale. Non-production costs are costs deducted as expenses during the current period.

Production costs are all the costs involved in the manufacture of goods. In the case of manufactured goods, these costs consist of direct material, direct labour and manufacturing overhead.

Non-production costs are taken directly to the income statement as expenses in the period in which they are incurred; such costs consist of selling and administrative expenses.

5.1 Production and non-production costs

The distinction between production and non-production costs is the basis of valuing inventory.

5.2 Example

A business has the following costs for a period:

	$
Materials	600
Labour	1,000
Production overheads	500
Administration overheads	700
	2,800

During the period 100 units are produced. If all of these costs were allocated to production units, each unit would be valued at $28.

This would be incorrect. Only **production** costs are allocated to units of inventory. Administrative overheads are **non-production** costs.

So each unit of inventory should be valued at $21((600 + 1,000 + 500)/100)

This affects both gross profit and the valuation of closing inventory. If during the period 80 units are sold at $40 each, the gross profit will be:

	$
Sales (80 × 40)	3,200
Cost of sales (80 × 21)	(1,680)
Gross profit	1,520

The value of closing (unsold) inventory will be $420 (20 × 21).

6 Cost codes

> Once costs have been classified, a coding system can be applied to make it easier to manage the cost data, both in manual systems and in computerised systems.

Coding is the way in which the classification system that we have been looking at is applied.

Step 1	Costs are classified.

Step 2	Costs are coded.

Each individual cost should be identifiable by its code. This is possible by building up the individual characteristics of the cost into the code.

The characteristics which are normally identified are as follows.

- The **nature** of the cost (materials, labour, overhead), which is known as a **subjective classification**

- The **type** of cost (direct, indirect and so on)

- The **cost centre** to which the cost should be allocated or **cost unit** which should be charged, which is known as an **objective classification**

- The **department** which the particular cost centre is in

6.1 Features of a good coding system

An efficient and effective coding system, whether manual or computerised, should incorporate the following features.

(a)   The code must be **easy to use and communicate**.

(b)   Each item should have a **unique code**.

(c)   The coding system must **allow for expansion**.

(d)   If there is conflict between the ease of using the code by the people involved and its manipulation on a computer, the **human interest should dominate**.

(e)   The code should be **flexible** so that small changes in a cost's classification can be incorporated without major changes to the coding system itself.

(f)   The coding system should provide a **comprehensive** system, whereby every recorded item can be suitably coded.

(g)   The coding system should be **brief**, to save clerical time in writing out codes and to save storage space in computer memory and on computer files. At the same time codes must be **long enough** to allow for the suitable coding of all items.

(h)   The likelihood of **errors** going undetected should be minimised.

(i)   There should be a readily available **index or reference book** of codes.

(j)   Existing codes should be **reviewed** regularly and out-of-date codes removed.

(k)   Code numbers should be **issued from a single central point**. Different people should not be allowed to add new codes to the existing list independently.

(l)   The code should be either **entirely numeric or entirely alphabetic**. In a computerised system, numeric characters are preferable. The use of dots, dashes, colons and so on should be avoided.

(m)   Codes should be **uniform** (that is, have the same length and the same structure) to assist in the detection of missing characters and to facilitate processing.

(n)   The coding system should avoid problems such as confusion between I and 1, O and 0 (zero), S and 5 and so on.

(o)   The coding system should, if possible, be **significant** (in other words, the actual code should signify something about the item being coded).

(p)   If the code consists of alphabetic characters, it should be derived from the item's description or name (that is, **mnemonics** should be used).

6.2 Types of code

6.2.1 Composite codes

The CIMA *Official Terminology* definition of a code describes a composite code.

'For example, in costing, the first three digits in the **composite code** 211.392 might indicate the **nature** of the expenditure (**subjective classification**) and the last three digits might indicate the **cost centre or cost unit to be charged (objective classification).**

So the digits 211 might refer to:

2   Materials
1   Raw materials
1   Timber

This would indicate to anyone familiar with the coding system that the expenditure was incurred on timber.

The digits 392 might refer to:

3   Direct cost
9   Factory alpha
2   Assembly department

This would indicate the expenditure was to be charged as a direct material cost to the assembly department in factory alpha.

6.2.2 Other types of code

Here are some other examples of codes.

(a)   **Sequence (or progressive) codes**

Numbers are given to items in ordinary numerical sequence, so that there is no obvious connection between an item and its code. For example:

000042	4cm nails
000043	Office stapler
000044	Hand wrench

(b)   **Group classification codes**

These are an improvement on simple sequences codes, in that a digit (often the first one) indicates the classification of an item. For example:

4NNNNN	Nails
5NNNNN	Screws
6NNNNN	Bolts

(Note. 'N' stands for another digit; 'NNNNN' indicates there are five further digits in the code.)

(c)   **Faceted codes**

These are a refinement of group classification codes, in that each digit of the code gives information about an item. For example:

(i)   The first digit:

    1   Nails
    2   Screws
    3   Bolts
        etc…

(ii)   The second digit:

    1   Steel
    2   Brass
    3   Copper
        etc…

(iii) The third digit:

    1   50mm
    2   60mm
    3   75mm
        etc…

A 60mm steel screw would have a code of 212.

(d)   **Significant digit codes**

These incorporate some digit(s) which is (are) part of the description of the item being coded. For example:

5000	Screws	5060	60mm screws
5050	50mm screws	5075	75mm screws

(e) **Hierarchical codes**

This is a type of faceted code where each digit represents a classification, and each digit further to the right represents a smaller subset than those to the left. For example:

3	=	Screws	32	=	Round headed screws
31	=	Flat headed screws	322	=	Steel (round headed) screws and so on

A coding system does not have to be structured entirely on any one of the above systems. It can mix the various features according to the items which need to be coded.

6.3 Example: coding systems

Formulate a coding system suitable for computer application for the cost accounts of a small manufacturing company.

Solution

A suggested computer-based four-digit numerical coding system is set out below.

Basic structure	Code number	Allocation
First division	1000-4999	This range provides for cost accounts and is divided into four main departmental sections with ten cost centre subsections in each department, allowing for a maximum of 99 accounts of each cost centre.
Second division	1000-1999	Department 1
	2000-2999	Department 2
	3000-3999	Department 3
	4000-4999	Department 4
Third division	100-999	Facility for ten cost centres in each department
Fourth division		Breakdown of costs in each cost centre
	01-39	Direct costs
	40-59	Variable costs
	60-79	Fixed costs
	80-99	Spare capacity

Codes 5000-9999 could be used for the organisation's financial accounts.

An illustration of the coding of steel screws might be as follows.

Department 2

Cost centre	1	2	3	4
Consumable stores	2109	2209	2309	2409

The four-digit codes above indicate the following.

- The first digit, 2, refers to the department.
- The second digit, 1, 2, 3 or 4, refers to the cost centre which incurred the cost.
- The last two digits, 09, refer to 'materials costs, steel screws'.

6.4 The advantages of a coding system

(a) A code is usually **briefer** than a description, thereby saving clerical time in a manual system and storage space in a computerised system.

(b) A code is **more precise** than a description and therefore **reduces ambiguity**.

(c) Coding **facilitates data processing**.

7 Cost units, cost objects and responsibility centres

7.1 Cost centres

> **Cost centres** are collecting places for costs before they are further analysed. Costs are further analysed into cost units once they have been traced to cost centres.

Costs consist of the costs of the following.

- Direct materials
- Direct labour
- Direct expenses
- Production overheads
- Administration overheads
- General overheads

When costs are incurred, they are generally allocated to a **cost centre**. Cost centres may include the following.

- A department

- A machine, or group of machines

- A project (eg the installation of a new computer system)

- Overhead costs eg rent, rates, electricity (which may then be allocated to departments or projects)

Cost centres are an essential 'building block' of a costing system. They are the starting point for the following.

(a) The classification of actual costs incurred.
(b) The preparation of budgets of planned costs.
(c) The comparison of actual costs and budgeted costs (management control).

7.2 Cost units

> A **cost unit** is a unit of product or service to which costs can be related. The cost unit is the basic control unit for costing purposes.

Once costs have been traced to cost centres, they can be further analysed in order to establish a **cost per cost unit**. Alternatively, some items of cost may be charged directly to a cost unit, for example direct materials and direct labour costs.

Examples of cost units include the following.

- Patient episode (in a hospital)
- Barrel (in the brewing industry)
- Room (in a hotel)

QUESTION   Cost units

Suggest suitable cost units which could be used to aid control within the following organisations.

(a) A hotel with 50 double rooms and 10 single rooms
(b) A hospital
(c) A road haulage business

ANSWER

(a)	Guest/night	(b)	Patient/night	(c)	Tonne/mile
	Bed occupied/night		Operation		Mile
	Meal supplied		Outpatient visit		

7.3 Cost objects

A **cost object** is any activity for which a separate measurement of costs is desired.

If the users of management information wish to know the cost of something, this something is called a **cost object**. Examples include the following.

- The cost of a product
- The cost of a service
- The cost of operating a department

7.4 Profit centres

Profit centres are similar to cost centres but are accountable for both **costs** *and* **revenues**.

We have seen that a cost centre is where costs are collected. Some organisations, however, work on a profit centre basis.

Profit centre managers should normally have control over how revenue is raised and how costs are incurred. Often, several cost centres will comprise one profit centre. The profit centre manager will be able to make decisions about both purchasing and selling and will be expected to do both as profitably as possible.

A profit centre manager will want information regarding both revenues and costs. He will be judged on the profit margin achieved by his division. In practice, it may be that there are fixed costs which he cannot control, so he should be judged on contribution, which is revenue less variable costs. In this case he will want information about which products yield the highest contribution.

7.5 Revenue centres

Revenue centres are similar to cost centres and profit centres but are accountable for **revenues only**.

Revenue centre managers should normally have control over how revenues are raised

A revenue centre manager is not accountable for costs. He will be aiming purely to maximise sales revenue. He will want information on markets and new products and he will look closely at pricing and the sales performance of competitors – in addition to monitoring revenue figures.

7.6 Investment centres

An **investment centre** is a profit centre with additional responsibilities for capital investment and possibly for financing, and whose performance is measured by its return on investment.

An investment centre manager will take the same decisions as a profit centre manager but he also has additional responsibility for investment. So he will be judged additionally on his handling of cash surpluses and he will seek to make only those investments which yield a higher percentage than the company's notional cost of capital. So the investment centre manager will want the same information as the profit centre manager and in addition he will require quite detailed appraisals of possible investments and information regarding the results of investments already undertaken. He will have to make decisions regarding the purchase or lease of non-current assets and the investment of cash surpluses. Most of these decisions involve large sums of money.

7.7 Responsibility centres

A **responsibility centre** is a department or organisational function whose performance is the direct responsibility of a specific manager.

Cost centres, revenue centres, profit centres and investment centres are also known as **responsibility centres**.

QUESTION

Investment centre

Which of the following is a characteristic of an investment centre?

A   Managers have control over marketing.
B   Management have a sales team.
C   Management have a sales team and are given a credit control function.
D   Managers can purchase capital assets.

ANSWER

The correct answer is D.

EXAM FOCUS POINT

This chapter has introduced a number of new terms and definitions. The topics covered in this chapter are key areas of the syllabus and are likely to be tested in the exam.

CHAPTER ROUNDUP

⤷ A **direct cost** is a cost that can be traced in full to the product, service or department being costed. An **indirect cost** (or overhead) is a cost that is incurred in the course of making a product, providing a service or running a department, but which cannot be traced directly and in full to the product, service or department.

⤷ **Classification by function** involves classifying costs as production/manufacturing costs, administration costs or marketing/selling and distribution costs.

⤷ A different way of analysing and classifying costs is into **fixed costs** and **variable costs**. Many items of expenditure are part-fixed and part-variable and hence are termed **semi-fixed** or **semi-variable** costs.

⤷ For the preparation of financial statements, costs are often classified as **production costs** and **non-production costs**. Production costs are costs identified with goods produced or purchased for resale. Non-production costs are costs deducted as expenses during the current period.

⤷ Once costs have been classified, a coding system can be applied to make it easier to manage the cost data, both in manual systems and in computerised systems.

⤷ **Cost centres** are collecting places for costs before they are further analysed. Costs are further analysed into cost units once they have been traced to cost centres.

⤷ A **cost unit** is a unit of product or service to which costs can be related. The cost unit is the basic control unit for costing purposes.

⤷ A **cost object** is any activity for which a separate measurement of costs is desired.

⤷ **Profit centres** are similar to cost centres but are accountable for both **costs** *and* **revenues**.

⤷ **Revenue centres** are similar to cost centres and profit centres but are accountable for **revenues only**. Revenue centre managers should normally have control over how revenues are raised.

⤷ An **investment centre** is a profit centre with additional responsibilities for capital investment and possibly for financing, and whose performance is measured by its return on investment.

⤷ A **responsibility centre** is a department or organisational function whose performance is the direct responsibility of a specific manager.

QUICK QUIZ

1   Give two examples of direct expenses.

2   Give an example of an administration overhead, a selling overhead and a distribution overhead.

3   What are functional costs?

4   What is the distinction between fixed and variable costs?

5   What are production costs and non-production costs?

6   What is a cost centre?

7   What is a cost unit?

8   What is a profit centre?

9   What is an investment centre?

BPP LEARNING MEDIA

ANSWERS TO QUICK QUIZ

1
- The hire of tools or equipment for a particular job
- Specific costs of the workforce used to make a product

2
- **Administration overhead** = Depreciation of office buildings and equipment
- **Selling overhead** = Printing and stationery (catalogues, price lists)
- **Distribution overhead** = Wages of packers, drivers and despatch clerks

3   Functional costs are classified as follows.

- **Production** or **manufacturing costs**
- **Administration costs**
- **Marketing** or **selling and distribution costs**

4   A **fixed cost** is a cost which is incurred for a particular period of time and which, within certain activity levels, is unaffected by changes in the level of activity.

A **variable cost** is a cost which tends to vary with the level of activity.

5   **Production costs** are costs identified with a finished product. Such costs are initially identified as part of the value of inventory. They become expenses only when the inventory is sold.

Non-production costs are costs that are deducted as expenses during the current period without ever being included in the value of inventory held.

6   A **cost centre** acts as a collecting place for certain costs before they are analysed further.

7   A **cost unit** is a unit of product or service to which costs can be related. The cost unit is the basic control unit for costing purposes.

8   A **profit centre** is similar to a cost centre but is accountable for **costs** and **revenues**.

9   An **investment centre** is a profit centre with additional responsibilities for capital investment and possibly financing.

Now try ...

Attempt the questions below from the **Exam Question Bank**

Number

Q10- Q14

Cost behaviour

So far in this text we have introduced you to the subject of management information and explained in general terms what it is and what it does. In Chapter 3 we considered the principal methods of classifying costs. In particular, we introduced the concept of the division of costs into those that vary directly with changes in activity levels (**variable costs**) and those that do not (**fixed costs**). This chapter examines further this two-way split of **cost behaviour** and explains one method of splitting semi-variable costs into these two elements, the **high-low** method.

TOPIC LIST	SYLLABUS REFERENCE
1 Introduction to cost behaviour	A3 (e)
2 Cost behaviour patterns	A3 (e), (g)
3 Determining the fixed and variable elements of semi-variable costs	A3 (h)
4 Linear equations	A3 (i)
5 Linear equations and graphs	A3 (i)

Study Guide	Intellectual level
A	**The nature, source and purpose of management information**	
3	**Cost classification**	
(e)	Explain and illustrate with examples classifications used in the analysis of the product/service costs including by function, direct and indirect, fixed and variable, stepped fixed and semi variable costs	S
(g)	Describe and illustrate graphically different types of cost behaviour	S
(h)	Use high-low analysis to separate the fixed and variable elements of total costs including situations involving semi variable and stepped fixed costs and changes in the variable cost per unit	S
(i)	Explain the structure of linear functions and equations	S

EXAM FOCUS POINT

Cost behaviour is a key area of the **Management Accounting** syllabus and you need to understand fixed and variable elements and the use of high-low analysis.

1 Introduction to cost behaviour

1.1 Cost behaviour and decision-making

Cost behaviour is the way in which costs are affected by changes in the volume of output.

Management decisions will often be based on how costs and revenues vary at different activity levels. Examples of such decisions are as follows.

- What should the **planned activity level** be for the next period?
- Should the **selling price** be reduced in order to sell more units?
- Should a particular component be **manufactured internally** or **bought in**?
- Should a **contract** be undertaken?

1.2 Cost behaviour and cost control

If the accountant does not know the level of costs which should have been incurred as a result of an organisation's activities, how can he or she hope to control costs?

1.3 Cost behaviour and budgeting

Knowledge of cost behaviour is obviously essential for the tasks of **budgeting**, **decision making** and **control accounting**.

EXAM FOCUS POINT

Remember that the behavioural analysis of costs is important for planning, control and decision-making.

1.4 Cost behaviour and levels of activity

There are many factors which may influence costs. The major influence is **volume of output**, or the **level of activity**. The level of activity may refer to one of the following.

- Number of units produced
- Value of items sold
- Number of items sold
- Number of invoices issued
- Number of units of electricity consumed

1.5 Cost behaviour principles

The basic principle of cost behaviour is that **as the level of activity rises, costs will usually rise**. It will cost more to produce 2,000 units of output than it will cost to produce 1,000 units.

This principle is common sense. The problem for the accountant, however, is to determine, for each item of cost, the way in which costs rise and by how much as the level of activity increases. For our purposes here, the level of activity for measuring cost will generally be taken to be the **volume of production**.

1.6 Example: cost behaviour and activity level

Hans Bratch has a fleet of company cars for sales representatives. Running costs have been estimated as follows.

(a) Cars cost $12,000 when new, and have a guaranteed trade-in value of $6,000 at the end of two years. Depreciation is charged on a straight-line basis.

(b) Petrol and oil cost 15 cents per mile.

(c) Tyres cost $300 per set to replace; replacement occurs after 30,000 miles.

(d) Routine maintenance costs $200 per car (on average) in the first year and $450 in the second year.

(e) Repairs average $400 per car over two years and are thought to vary with mileage. The average car travels 25,000 miles per annum.

(f) Tax, insurance, membership of motoring organisations and so on cost $400 per annum per car.

Required

Calculate the average cost per annum of cars which travel 15,000 miles per annum and 30,000 miles per annum.

Solution

Costs may be analysed into fixed, variable and stepped cost items, a stepped cost being a cost which is fixed in nature but only within certain levels of activity.

(a) **Fixed costs**

	$ per annum
Depreciation $(12,000 – 6,000) ÷ 2	3,000
Routine maintenance $(200 + 450) ÷ 2	325
Tax, insurance etc	400
	3,725

(b) **Variable costs**

	Cents per mile
Petrol and oil	15.0
Repairs ($400 ÷ 50,000 miles)*	0.8
	15.8

* If the average car travels 25,000 miles per annum, it will be expected to travel 50,000 miles over two years (this will correspond with the repair bill of $400 over two years).

(c)   Step costs are tyre replacement costs, which are $300 at the end of every 30,000 miles.

(i)   If the car travels less than or exactly 30,000 miles in two years, the tyres will not be changed. Average cost of tyres per annum = $0.

(ii)   If a car travels more than 30,000 miles and up to (and including) 60,000 miles in two years, there will be one change of tyres in the period. Average cost of tyres per annum = $150 ($300 ÷ 2).

(iii)   If a car exceeds 60,000 miles in two years (up to 90,000 miles) there will be two tyre changes. Average cost of tyres per annum = $300 ($600 ÷ 2).

The estimated costs per annum of cars travelling 15,000 miles per annum and 30,000 miles per annum would therefore be as follows.

	15,000 miles per annum $	30,000 miles per annum $
Fixed costs	3,725	3,725
Variable costs (15.8c per mile)	2,370	4,740
Tyres	–	150
Cost per annum	6,095	8,615

2 Cost behaviour patterns

2.1 Fixed costs

A **fixed cost** is a cost which tends to be unaffected by increases or decreases in the volume of output.

Fixed costs are a **period charge**, in that they relate to a span of time; as the time span increases, so too will the fixed costs (which are sometimes referred to as period costs for this reason). It is important to understand that **fixed costs always have a variable element**, since an increase or decrease in production may also bring about an increase or decrease in fixed costs.

A sketch graph of fixed cost would look like this.

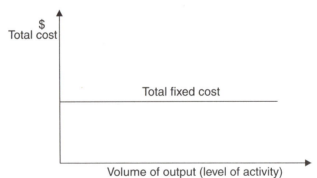

Examples of a fixed cost would be as follows.

- The salary of the managing director (per month or per annum)
- The rent of a single factory building (per month or per annum)
- Straight line depreciation of a single machine (per month or per annum)

2.2 Step costs

A **step cost** is a cost which is fixed in nature but only within certain levels of activity.

Consider the depreciation of a machine which may be fixed if production remains below 1,000 units per month. If production exceeds 1,000 units, a second machine may be required, and the cost of depreciation (on two machines) would go up a step. A sketch graph of a step cost could look like this.

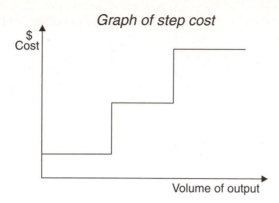

Graph of step cost

Other examples of step costs are as follows.

(a)   Rent is a step cost in situations where accommodation requirements increase as output levels get higher.

(b)   Basic pay of employees is nowadays usually fixed, but as output rises, more employees (direct workers, supervisors, managers and so on) are required.

(c)   Royalties.

2.3 Variable costs

A **variable cost** is a cost which tends to vary directly with the volume of output. The variable cost per unit is the same amount for each unit produced.

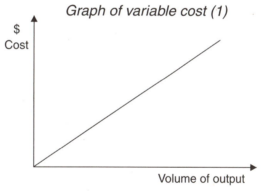

Graph of variable cost (1)

A constant variable cost per unit implies that the price per unit of say, material purchased is constant, and that the rate of material usage is also constant.

(a)   The most important variable cost is the **cost of raw materials** (where there is no discount for bulk purchasing since bulk purchase discounts reduce the cost of purchases).

(b)   **Direct labour costs** are, for very important reasons, classed as a variable cost even though basic wages are usually fixed.

(c)   **Sales commission** is variable in relation to the volume or value of sales.

(d)   **Bonus payments** for productivity to employees might be variable once a certain level of output is achieved, as the following diagram illustrates.

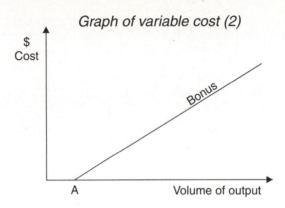

Graph of variable cost (2)

Up to output A, no bonus is earned.

Imagine if, up to a given level of activity, the purchase price per unit of raw material is constant. After that point, a quantity discount is given so the price per unit is lower for further purchases and also retrospectively to all units already purchased. The graph would be as follows.

Graph of variable cost (3)

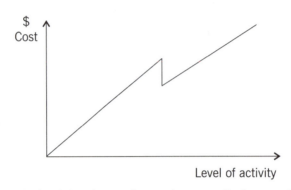

Imagine if, up to a given level of activity, the purchase price per unit of raw material is constant. After that point, a discount is given so that the price per unit is lower for further purchases but not for the units already purchased. The graph would be as follows.

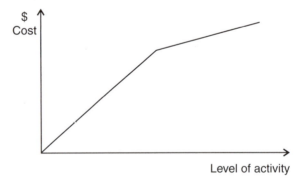

2.4 Non-linear or curvilinear variable costs

If the relationship between total variable cost and volume of output can be shown as a curved line on a graph, the relationship is said to be **curvilinear**.

Two typical relationships are as follows.

(a)

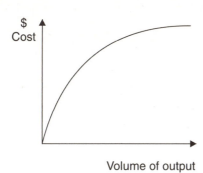

Volume of output

(b)

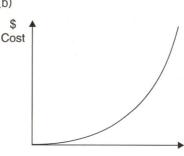

Volume of output

Each extra unit of output in graph (a) causes a **less than proportionate** increase in cost whereas in graph (b), each extra unit of output causes **a more than proportionate** increase in cost.

The cost of a piecework scheme for individual workers with differential rates could behave in a **curvilinear** fashion if the rates increase by small amounts at progressively higher output levels.

2.5 Semi-variable costs (or semi-fixed costs or mixed costs)

A **semi-variable/semi-fixed/mixed cost** is a cost which contains both fixed and variable components and so is partly affected by changes in the level of activity.

Examples of these costs include the following.

(a) **Electricity and gas bills**

    (i)   Fixed cost = standing charge
    (ii)   Variable cost = charge per unit of electricity used

(b) **Salesman's salary**

    (i)   Fixed cost = basic salary
    (ii)   Variable cost = commission on sales made

(c) **Costs of running a car**

    (i)   Fixed cost = road tax, insurance
    (ii)   Variable costs = petrol, oil, repairs (which vary with miles travelled)

2.6 Other cost behaviour patterns

Other cost behaviour patterns may be appropriate to certain cost items. Examples of two other cost behaviour patterns are shown below.

(a) *Cost behaviour pattern (1)*

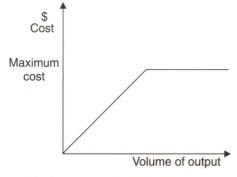

(b) *Cost behaviour pattern (2)*

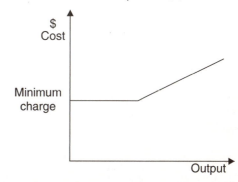

- Graph (a) represents an item of cost which is variable with output up to a certain maximum level of cost.

- Graph (b) represents a cost which is variable with output, subject to a minimum (fixed) charge.

2.7 Cost behaviour and cost per unit

The following table relates to different levels of production of the zed. The variable cost of producing a zed is $5. Fixed costs are $5,000.

	1 zed $	10 zeds $	50 zeds $
Total variable cost	5	50	250
Variable cost per unit	5	5	5
Total fixed cost	5,000	5,000	5,000
Fixed cost per unit	5,000	500	100
Total cost (fixed and variable)	5,005	5,050	5,250
Total cost per unit	5,005	505	105

What happens when activity levels rise can be summarised as follows.

- The variable cost per unit remains constant
- The fixed cost per unit falls
- The total cost per unit falls

This may be illustrated graphically as follows.

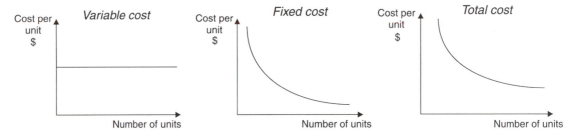

QUESTION

Fixed, variable, mixed costs

Are the following likely to be fixed, variable or mixed costs?

(a)   Telephone bill
(b)   Annual salary of the chief accountant
(c)   The management accountant's annual membership fee to ACCA (paid by the company)
(d)   Cost of materials used to pack 20 units of product X into a box
(e)   Wages of warehousemen

ANSWER

(a)   Mixed
(b)   Fixed
(c)   Fixed
(d)   Variable
(e)   Variable

EXAM FOCUS POINT

An exam question may give you a graph and require you to extract information from it.

2.8 Assumptions about cost behaviour

Assumptions about cost behaviour include the following.

(a)   Within the normal or **relevant range** of output, costs are often assumed to be either **fixed**, **variable** or **semi-variable** (mixed).

(b)   Departmental costs within an organisation are assumed to be **mixed costs**, with a **fixed** and a **variable** element.

(c)   Departmental costs are assumed to rise in a straight line as the volume of activity increases. In other words, these costs are said to be **linear**.

The **high-low method** of determining fixed and variable elements of mixed costs relies on the assumption that mixed costs are linear. We shall now go on to look at this method of cost determination.

3 Determining the fixed and variable elements of semi-variable costs

3.1 Analysing costs

> The fixed and variable elements of semi-variable costs can be determined by the **high-low method**.

It is generally assumed that costs are one of the following.

- Variable
- Fixed
- Semi-variable

Cost accountants tend to separate semi-variable costs into their variable and fixed elements. They therefore generally tend to treat costs as either **fixed** or **variable**.

There are several methods for identifying the fixed and variable elements of semi-variable costs. Each method is only an estimate, and each will produce different results. One of the principal methods is the **high-low method.**

3.2 High-low method

Follow the steps below to estimate the fixed and variable elements of semi-variable costs.

Step 1	Review records of costs in previous periods.
	• Select the period with the **highest** activity level.
	• Select the period with the **lowest** activity level.

Step 2	Determine the following.
	• Total cost at high activity level
	• Total cost at low activity level
	• Total units at high activity level
	• Total units at low activity level

Step 3	Calculate the following.
	$$\frac{\text{Total cost at high activity level} - \text{total cost at low activity level}}{\text{Total units at high activity level} - \text{total units at low activity level}}$$
	= variable cost per unit (v)

Step 4	The fixed costs can be determined as follows. (Total cost at high activity level) −(total units at high activity level × variable cost per unit)

The following graph demonstrates the high-low method.

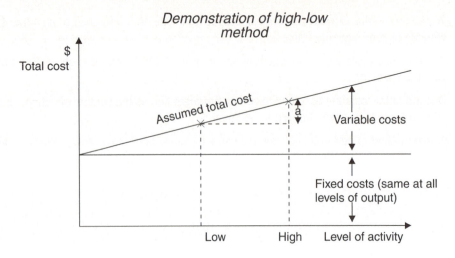

Demonstration of high-low method

3.3 Example: The high-low method

DG Co has recorded the following total costs during the last five years.

Year	Output volume Units	Total cost $
20X0	65,000	145,000
20X1	80,000	162,000
20X2	90,000	170,000
20X3	60,000	140,000
20X4	75,000	160,000

Required

Calculate the total cost that should be expected in 20X5 if output is 85,000 units.

Solution

Step 1
- Period with highest activity = 20X2
- Period with lowest activity = 20X3

Step 2
- Total cost at high activity level = 170,000
- Total cost at low activity level = 140,000
- Total units at high activity level = 90,000
- Total units at low activity level = 60,000

Step 3   Variable cost per unit

$$= \frac{\text{total cost at high activity level} - \text{total cost at low activity level}}{\text{total units at high activity level} - \text{total units at low activity level}}$$

$$= \frac{170,000 - 140,000}{90,000 - 60,000} = \frac{30,000}{30,000} = \$1 \text{ per unit}$$

Step 4   Fixed costs = (total cost at high activity level) – (total units at high activity level × variable cost per unit)

= 170,000 – (90,000 × 1) = 170,000 – 90,000 = $80,000

Therefore the costs in 20X5 for output of 85,000 units are as follows.

		$
Variable costs = 85,000 × $1		85,000
Fixed costs		80,000
		165,000

EXAM FOCUS POINT

Remember that the high-low method refers to the highest and lowest volume and not the highest and lowest cost.

3.4 Example: The high-low method with stepped fixed costs

The following data relate to the overhead expenditure of contract cleaners (for industrial cleaning) at two activity levels.

Square metres cleaned	12,750	15,100
Overheads	$73,950	$83,585

When more than 14,000 square metres are industrially cleaned, there will be a step up in fixed costs of $4,700.

Required

Calculate the estimated total cost if 14,500 square metres are to be industrially cleaned.

Solution

Before we can compare high output costs with low output costs in the normal way, we must eliminate the part of the high output costs that are due to the step up in fixed costs:

Total cost for 15,100 without step up in fixed costs = $83,585 – $4,700 = $78,885

We can now proceed in the normal way using the revised cost above.

	Units			$
High output	15,100	Total cost		78,885
Low output	12,750	Total cost		73,950
	2,350			4,935

$$\text{Variable cost} = \frac{\$4,935}{2,350}$$

$$= \$2.10 \text{ per square metre}$$

Before we can calculate the total cost for 14,500 square metres we need to find the fixed costs. As the fixed costs for 14,500 square metres will include the step up of $4,700, we can use the activity level of 15,100 square metres for the fixed cost calculation:

	$
Total cost (15,100 square metres) (this includes the step up in fixed costs)	83,585
Total variable costs (15,100 x $2.10)	31,710
Total fixed costs	51,875

Estimated overhead expenditure if 14,500 square metres are to be industrially cleaned:

	$
Fixed costs	51,875
Variable costs (14,500 × $2.10)	30,450
	82,325

3.5 Example: The high-low method with a change in the variable cost per unit

Same data as the previous question.

Additionally, a round of wage negotiations have just taken place which will cost an additional $1 per square metre.

Solution

Estimated overheads to clean 14,500 square metres.

	Per square metre $
Variable cost	2.10
Additional variable cost	1.00
Total variable cost	3.10

Cost for 14,500 square metres:

	$
Fixed	51,875
Variable costs (14,500 × $3.10)	44,950
	96,825

QUESTION

High-low method

The Valuation Department of a large firm of surveyors wishes to develop a method of predicting its total costs in a period. The following past costs have been recorded at two activity levels.

	Number of valuations (V)	Total cost (TC)
Period 1	420	82,200
Period 2	515	90,275

The total cost model for a period could be represented as follows.

A	TC = $46,500 + 85V	C	TC = $46,500 – 85V
B	TC = $42,000 + 95V	D	IC = $51,500 – 95V

ANSWER

The correct answer is A.

	Valuations V	Total cost $
Period 2	515	90,275
Period 1	420	82,200
Change due to variable cost	95	8,075

∴ Variable cost per valuation = $8,075/95 = $85.

Period 2: fixed cost = $90,275 – (515 × $85)
= $46,500

Using good MCQ technique, you should have managed to eliminate C and D as incorrect options straightaway. The variable cost must be added to the fixed cost, rather than subtracted from it. Once you had calculated the variable cost as $85 per valuation (as shown above), you should have been able

to select option A without going on to calculate the fixed cost (we have shown this calculation above for completeness).

4 Linear equations

4.1 Introduction

A linear equation is a straight line and has the general form y = a + bx

A linear equation has the general form y = a + bx

where

y   is the dependent variable whose value depends upon the value of x;

x   is the independent variable whose value helps to determine the corresponding value of y;

a   is a constant, that is, a fixed amount;

b   is also a constant, being the coefficient of x (that is, the number by which the value of x should be multiplied to derive the value of y).

Let us establish some basic linear equations. Suppose that it takes Joe Bloggs 15 minutes to walk one mile. How long does it take Joe to walk two miles? Obviously it takes him 30 minutes. How did you calculate the time? You probably thought that if the distance is doubled then the time must be doubled. How do you explain (in words) the relationships between the distance walked and the time taken? One explanation would be that every mile walked takes 15 minutes.

That is an explanation in words. Can you explain the relationship with an equation?

First you must decide which is the dependent variable and which is the independent variable. In other words, does the time taken depend on the number of miles walked or does the number of miles walked depend on the time it takes to walk a mile? Obviously the time depends on the distance. We can therefore let y be the dependent variable (time taken in minutes) and x be the independent variable (distance walked in miles).

We now need to determine the constants a and b. There is no fixed amount so a = 0. To ascertain b, we need to establish the number of times by which the value of x should be multiplied to derive the value of y. Obviously y = 15x where y is in minutes. If y were in hours then y = $^{x}/_{4}$.

4.2 Example: Deriving a linear equation

A salesman's weekly wage is made up of a basic weekly wage of $100 and commission of $5 for every item he sells. Derive an equation which describes this scenario.

Solution

$$
\begin{aligned}
x &= \text{number of items sold} \\
y &= \text{weekly wage} \\
a &= \$100 \\
b &= \$5 \\
\therefore \quad y &= 5x + 100
\end{aligned}
$$

Note that the letters used in an equation do not have to be x and y. It may be sensible to use other letters, for example we could use p and q if we are describing the relationship between the price of an item and the quantity demanded.

5 Linear equations and graphs

5.1 The rules for drawing graphs

One of the clearest ways of presenting the relationship between two variables is by plotting a linear equation as a straight line on a graph.

A graph has a horizontal axis, the x axis and a vertical axis, the y axis. The x axis is used to represent the independent variable and the y axis is used to represent the dependent variable.

If calendar time is one variable, it is always treated as the independent variable. When time is represented on the x axis of a graph, we have a time series.

(a) If the data to be plotted are derived from calculations, rather than given in the question, make sure that there is a neat table in your working papers.

(b) The scales on each axis should be selected so as to use as much of the graph paper as possible. Do not cramp a graph into one corner.

(c) In some cases it is best not to start a scale at zero so as to avoid having a large area of wasted paper. This is perfectly acceptable as long as the scale adopted is clearly shown on the axis. One way of avoiding confusion is to break the axis concerned, as follows.

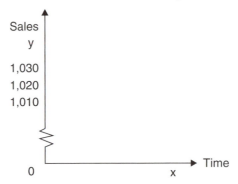

(d) The scales on the x axis and the y axis should be marked. For example, if the y axis relates to amounts of money, the axis should be marked at every $1, or $100 or $1,000 interval or at whatever other interval is appropriate. The axes must be marked with values to give the reader an idea of how big the values on the graph are.

(e) A graph should not be overcrowded with too many lines. Graphs should always give a clear, neat impression.

(f) A graph must always be given a title, and where appropriate, a reference should be made to the source of data.

5.2 Example: Drawing graphs

Plot the graphs for the following relationships.

(a) $y = 4x + 5$
(b) $y = 10 - x$

In each case consider the range of values from x = 0 to x = 10

Solution

The first step is to draw up a table for each equation. Although the problem mentions x = 0 to x = 10, it is not necessary to calculate values of y for x = 1, 2, 3 etc. A graph of a linear equation can actually be drawn from just two (x, y) values but it is always best to calculate a number of values in case you make an arithmetical error. We have calculated six values. You could settle for three or four.

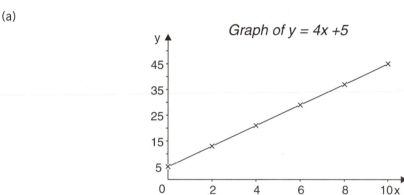

	(a)			*(b)*	
x		y	x		y
0		5	0		10
2		13	2		8
4		21	4		6
6		29	6		4
8		37	8		2
10		45	10		0

(a)

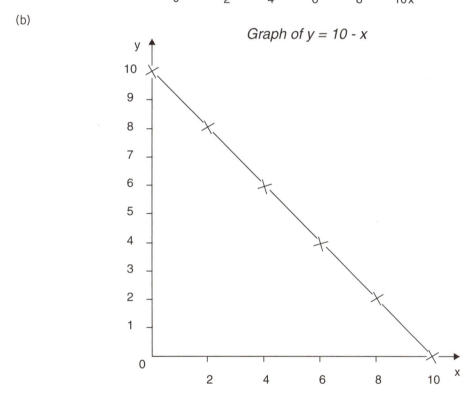

(b)

5.3 The intercept and the slope

The graph of a linear equation is determined by two things, the gradient (or slope) of the straight line and the point at which the straight line crosses the y axis.

The point at which the straight line crosses the y axis is known as the intercept. Look back at Paragraph 5.2(a). The intercept of y = 4x + 5 is (0, 5) and the intercept of y = 10 – x is (0, 10). It is no coincidence that the intercept is the same as the constant represented by a in the general form of the equation y = a + bx. a is the value y takes when x = 0, in other words a constant, and so is represented on a graph by the point (0, a).

The gradient of the graph of a linear equation is $(y_2 - y_1)/(x_2 - x_1)$ where (x_1, y_1) and (x_1, x_2) are two points on the straight line.

The slope of y = 4x + 5 = (21 – 13)/(4–2) = 8/2 = 4 where $(x_1, y_1) = (2, 13)$ and $(x_2, y_2) = (4,21)$

The slope of $y = 10 - x = (6 - 8)/(4 - 2) = -2/2 = -1$.

Note that the gradient of $y = 4x + 5$ is positive whereas the gradient of $y = 10 - x$ is negative. A positive gradient slopes upwards from left to right whereas a negative gradient slopes downwards from right to left. The greater the value of the gradient, the steeper the slope.

Just as the intercept can be found by inspection of the linear equation, so can the gradient. It is represented by the coefficient of x (b in the general form of the equation). The slope of the graph $y = 7x - 3$ in therefore 7 and the slope of the graph $y = 3,597 - 263 x$ is -263.

5.4 Example: intercept and slope

Find the intercept and slope of the graphs of the following linear equations.

(a) $y = \dfrac{x}{10} - \dfrac{1}{3}$

(b) $4y = 16x - 12$

Solution

(a)   Intercept $= a = -\dfrac{1}{3}$ ie $(0, -\dfrac{1}{3})$

Slope $= b = \dfrac{1}{10}$

(b) $4y = 16x - 12$

Equation must be form $y = a + bx$

$y = -\dfrac{12}{4} + \dfrac{16}{4} x = -3 + 4x$

Intercept $= a = -3$ ie $(0, -3)$

Slope $= 4$

CHAPTER ROUNDUP

- **Cost behaviour** is the way in which costs are affected by changes in the volume of output.

- The basic principle of cost behaviour is that **as the level of activity rises, costs will usually rise**. It will cost more to produce 2,000 units of output than it will to produce 1,000 units.

- A **fixed cost** is a cost which tends to be unaffected by increases or decreases in the volume of output.

- A **step cost** is a cost which is fixed in nature but only within certain levels of activity.

- A **variable cost** is a cost which tends to vary directly with the volume of output. The variable cost per unit is the same amount for each unit produced.

- If the relationship between total variable cost and volume of output can be shown as a curved line on a graph, the relationship is said to be **curvilinear**.

- A **semi-variable/semi-fixed/mixed cost** is a cost which contains both fixed and variable components and so is partly affected by changes in the level of activity.

- The fixed and variable elements of semi-variable costs can be determined by the **high-low method**.

- A linear equation is a straight line and has the general form $y = a + bx$

  where

- y is the dependent variable whose value depends upon the value of x

- x is the independent variable whose value helps to determine the corresponding value of y

- a is a constant, that is, a fixed amount

- b is also a constant, being the coefficient of x (that is, the number by which the value of x should be multiplied to derive the value of y)

QUICK QUIZ

1   Cost behaviour is ....

2   The basic principle of cost behaviour is that as the level of activity rises, costs will usually rise/fall.

3   Fill in the gaps for each of the graph titles below.

(a)

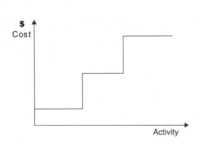

Graph of a ....cost

Example:

(b)

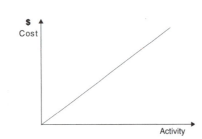

Graph of a ....cost

Example:

(c)

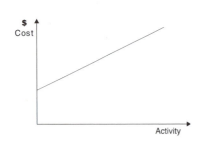

Graph of a ....cost

Example:

(d)

Graph of a ....cost

Example:

4   Costs are assumed to be either fixed, variable or semi-variable within the normal or relevant range of output.

True   ☐

False   ☐

5   The costs of operating the canteen at 'Eat a lot Company' for the past three months is as follows.

Month	Cost $	Employees
1	72,500	1,250
2	75,000	1,300
3	68,750	1,175

Calculate

(a)   Variable cost (per employee per month)
(b)   Fixed cost per month

ANSWERS TO QUICK QUIZ

1   The variability of input costs with activity undertaken.

2   Rise

3   (a)   Step cost. Example: rent, supervisors' salaries
      (b)   Variable cost. Example: raw materials, direct labour
      (c)   Semi-variable cost. Example: electricity and telephone
      (d)   Fixed. Example: rent, depreciation (straight-line)

4   True

5   (a)   Variable cost = $50 per employee per month
      (b)   Fixed costs = $10,000 per month

	Activity	Cost $
High	1,300	75,000
Low	1,175	68,750
	125	6,250

Variable cost per employee = $6,250/125 = $50

For 1,175 employees, total cost = $68,750

Total cost	= variable cost + fixed cost
$68,750	= (1,175 × $50) + fixed cost

∴ Fixed cost   = $68,750 – $58,750
                 = $10,000

Now try ...

Attempt the questions below from the **Exam Question Bank**

Number

Q15 – Q19

BPP
LEARNING MEDIA

In this chapter we will look at how the management accountant might present management information. Your syllabus requires you to prepare reports, graphs and tables but this is very difficult to examine in a computer based exam. The focus, therefore, should be on **interpreting reports** and understanding what **format** would be suitable depending on the purpose of the report.

Presenting information

TOPIC LIST	SYLLABUS REFERENCE
1 Presenting, disseminating and interpreting information	A4 (a)
2 Written reports	A4 (a)
3 Planning a report	A4 (a)
4 The format of reports	A4 (a)
5 Presenting and interpreting information in tables	A4 (b), (c)
6 Presenting and interpreting information in charts	A4 (b), (c)

Study Guide	Intellectual level
A **The nature, source and purpose of management information**	
4 **Presenting information**	
(a) Prepare written reports representing management information in suitable formats according to purpose	S
(b) Present information using tables, charts and graphs (bar charts, line graphs, pie charts and scatter graphs)	S
(c) Interpret information (including the above tables, charts and graphs) presented in management reports	S

1 Presenting, disseminating and interpreting information

As we saw in Chapter 1, the management accountant is involved in the **presentation**, **dissemination** and **interpretation** of information. In this chapter we will be looking at the ways in which information can be presented, disseminated and interpreted.

QUESTION

Information manager

Why might the management accountant be known as the information manager?

ANSWER

The management accountant is called the information manager because management accounting is concerned with the collection of data, its analysis and processing into information, and the interpretation and communication of that information so as to assist management with planning, control and decision making.

2 Written reports

The purpose of a **report** must be clear, and certain general principles should be followed in planning and giving structure to a report.

Stylistic qualities of reports include objectivity and balance and ease of understanding.

To keep the main body of the report short enough to hold the reader's interest, detailed explanations, charts and tables of figures should be put into **appendices**. The main body of the report should make cross-reference to the appendices in appropriate places.

2.1 What is a report?

There are a variety of formats and styles of reports.

(a) You may think of reports as **extensive, complex documents**, but a **single page may be sufficient** in many contexts.

(b) **Routine reports are produced at regular intervals**. An example of a routine report is a budgetary control report, the preparation of which we will be looking at later in this text. **Special reports may be commissioned for 'one-off' planning and decision-making purposes** such as a report on a proposed project or particular issue.

(c) Reports may be **for professional purposes**, or they may be **for a wider audience** who will not all necessarily understand or require the same information.

Reports are meant to be **useful**. The information contained in a business report might be used in several ways.

(a)   **To assist management**, as they rarely have time to carry out their own detailed investigations into the matters on which they make decisions; their time, moreover, is extremely expensive.

(b)   **As a permanent record and source of reference**, should details need to be confirmed or recalled in the future.

(c)   **To convey information** or suggestions/ideas to other interested parties (eg in a report for a committee).

2.2 Reports and their purpose

Reports are usually intended to **initiate a decision or action**. The decisions or actions might be the following types.

(a)   **Control action**. If the report describes what has happened in the past, a control action may be taken in an attempt to prevent a repeat of this behaviour.

(b)   **Planning decisions**. Reports that are commissioned to advise on a certain course of action will include a **recommendation** about what decision should be taken.

2.3 The report and the report users

(a)   A special **'one-off' report** will be **commissioned by a manager**, who will then expect to **make a decision** on the basis of what the report tells him. For example, the board of directors of a company might call for a report on the financial viability of a new product or investment, and they will expect to decide whether or not to undertake the product development or the investment on the basis of the report's findings.

(b)   **Routine reports,** such as performance reports, might be **required because they are a part of established procedures.** The managers receiving the reports will not have commissioned them specifically, but they will be expected to act on anything out-of-the-ordinary that the report tells them.

(c)   **Some reports arise out of a particular event**, on which regulations prescribe the writing of a report. For example, a leaving report must be written following an employee's resignation.

(d)   **Individual responsibilities** often include the requirement to write reports. The secretary at a meeting will have to report to members the procedures and decisions taken.

Whether the report is 'one-off' or routine, there is an **obligation on the part of the person requesting the report to state the use to which it will be put.** In other words, the purpose of the report must be clear to both its writers and its users.

The report writer should communicate information in an unbiased way. Information should be communicated impartially, so that the report user can make his own judgements. This has the following implications.

(a)   Any assumptions, evaluations and recommendations by the report writer should be clearly 'signalled' as such.

(b)   Points should not be over-weighted (or omitted as irrelevant) without honestly evaluating how **objective** the selection is.

(c)   Facts and findings should be **balanced** against each other.

(d)   A firm **conclusion** should, if possible, be reached. It should be clear how and why it was reached.

QUESTION   Report writing

When writing a report, what can you do to ensure that the particular needs and abilities of the users of your report will be met?

ANSWER

(a)   Avoid 'jargon', overly technical terms and specialist knowledge the user may not share.

(b)   Keep vocabulary, sentence and paragraph structures as simple as possible, for clarity (without patronising an intelligent user).

(c)   Bear in mind the type and level of detail that will interest the user and be relevant to his/her purpose.

(d)   In a business context, the user may range from senior manager to junior supervisor, to non-managerial employee (such as in the case of minutes of a meeting) to complete layman (customer, press and so on). Vocabulary, syntax and presentation, the amount of detail gone into, the technical matter included and the formality of the report structure should all be influenced by such concerns.

2.4 Timeliness

As with all information a report may be of no use at all if it is not produced **on time**. There is no point in presenting a report to influence a decision if the decision has already been made. The timescales within which the report user is working must be known, and the time available to produce the report planned accordingly.

3 Planning a report

QUESTION   Report planning

Which of the following questions should you ask yourself before writing a report?

(a)   Who is the user?
(b)   What type of report will be most useful to him/her?
(c)   What exactly does he/she need to know, and for what purpose?
(d)   How much information is required, how quickly and at what cost?
(e)   Do you need to give judgements, recommendations etc (or just information)?

A   a, b, c
B   b, e
C   c, d, e
D   a, b, c, d, e

ANSWER

D   All of these are important and you should know the answers before you embark on writing your report.

4 The format of reports

4.1 General principles

When a **formal request is made by a superior for a report** to be prepared, such as in a formally-worded memorandum or letter, it is likely the **format and style of the report** expected is to be **formal as well**.

An **informal request** for a report – 'Can you jot down a few ideas for me about...' or 'Let me know what happens, will you?' – **will result in an informal report**, in which the structure will be less rigid, and the style slightly more personal (depending on the relationship perceived to exist between the writer and user).

If in doubt, it is better (more courteous and effective) to be too formal than informal.

The purpose of reports and their subject matter vary widely, but there are certain **generally accepted principles of report writing**.

Feature	Detail
Title	The title should be as short as possible whilst indicating clearly what the report is about.
Identification of report writer, report user and date	**If the report is extensive**, it should open with a list of contents.
Contents page	
Terms of reference	The introductory section of the report should include the terms of reference. The terms of reference will explain not only the **purpose** of the report but also any **restrictions** on its **scope**. When **timescale** is important, this too should be specified.
Sources of information	Sources of information should be acknowledged in the report. Alternatively, if the report is based on primary research, the nature of the fact-finding should be explained, perhaps in an appendix to the report.
Sections	The main body of the report should be divided into sections, each with a clear heading. These headings (or sub-headings) should if possible be standardised when reports are produced regularly (such as budgetary control reports). Paragraphs should be numbered, for ease of reference. Each paragraph should be concerned with just one basic idea.
Appendices	To keep the main body of the report short enough to hold the reader's interest, detailed explanations, charts and tables of figures should be put into appendices. The main body of the report should make cross-references to the appendices in appropriate places.
Summary of recommendations	A report will usually contain **conclusions or recommendations** about the **course of action** to be taken by the report user. These conclusions or recommendations should perhaps be stated at the beginning of the report (after the introduction and statement of terms of reference). The main body of the report can then follow and should lead the report user through the considerations that led the report writer to these conclusions. The conclusions or recommendations should then be re-stated at the end of the main body of the report.
Prominence of important items	The most significant items in a report should be given prominence.

We are going to look at three main types of report.

(a) The short formal report
(b) The short informal report
(c) The memorandum report

You should not feel bound to use the following headings in a report in an exam, but the guidelines on report sections may be helpful, should you wish to follow them.

4.2 The short formal report

The short formal report is **used in formal contexts** such as where middle management is reporting to senior management. It should be laid out according to certain basic guidelines. It will be split into logical sections, each referenced and headed appropriately.

SHORT FORMAL REPORT

TITLE   At the top of every report (or on a title page, for lengthy ones) appears the title of the report (its subject) and, as appropriate, *who* has prepared it, *for whom* it is intended, the *date* of completion, and the *status* of the report ('Confidential' or 'Urgent').

I   TERMS OF REFERENCE or INTRODUCTION

        Here is laid out the scope and purpose of the report: what is to be investigated, what kind of information is required, whether recommendations are to be made etc.

II   PROCEDURE or METHOD

        This outlines the steps taken to make an investigation, collect data etc. Telephone calls or visits made, documents consulted, computations made etc should be briefly described, with the names of other people involved.

III   FINDINGS

        In this section the information itself is set out. The content should be clearly structured in chronological order, order of importance, or any other *logical* relationship.

IV   CONCLUSIONS

        This section allows for a summary of main findings.

V   RECOMMENDATIONS

        Here, if asked to do so in the terms of reference, the writer of the report may suggest the solution to the problem investigated so that the recipient will be able to make a decision if necessary.

4.3 The short informal report

The short informal report is used **for less complex and lower-level information.** You, as assistant management accountant (or similar), could be asked to prepare such a report for the Management Accounts Manager.

The structure of the informal report is less developed: it will be shorter and less complex in any case, so will not require elaborate referencing and layout. There will be three main sections, each of which may be headed in any way appropriate to the context in which the report is written.

SHORT INFORMAL REPORT

To: (the name and title of the person to whom the report is addressed)

From: (the name and title of the report writer)

Date:

Reference: (if necessary)

Subject: (brief description of the reason for or content of the report)

1   **Background or Situation or Introduction**

     This sets the context of the report. Include anything that will help the reader to understand the rest of the report: the reason why it was requested, the current situation, and any other background information on people and things that will be mentioned in the following detailed section. This section may also contain the equivalent of 'terms of reference' and 'procedure' ('method').

2   **Findings or Analysis of the situation**

     Here is set out the detailed information gathered, narrative of events or other substance of the report as required by the user. This section may or may not require subheadings: concise prose paragraphs may be sufficient.

3   **Action or Solution or Conclusion**

     The main thrust of the findings may be summarised in this section and conclusions drawn, together with a note of the outcome of events, or action required, or recommendations as to how a problem might be solved.

4.4 The memorandum report

In informal reporting situations within an organisation, the 'short informal report' may well be presented in A4 memorandum format, which incorporates title headings and can thereafter be laid out at the writer's discretion. An ordinary memorandum **may be used for flexible, informal reports**: aside from the convenient title headings, there **are no particular requirements for structure, headings or layout**. The writer may consider whatever is logical, convenient and attractive for the reader.

5   Presenting and interpreting information in tables

Tables are a simple way of presenting information about two variables.

A **table** is a matrix of information in rows and columns, with the rows and columns having titles.

Since a table is **two-dimensional**, it can only show two variables. For example, the resources required to produce items in a factory could be tabulated, with one dimension (rows or columns) representing the items produced and the other dimension representing the resources.

Resources for production: all figures in pounds

| | *Products* | | | | |
	Athens	*Benidorm*	*Corfu*	*Dassia*	*Total*
Resources					
Direct material M_1	X	X	X	X	X
Direct material M_2	X	X	X	X	X
Direct labour grade S_1	X	X	X	X	X
Direct labour grade S_2	X	X	X	X	X
Direct expenses	X	X	X	X	X
Overheads	X	X	X	X	X
Total	X̄	X̄	X̄	X̄	X̄

5.1 Guidelines for tabulation

Once you have established what the table's two dimensions are, you should apply the following guidelines when presenting information in tabular form.

(a)   The table should be given a clear **title**.
(b)   All columns should be **clearly labelled**.
(c)   Where appropriate, there should be clear **sub-totals**.
(d)   A **total column** may be presented (usually the right-hand column.)
(e)   A **total figure** is often advisable at the bottom of each column of figures.
(f)   Information presented should be easy to read.

5.2 Example: tables

The total sales revenue of a certain trading company in year 8 was $10,000,000. Sales were made to three different regions, central, north and south. $6,000,000 of sales were to the central region and $3,000,000 were to the north region. The organisation makes four products, the L, the U, the C and the Y. Sales of the L totalled $1,100,000, sales of the U also totalled $1,100,000, while sales of the C totalled $2,900,000.

Sales to the central region were $3,500,000 of the Y, $1,500,000 of the C and $500,000 of the L, whilst in the north region, sales of the Y totalled $1,000,000, sales of the C totalled $1,100,000 and sales of the L $500,000.

Required

Draw up a table to show all the details of sales in the organisation and interpret the data by providing suitable secondary statistics to describe the distribution of sales across the three regions.

5.3 Solution

The basic table required has the following two dimensions.

(a)   Regions
(b)   Products

Secondary statistics are supporting figures that are **supplementary,** and which clarify or amplify the main pieces of information. A major example of secondary statistics is **percentages**. In this example, we could show one of the following.

(a)   The percentage of the total sales in each region of each product
(b)   The percentage of the total sales of each product made in each region

In this example, (a) has been selected but you might consider that (b) would be more suitable. Either could be suitable, depending of course on what purposes the information is being collected and presented for.

Analysis of sales

Products	Central $m	Central %	North $m	North %	South $m	South %	Total $m	Total %
L	0.5	8.3	0.5	16.7	0.1**	10	1.1	11
U	0.5*	8.3	0.4*	13.3	0.2**	20	1.1	11
C	1.5	25.0	1.1	36.7	0.3**	30	2.9	29
Y	3.5	58.4	1.0	33.3	0.4**	40	4.9*	49
Total	6.0	100.0	3.0	100.0	1.0	100	10.0	100

*   Balancing figure to make up the column total
**   Balancing figure then needed to make up the row total

The percentages calculated allow us to **interpret** the information in the table. For example, we can see that nearly 50% of the organisation's sales are of product Y, and that 25% of the Central region's sales are of product C. The percentages highlight additional information which was not readily discernible from the absolute figures.

If we had selected approach (b) however, different features would have been highlighted. We would have known, for example, the percentage of sales of the L made to the Southern region.

QUESTION

Table

Draw up a table using the information in the example but this time interpret the information by adopting approach (b).

ANSWER

Analysis of sales
Products

Regions	L $m	L %	U $m	U %	C $m	C %	Y $m	Y %	Total $m	Total %
Central	0.5	0.455	0.5	0.454	1.5	0.517	3.5	0.714	6.0	60
North	0.5	0.455	0.4	0.364	1.1	0.379	1.0	0.204	3.0	30
South	0.1	0.090	0.2	0.182	0.3	0.104	0.4	0.082	1.0	10
	1.1	1.000	1.1	1.000	2.9	1.000	4.9	1.000	10.0	100

6 Presenting and interpreting information in charts

Bar charts often convey the meaning or significance of data more clearly than would a table.

There are three main types of bar chart: **simple**, **component** (including percentage component) and **multiple** (or compound).

Instead of presenting information in a table, it might be preferable to give a visual display in the form of a **chart**.

The purpose of a chart is to convey the information in a way that will demonstrate its meaning or significance more clearly than a table would. Charts are not always more appropriate than tables. The **most suitable way of presenting information** will depend on the following.

(a)   **What the information is intended to show**. Visual displays usually make one or two points quite forcefully, whereas tables usually give more detailed information.

(b)   **Who is going to use the information**. Some individuals might understand visual displays more readily than tables.

6.1 Bar charts

A **bar chart** is a method of presenting information in which quantities are shown in the form of bars on a chart, the length of the bars being proportional to the quantities.

The bar chart is one of the most common methods of presenting information in a visual form. There are three main types of bar chart.

(a)   **Simple** bar charts
(b)   **Component** bar charts, including **percentage component** bar charts
(c)   **Multiple** (or compound) bar charts

6.2 Simple bar charts

A **simple bar chart** is a chart consisting of one or more bars, in which the length of each bar indicates the magnitude of the corresponding information.

6.3 Example: a simple bar chart

Barker Ltd's total sales for the years from year 1 to year 6 are as follows.

Year	Sales
	Units
1	8,000
2	12,000
3	11,000
4	14,000
5	16,000
6	17,000

The information could be shown on a simple bar chart as follows.

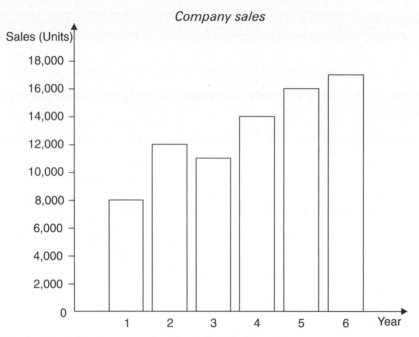

Company sales

Each axis of the chart must be clearly **labelled**, and there must be a **scale**. This is vital when the reader comes to interpret the bar chart. Here, the y axis includes a scale for the level of sales, and so readers of the bar chart can see not only that sales levels have been **rising** year by year (with year 3 being an exception) but also **what** the actual sales levels have been each year.

Simple bar charts serve two interpretation purposes.

(a)   They show the actual magnitude of each item.
(b)   They enable one to compare magnitudes, by comparing the lengths of bars on the chart.

6.4 Component bar charts

A **component bar chart** is a bar chart that gives a breakdown of each total into its components.

6.5 Example: a component bar chart

Barker's sales for years 7 to 9 are as follows.

	Year 7 Units	Year 8 Units	Year 9 Units
Region 1	10,000	12,000	17,000
Region 2	9,000	10,000	10,000
Region 3	5,000	6,000	7,000
Total	24,000	28,000	34,000

An interpretation of a component bar chart would show the following.

(a)   How total sales have changed from year to year
(b)   The components of each year's total

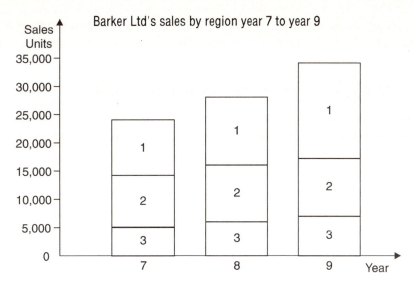

In this diagram the growth in sales is illustrated and the significance of growth in region 1 sales as the reason for the total sales growth is also fairly clear. The growth in region 1 sales would have been even clearer if region 1 had been drawn as the bottom element in each bar instead of the top one.

6.6 Percentage component bar charts

The **difference** between a **component bar chart** and a **percentage component bar chart** is that with a **component bar chart**, the total length of **each bar** (and the length of each component in it) **indicates magnitude**. A bigger amount is shown by a longer bar. With a **percentage component bar chart, total magnitudes are not shown**. If two or more bars are drawn on the chart, the total length of each bar is the same. The only varying lengths in a percentage component bar chart are the lengths of the sections of a bar, which vary according to the relative sizes of the components.

6.7 Example: a percentage component bar chart

The information in the previous example of sales of Barker could have been shown in a percentage component bar chart as follows.

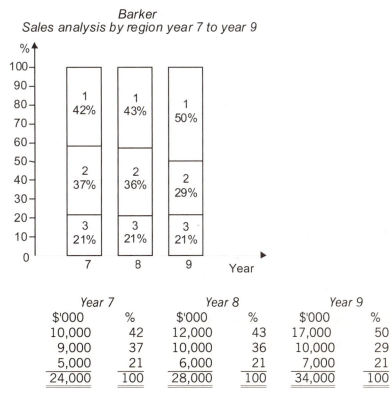

Working

	Year 7		Year 8		Year 9	
	$'000	%	$'000	%	$'000	%
Region 1	10,000	42	12,000	43	17,000	50
Region 2	9,000	37	10,000	36	10,000	29
Region 3	5,000	21	6,000	21	7,000	21
Total	24,000	100	28,000	100	34,000	100

This chart shows that sales in region 3 have remained a steady proportion of total sales, but the proportion of sales in region 1 in total sales has gone up quite considerably, while the proportion of sales in region 2 has fallen correspondingly.

6.8 Multiple bar charts (compound bar charts)

A **multiple bar chart** (or **compound bar chart**) is a bar chart in which two or more separate bars are used to present sub-divisions of information.

6.9 Example: a multiple bar chart

The information on Barker's sales could be shown in a multiple bar chart as follows.

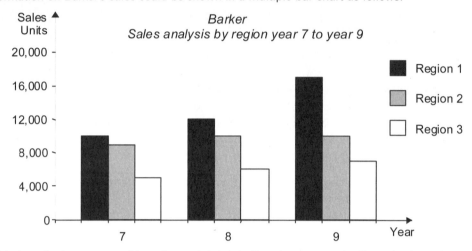

A multiple bar chart uses several bars for each total. In the above example, the sales in each year are shown as three separate bars, one for each region 1, 2 and 3.

Multiple bar charts are sometimes drawn with the bars horizontal instead of vertical.

Multiple bar charts present similar information to component bar charts, except for the following.

(a)   Multiple bar charts do not show the grand total (in the above example, the total sales each year) whereas component bar charts do.

(b)   Multiple bar charts illustrate the comparative magnitudes of the components more clearly than component bar charts.

6.10 Pie charts

A pie chart is a chart which is used to show pictorially the relative size of component elements of a total.

It is called a pie chart because it is **circular**, and so has the **shape of a pie** in a round pie dish. The 'pie' is then cut into slices with each slice representing part of the total.

Pie charts have sectors of varying sizes, and you need to be able to draw sectors fairly accurately. To do this, you need a **protractor**. Working out sector sizes involves converting parts of the total into **equivalent degrees of a circle**. A complete 'pie' = 360°: the number of degrees in a circle = 100% of whatever you are showing. An element which is 50% of your total will therefore occupy a segment of 180°, and so on.

6.10.1 Using shading and colour

Two pie charts are shown as follows.

Breakdown of air and noise pollution complaints, 1

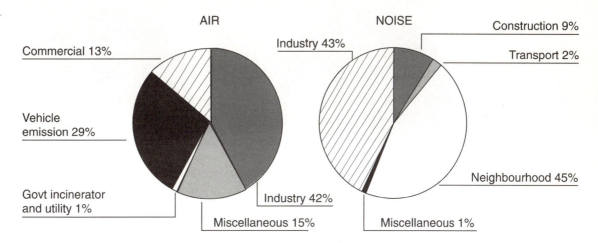

- **Shading** distinguishes the segments from each other
- **Colour** can also be used to distinguish segments

6.10.2 Example: Pie charts

The costs of materials at the Cardiff Factory and the Swansea Factory during January 20X0 were as follows.

	Cardiff factory		Swansea factory	
	$'000	%	$'000	%
Material W	70	35	50	20
Material A	30	15	125	50
Material L	90	45	50	20
Material E	10	5	25	10
	200	100	250	100

Show the costs for the factories in pie charts.

Solution

To convert the components into degrees of a circle, we can use either the **percentage figures** or the **actual cost figures**.

Using the percentage figures

The total percentage is 100%, and the total number of degrees in a circle is 360°. To convert from one to the other, we multiply each percentage value by 360/100% = 3.6.

	Cardiff factory		Swansea factory	
	%	Degrees	%	Degrees
Material W	35	126	20	72
Material A	15	54	50	180
Material L	45	162	20	72
Material E	5	18	10	36
	100	360	100	360

Using the actual cost figures

	Cardiff factory		Swansea factory	
	$'000	Degrees	$'000	Degrees
Material W (70/200 × 360°)	70	126	50	72
Material A	30	54	125	180
Material L	90	162	50	72
Material E	10	18	25	36
	200	360	250	360

A pie chart could be drawn for each factory.

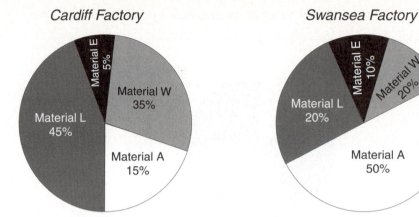

(a)   If the pie chart is drawn manually, a protractor must be used to measure the degrees accurately to obtain the correct sector sizes.

(b)   Using a computer makes the process much simpler, especially using a spreadsheet. You just draw up the data in a spreadsheet and click on the chart button to create a visual representation of what you want. Note that you can only use colour effectively if you have a colour printer!

6.10.3 Advantages of pie charts

*   They give a simple pictorial display of the relative sizes of elements of a total
*   They show clearly when one element is much bigger than others
*   They can clearly show differences in the elements of two different totals

6.10.4 Disadvantages of pie charts

(a)   They only show the relative sizes of elements. In the example of the two factories, for instance, the pie charts do not show that costs at the Swansea factory were $50,000 higher in total than at the Cardiff factory.

(b)   They involve **calculating degrees of a circle** and drawing sectors accurately, and this can be time consuming unless computer software is used.

(c)   It is often **difficult to compare sector sizes** easily. For example, suppose that the following two pie charts are used to show the elements of a company's sales.

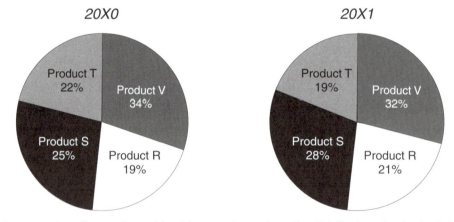

Without the percentage figures, it would not be easy to see how the distribution of sales had changed between 20X0 and 20X1.

QUESTION

Pie charts

The European division of Scent to You, a flower delivery service has just published its accounts for the year ended 30 June 20X0. The sales director made the following comments.

'Our total sales for the year were $1,751,000, of which $787,000 were made in the United Kingdom, $219,000 in Italy, $285,000 in France and $92,000 in Germany. Sales in Spain and Holland

amounted to $189,000 and $34,000 respectively, whilst the rest of Europe collectively had sales of $145,000 in the twelve months to 30 June 20X0.'

Required

Present the above information in the form of a pie chart. Show all of your workings.

ANSWER

Workings

	Sales $'000		Degrees
United Kingdom	787	(787/1,751 × 360)	162
Italy	219		45
France	285		58
Germany	92		19
Spain	189		39
Rest of Europe	145		30
Holland	34		7
	1,751		360

Scent to You
Sales for the year ended 30 June 20X0

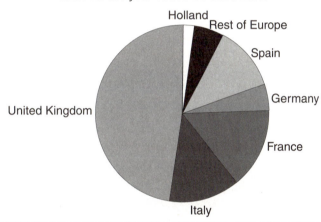

EXAM FOCUS POINT

A computer based exam cannot require you to draw charts so questions will focus on labelling, calculating values, choosing an appropriate chart and coming to conclusions using charts.

6.11 Scatter diagrams

Scatter diagrams are graphs which are used to exhibit data, (rather than equations) in order to compare the way in which two variables vary with each other.

6.12 Constructing a scatter diagram

The x axis of a scatter diagram is used to represent the independent variable and the y axis represents the dependent variable.

To construct a scatter diagram or scattergraph, we must have several pairs of data, with each pair showing the value of one variable and the corresponding value of the other variable. Each pair is plotted on a graph. The resulting graph will show a number of pairs, scattered over the graph. The scattered points might or might not appear to follow a trend.

6.13 Example: Scatter diagram

The output at a factory each week for the last ten weeks, and the cost of that output, were as follows.

Week	1	2	3	4	5	6	7	8	9	10
Output (units)	10	12	10	8	9	11	7	12	9	14
Cost ($)	42	44	38	34	38	43	30	47	37	50

Required

Plot the data given on a scatter diagram.

Solution

The data could be shown on a scatter diagram as follows.

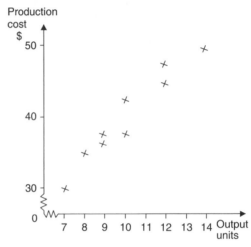

(a)   The cost depends on the volume of output: volume is the independent variable and is shown on the x axis.

(b)   You will notice from the graph that the plotted data, although scattered, lie approximately on a rising trend line, with higher total costs at higher output volumes. (The lower part of the axes have been omitted, so as not to waste space. The break in the axes is indicated by the jagged lines.)

6.14 The trend line

For the most part, scatter diagrams are used to try to identify **trend lines**.

If a trend can be seen in a scatter diagram, the next step is to try to draw a trend line.

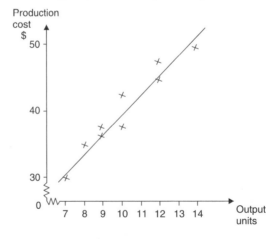

6.14.1 Using trend lines to make predictions

(a)   In the previous example, we have drawn a trend line from the scatter diagram of output units and production cost. This trend line might turn out to be, say, $y = 10 + 3x$. We could then use this trend line to establish what we think costs ought to be, approximately, if output were, say, 10 units or 15 units in any week. (These 'expected' costs could subsequently be compared with the actual costs, so that managers could judge whether actual costs were higher or lower than they ought to be.)

(b)   If a scatter diagram is used to record sales over time, we could draw a trend line, and use this to forecast sales for next year.

6.14.2 Adding trend lines to scatter diagrams

The trend line could be a straight line, or a curved line. The simplest technique for drawing a trend line is to make a visual judgement about what the closest-fitting trend line seems to be, the 'line of best fit'.

Here is another example of a scatter diagram with a trend line added.

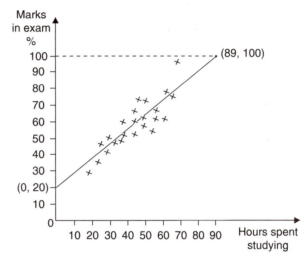

The equation of a straight line is given by **y = a + bx**, where **a** is the **intercept** on the y axis and **b** is the **gradient**.

The line passes through the point x = 0, y = 20, so a = 20. The line also passes through x = 89, y = 100, so:

$$100 = 20 + (b \times 89)$$

$$b = \frac{(100 - 20)}{89}$$
$$= 0.9$$

The line is y = 20 + 0.9x

We will look at this in more detail in Chapter 14 on forecasting.

QUESTION

The quantities of widgets produced by WDG Co during the year ended 31 October 20X9 and the related costs were as follows.

Month	Production Thousands	Factory cost $'000
20X8		
November	7	45
December	10	59
20X9		
January	13	75
February	14	80
March	11	65
April	7	46
May	5	35
June	4	30

Month	Production	Factory cost
	Thousands	$'000
July	3	25
August	2	20
September	1	15
October	5	35

You may assume that the value of money remained stable throughout the year.

Required

(a)   Draw a scatter diagram related to the data provided above, and plot on it the line of best fit.

(b)   Now answer the following questions.

   (i)   What would you expect the factory cost to have been if 12,000 widgets had been produced in a particular month?

   (ii)   What is your estimate of WDG's monthly fixed cost?

ANSWER

Your answers to parts (b)(i) and (ii) may have been slightly different from those given here, but they should not have been very different, because the data points lay very nearly along a straight line.

(a)   WDG Co – Scatter diagram of production and factory costs, November 20X8-October 20X9

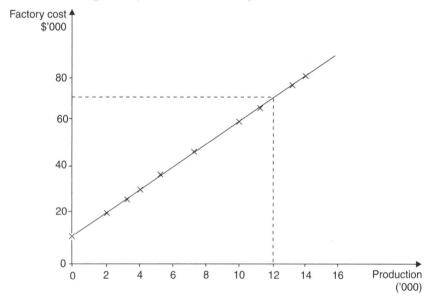

(b)   (i)   The estimated factory cost for a production of 12,000 widgets is $70,000.

   (ii)   The monthly fixed costs are indicated by the point where the line of best fit meets the vertical axis (costs at zero production). The fixed costs are estimated as $10,000 a month.

CHAPTER ROUNDUP

↳ The purpose of a **report** must be clear, and certain general principles should be followed in planning and giving structure to a report.

↳ Stylistic qualities of reports include objectivity and balance and ease of understanding.

↳ To keep the main body of the report short enough to hold the reader's interest, detailed explanations, charts and tables of figures should be put into **appendices**. The main body of the report should make cross-reference to the appendices in appropriate places.

↳ **Tables** are a simple way of presenting information about two variables.

↳ Bar charts often convey the meaning or significance of data more clearly than would a table.

↳ There are three main types of bar chart: **simple**, **component** (including percentage component) and **multiple** (or compound).

↳ **Scatter diagrams** are graphs which are used to exhibit data, (rather than equations) in order to compare the way in which two variables vary with each other.

QUICK QUIZ

1 Why is it important to space out a report?
2 When should appendices be used in reports?
3 When would a memorandum report be used?
4 What are the main guidelines for tabulation?
5 Name the three main types of bar chart.

ANSWERS TO QUICK QUIZ

1   Intelligent use of spacing separates headings from the body of the text for easy scanning, and also makes a large block more attractive and 'digestible'.

2   Appendices should be used if the report will be too long and detailed to hold the reader's interest.

3   A memorandum would be used for flexible, informal reports.

4   (a)   The table should be given a clear title.
    (b)   All columns should be clearly labelled.
    (c)   The information should be inserted into the appropriate places in the table.
    (d)   Where appropriate, there should be clear sub-totals.
    (e)   A total column may be presented; this would usually be the right-hand column.
    (f)   A total figure is often advisable at the bottom of each column of figures.
    (g)   Tables should not be packed with too much information so that reading the table is difficult.

5   (a)   Simple bar charts
    (b)   Component bar charts, including percentage component bar charts
    (c)   Multiple (or compound) bar charts

Now try ...

Attempt the questions below from the **Exam Question Bank**

Number

Q20 – Q22

part

B

Cost accounting techniques

CHAPTER

06

The investment in inventory is a very important one for most businesses, both in terms of monetary value and relationships with customers (no inventory, no sale, loss of customer goodwill). It is therefore vital that management establish and maintain an **effective inventory control system**.

This chapter will concentrate on a **inventory control system** for materials, but similar problems and considerations apply to all forms of inventory.

Accounting for materials

Study Guide		Intellectual level
B	**Cost accounting techniques**	
1	**Accounting for material, labour and overheads**	
(a)(i)	Describe the different procedures and documents necessary for the ordering, receiving and issuing of materials from inventory	K
(a)(ii)	Describe the control procedures used to monitor physical and 'book' inventory and to minimise discrepancies and losses	K
(a)(iii)	Interpret the entries and balances in the material inventory account	S
(a)(iv)	Identify, explain and calculate the costs of ordering and holding inventory (including buffer inventory)	S
(a)(v)	Calculate and interpret optimal reorder quantities	S
(a)(vi)	Calculate and interpret optimal reorder quantities when discounts apply	S
(a)(vii)	Produce calculations to minimise inventory costs when inventory is gradually replenished	S
(a)(viii)	Describe and apply appropriate methods for establishing reorder levels where demand in the lead time is constant	S
(a)(ix)	Calculate the value of closing inventory and material issues using LIFO, FIFO and average methods	S

EXAM FOCUS POINT

Material costs is another key area of the syllabus so expect questions on this topic. Make sure you understand and can use the EOQ formula. It will be given to you in the exam.

1 What is inventory control?

1.1 Introduction

Inventory control includes the functions of inventory ordering and purchasing, receiving goods into store, storing and issuing inventory and controlling levels of inventory.

Classifications of inventories

- Raw materials
- Work in progress
- Spare parts/consumables
- Finished goods

This chapter will concentrate on an **inventory control system** for materials, but similar problems and considerations apply to all forms of inventory. Controls should cover the following functions.

- The **ordering** of inventory
- The **purchase** of inventory
- The **receipt** of goods into store
- **Storage**
- The **issue** of inventory and maintenance of inventory at the most appropriate level

1.2 Qualitative aspects of inventory control

We may wish to **control inventory** for the following reasons.

- Holding costs of inventory may be expensive.
- Production will be disrupted if we run out of raw materials.
- Unused inventory with a short shelf life may incur unnecessary expenses.

If manufactured goods are made out of low quality materials, the end product will be of low quality also. It may therefore be necessary to control the quality of inventory, in order to maintain a good reputation with consumers.

2 The ordering, receipt and issue of raw materials

Technical competence 2 requires you to demonstrate you are competent in verifying and recording purchases and payments from originating documents. The knowledge you gain in this chapter will help you demonstrate your competence in this area.

2.1 Ordering and receiving materials

Every movement of a material in a business should be documented using the following as appropriate: purchase requisition; purchase order; GRN; materials requisition note; materials transfer note and materials returned note.

Proper records must be kept of the physical procedures for ordering and receiving a consignment of materials to ensure the following.

- That enough inventory is held
- That there is no duplication of ordering
- That quality is maintained
- That there is adequate record keeping for accounts purposes

2.2 Purchase requisition

Current inventories run down to the level where a reorder is required. The stores department issues a **purchase requisition** which is sent to the purchasing department, authorising the department to order further inventory. An example of a purchase requisition is shown below.

PURCHASE REQUISITION	Req. No.	
Department/job number: Suggested Supplier:	Date	
	Requested by: Latest date required:	

Quantity	Code number	Description	Estimated Cost	
			Unit	$

Authorised signature:

2.3 Purchase order

The purchasing department draws up a **purchase order** which is sent to the supplier. (The supplier may be asked to return an acknowledgement copy as confirmation of his acceptance of the order.) Copies of

the purchase order must be sent to the accounts department and the storekeeper (or receiving department).

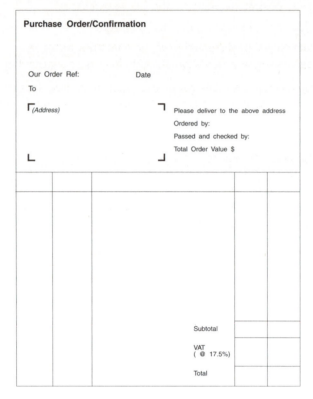

2.4 Quotations

The purchasing department may have to obtain a number of quotations if either a new inventory line is required, the existing supplier's costs are too high or the existing supplier no longer stocks the goods needed. Trade discounts (reduction in the price per unit given to some customers) should be negotiated where possible.

2.5 Delivery note

The supplier delivers the consignment of materials, and the storekeeper signs a **delivery note** for the carrier. The packages must then be checked against the copy of the purchase order, to ensure that the supplier has delivered the types and quantities of materials which were ordered. (Discrepancies would be referred to the purchasing department.)

2.6 Goods received note

If the delivery is acceptable, the storekeeper prepares a **goods received note (GRN)**, an example of which is shown below.

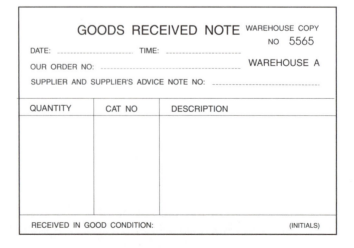

A copy of the **GRN** is sent to the accounts department, where it is matched with the copy of the purchase order. The supplier's invoice is checked against the purchase order and GRN, and the necessary steps are taken to pay the supplier. The invoice may contain details relating to discounts such as trade discounts, quantity discounts (order in excess of a specified amount) and settlement discounts (payment received within a specified number of days).

QUESTION

Ordering materials

What are the possible consequences of a failure of control over ordering and receipt of materials?

ANSWER

(a)   Incorrect materials being delivered, disrupting operations
(b)   Incorrect prices being paid
(c)   Deliveries other than at the specified time (causing disruption)
(d)   Insufficient control over quality
(e)   Invoiced amounts differing from quantities of goods actually received or prices agreed

You may, of course, have thought of equally valid consequences.

2.7 Materials requisition note

Materials can only be issued against a **materials/stores requisition**. This document must record not only the quantity of goods issued, but also the cost centre or the job number for which the requisition is being made. The materials requisition note may also have a column, to be filled in by the cost department, for recording the cost or value of the materials issued to the cost centre or job.

Materials requisition note			
Date required _ _ _ _ _ _ _ _ .		Cost centre No/ Job No _ _ _ _ _ _ _ _ _ _ _ .	
Quantity	Item code	Description	$
Signature of requisitioning Manager/ Foreman _		Date _ _ _ _ _ _	

2.8 Materials transfers and returns

Where materials, having been issued to one job or cost centre, are later transferred to a different job or cost centre, without first being returned to stores, a **materials transfer note** should be raised. Such a note must show not only the job receiving the transfer, but also the job from which it is transferred. This enables the appropriate charges to be made to jobs or cost centres.

Material returns must also be documented on a **materials returned note**. This document is the 'reverse' of a requisition note, and must contain similar information. In fact it will often be almost identical to a requisition note. It will simply have a different title and perhaps be a distinctive colour, such as red, to highlight the fact that materials are being returned.

2.9 Computerised inventory control systems

Many inventory control systems these days are computerised. Computerised inventory control systems vary greatly, but most will have the features outlined below.

(a) **Data must be input into the system**. For example, details of goods received may simply be written on to a GRN for later entry into the computer system. Alternatively, this information may be keyed in directly to the computer: a GRN will be printed and then signed as evidence of the transaction, so that both the warehouse and the supplier can have a hard copy record in case of dispute. Some systems may incorporate the use of devices such as bar code readers.

Other types of transaction which will need to be recorded include the following.

(i) **Transfers** between different categories of inventory (for example from work in progress to finished goods)

(ii) **Despatch**, resulting from a sale, of items of finished goods to customers

(iii) **Adjustments** to inventory records if the amount of inventory revealed in a physical inventory count differs from the amount appearing on the inventory records

(b) **An inventory master file is maintained**. This file will contain details for every category of inventory and will be updated for new inventory lines. A database file may be maintained.

QUESTION
Inventory master file

What type of information do you think should be held on an inventory master file?

ANSWER

Here are some examples.

(a)	Inventory code number, for reference	(e)	Cost per unit
(b)	Brief description of inventory item	(f)	Selling price per unit (if finished goods)
(c)	Reorder level	(g)	Amount in inventory
(d)	Reorder quantity	(h)	Frequency of usage

The file may also hold details of inventory movements over a period, but this will depend on the type of system in operation. In a **batch system**, transactions will be grouped and input in one operation and details of the movements may be held in a separate transactions file, the master file updated in total only. In an **on-line system**, transactions may be input directly to the master file, where the record of movements is thus likely to be found. Such a system will mean that the inventory records are constantly up to date, which will help in monitoring and controlling inventory.

The system may generate orders automatically once the amount in inventory has fallen to the reorder level.

(c) **The system will generate outputs**. These may include, depending on the type of system, any of the following.

(i) **Hard copy** records, for example a printed GRN, of transactions entered into the system.

(ii) Output on a **VDU** screen in response to an enquiry (for example the current level of a particular line of inventory, or details of a particular transaction).

(iii) Various **printed reports**, devised to fit in with the needs of the organisation. These may include inventory movement reports, detailing over a period the movements on all inventory lines, listings of GRNs, despatch notes and so forth.

A computerised inventory control system is usually able to give more up to date information and more flexible reporting than a manual system but remember that both manual and computer based inventory control systems need the same types of data to function properly.

3 The storage of raw materials

3.1 Objectives of storing materials

- Speedy **issue** and **receipt** of materials
- Full **identification** of all materials at all times
- Correct **location** of all materials at all times
- **Protection** of materials from damage and deterioration
- Provision of **secure stores** to avoid pilferage, theft and fire
- **Efficient** use of storage space
- **Maintenance** of correct inventory levels
- Keeping correct and up-to-date **records** of receipts, issues and inventory levels

3.2 Recording inventory levels

One of the objectives of storekeeping is to maintain accurate records of current inventory levels. This involves the accurate recording of inventory movements (issues from and receipts into stores). The most frequently encountered system for recording inventory movements is the use of bin cards and stores ledger accounts.

3.2.1 Bin cards

A **bin card** shows the level of inventory of an item at a particular stores location. It is kept with the actual inventory and is updated by the storekeeper as inventories are received and issued. A typical bin card is shown below.

Bin card

Part code no _ _ _ _ _ _ _ _ _ _ _ _ Location _ _ _ _ _ _ _ _ _ _ _ _ _ _ _ _ _ _

Bin number _ _ _ _ _ _ _ _ _ _ _ _ _ Stores ledger no _ _ _ _ _ _ _ _ _ _ _ _ _ _

Receipts			Issues			Inventory balance
Date	Quantity	G.R.N. No.	Date	Quantity Req. No.		

The use of bin cards is decreasing, partly due to the difficulty in keeping them updated and partly due to the merging of inventory recording and control procedures, frequently using computers.

3.2.2 Stores ledger accounts

A typical stores ledger account is shown below. Note that it shows the value of inventory.

Stores ledger account

Material _ _ _ _ _ _ _ _ _ _ _ _ _ _ _ _ _ _ . Maximum Quantity _ _ _ _ _ _ _ _ _ _ _ _ _ _

Code _ _ _ _ _ _ _ _ _ _ _ _ _ _ _ _ _ _ _ Minimum Quantity _ _ _ _ _ _ _ _ _ _ _ _ _ _ _

Date	Receipts				Issues				Inventory		
	G.R.N No.	Quantity	Unit price $	Amount $	Stores Req. No	Quantity	Unit price $	Amount $	Quantity	Unit price $	Amount $

The above illustration shows a card for a manual system, but even when the inventory records are computerised, the same type of information is normally included in the computer file. The running balance on the stores ledger account allows inventory levels and valuation to be monitored.

3.2.3 Free inventory

Managers need to know the **free inventory balance** in order to obtain a full picture of the current inventory position of an item. Free inventory represents what is really **available for future use** and is calculated as follows.

Materials in inventory	X
+ Materials on order from suppliers	X
− Materials requisitioned, not yet issued	(X)
Free inventory balance	X̲

Knowledge of the level of physical inventory assists inventory issuing, inventory counting and controlling maximum and minimum inventory levels: knowledge of the level of free inventory assists ordering.

QUESTION

Units on order

A wholesaler has 8,450 units outstanding for Part X100 on existing customers' orders; there are 3,925 units in inventory and the calculated free inventory is 5,525 units.

How many units does the wholesaler have on order with his supplier?

A 9,450   B 10,050   C 13,975   D 17,900

ANSWER

Free inventory balance	=	units in inventory + units on order − units ordered, but not yet issued
5,525	=	3,925 + units on order − 8,450
Units on order	=	10,050

The correct answer is B.

3.3 Identification of materials: inventory codes (materials codes)

Materials held in stores are **coded** and **classified**. Advantages of using code numbers to identify materials are as follows.

(a)   Ambiguity is avoided.

(b)   Time is saved. Descriptions can be lengthy and time-consuming.

(c)   Production efficiency is improved. The correct material can be accurately identified from a code number.

(d)   Computerised processing is made easier.

(e)   Numbered code systems can be designed to be flexible, and can be expanded to include more inventory items as necessary.

The digits in a code can stand for the type of inventory, supplier, department and so forth.

3.4 The inventory count (stocktake)

The **inventory count (stocktake)** involves counting the physical inventory on hand at a certain date, and then checking this against the balance shown in the inventory records. The inventory count can be carried out on a **continuous** or **periodic** basis.

Periodic stocktaking is a process whereby all inventory items are physically counted and valued at a set point in time, usually at the end of an accounting period.

Continuous stocktaking is counting and valuing selected items at different times on a rotating basis. This involves a specialist team counting and checking a number of inventory items each day, so that each item is checked at least once a year. Valuable items or items with a high turnover could be checked more frequently.

3.4.1 Advantages of continuous stocktaking compared to periodic stocktaking

(a)   The annual stocktaking is unnecessary and the disruption it causes is avoided.

(b)   Regular skilled stocktakers can be employed, reducing likely errors.

(c)   More time is available, reducing errors and allowing investigation.

(d)   Deficiencies and losses are revealed sooner than they would be if stocktaking were limited to an annual check.

(e)   Production hold-ups are eliminated because the stores staff are at no time so busy as to be unable to deal with material issues to production departments.

(f)   Staff morale is improved and standards raised.

(g)   Control over inventory levels is improved, and there is less likelihood of overstocking or running out of inventory.

3.4.2 Inventory discrepancies

There will be occasions when inventory checks disclose discrepancies between the physical amount of an item in inventory and the amount shown in the inventory records. When this occurs, the cause of the discrepancy should be investigated, and appropriate action taken to ensure that it does not happen again.

3.4.3 Perpetual inventory

Perpetual inventory refers to an inventory recording system whereby the records (bin cards and stores ledger accounts) are updated for each receipt and issue of inventory as it occurs.

This means that there is a continuous record of the balance of each item of inventory. The balance on the stores ledger account therefore represents the inventory on hand and this balance is used in the calculation of closing inventory in monthly and annual accounts. In practice, physical inventories may not agree with recorded inventories and therefore continuous stocktaking is necessary to ensure that the perpetual inventory system is functioning correctly and that minor inventory discrepancies are corrected.

3.4.4 Obsolete, deteriorating and slow-moving inventories and wastage

Obsolete inventories are those items which have become out-of-date and are no longer required. Obsolete items are written off and disposed of.

Inventory items may be wasted because, for example, they get broken. All **wastage** should be noted on the inventory records immediately so that physical inventory equals the inventory balance on records and the cost of the wastage written off.

Slow-moving inventories are inventory items which are likely to take a long time to be used up. For example, 5,000 units are in inventory, and only 20 are being used each year. This is often caused by overstocking. Managers should investigate such inventory items and, if it is felt that the usage rate is unlikely to increase, excess inventory should be written off as for obsolete inventory, leaving perhaps four or five years' supply in inventory.

4 Inventory control levels

4.1 Inventory costs

Inventory costs include purchase costs, holding costs, ordering costs and costs of running out inventory.

The costs of purchasing inventory are usually one of the largest costs faced by an organisation and, once obtained, inventory has to be carefully controlled and checked.

4.1.1 Reasons for holding inventories

- To ensure sufficient goods are available to meet expected demand
- To provide a buffer between processes
- To meet any future shortages
- To take advantage of bulk purchasing discounts
- To absorb seasonal fluctuations and any variations in usage and demand
- To allow production processes to flow smoothly and efficiently
- As a necessary part of the production process (such as when maturing cheese)
- As a deliberate investment policy, especially in times of inflation or possible shortages

4.1.2 Holding costs

If inventories are too high, **holding costs** will be incurred unnecessarily. Such costs occur for a number of reasons.

(a) **Costs of storage and stores operations.** Larger inventories require more storage space and possibly extra staff and equipment to control and handle them.

(b) **Interest charges**. Holding inventories involves the tying up of capital (cash) on which interest must be paid.

(c) **Insurance costs**. The larger the value of inventories held, the greater insurance premiums are likely to be.

(d) **Risk of obsolescence**. The longer a inventory item is held, the greater is the risk of obsolescence.

(e) **Deterioration**. When materials in store deteriorate to the extent that they are unusable, they must be thrown away with the likelihood that disposal costs would be incurred.

4.1.3 Costs of obtaining inventory

On the other hand, if inventories are kept low, small quantities of inventory will have to be ordered more frequently, thereby increasing the following **ordering or procurement costs**.

(a) **Clerical and administrative costs** associated with purchasing, accounting for and receiving goods

(b) **Transport costs**

(c) **Production run costs**, for inventory which is manufactured internally rather than purchased from external sources

4.1.4 Stockout costs (running out of inventory)

An additional type of cost which may arise if inventory are kept too low is the type associated with running out of inventory. There are a number of causes of **stockout costs**.

- Lost contribution from lost sales
- Loss of future sales due to disgruntled customers
- Loss of customer goodwill
- Cost of production stoppages
- Labour frustration over stoppages
- Extra costs of urgent, small quantity, replenishment orders

4.1.5 Objective of inventory control

The overall objective of inventory control is, therefore, to maintain inventory levels so that the total of the following costs is minimised.

- Holding costs
- Stockout costs
- Ordering costs

4.2 Inventory control levels

Inventory control levels can be calculated in order to maintain inventories at the optimum level. The three critical control levels are reorder level, minimum level and maximum level.

Based on an analysis of past inventory usage and delivery times, inventory control levels can be calculated and used to maintain inventory at their optimum level (in other words, a level which minimises costs). These levels will determine 'when to order' and 'how many to order'.

4.2.1 Reorder level

When inventories reach this level, an order should be placed to replenish inventories. The reorder level is determined by consideration of the following.

- The maximum rate of consumption   • The maximum lead time

The maximum lead time is the time between placing an order with a supplier, and the inventory becoming available for use

FORMULA TO LEARN

Reorder level = maximum usage × maximum lead time

4.2.2 Minimum level

This is a warning level to draw management attention to the fact that inventories are approaching a dangerously low level and that stockouts are possible.

FORMULA TO LEARN

Minimum level = reorder level – (average usage × average lead time)

4.2.3 Maximum level

This also acts as a warning level to signal to management that inventories are reaching a potentially wasteful level.

FORMULA TO LEARN

Maximum level = reorder level + reorder quantity – (minimum usage × minimum lead time)

This graph shows the varying levels of inventory over a time period.

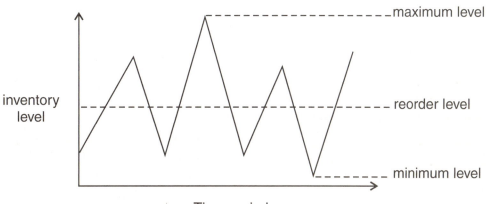

QUESTION

Maximum inventory level

A large retailer with multiple outlets maintains a central warehouse from which the outlets are supplied. The following information is available for Part Number SF525.

Average usage	350 per day
Minimum usage	180 per day
Maximum usage	420 per day
Lead time for replenishment	11-15 days
Re-order quantity	6,500 units
Re-order level	6,300 units

(a) Based on the data above, what is the maximum level of inventory?

  A 5,250 B 6,500 C 10,820 D 12,800

(b) Based on the data above, what is the approximate number of Part Number SF525 carried as buffer inventory?

  A 200 B 720 C 1,680 D 1,750

ANSWER

(a) Maximum inventory level = reorder level + reorder quantity – (min usage × min lead time)
  = 6,300 + 6,500 – (180 × 11)
  = 10,820

The correct answer is C.

Using good MCQ technique, if you were resorting to a guess you should have eliminated option A. The maximum inventory level cannot be less than the reorder quantity.

(b) Buffer inventory = minimum level

  Minimum level = reorder level – (average usage × average lead time)
    = 6,300 – (350 × 13) = 1,750.

The correct answer is D.

Option A could again be easily eliminated. With minimum usage of 180 per day, a buffer inventory of only 200 would not be much of a buffer!

4.2.4 Reorder quantity

This is the quantity of inventory which is to be ordered when inventory reaches the reorder level. If it is set so as to minimise the total costs associated with holding and ordering inventory, then it is known as the economic order quantity.

4.2.5 Average inventory

The formula for the average inventory level assumes that inventory levels fluctuate evenly between the minimum (or safety) inventory level and the highest possible inventory level (the amount of inventory immediately after an order is received, ie safety inventory + reorder quantity).

FORMULA TO LEARN

Average inventory = safety inventory + ½ reorder quantity

QUESTION

Average inventory

A component has a safety inventory of 500, a re-order quantity of 3,000 and a rate of demand which varies between 200 and 700 per week. The average inventory is approximately

A 2,000   B 2,300   C 2,500   D 3,500

ANSWER

A   Average inventory   = safety inventory + ½ reorder quantity
                                   = 500 + (0.5 × 3,000)
                                   = 2,000

4.3 Economic order quantity (EOQ)

The **economic order quantity (EOQ)** is the order quantity which minimises inventory costs. The EOQ can be calculated using a table, graph or formula.

Economic order theory assumes that the average inventory held is equal to one half of the reorder quantity (although as we saw in the last section, if an organisation maintains some sort of buffer or safety inventory then average inventory = buffer inventory + half of the reorder quantity). We have seen that there are certain costs associated with holding inventory. These costs tend to increase with the level of inventories, and so could be reduced by ordering smaller amounts from suppliers each time.

On the other hand, as we have seen, there are costs associated with ordering from suppliers: documentation, telephone calls, payment of invoices, receiving goods into stores and so on. These costs tend to increase if small orders are placed, because a larger number of orders would then be needed for a given annual demand.

4.3.1 Example: Economic order quantity

Suppose a company purchases raw material at a cost of $16 per unit. The annual demand for the raw material is 25,000 units. The holding cost per unit is $6.40 and the cost of placing an order is $32.

We can tabulate the annual relevant costs for various order quantities as follows.

Order quantity (units)		100	200	300	400	500	600	800	1,000
Average inventory (units)	(a)	50	100	150	200	250	300	400	500
Number of orders	(b)	250	125	83	63	50	42	31	25
		$	$	$	$	$	$	$	$
Annual holding cost	(c)	320	640	960	1,280	1,600	1,920	2,560	3,200
Annual order cost	(d)	8,000	4,000	2,656	2,016	1,600	1,344	992	800
Total relevant cost		8,320	4,640	3,616	3,296	3,200	3,264	3,552	4,000

Notes

(a)   Average inventory = Order quantity ÷ 2 (ie assuming no safety inventory)
(b)   Number of orders = annual demand ÷ order quantity
(c)   Annual holding cost = Average inventory × $6.40
(d)   Annual order cost = Number of orders × $32

You will see that the economic order quantity is 500 units. At this point the total annual relevant costs are at a minimum.

4.3.2 Example: Economic order quantity graph

We can present the information tabulated in Paragraph 4.3.1 in graphical form. The vertical axis represents the relevant annual costs for the investment in inventories, and the horizontal axis can be used to represent either the various order quantities or the average inventory levels; two scales are actually shown on the horizontal axis so that both items can be incorporated. The graph shows that, as the average inventory level and order quantity increase, the holding cost increases. On the other hand, the ordering costs decline as inventory levels and order quantities increase. The total cost line represents the sum of both the holding and the ordering costs.

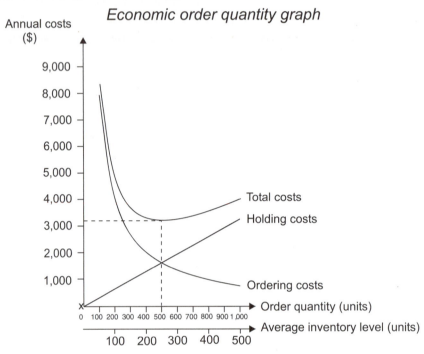

Economic order quantity graph

Note that the total cost line is at a minimum for an order quantity of 500 units and occurs at the point where the ordering cost curve and holding cost curve intersect. **The EOQ is therefore found at the point where holding costs equal ordering costs.**

4.3.3 EOQ formula

The formula for the EOQ will be provided in your examination.

FORMULA TO LEARN

$$EOQ = \sqrt{\frac{2C_0D}{C_H}} \quad \text{(given to you in the exam)}$$

where
C_H = cost of holding one unit of inventory for one time period
C_0 = cost of ordering a consignment from a supplier
D = demand during the time period

QUESTION

EOQ

Calculate the EOQ using the formula and the information in Paragraph 4.3.1.

ANSWER

$$EOQ = \sqrt{\frac{2 \times \$32 \times 25,000}{\$6.40}}$$

$$= \sqrt{250,000}$$

$$= 500 \text{ units}$$

QUESTION

EOQ and holding costs

A manufacturing company uses 25,000 components at an even rate during a year. Each order placed with the supplier of the components is for 2,000 components, which is the economic order quantity. The company holds a buffer inventory of 500 components. The annual cost of holding one component in inventory is $2.

What is the total annual cost of holding inventory of the component?

A $2,000   B $2,500   C $3,000   D $4,000

ANSWER

The correct answer is C.

[Buffer inventory + (EOQ/2)] x Annual holding cost per component

= [500 + (2,000/2)] x $2

= $3,000

EXAM FOCUS POINT

Make sure you understand how to use the EOQ formula for different purposes such as this.

4.4 Economic batch quantity (EBQ)

The **economic batch quantity** (EBQ) is a modification of the EOQ and is used when resupply is gradual instead of instantaneous.

$$EBQ = \sqrt{\frac{2C_0 D}{C_H(1 - D/R)}}$$

Typically, a manufacturing company might hold inventories of a finished item, which is produced in batches. Once the order for a new batch has been placed, and the production run has started, finished output might be used before the batch run has been completed.

4.4.1 Example: Economic batch quantity

If the daily demand for an item of inventory is ten units, and the storekeeper orders 100 units in a batch. The rate of production is 50 units a day.

(a)   On the first day of the batch production run, the stores will run out of its previous inventories, and re-supply will begin. 50 units will be produced during the day, and ten units will be consumed. The closing inventory at the end of day 1 will be 50 – 10 = 40 units.

(b)   On day 2, the final 50 units will be produced and a further ten units will be consumed. Closing inventory at the end of day 2 will be (40 + 50 –10) = 80 units.

(c)   In eight more days, inventories will fall to zero.

The minimum inventory in this example is zero, and the maximum inventory is 80 units. The maximum inventory is the quantity ordered (Q = 100) minus demand during the period of the batch production run which is Q × D/R, where

D   is the rate of demand   R   is the rate of production
Q   is the quantity ordered.

In our example, the maximum inventory is $(100 - \dfrac{10}{50} \times 100) = 100 - 20 = 80$ units.

The maximum inventory level, given gradual re-supply, is thus $Q - \dfrac{QD}{R} = Q(1 - D/R)$.

4.4.2 Example: Economic batch quantity graph

The position in Paragraph 4.4.1 can be represented graphically as follows. (Don't worry if this graph is not helpful for you. The main thing is to be able to apply the formula in the exam.)

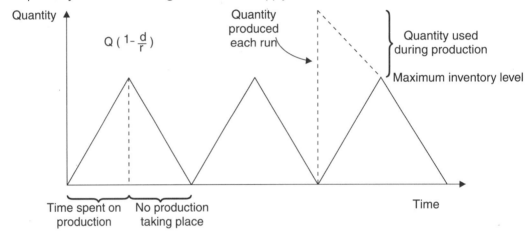

An amended EOQ (economic batch quantity, or EBQ) formula is required because average inventories are not Q/2 but Q(1 – D/R)/2.

4.4.3 EBQ Formula

EBQ is $\sqrt{\dfrac{2C_o D}{C_H (1 - D/R)}}$ (given in exam)

where R   = the production rate per time period (which must exceed the inventory usage)
        Q   = the amount produced in each batch
        D   = the usage per time period
        C_o = the set up cost per batch
        C_H = the holding cost per unit of inventory per time period

QUESTION   Economic production run

A company is able to manufacture its own components for inventory at the rate of 4,000 units a week. Demand for the component is at the rate of 2,000 units a week. Set up costs for each production run are $50. The cost of holding one unit of inventory is $0.001 a week.

Required

Calculate the economic production run.

ANSWER

$$Q = \sqrt{\frac{2 \times 50 \times 2,000}{0.001(1 - 2,000/4,000)}} = 20,000 \text{ units (giving an inventory cycle of 10 weeks)}$$

4.5 Bulk discounts

The solution obtained from using the simple EOQ formula may need to be modified if bulk discounts (also called quantity discounts) are available. The following graph shows the effect that discounts granted for orders of certain sizes may have on total costs.

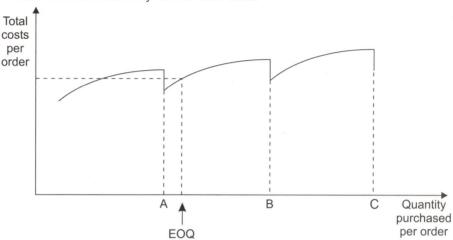

The graph above shows the following.

- Differing bulk discounts are given when the order quantity exceeds A, B and C
- The minimum total cost (ie when quantity B is ordered rather than the EOQ)

To decide mathematically whether it would be worthwhile taking a discount and ordering larger quantities, it is necessary to **minimise** the total of the following.

- Total material costs
- Ordering costs
- Inventory holding costs

The **total cost** will be **minimised** at one of the following.

- At the **pre-discount EOQ level**, so that a discount is not worthwhile
- At the **minimum order size** necessary to earn the discount

4.5.1 Example: Bulk discounts

The annual demand for an item of inventory is 45 units. The item costs $200 a unit to purchase, the holding cost for one unit for one year is 15% of the unit cost and ordering costs are $300 an order.

The supplier offers a 3% discount for orders of 60 units or more, and a discount of 5% for orders of 90 units or more.

Required

Calculate the cost-minimising order size.

Solution

(a) The EOQ ignoring discounts is $\sqrt{\dfrac{2 \times 300 \times 45}{15\% \text{ of } 200}} = 30$

	$
Purchases (no discount) 45 × $200	9,000
Holding costs (W1)	450
Ordering costs (W2)	450
Total annual costs	9,900

Workings

(1) **Holding costs**

Holding costs = Average stock × holding cost for one unit of inventory per annum

Average inventory = Order quantity ÷ 2
= 30 ÷ 2 = 15 units

Holding cost for one unit of inventory per annum = 15% × $200
= $30

∴ Holding costs = 15 units × $30
= $450

(2) **Ordering costs**

Ordering costs = Number of orders × ordering costs per order ($300)

Number of orders = Annual demand ÷ order quantity
= 45 ÷ 30
= 1.5 orders

∴ ordering costs = 1.5 orders × $300
= $450

(b) With a discount of 3% and an order quantity of 60, units costs are as follows.

	$
Purchases $9,000 × 97%	8,730
Holding costs (W3)	873
Ordering costs (W4)	225
Total annual costs	9,828

Workings

(3) **Holding costs**

Holding costs = Average inventory × holding cost for one unit of inventory per annum

Average inventory = Order quantity ÷ 2
= 60 ÷ 2 = 30 units

Holding cost for one unit of inventory per annum = 15% × 97% × $200 = $29.10

Note. 97% = 100% – 3% discount

∴ Holding costs = 30 units × $29.10
= $873

(4) **Ordering costs**

Ordering costs = Number of orders × ordering costs per order ($300)

Number of orders = Annual demand ÷ order quantity
= 45 ÷ 60
= 0.75 orders

∴ Ordering costs = 0.75 orders × $300
= $225

(c)   With a discount of 5% and an order quantity of 90, units costs are as follows.

	$
Purchases $9,000 × 95%	8,550.0
Holding costs (W5)	1,282.5
Ordering costs (W6)	150.0
Total annual costs	9,982.5

Workings

(5)   **Holding costs**

Holding costs = Average inventory × holding cost for one unit of inventory per annum

Average inventory = order quantity ÷ 2
= 90 ÷ 2
= 45 units

Holding cost for one unit of inventory per annum = 15% × 95% × $200
= $28.50

Note. 95% = 100% − 5% discount

∴ Holding costs = 45 units × $28.50
= $1,282.50

(6)   **Ordering costs**

Ordering costs = Number of orders × ordering costs per order ($300)

Number of orders = Annual demand ÷ order quantity
= 45 ÷ 90
= 0.5 orders

∴ ordering costs = 0.5 orders × $300
= $150

The cheapest option is to order 60 units at a time.

Note that the value of C_H varied according to the size of the discount, because C_H was a percentage of the purchase cost. This means that **total holding costs are reduced because of a discount**. This could easily happen if, for example, most of C_H was the cost of insurance, based on the cost of inventory held.

QUESTION

Discounts

A company uses an item of inventory as follows.

Purchase price:	$96 per unit
Annual demand:	4,000 units
Ordering cost:	$300
Annual holding cost:	10% of purchase price
Economic order quantity:	500 units

Required

Ascertain whether the company should order 1,000 units at a time in order to secure an 8% discount.

ANSWER

The total annual cost at the economic order quantity of 500 units is as follows.

	$
Purchases 4,000 × $96	384,000
Ordering costs $300 × (4,000/500)	2,400
Holding costs $96 × 10% × (500/2)	2,400
	388,800

The total annual cost at an order quantity of 1,000 units would be as follows.

	$
Purchases $384,000 × 92%	353,280
Ordering costs $300 × (4,000/1,000)	1,200
Holding costs $96 × 92% × 10% × (1,000/2)	4,416
	358,896

The company should order the item 1,000 units at a time, saving $(388,800 – 358,896) = $29,904 a year.

4.6 Other systems of stores control and reordering

4.6.1 Order cycling method

Under the order cycling method, quantities on hand of each stores item are reviewed periodically (every 1, 2 or 3 months). For low-cost items, a technique called the 90-60-30 day technique can be used, so that when inventories fall to 60 days' supply, a fresh order is placed for a 30 days' supply so as to boost inventories to 90 days' supply. For high-cost items, a more stringent stores control procedure is advisable so as to keep down the costs of inventory holding.

4.6.2 Two-bin system

The two-bin system of stores control (or visual method of control) is one whereby each stores item is kept in two storage bins. When the first bin is emptied, an order must be placed for re-supply; the second bin will contain sufficient quantities to last until the fresh delivery is received. This is a simple system which is not costly to operate but it is not based on any formal analysis of inventory usage and may result in the holding of too much or too little inventory.

4.6.3 Classification of materials

Materials items may be classified as expensive, inexpensive or in a middle-cost range. Because of the practical advantages of simplifying stores control procedures without incurring unnecessary high costs, it may be possible to segregate materials for selective stores control.

(a) Expensive and medium-cost materials are subject to careful stores control procedures to minimise cost.

(b) Inexpensive materials can be stored in large quantities because the cost savings from careful stores control do not justify the administrative effort required to implement the control.

This selective approach to stores control is sometimes called the **ABC method** whereby materials are classified A, B or C according to their expense-group A being the expensive, group B the medium-cost and group C the inexpensive materials.

4.6.4 Pareto (80/20) distribution

A similar selective approach to stores control is the **Pareto (80/20) distribution** which is based on the finding that in many stores, 80% of the value of stores is accounted for by only 20% of the stores items, and inventories of these more expensive items should be controlled more closely.

5 | Accounting for material costs

We will use an example to illustrate how to account for the purchase and issue of raw materials.

5.1 Example – material control account

Bossy Co manufactures a single product and has the following transactions for material during a particular period:

(1) Raw materials of $500,000 were purchased on credit from a supplier (Timid Co).
(2) Raw materials costing $10,000 were returned to the same supplier due to defects.
(3) The total stores requisitions for direct material for the period were $400,000.
(4) Total issues for indirect materials during the period were $15,000.
(5) $5,000 of unused material was returned to stores from production.

Required

Prepare the material control account for the period, showing clearly how each transaction is treated.

Solution

Notes on transactions:

(1) All raw material purchases are entered into the material control account as a debit entry – the corresponding credit goes to the payables control account.

(2) Any returns of material are treated in the opposite way to purchases of material.

(3) Direct material is directly related to production. The material control account will be reduced (credited) by the amount of material being issued. On-going production is represented by a Work in Progress account in the ledger system.

(4) Indirect materials are not directly related to production so will not affect the Work in Progress account. Such materials are classed as factory overheads and will therefore be entered into a Factory Overheads account.

(5) The unused material returned to stores (inventory) will increase materials inventory and will therefore be a debit entry in the material control account. As it is being returned from production, the corresponding credit entry will be in the Work in Progress account.

MATERIAL CONTROL ACCOUNT

	$		$
(1) Payables control account	500,000	(2) Payables control account	10,000
(2) Work in Progress account	5,000	(3) Work in Progress account	400,000
		(4) Factory Overheads account	15,000
		Closing inventory (bal. figure)	80,000
	505,000		505,000

Any **increases** in materials inventory will result in a **debit** entry in the material control account whilst any **reductions** in materials inventory will be shown as a **credit** entry in the material control account.

QUESTION

Accounting for materials

Doodaa Co issued $100,000 of material from stores, 25% of which did not relate directly to production. How would the transaction be recorded in Doodaa's ledger accounts?

A	Debit: Work in Progress	$100,000	Credit: Material Control Account	$100,000
B	Debit: Material Control Account	$100,000	Credit: Work in Progress	$100,000
C	Debit: Work in Progress Debit: Factory Overheads	$75,000 $25,000	Credit: Material Control Account	$100,000
D	Debit: Material Control Account	$100,000	Credit: Work in Progress Credit: Factory Overheads	$75,000 $25,000

ANSWER

The correct answer is C.

Materials inventory is being reduced as materials are being issued therefore the Material Control Account is credited with $100,000. 25% of the total ($25,000) did not relate to production and should therefore be debited to Factory Overheads. The remaining $75,000 which relates directly to production

should be debited to Work in Progress. The total debit entries equal the total credit entries, which should always be the case.

6 Inventory valuation

The correct **pricing of issues and valuation of inventory** are of the utmost importance because they have a direct effect on the calculation of profit. Several different methods can be used in practice.

6.1 Valuing inventory in financial accounts

You may be aware from your studies for the Foundations of Financial Accounting paper that, for financial accounting purposes, inventories are valued at the **lower of cost and net realisable value**. In practice, inventories will probably be valued at cost in the stores records throughout the course of an accounting period. Only when the period ends will the value of the inventory in hand be reconsidered so that items with a net realisable value below their original cost will be revalued downwards, and the inventory records altered accordingly.

6.2 Charging units of inventory to cost of production or cost of sales

It is important to be able to distinguish between the way in which the physical items in inventory are actually issued. In practice a storekeeper may issue goods in the following way.

- The oldest goods first
- The latest goods received first
- Randomly
- Those which are easiest to reach

By comparison the cost of the goods issued must be determined on a **consistently applied basis**, and must ignore the likelihood that the materials issued will be costed at a price different to the amount paid for them.

This may seem a little confusing at first, and it may be helpful to explain the point further by looking at an example.

6.3 Example: inventory valuation

Suppose that there are three units of a particular material in inventory.

Units	Date received	Purchase cost
A	June 20X1	$100
B	July 20X1	$106
C	August 20X1	$109

In September, one unit is issued to production. As it happened, the physical unit actually issued was B. The accounting department must put a value or cost on the material issued, but the value would not be the cost of B, $106. The principles used to value the materials issued are not concerned with the actual unit issued, A, B, or C. Nevertheless, the accountant may choose to make one of the following assumptions.

(a) The unit issued is valued as though it were the earliest unit in inventory, ie at the purchase cost of A, $100. This valuation principle is called **FIFO**, or **first in, first out**.

(b) The unit issued is valued as though it were the most recent unit received into inventory, ie at the purchase cost of C, $109. This method of valuation is **LIFO**, or **last in, first out**.

(c) The unit issued is valued at an **average** price of A, B and C, ie $105.

(It may be that each item of inventory is marked with the purchase cost, as it is received. This method is known as the specific price method. In the majority of cases this method is not practical.)

6.4 A chapter example

In the following sections we will consider each of the pricing methods detailed above (and a few more), using the following transactions to illustrate the principles in each case.

TRANSACTIONS DURING MAY 20X6

	Quantity	Unit cost	Total cost	Market value per unit on date of transaction
	Units	$	$	$
Opening balance, 1 May	100	2.00	200	
Receipts, 3 May	400	2.10	840	2.11
Issues, 4 May	200			2.11
Receipts, 9 May	300	2.12	636	2.15
Issues, 11 May	400			2.20
Receipts, 18 May	100	2.40	240	2.35
Issues, 20 May	100			2.35
Closing balance, 31 May	200			2.38
			1,916	

---

7 FIFO (first in, first out)

FIFO assumes that materials are issued out of inventory in the order in which they were delivered into inventory: issues are priced at the cost of the earliest delivery remaining in inventory.

7.1 Example: FIFO

Using **FIFO**, the cost of issues and the closing inventory value in the transactions in section 6.4 would be as follows.

Date of issue	Quantity issued	Value		
	Units		$	$
4 May	200	100 o/s at $2	200	
		100 at $2.10	210	
				410
11 May	400	300 at $2.10	630	
		100 at $2.12	212	
				842
20 May	100	100 at $2.12		212
Cost of issues				1,464
Closing inventory value	200	100 at $2.12	212	
		100 at $2.40	240	
				452
				1,916

Notes

(a) The cost of materials issued plus the value of closing inventory equals the cost of purchases plus the value of opening inventory ($1,916).

(b) The market price of purchased materials is rising dramatically. In a period of inflation, there is a tendency with FIFO for materials to be issued at a cost lower than the current market value, although closing inventories tend to be valued at a cost approximating to current market value. FIFO is therefore essentially a **historical cost method**, materials included in cost of production being valued at historical cost.

7.2 Advantages and disadvantages of the FIFO method

Advantages	Disadvantages
It is a logical pricing method which probably represents what is physically happening: in practice the oldest inventory is likely to be used first.	FIFO can be cumbersome to operate because of the need to identify each batch of material separately.
It is easy to understand and explain to managers.	Managers may find it difficult to compare costs and make decisions when they are charged with varying prices for the same materials.
The inventory valuation can be near to a valuation based on replacement cost.	In a period of high inflation, inventory issue prices will lag behind current market value.

QUESTION

FIFO

Complete the table below in as much detail as possible using the information in Sections 6.4 and 7.1.

Date	Receipts			Issues			Inventory		
	Quantity	Unit price $	Amount $	Quantity	Unit price $	Amount $	Quantity	Unit price $	Amount $

ANSWER

Date	Receipts			Issues			Inventory		
	Quantity	Unit price $	Amount $	Quantity	Unit price $	Amount $	Quantity	Unit price $	Amount $
1.5.X3							100	2.00	200.00
3.5.X3	400	2.10	840.00				100	2.00	200.00
							400	2.10	840.00
							500		1,040.00
4.5.X3				100	2.00	200.00			
				100	2.10	210.00	300	2.10	630.00
9.5.X3	300	2.12	636.00				300	2.10	630.00
							300	2.12	636.00
							600		1,266.00

Date	Receipts Qty	Receipts Unit price	Receipts Amount	Issues Qty	Issues Unit price	Issues Amount	Balance Qty	Balance Unit price	Balance Amount
11.5.X3				300	2.10	630.00			
				100	2.12	212.00	200	2.12	424.00
18.5.X3	100	2.40	240.00				200	2.12	424.00
							100	2.40	240.00
							300		664.00
20.5.X3				100	2.12	212.00	100	2.12	212.00
							100	2.40	240.00
31.5.X3							200		452.00

Note that this type of record is called a **perpetual inventory system** as it shows each receipt and issue of inventory as it occurs.

8 LIFO (last in, first out)

> **LIFO** assumes that materials are issued out of inventory in the reverse order to which they were delivered: the most recent deliveries are issued before earlier ones, and issues are priced accordingly.

8.1 Example: LIFO

Using LIFO, the cost of issues and the closing inventory value in the example above would be as follows.

Date of issue	Quantity issued Units	Valuation	$	$
4 May	200	200 at $2.10		420
11 May	400	300 at $2.12	636	
		100 at $2.10	210	
				846
20 May	100	100 at $2.40		240
Cost of issues				1,506
Closing inventory value	200	100 at $2.10	210	
		100 at $2.00	200	
				410
				1,916

Notes

(a) The cost of materials issued plus the value of closing inventory equals the cost of purchases plus the value of opening inventory ($1,916).

(b) In a period of inflation there is a tendency with **LIFO** for the following to occur.

    (i) Materials are issued at a price which approximates to current market value (or **economic cost**).

    (ii) Closing inventories become undervalued when compared to market value.

8.2 Advantages and disadvantages of the **LIFO** method

Advantages	Disadvantages
Inventories are issued at a price which is close to current market value.	The method can be cumbersome to operate because it sometimes results in several batches being only part-used in the inventory records before another batch is received.
Managers are continually aware of recent costs when making decisions, because the costs being charged to their department or products will be current costs.	LIFO is often the opposite to what is physically happening and can therefore be difficult to explain to managers.
	As with FIFO, decision making can be difficult because of the variations in prices.

8.3 Changing from LIFO to FIFO or from FIFO to LIFO

You may get an assessment question which asks you what would happen to closing inventory values or gross profits if a business changed its method from LIFO to FIFO or vice versa. You may find it easier to think about this using diagrams.

Let's consider a very simple example where four barrels of inventory are purchased during a month of rising prices, and two are used. There is no opening inventory.

		Cost		
Jan 1st		$100 per barrel	**LIFO** – these barrels would be left as **closing inventory $250**	**FIFO** – these barrels would be issued to **production** first (and charged to cost of sales) **$250)**
Jan 19th		$150 per barrel		
Jan 20th		$200 per barrel	**LIFO** – these barrels would be issued to **production** first (and charged to cost of sales) **$450**	**FIFO** – these barrels would be left as **closing inventory $450**
Jan 31st		$250 per barrel		

Notice the rising prices

As you can see, during a period of rising prices, the closing inventory value using LIFO would be $250 and using FIFO would be higher at $450. The charge to cost of sales will be lower using FIFO and therefore the gross profit will be higher.

9 AVCO (cumulative weighted average pricing)

The cumulative weighted average pricing method (or AVCO) calculates a **weighted average price** for all units in inventory. Issues are priced at this average cost, and the balance of inventory remaining would have the same unit valuation. The average price is determined by dividing the total cost by the total number of units.

A new weighted average price is calculated whenever a new delivery of materials is received into store. This is the key feature of cumulative weighted average pricing.

9.1 Example: AVCO

In our example, issue costs and closing inventory values would be as follows.

Date	Received Units	Issued Units	Balance Units	Total inventory value $	Unit cost $	$
Opening inventory			100	200	2.00	
3 May	400			840	2.10	
			* 500	1,040	2.08	
4 May		200		(416)	2.08	416
			300	624	2.08	
9 May	300			636	2.12	
			* 600	1,260	2.10	
11 May		400		(840)	2.10	840
			200	420	2.10	
18 May	100			240	2.40	
			* 300	660	2.20	
20 May		100		(220)	2.20	220
						1,476
Closing inventory value			200	440	2.20	440
						1,916

* A new inventory value per unit is calculated whenever a new receipt of materials occurs.

Notes

(a)   The cost of materials issued plus the value of closing inventory equals the cost of purchases plus the value of opening inventory ($1,916).

(b)   In a period of inflation, using the cumulative weighted average pricing system, the value of material issues will rise gradually, but will tend to lag a little behind the current market value at the date of issue. Closing inventory values will also be a little below current market value.

9.2 Advantages and disadvantages of AVCO

Advantages	Disadvantages
Fluctuations in prices are smoothed out, making it easier to use the data for decision making.	The resulting issue price is rarely an actual price that has been paid, and can run to several decimal places.
It is easier to administer than FIFO and LIFO, because there is no need to identify each batch separately.	Prices tend to lag a little behind current market values when there is gradual inflation.

QUESTION

Inventory valuation methods

Shown below is an extract from records for inventory code no 988988.

Date		Receipts				Issues				Balance		
	Qty	Value $	Total $	Qty	Value $	Total $	Qty	Value $	Total $
5 June							30	2.50	75
8 June	20	3.00	60						
10 June				10		A			
14 June				20		B			
18 June	40	2.40	96						
20 June				6		C			D

(a) The values that would be entered on the stores ledger card for A, B, C and D in a cumulative weighted average pricing system would be:

A $ ☐   C $ ☐

B $ ☐   D $ ☐

(b) The values that would be entered on the stores ledger card for A, B, C and D in a LIFO system would be:

A $ ☐   C $ ☐

B $ ☐   D $ ☐

ANSWER

(a) A $ 27   C $ 15

     B $ 54   D $ 135

Workings

				$
8 June	Inventory balance	30	units @ $2.50	75
		20	units @ $3.00	60
		50		135

Weighted average price = $135/50 = $2.70

| **10 June** | Issues | 10 | units × $2.70 | $27 |
| **14 June** | Issues | 20 | units × $2.70 | $54 |

18 June	Inventory balance	20	units @ $2.70	54
	Remaining receipts	40	units @ $2.40	96
		60		150

Weighted average price = $150/60 = = $2.50

| **20 June** | Issues | 6 | units × $2.50 | $15 |
| | Inventory balance | 54 | units × $2.50 | $135 |

(b) A $ [30]   C $ [14.40]

    B $ [55]   D $ [131.60]

Workings

10 June		10	units × $3.00	$30
14 June	Remaining	10	units × $3.00	$30
		10	units × $2.50	$25
				$55
20 June	Issues:	6	units × $2.40	$14.40
	Balance:	34	units × $2.40	81.60
		20	units × $2.50	50.00
		54		131.60

9.3 Periodic weighted average

The periodic weighted average pricing method calculates an average price at the end of the period, based on the total purchases in that period.

$$\text{Periodic weighted average} = \frac{\text{Cost of opening inventory} + \text{total cost of receipts}}{\text{Units of opening inventory} + \text{total units received}}$$

9.3.1 Example: Periodic weighted average

A wholesaler had the following receipts and issues during May.

	Receipts units	Issues units	$/unit
4 May	800		30
6 May		400	
13 May	600		35
14 May		400	
23 May	600		40
25 May		400	
29 May		400	
	2,000	1,600	

Calculate the value of closing inventory at the end of May using the periodic weighted average.

$$\text{Periodic weighted average} = \frac{(800 \times \$30) + (600 \times \$35) + (600 \times \$40)}{800 + 600 + 600}$$

$$= \$34.50 \text{ per unit}$$

Value of closing inventory = 400 units × $34.50

$$= \$13,800$$

EXAM FOCUS POINT

As this method is easier than the cumulative weighted average method you are less likely to get a question on it in the exam! Make sure you use the cumulative weighted average method unless the exam question specifically mentions the periodic weighted average.

CHAPTER ROUNDUP

↳ **Inventory control** includes the functions of inventory ordering and purchasing, receiving goods into store, storing and issuing inventory and controlling the levels of inventory.

↳ Every movement of material in a business should be documented using the following as appropriate: purchase requisition, purchase order, GRN, materials requisition note, materials transfer note and materials returned note.

↳ The **inventory count (stocktake)** involves counting the physical inventory on hand at a certain date, and then checking this against the balance shown in the inventory records. The inventory count can be carried out on a **continuous** or **periodic** basis.

↳ **Perpetual inventory** refers to an inventory recording system whereby the records (bin cards and stores ledger accounts) are updated for each receipt and issue of inventory as it occurs.

↳ **Obsolete inventories** are those items which have become out-of-date and are no longer required. Obsolete items are written off and disposed of.

↳ **Inventory costs** include purchase costs, holding costs, ordering costs and costs of running out of inventory.

↳ **Inventory control levels** can be calculated in order to maintain inventories at the optimum level. The three critical control levels are reorder level, minimum level and maximum level.

↳ The **economic order quantity** (EOQ) is the order quantity which minimises inventory costs. The EOQ can be calculated using a table, graph or formula.

$$EOQ = \sqrt{\frac{2C_oD}{C_H}}$$

↳ The **economic batch quantity (EBQ)** is a modification of the EOQ and is used when resupply is gradual instead of instantaneous.

$$EBQ = \sqrt{\frac{2C_oD}{C_H(1-D/R)}}$$

↳ Any **increases** in materials inventory will result in a **debit** entry in the material control account whilst any **reductions** in materials inventory will be shown as a **credit** entry in the material control account.

↳ The correct **pricing of issues and valuation of inventory** are of the utmost importance because they have a direct effect on the calculation of profit. Several different methods can be used in practice.

↳ **FIFO** assumes that materials are issued out of inventory in the order in which they were delivered into inventory: issues are priced at the cost of the earliest delivery remaining in inventory.

↳ **LIFO** assumes that materials are issued out of inventory in the reverse order to which they were delivered: the most recent deliveries are issued before earlier ones, and issues are priced accordingly.

↳ The cumulative weighted average pricing method (or AVCO) calculates a **weighted average price** for all units in inventory. Issues are priced at this average cost, and the balance of inventory remaining would have the same unit valuation. The average price is determined by dividing the total cost by the total number of units.

A new weighted average price is calculated whenever a new delivery of materials is received into store. This is the key feature of cumulative weighted average pricing.

QUICK QUIZ

1 List six objectives of storekeeping.

- ....
- ....
- ....
- ....
- ....
- ....

2 Free inventory represents...

3 Free inventory is calculated as follows. (Delete as appropriate)

(a)	+ –	Materials in inventory		X
(b)	+ –	Materials in order		X
(c)	+ –	Materials requisitioned (not yet issued)		X
		Free inventory balance		X

4 How does periodic inventory counting differ from continuous inventory counting?

5 Match up the following.

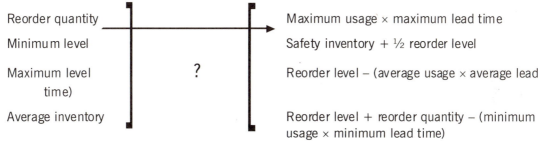

Reorder quantity

Minimum level

Maximum level time)

Average inventory

?

Maximum usage × maximum lead time

Safety inventory + ½ reorder level

Reorder level – (average usage × average lead time)

Reorder level + reorder quantity – (minimum usage × minimum lead time)

6 $EOQ = \sqrt{\dfrac{2C_o D}{C_H}}$

Where

(a) C_H = ...
(b) C_o = ...
(c) D = ...

7 When is the economic batch quantity used?

8 Which of the following are true?

I With FIFO, the inventory valuation will be very close to replacement cost.

II With LIFO, inventories are issued at a price which is close to the current market value.

III Decision making can be difficult with both FIFO and LIFO because of the variations in prices.

IV A disadvantage of the weighted average method of inventory valuation is that the resulting issue price is rarely an actual price that has been paid and it may be calculated to several decimal places.

A I and II only
B I, II and III only
C I and III only
D I, II, III and IV

9 LIFO is essentially an historical cost method.

True ☐

False ☐

10 *Fill in the blanks.*

When using .... method of inventory valuation, issues are at a price which approximates to economic cost.

1 • Speedy **issue** and **receipt** of materials
   • Full **identification** of all materials at all times
   • Correct **location** of all materials at all times
   • **Protection** of materials from damage and deterioration
   • Provision of **secure stores** to avoid pilferage, theft and fire
   • **Efficient** use of storage space
   • **Maintenance** of correct inventory levels
   • Keeping correct and up-to-date **records** of receipts, issues and inventory levels

2 Inventory that is readily available for future use.

3 (a) +
  (b) +
  (c) –

4 **Periodic inventory counting.** All inventory items physically counted and valued, usually annually.

   Continuous inventory counting. Counting and valuing selected items at different times of the year (at least once a year).

5

Reorder quantity ⟶ Maximum usage × maximum lead time

Minimum level ⟶ Safety inventory + ½ reorder level

Maximum level ⟶ Reorder level – (average usage × average lead time)

Average inventory ⟶ Reorder level + reorder quantity – (minimum usage × minimum lead time)

6 (a) Cost of holding one unit of inventory for one time period
  (b) Cost of ordering a consignment from a supplier
  (c) Demand during the time period

7 When resupply of a product is gradual instead of instantaneous.

8 D All of the statements are true

9 False. FIFO is an historical cost method

10 LIFO

Now try ...

Attempt the questions below from the **Exam Question Bank**

Number

Q23 – Q28

CHAPTER

07

Just as management need to control inventories and operate an appropriate valuation policy in an attempt to control material costs, so too must they be aware of the most suitable **remuneration policy** for their organisation. We will be looking at a number of methods of remuneration and will consider the various types of **incentive scheme** that exist. We will also examine the procedures and documents required for the accurate **recording of labour costs**. **Labour turnover** will be studied too.

Accounting for labour

TOPIC LIST	SYLLABUS REFERENCE
1 Measuring labour activity	B1 (b)(vi)
2 Remuneration methods	B1 (b)(iv)
3 Recording labour costs	B1 (b)(ii)
4 Labour turnover	B1 (b)(v)
5 Accounting for labour costs	B1 (b)(i)(iii)(vii)

Study Guide	Intellectual level
B **Cost accounting techniques**	
1 **Accounting for material, labour and overheads**	S
(b)(i) Calculate direct and indirect labour costs	K
(b)(ii) Explain the methods used to relate input labour costs to work done	
(b)(iii) Prepare the journal and ledger entries to record labour cost inputs and outputs	S
(b)(iv) Describe different remuneration methods: time-based systems, piecework systems and individual and group incentive schemes	K
(b)(v) Calculate the level, and analyse the costs and causes of labour turnover	S
(b)(vi) Explain and calculate labour efficiency, capacity and production volume ratios	S
(b)(vii) Interpret the entries in the labour account	S

EXAM FOCUS POINT

You may get a question just on labour costs or on working out an employee's pay or you may have to deal with labour as a component of variable cost or overhead.

---

1 Measuring labour activity

Production and productivity are common methods of measuring labour activity.

1.1 Production and productivity

Production is the quantity or volume of output produced. **Productivity** is a measure of the efficiency with which output has been produced. An increase in production without an increase in productivity will not reduce unit costs

1.2 Example: Production and productivity

Suppose that an employee is expected to produce three units in every hour that he works. The standard rate of productivity is three units per hour, and one unit is valued at $^1/_3$ of a standard hour of output. If, during one week, the employee makes 126 units in 40 hours of work the following comments can be made.

(a)   **Production** in the week is 126 units.

(b)   **Productivity** is a relative measure of the hours actually taken and the hours that should have been taken to make the output.

(i)	**Either**, 126 units should take	42 hours
	But did take	40 hours
	Productivity ratio = 42/40 × 100% =	105%
(ii)	**Or alternatively**, in 40 hours, he should make (× 3)	120 units
	But did make	126 units
	Productivity ratio = 126/120 × 100% =	105%

A productivity ratio greater than 100% indicates that actual efficiency is better than the expected or 'standard' level of efficiency.

Standard hour of production is a concept used in standard costing, and means the number of units that can be produced by one worker working in the standard way at the standard rate for one hour.

1.3 Planning and controlling production and productivity

Management will wish to **plan** and **control** both production levels and labour productivity.

(a)   **Production levels can be raised** as follows.

      (i)   Working overtime
      (ii)   Hiring extra staff
      (iii)   Sub-contracting some work to an outside firm
      (iv)   Managing the work force so as to achieve more output.

(b)   **Production levels can be reduced** as follows.

      (i)   Cancelling overtime
      (ii)   Laying off staff

(c)   **Productivity**, if improved, will enable a company to achieve its production targets in fewer hours of work, and therefore at a lower cost.

1.4 Productivity and its effect on cost

Improved productivity is an important means of reducing total unit costs. In order to make this point clear, a simple example will be used.

1.4.1 Example: Productivity and its effect on cost

Clooney Co has a production department in its factory consisting of a work team of just two men, Doug and George. Doug and George each work a 40 hour week and refuse to do any overtime. They are each paid $100 per week and production overheads of $400 per week are charged to their work.

(a)   In week one, they produce 160 units of output between them. Productivity is measured in units of output per man hour.

Production	160 units
Productivity (80 man hours)	2 units per man hour
Total cost	$600 (labour plus overhead)
Cost per man hour	$7.50
Cost per unit	$3.75

(b)   In week two, management pressure is exerted on Doug and George to increase output and they produce 200 units in normal time.

Production	200 units (up by 25%)
Productivity	2.5 units per man hour (up by 25%)
Total cost	$600
Cost per man hour	$7.50 (no change)
Cost per unit	$3.00 (a saving of 20% on the previous cost; 25% on the new cost)

(c)   In week three, Doug and George agree to work a total of 20 hours of overtime for an additional $50 wages. Output is again 200 units and overhead charges are increased by $100.

Production	200 units (up 25% on week one)
Productivity (100 man hours)	2 units per hour (no change on week one)
Total cost ($600 + $50 + $100)	$750
Cost per unit	$3.75

(d)   Conclusions

    (i)   An increase in production without an increase in productivity will not reduce unit costs (week one compared with week three).

    (ii)   An **increase in productivity will reduce unit costs** (week one compared with week two).

1.4.2 Automation

Labour cost control is largely concerned with **productivity**. Rising wage rates have increased automation, which in turn has improved productivity and reduced costs.

Where **automation** is introduced, productivity is often, but misleadingly, measured in terms of **output per man-hour**.

1.4.3 Example: Automation

Suppose, for example, that a work-team of six men (240 hours per week) is replaced by one machine (40 hours per week) and a team of four men (160 hours per week), and as a result output is increased from 1,200 units per week to 1,600 units.

	Production	Man hours	Productivity
Before the machine	1,200 units	240	5 units per man hour
After the machine	1,600 units	160	10 units per man hour

Labour productivity has doubled because of the machine, and employees would probably expect extra pay for this success. For control purposes, however, it is likely that a new measure of productivity is required, **output per machine hour**, which may then be measured against a standard output for performance reporting.

1.5 Efficiency, capacity and production volume ratios

Other measures of labour activity include the following.

- Production volume ratio, or activity ratio
- Efficiency ratio (or productivity ratio)
- Capacity ratio

Efficiency ratio	× **Capacity ratio**	= **Production volume ratio**
$\dfrac{\text{Expected hours to make output}}{\text{Actual hours taken}}$	$\times \dfrac{\text{Actual hours worked}}{\text{Hours budgeted}}$	$= \dfrac{\text{Output measured in expected or standard hours}}{\text{Hours budgeted}}$

These ratios are usually expressed as percentages.

1.5.1 Example: Labour activity ratios

Rush and Fluster Co budgets to make 25,000 standard units of output (in four hours each) during a budget period of 100,000 hours.

Actual output during the period was 27,000 units which took 120,000 hours to make.

Required

Calculate the efficiency, capacity and production volume ratios.

Solution

(a)   Efficiency ratio $\dfrac{(27,000 \times 4) \text{ hours}}{120,000} \times 100\% = 90\%$

(b)   Capacity ratio $\dfrac{120,000 \text{ hours}}{100,000 \text{ hours}} \times 100\% = 120\%$

(c)   Production volume ratio $\dfrac{(27{,}000 \times 4)\ \text{hours}}{100{,}000} \times 100\% = 108\%$

(d)   The production volume ratio of 108% (more output than budgeted) is explained by the 120% capacity working, offset to a certain extent by the poor efficiency (90% × 120% = 108%).

Where efficiency standards are associated with remuneration schemes they generally allow 'normal time' (that is, time required by the average person to do the work under normal conditions) plus an allowance for rest periods and possible delays. There should therefore be a readily achievable standard of efficiency (otherwise any remuneration scheme will fail to motivate employees), but without being so lax that it makes no difference to the rate at which work is done.

2 Remuneration methods

> There are three basic groups of **remuneration** method: **time work**, **piecework schemes** and **bonus/incentive schemes**.

Labour remuneration methods have an effect on the following.

*   The cost of finished products and services.
*   The morale and efficiency of employees.

2.1 Time work

KEY TERM

The most common form of **time work** is a **day-rate system** in which wages are calculated by the following formula.

Wages = Hours worked × rate of pay per hour

2.1.1 Overtime premiums

If an employee works for more hours than the basic daily requirement he may be entitled to an **overtime payment**. Hours of overtime are usually paid at a **premium rate**. For instance, if the basic day-rate is $4 per hour and overtime is paid at time-and-a-quarter, eight hours of overtime would be paid the following amount.

	$
Basic pay (8 × $4)	32
Overtime premium (8 × $1)	8
Total (8 × $5)	40

The **overtime premium** is the extra rate per hour which is paid, not the whole of the payment for the overtime hours.

If employees work unsocial hours, for instance overnight, they may be entitled to a **shift premium**. The extra amount paid per hour, above the basic hourly rate, is the **shift premium**.

2.1.2 Summary of day-rate systems

(a)   They are easy to understand.

(b)   They do not lead to very complex negotiations when they are being revised.

(c)   They are most appropriate when the quality of output is more important than the quantity, or where there is no basis for payment by performance.

(d)   There is no incentive for employees who are paid on a day-rate basis to improve their performance.

2.2 Piecework schemes

FORMULA TO LEARN

In a **piecework scheme**, wages are calculated by the following formula.

Wages = Units produced × Rate of pay per unit

Suppose for example, an employee is paid $1 for each unit produced and works a 40 hour week. Production overhead is added at the rate of $2 per direct labour hour.

Weekly production Units	Pay (40 hours) $	Overhead $	Conversion cost $	Conversion cost per unit $
40	40	80	120	3.00
50	50	80	130	2.60
60	60	80	140	2.33
70	70	80	150	2.14

As his output increases, his wage increases and at the same time unit costs of output are reduced.

It is normal for pieceworkers to be offered a **guaranteed minimum wage**, so that they do not suffer loss of earnings when production is low through no fault of their own.

If an employee makes several different types of product, it may not be possible to add up the units for payment purposes. Instead, a **standard time allowance** is given for each unit to arrive at a total of piecework hours for payment.

QUESTION
Weekly pay

Penny Pincher is paid 50c for each towel she weaves, but she is guaranteed a minimum wage of $60 for a 40 hour week. In a series of four weeks, she makes 100, 120, 140 and 160 towels.

Required

Calculate her pay each week, and the conversion cost per towel if production overhead is added at the rate of $2.50 per direct labour hour.

ANSWER

Week	Output Units	Pay $	Production overhead $	Conversion cost $	Unit conversion cost $
1	100 (minimum)	60	100	160	1.60
2	120	60	100	160	1.33
3	140	70	100	170	1.21
4	160	80	100	180	1.13

There is no incentive to Penny Pincher to produce more output unless she can exceed 120 units in a week. The guaranteed minimum wage in this case is too high to provide an incentive.

2.2.1 Example: Piecework

An employee is paid $5 per piecework hour produced. In a 35 hour week he produces the following output.

	Piecework time allowed per unit
3 units of product A	2.5 hours
5 units of product B	8.0 hours

Required

Calculate the employee's pay for the week.

Solution

Piecework hours produced are as follows.

Product A	3 × 2.5 hours	7.5 hours
Product B	5 × 8 hours	40.0 hours
Total piecework hours		47.5 hours

Therefore employee's pay = 47.5 × $5 = $237.50 for the week.

2.2.2 Differential piecework scheme

Differential piecework schemes offer an incentive to employees to increase their output by paying higher rates for increased levels of production. For example:

up to 80 units per week, rate of pay per unit	=	$1.00
80 to 90 units per week, rate of pay per unit	=	$1.20
above 90 units per week, rate of pay per unit	=	$1.30

Employers should obviously be careful to make it clear whether they intend to pay the increased rate on all units produced, or on the extra output only.

2.2.3 Summary of piecework schemes

- They enjoy fluctuating popularity.
- They are occasionally used by employers as a means of increasing pay levels.
- They are often seen to drive employees to work too hard to earn a satisfactory wage.

Careful inspection of output is necessary to ensure that quality doesn't fall as production increases.

2.3 Bonus/incentive schemes

2.3.1 Introduction

In general, **bonus schemes** were introduced to compensate workers paid under a time-based system for their inability to increase earnings by working more efficiently. Various types of incentive and bonus schemes have been devised which encourage greater productivity. The characteristics of such schemes are as follows.

(a)   Employees are paid more for their efficiency.

(b)   The profits arising from productivity improvements are shared between employer and employee.

(c)   Morale of employees is likely to improve since they are seen to receive extra reward for extra effort.

A bonus scheme must satisfy certain conditions to operate successfully.

(a)   Its **objectives** should be **clearly stated** and **attainable** by the employees.

(b)   The **rules** and conditions of the scheme should be **easy to understand**.

(c)   It must **win** the full **acceptance** of everyone concerned.

(d)   It should be seen to be **fair to employees and employers**.

(e)   The bonus should ideally be **paid soon after the extra effort has been made** by the employees.

(f)   **Allowances** should be made for external factors outside the employees' control which reduce their productivity (machine breakdowns, material shortages).

(g)   Only those employees who make the extra effort should be rewarded.

(h)   The scheme must be **properly communicated** to employees.

We shall be looking at the following types of incentive schemes in detail.

- High day rate system
- Individual bonus schemes
- Group bonus schemes

- Profit sharing schemes
- Incentive schemes involving shares
- Value added incentive schemes

Some organisations employ a variety of incentive schemes. A scheme for a production labour force may not necessarily be appropriate for white-collar workers. An organisation's incentive schemes may be regularly reviewed, and altered as circumstances dictate.

2.4 High day-rate system

A **high day-rate system** is a system where employees are paid a high hourly wage rate in the expectation that they will work more efficiently than similar employees on a lower hourly rate in a different company.

2.4.1 Example: High day-rate system

For example if an employee would make 100 units in a 40 hour week if he were paid $2 per hour, but 120 units if he were paid $2.50 per hour, and if production overhead is added to cost at the rate of $2 per direct labour hour, costs per unit of output would be as follows.

(a)   Costs per unit of output on the low day-rate scheme would be:

$$\frac{(40 \times \$4)}{100} = \$1.60 \text{ per unit}$$

(b)   Costs per unit of output on the high day-rate scheme would be:

$$\frac{(40 \times \$4.50)}{120} = \$1.50 \text{ per unit}$$

(c)   Note that in this example the labour cost per unit is lower in the first scheme (80c) than in the second (83.3c), but the unit conversion cost (labour plus production overhead) is higher because overhead costs per unit are higher at 80c than with the high day-rate scheme (66.7c).

(d)   In this example, the high day-rate scheme would reward both employer (a lower unit cost by 10c) and employee (an extra 50c earned per hour).

2.4.2 Advantages and disadvantages of high day rate schemes

There are two **advantages** of a high day-rate scheme over other incentive schemes.

(a)   It is **simple** to calculate and **easy** to understand.
(b)   It **guarantees** the employee a consistently **high wage**.

The **disadvantages** of such schemes are as follows.

(a)   **Employees cannot earn more than the fixed hourly rate for their extra effort**. In the previous example, if the employee makes 180 units instead of 120 units in a 40 hour week on a high day-rate pay scheme, the cost per unit would fall to $1 but his wage would be the same – 40 hours at $4.50. All the savings would go to benefit the company and none would go to the employee.

(b)   **There is no guarantee that the scheme will work consistently**. The high wages may become the accepted level of pay for normal working, and supervision may be necessary to ensure that a high level of productivity is maintained. Unit costs would rise.

(c)   **Employees may prefer to work at a normal rate of output**, even if this entails accepting the lower wage paid by comparable employers.

2.5 Individual bonus schemes

An **individual bonus scheme** is a remuneration scheme whereby **individual** employees qualify for a bonus on top of their basic wage, with each person's bonus being calculated separately.

(a)   The bonus is **unique** to the individual. It is not a share of a group bonus.

(b)   The individual can earn a bonus by working at an **above-target** standard of efficiency.

(c)   The individual earns a **bigger bonus the greater his efficiency**, although the bonus scheme might incorporate quality safeguards, to prevent individuals from sacrificing quality standards for the sake of speed and more pay.

To be successful, however, an **individual bonus scheme** must take account of the following factors.

(a)   Each individual should be rewarded for the **work done by that individual**. This means that each person's output and time must be measured separately. Each person must therefore work without the assistance of anyone else.

(b)   Work should be **fairly routine**, so that standard times can be set for jobs.

(c)   The bonus should be **paid soon after the work is done**, to provide the individual with the incentive to try harder.

2.6 Group bonus schemes

A **group bonus scheme** is an incentive plan which is related to the output performance of an entire group of workers, a department, or even the whole factory.

Where individual effort cannot be measured, and employees work as a team, an individual incentive scheme is impracticable but a **group bonus scheme** would be feasible.

The other **advantages** of group bonus schemes are as follows.

(a)   They are **easier to administer** because they reduce the clerical effort required to measure output and calculate individual bonuses.

(b)   They **increase co-operation** between fellow workers.

(c)   They have been found to **reduce** accidents, spoilage, waste and absenteeism.

Serious **disadvantages** would occur in the following circumstances.

(a)   The employee groups demand **low efficiency standards** as a condition of accepting the scheme.

(b)   Individual employees are browbeaten by their fellow workers for working too slowly.

3 Recording labour costs

Labour attendance time is recorded on, for example, an attendance record or clock card. Job time may be recorded on daily time sheets, weekly time sheets or job cards depending on the circumstances. The manual recording of times on time sheets or job cards is, however, liable to error or even deliberate deception and may be unreliable. The labour cost of pieceworkers is recorded on a piecework ticket/operation card.

3.1 Organisation for controlling and measuring labour costs

Several departments and management groups are involved in the collection, recording and costing of labour. These include the following.

- Personnel
- Production planning
- Timekeeping

- Wages
- Cost accounting

3.2 Personnel department

The **personnel department** is responsible for the following:

- Engagement, transfer and discharge of employees.
- Classification and method of remuneration.

The department is headed by a **professional personnel officer** trained in personnel management, labour laws, company personnel policy and industry conditions who should have an understanding of the needs and problems of the employees.

When a person is engaged a **personnel record card** should be prepared showing full personal particulars, previous employment, medical category and wage rate. Other details to be included are social security number, address, telephone number, transfers, promotions, changes in wage rates, sickness and accidents and, when an employee leaves, the reason for leaving.

Personnel departments sometimes **maintain records of overtime and shift working**. Overtime has to be sanctioned by the works manager or personnel office who advise the time-keepers who control the time booked.

The personnel department is responsible for issuing **reports to management** on normal and overtime hours worked, absenteeism and sickness, lateness, labour turnover and disciplinary action.

3.3 Production planning department

This department is responsible for the following.

- Scheduling work
- Issuing job orders to production departments
- Chasing up jobs when they run late

3.4 Timekeeping department

The **timekeeping department** is responsible for recording the attendance time and job time of the following.

- The time spent in the factory by each worker
- The time spent by each worker on each job

Such timekeeping provides basic data for statutory records, payroll preparation, labour costs of an operation or overhead distribution (where based on wages or labour hours) and statistical analysis of labour records for determining productivity and control of labour costs.

3.5 Attendance time

The bare minimum record of employees' time is a simple **attendance record** showing days absent because of holiday, sickness or other reason. A typical record of attendance is shown as follows.

	1	2	3	4	5	6	7	8	9	10	11	12	13	14	15	16	17	18	19	20	21	22	23	24	25	26	27	28	29	30	31
JAN																															
FEB																															
MAR																															
APR																															
MAY																															
JUNE																															
JULY																															
AUG																															
SEPT																															
OCT																															
NOV																															
DEC																															

NAME: A.N. OTHER   *DEPT:* 072   *NI REF:* WD 4847 41C   *LEAVE ENTITLEMENT:* 20

Illness: I
Industrial Accident: IA
Maternity: M

Leave: L
Unpaid Leave: UL
Special Leave: SL

Training: T
Jury Service: J

Note overleaf: (1) The reasons for special leave (eg bereavement).

(2) Ensure training is noted on personnel card.

RECORD OF ATTENDANCE

It is also necessary to have a record of the following.

- Time of arrival
- Time of breaks
- Time of departure

These may be recorded as follows.

- In a signing-in book
- By using a time recording clock which stamps the time on a clock card
- By using swipe cards (which make a computer record)

An example of a clock card is shown as follows.

No				Ending	
Name					
HOURS	RATE	AMOUNT	DEDUCTIONS		
Basic			Tax		
O/T			Insurance		
Others			Other		
			Total deduction		
Total					
Less deductions					
Net due					
Time	Day		Basic time	Overtime	
1230 T					
0803 T					
1700 M					
1305 M					
1234 M					
0750 M					
Signature _ _ _ _ _ _ _ _ _ _ _					

3.6 Job time

Continuous production. Where **routine, repetitive** work is carried out it might not be practical to record the precise details. For example if a worker stands at a conveyor belt for seven hours his work can be measured by keeping a note of the number of units that pass through his part of the process during that time.

Job costing. When the work is not of a repetitive nature the records required might be one or several of the following.

(a) **Daily time sheets**. A time sheet is filled in by the employee as a record of how their time has been spent. The total time on the time sheet should correspond with time shown on the attendance record.

(b) **Weekly time sheets**. These are similar to daily time sheets but are passed to the cost office at the end of the week. An example of a weekly timesheet is shown below.

Time Sheet No. _ _ _ _ _ _ _ _ _ _ _ _ _ _ _ _ _							
Employee Name _ _ _ _ _ _ _ _ _ Clock Code _ _ _ _ _ _ _ _ _ Dept _ _ _ _ _ _ _							
Date _ _ _ _ _ _ _ _ _ _ _ _ _ _ _ _ _ _ Week No. _ _ _ _ _ _ _ _ _ _ _ _ _							
Job No.	Start Time	Finish Time	Qty	Checker	Hrs	Rate	Extension

(c) **Job cards**. Cards are prepared for each job or batch. When an employee works on a job he or she records on the job card the time spent on that job. Job cards are therefore likely to contain entries relating to numerous employees. On completion of the job it will contain a full record of the times and quantities involved in the job or batch. A typical job card is shown as follows.

JOB CARD			
Department _ Job no _ .			
Date _ . Operation no. _			
Time allowance _ _ _ _ _ _ _ _ _ _ _ _ _ _ _ _ _ _ Time started _ _ _ _ _ _ _ _ _ _ _ _ _ _ _ _ _ _ _			
	Time finished _ _ _ _ _ _ _ _ _ _ _ _ _ _ _ _ _ _ _ .		
	Hours on the job _ _ _ _ _ _ _ _ _ _ _ _ _ _ _ _ _ _		
Description of job	Hours	Rate	Cost
Employee no_ Certified by _			
Signature _			

A job card will be given to the employee, showing the work to be done and the expected time it should take. The employee will record the time started and time finished for each job. Breaks for tea and lunch may be noted on the card, as standard times, by the production planning department. The hours actually taken and the cost of those hours will be calculated by the accounting department.

Piecework. The wages of pieceworkers and the labour cost of work done by them is determined from what is known as a **piecework ticket** or an **operation card**. The card records the total number of items (or 'pieces') produced and the number of rejects. Payment is only made for 'good' production.

OPERATION CARD				
Operator's Name _____		Total Batch Quantity _____		
Clock No _____		Start Time _____		
Pay week No _____ Date _____		Stop Time _____		
Part No _____		Works Order No _____		
Operation _____		Special Instructions _____		
Quantity Produced	No Rejected	Good Production	Rate	$
Inspector _____		Operative _____		
Foreman _____		Date _____		
PRODUCTION CANNOT BE CLAIMED WITHOUT A PROPERLY SIGNED CARD				

Note that the attendance record of a pieceworker is required for calculations of holidays, sick pay and so on.

Other types of work. Casual workers are paid from job cards or time sheets. Time sheets are also used where outworkers are concerned.

Office work can be measured in a similar way, provided that the work can be divided into distinct jobs. Firms of accountants and advertising agencies, for example, book their staff time to individual clients and so make use of time sheets for salaried staff.

3.7 Salaried labour

Even though salaried staff are paid a flat rate monthly, they may be required to prepare timesheets. The reasons are as follows.

(a)   Timesheets provide management with information (eg product costs).

(b)   Timesheet information may provide a basis for billing for services provided (eg service firms where clients are billed based on the number of hours work done).

(c)   Timesheets are used to record hours spent and so support claims for overtime payments by salaried staff.

An example of a timesheet (as used in the service sector) is shown as follows.

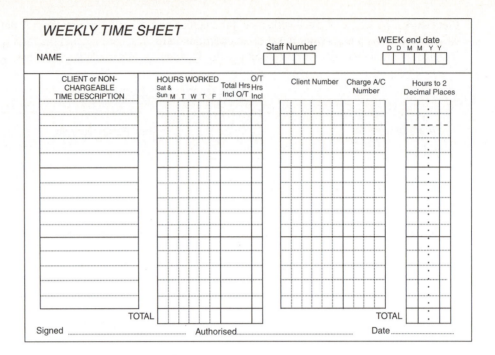

3.8 Idle time

> **Idle time** has a cost because employees will still be paid their basic wage or salary for these unproductive hours and so there should be a record of idle time.

Idle time occurs when employees cannot get on with their work, through no fault of their own. Examples are as follows.

- Machine breakdowns
- Shortage of work

A record of idle time may simply comprise an entry on time sheets coded to 'idle time' generally, or separate idle time cards may be prepared. A supervisor might enter the time of a stoppage, its cause, its duration and the employees made idle on an idle time record card. Each stoppage should have a reference number which can be entered on time sheets or job cards.

3.9 Wages department

Responsibilities of the payroll department include the following.

- Preparation of the payroll and payment of wages.
- Maintenance of employee records.
- Summarising wages cost for each cost centre.
- Summarising the hours worked for each cost centre.
- Summarising other payroll information eg bonus payment, pensions etc.
- Providing an internal check for the preparation and payout of wages.

Attendance cards are the basis for payroll preparation. For **time workers**, the gross wage is the product of time attended and rate of pay. To this is added any overtime premium or bonus. For **piece workers**, gross wages are normally obtained by the product of the number of good units produced and the unit rate, with any premiums, bonuses and allowances for incomplete jobs added.

After calculation of net pay, a pay slip is prepared showing all details of earnings and deductions. The wage envelope or the attendance card may be used for this purpose.

When the payroll is complete, a coin and note analysis is made and a cheque drawn to cover the total amount. On receipt of the cash, the pay envelopes are made up and sealed. A receipt is usually obtained on payout (the attendance card can be used). Wages of absentees are retained until claimed by an authorised person.

Internal checks are necessary to prevent fraud. One method is to distribute the payroll work so that no person deals completely with any transaction. All calculations should be checked on an adding machine where possible. Makeup of envelopes should not be done by persons who prepare the payroll. The cashier should reconcile his analysis with the payroll summary.

3.10 Cost accounting department

The cost accounting department has the following responsibilities.

- The accumulation and classification of all cost data (which includes labour costs).
- Preparation of cost data reports for management.
- Analysing labour information on time cards and payroll.

In order to establish the labour cost involved in products, operations, jobs and cost centres, the following documents are used.

- Clock cards
- Idle time cards
- Job cards
- Payroll

Analyses of labour costs are used for the following.

(a) Charging wages directly attributable to production to the appropriate job or operation.

(b) Charging wages which are not directly attributable to production as follows.

  (i) Idle time of production workers is charged to indirect costs as part of the overheads.

  (ii) Wages costs of supervisors, or store assistants are charged to the overhead costs of the relevant department.

(c) Producing idle time reports which show a summary of the hours lost through idle time, and the cause of the idle time. Idle time may be analysed as follows.

  (i) Controllable eg lack of materials.
  (ii) Uncontrollable eg power failure.

3.11 Idle time ratio

FORMULA TO LEARN

$$\text{Idle time ratio} = \frac{\text{Idle hours}}{\text{Total hours}} \times 100\%$$

The idle time ratio is useful because it shows the proportion of available hours which were lost as a result of idle time.

4 Labour turnover

Labour turnover is the rate at which employees leave a company and this rate should be kept as low as possible. The cost of labour turnover can be divided into **preventative** and **replacement costs**.

EXAM FOCUS POINT

Make sure that you know how to calculate labour turnover.

4.1 The reasons for labour turnover

Some employees will leave their job and go to work for another company or organisation. Sometimes the reasons are unavoidable.

- Illness or accidents
- A family move away from the locality
- Marriage, pregnancy or difficulties with child care provision
- Retirement or death

Other causes of labour turnover are to some extent controllable.

- Paying a lower wage rate than is available elsewhere.
- Requiring employees to work in unsafe or highly stressful conditions.
- Requiring employees to work uncongenial hours.
- Poor relationships between management and staff.
- Lack of opportunity for career enhancement.
- Requiring employees to work in inaccessible places (eg no public transport).
- Discharging employees for misconduct, bad timekeeping or unsuitability.

4.2 Measuring labour turnover

Labour turnover is a measure of the number of employees leaving/being recruited in a period of time expressed as a percentage of the total labour force.

FORMULA TO LEARN

$$\text{Labour turnover rate} = \frac{\text{Replacements}}{\text{Average number of employees in period}} \times 100\%$$

4.3 Example : Labour turnover rate

Revolving Doors Inc had a staff of 2,000 at the beginning of 20X1 and, owing to a series of redundancies caused by the recession, 1,000 at the end of the year. Voluntary redundancy was taken by 1,500 staff at the end of June, 500 more than the company had anticipated, and these excess redundancies were immediately replaced by new joiners.

The labour turnover rate is calculated as follows.

$$\text{Rate} = \frac{500}{(2,000 + 1,000) \div 2} \times 100\% = 33\%$$

4.4 The costs of labour turnover

The costs of labour turnover can be large and management should attempt to keep labour turnover as low as possible so as to minimise these costs. The **cost of labour turnover** may be divided into the following.

- Preventative costs
- Replacement costs

4.4.1 Replacement costs

These are the costs incurred as a result of hiring new employees. and they include the following.

- Cost of selection and placement
- Inefficiency of new labour; productivity will be lower
- Costs of training
- Loss of output due to delay in new labour becoming available
- Increased wastage and spoilage due to lack of expertise among new staff

- The possibility of more frequent accidents at work
- Cost of tool and machine breakages

4.4.2 Preventative costs

These are costs incurred in order to prevent employees leaving and they include the following.

- Cost of personnel administration incurred in maintaining good relationships
- Cost of medical services including check-ups, nursing staff and so on
- Cost of welfare services, including sports facilities and canteen meals
- Pension schemes providing security to employees

4.5 The prevention of high labour turnover

Labour turnover will be reduced by the following actions.

- Paying satisfactory wages
- Offering satisfactory hours and conditions of work
- Creating a good informal relationship between members of the workforce
- Offering good training schemes and a well-understood career or promotion ladder
- Improving the content of jobs to create job satisfaction
- Proper planning so as to avoid redundancies
- Investigating the cause of an apparently high labour turnover

5 Accounting for labour costs

We will use an example to briefly review the principal bookkeeping entries for wages.

5.1 Example: The wages control account

The following details were extracted from a weekly payroll for 750 employees at a factory.

Analysis of gross pay

	Direct workers $	Indirect workers $	Total $
Ordinary time	36,000	22,000	58,000
Overtime: basic wage	8,700	5,430	14,130
premium	4,350	2,715	7,065
Shift allowance	3,465	1,830	5,295
Sick pay	950	500	1,450
Idle time	3,200	–	3,200
	56,665	32,475	89,140
Net wages paid to employees	$45,605	$24,220	$69,825

Required

Prepare the wages control account for the week.

Solution

(a) **The wages control account** acts as a sort of 'collecting place' for net wages paid and deductions made from gross pay. The gross pay is then analysed between direct and indirect wages.

(b) The first step is to determine which wage costs are **direct** and which are **indirect**. The direct wages will be debited to the work in progress account and the indirect wages will be debited to the production overhead account.

(c) There are in fact only two items of direct wages cost in this example, the ordinary time ($36,000) and the basic overtime wage ($8,700) paid to direct workers. All other payments (including the overtime premium) are indirect wages.

BPP
LEARNING MEDIA

(d)   The net wages paid are debited to the control account, and the balance then represents the deductions which have been made for tax, social insurance, and so on.

WAGES CONTROL ACCOUNT

	$		$
Bank: net wages paid	69,825	Work in progress – direct labour	44,700
Deductions control accounts*		Production overhead control:	
($89,140 – $69,825)	19,315	Indirect labour	27,430
		Overtime premium	7,065
		Shift allowance	5,295
		Sick pay	1,450
		Idle time	3,200
	89,140		89,140

* In practice there would be a separate deductions control account for each type of deduction made (for example, tax and social insurance).

5.2 Direct and indirect labour costs

We had a brief look at direct and indirect labour costs in Chapter 3. Have a go at the following questions to remind yourself about the classification of labour costs.

QUESTION

Direct and indirect costs

A direct labour employee's wage in week 5 consists of the following.

		$
(a)	Basic pay for normal hours worked, 36 hours at $4 per hour =	144
(b)	Pay at the basic rate for overtime, 6 hours at $4 per hour =	24
(c)	Overtime shift premium, with overtime paid at time-and-a-quarter ¼ × 6 hours × $4 per hour =	6
(d)	A bonus payment under a group bonus (or 'incentive') scheme – bonus for the month =	30
	Total gross wages in week 5 for 42 hours of work	204

Required

Establish which costs are direct costs and which are indirect costs.

ANSWER

Items (a) and (b) are direct labour costs of the items produced in the 42 hours worked in week 5.

Overtime premium, item (c), is usually regarded as an overhead expense, because it is 'unfair' to charge the items produced in overtime hours with the premium. Why should an item made in overtime be more costly just because, by chance, it was made after the employee normally clocks off for the day?

Group bonus scheme payments, item (d), are usually overhead costs, because they cannot normally be traced directly to individual products or jobs.

In this example, the direct labour employee costs were $168 in direct costs and $36 in indirect costs.

QUESTION

Overtime

Jaffa Co employs two types of labour: skilled workers, considered to be direct workers, and semi-skilled workers considered to be indirect workers. Skilled workers are paid $10 per hour and semi-skilled $5 per hour.

The skilled workers have worked 20 hours overtime this week, 12 hours on specific orders and 8 hours on general overtime. Overtime is paid at a rate of time and a quarter.

The semi-skilled workers have worked 30 hours overtime, 20 hours for a specific order at a customer's request and the rest for general purposes. Overtime again is paid at time and a quarter.

What would be the total overtime pay considered to be a direct cost for this week?

A $275   C $375
B $355   D $437.50

ANSWER

		Direct cost $	Indirect cost $
Skilled workers			
Specific overtime	(12 hours × $10 × 1.25)	150	
General overtime	(8 hours × $10 × 1)	80	
	(8 hours × $10 × 0.25)		20
Semi-skilled workers			
Specific overtime	(20 hours × $5 × 1.25)	125	
General overtime	(10 hours × $5 × 1.25)		62.50
		355	82.50

The correct answer is therefore B.

If you selected option A, you forgot to include the direct cost of the general overtime of $80 for the skilled workers.

If you selected option C, you included the overtime premium for skilled workers' general overtime of $20.

If you selected option D, you calculated the total of direct cost + indirect cost instead of the direct cost.

EXAM FOCUS POINT

The study guide for this paper states that candidates should be able to calculate direct and indirect labour costs.

CHAPTER ROUNDUP

↳ **Production** is the quantity or volume of output produced. **Productivity** is a measure of the efficiency with which output has been produced. An increase in production without an increase in productivity will not reduce unit costs.

↳ There are three basic groups of **remuneration** method: **time work**, **piecework schemes** and **bonus/incentive** schemes.

↳ Labour attendance time is recorded on, for example, an attendance record or clock card. Job time may be recorded on daily time sheets, weekly time sheets or job cards depending on the circumstances. The manual recording of times on time sheets or job cards, is however, liable to error or even deliberate deception and may be unreliable. The labour cost of pieceworkers is recorded on a piecework ticket/operation card.

↳ **Idle time** has a cost because employees will still be paid their basic wage or salary for these unproductive hours and so there should be a record of idle time.

↳ **Labour turnover** is the rate at which employees leave a company and this rate should be kept as low as possible. The cost of labour turnover can be divided into **preventative** and **replacement** costs.

QUICK QUIZ

1   Distinguish between the terms production and productivity.

2   When does idle time occur?

3   What are the responsibilities of a typical wages department?

4   Define the idle time ratio.

5   List six methods of reducing labour turnover.

BPP
LEARNING MEDIA

1
- **Production** is the quantity or volume of output produced
- **Productivity** is a measure of the efficiency with which output has been produced

2   **Idle time** occurs when employees cannot get on with their work, through no fault of their own, for example when machines break down or there is a shortage of work.

3
- Preparation of the payroll and payment of wages
- Maintenance of employee records
- Summarising wages cost for each cost centre
- Summarising the hours worked for each cost centre
- Summarising other payroll information, eg bonus payment, pensions etc
- Providing an internal check for the preparation and payout of wages

4   Idle time ratio $= \dfrac{\text{Idle hours}}{\text{Total hours}} \times 100\%$

5   Any six from:
- Paying satisfactory wages
- Offering satisfactory hours and conditions of work
- Creating a good informal relationship between members of the workforce
- Offering good training schemes and a well-understood career or promotion ladder
- Improving the content of jobs to create job satisfaction
- Proper planning so as to avoid redundancies
- Investigating the cause of an apparently high labour turnover

---

Now try ...

Attempt the questions below from the **Exam Question Bank**

Number

Q29 – Q34

BPP
LEARNING MEDIA

Absorption costing is a method of accounting for overheads. It is basically a method of sharing out overheads incurred amongst units produced.

This chapter begins by explaining why absorption costing might be necessary and then provides an overview of how the cost of a unit of product is built up under a system of absorption costing. A detailed analysis of this costing method is then provided, covering the three stages of absorption costing: **allocation**, **apportionment** and **absorption**.

Accounting for overheads

TOPIC LIST	SYLLABUS REFERENCE
1 Overheads	B1(c)(i)
2 Absorption costing: an introduction	B1(c)(i)(ii)
3 Overhead allocation	B1(c)((iii)
4 Overhead apportionment	B1(c)(iii)(iv)
5 Overhead absorption	B1(c)(v)
6 Blanket absorption rates and departmental absorption rates	B1(c)(v)
7 Over and under absorption of overheads	B1(c)(vii)
8 Ledger entries relating to overheads	B1(c)(vi)

EXAM FOCUS POINT

Overhead apportionment and absorption is one of the most important topics in your Management Accounting studies and is almost certain to appear in the exam. Make sure that you study the contents of this chapter and work through the calculations very carefully.

1 Overheads

Overhead is the cost incurred in the course of making a product, providing a service or running a department, but which cannot be traced directly and in full to the product, service or department.

Overhead is actually the total of the following.

- Indirect materials
- Indirect labour
- Indirect expenses

The total of these indirect costs is usually split into the following categories.

- **Production**
- **Administration**
- **Selling and distribution**

In cost accounting there are two schools of thought as to the correct method of dealing with overheads.

- Absorption costing
- Marginal costing

BPP
LEARNING MEDIA

2 Absorption costing: an introduction

> **The objective of absorption costing** is to include in the total cost of a product an appropriate share of the organisation's total overhead. An appropriate share is generally taken to mean an amount which reflects the amount of time and effort that has gone into producing a unit or completing a job.

An organisation with one production department that produces identical units will divide the total overheads among the total units produced. **Absorption costing is a method for sharing overheads between different products on a fair basis**.

2.1 Is absorption costing necessary?

Suppose that a company makes and sells 100 units of a product each week. The prime cost per unit is $6 and the unit sales price is $10. Production overhead costs $200 per week and administration, selling and distribution overhead costs $150 per week. The weekly profit could be calculated as follows.

	$	$
Sales (100 units × $10)		1,000
Prime costs (100 × $6)	600	
Production overheads	200	
Administration, selling and distribution costs	150	
		950
Profit		50

In absorption costing, overhead costs will be added to each unit of product manufactured and sold.

	$ per unit
Prime cost per unit	6
Production overhead ($200 per week for 100 units)	2
Full factory cost	8

The weekly profit would be calculated as follows.

	$
Sales	1,000
Less factory cost of sales	800
Gross profit	200
Less administration, selling and distribution costs	150
Net profit	50

Sometimes, but not always, the overhead costs of administration, selling and distribution are also added to unit costs, to obtain a full cost of sales.

	$ per unit
Prime cost per unit	6.00
Factory overhead cost per unit	2.00
Administration, selling and distribution costs per unit	1.50
Full cost of sales	9.50

The weekly profit would be calculated as follows.

	$
Sales	1,000
Less full cost of sales	950
Profit	50

It may already be apparent that the weekly profit is $50 no matter how the figures have been presented. So, how does absorption costing serve any useful purpose in accounting?

The **theoretical justification** for using absorption costing is that all production overheads are incurred in the production of the organisation's output and so each unit of the product receives some benefit from these costs. Each unit of output should therefore be charged with some of the overhead costs.

2.2 Practical reasons for using absorption costing

The main reasons for using absorption costing are for inventory valuations, pricing decisions, and establishing the profitability of different products.

(a) **Inventory valuations**. Inventory in hand must be valued for two reasons.

    (i)   For the closing inventory figure in the statement of financial position

    (ii)   For the cost of sales figure in the income statement

    The valuation of inventory will affect profitability during a period because of the way in which the cost of sales is calculated.

        The cost of goods produced
    +   the value of opening inventories
    −   the value of closing inventories
    =   the cost of goods sold.

    In our example, closing inventories might be valued at prime cost ($6), but in absorption costing, they would be valued at a fully absorbed factory cost, $8 per unit. (They would not be valued at $9.50, the full cost of sales, because the only costs incurred in producing goods for finished inventory are factory costs.)

(b) **Pricing decisions**. Many companies attempt to fix selling prices by calculating the full cost of production or sales of each product, and then adding a margin for profit. In our example, the company might have fixed a gross profit margin at 25% on factory cost, or 20% of the sales price, in order to establish the unit sales price of $10. 'Full cost plus pricing' can be particularly useful for companies which do jobbing or contract work, where each job or contract is different, so that a standard unit sales price cannot be fixed. Without using absorption costing, a full cost is difficult to ascertain.

(c) **Establishing the profitability of different products**. This argument in favour of absorption costing is more contentious, but is worthy of mention here. If a company sells more than one product, it will be difficult to judge how profitable each individual product is, unless overhead costs are shared on a fair basis and charged to the cost of sales of each product.

2.3 International Accounting Standard 2 (IAS 2)

Absorption costing is recommended in financial accounting by IAS 2 *Inventories*. IAS 2 deals with **financial accounting systems**. The cost accountant is (in theory) free to value inventories by whatever method seems best, but where companies integrate their financial accounting and cost accounting systems into a single system of accounting records, the valuation of closing inventories will be determined by IAS 2.

IAS 2 states that costs of all inventories should comprise those costs which have been incurred in the normal course of business in **bringing the inventories to their 'present location and condition'**. These costs incurred will include all related production overheads, even though these overheads may accrue on a time basis. In other words, in financial accounting, closing inventories should be valued at full factory cost, and it may therefore be convenient and appropriate to value inventories by the same method in the cost accounting system.

2.4 Absorption costing stages

The three stages of absorption costing are:

- 1 Allocation
- 2 Apportionment
- 3 Absorption

We shall now begin our study of absorption costing by looking at the process of **overhead allocation**.

BPP
LEARNING MEDIA

3 Overhead allocation

3.1 Introduction

Allocation is the process by which whole cost items are charged direct to a cost unit or cost centre.

Cost centres may be one of the following types.

(a) A **production department**, to which production overheads are charged

(b) A **production area service department**, to which production overheads are charged

(c) An **administrative department**, to which administration overheads are charged

(d) A **selling** or a **distribution department**, to which sales and distribution overheads are charged

(e) An **overhead cost centre**, to which items of expense which are shared by a number of departments, such as rent and rates, heat and light and the canteen, are charged

The following costs would therefore be charged to the following cost centres via the process of allocation.

- Direct labour will be charged to a production cost centre.
- The cost of a warehouse security guard will be charged to the warehouse cost centre.
- Paper (recording computer output) will be charged to the computer department.
- Costs such as the canteen are charged direct to various overhead cost centres.

3.2 Example: Overhead allocation

Consider the following costs of a company.

Wages of the foreman of department A	$200
Wages of the foreman of department B	$150
Indirect materials consumed in department A	$50
Rent of the premises shared by departments A and B	$300

The cost accounting system might include three overhead cost centres.

Cost centre:	101	Department A
	102	Department B
	201	Rent

Overhead costs would be allocated directly to each cost centre, ie $200 + $50 to cost centre 101, $150 to cost centre 102 and $300 to cost centre 201. The rent of the factory will be subsequently shared between the two production departments, but for the purpose of day to day cost recording, the rent will first of all be charged in full to a separate cost centre.

4 Overhead apportionment

Apportionment is a procedure whereby indirect costs are spread fairly between cost centres. Service cost centre costs may be apportioned to production cost centres by using the reciprocal method.

The following question will be used to illustrate the overhead apportionment process.

4.1 Example: Overhead apportionment - Swotathon

Swotathon Inc has two production departments (A and B) and two service departments (maintenance and stores). Details of next year's budgeted overheads are shown below.

	Total ($)		Total ($)
Heat and light	19,200	Rent and rates	38,400
Repair costs	9,600	Canteen	9,000
Machinery Depreciation	54,000	Machinery insurance	25,000

Details of each department are as follows.

	A	B	Maintenance	Stores	Total
Floor area (m²)	6,000	4,000	3,000	2,000	15,000
Machinery book value ($)	48,000	20,000	8,000	4,000	80,000
Number of employees	50	40	20	10	120
Allocated overheads ($)	**15,000**	**20,000**	**12,000**	**5,000**	**50,000**

Service departments' services were used as follows.

	A	B	Maintenance	Stores	Total
Maintenance hours worked	5,000	4,000	----	1,000	10,000
Number of stores requisitions	3,000	1,000	----	----	4,000

4.2 Stage 1: Apportioning general overheads

Overhead apportionment follows on from overhead allocation. The first stage of overhead apportionment is to identify all overhead costs as production department, production service department, administration or selling and distribution overhead. The costs for heat and light, rent and rates, the canteen and so on (ie costs allocated to general overhead cost centres) must therefore be shared out between the other cost centres.

4.2.1 Bases of apportionment

It is considered important that overhead costs should be shared out on a **fair basis**. You will appreciate that because of the complexity of items of cost it is rarely possible to use only one method of apportioning costs to the various departments of an organisation. The bases of apportionment for the most usual cases are given below.

Overhead to which the basis applies	Basis
Rent, rates, heating and light, repairs and depreciation of buildings	Floor area occupied by each cost centre
Depreciation, insurance of equipment	Cost or book value of equipment
Personnel office, canteen, welfare, wages and cost offices, first aid	Number of employees, or labour hours worked in each cost centre

Note that heating and lighting may also be apportioned using volume of space occupied by each cost centre.

4.2.2 Example: Swotathon

Using the Swotathon question above, show how overheads should be apportioned between the four departments.

Solution

Item of cost	Basis of apportionment	A $	B $	Mainten-ance $	Stores $	Total $
Heat and light	Floor area (W1)	7,680	5,120	3,840	2,560	19,200
Repair costs	Floor area (W1)	3,840	2,560	1,920	1,280	9,600
Machine depⁿ	Machinery value (W2)	32,400	13,500	5,400	2,700	54,000
Rent and rates	Floor area (W1)	15,360	10,240	7,680	5,120	38,400
Canteen	No of employees (W3)	3,750	3,000	1,500	750	9,000
Machine insurance	Machinery value (W2)	15,000	6,250	2,500	1,250	25,000
Total		78,030	40,670	22,840	13,660	

Workings

(1)   Overhead apportioned by floor area

Overhead apportioned to department $= \dfrac{\text{Floor area occupied by department}}{\text{Total floor area}} \times \text{total overhead}$

For example:

Heat and light apportioned to Dept A $= \dfrac{6{,}000}{15{,}000} \times 19{,}200 = \$7{,}680$

(2)   Overheads apportioned by machinery value

Overheads apportioned to department $= \dfrac{\text{Value of department's machinery}}{\text{Total value of machinery}} \times \text{total overhead}$

(3)   Overheads apportioned by number of employees

Overheads apportioned to department $= \dfrac{\text{No of employees in department}}{\text{Total no of employees}} \times \text{total overhead}$

4.3 Stage 2 – Apportion service department costs

Only production departments produce goods that will ultimately be sold. In order to calculate a correct price for these goods, we must determine the **total cost** of producing each unit – that is, not just the cost of the labour and materials that are directly used in production, but also the **indirect** costs of services provided by such departments as maintenance, stores and canteen.

Our aim is to apportion all the **service** department costs to the **production** departments, in one of three ways.

(a)   The **direct** method, where the service centre costs are apportioned to production departments only.

(b)   The **step-down** method, where each service centre's costs are not only apportioned to production departments but to some (but not all) of the other service centres that make use of the services provided.

(c)   The **repeated distribution** (or **reciprocal**) method, where service centre costs are apportioned to both the production departments and service departments that use the services. The service centre costs are then gradually apportioned to the production departments. This method is used only when service departments work for each other – that is, **service departments use each other's services** (for example, the maintenance department will use the canteen, whilst the canteen may rely on the maintenance department to ensure its equipment is functioning properly or to replace bulbs, plugs, and so on).

EXAM FOCUS POINT

Remember that **all** service department costs must be allocated – that is, both **general overheads** that were apportioned and those overheads that are **specific** to the individual departments.

4.3.1 Basis of apportionment

Whichever method is used to apportion service cost centre costs, **the basis of apportionment must be fair**. A different apportionment basis may be applied for each service cost centre. This is demonstrated in the following table.

Service cost centre	Possible basis of apportionment
Stores	Number or cost value of material requisitions
Maintenance	Hours of maintenance work done for each cost centre
Production planning	Direct labour hours worked in each production cost centre

4.3.2 Direct method of reapportionment

The **direct method of reapportionment** involves apportioning the costs of each service cost centre **to production cost centres only**.

This method is most easily explained by working through the following example.

4.3.3 Example: Swotathon direct method (ignores inter-service department work)

	A $	B $	Maintenance $	Stores $
Allocated costs (from Section 4.1)	15,000	20,000	12,000	5,000
General costs (from Section 4.2.2)	78,030	40,670	22,840	13,660
	93,030	60,670	34,840	18,660

Service departments' services were used as follows.

	A	B	Maintenance	Stores	Total
Maintenance hours used	5,000	4,000	–	1,000	10,000
Number of stores requisitions	3,000	1,000	1,000	–	5,000

Required

Calculate the total production overhead costs of Departments A and B using the direct method of reapportionment.

Solution

Service department	Basis of apportionment	Total cost $	Dept A $	Dept B $
Maintenance	Maintenance hours (W1)	34,840	19,356	15,484
Stores	Number of requisitions (W2)	18,660	13,995	4,665
		53,500	33,351	20,149
Previously allocated costs		153,700	93,030	60,670
Total overhead		207,200	126,381	80,819

Workings

(1) **Maintenance department overheads**

These are reapportioned as follows.

Total hours worked in Departments A and B = 5,000 + 4,000 = 9,000 hours

$$\text{Reapportioned to Department A} = \frac{5,000}{9,000} \times \$34,840 = \$19,356$$

$$\text{Reapportioned to Department B} = \frac{4,000}{9,000} \times \$34,840 = \$15,484$$

(2) **Stores department overheads**
These are reapportioned as follows.

Total number of stores requisitions	= 3,000 + 1,000
(for Departments A and B)	= 4,000

Reapportioned to Department A $= \dfrac{3,000}{4,000} \times \$18,660 = \$13,995$

Reapportioned to Department B $= \dfrac{1,000}{4,000} \times \$18,660 = \$4,665$

The total overhead has now been shared, on a fair basis, between the two production departments.

QUESTION

Reapportionment (1)

The following table shows the overheads apportioned to the five departments in Baldwin Co.

	Total $	Machine shop A $	Machine shop B $	Assembly $	Canteen $	Mainten-ance $
Indirect wages	78,560	8,586	9,190	15,674	29,650	15,460
Consumable materials	16,900	6,400	8,700	1,200	600	–
Rent and rates	16,700	3,711	4,453	5,567	2,227	742
Insurance	2,400	533	640	800	320	107
Power	8,600	4,730	3,440	258	–	172
Heat and light	3,400	756	907	1,133	453	151
Depreciation	40,200	20,100	17,900	2,200	–	–
	166,760	44,816	45,230	26,832	33,250	16,632

Other information:

	Total	Machine shop A	Machine shop B	Assembly	Canteen	Mainten-ance
Power usage – technical estimates (%)	100	55	40	3	–	2
Direct labour (hours)	35,000	8,000	6,200	20,800	–	–
Machine usage (hours)	25,200	7,200	18,000	–	–	–
Area (square metres)	45,000	10,000	12,000	15,000	6,000	2,000

Required

Using the bases which you consider to be the most appropriate, calculate overhead totals for Baldwin Co's three production departments, Machine Shop A, Machine Shop B and Assembly.

ANSWER

	Total $	A $	B $	Assembly $	Canteen $	Mainten-ance $	Basis of appor-tionment
Total overheads	166,760	44,816	45,230	26,832	33,250	16,632	
Reapportion (W1)	–	7,600	5,890	19,760	(33,250)	–	Dir labour
Reapportion (W2)	–	4,752	11,880	–	–	(16,632)	Mac usage
Totals	166,760	57,168	63,000	46,592	–	–	

Workings

(1) **Canteen overheads**

Total direct labour hours = 35,000

Machine shop A $= \dfrac{8,000}{35,000} \times \$33,250 = \$7,600$

Machine shop B $= \dfrac{6,200}{35,000} \times \$33,250 = \$5,890$

$$\text{Assembly} = \frac{20,800}{35,000} \times \$33,250 = \$19,760$$

(2) **Maintenance overheads**

Total machine hours = 25,200

$$\text{Machine shop A} = \frac{7,200}{25,200} \times \$16,632 = \$4,752$$

$$\text{Machine shop B} = \frac{18,000}{25,200} \times \$16,632 = \$11,880$$

The total overhead has now been shared, on a fair basis, between the three production departments.

4.3.4 Step down method of reapportionment

This method works as follows.

Step 1	Reapportion one of the service cost centre's overheads to all of the other centres which make use of its services (production and service).

Step 2	Reapportion the overheads of the remaining service cost centre to the production departments only. The other service cost centre is ignored.

4.3.5 Example: Swotathon step down method

	A $	B $	Maintenance $	Stores $
Allocated costs (from Section 4.1)	15,000	20,000	12,000	5,000
General costs (from Section 4.2.2)	78,030	40,670	22,840	13,660
	93,030	60,670	34,840	18,660

Service departments' services were used as follows.

	A	B	Maintenance	Stores	Total
Maintenance hours used	5,000	4,000	–	1,000	10,000
	(50%)*	(40%)		(10%)	(100%)
Number of stores requisitions	3,000**	1,000	1,000	–	5,000
	(60%)	(20%)	(20%)		(100%)

* 5,000/10,000 × 100% = 50%, 4,000/10,000 = 40%, 1,000/10,000 = 10%
** 3,000/5,000 × 100% = 60%, 1,000/5,000 = 20%

Required
Apportion the service department overhead costs using the step down method of apportionment, starting with the stores department.

Solution

	A $	B $	Maintenance $	Stores $
Overhead costs (general and allocated)	93,030	60,670	34,840	18,660
Apportion stores (60%/20%/20%)	11,196	3,732	3,732	(18,660)
			38,572	
Apportion maintenance (5/9 / 4/9)	21,429	17,143	(38,572)	
	125,655	81,545	–	–

If the first apportionment had been the maintenance department, then the overheads of $34,840 would have been apportioned as follows.

	A $	B $	Maintenance $	Stores $
Overhead costs (general and allocated)	93,030	60,670	34,840	18,660
Apportion maintenance (50%/40%/10%)	17,420	13,936	(34,840)	3,484
			-	22,144
Apportion stores (3/4 / 1/4)	16,608	5,536		(22,144)
	127,058	80,142	-	-

Note. Notice how the final results differ, depending upon whether the stores department or the maintenance department is apportioned first.

If one service cost centre, compared with the other(s), has higher overhead costs and carries out a bigger proportion of work for the other service cost centre(s), then the overheads of this service centre should be reapportioned first.

QUESTION

Reapportionment (2)

Elm Co has two service departments serving two production departments. Overhead costs apportioned to each department are as follows.

Production 1 $	Production 2 $	Service 1 $	Service 2 $
97,428	84,947	9,384	15,823

Service 1 department is expected to work a total of 40,000 hours for the other departments, divided as follows.

	Hours
Production 1	20,000
Production 2	15,000
Service 2	5,000

Service 2 department is expected to work a total of 12,000 hours for the other departments, divided as follows.

	Hours
Production 1	3,000
Production 2	8,000
Service 1	1,000

Required

The finance director has asked you to reapportion the costs of the two service departments using the direct method of apportionment.

ANSWER

Direct apportionment method	Production 1 $	Production 2 $	Service 1 $	Service 2 $
	97,428	84,947	9,384	15,823
Apportion Service 1 costs (20:15)	5,362	4,022	(9,384)	–
	102,790	88,969	–	15,823
Apportion Service 2 costs (3:8)	4,315	11,508	–	(15,823)
	107,105	100,477	–	–

QUESTION

Stepdown method

When you show the finance director how you have reapportioned the costs of the two service departments, he says 'Did I say that we used the direct method? Well, I meant to say the step down method.'

Required

Prove to the finance director that you know how to use the step down method. (**Note.** Apportion the overheads of service department 1 first.)

ANSWER

Step down method	Production 1 $	Production 2 $	Service 1 $	Service 2 $
	97,428	84,947	9,384	15,823
Apportion Service 1 costs (20:15:5)	4,692	3,519	(9,384)	1,173
	102,120	88,466	–	16,996
Apportion Service 2 costs (3:8)	4,635	12,361	–	(16,996)
	106,755	100,827	–	–

4.4 The reciprocal (repeated distribution) method of apportionment

4.4.1 Example: Swotathon using repeated distribution method

	A $	B $	Maintenance $	Stores $
Allocated costs (from Section 4.1)	15,000	20,000	12,000	5,000
General costs (from Section 4.2.2)	78,030	40,670	22,840	13,660
	93,030	60,670	34,840	18,660

	A	B	Maintenance	Stores	Total
Maintenance hours used	5,000	4,000	–	1,000	10,000
Number of stores requisitions	3,000	1,000	1,000	–	5,000

Show how the Maintenance and Stores departments' overheads would be apportioned to the two production departments and calculate total overheads for each of the production departments.

Solution

Remember to apportion both the general and allocated overheads. The bases of apportionment for Maintenance and Stores are the same as for the above examples (that is, maintenance hours worked and number of stores requisitions).

	A $	B $	Maintenance $	Stores $
Total overheads (general and allocated)	93,030	60,670	34,840	18,660
Apportion maintenance (note (a))	17,420	13,936	(34,840)	3,484
			NIL	22,144
Apportion stores (note (b))	13,286	4,429	4,429	(22,144)
			4,429	NIL
Apportion maintenance	2,215	1,772	(4,429)	442
			NIL	442
Apportion stores (note (c))	332	110	NIL	(442)
Total overheads	126,283	80,917	NIL	NIL

Notes

(a)   It does not matter which department you choose to apportion first.

Apportioned as follows:

$$\frac{\text{Maintenance hours worked in department}}{\text{Total maintenance hours worked}} \times \$34,840$$

$$\text{Production department A} = \frac{5,000}{10,000} \times \$34,840 = \$17,420$$

$$\text{Production department B} = \frac{4,000}{10,000} \times \$34,840 = \$13,936$$

$$\text{Stores department} = \frac{1,000}{10,000} \times \$34,840 = \$3,484$$

(b)   Stores overheads are apportioned as follows:

$$\frac{\text{Number of stores requisitions for department}}{\text{Total number of stores requisitions}} \times \$22,144$$

$$\text{Production department A} \quad = \frac{3,000}{5,000} \times \$22,144 = \$13,286$$

$$\text{Production department B} \quad = \frac{1,000}{5,000} \times \$22,144 = \$4,429$$

$$\text{Maintenance} \quad = \frac{1,000}{5,000} \times \$22,144 = \$4,429$$

(c)   The problem with the repeated distribution method is that you can keep performing the same calculations many times. When you are dealing with a small number (such as $442 above) you can take the decision to apportion the figure between the production departments only. In this case, we ignore the stores requisitions for Maintenance and base the apportionment on the total stores requisitions for the production departments (that is, 4,000). The amount apportioned to production department A was calculated as follows.

$$\frac{\text{Stores requisitions for A}}{\text{Total stores requisitions (A+B)}} \times \text{Stores overheads} = \frac{3,000}{4,000} \times \$442 = £332$$

4.5 The reciprocal (algebraic) method of apportionment

The results of the reciprocal method of apportionment may also be obtained using **algebra** and **simultaneous equations**.

4.5.1 Example: Swotathon using the algebraic method of apportionment

Whenever you are using equations you must define each variable.

Let   M = total overheads for the Maintenance department
       S = total overheads for the Stores department

Remember that total overheads for the Maintenance department consist of general overheads apportioned, allocated overheads and the share of Stores overheads (20%).

Similarly, total overheads for Stores will be the total of general overheads apportioned, allocated overheads and the 10% share of Maintenance overheads.

M = 0.2S + $34,840	(1)	($34,840 was calculated in section 4.4)	
S = 0.1M + $18,660	(2)	($18,660 was calculated in section 4.4)	

We now solve the equations.

Multiply equation (1) by 5 to give us

5M = S + 174,200	(3), which can be rearranged as
S = 5M − 174,200	(4)

Subtract equation (2) from equation (4)

S = 5M − 174,200	(4)
S = 0.1M + 18,660	(2)

0 = 4.9M − 192,860

4.9M = 192,860

$$M = \frac{192,860}{4.9} = \$39,359$$

Substitute M = 39,359 into equation (2)

S = 0.1 × 39,359 + 18,660
S = 3,936 + 18,660 = 22,596

These overheads can now be apportioned to the production departments using the proportions above.

	A	B	Maintenance	Stores
	$	$	$	$
Overhead costs	93,030	60,670	34,840	18,660
Apportion maintenance (50%/40%/10%)	19,680	15,743	(39,359)	3,936
Apportion stores (60%/20%/20%)	13,558	4,519	4,519	(22,596)
Total	126,268	80,932	Nil	Nil

You will notice that the total overheads for production departments A and B are the same regardless of the method used (difference is due to rounding).

EXAM FOCUS POINT

You must never ignore the existence of reciprocal services unless a question specifically instructs you to do so.

4.6 A full example for you to try

Now that we have worked through the various stages of overhead apportionment, you should try this question to ensure you understand the techniques.

QUESTION

Reapportionment

Sandstorm is a jobbing engineering concern which has three production departments (forming, machines and assembly) and two service departments (maintenance and general).

The following analysis of overhead costs has been made for the year just ended.

	$	$
Rent and rates		8,000
Power		750
Light, heat		5,000
Repairs, maintenance:		
Forming	800	
Machines	1,800	
Assembly	300	
Maintenance	200	
General	100	
		3,200
Departmental expenses:		
Forming	1,500	
Machines	2,300	
Assembly	1,100	
Maintenance	900	
General	1,500	
		7,300
Depreciation:		
Plant		10,000
Fixtures and fittings		250
Insurance:		
Plant		2,000
Buildings		500
Indirect labour:		
Forming	3,000	
Machines	5,000	
Assembly	1,500	
Maintenance	4,000	
General	2,000	
		15,500
		52,500

Other available data are as follows.

	Floor area sq. ft	Plant value $	Fixtures & fittings $	Effective horse-power	Direct cost for year $	Labour hours worked	Machine hours worked
Forming	2,000	25,000	1,000	40	20,500	14,400	12,000
Machines	4,000	60,000	500	90	30,300	20,500	21,600
Assembly	3,000	7,500	2,000	15	24,200	20,200	2,000
Maintenance	500	7,500	1,000	5			
General	500	–	500	–	–	–	–
	10,000	100,000	5,000	150	75,000	55,100	35,600

Service department costs are apportioned as follows.

	Maintenance %	General %
Forming	20	20
Machines	50	60
Assembly	20	10
General	10	–
Maintenance	–	10
	100	100

Required

Using the data provided prepare an analysis showing the distribution of overhead costs to departments. Reapportion service cost centre costs using the reciprocal method.

ANSWER

Analysis of distribution of actual overhead costs

	Basis	Forming $	Machines $	Assembly $	Maint. $	General $	Total $
Directly allocated overheads:							
Repairs, maintenance		800	1,800	300	200	100	3,200
Departmental expenses		1,500	2,300	1,100	900	1,500	7,300
Indirect labour		3,000	5,000	1,500	4,000	2,000	15,500
Apportionment of other overheads:							
Rent, rates	1	1,600	3,200	2,400	400	400	8,000
Power	2	200	450	75	25	0	750
Light, heat	1	1,000	2,000	1,500	250	250	5,000
Depreciation of plant	3	2,500	6,000	750	750	0	10,000
Depreciation of F and F	4	50	25	100	50	25	250
Insurance of plant	3	500	1,200	150	150	0	2,000
Insurance of buildings	1	100	200	150	25	25	500
		11,250	22,175	8,025	6,750	4,300	52,500

Basis of apportionment:

1	floor area	3	plant value
2	effective horsepower	4	fixtures and fittings value

Apportionment of service department overheads to production departments, using the reciprocal method.

	Forming $	Machines $	Assembly $	Maintenance $	General $	Total $
Overheads	11,250	22,175	8,025	6,750	4,300	52,500
	1,350	3,375	1,350	(6,750)	675	
					4,975	
	995	2,985	498	497	(4,975)	
	99	249	99	(497)	50	
	10	30	5	5	(50)	
	1	3	1	(5)		
	13,705	28,817	9,978	0	0	52,500

EXAM FOCUS POINT

Remember that you will never be asked a question of this length in the real exam. However, exam questions may, for example, give you the total general and allocated overheads, and ask you to apportion service department overheads to production departments.

QUESTION
Apportioning service department overheads

Spaced Out Co has two production departments (F and G) and two service departments (Canteen and Maintenance). Total allocated and apportioned general overheads for each department are as follows.

F	G	Canteen	Maintenance
$125,000	$80,000	$20,000	$40,000

Canteen and Maintenance perform services for both production departments and Canteen also provides services for Maintenance in the following proportions.

	F	G	Canteen	Maintenance
% of Canteen to	60	25	-	15
% of Maintenance to	65	35	-	-

What would be the total overheads for production department G once the service department costs have been apportioned?

A $90,763   B $100,500   C $99,000   D $100,050

ANSWER

The correct answer is D.

Total Maintenance overheads = $40,000 + 15% of Canteen overheads
= $40,000 + 15% of $20,000
= $43,000

Of which 35% are apportioned to G = $15,050

Canteen costs apportioned to G = 25% of $20,000 = $5,000

Total overheads for G = $80,000 + 15,050 + 5,000 = $100,050

5 Overhead absorption

5.1 Introduction

> **Overhead absorption** is the process whereby overhead costs allocated and apportioned to production cost centres are added to unit, job or batch costs. Overhead absorption is sometimes called **overhead recovery.**

Having allocated and/or apportioned all overheads, the next stage in the costing treatment of overheads is to add them to, or **absorb them into, cost units.**

Overheads are usually added to cost units using a **predetermined overhead absorption rate**, which is calculated using figures from the budget.

5.2 Calculation of overhead absorption rates

Step 1	Estimate the overhead likely to be incurred during the coming period.
Step 2	Estimate the activity level for the period. This could be total hours, units, or direct costs or whatever it is upon which the overhead absorption rates are to be based.
Step 3	Divide the estimated overhead by the budgeted activity level. This produces the overhead absorption rate.
Step 4	Absorb the overhead into the cost unit by applying the calculated absorption rate.

5.3 Example: The basics of absorption costing

Athena Co makes two products, the Greek and the Roman. Greeks take 2 labour hours each to make and Romans take 5 labour hours. What is the overhead cost per unit for Greeks and Romans respectively if overheads are absorbed on the basis of labour hours?

Solution

Step 1	Estimate the overhead likely to be incurred during the coming period
	Athena Co estimates that the total overhead will be $50,000

Step 2	Estimate the activity level for the period
	Athena Co estimates that a total of 100,000 direct labour hours will be worked

Step 3 Divide the estimated overhead by the budgeted activity level

$$\text{Absorption rate} = \frac{\$50,000}{100,000 \text{ hrs}} = \$0.50 \text{ per direct labour hour}$$

Step 4 Absorb the overhead into the cost unit by applying the calculated absorption rate

	Greek	Roman
Labour hours per unit	2	5
Absorption rate per labour hour	$0.50	$0.50
Overhead absorbed per unit	$1	$2.50

It should be obvious to you that, even if a company is trying to be 'fair', there is a great lack of precision about the way an absorption base is chosen.

This arbitrariness is one of the main criticisms of absorption costing, and if absorption costing is to be used (because of its other virtues) then it is important that **the methods used are kept under regular review.** Changes in working conditions should, if necessary, lead to changes in the way in which work is accounted for.

For example, a labour intensive department may become mechanised. If a direct labour hour rate of absorption had been used previous to the mechanisation, it would probably now be more appropriate to change to the use of a machine hour rate.

5.4 Choosing the appropriate absorption base

The different **bases of absorption** (or 'overhead recovery rates') are as follows.

- A percentage of direct materials cost
- A percentage of direct labour cost
- A percentage of prime cost
- A rate per machine hour
- A rate per direct labour hour
- A rate per unit
- A percentage of factory cost (for administration overhead)
- A percentage of sales or factory cost (for selling and distribution overhead)

The choice of an absorption basis is a matter of judgement and common sense, what is required is an **absorption basis** which realistically reflects the characteristics of a given cost centre and which avoids undue anomalies.

Many factories use a **direct labour hour rate** or **machine hour rate** in preference to a rate based on a percentage of direct materials cost, wages or prime cost.

(a) A **direct labour** hour basis is most appropriate in a **labour intensive** environment.

(b) A **machine hour** rate would be used in departments where production is controlled or dictated by machines.

(c) A **rate per unit** would be effective only if all units were identical.

5.5 Example: Overhead absorption

The budgeted production overheads and other budget data of Bridge Cottage Co are as follows.

Budget	Production dept A	Production dept B
Overhead cost	$36,000	$5,000
Direct materials cost	$32,000	
Direct labour cost	$40,000	
Machine hours	10,000	
Direct labour hours	18,000	
Units of production		1,000

Required

Calculate the absorption rate using the various bases of apportionment.

Solution

Department A

(i)   Percentage of direct materials cost $\dfrac{\$36,000}{\$32,000} \times 100\% = 112.5\%$

(ii)   Percentage of direct labour cost $\dfrac{\$36,000}{\$40,000} \times 100\% = 90\%$

(iii)   Percentage of prime cost $\dfrac{\$36,000}{\$72,000} \times 100\% = 50\%$

(iv)   Rate per machine hour $\dfrac{\$36,000}{10,000 \text{ hrs}} = \$3.60$ per machine hour

(v)   Rate per direct labour hour $\dfrac{\$36,000}{18,000 \text{ hrs}} = \$2$ per direct labour hour

The department B absorption rate will be based on units of output.

$\dfrac{\$5,000}{1,000 \text{ units}} = \$5$ per unit produced

5.6 Bases of absorption

The choice of the basis of absorption is significant in determining the cost of individual units, or jobs, produced. Using the previous example, suppose that an individual product has a material cost of $80, a labour cost of $85, and requires 36 labour hours and 23 machine hours to complete. The overhead cost of the product would vary, depending on the basis of absorption used by the company for overhead recovery.

(a)   As a percentage of direct material cost, the overhead cost would be

     112.5% × $80   = $90.00

(b)   As a percentage of direct labour cost, the overhead cost would be

     90% × $85   = $76.50

(c)   As a percentage of prime cost, the overhead cost would be 50% × $165   = $82.50

(d)   Using a machine hour basis of absorption, the overhead cost would be

     23 hrs × $3.60   = $82.80

(e)   Using a labour hour basis, the overhead cost would be 36 hrs × $2   = $72.00

In theory, each basis of absorption would be possible, but the company should choose a basis for its own costs which seems to be **'fairest'**.

6 Blanket absorption rates and departmental absorption rates

6.1 Introduction

A **blanket overhead absorption rate** is an absorption rate used throughout a factory and for all jobs and units of output irrespective of the department in which they were produced.

For example, if total overheads were $500,000 and there were 250,000 direct machine hours during the period, the **blanket overhead rate** would be $2 per direct machine hour and all jobs passing through the factory would be charged at that rate.

Blanket overhead rates are not appropriate in the following circumstances.

- There is more than one department.
- Jobs do not spend an equal amount of time in each department.

If a single factory overhead absorption rate is used, some products will receive a higher overhead charge than they ought 'fairly' to bear, whereas other products will be under-charged.

If **a separate absorption rate** is used for each department, charging of overheads will be fair and the full cost of production of items will represent the amount of the effort and resources put into making them.

6.2 Example: Separate absorption rates

The Old Grammar School has two production departments, for which the following budgeted information is available.

	Department A	Department B	Total
Budgeted overheads	$360,000	$200,000	$560,000
Budgeted direct labour hours	200,000 hrs	40,000 hrs	240,000 hrs

If a single factory overhead absorption rate is applied, the rate of overhead recovery would be:

$$\frac{\$560,000}{240,000 \text{ hours}} = \$2.33 \text{ per direct labour hour}$$

If separate departmental rates are applied, these would be:

$$Department\ A = \frac{\$360,000}{200,000 \text{ hours}} = \$1.80 \text{ per direct labour hour}$$

$$Department\ B = \frac{\$200,000}{40,000 \text{ hours}} = \$5 \text{ per direct labour hour}$$

Department B has a higher overhead rate of cost per hour worked than department A.

Now let us consider two separate jobs.

Job X has a prime cost of $100, takes 30 hours in department B and does not involve any work in department A.

Job Y has a prime cost of $100, takes 28 hours in department A and 2 hours in department B.

What would be the factory cost of each job, using the following rates of overhead recovery?

(a) A single factory rate of overhead recovery
(b) Separate departmental rates of overhead recovery

Solution

			Job X $		Job Y $
(a)	**Single factory rate**				
	Prime cost		100		100
	Factory overhead (30 × $2.33)		70		70
	Factory cost		170		170

				Job X $		Job Y $
(b)	**Separate departmental rates**					
	Prime cost			100		100.00
	Factory overhead:	department A		0	(28 × $1.80)	50.40
		department B	(30 × $5)	150	(2 × $5)	10.00
	Factory cost			250		160.40

Using a single factory overhead absorption rate, both jobs would cost the same. However, since job X is done entirely within department B where overhead costs are relatively higher, whereas job Y is done mostly within department A, where overhead costs are relatively lower, it is arguable that job X should cost more than job Y. This will occur if separate departmental overhead recovery rates are used to reflect the work done on each job in each department separately.

If all jobs do not spend approximately the same time in each department then, to ensure that all jobs are charged with their fair share of overheads, it is necessary to establish **separate overhead rates for each department**.

QUESTION

Machine hour absorption rate

The following data relate to one year in department A.

Budgeted machine hours	25,000
Actual machine hours	21,875
Budgeted overheads	$350,000
Actual overheads	$350,000

Based on the data above, what is the machine hour absorption rate as conventionally calculated?

A $12   B $14   C $16   D $18

ANSWER

Don't forget, if your calculations produce a solution which does not correspond with any of the options available, then eliminate the unlikely options and make a guess from the remainder. Never leave out a multiple choice question.

A common pitfall is to think 'we haven't had answer A for a while, so I'll guess that'. The examiner is *not* required to produce an even spread of A, B, C and D answers in the examination. There is no reason why the answer to *every* question cannot be D!

The correct answer in this case is B.

$$\text{Overhead absorption rate} = \frac{\text{Budgeted overheads}}{\text{Budgeted machine hours}} = \frac{\$350,000}{25,000} = \$14 \text{ per machine hour}$$

7 Over and under absorption of overheads

7.1 Introduction

> **Over** and **under absorption** of overheads occurs because the predetermined overhead absorption rates are based on estimates.

The rate of overhead absorption is based on estimates (of both numerator and denominator) and it is quite likely that either one or both of the estimates will not agree with what actually occurs.

(a) **Over absorption** means that the overheads charged to the cost of sales are greater then the overheads actually incurred.

(b) **Under absorption** means that insufficient overheads have been included in the cost of sales.

It is almost inevitable that at the end of the accounting year there will have been an over absorption or under absorption of the overhead actually incurred.

7.2 Example: Over and under absorption

Suppose that the budgeted overhead in a production department is $80,000 and the budgeted activity is 40,000 direct labour hours. The overhead recovery rate (using a direct labour hour basis) would be $2 per direct labour hour.

Actual overheads in the period are, say $84,000 and 45,000 direct labour hours are worked.

	$
Overhead incurred (actual)	84,000
Overhead absorbed (45,000 × $2)	90,000
Over absorption of overhead	6,000

In this example, the cost of produced units or jobs has been charged with $6,000 more than was actually spent. An adjustment to reconcile the overheads charged to the actual overhead is necessary and the over-absorbed overhead will be credited to the profit and loss account at the end of the accounting period.

7.3 The reasons for under-/over-absorbed overhead

The overhead absorption rate is predetermined from budget estimates of overhead cost and the expected volume of activity. Under– or over-recovery of overhead will occur in the following circumstances.

* Actual overhead costs are different from budgeted overheads
* The actual activity level is different from the budgeted activity level
* Actual overhead costs *and* actual activity level differ from the budgeted costs and level

7.4 Example: Reasons for under-/over-absorbed overhead

Pembridge Co has a budgeted production overhead of $50,000 and a budgeted activity of 25,000 direct labour hours and therefore a recovery rate of $2 per direct labour hour.

Required

Calculate the under-/over-absorbed overhead, and the reasons for the under-/over-absorption, in the following circumstances.

(a) Actual overheads cost $47,000 and 25,000 direct labour hours are worked.
(b) Actual overheads cost $50,000 and 21,500 direct labour hours are worked.
(c) Actual overheads cost $47,000 and 21,500 direct labour hours are worked.

Solution

(a)

	$
Actual overhead	47,000
Absorbed overhead (25,000 × $2)	50,000
Over-absorbed overhead	3,000

The reason for the over absorption is that although the actual and budgeted direct labour hours are the same, actual overheads cost less than expected.

(b)

	$
Actual overhead	50,000
Absorbed overhead (21,500 × $2)	43,000
Under-absorbed overhead	7,000

The reason for the under absorption is that although budgeted and actual overhead costs were the same, fewer direct labour hours were worked than expected.

(c)

	$
Actual overhead	47,000
Absorbed overhead (21,500 × $2)	43,000
Under-absorbed overhead	4,000

The reason for the under absorption is a combination of the reasons in (a) and (b).

The distinction between **overheads incurred** (actual overheads) and **overheads absorbed** is an important one which you must learn and understand. The difference between them is known as under– or over-absorbed overheads.

QUESTION
Under-/over-absorbed overhead

The budgeted and actual data for River Arrow Products Co for the year to 31 March 20X5 are as follows.

	Budgeted	Actual
Direct labour hours	9,000	9,900
Direct wages	$34,000	$35,500
Machine hours	10,100	9,750
Direct materials	$55,000	$53,900
Units produced	120,000	122,970
Overheads	$63,000	$61,500

The cost accountant of River Arrow Products Co has decided that overheads should be absorbed on the basis of labour hours.

Required

Calculate the amount of under– or over-absorbed overheads for River Arrow Products Co for the year to 31 March 20X5.

ANSWER

$$\text{Overhead absorption rate} = \frac{\$63,000}{9,000} = \$7 \text{ per hour}$$

Overheads absorbed by production = 9,900 × $7 = $69,300

	$
Actual overheads	61,500
Overheads absorbed	69,300
Over-absorbed overheads	7,800

You may find the following graph helpful to your understanding.

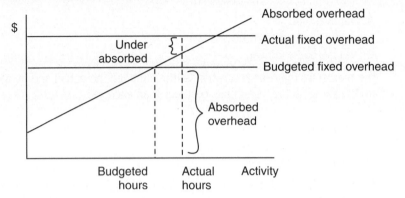

You can see from the graph that when we absorb overheads, we are really treating them as variable costs. They are, however, fixed costs. The graph highlights the fact that if we treat fixed costs as variable costs, this will result in under- or over-absorption.

EXAM FOCUS POINT

You can always work out whether overheads are under– or over-absorbed by using the following rule.

- If Actual overhead incurred – Absorbed overhead = NEGATIVE (N), then overheads are over-absorbed (O) (NO)

- If Actual overhead incurred – Absorbed overhead = POSITIVE (P), then overheads are under-absorbed (U) (PU)

So, remember the NOPU rule when you go into your examination and you won't have any trouble in deciding whether overheads are under– or over-absorbed!

QUESTION
Budgeted overhead absorption rate

A management consultancy recovers overheads on chargeable consulting hours. Budgeted overheads were $615,000 and actual consulting hours were 32,150. Overheads were under-recovered by $35,000.

If actual overheads were $694,075 what was the budgeted overhead absorption rate per hour?

A $19.13   B $20.50   C $21.59   D $22.68

ANSWER

	$
Actual overheads	694,075
Under-recoverable overheads	35,000
Overheads recovered for 32,150 hours at budgeted overhead absorption rate (x)	659,075

$$32,150 \ x \ = \ 659,075$$

$$x \ = \ \frac{659,075}{32,150} = \$20.50$$

The correct option is B.

8 Ledger entries relating to overheads

8.1 Introduction

The bookkeeping entries for overheads are not as straightforward as those for materials and labour. We shall now consider the way in which overheads are dealt with in a cost accounting system.

When an absorption costing system is in use we now know that the amount of overhead included in the cost of an item is absorbed at a predetermined rate. The entries made in the cash book and the nominal ledger, however, are the actual amounts.

You will remember that it is highly unlikely that the actual amount and the predetermined amount will be the same. The difference is called **under– or over-absorbed overhead**. To deal with this in the cost accounting books, therefore, we need to have an account to collect under– or over-absorbed amounts for each type of overhead.

8.2 Example: The under-/over-absorbed overhead account

Mariott's Motorcycles absorbs production overheads at the rate of $0.50 per operating hour and administration overheads at 20% of the production cost of sales. Actual data for one month was as follows.

Administration overheads	$32,000
Production overheads	$46,500
Operating hours	90,000
Production cost of sales	$180,000

What entries need to be made for overheads in the ledgers?

Solution

PRODUCTION OVERHEADS

	DR $		CR $
Cash	46,500	Absorbed into WIP (90,000 × $0.50)	45,000
		Under absorbed overhead	1,500
	46,500		46,500

ADMINISTRATION OVERHEADS

	DR $		CR $
Cash	32,000	To cost of sales (180,000 × 0.2)	36,000
Over-absorbed overhead	4,000		
	36,000		36,000

UNDER-/OVER-ABSORBED OVERHEADS

	DR $		CR $
Production overhead	1,500	Administration overhead	4,000
Balance to profit and loss account	2,500		
	4,000		4,000

Less production overhead has been absorbed than has been spent so there is **under-absorbed overhead** of $1,500. More administration overhead has been absorbed (into cost of sales, note, not into WIP) and so there is **over-absorbed overhead** of $4,000. The net over-absorbed overhead of $2,500 is a credit in the income statement.

CHAPTER ROUNDUP

↪ **Overhead** is the cost incurred in the course of making a product, providing a service or running a department, but which cannot be traced directly and in full to the product, service or department.

↪ The **objective of absorption costing** is to include in the total cost of a product an appropriate share of the organisation's total overhead. An appropriate share is generally taken to mean an amount which reflects the amount of time and effort that has gone into producing a unit or completing a job.

↪ The main reasons for using absorption costing are for **inventory valuations, pricing decisions** and **establishing the profitability of different products.**

↪ The three stages of absorption costing are:

– 1 Allocation   – 3 Absorption
– 2 Apportionment

↪ **Allocation** is the process by which whole cost items are charged direct to a cost unit or cost centre.

↪ **Apportionment** is a procedure whereby indirect costs are spread fairly between cost centres. Service cost centre costs may be apportioned to production cost centres by using the reciprocal method.

↪ The results of the reciprocal method of apportionment may also be obtained using **algebra** and **simultaneous equations**.

↪ **Overhead absorption** is the process whereby overhead costs allocated and apportioned to production cost centres are added to unit, job or batch costs. Overhead absorption is sometimes called **overhead recovery**.

↪ A **blanket overhead absorption rate** is an absorption rate used throughout a factory and for all jobs and units of output irrespective of the department in which they were produced.

↪ **Over** and **under absorption of overheads** occurs because the predetermined overhead absorption rates are based on estimates.

QUICK QUIZ

1   What is allocation?

2   Name the three stages in charging overheads to units of output.

3   Match the following overheads with the most appropriate basis of apportionment.

Overhead		**Basis of apportionment**	
(a)	Depreciation of equipment	(1)	Direct machine hours
(b)	Heat and light costs	(2)	Number of employees
(c)	Canteen	(3)	Book value of equipment
(d)	Insurance of equipment	(4)	Floor area

4   A direct labour hour basis is most appropriate in which of the following environments?

    A   Machine-intensive   C   When all units produced are identical

    B   Labour-intensive   D   None of the above

5   What is the problem with using a single factory overhead absorption rate?

6   How is under-/over-absorbed overhead accounted for?

7   Why does under– or over-absorbed overhead occur?

1   The process whereby whole cost items are charged direct to a cost unit or cost centre.

2   •   Allocation   •   Absorption
    •   Apportionment

3   (a)   (3)   (c)   (2)
    (b)   (4)   (d)   (3)

4   B

5   Because some products will receive a higher overhead charge than they ought 'fairly' to bear and other products will be undercharged.

6   Under-/over-absorbed overhead is written as an adjustment to the income statement at the end of an accounting period.

    •   Over-absorbed overhead → credit in income statement
    •   Under-absorbed overhead → debit in income statement

7   •   Actual overhead costs are different from budgeted overheads
    •   The actual activity level is different from the budgeted activity level
    •   Actual overhead costs *and* actual activity level differ from the budgeted costs and level

Now try ...

Attempt the questions below from the **Exam Question Bank**

Number

Q35 – Q40

CHAPTER

09

This chapter defines **marginal costing** and compares it with absorption costing. Whereas absorption costing recognises fixed costs (usually fixed production costs) as part of the cost of a unit of output and hence as product costs, marginal costing treats all fixed costs as period costs. Two such different costing methods obviously each have their supporters and so we will be looking at the arguments both in favour of and against each method. Each costing method, because of the different inventory valuation used, produces a different profit figure and we will be looking at this particular point in detail.

Absorption and marginal costing

EXAM FOCUS POINT

You may see questions in your examination which require you to calculate profit or losses using absorption and marginal costing.

1 Marginal cost and marginal costing

1.1 Introduction

Marginal cost is the variable cost of one unit of product or service.

Marginal costing is an alternative method of costing to absorption costing. In marginal costing, only variable costs are charged as a cost of sale and a contribution is calculated (sales revenue minus variable cost of sales). Closing inventories of work in progress or finished goods are valued at marginal (variable) production cost. Fixed costs are treated as a period cost, and are charged in full to the profit and loss account of the accounting period in which they are incurred.

The **marginal production cost** per unit of an item usually consists of the following.

- Direct materials
- Direct labour
- Variable production overheads

Direct labour costs might be excluded from marginal costs when the work force is a given number of employees on a fixed wage or salary. Even so, it is not uncommon for direct labour to be treated as a variable cost, even when employees are paid a basic wage for a fixed working week. If in doubt, you should treat direct labour as a variable cost unless given clear indications to the contrary. Direct labour is often a step cost, with sufficiently short steps to make labour costs act in a variable fashion.

The **marginal cost of sales** usually consists of the marginal cost of production adjusted for inventory movements plus the variable selling costs, which would include items such as sales commission, and possibly some variable distribution costs.

1.2 Contribution

> **Contribution** is an important measure in marginal costing, and it is calculated as the difference between sales value and marginal or variable cost of sales.

Contribution is of fundamental importance in marginal costing, and the term 'contribution' is really short for 'contribution towards covering fixed overheads and making a profit'.

2 The principles of marginal costing

The principles of marginal costing are as follows.

(a) **Period fixed costs are the same, for any volume of sales and production** (provided that the level of activity is within the 'relevant range'). Therefore, by selling an extra item of product or service the following will happen.

(i)   Revenue will increase by the sales value of the item sold.
(ii)   Costs will increase by the variable cost per unit.
(iii)   Profit will increase by the amount of contribution earned from the extra item.

(b) Similarly, if the volume of sales falls by one item, the profit will fall by the amount of contribution earned from the item.

(c) **Profit measurement should therefore be based on an analysis of total contribution**. Since fixed costs relate to a period of time, and do not change with increases or decreases in sales volume, it is misleading to charge units of sale with a share of fixed costs. Absorption costing is therefore misleading, and it is more appropriate to deduct fixed costs from total contribution for the period to derive a profit figure.

(d) When a unit of product is made, the extra costs incurred in its manufacture are the **variable production costs**. Fixed costs are unaffected, and no extra fixed costs are incurred when output is increased. It is therefore argued that **the valuation of closing inventories should be at variable production cost** (direct materials, direct labour, direct expenses (if any) and variable production overhead) because these are the only costs properly attributable to the product.

2.1 Example: Marginal costing principles

Rain Until September Co makes a product, the Splash, which has a variable production cost of $6 per unit and a sales price of $10 per unit. At the beginning of September 20X0, there were no opening inventories and production during the month was 20,000 units. Fixed costs for the month were $45,000 (production, administration, sales and distribution). There were no variable marketing costs.

Required

Calculate the contribution and profit for September 20X0, using marginal costing principles, if sales were as follows.

(a)   10,000 Splashes   (c)   20,000 Splashes
(b)   15,000 Splashes

Solution

The stages in the profit calculation are as follows.

- To **identify the variable cost of sales, and then the contribution**.
- Deduct fixed costs from the total contribution to derive the profit.
- Value all closing inventories at marginal production cost ($6 per unit).

	10,000 Splashes		15,000 Splashes		20,000 Splashes	
	$	$	$	$	$	$
Sales (at $10)		100,000		150,000		200,000
Opening inventory	0		0		0	
Variable production cost	120,000					
			120,000		120,000	
	120,000		120,000		120,000	
Less value of closing						
inventory (at marginal cost)	60,000		30,000		–	
Variable cost of sales		60,000		90,000		120,000
Contribution		40,000		60,000		80,000
Less fixed costs		45,000		45,000		45,000
Profit/(loss)		(5,000)		15,000		35,000
Profit (loss) per unit		$(0.50)		$1		$1.75
Contribution per unit		$4		$4		$4

The conclusions which may be drawn from this example are as follows.

(a) The **profit per unit varies** at differing levels of sales, because the average fixed overhead cost per unit changes with the volume of output and sales.

(b) The **contribution per unit is constant** at all levels of output and sales. Total contribution, which is the contribution per unit multiplied by the number of units sold, increases in direct proportion to the volume of sales.

(c) Since the **contribution per unit does not change**, the most effective way of calculating the expected profit at any level of output and sales would be as follows.

  (i) First calculate the total contribution.
  (ii) Then deduct fixed costs as a period charge in order to find the profit.

(d) In our example the expected profit from the sale of 17,000 Splashes would be as follows.

	$
Total contribution (17,000 × $4)	68,000
Less fixed costs	45,000
Profit	23,000

  (i) If total contribution **exceeds fixed costs**, a profit is made
  (ii) If total contribution **exactly equals fixed costs**, no profit or loss is made
  (iii) If total contribution is **less than fixed costs**, there will be a loss

QUESTION
Marginal costing principles

Mill Stream makes two products, the Mill and the Stream. Information relating to each of these products for April 20X1 is as follows.

	Mill	Stream
Opening inventory	nil	nil
Production (units)	15,000	6,000
Sales (units)	10,000	5,000
Sales price per unit	$20	$30
Unit costs	$	$
Direct materials	8	14
Direct labour	4	2
Variable production overhead	2	1
Variable sales overhead	2	3

Fixed costs for the month	$
Production costs	40,000
Administration costs	15,000
Sales and distribution costs	25,000

Required

(a)   Using marginal costing principles and the method in 2.1(d) above, calculate the profit in April 20X1.

(b)   Calculate the profit if sales had been 15,000 units of Mill and 6,000 units of Stream.

ANSWER

(a)

	$
Contribution from Mills (unit contribution = $20 − $16 = $4 × 10,000)	40,000
Contribution from Streams (unit contribution = $30 − $20 = $10 × 5,000)	50,000
Total contribution	90,000
Fixed costs for the period	80,000
Profit	10,000

(b)   At a higher volume of sales, profit would be as follows.

	$
Contribution from sales of 15,000 Mills (× $4)	60,000
Contribution from sales of 6,000 Streams (× $10)	60,000
Total contribution	120,000
Less fixed costs	80,000
Profit	40,000

2.2 Profit or contribution information

The main advantage of **contribution information** (rather than profit information) is that it allows an easy calculation of profit if sales increase or decrease from a certain level. By comparing total contribution with fixed overheads, it is possible to determine whether profits or losses will be made at certain sales levels. **Profit information**, on the other hand, does not lend itself to easy manipulation but note how easy it was to calculate profits using contribution information in the question entitled *Marginal costing principles*. **Contribution information** is more useful for **decision making** than profit information.

3   Marginal costing and absorption costing and the calculation of profit

3.1 Introduction

In **marginal costing**, fixed production costs are treated as **period costs** and are written off as they are incurred. In **absorption costing**, fixed production costs are absorbed into the cost of units and are carried forward in inventory to be charged against sales for the next period. Inventory values using absorption costing are therefore greater than those calculated using marginal costing.

Marginal costing as a cost accounting system is significantly different from absorption costing. It is an **alternative method** of accounting for costs and profit, which rejects the principles of absorbing fixed overheads into unit costs.

Marginal costing	Absorption costing
Closing inventories are valued at marginal production cost.	Closing inventories are valued at full production cost.
Fixed costs are period costs.	Fixed costs are absorbed into unit costs.
Cost of sales does not include a share of fixed overheads.	Cost of sales does include a share of fixed overheads (see note below).

Note. The share of fixed overheads included in cost of sales are from the previous period (in opening inventory values). Some of the fixed overheads from the current period will be excluded by being carried forward in closing inventory values.

In **marginal costing**, it is necessary to identify the following.

- Variable costs
- Contribution
- Fixed costs

In **absorption costing** (sometimes known as **full costing**), it is not necessary to distinguish variable costs from fixed costs.

3.2 Example: Marginal and absorption costing compared

The following example will be used to lead you through the various steps in calculating marginal and absorption costing profits, and will highlight the differences between the two techniques.

Big Woof Co manufactures a single product, the Bark, details of which are as follows.

Per unit	$
Selling price	180.00
Direct materials	40.00
Direct labour	16.00
Variable overheads	10.00

Annual fixed production overheads are budgeted to be $1.6 million and Big Woof expects to produce 1,280,000 units of the Bark each year. Overheads are absorbed on a per unit basis. Actual overheads are $1.6 million for the year.

Budgeted fixed selling costs are $320,000 per quarter.

Actual sales and production units for the first quarter of 20X8 are given below.

	January – March
Sales	240,000
Production	280,000

There is no opening inventory at the beginning of January.

Prepare income statements for the quarter, using

(a) Marginal costing
(b) Absorption costing

Solution

Step 1	Calculate the overhead absorption rate per unit

Remember that overhead absorption rate is based only on budgeted figures.

$$\text{Overhead absorption rate} = \frac{\text{Budgeted fixed overheads}}{\text{Budgeted units}}$$

Also be careful with your calculations. You are dealing with a three month period but the figures in the question are for a whole year. You will have to convert these to quarterly figures.

$$\text{Budgeted overheads (quarterly)} = \frac{\$1.6\,\text{million}}{4} = \$400,000$$

$$\text{Budgeted production (quarterly)} = \frac{1,280,000}{4} = 320,000 \text{ units}$$

$$\text{Overhead absorption rate per unit} = \frac{\$400,000}{320,000} = \$1.25 \text{ per unit}$$

Step 2   **Calculate total cost per unit**

Total cost per unit (absorption costing)	=	Variable cost + fixed production cost
	=	(40 + 16 + 10) + 1.25
	=	$67.25

Total cost per unit (marginal costing) = Variable cost per unit = $66

Step 3   **Calculate closing inventory in units**

Closing inventory = Opening inventory + production – sales
Closing inventory = 0 + 280,000 – 240,000 = 40,000 units

Step 4   **Calculate under/over absorption of overheads**

This is based on the difference between actual production and budgeted production.

Actual production = 280,000 units

Budgeted production = 320,000 units (see step 1 above)

Under-production = 40,000 units

As Big Woof produced 40,000 fewer units than expected, there will be an under-absorption of overheads of 40,000 x $1.25 (see step 1 above) = $50,000. This will be added to production costs in the income statement.

Step 5   **Produce income statements**

	Marginal costing		*Absorption costing*	
	$'000	$'000	$'000	$'000
Sales (240,000 x $180)		43,200		43,200
Less Cost of Sales				
Opening inventory	0		0	
Add Production cost				
280,000 x $66	18,480			
280,000 x $67.25			18,830	
Less Closing inventory				
40,000 x $66	(2,640)			
40,000 x $67.25			(2,690)	
	———	(15,840)	16,140	
Add Under absorbed O/H			50	
			———	(16,190)
Contribution		27,360		
Gross profit				27,010
Less				
Fixed production O/H	400		Nil	
Fixed selling O/H	320		320	
	———	(720)	———	(320)
Net profit		26,640		26,690

3.3 No changes in inventory

You will notice from the above calculations that there are **differences** between marginal and absorption costing profits. Before we go on to reconcile the profits, how would the profits for the two different techniques differ if there were **no changes** between opening and closing inventory (that is, if production = sales)?

For the first quarter we will now assume that sales were 280,000 units.

	Marginal costing		Absorption costing	
	$000	$000	$000	$000
Sales (280,000 x $180)		50,400		50,400
Less Cost of Sales				
Opening inventory	0			
Add Production cost				
280,000 x $66	18,480			
280,000 x $67.25			18,830	
Less Closing inventory	NIL		NIL	
		(18,480)	18,830	
Add Under absorbed O/H			50	
				(18,880)
Contribution		31,920		
Gross profit				31,520
Less				
Fixed production O/H	400			
Fixed selling O/H	320		320	
		(720)		(320)
Net profit		31,200		31,200

You will notice that there are now no differences between the two profits. The difference in profits is due to changes in inventory levels during the period.

QUESTION

AC versus MC

The overhead absorption rate for product X is $10 per machine hour. Each unit of product X requires five machine hours. Inventory of product X on 1.1.X1 was 150 units and on 31.12.X1 it was 100 units. What is the difference in profit between results reported using absorption costing and results reported using marginal costing?

A   The absorption costing profit would be $2,500 less
B   The absorption costing profit would be $2,500 greater
C   The absorption costing profit would be $5,000 less
D   The absorption costing profit would be $5,000 greater

ANSWER

Difference in profit = **change** in inventory levels × fixed overhead absorption per unit = (150 – 100) × $10 × 5 = $2,500 **lower** profit, because inventory levels **decreased**. The correct answer is therefore option A.

The key is the change in the volume of inventory. Inventory levels have **decreased** therefore absorption costing will report a **lower** profit. This eliminates options B and D.

Option C is incorrect because it is based on the closing inventory only (100 units × $10 × 5 hours).

4 Reconciling profits

4.1 Introduction

Reported profit figures using marginal costing or absorption costing will differ if there is any change in the level of inventories in the period. If production is equal to sales, there will be no difference in calculated profits using the costing methods.

The difference in profits reported under the two costing systems is due to the different inventory valuation methods used.

If inventory levels increase between the beginning and end of a period, absorption costing will report the higher profit. This is because some of the fixed production overhead incurred during the period will be carried forward in closing inventory (which reduces cost of sales) to be set against sales revenue in the following period instead of being written off in full against profit in the period concerned.

If inventory levels decrease, **absorption costing will report the lower profit** because as well as the fixed overhead incurred, fixed production overhead which had been carried forward in opening inventory is released and is also included in cost of sales.

4.2 Example: Reconciling profits

The profits reported under absorption costing and marginal costing for January – March in the Big Woof question above can be reconciled as follows.

	$'000
Marginal costing profit	26,640
Adjust for fixed overhead included in inventory:	
Inventory increase of 40,000 units × $1.25	50
Absorption costing profit	26,690

4.3 Reconciling profits – a shortcut

A quick way to establish the difference in profits without going through the whole process of drawing up the income statements is as follows.

Difference in profits = change in inventory level x overhead absorption rate per unit

If inventory levels have **gone up** (that is, closing inventory > opening inventory) then **absorption costing** profit will be **greater** than **marginal costing** profit.

If inventory levels have **gone down** (that is, closing inventory < opening inventory) then **absorption costing** profit will be **less** than **marginal costing** profit.

In the Big Woof example above

Change in inventory = 40,000 units (an increase)

Overhead absorption rate = $1.25 per unit

We would expect absorption costing profit to be **greater** than marginal costing profit by 40,000 x $1.25 = **$50,000**. If you check back to the answer, you will find that this is the case.

QUESTION
Absorption costing profit

When opening inventories were 8,500 litres and closing inventories 6,750 litres, a firm had a profit of $62,100 using marginal costing.

Assuming that the fixed overhead absorption rate was $3 per litre, what would be the profit using absorption costing?

A $41,850   B $56,850   C $67,350   D $82,350

ANSWER

Difference in profit = (8,500 – 6,750) × $3 = $5,250

Absorption costing profit = $62,100 – $5,250 = $56,850

The correct answer is B.

Since inventory levels reduced, the absorption costing profit will be lower than the marginal costing profit. You can therefore eliminate options C and D.

QUESTION

Last month a manufacturing company's profit was $2,000, calculated using absorption costing principles. If marginal costing principles has been used, a loss of $3,000 would have occurred. The company's fixed production cost is $2 per unit. Sales last month were 10,000 units.

What was last month's production (in units)?

A 7,500   B 9,500   C 10,500   D 12,500

ANSWER

The correct answer is D.

Any difference between marginal and absorption costing profit is due to changes in inventory.

	$
Absorption costing profit	2,000
Marginal costing loss	(3,000)
Difference	5,000

Change in inventory = Difference in profit/fixed product cost per unit

= $5,000/$2 = 2,500 units

Marginal costing loss is lower than absorption costing profit therefore inventory has gone up – that is, production was greater than sales by 2,500 units.

Production = 10,000 units (sales) + 2,500 units = 12,500 units

EXAM FOCUS POINT

Don't overlook the fact that there might be a **loss** rather than a profit.

The effect on profit of using the two different costing methods can be confusing. You *must* get it straight in your mind before the examination. Remember that if opening inventory values are greater than closing inventory values, marginal costing shows the greater profit.

5 Marginal costing versus absorption costing

Absorption costing is most often used for routine profit reporting and must be used for financial accounting purposes. **Marginal costing** provides better management information for planning and decision making. There are a number of arguments both for and against each of the costing systems.

The following diagram summarises the arguments in favour of both marginal and absorption costing.

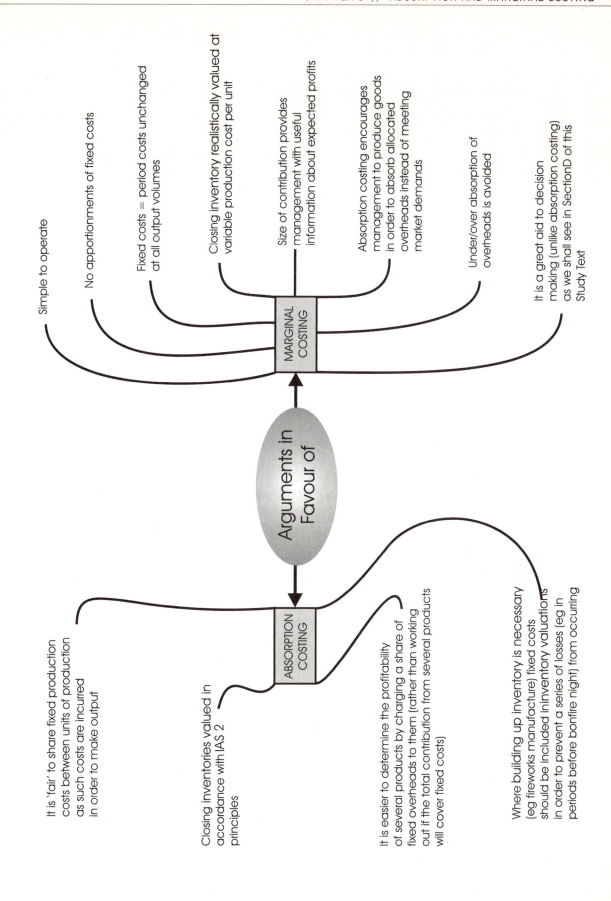

Simple to operate

No apportionments of fixed costs

Fixed costs = period costs unchanged at all output volumes

Closing inventory realistically valued at variable production cost per unit

Size of contribution provides management with useful information about expected profits

Absorption costing encourages management to produce goods in order to absorb allocated overheads instead of meeting market demands

Under/over absorption of overheads is avoided

It is a great aid to decision making (unlike absorption costing) as we shall see in SectionD of this Study Text

MARGINAL COSTING

Arguments in Favour of

ABSORPTION COSTING

It is 'fair' to share fixed production costs between units of production as such costs are incurred in order to make output

Closing inventories valued in accordance with IAS 2 principles

It is easier to determine the profitability of several products by charging a share of fixed overheads to them (rather than working out if the total contribution from several products will cover fixed costs)

Where building up inventory is necessary (eg fireworks manufacture) fixed costs should be included in inventory valuations in order to prevent a series of losses (eg in periods before bonfire night) from occurring

CHAPTER ROUNDUP

↳ **Marginal cost** is the variable cost of one unit of product or service.

↳ **Contribution** is an important measure in marginal costing, and it is calculated as the difference between sales value and marginal or variable cost of sales.

↳ In **marginal costing**, fixed production costs are treated as **period costs** and are written off as they are incurred. In **absorption costing**, fixed production costs are absorbed into the cost of units and are carried forward in inventory to be charged against sales for the next period. Inventory values using absorption costing are therefore greater than those calculated using marginal costing.

↳ **Reported profit figures using marginal costing or absorption costing will differ if there is any change in the level of inventories in the period.** If production is equal to sales, there will be no difference in calculated profits using these costing methods.

↳ **Absorption costing** is most often used for routine profit reporting and must be used for financial accounting purposes. **Marginal costing** provides better management information for planning and decision making. There are a number of arguments both for and against each of the costing systems.

QUICK QUIZ

1   What is marginal costing?

2   What is a period cost in marginal costing?

3   Sales value – marginal cost of sales = ...

4   Marginal costing and absorption costing are different techniques for assessing profit in a period. If there are changes in inventory during a period, marginal costing and absorption costing give different results for profit obtained.

Which of the following statements are true?

I   If inventory levels increase, marginal costing will report the higher profit.

II   If inventory levels decrease, marginal costing will report the lower profit.

III   If inventory levels decrease, marginal costing will report the higher profit.

IV   If the opening and closing inventory volumes are the same, marginal costing and absorption costing will give the same profit figure.

A   All of the above   C   I and IV
B   I, II and IV   D   III and IV

5   Which of the following are arguments in favour of marginal costing?

(a)   Closing inventory is valued in accordance with IAS 2.
(b)   It is simple to operate.
(c)   There is no under or over absorption of overheads.
(d)   Fixed costs are the same regardless of activity levels.
(e)   The information from this costing method may be used for decision making.

ANSWERS TO QUICK QUIZ

1   Marginal costing is an alternative method of costing to absorption costing. In marginal costing, only variable costs are charged as a cost of sale and a contribution is calculated (sales revenue – variable cost of sales).

2   A fixed cost

3   Contribution

4   D

5   (b), (c), (d), (e)

Now try ...

Attempt the questions below from the **Exam Question Bank**

Number

Q41 – Q45

10

Job, batch and service costing

The first costing method that we shall be looking at is **job costing**. We will see the circumstances in which job costing should be used and how the costs of jobs are calculated. We will look at how the **costing of individual jobs** fits in with the recording of total costs in control accounts and then we will move on to **batch costing**, the procedure for which is similar to job costing.

Service costing deals with **specialist services** supplied to third parties or an **internal service** supplied within an organisation.

TOPIC LIST	SYLLABUS REFERENCE
1 Costing methods	B3 (a)(i)
2 Job costing	B3 (a)(i), (ii), (iii), (iv)
3 Batch costing	B3 (a)(i), (ii), (iii), (iv)
4 Service costing	B3 (c)(i), (ii), (iii)

1   Costing methods

A **costing method** is designed to suit the way goods are processed or manufactured or the way services are provided.

Each organisation's costing method will have unique features but costing methods of firms in the same line of business will more than likely have common aspects. Organisations involved in completely different activities, such as hospitals and car part manufacturers, will use very different methods.

We will be considering these important costing methods in this chapter.

- Job
- Batch
- Service

2   Job costing

2.1 Introduction

Job costing is a costing method applied where work is undertaken to customers' special requirements and each order is of comparatively short duration.

A job is a cost unit which consists of a single order or contract.

The work relating to a job moves through processes and operations as a **continuously identifiable unit**. Job costing is most commonly applied within a factory or workshop, but may also be applied to property repairs and internal capital expenditure.

BPP LEARNING MEDIA

2.2 Procedure for the performance of jobs

The normal procedure in jobbing concerns involves:

(a)   The prospective customer approaches the supplier and indicates the **requirements** of the job.

(b)   A representative sees the prospective customer and agrees with him the **precise details** of the items to be supplied. For example the quantity, quality, size and colour of the goods, the date of delivery and any special requirements.

(c)   The estimating department of the organisation then **prepares an estimate for the job**. This will be based on the cost of the materials to be used, the labour expense expected, the cost overheads, the cost of any additional equipment needed specially for the job, and finally the supplier's **profit margin**. The total of these items will represent the **quoted selling price**.

(d)   If the estimate is accepted the job can be **scheduled**. All materials, labour and equipment required will be 'booked' for the job. In an efficient organisation, the start of the job will be timed to ensure that while it will be ready for the customer by the promised date of delivery it will not be loaded too early, otherwise storage space will have to be found for the product until the date it is required by (and was promised to) the customer.

2.3 Job cost sheets/cards

Costs for each job are collected on a **job cost sheet** or **job card**.

With other methods of costing, it is usual to produce for inventory; this means that management must decide in advance how many units of each type, size, colour, quality and so on will be produced during the coming year, regardless of the identity of the customers who will eventually buy the product. In job costing, because production is usually carried out in accordance with the **special requirements of each customer**, it is **usual for each job to differ in one or more respects from another job.**

A separate record must therefore be maintained to show the details of individual jobs. Such records are often known as **job cost sheets** or **job cost cards**. An example is shown on the next page.

Either the **detail of relatively small jobs** or a **summary** of direct materials, direct labour and so on **for larger jobs** will be shown on a job cost sheet.

2.4 Job cost information

Material costs for each job are determined from **material requisition notes**. **Labour times** on each job are recorded on a **job ticket**, which is then costed and recorded on the job cost sheet. Some labour costs, such as overtime premium or the cost of rectifying sub-standard output, might be charged either directly to a job or else as an overhead cost, depending on the circumstances in which the costs have arisen. **Overhead** is absorbed into the cost of jobs using the predetermined overhead absorption rates.

Information for the direct and indirect costs will be gathered as follows.

2.4.1 Direct material cost

(a)   The estimated cost will be calculated by valuing all items on the **bill of materials**. Materials that have to be specially purchased for the job in question will need to be priced by the purchasing department.

(b)   The actual cost of materials used will be calculated by valuing materials issues notes for those issues from store for the job and/or from invoices for materials specially purchased. All documentation should indicate the job number to which it relates.

2.4.2 Direct labour cost

(a)   The estimated **labour time requirement** will be calculated from past experience of similar types of work or work study engineers may prepare estimates following detailed specifications. Labour rates will need to take account of any increases, overtime and bonuses.

(b)   The actual labour hours will be available from either time sheets or job tickets/cards, using job numbers where appropriate to indicate the time spent on each job. The actual labour cost will be calculated using the hours information and current labour rates (plus bonuses, overtime payments and so on).

2.4.3 Direct expenses

(a)   The estimated cost of **any expenses likely** to be incurred can be obtained from a supplier.

(b)   The details of actual direct expenses incurred can be taken from invoices.

JOB COST CARD														Job No. B641			
Customer Mr J White						Customer's Order No.								Vehicle make Peugot 205 GTE			
Job Description Repair damage to offside front door																	
Estimate Ref. 2599						Invoice No.								Vehicle reg. no. G 614 SOX			
Quoted price $338.68						Invoice price $355.05								Date to collect 14.6.00			

Material						Labour								Overheads			
Date	Req. No.	Qty.	Price	Cost		Date	Emp-loyee	Cost Ctre	Hrs.	Rate	Bonus	Cost		Hrs	OAR	Cost	
				$	c							$	c			$	c
12.6	36815	1	75.49	75	49	12.6	018	B	1.98	6.50	-	12	87	7.9	2.50	19	75
12.6	36816	1	33.19	33	19	13.6	018	B	5.92	6.50	-	38	48				
12.6	36842	5	6.01	30	05						13.65	13	65				
13.6	36881	5	3.99	19	95												
Total C/F				158	68	Total C/F						65	00	Total C/F		19	75

Expenses						Job Cost Summary		Actual		Estimate	
			Cost					$	c	$	c
Date	Ref.	Description	$	c		Direct Materials B/F		158	68	158	68
						Direct Expenses B/F		50	00		
						Direct Labour B/F		65	00	180	00
12.6	-	N. Jolley Panel-beating	50	-		Direct Cost		273	68		
						Overheads B/F		19	75		
								293	43		
						Admin overhead (add 10%)		29	34		
						= Total Cost		322	77	338	68
						Invoice Price		355	05		
Total C/F			50	-		Job Profit/Loss		32	28		

Comments
Job Cost Card Completed by _____

(Note that the abbreviations of b/f and c/f in the above cost card mean 'brought forward' and 'carried forward'.)

2.4.4 Production overheads

(a)   The **estimated production overheads** to be included in the job cost will be calculated from **overhead absorption rates** in operation and the estimate of the basis of the absorption rate (for example, direct labour hours). This assumes the job estimate is to include overheads (in a competitive environment management may feel that if overheads are to be incurred irrespective of whether or not the job is taken on, the minimum estimated quotation price should be based on variable costs only).

(b)   The actual production overhead to be included in the job cost will be calculated from the overhead absorption rate and the actual results (such as labour hours coded to the job in question). **Inaccurate overhead absorption rates can seriously harm an organisation**; if jobs are over priced, customers will go elsewhere and if jobs are under priced revenue will fail to cover costs.

2.4.5 Administration, selling and distribution overheads

The organisation may absorb **non-production overheads** using any one of a variety of methods (percentage on full production cost, for example) and estimates of these costs and the actual costs should be included in the estimated and actual job cost.

2.5 Rectification costs

If the finished output is found to be sub-standard, it may be possible to rectify the fault. The sub-standard output will then be returned to the department or cost centre where the fault arose.

Rectification costs can be treated in two ways.

(a)   If rectification work is not a frequent occurrence, but arises on occasions with specific jobs to which it can be traced directly, then the rectification costs should be **charged as a direct cost to the jobs concerned.**

(b)   If rectification is regarded as a normal part of the work carried out generally in the department, then the rectification costs should be **treated as production overheads**. This means that they would be included in the total of production overheads for the department and absorbed into the cost of all jobs for the period, using the overhead absorption rate.

2.6 Work in progress

At the year end, the **value of work in progress** is simply the **sum of the costs incurred on incomplete jobs** (provided that the costs are lower than the net realisable value of the customer order).

2.7 Pricing the job

The usual method of fixing prices in a jobbing concern is **cost plus pricing**.

Cost plus pricing means that a desired profit margin is added to total costs to arrive at the selling price.

The estimated profit will depend on the particular circumstance of the job and organisation in question. In competitive situations the profit may be small but if the organisation is sure of securing the job the margin may be greater. In general terms, the profit earned on each job should **conform to the requirements of the organisation's overall business plan**.

The final price quoted will, of course, be affected by what competitors charge and what the customer will be willing to pay.

EXAM FOCUS POINT

An exam question about job costing may ask you to accumulate costs to arrive at a job cost, and then to determine a job price by adding a certain amount of profit. The selling price can be expressed as a percentage **margin** or a percentage **mark-up**.

For example, a selling price based on a 20% margin means that profit is 20% of **selling price**.

	%
Cost of job	80
+ profit	20
= selling price	100

A selling price based on a 20% mark-up means that profit is 20% of **cost**.

	%
Cost of job	100
+ profit	20
= selling price	120

2.7.1 Example: Selling price and unit cost

Product CT's unit cost is $150. A selling price is set based on a margin of 20%.

What is the selling price?

Solution

	$	%
Cost	150	80
Profit	?	20
Selling price	?	100

Therefore selling price = $150 ÷ 80% = $187.50

2.7.2 Example: Selling price and unit cost (2)

Product HM's unit cost is $650. The mark up is 20%.

What is the selling price?

Solution

	$	%
Cost	650	100
Profit	?	20
Selling price	?	120

Therefore selling price = $650 × 120% = $780

2.7.1 Example: Selling price and unit cost (3)

Product JT's selling price is $935. The mark up is 10%.

What is the unit cost?

Solution

	$	%
Cost	?	100
Profit	?	10
Selling price	935	110

Therefore unit cost = $935 ÷ 110% = $850

2.8 Job costing and computerisation

Job cost sheets exist in manual systems, but it is **increasingly likely** that in large organisations the **job costing system will be computerised**, using accounting software specifically designed to deal with job costing requirements. A computerised job accounting system is likely to contain the following features.

(a) Every job will be given a **job code number**, which will determine how the data relating to the job is stored.

(b) A separate set of **codes will be given for the type of costs** that any job is likely to incur. Thus, 'direct wages', say, will have the same code whichever job they are allocated to.

(c) In a sophisticated system, **costs can be analysed both by job** (for example all costs related to Job 456), **but also by type** (for example direct wages incurred on all jobs). It is thus easy to perform control analysis and to make comparisons between jobs.

(d) A job costing system might have facilities built into it which incorporate other factors relating to the performance of the job. In complex jobs, sophisticated planning techniques might be employed to ensure that the job is performed in the minimum time possible: time management features may be incorporated into job costing software.

2.9 Example: Job costing

Fateful Morn is a jobbing company. On 1 June 20X2, there was one uncompleted job in the factory. The job card for this work is summarised as follows.

Job Card, Job No 6832

	$
Costs to date	
Direct materials	630
Direct labour (120 hours)	350
Factory overhead ($2 per direct labour hour)	240
Factory cost to date	1,220

During June, three new jobs were started in the factory, and costs of production were as follows.

Direct materials		$
Issued to:	Job 6832	2,390
	Job 6833	1,680
	Job 6834	3,950
	Job 6835	4,420
Damaged inventory written off from stores		2,300

Material transfers	$
Job 6834 to Job 6833	250
Job 6832 to 6834	620

Materials returned to store	$
From Job 6832	870
From Job 6835	170

Direct labour hours recorded

Job 6832	430 hrs
Job 6833	650 hrs
Job 6834	280 hrs
Job 6835	410 hrs

The cost of labour hours during June 20X2 was $3 per hour, and production overhead is absorbed at the rate of $2 per direct labour hour. Production overheads incurred during the month amounted to $3,800. Completed jobs were delivered to customers as soon as they were completed, and the invoiced amounts were as follows.

Job 6832	$5,500
Job 6834	$8,000
Job 6835	$7,500

Administration and marketing overheads are added to the cost of sales at the rate of 20% of factory cost. Actual costs incurred during June 20X2 amounted to $3,200.

Required

(a) Prepare the job accounts for each individual job during June 20X2; (the accounts should only show the cost of production, and not the full cost of sale).

(b) Prepare the summarised job cost cards for each job, and calculate the profit on each completed job.

Solution

(a) **Job accounts**

JOB 6832

	$		$
Balance b/f	1,220	Job 6834 a/c	620
Materials (stores a/c)	2,390	(materials transfer)	
Labour (wages a/c)	1,290	Stores a/c (materials returned)	870
Production overhead (o'hd a/c)	860	Cost of sales a/c (balance)	4,270
	5,760		5,760

JOB 6833

	$		$
Materials (stores a/c)	1,680	Balance c/f	5,180
Labour (wages a/c)	1,950		
Production overhead (o'hd a/c)	1,300		
Job 6834 a/c (materials transfer)	250		
	5,180		5,180

JOB 6834

	$		$
Materials (stores a/c)	3,950	Job 6833 a/c (materials transfer)	250
Labour (wages a/c)	840		
Production overhead (o'hd a/c)	560	Cost of sales a/c (balance)	5,720
Job 6832 a/c (materials transfer)	620		
	5,970		5,970

JOB 6835

	$		$
Materials (stores a/c)	4,420	Stores a/c (materials returned)	170
Labour (wages a/c)	1,230		
Production overhead (o'hd a/c)	820	Cost of sales a/c (balance)	6,300
	6,470		6,470

(b) **Job cards, summarised**

	Job 6832	Job 6833	Job 6834	Job 6835
	$	$	$	$
Materials	1,530*	1,930	4,320**	4,250
Labour	1,640	1,950	840	1,230
Production overhead	1,100	1,300	560	820
Factory cost	4,270	5,180 (c/f)	5,720	6,300
Admin & marketing o'hd (20%)	854		1,144	1,260
Cost of sale	5,124		6,864	7,560
Invoice value	5,500		8,000	7,500
Profit/(loss) on job	376		1,136	(60)

*$(630 + 2,390 − 620 − 870)
**$(3,950 + 620 − 250)

2.10 Job costing for internal services

It is possible to use a job costing system **to control the costs of an internal service department**, such as the maintenance department or the printing department.

If a job costing system is used it is possible to **charge the user departments for the cost of specific jobs carried out, rather than apportioning the total costs of these service departments** to the user departments using an arbitrarily determined apportionment basis.

An internal job costing system for service departments will have the following advantages.

Advantages	Comment
Realistic apportionment	The identification of expenses with jobs and the subsequent charging of these to the department(s) responsible means that costs are borne by those who incurred them.
Increased responsibility and awareness	User departments will be aware that they are charged for the specific services used and may be more careful to use the facility more efficiently. They will also appreciate the true cost of the facilities that they are using and can take decisions accordingly.
Control of service department costs	The service department may be restricted to charging a standard cost to user departments for specific jobs carried out or time spent. It will then be possible to measure the efficiency or inefficiency of the service department by recording the difference between the standard charges and the actual expenditure.
Planning information	This information will ease the planning process, as the purpose and cost of service department expenditure can be separately identified.

QUESTION

Total job cost

A furniture-making business manufactures quality furniture to customers' orders. It has three production departments (A, B and C) which have overhead absorption rates (per direct labour hour) of $12.86, $12.40 and $14.03 respectively.

Two pieces of furniture are to be manufactured for customers. Direct costs are as follows.

	Job XYZ	Job MNO
Direct material	$154	$108
Direct labour	20 hours dept A	16 hours dept A
	12 hours dept B	10 hours dept B
	10 hours dept C	14 hours dept C

Labour rates are as follows: $3.80(A); $3.50 (B); $3.40 (C)

Calculate the total cost of each job.

ANSWER

		Job XYZ $		Job MNO $
Direct material		154.00		108.00
Direct labour: dept A	(20 × 3.80)	76.00	(16 × 3.80)	60.80
dept B	(12 × 3.50)	42.00	(10 × 3.50)	35.00
dept C	(10 × 3.40)	34.00	(14 × 3.40)	47.60
Total direct cost		306.00		251.40
Overhead: dept A	(20 × 12.86)	257.20	(16 × 12.86)	205.76
dept B	(12 × 12.40)	148.80	(10 × 12.40)	124.00
dept C	(10 × 14.03)	140.30	(14 × 14.03)	196.42
Total cost		852.30		777.58

QUESTION

Closing work in progress

A firm uses job costing and recovers overheads on direct labour.

Three jobs were worked on during a period, the details of which are as follows.

	Job 1 $	Job 2 $	Job 3 $
Opening work in progress	8,500	0	46,000
Material in period	17,150	29,025	0
Labour for period	12,500	23,000	4,500

The overheads for the period were exactly as budgeted, $140,000.

Jobs 1 and 2 were the only incomplete jobs.

What was the value of closing work in progress?

A $81,900   B $90,175   C $140,675   D $214,425

ANSWER

Total labour cost = $12,500 + $23,000 + $4,500 = $40,000

$$\text{Overhead absorption rate} = \frac{\$140,000}{\$40,000} \times 100\% = 350\% \text{ of direct labour cost}$$

Closing work in progress valuation

		Job 1 $		Job 2 $	Total $
Costs given in question		38,150		52,025	90,175
Overhead absorbed	(12,500 × 350%)	43,750	(23,000 × 350%)	80,500	124,250
					214,425

Option D is correct.

We can eliminate option B because $90,175 is simply the total of the costs allocated to Jobs 1 and 2, with no absorption of overheads. Option A is an even lower cost figure, therefore it can also be eliminated.

Option C is wrong because it is a simple total of all allocated costs, including Job 3 which is not incomplete.

3 Batch costing

3.1 Introduction

Batch costing is similar to job costing in that each batch of similar articles is separately identifiable. The **cost per unit** manufactured in a batch is the total batch cost divided by the number of units in the batch.

A **batch** is a group of similar articles which maintains its identity during one or more stages of production and is treated as a cost unit.

In general, the **procedures for costing batches are very similar to those for costing jobs**.

(a)   The **batch is treated as a job during production** and the costs are collected in the manner already described in this chapter.

(b)   Once the batch has been completed, the cost per unit can be calculated as the total batch cost divided into the number of units in the batch.

3.2 Example: Batch costing

Rio manufactures Brazils to order and has the following budgeted overheads for the year, based on normal activity levels.

Production departments	Budgeted Overheads $	Budgeted activity
Welding	12,000	3,000 labour hours
Assembly	20,000	2,000 labour hours

Selling and administrative overheads are 25% of factory cost. An order for 500 Brazils, made as Batch 38, incurred the following costs.

Materials $24,000

Labour   200 hours in the Welding Department at $5 per hour
400 hours in the Assembly Department at $10 per hour

$1,000 was paid for the hire of x-ray equipment for testing the accuracy of the welds.

Required

Calculate the cost per unit for Batch 38.

Solution

The first step is to calculate the overhead absorption rate for the production departments.

$$\text{Welding} \quad = \quad \frac{\$12,000}{3,000} \quad = \quad \$4 \text{ per labour hour}$$

$$\text{Assembly} \quad = \quad \frac{\$20,000}{2,000} \quad = \quad \$10 \text{ per labour hour}$$

Total cost – Batch 38

		$	$
Direct material			24,000
Direct expense			1,000
Direct labour	200 × $5 =	1,000	
	400 × $10 =	4,000	
			5,000
Prime cost			30,000
Overheads	200 × $4 =	800	
	400 × $10 =	4,000	
			4,800
Factory cost			34,800
Selling and administrative cost (25% of factory cost)			8,700
Total cost			43,500

$$\text{Cost per unit} = \frac{\$43,500}{500} = \$87$$

4 Service costing

4.1 What is service costing?

Service costing can be used by companies operating in a service industry or by companies wishing to establish the cost of services carried out by some of their departments. Service organisations do not make or sell tangible goods.

Service costing (or **function costing**) is a costing method concerned with establishing the costs, not of items of production, but of services rendered.

Service costing is used in the following circumstances.

(a)   A company operating in a service industry will cost its services, for which sales revenue will be earned; examples are electricians, car hire services, road, rail or air transport services and hotels.

(b)   A company may wish to establish the cost of services carried out by some of its departments; for example the costs of the vans or lorries used in distribution, the costs of the computer department, or the staff canteen.

4.2 Service costing versus product costing (such as job or process costing)

(a)   With many services, the cost of direct materials consumed will be relatively small compared to the labour, direct expenses and overheads cost. In product costing the direct materials are often a greater proportion of the total cost.

(b)   Although many services are revenue-earning, others are not (such as the distribution facility or the staff canteen). This means that the purpose of service costing may not be to establish a profit or loss (nor to value closing inventories for the statement of financial position) but may rather be to provide management information about the comparative costs or efficiency of the services, with a view to helping managers to budget for their costs using historical data as a basis for estimating costs in the future and to control the costs in the service departments.

(c)   The procedures for recording material costs, labour hours and other expenses will vary according to the nature of the service.

4.3 Specific characteristics of services

Specific characteristics of services

- **S**imultaneity
- **H**eterogeneity
- **I**ntangibility
- **P**erishability

Consider the service of providing a haircut.

(a) The production and consumption of a haircut are **simultaneous,** and therefore it cannot be inspected for quality in advance, nor can it be returned if it is not what was required.

(b) A haircut is **heterogeneous** and so the exact service received will vary each time: not only will two hairdressers cut hair differently, but a hairdresser will not consistently deliver the same standard of haircut.

(c) A haircut is **intangible** in itself, and the performance of the service comprises many other intangible factors, like the music in the salon, the personality of the hairdresser, the quality of the coffee.

(d) Haircuts are **perishable,** that is, they cannot be stored. You cannot buy them in bulk, and the hairdresser cannot do them in advance and keep them stocked away in case of heavy demand. The incidence of work in progress in service organisations is less frequent than in other types of organisation.

Note the mnemonic **SHIP** for remembering the specific characteristics of services.

4.4 Unit cost measures

The main problem with service costing is the **difficulty in defining a realistic cost unit** that represents a suitable measure of the service provided. Frequently, a composite cost unit may be deemed more appropriate. Hotels, for example, may use the 'occupied bed-night' as an appropriate unit for cost ascertainment and control.

Typical cost units used by companies operating in a service industry are shown below.

Service	Cost unit
Road, rail and air transport services	Passenger/mile or kilometre, ton/mile, tonne/kilometre
Hotels	Occupied bed-night
Education	Full-time student
Hospitals	Patient
Catering establishment	Meal served

QUESTION
Internal services

Can you think of examples of cost units for internal services such as canteens, distribution and maintenance?

ANSWER

Service	Cost unit
Canteen	Meal served
Vans and lorries used in distribution	Mile or kilometre, ton/mile, tonne/kilometre
Maintenance	Man hour

Each organisation will need to ascertain the **cost unit** most appropriate to its activities. If a number of organisations within an industry use a common cost unit, then valuable comparisons can be made between similar establishments. This is particularly applicable to hospitals, educational establishments and local authorities. Whatever cost unit is decided upon, the calculation of a cost per unit is as follows.

FORMULA TO LEARN

$$\text{Cost per service unit} = \frac{\text{Total costs for period}}{\text{Number of service units in the period}}$$

4.5 Service cost analysis

Service cost analysis should be performed in a manner which ensures that the following objectives are attained.

(a) Planned costs should be compared with actual costs.

Differences should be investigated and corrective action taken as necessary.

(b) A cost per unit of service should be calculated.

If each service has a number of variations (such as maintenance services provided by plumbers, electricians and carpenters) then the calculation of a cost per unit of each service may be necessary.

(c) The cost per unit of service should be used as part of the control function.

For example, costs per unit of service can be compared, month by month, period by period, year by year and so on and any unusual trends can be investigated.

(d) Prices should be calculated for services being sold to third parties.

The procedure is similar to job costing. A mark-up is added to the cost per unit of service to arrive at a selling price.

(e) Costs should be analysed into fixed, variable and semi-variable costs to help assist management with planning, control and decision making.

4.6 Service cost analysis in internal service situations

Service department costing is also used to establish a specific cost for an internal service which is a service provided by one department for another, rather than sold externally to customers eg canteen, maintenance.

4.6.1 Transport costs

'**Transport costs**' is a term used here to refer to the costs of the transport services used by a company, rather than the costs of a transport organisation, such as a rail network.

If a company has a fleet of lorries or vans which it uses to distribute its goods, it is useful to know how much the department is costing for a number of reasons.

(a) Management should be able to budget for expected costs, and to control actual expenditure on transport by comparing actual costs with budgeted costs.

(b) The company may charge customers for delivery or 'carriage outwards' costs, and a charge based on the cost of the transport service might be appropriate.

(c) If management knows how much its own transport is costing, a comparison can be made with alternative forms of transport to decide whether a cheaper or better method of delivery can be found.

(d) Similarly, if a company uses, say, a fleet of lorries, knowledge of how much transport by lorry costs should help management to decide whether another type of vehicle, say vans, would be cheaper to use.

Transport costs may be analysed to provide the cost of operating one van or lorry each year, but it is more informative to analyse costs as follows.

(a)   The cost per mile or kilometre travelled.

(b)   The cost per ton/mile or tonne/kilometre (the cost of carrying one tonne of goods for one kilometre distance) or the cost per kilogram/metre.

For example, suppose that a company lorry makes five deliveries in a week.

Delivery	Tonnes carried	Distance (one way) Kilometres	Tonne/kilometres carried
1	0.4	180	72
2	0.3	360	108
3	1.2	100	120
4	0.8	250	200
5	1.0	60	60
			560

If the costs of operating the lorry during the week are known to be $840, the cost per tonne/kilometre would be:

$$\frac{\$840}{560 \text{ tonne/kilometre}} = \$1.50 \text{ per tonne/kilometre}$$

Transport costs might be collected under five broad headings.

(a)   **Running costs** such as petrol, oil, drivers' wages
(b)   **Loading costs** (the labour costs of loading the lorries with goods for delivery)
(c)   **Servicing, repairs**, spare parts and tyre usage
(d)   **Annual direct expenses** such as road tax, insurance and depreciation
(e)   **Indirect costs of the distribution department** such as the wages of managers

The role of the cost accountant is to provide a system for **recording and analysing costs**. Just as production costs are recorded by means of material requisition notes, labour time sheets and so on, so too must transport costs be recorded by means of log sheets or time sheets, and material supply notes.

The purpose of a lorry driver's log sheet is to record distance travelled, or the number of tonne/kilometres and the drivers' time.

4.6.2 Canteen costs

Another example of service costing is the cost of a company's **canteen services**. A feature of canteen costing is that some revenue is earned when employees pay for their meals, but the prices paid will be insufficient to cover the costs of the canteen service. The company will subsidise the canteen and a major purpose of canteen costing is to establish the size of the subsidy.

If the costs of the canteen service are recorded by a system of service cost accounting, the likely headings of expense would be as follows.

(a)   **Food and drink**: separate canteen stores records may be kept, and the consumption of food and drink recorded by means of 'materials issues' notes.

(b)   **Labour costs of the canteen staff**: hourly paid staff will record their time at work on a time card or time sheet. Salaried staff will be a 'fixed' cost each month.

(c)   **Consumable stores** such as crockery, cutlery, glassware, table linen and cleaning materials will also be recorded in some form of inventory control system.

(d)   **The cost of gas and electricity** may be separately metered; otherwise an apportionment of the total cost of such utilities for the building as a whole will be made to the canteen department.

(e)   Asset records will be kept and **depreciation charges** made for major items of equipment like ovens and furniture.

(f)   An apportionment of other **overhead costs** of the building (rent and rates, building insurance and maintenance and so on) may be charged against the canteen.

Cash income from canteen sales will also be recorded.

4.6.3 Example: Service cost analysis

Suppose that a canteen recorded the following costs and revenue during the month.

	$
Food and drink	11,250
Labour	11,250
Heating and lighting	1,875
Repairs and consumable stores	1,125
Financing costs	1,000
Depreciation	750
Other apportioned costs	875
Revenue	22,500

The canteen served 37,500 meals in the month.

The size of the subsidy could be easily identified as follows:

	$
The total costs of the canteen	28,125
Revenue	22,500
Loss, to be covered by the company	5,625

The cost per meal averages 75c and the revenue per meal 60c. If the company decided that the canteen should pay its own way, without a subsidy, the average price of a meal would have to be raised by 15 cents.

4.7 The usefulness of costing services that do not earn revenue

4.7.1 Purposes of service costing

The techniques for costing services are similar to the techniques for costing products, but why should we want to establish a cost for 'internal' services, services that are provided by one department for another, rather than sold externally to customers? In other words, what is the purpose of service costing for non-revenue-earning services?

Service costing has two basic purposes.

(a)   **To control the costs in the service department**. If we establish a distribution cost per tonne kilometre, a canteen cost per employee, or job costs of repairs, we can establish control measures in the following ways.

   (i)   Comparing actual costs against a target or standard
   (ii)   Comparing current actual costs against actual costs in previous periods

(b)   **To control the costs of the user departments**, and prevent the unnecessary use of services. If the costs of services are charged to the user departments in such a way that the charges reflect the use actually made by each department of the service department's services then the following will occur.

   (i)   The overhead costs of user departments will be established more accurately; indeed some service department variable costs might be identified as directly attributable costs of the user department.

   (ii)   If the service department's charges for a user department are high, the user department might be encouraged to consider whether it is making an excessively costly and wasteful use of the service department's service.

   (iii) The user department might decide that it can obtain a similar service at a lower cost from an external service company.

4.7.2 Example: costing internal services

(a)   If maintenance costs in a factory are costed as jobs (that is, if each bit of repair work is given a job number and costed accordingly) repair costs can be charged to the departments on the basis of repair jobs actually undertaken, instead of on a more generalised basis, such as apportionment according to machine hour capacity in each department. Departments with high repair costs

could then consider their high incidence of repairs, the age and reliability of their machines, or the skills of the machine operatives.

(b) If IT costs are charged to a user department on the basis of a cost per hour, the user department would assess whether it was getting good value from its use of the IT department and whether it might be better to outsource some if its IT work.

4.8 Service cost analysis in service industry situations

4.8.1 Distribution costs

Example: service cost analysis in the service industry

This example shows how a rate per tonne/kilometre can be calculated for a distribution service.

Rick Shaw operates a small fleet of delivery vehicles. Standard costs have been established as follows.

Loading	1 hour per tonne loaded
Loading costs:	
Labour (casual)	$2 per hour
Equipment depreciation	$80 per week
Supervision	$80 per week
Drivers' wages (fixed)	$100 per man per week
Petrol	10c per kilometre
Repairs	5c per kilometre
Depreciation	$80 per week per vehicle
Supervision	$120 per week
Other general expenses (fixed)	$200 per week

There are two drivers and two vehicles in the fleet.

During a slack week, only six journeys were made.

Journey	Tonnes carried (one way)	One-way distance of journey Kilometres
1	5	100
2	8	20
3	2	60
4	4	50
5	6	200
6	5	300

Required

Calculate the expected average full cost per tonne/kilometre for the week.

Solution

Variable costs	Journey	1	2	3	4	5	6
		$	$	$	$	$	$
Loading labour		10	16	4	8	12	10
Petrol (both ways)		20	4	12	10	40	60
Repairs (both ways)		10	2	6	5	20	30
		40	22	22	23	72	100

Total costs

	$
Variable costs (total for journeys 1 to 6)	279
Loading equipment depreciation	80
Loading supervision	80
Drivers' wages	200
Vehicles depreciation	160
Drivers' supervision	120
Other costs	200
	1,119

Journey	Tonnes	One way distance Kilometres	Tonne/kilometres
1	5	100	500
2	8	20	160
3	2	60	120
4	4	50	200
5	6	200	1,200
6	5	300	1,500
			3,680

Cost per tonne/kilometre $\dfrac{\$1,119}{3,680} = \$0.304$

Note that the large element of fixed costs may distort this measure but that a variable cost per tonne/kilometre of $279/3,680 = $0.076 may be useful for budgetary control.

4.8.2 Education

The techniques described in the preceding paragraphs can be applied, in general, to any service industry situation. Attempt the following question about education.

QUESTION   Suitable cost unit

A university with annual running costs of $3 million has the following students.

Classification	Number	Attendance weeks per annum	Hours per week
3 year	2,700	30	28
4 year	1,500	30	25
Sandwich	1,900	35	20

Required

Calculate a cost per suitable cost unit for the university to the nearest cent.

ANSWER

We need to begin by establishing a cost unit for the university. Since there are three different categories of students we cannot use 'a student' as the cost unit. Attendance hours would seem to be the most appropriate cost unit. The next step is to calculate the number of units.

Number of students	Weeks	Hours	Total hours per annum
2,700	× 30	× 28	= 2,268,000
1,500	× 30	× 25	= 1,125,000
1,900	× 35	× 20	= 1,330,000
			4,723,000

The cost per unit is calculated as follows.

$$\text{Cost per unit} = \frac{\text{Total cost}}{\text{Number of units}} = \$\left(\frac{3,000,000}{4,723,000}\right) = \underline{\$0.64}$$

QUESTION

Service costing

State which of the following are characteristics of service costing.

(i)   High levels of indirect costs as a proportion of total costs
(ii)   Use of composite cost units
(iii)   Use of equivalent units

A   (i) only   C   (ii) only
B   (i) and (ii) only   D   (ii) and (iii) only

ANSWER

B   In service costing it is difficult to identify many attributable direct costs. Many costs must be shared over several cost units, therefore characteristic (i) does apply. Composite cost units such as tonne-mile or room-night are often used, therefore characteristic (ii) does apply. Equivalent units are more often used in costing for tangible products, therefore characteristic (iii) does not apply. The correct answer is therefore B.

CHAPTER ROUNDUP

↳ A **costing method** is designed to suit the way goods are processed or manufactured or the way services are provided.

↳ **Job costing** is a costing method applied where work is undertaken to customers' special requirements and each order is of comparatively short duration.

↳ Costs for each job are collected on a **job cost sheet** or **job card.**

↳ **Material costs** for each job are determined from **material requisition notes**. **Labour times** on each job are recorded on a **job ticket**, which is then costed and recorded on the job cost sheet. Some labour costs, such as overtime premium or the cost of rectifying sub-standard output, might be charged either directly to a job or else as an overhead cost, depending on the circumstances in which the costs have arisen. **Overhead** is absorbed into the cost of jobs using the predetermined overhead absorption rates.

↳ The usual method of fixing prices within a jobbing concern is **cost plus pricing**.

↳ It is possible to use a job costing system **to control the costs of an internal service department**, such as the maintenance department or the printing department.

↳ **Batch costing** is similar to job costing in that each batch of similar articles is separately identifiable. The **cost per unit** manufactured in a batch is the total batch cost divided by the number of units in the batch.

↳ Service costing can be used by companies operating in a service industry or by companies wishing to establish the cost of services carried out by some of their departments. Service organisations do not make or sell tangible goods.

↳ Specific characteristics of services

   – **S**imultaneity
   – **H**eterogeneity
   – **I**ntangibility
   – **P**erishability

↳ The main problem with service costing is the difficulty in **defining a realistic cost unit** that represents a suitable measure of the service provided. Frequently, a composite cost unit may be deemed more appropriate. Hotels, for example, may use the 'occupied bed-night' as an appropriate cost unit for ascertainment and control.

↳ Service department costing is also used to establish a specific cost for an internal service which is a service provided by one department for another, rather than sold externally to customers eg canteen, maintenance.

QUICK QUIZ

1   How are the material costs for each job determined?

2   Which of the following are not characteristics of job costing?

    I   Customer driven production
    II   Complete production possible within a single accounting period
    III   Homogeneous products

    A   I and II only   C   II and III only
    B   I and III only   D   III only

3   The cost of a job is $100,000

    (a)   If profit is 25% of the job cost, the price of the job = $.................
    (b)   If there is a 25% margin, the price of the job = $....................

4   What is a batch?

5   How would you calculate the cost per unit of a completed batch?

6   Define service costing

7   Match up the following services with their typical cost units

Service		Cost unit
Hotels		Patient-day
Education	?	Meal served
Hospitals		Full-time student
Catering organisations		Occupied bed-night

8   What is the advantage of organisations within an industry using a common cost unit?

9   Cost per service unit = ...

10   Service department costing is used to establish a specific cost for an 'internal service' which is a service provided by one department for another.

    True   ☐

    False   ☐

ANSWERS TO QUICK QUIZ

1   From materials requisition notes, or from suppliers' invoices if materials are purchased specifically for a particular job.

2   D

3   (a) $100,000 + (25% × $100,000) = $100,000 + $25,000 = $125,000

    (b)   Let price of job = x

$$\therefore \text{Profit} = 25\% \times x \text{ (selling price)}$$
$$\text{If profit} = 0.25x$$
$$x - 0.25x = \text{cost of job}$$
$$0.75x = \$100,000$$
$$x = \frac{\$100,000}{0.75}$$
$$= \$133,333$$

4   A group of similar articles which maintains its identity during one or more stages of production and is treated as a cost unit.

5   $$\frac{\text{Total batch cost}}{\text{Number of units in the batch}}$$

6   Cost accounting for services or functions eg canteens, maintenance, personnel (service centres/functions).

7   **Service**   **Cost unit**

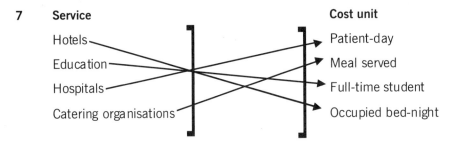

8   It is easier to make comparisons.

9   Cost per service unit = $$\frac{\text{Total costs for period}}{\text{Number of service units in the period}}$$

10   True

Now try ...

Attempt the questions below from the **Exam Question Bank**

Number

Q46 – Q49

CHAPTER

11

In this chapter we will consider **process costing**. The chapter will consider the topic from basics, looking at how to account for the most simple of processes. We then move on to how to account for any **losses** which might occur, as well as what to do with any **scrapped units** which are sold. We also consider how to deal with any **closing work in progress** and then look at two methods of valuing **opening work in progress**. Valuation of both opening and closing work in progress hinges on the concept of **equivalent units**, which will be explained in detail.

Process costing

EXAM FOCUS POINT

Expect several questions on process costing. The exam questions may be shorter than the examples and questions in this chapter, but if you have worked through some long questions you will have covered whatever can come up in the exam.

1 The basics of process costing

1.1 Introduction to process costing

Process costing is a costing method used where it is not possible to identify separate units of production, or jobs, usually because of the continuous nature of the production processes involved.

It is common to identify process costing with **continuous production** such as the following.

- Oil refining
- Paper
- Foods and drinks
- Chemicals

Process costing may also be associated with the continuous production of large volumes of low-cost items, such as **cans** or **tins**.

1.2 Features of process costing

(a)   The **output** of one process becomes the **input** to the next until the finished product is made in the final process.

(b)   The continuous nature of production in many processes means that there will usually be **closing work in progress which must be valued**. In process costing it is not possible to build up cost records of the cost per unit of output or the cost per unit of closing inventory because production in progress is an **indistinguishable homogeneous mass**.

(c)   There is often a **loss in process** due to spoilage, wastage, evaporation and so on.

(d)   Output from production may be a single product, but there may also be a **by-product** (or by-products) and/or **joint products.**

The aim of this chapter is to describe how cost accountants keep a set of accounts to record the costs of production in a processing industry. The aim of the set of accounts is to derive a cost, or valuation, for output and closing inventory.

1.3 Process accounts

Where a series of separate processes is required to manufacture the finished product, the output of one process becomes the input to the next until the final output is made in the final process. If two processes are required the accounts would look like this.

PROCESS 1 ACCOUNT

	Units	$		Units	$
Direct materials	1,000	50,000	Output to process 2	1,000	90,000
Direct labour		20,000			
Production overhead		20,000			
	1,000	90,000		1,000	90,000

PROCESS 2 ACCOUNT

	Units	$		Units	$
Materials from process 1	1,000	90,000	Output to finished goods	1,000	150,000
Added materials		30,000			
Direct labour		15,000			
Production overhead		15,000			
	1,000	150,000		1,000	150,000

Note that direct labour and production overhead may be treated together in an examination question as **conversion cost**.

Added materials, labour and overhead in process 2 are added gradually throughout the process. Materials from process 1, in contrast, will often be introduced in full at the start of process 2.

The 'units' columns in the process accounts are for **memorandum purposes** only and help you to ensure that you do not miss out any entries.

1.4 Framework for dealing with process costing

Process costing is centred around **four key steps**. The exact work done at each step will depend on whether there are normal losses, scrap, opening and closing work in progress.

Step 1   Determine output and losses
Step 2   Calculate cost per unit of output, losses and WIP
Step 3   Calculate total cost of output, losses and WIP
Step 4   Complete accounts

Let's look at these steps in more detail

Step 1	**Determine output and losses.** This step involves the following.

- Determining expected output
- Calculating normal loss and abnormal loss and gain
- Calculating equivalent units if there is closing or opening work in progress

Step 2	**Calculate cost per unit of output, losses and WIP.** This step involves calculating cost per unit or cost per equivalent unit.

Step 3	**Calculate total cost of output, losses and WIP.** In some examples this will be straightforward; however in cases where there is closing and/or opening work-in-progress a **statement of evaluation** will have to be prepared.

Step 4	**Complete accounts.** This step involves the following.

- Completing the process account
- Writing up the other accounts required by the question

2 Losses in process costing

2.1 Introduction

Losses may occur in process. If a certain level of loss is expected, this is known as **normal loss**. If losses are greater than expected, the extra loss is **abnormal loss**. If losses are less than expected, the difference is known as **abnormal gain**.

Normal loss is the loss expected during a process. It is not given a cost.

Abnormal loss is the extra loss resulting when actual loss is greater than normal or expected loss, and it is given a cost.

Abnormal gain is the gain resulting when actual loss is less than the normal or expected loss, and it is given a 'negative cost'.

Since normal loss is not given a cost, the cost of producing these units is borne by the 'good' units of output.

Abnormal loss and gain units are valued at the same unit rate as 'good' units. Abnormal events do not therefore affect the cost of good production. Their costs are **analysed separately** in an **abnormal loss or abnormal gain account**.

2.2 Example: abnormal losses and gains

Suppose that input to a process is 1,000 units at a cost of $4,500. Normal loss is 10% and there are no opening or closing stocks. Determine the accounting entries for the cost of output and the cost of the loss if actual output were as follows.

(a)   860 units (so that actual loss is 140 units)
(b)   920 units (so that actual loss is 80 units)

Solution

Before we demonstrate the use of the 'four-step framework' we will summarise the way that the losses are dealt with.

(a) Normal loss is given no share of cost.

(b) The cost of output is therefore based on the **expected** units of output, which in our example amount to 90% of 1,000 = 900 units.

(c) Abnormal loss is given a cost, which is written off to the profit and loss account via an abnormal loss/gain account.

(d) Abnormal gain is treated in the same way, except that being a gain rather than a loss, it appears as a **debit** entry in the process account (whereas a loss appears as a **credit** entry in this account).

(a) **Output is 860 units**

Step 1   Determine output and losses

If actual output is 860 units and the actual loss is 140 units:

	Units
Actual loss	140
Normal loss (10% of 1,000)	100
Abnormal loss	40

Step 2   Calculate cost per unit of output and losses

The cost per unit of output and the cost per unit of abnormal loss are based on expected output.

$$\frac{\text{Costs incurred}}{\text{Expected output}} = \frac{\$4,500}{900 \text{ units}} = \$5 \text{ per unit}$$

Step 3   Calculate total cost of output and losses

Normal loss is not assigned any cost.

	$
Cost of output (860 × $5)	4,300
Normal loss	0
Abnormal loss (40 × $5)	200
	4,500

Step 4   Complete accounts

PROCESS ACCOUNT

	Units	$		Units		$
Cost incurred	1,000	4,500	Normal loss	100		0
			Output (finished goods a/c)	860	(× $5)	4,300
			Abnormal loss	40	(× $5)	200
	1,000	4,500		1,000		4,500

ABNORMAL LOSS ACCOUNT

	Units	$		Units	$
Process a/c	40	200	Income statement	40	200

(b) **Output is 920 units**

Step 1   Determine output and losses

If actual output is 920 units and the actual loss is 80 units:

	Units
Actual loss	80
Normal loss (10% of 1,000)	100
Abnormal gain	20

Step 2   Calculate cost per unit of output and losses

The cost per unit of output and the cost per unit of abnormal gain are based on **expected** output.

$$\frac{\text{Costs incurred}}{\text{Expected output}} = \frac{\$4,500}{900\,\text{units}} = \$5 \text{ per unit}$$

(Whether there is abnormal loss or gain does not affect the valuation of units of output. The figure of $5 per unit is exactly the same as in the previous paragraph, when there were 40 units of abnormal loss.)

Step 3   Calculate total cost of output and losses

	$
Cost of output (920 × $5)	4,600
Normal loss	0
Abnormal gain (20 × $5)	(100)
	4,500

Step 4   Complete accounts

PROCESS ACCOUNT

	Units	$		Units	$
Cost incurred	1,000	4,500	Normal loss	100	0
Abnormal gain a/c	20 (x $5)	100	Output (finished goods a/c)	920 (x $5)	4,600
	1,020	4,600		1,020	4,600

ABNORMAL GAIN

	Units	$		Units	$
Income statement	20	100	Process a/c	20	100

QUESTION   Abnormal losses and gains

Shiny Co has two processes, Y and Z. There is an expected loss of 5% of input in process Y and 7% of input in process Z. Activity during a four week period is as follows.

	Y	Z
Material input (kg)	20,000	28,000
Output (kg)	18,500	26,100

Is there an abnormal gain or abnormal loss for each process?

	Y	Z
A	Abnormal loss	Abnormal loss
B	Abnormal gain	Abnormal loss
C	Abnormal loss	Abnormal gain
D	Abnormal gain	Abnormal gain

ANSWER

The correct answer is C.

	Y		Z	
Input (kg)	20,000		28,000	
Normal loss (kg)	1,000	(5% of 20,000)	1,960	(7% of 28,000)
Expected output	19,000		26,040	
Actual output	18,500		26,100	
Abnormal loss/gain	500	(loss)	60	(gain)

2.3 Example: Abnormal losses and gains again

During a four-week period, period 3, costs of input to a process were $29,070. Input was 1,000 units, output was 850 units and normal loss is 10%.

During the next period, period 4, costs of input were again $29,070. Input was again 1,000 units, but output was 950 units.

There were no units of opening or closing inventory.

Required

Prepare the process account and abnormal loss or gain account for each period.

Solution

Step 1 Determine output and losses

Period 3

	Units
Actual output	850
Normal loss (10% × 1,000)	100
Abnormal loss	50
Input	1,000

Period 4

	Units
Actual output	950
Normal loss (10% × 1,000)	100
Abnormal gain	(50)
Input	1,000

Step 2 **Calculate cost per unit of output and losses**

For each period the cost per unit is based on expected output.

$$\frac{\text{Cost of input}}{\text{Expected units of output}} = \frac{\$29,070}{900} = \$32.30 \text{ per unit}$$

Step 3 **Calculate total cost of output and losses**

Period 3

	$
Cost of output (850 × $32.30)	27,455
Normal loss	0
Abnormal loss (50 × $32.30)	1,615
	29,070

Period 4

	$
Cost of output (950 × $32.30)	30,685
Normal loss	0
Abnormal gain (50 × $32.30)	1,615
	29,070

Step 4   **Complete accounts**

PROCESS ACCOUNT

	Units	$		Units	$
Period 3					
Cost of input	1,000	29,070	Normal loss	100	0
			Finished goods a/c	850	27,455
			(× $32.30)		
			Abnormal loss a/c	50	1,615
			(× $32.30)		
	1,000	29,070		1,000	29,070
Period 4					
Cost of input	1,000	29,070	Normal loss	100	0
Abnormal gain a/c	50	1,615	Finished goods a/c	950	30,685
(× $32.30)			(× $32.30)		
	1,050	30,685		1,050	30,685

ABNORMAL LOSS OR GAIN ACCOUNT

	$		$
Period 3		*Period 4*	
Abnormal loss in process a/c	1,615	Abnormal gain in process a/c	1,615

A nil balance on this account will be carried forward into period 5.

If there is a closing balance in the abnormal loss or gain account when the profit for the period is calculated, this balance is taken to the income statement: an abnormal gain will be a credit to the income statement and an abnormal loss will be a debit to the income statement.

QUESTION

Process account

3,000 units of material are input to a process. Process costs are as follows.

Material	$11,700
Conversion costs	$6,300

Output is 2,000 units. Normal loss is 20% of input.

Required

Prepare a process account and the appropriate abnormal loss/gain account.

ANSWER

Step 1   **Determine output and losses**

We are told that output is 2,000 units.
Normal loss = 20% × 3,000 = 600 units
Abnormal loss = (3,000 – 600) – 2,000 = 400 units

Step 2   **Calculate cost per unit of output and losses**

$$\text{Cost per unit} = \frac{\$(11,700+6,300)}{2,400} = \$7.50$$

Step 3 **Calculate total cost of output and losses**

		$
Output	(2,000 × $7.50)	15,000
Normal loss		0
Abnormal loss	(400 × $7.50)	3,000
		18,000

Step 4 **Complete accounts**

PROCESS ACCOUNT

	Units	$		Units	$
Material	3,000	11,700	Output	2,000	15,000
Conversion costs		6,300	Normal loss	600	
			Abnormal loss	400	3,000
	3,000	18,000		3,000	18,000

ABNORMAL LOSS ACCOUNT

	$		$
Process a/c	3,000	Income statement	3,000

QUESTION

Finished output

Charlton Co manufactures a product in a single process operation. Normal loss is 10% of input. Loss occurs at the end of the process. Data for June are as follows.

Opening and closing inventories of work in progress	Nil
Cost of input materials (3,300 units)	$59,100
Direct labour and production overhead	$30,000
Output to finished goods	2,750 units

The full cost of finished output in June was

A $74,250   B $81,000   C $82,500   D $89,100

ANSWER

Step 1 **Determine output and losses**

	Units
Actual output	2,750
Normal loss (10% × 3,300)	330
Abnormal loss	220
	3,300

Step 2 **Calculate cost per unit of output and losses**

$$\frac{\text{Cost of input}}{\text{Expected units of output}} = \frac{\$89,100}{3,300 - 330} = \$30 \text{ per unit}$$

Step 3 **Calculate total cost of output and losses**

	$
Cost of output (2,750 × $30)	82,500 **(The correct answer is C)**
Normal loss	0
Abnormal loss (220 × $30)	6,600
	89,100

If you were reduced to making a calculated guess, you could have eliminated option D. This is simply the total input cost, with no attempt to apportion some of the cost to the abnormal loss.

Option A is incorrect because it results from allocating a full unit cost to the normal loss: remember that normal loss does not carry any of the process cost.

Option B is incorrect because it results from calculating a 10% normal loss based on *output* of 2,750 units (275 units normal loss), rather than on *input* of 3,300 units.

3 Losses with scrap value

Scrap is 'Discarded material having some value.'

Loss or spoilage may have scrap value.

- The **scrap value** of normal loss is usually deducted from the cost of materials.
- The **scrap value** of abnormal loss (or abnormal gain) is usually set off against its cost, in an abnormal loss (abnormal gain) account.

As the questions that follow will show, the three steps to remember are these.

Step 1	Separate the **scrap value** of **normal loss** from the **scrap value** of **abnormal loss** or **gain**.
Step 2	In effect, subtract the scrap value of normal loss from the cost of the process, by crediting it to the process account (as a 'value' for normal loss).
Step 3	*Either* subtract the value of abnormal loss scrap from the cost of abnormal loss, by crediting the abnormal loss account.
	or subtract the cost of the abnormal gain scrap from the value of abnormal gain, by debiting the abnormal gain account.

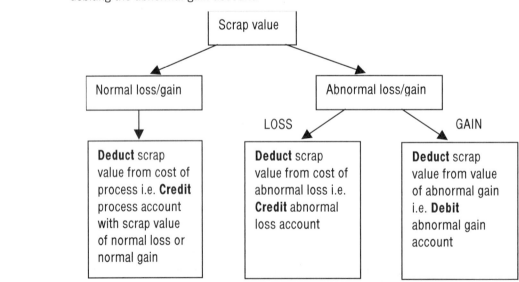

BPP LEARNING MEDIA

QUESTION

Losses and scrap

3,000 units of material are input to a process. Process costs are as follows.

Material	$11,700
Conversion costs	$6,300

Output is 2,000 units. Normal loss is 20% of input.

The units of loss could be sold for $1 each. Prepare appropriate accounts.

ANSWER

Step 1   Determine output and losses

Input	3,000 units
Normal loss (20% of 3,000)	600 units
Expected output	2,400 units
Actual output	2,000 units
Abnormal loss	400 units

Step 2   Calculate cost per unit of output and losses

	$
Scrap value of normal loss	600
Scrap value of abnormal loss	400
Total scrap (1,000 units × $1)	1,000

$$\text{Cost per expected unit} = \frac{\$((11,700-600)+6,300)}{2,400} = \$7.25$$

Step 3   Calculate total cost of output and losses

		$
Output	(2,000 × $7.25)	14,500
Normal loss	(600 × $1.00)	600
Abnormal loss	(400 × $7.25)	2,900
		18,000

Step 4   Complete accounts

PROCESS ACCOUNT

	Units	$		Units	$
Material	3,000	11,700	Output	2,000	14,500
Conversion costs		6,300	Normal loss	600	600
			Abnormal loss	400	2,900
	3,000	18,000		3,000	18,000

ABNORMAL LOSS ACCOUNT

	$		$
Process a/c	2,900	Scrap a/c	400
		Inc statement	2,500
	2,900		2,900

SCRAP ACCOUNT

	$		$
Normal loss	600	Cash	1,000
Abnormal loss	400		
	1,000		1,000

QUESTION

JJ has a factory which operates two production processes, cutting and pasting. Normal loss in each process is 10%. Scrapped units out of the cutting process sell for $3 per unit whereas scrapped units out of the pasting process sell for $5. Output from the cutting process is transferred to the pasting process: output from the pasting process is finished output ready for sale.

Relevant information about costs for control period 7 are as follows.

	Cutting process		Pasting process	
	Units	$	Units	$
Input materials	18,000	54,000		
Transferred to pasting process	16,000			
Materials from cutting process			16,000	
Added materials			14,000	70,000
Labour and overheads		32,400		135,000
Output to finished goods			28,000	

Required

Prepare accounts for the cutting process, the pasting process, abnormal loss, abnormal gain and scrap.

ANSWER

(a)   *Cutting process*

Step 1   **Determine output and losses**

The normal loss is 10% of 18,000 units = 1,800 units, and the actual loss is (18,000 – 16,000) = 2,000 units. This means that there is abnormal loss of 200 units.

Actual output	16,000 units
Abnormal loss	200 units
Expected output (90% of 18,000)	16,200 units

Step 2   **Calculate cost per unit of output and losses**

(i)   The total value of scrap is 2,000 units at $3 per unit = $6,000. We must split this between the scrap value of normal loss and the scrap value of abnormal loss.

	$
Normal loss (1,800 × $3)	5,400
Abnormal loss (200 × $3)	600
Total scrap (2,000 units × $3)	6,000

(ii)   The scrap value of normal loss is first deducted from the materials cost in the process, in order to calculate the output cost per unit and then credited to the process account as a 'value' for normal loss. The cost per unit in the cutting process is calculated as follows.

	Total cost		Cost per expected unit of output
	$		$
Materials	54,000		
Less normal loss scrap value*	5,400		
	48,600	(÷ 16,200)	3.00
Labour and overhead	32,400	(÷ 16,200)	2.00
Total	81,000	(÷ 16,200)	5.00

* It is usual to set this scrap value of normal loss against the cost of materials.

Step 3   **Calculate total cost of output and losses**

		$
Output	(16,000 units × $5)	80,000
Normal loss	(1,800 units × $3)	5,400
Abnormal loss	(200 units × $5)	1,000
		86,400

Step 4   **Complete accounts**

PROCESS 1 ACCOUNT

	Units	$		Units	$
Materials	18,000	54,000	Output to pasting process *	16,000	80,000
Labour and			Normal loss (scrap a/c) **	1,800	5,400
overhead		32,400	Abnormal loss a/c *	200	1,000
	18,000	86,400		18,000	86,400

* At $5 per unit   ** At $3 per unit

(b)   *Pasting process*

Step 1   **Determine output and losses**

The normal loss is 10% of the units processed = 10% of (16,000 + 14,000) = 3,000 units. The actual loss is (30,000 − 28,000) = 2,000 units, so that there is abnormal gain of 1,000 units. These are *deducted* from actual output to determine expected output.

	Units
Actual output	28,000
Abnormal gain	(1,000)
Expected output (90% of 30,000)	27,000

Step 2   **Calculate cost per unit of output and losses**

(i)   The total value of scrap is 2,000 units at $5 per unit = $10,000. We must split this between the scrap value of normal loss and the scrap value of abnormal gain. Abnormal gain's scrap value is 'negative'.

		$
Normal loss scrap value	3,000 units × $5	15,000
Abnormal gain scrap value	1,000 units × $5	(5,000)
Scrap value of actual loss	2,000 units × $5	10,000

(ii)   The scrap value of normal loss is first deducted from the cost of materials in the process, in order to calculate a cost per unit of output, and then credited to the process account as a 'value' for normal loss. The cost per unit in the pasting process is calculated as follows.

	Total cost		Cost per expected unit of output
	$		$
Materials:			
Transfer from	80,000		
cutting process	80,000		
Added in pasting process	70,000		
	150,000		
Less scrap value of			
normal loss	15,000		
	135,000	(÷ 27,000)	5
Labour and overhead	135,000	(÷ 27,000)	5
	270,000	(÷ 27,000)	10

Step 3   **Calculate total cost of output and losses**

		$
Output	(28,000 units × $10)	280,000
Normal loss	(3,000 units × $5)	15,000
		295,000
Abnormal gain	(1,000 units × $10)	(10,000)
		285,000

Step 4   **Complete accounts**

PASTING PROCESS ACCOUNT

	Units	$		Units	$
From cutting process	16,000	80,000	Finished output*	28,000	280,000
Added materials	14,000	70,000			
Labour and o/hd		135,000	Normal loss	3,000	15,000
	30,000	285,000	(scrap a/c)		
Abnormal gain a/c		10,000			
	1,000*				
	31,000	295,000		31,000	295,000

* At $10 per unit

(c) and (d)

Abnormal loss and abnormal gain accounts

For each process, one or the other of these accounts will record three items.

(i) The cost/value of the abnormal loss/gain (corresponding entry to that in the process account).

(ii) The scrap value of the abnormal loss or gain, to set off against it.

(iii) A balancing figure, which is written to the income statement as an adjustment to the profit figure.

ABNORMAL LOSS ACCOUNT

	Units	$		$
Cutting process	200	1,000	Scrap a/c (scrap value of ab. loss)	600
			Income statement (balance)	400
		1,000		1,000

ABNORMAL GAIN ACCOUNT

	$		Units	$
Scrap a/c (scrap value of abnormal gain units)	5,000	Pasting process	1,000	10,000
Income statement (balance)	5,000			
	10,000			10,000

(e)   **Scrap account**

This is credited with the cash value of actual units scrapped. The other entries in the account should all be identifiable as corresponding entries to those in the process accounts, and abnormal loss and abnormal gain accounts.

SCRAP ACCOUNT

	$		$
Normal loss:		Cash:	
Cutting process (1,800 × $3)	5,400	Sale of cutting process scrap (2,000 × $3)	6,000
Pasting process (3,000 × $5)	15,000	Sale of pasting process scrap (2,000 × $5)	10,000
Abnormal loss a/c	600	Abnormal gain a/c	5,000
	21,000		21,000

Abnormal losses and gains never affect the cost of good units of production. The scrap value of abnormal losses is **not** credited to the process account, and abnormal loss and gain units carry the same **full cost** as a good unit of production.

4 Losses with a disposal cost

4.1 Introduction

You must also be able to deal with losses which have a **disposal cost**.

The basic calculations required in such circumstances are as follows.

(a) Increase the process costs by the cost of disposing of the units of normal loss and use the resulting cost per unit to value good output and abnormal loss/gain.

(b) The normal loss is given no value in the process account.

(c) Include the disposal costs of normal loss on the debit side of the process account.

(d) Include the disposal costs of abnormal loss in the abnormal loss account and hence in the transfer of the cost of abnormal loss to the income statement.

4.2 Example: Losses with a disposal cost

Suppose that input to a process was 1,000 units at a cost of $4,500. Normal loss is 10% and there are no opening and closing inventories. Actual output was 860 units and loss units had to be disposed of at a cost of $0.90 per unit.

Normal loss = 10% × 1,000 = 100 units. ∴ Abnormal loss = 900 – 860 = 40 units

$$\text{Cost per unit} = \frac{\$4,500 + (100 \times \$0.90)}{900} = \$5.10$$

The relevant accounts would be as follows.

PROCESS ACCOUNT

	Units	$		Units	$
Cost of input	1,000	4,500	Output	860	4,386
Disposal cost of			Normal loss	100	
normal loss		90	Abnormal loss	40	204
	1,000	4,590		1,000	4,590

ABNORMAL LOSS ACCOUNT

	$		$
Process a/c	204	Income statement	240
Disposal cost (40 × $0.90)	36		
	240		240

5 Valuing closing work in progress

5.1 Introduction

When units are partly completed at the end of a period (and hence there is closing work in progress), it is necessary to calculate the **equivalent units of production** in order to determine the cost of a completed unit.

EXAM FOCUS POINT

The Study Guide states that losses and work in progress in the same process will not be examined.

In the examples we have looked at so far we have assumed that opening and closing inventories of work in process have been nil. We must now look at more realistic examples and consider how to allocate the costs incurred in a period between completed output (that is, finished units) and partly completed closing inventory.

Some examples will help to illustrate the problem, and the techniques used to share out (apportion) costs between finished output and closing inventories.

Suppose that we have the following account for Process 2 for period 9.

PROCESS ACCOUNT

	Units	$		Units	$
Materials	1,000	6,200	Finished goods	800	?
Labour and overhead		2,850	Closing WIP	200	?
	1,000	9,050		1,000	9,050

How do we value the finished goods and closing work in process?

With any form of process costing involving closing WIP, we have to apportion costs between output and closing WIP. To apportion costs 'fairly' we make use of the concept of **equivalent units of production**.

5.2 Equivalent units

Equivalent units are notional whole units which represent incomplete work, and which are used to apportion costs between work in process and completed output.

We will assume that in the example above the degree of completion is as follows.

(a) **Direct materials**. These are added in full at the start of processing, and so any closing WIP will have 100% of their direct material content. (This is not always the case in practice. Materials might be added gradually throughout the process, in which case closing inventory will only be a certain percentage complete as to material content. We will look at this later in the chapter.)

(b) **Direct labour and production overhead.** These are usually assumed to be incurred at an even rate through the production process, so that when we refer to a unit that is 50% complete, we mean that it is half complete for labour and overhead, although it might be 100% complete for materials.

Let us also assume that the closing WIP is 100% complete for materials and 25% complete for labour and overhead.

How would we now put a value to the finished output and the closing WIP?

In **Step 1** of our framework, we have been told what output and losses are. However we also need to calculate **equivalent units**.

STATEMENT OF EQUIVALENT UNITS

		Materials		Labour and overhead	
	Total units	Degree of completion	Equivalent units	Degree of completion	Equivalent units
Finished output	800	100%	800	100%	800
Closing WIP	200	100%	200	25%	50
	1,000		1,000		850

In **Step 2** the important figure is **average cost per equivalent unit**. This can be calculated as follows.

STATEMENT OF COSTS PER EQUIVALENT UNIT

	Materials	Labour and overhead
Costs incurred in the period	$6,200	$2,850
Equivalent units of work done	1,000	850
Cost per equivalent unit (approx)	$6.20	$3.3529

To calculate total costs for **Step 3**, we prepare a statement of evaluation to show how the costs should be apportioned between finished output and closing WIP.

STATEMENT OF EVALUATION

	Materials			Labour and overheads			
Item	Equivalent units	Cost per equivalent units $	Cost $	Equiv units	Cost per equiv units $	Cost $	Total cost $
Finished output	800	6.20	4,960	800	3.3529	2,682	7,642
Closing WIP	200	6.20	1,240	50	3.3529	168	1,408
	1,000		6,200	850		2,850	9,050

The process account (work in progress, or work in process account) would be shown as follows.

PROCESS ACCOUNT

	Units	$		Units	$
Materials	1,000	6,200	Finished goods	800	7,642
Labour overhead		2,850	Closing WIP	200	1,408
	1,000	9,050		1,000	9,050

QUESTION

Equivalent units for closing WIP

Ally Co has the following information available on Process 9.

PROCESS 9 ACCOUNT

		$			$
Input	10,000kg	59,150	Finished goods	8,000kg	52,000
			Closing WIP	2,000kg	7,150
		59,150			59,150

How many equivalent units were there for Closing WIP?

A   1,000   C   2,000
B   1,100   D   8,000

ANSWER

The correct answer is B.

This question requires you to **work backwards**. You can calculate the cost per unit using the Finished Goods figures.

$$\text{Cost per unit} = \frac{\text{Cost of finished goods}}{\text{Number of kg}} = \frac{52,000}{8,000} = \$6.50$$

If 2,000kg (Closing WIP figure) were fully complete total cost would be

2,000 x $6.50 = $13,000

Actual cost of Closing WIP = $7,150

Degree of completion = $\dfrac{7,150}{13,000}$ = 55%

Therefore equivalent units = 55% of 2,000 = 1,100kg

QUESTION
Equivalent units

Ashley Co operates a process costing system. The following details are available for Process 2.

Materials input at beginning of process   12,000 kg, costing $18,000
Labour and overheads added $28,000

10,000kg were completed and transferred to the Finished Goods account. The remaining units were 60% complete with regard to labour and overheads. There were no losses in the period.

What is the value of Closing WIP in the process account?

A	$4,800	C	$7,667
B	$6,000	D	$8,000

ANSWER

The correct answer is B.

STATEMENT OF EQUIVALENT UNITS

	Units	Material Degree of completion	Equivalent units	Units	Labour Degree of completion	Equivalent units
Finished goods	10,000	100%	10,000	10,000	100%	10,000
Closing WIP	2,000	100%	2,000	2,000	60%	1,200
	12,000		12,000	12,000		11,200

COSTS PER EQUIVALENT UNIT

	Material	Labour
Total cost	$18,000	$28,000
Equivalent units	12,000	11,200
Cost per unit	$1.50	$2.50

Total cost per unit = $4.00

Value of Closing WIP = ($1.50 x 2,000) + ($2.50 x 1,200) = $6,000

5.3 Different rates of input

In many industries, materials, labour and overhead may be **added at different rates** during the course of production.

(a)   Output from a previous process (for example the output from process 1 to process 2) may be introduced into the subsequent process all at once, so that closing inventory is 100% complete in respect of these materials.

(b)   Further materials may be added gradually during the process, so that closing inventory is only partially complete in respect of these added materials.

(c)   Labour and overhead may be 'added' at yet another different rate. When production overhead is absorbed on a labour hour basis, however, we should expect the degree of completion on overhead to be the same as the degree of completion on labour.

When this situation occurs, **equivalent units**, and a **cost per equivalent unit**, should be calculated separately for each type of material, and also for conversion costs.

5.4 Example: Equivalent units and different degrees of completion

Suppose that Columbine Co is a manufacturer of processed goods, and that results in process 2 for April 20X3 were as follows.

Opening inventory	NIL
Material input from process 1	4,000 units

Costs of input:

	$
Material from process 1	6,000
Added materials in process 2	1,080
Conversion costs	1,720

Output is transferred into the next process, process 3.

Closing work in process amounted to 800 units, complete as to:

Process 1 material	100%
Added materials	50%
Conversion costs	30%

Required

Prepare the account for process 2 for April 20X3.

Solution

(a)   STATEMENT OF EQUIVALENT UNITS (OF PRODUCTION IN THE PERIOD)

			Equivalent units of production					
			Process 1 material		Added materials		Labour and overhead	
Input	*Output*	*Total*						
Units		Units	Units	%	Units	%	Units	%
4,000	Completed production	3,200	3,200	100	3,200	100	3,200	100
	Closing inventory	800	800	100	400	50	240	30
4,000		4,000	4,000		3,600		3,440	

(b)   STATEMENT OF COST (PER EQUIVALENT UNIT)

Input	*Cost*	*Equivalent production in units*	*Cost per unit*
	$		$
Process 1 material	6,000	4,000	1.50
Added materials	1,080	3,600	0.30
Labour and overhead	1,720	3,440	0.50
	8,800		2.30

(c)   STATEMENT OF EVALUATION (OF FINISHED WORK AND CLOSING INVENTORIES)

Production	*Cost element*	*Number of equivalent units*	*Cost per equivalent unit*	*Total*	*Cost*
			$	$	$
Completed production		3,200	2.30		7,360
Closing inventory:	process 1 material	800	1.50	1,200	
	added material	400	0.30	120	
	labour and overhead	240	0.50	120	
					1,440
					8,800

BPP
LEARNING MEDIA

(d)   PROCESS ACCOUNT

	Units	$		Units	$
Process 1 material	4,000	6,000	Process 3 a/c	3,200	7,360
Added material		1,080			
Conversion costs		1,720	Closing inventory c/f	800	1,440
	4,000	8,800		4,000	8,800

6 Valuing opening work in progress: FIFO method

6.1 Introduction

> Account can be taken of opening work in progress using either the **FIFO** method or the **weighted average cost method**.

Opening work in progress is partly complete at the beginning of a period and is valued at the cost incurred to date. In the example in Paragraph 4.4, closing work in progress of 800 units at the end of April 20X3 would be carried forward as opening inventory, value $1,440, at the beginning of May 20X3.

It therefore follows that the work required to complete units of opening inventory is 100% minus the work in progress done in the previous period. For example, if 100 units of opening inventory are 70% complete at the beginning of June 20X2, the equivalent units of production would be as follows.

Equivalent units in previous period	(May 20X2) (70%)	=	70
Equivalent units to complete work in current period	(June 20X2) (30%)	=	30
Total work done			100

The FIFO method of valuation deals with production on a first in, first out basis. The assumption is that the first units completed in any period are the units of opening inventory that were held at the beginning of the period.

6.2 Example: WIP and FIFO

Suppose that information relating to process 1 of a two-stage production process is as follows, for August 20X2.

Opening inventory 500 units: degree of completion	60%
Cost to date	$2,800

Costs incurred in August 20X2	$
Direct materials (2,500 units introduced)	13,200
Direct labour	6,600
Production overhead	6,600
	26,400

Closing inventory 300 units: degree of completion	80%

There was no loss in the process.

Required

Prepare the process 1 account for August 20X2.

Solution

As the term implies, first in, first out means that in August 20X2 the first units completed were the units of opening inventory.

Opening inventories: work done to date =	60%
plus work done in August 20X2 =	40%

The cost of the work done up to 1 August 20X2 is known to be $2,800, so that the cost of the units completed will be $2,800 plus the cost of completing the final 40% of the work on the units in August 20X2.

Once the opening inventory has been completed, all other finished output in August 20X2 will be work started as well as finished in the month.

	Units
Total output in August 20X2 *	2,700
Less opening inventory, completed first	500
Work started and finished in August 20X2	2,200

(* Opening inventory plus units introduced minus closing inventory = 500 + 2,500 – 300)

What we are doing here is taking the total output of 2,700 units, and saying that we must divide it into two parts as follows.

(a) The opening inventory, which was first in and so must be first out.
(b) The rest of the units, which were 100% worked in the period.

Dividing finished output into two parts in this way is a necessary feature of the FIFO valuation method.

Continuing the example, closing inventory of 300 units will be started in August 20X2, but not yet completed.

The total cost of output to process 2 during 20X2 will be as follows.

		$	
Opening inventory	cost brought forward	2,800	(60%)
	plus cost incurred during August 20X2, to complete	x	(40%)
		2,800 + x	
Fully worked 2,200 units		y	
Total cost of output to process 2, FIFO basis		2,800 + x + y	

Equivalent units will again be used as the basis for apportioning **costs incurred during August 20X2**. Be sure that you understand the treatment of 'opening inventory units completed', and can relate the calculations to the principles of FIFO valuation.

Step 1   **Determine output and losses**

STATEMENT OF EQUIVALENT UNITS

	Total units		Equivalent units of production in August 20X2
Opening inventory units completed	500	(40%)	200
Fully worked units	2,200	(100%)	2,200
Output to process 2	2,700		2,400
Closing inventory	300	(80%)	240
	3,000		2,640

Step 2   **Calculate cost per unit of output and losses**

The cost per equivalent unit in August 20X2 can now be calculated.

STATEMENT OF COST PER EQUIVALENT UNIT

$$\frac{\text{Cost incurred}}{\text{Equivalent units}} = \frac{\$26,400}{2,640}$$

Cost per equivalent unit = $10

Step 3 **Calculate total costs of output, losses and WIP**

STATEMENT OF EVALUATION

	Equivalent units	Valuation $
Opening inventory, work done in August 20X2	200	2,000
Fully worked units	2,200	22,000
Closing inventory	240	2,400
	2,640	26,400

The total value of the completed opening inventory will be $2,800 (brought forward) plus $2,000 added in August before completion = $4,800.

Step 4 **Complete accounts**

PROCESS 1 ACCOUNT

	Units	$		Units	$
Opening inventory	500	2,800	Output to process 2:		
Direct materials	2,500	13,200	Opening inventory	500	4,800
Direct labour		6,600	Fully worked units	2,200	22,000
Production o'hd		6,600		2,700	26,800
			Closing inventory	300	2,400
	3,000	29,200		3,000	29,200

We now know that the value of x is $(4,800 − 2,800) = $2,000 and the value of y is $22,000.

QUESTION

FIFO and equivalent units

Walter Co uses the FIFO method of process costing. At the end of a four week period, the following information was available for process P.

Opening WIP	2,000 units (60% complete) costing $3,000 to date
Closing WIP	1,500 units (40% complete)
Transferred to next process	7,000 units

How many units were started and completed during the period?

A	5,000 units	C	8,400 units
B	7,000 units	D	9,000 units

ANSWER

The correct answer is A.

As we are dealing with the FIFO method, Opening WIP must be completed first.

Total output	7,000 units
Less Opening WIP (completed first)	2,000 units
Units started and completed during the period	5,000 units

QUESTION

Closing WIP – FIFO

The following information relates to process 3 of a three-stage production process for the month of January 20X4.

Opening inventory

300 units complete as to:

		$
materials from process 2	100%	4,400
added materials	90%	1,150
labour	80%	540
production overhead	80%	810
		6,900

In January 20X4, a further 1,800 units were transferred from process 2 at a valuation of $27,000. Added materials amounted to $6,600 and direct labour to $3,270. Production overhead is absorbed at the rate of 150% of direct labour cost. Closing inventory at 31 January 20X4 amounted to 450 units, complete as to:

process 2 materials	100%
added materials	60%
labour and overhead	50%

Required

Prepare the process 3 account for January 20X4 using FIFO valuation principles.

ANSWER

Step 1 **Statement of equivalent units**

	Total units	Process 2 materials		Added materials		Conversion costs
Opening inventory	300	0	(10%)	30	(20%)	60
Fully worked units *	1,350	1,350		1,350		1,350
Output to finished goods	1,650	1,350		1,380		1,410
Closing inventory	450	450	(60%)	270	(50%)	225
	2,100	1,800		1,650		1,635

* Transfers from process 2, minus closing inventory.

Step 2 **Statement of costs per equivalent unit**

	Total cost $	Equivalent units	Cost per equivalent unit $
Process 2 materials	27,000	1,800	15.00
Added materials	6,600	1,650	4.00
Direct labour	3,270	1,635	2.00
Production overhead (150% of $3,270)	4,905	1,635	3.00
			24.00

Step 3 **Statement of evaluation**

	Process 2 materials $		Additional materials $		Labour $		Overhead $		Total $
Opening inventory cost b/f	4,400		1,150		540		810		6,900
Added in Jan 20X4	–	(30x$4)	120	(60x$2)	120	(60x$3)	180		420
	4,400		1,270		660		990		7,320
Fully worked units	20,250		5,400		2,700		4,050		32,400
Output to finished Goods	24,650		6,670		3,360		5,040		39,720
Closing inventory (450x$15)	6,750	(270x$4)	1,080	(225x$2)	450	(225x$3)	675		8,955
	31,400		7,750		3,810		5,715		48,675

Step 4 **Complete accounts**

PROCESS 3 ACCOUNT

	Units	$		Units	$
Opening inventory b/f	300	6,900	Finished goods a/c	1,650	39,720
Process 2 a/c	1,800	27,000			
Stores a/c		6,600			
Wages a/c		3,270			
Production o'hd a/c		4,905	Closing inventory c/f	450	8,955
	2,100	48,675		2,100	48,675

QUESTION

Equivalent units and FIFO

Cheryl Co operates a FIFO process costing system. The following information is available for last month.

Opening work in progress	2,000 units valued at	$3,000
Input	60,000 units costing	$30,000
Conversion costs		$20,000
Units transferred to next process	52,000 units	
Closing work in progress	10,000 units	

Opening work in progress was 100% complete with regard to input materials and 70% complete as to conversion. Closing work in progress was complete with regard to input materials and 80% complete as to conversion.

What was the number of equivalent units with regard to conversion costs?

A   44,000   C   52,000
B   50,600   D   58,600

ANSWER

The correct answer is D.

		Units
Opening work in progress	30% of 2,000 units still to be completed	600
Closing work in progress	80% of 10,000 units completed	8,000
Units started and completed	(Opening WIP + input – closing WIP) – opening WIP	50,000
		58,600

7 Valuing opening work in progress: weighted average cost method

7.1 Introduction

An alternative to FIFO is the **weighted average cost method of inventory valuation** which calculates a weighted average cost of units produced from both opening inventory and units introduced in the current period.

By this method **no distinction is made between units of opening inventory and new units introduced** to the process during the accounting period. The cost of opening inventory is added to costs incurred during the period, and completed units of opening inventory are each given a value of one full equivalent unit of production.

7.2 Example: Weighted average cost method

Magpie produces an item which is manufactured in two consecutive processes. Information relating to process 2 during September 20X3 is as follows.

Opening inventory 800 units

Degree of completion:		$
process 1 materials	100%	4,700
added materials	40%	600
conversion costs	30%	1,000
		6,300

During September 20X3, 3,000 units were transferred from process 1 at a valuation of $18,100. Added materials cost $9,600 and conversion costs were $11,800.

Closing inventory at 30 September 20X3 amounted to 1,000 units which were 100% complete with respect to process 1 materials and 60% complete with respect to added materials. Conversion cost work was 40% complete.

Magpie uses a weighted average cost system for the valuation of output and closing inventory.

Required

Prepare the process 2 account for September 20X3.

Solution

Step 1   Opening inventory units count as a full equivalent unit of production when the weighted average cost system is applied. Closing inventory equivalent units are assessed in the usual way.

STATEMENT OF EQUIVALENT UNITS

	Total units		Process 1 material		Added material		Conversion costs
Opening inventory	800	(100%)	800		800		800
Fully worked units*	2,000	(100%)	2,000		2,000		2,000
Output to finished goods	2,800		2,800		2,800		2,800
Closing inventory	1,000	(100%)	1,000	(60%)	600	(40%)	400
	3,800		3,800		3,400		3,200

(*3,000 units from process 1 minus closing inventory of 1,000 units)

Step 2   The cost of opening inventory is added to costs incurred in September 20X3, and a cost per equivalent unit is then calculated.

STATEMENT OF COSTS PER EQUIVALENT UNIT

	Process 1 material $	Added materials $	Conversion costs $
Opening inventory	4,700	600	1,000
Added in September 20X3	18,100	9,600	11,800
Total cost	22,800	10,200	12,800
Equivalent units	3,800 units	3,400 units	3,200 units
Cost per equivalent unit	$6	$3	$4

Step 3 STATEMENT OF EVALUATION

	Process 1 material $	Added materials $	Conversion costs $	Total cost $
Output to finished goods				
(2,800 units)	16,800	8,400	11,200	36,400
Closing inventory	6,000	1,800	1,600	9,400
				45,800

Step 4 PROCESS 2 ACCOUNT

	Units	$		Units	$
Opening inventory b/f	800	6,300	Finished goods a/c	2,800	36,400
Process 1 a/c	3,000	18,100			
Added materials		9,600			
Conversion costs		11,800	Closing inventory c/f	1,000	9,400
	3,800	45,800		3,800	45,800

7.3 Which method should be used?

FIFO inventory valuation is more common than the weighted average method, and should be used unless an indication is given to the contrary. You may find that you are presented with limited information about the opening inventory, which forces you to use either the FIFO or the weighted average method. The rules are as follows.

(a)   If you are told the degree of completion of each element in opening inventory, but not the value of each cost element, then you must use the **FIFO method**.

(b)   If you are not given the degree of completion of each cost element in opening inventory, but you are given the value of each cost element, then you must use the **weighted average method.**

QUESTION   Equivalent units

During August, a factory commenced work on 20,000 units. At the start of the month there were no partly finished units but at the end of the month there were 2,000 units which were only 40% complete. Costs in the month were $3,722,400.

(a)   How many equivalent units of closing WIP were there in the month?

A	20,000	C	18,000
B	2,000	D	800

(b)   What is the total value of fully completed output which would show in the process account?

A	$3,960,000	C	$3,722,400
B	$3,564,000	D	$3,350,160

ANSWER

(a)   D   Equivalent units of WIP = 40% × 2,000 = 800

(b)   B

Total finished output	18,000	units

Total equivalent units =	
18,000 100%	18,000
2,000 × 40%	800
	18,800

Cost per equivalent unit = 3,722,400/18,800 =	$198

∴ Value of fully completed output:

18,000 × 198 =	$3,564,000

CHAPTER ROUNDUP

↳ **Process costing** is a costing method used where it is not possible to identify separate units of production or jobs, usually because of the continuous nature of the production processes involved.

↳ Process costing is centred around **four key steps**. The exact work done at each step will depend on whether there are normal losses, scrap, opening and closing work in progress.

    Step 1.   Determine output and losses
    Step 2.   Calculate cost per unit of output, losses and WIP
    Step 3.   Calculate total cost of output, losses and WIP
    Step 4.   Complete accounts

↳ **Losses** may occur in process. If a certain level of loss is expected, this is known as **normal loss**. If losses are greater than expected, the extra loss is **abnormal loss**. If losses are less than expected, the difference is known as **abnormal gain**.

↳ The **scrap value** of normal loss is usually deducted from the cost of materials.

↳ The **scrap value** of abnormal loss (or abnormal gain) is usually set off against its cost, in an abnormal loss (abnormal gain) account

↳ Abnormal losses and gains never affect the cost of good units of production. The scrap value of abnormal loss is **not** credited to the process account, and abnormal loss and gain units carry the same **full cost** as a good unit of production.

↳ When units are partly completed at the end of a period (and hence there is closing work in progress), it is necessary to calculate the **equivalent units of production** in order to determine the cost of a completed unit.

↳ Account can be taken of opening work in progress using either the **FIFO** method or the **weighted average cost method**.

QUICK QUIZ

1   Define process costing.

2   Process costing is centred around four key steps.

    Step 1.   ....

    Step 2.   ....

    Step 3.   ....

    Step 4.   ....

3   Abnormal gains result when actual loss is less than normal or expected loss.

    True   ☐

    False   ☐

4

    Normal loss (no scrap value)   Same value as good output (positive cost)

    Abnormal loss   **?**   No value

    Abnormal gain   Same value as good output (negative cost)

5   How is revenue from scrap treated?

    A   As an addition to sales revenue   C   As a bonus to employees
    B   As a reduction in costs of processing   D   Any of the above

BPP
LEARNING MEDIA

6 What is an equivalent unit?

7 When there is closing WIP at the end of a process, what is the first step in the four-step approach to process costing questions and why must it be done?

8 What is the weighted average cost method of inventory valuation?

9 Unless given an indication to the contrary, the weighted average cost method of inventory valuation should be used to value opening WIP.

True ☐

False ☐

1 **Process costing** is a costing method used where it is not possible to identify separate units of production, or jobs, usually because of the continuous nature of the production processes involved.

2
Step 1.	Determine output and losses
Step 2.	Calculate cost per unit of output, losses and WIP
Step 3.	Calculate total cost of output, losses and WIP
Step 4.	Complete accounts

3 True

4

Normal loss (no scrap value) → Same value as good output (positive cost)

Abnormal loss → No value

Abnormal gain → Same value as good output (negative cost)

5 B

6 An **equivalent unit** is a notional whole unit which represents incomplete work, and which is used to apportion costs between work in process and completed output.

7 **Step 1.** It is necessary to calculate the equivalent units of production (by drawing up a statement of equivalent units). Equivalent units of production are notional whole units which represent incomplete work and which are used to apportion costs between work in progress and completed output.

8 A method where no distinction is made between units of opening inventory and new units introduced to the process during the current period.

9 False. FIFO inventory valuation is more common than the weighted average method and should be used unless an indication is given to the contrary.

Now try ...

Attempt the questions below from the **Exam Question Bank**

Number

Q50 – Q54

CHAPTER

12

You should now be aware of the most simple and the more complex areas of process costing. In this chapter we are going to turn our attention to the methods of accounting for **joint products** and **by-products** which arise as a result of a **continuous process**.

Process costing, joint products and by-products

Study Guide	Intellectual level
B **Cost accounting techniques**	
3 **Cost accounting methods**	
(b)(x) Distinguish between by-products and joint products	K
(b)(xi) Value by-products and joint products at the point of separation	S
(b)(xii) Prepare process accounts in situations where by-products and/or joint products occur	S

EXAM FOCUS POINT

Make sure you understand all the basics here.

1 Joint products and by-products

1.1 Introduction

Joint products are two or more products separated in a process, each of which has a **significant value** compared to the other. A **by-product** is an incidental product from a process which has an **insignificant value** compared to the main product.

KEY TERM

Joint products are two or more products which are output from the same processing operation, but which are indistinguishable from each other up to their point of separation.

A by-product is a supplementary or secondary product (arising as the result of a process) whose value is small relative to that of the principal product.

(a) Joint products have a **substantial sales value**. Often they require further processing before they are ready for sale. Joint products arise, for example, in the oil refining industry where diesel fuel, petrol, paraffin and lubricants are all produced from the same process.

(b) The distinguishing feature of a by-product is its **relatively low sales value** in comparison to the main product. In the timber industry, for example, by-products include sawdust, small offcuts and bark.

What exactly separates a joint product from a by-product?

(a) A **joint product** is regarded as an important saleable item, and so it should be **separately costed**. The profitability of each joint product should be assessed in the cost accounts.

(b) A **by-product** is not important as a saleable item, and whatever revenue it earns is a 'bonus' for the organisation. Because of their relative insignificance, by-products are **not separately costed**.

EXAM FOCUS POINT

The study guide states that you must be able to 'distinguish between by-products and joint products'.

1.2 Problems in accounting for joint products

The point at which **joint products** and **by-products** become separately identifiable is known as the **split-off point** or **separation point**. Costs incurred up to this point are called **common costs** or **joint costs**.

Costs incurred prior to this point of separation are **common** or **joint costs**, and these need to be allocated (apportioned) in some manner to each of the joint products. In the following sketched example, there are two different split-off points.

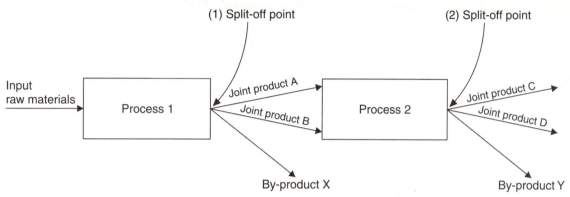

Problems in accounting for joint products are basically of two different sorts.

(a)   How common costs should be apportioned between products, in order to put a value to closing inventories and to the cost of sale (and profit) for each product.

(b)   Whether it is more profitable to sell a joint product at one stage of processing, or to process the product further and sell it at a later stage.

2 Dealing with common costs

2.1 Introduction

The main methods of apportioning joint costs, each of which can produce significantly different results are as follows.

- Physical measurement
- Relative sales value apportionment method; sales value at split-off point

The problem of costing for joint products concerns **common costs**, that is those common processing costs shared between the units of eventual output up to their 'split-off point'. Some method needs to be devised for sharing the common costs between the individual joint products for the following reasons.

(a)   To put a value to closing inventories of each joint product.
(b)   To record the costs and therefore the profit from each joint product.
(c)   Perhaps to assist in pricing decisions.

Here are some examples of the common costs problem.

(a)   How to spread the common costs of oil refining between the joint products made (petrol, naphtha, kerosene and so on).

(b)   How to spread the common costs of running the telephone network between telephone calls in peak and cheap rate times, or between local and long distance calls.

Various methods that might be used to establish a basis for apportioning or allocating common costs to each product are as follows.

- Physical measurement
- Relative sales value apportionment method; sales value at split-off point

2.2 Dealing with common costs: physical measurement

With physical measurement, **the common cost is apportioned to the joint products on the basis of the proportion that the output of each product bears by weight or volume to the total output.** An example of this would be the case where two products, product 1 and product 2, incur common costs to the point of separation of $3,000 and the output of each product is 600 tons and 1,200 tons respectively.

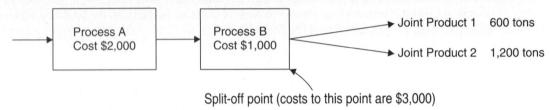

Split-off point (costs to this point are $3,000)

Product 1 sells for $4 per ton and product 2 for $2 per ton.

The division of the common costs ($3,000) between product 1 and product 2 could be based on the tonnage of output.

	Product 1		Product 2	Total
Output	600 tons	+	1,200 tons	1,800 tons
Proportion of common cost	$\dfrac{600}{1,800}$	+	$\dfrac{1,200}{1,800}$	
	$		$	$
Apportioned cost	1,000		2,000	3,000
Sales	2,400		2,400	4,800
Profit	1,400		400	1,800
Profit/sales ratio	58.3%		16.7%	37.5%

Physical measurement has the following limitations.

(a) Where the products separate during the processes into different states, for example where one product is a gas and another is a liquid, this method is unsuitable.

(b) This method does not take into account the relative income-earning potentials of the individual products, with the result that one product might appear very profitable and another appear to be incurring losses.

2.3 Dealing with common costs: sales value at split-off point

> The **relative sales value method** is the most widely used method of apportioning joint costs because (ignoring the effect of further processing costs) it assumes that all products achieve the same profit margin.

With relative sales value apportionment of common costs, **the cost is allocated according to the product's ability to produce income**. This method is most widely used because the assumption that some profit margin should be attained for all products under normal marketing conditions is satisfied. The common cost is apportioned to each product in the proportion that the sales (market) value of that product bears to the sales value of the total output from the particular processes concerned. Using the previous example where the sales price per unit is $4 for product 1 and $2 for product 2.

(a) Common costs of processes to split-off point $3,000
(b) Sales value of product 1 at $4 per ton $2,400
(c) Sales value of product 2 at $2 per ton $2,400

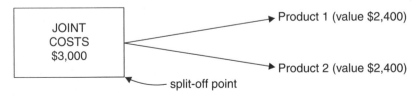

	Product 1	Product 2	Total
Sales	$2,400	$2,400	$4,800
Proportion of common cost apportioned	$\left(\dfrac{2,400}{4,800}\right)$	$\left(\dfrac{2,400}{4,800}\right)$	
	$	$	$
Apportioned cost	1,500	1,500	3,000
Sales	2,400	2,400	4,800
Profit	900	900	1,800
Profit/sales ratio	37.5%	37.5%	37.5%

A comparison of the gross profit margin resulting from the application of the above methods for allocating common costs will illustrate the greater acceptability of the relative sales value apportionment method. Physical measurement gives a higher profit margin to product 1, not necessarily because product 1 is highly profitable, but because it has been given a smaller share of common costs.

QUESTION

Joint products

In process costing, a joint product is

A   A product which is produced simultaneously with other products but which is of lesser value than at least one of the other products

B   A product which is produced simultaneously with other products and is of similar value to at least one of the other products

C   A product which is produced simultaneously with other products but which is of greater value than any of the other products

D   A product produced jointly with another organisation

ANSWER

The correct answer is B, a product which is of similar value to at least one of the other products.

QUESTION

Sales value method

Two products (W and X) are created from a joint process. Both products can be sold immediately after split-off. There are no opening inventories or work in progress. The following information is available for last period.

Total joint production costs $776,160

Product	Production units	Sales units	Selling price per unit
W	12,000	10,000	$10
X	10,000	8,000	$12

Using the sales value method of apportioning joint production costs, what was the value of the closing inventory of product X for last period?

A $68,992
B $70,560
C $76,032
D $77,616

ANSWER

The correct answer is D.

Sales value of production:

Product W	(12,000 × $10)	$120,000
Product X	(10,000 × $12)	$120,000

Therefore joint costs are apportioned in the ratio 1:1.

Amount apportioned to product X (776,160/2) $388,080

The $388,080 is the total cost of producing 10,000 units of X. This gives a cost per unit of $388,080/10,000 = $38.808 per unit.

10,000 units were made but only 8,000 units were sold. This means that we have 10,000 – 8,000 = 2,000 units left in inventory.

2,000 x $38.808 = $77,616

Alternatively:

20% of X's production is in closing inventory = 20% of $388,080 = $77,616

EXAM FOCUS POINT

Make sure you split the joint costs according to **sales value of production** rather than individual selling prices or sales value of sales.

3 Joint products in process accounts

This example illustrates how joint products are incorporated into process accounts.

3.1 Example: joint products and process accounts

Three joint products are manufactured in a common process, which consists of two consecutive stages. Output from process 1 is transferred to process 2, and output from process 2 consists of the three joint products, Hans, Nils and Bumpsydaisies. All joint products are sold as soon as they are produced.

Data for period 2 of 20X6 are as follows.

	Process 1	*Process 2*
Opening and closing inventory	None	None
Direct material		
(30,000 units at $2 per unit)	$60,000	–
Conversion costs	$76,500	$226,200
Normal loss	10% of input	10% of input
Scrap value of normal loss	$0.50 per unit	$2 per unit
Output	26,000 units	10,000 units of Han
		7,000 units of Nil
		6,000 units of Bumpsydaisy

Selling prices are $18 per unit of Han, $20 per unit of Nil and $30 per unit of Bumpsydaisy.

Required

(a) Prepare the Process 1 account.
(b) Prepare the Process 2 account using the sales value method of apportionment.
(c) Prepare a profit statement for the joint products.

Solution

(a) **Process 1 equivalent units**

	Total units	Equivalent units
Output to process 2	26,000	26,000
Normal loss	3,000	0
Abnormal loss (balance)	1,000	1,000
	30,000	27,000

Costs of process 1

	$
Direct materials	60,000
Conversion costs	76,500
	136,500
Less scrap value of normal loss (3,000 × $0.50)	1,500
	135,000

$$\text{Cost per equivalent unit} = \frac{\$135,000}{27,000} = \$5$$

PROCESS 1 ACCOUNT

	$		$
Direct materials	60,000	Output to process 2 (26,000 × $5)	130,000
Conversion costs	76,500	Normal loss (scrap value)	1,500
		Abnormal loss a/c (1,000 × $5)	5,000
	136,500		136,500

(b) **Process 2 equivalent units**

	Total units	Equivalent units
Units of Hans produced	10,000	10,000
Units of Nils produced	7,000	7,000
Units of Bumpsydaisies produced	6,000	6,000
Normal loss (10% of 26,000)	2,600	0
Abnormal loss (balance)	400	400
	26,000	23,400

Costs of process 2

	$
Material costs – from process 1	130,000
Conversion costs	226,200
	356,200
Less scrap value of normal loss (2,600 × $2)	5,200
	351,000

$$\text{Cost per equivalent unit} \; \frac{\$351,000}{23,400} = \$15$$

Cost of good output (10,000 + 7,000 + 6,000) = 23,000 units × $15 = $345,000

The sales value of joint products, and the apportionment of the output costs of $345,000, is as follows.

	Sales value $	%	Costs (process 2) $
Hans (10,000 × $18)	180,000	36	124,200
Nils (7,000 × $20)	140,000	28	96,600
Bumpsydaisy (6,000 × $30)	180,000	36	124,200
	500,000	100	345,000

PROCESS 2 ACCOUNT

	$		$
Process 1 materials	130,000	Finished goods accounts	
Conversion costs	226,200	– Hans	124,200
		– Nils	96,600
		– Bumpsydaisies	124,200
		Normal loss (scrap value)	5,200
		Abnormal loss a/c	6,000
	356,200		356,200

(c) PROFIT STATEMENT

	Hans	Nils	Bumpsydaisies
	$'000	$'000	$'000
Sales	180.0	140.0	180.0
Costs	124.2	96.6	124.2
Profit	55.8	43.4	55.8
Profit/ sales ratio	31%	31%	31%

QUESTION
Unit basis of apportionment

Prepare the Process 2 account and a profit statement for the joint products in the above example using the units basis of apportionment.

ANSWER

PROCESS 2 ACCOUNT

	$		$
Process 1 materials	130,000	Finished goods accounts	
Conversion costs	226,200	– Hans (10,000 × $15)	150,000
		– Nils (7,000 × $15)	105,000
		– Bumpsydaisies (6,000 × $15)	90,000
		Normal loss (scrap value)	5,200
		Abnormal loss a/c	6,000
	356,200		356,200

PROFIT STATEMENT

	Hans	Nils	Bumpsydaisies
	$'000	$'000	$'000
Sales	180	140	180
Costs	150	105	90
Profit	30	35	90
Profit/ sales ratio	16.7%	25%	50%

QUESTION
Joint costs and process costing

Polly Co operates a process costing system, the final output from which is three different products: Bolly, Dolly and Folly. Details of the three products for March are as follows.

	Bolly	Dolly	Folly
Selling price per unit	$25	$18	$32
Output for March	6,000 units	10,000 units	4,000 units

22,000 units of material were input to the process, costing $242,000. Conversion costs were $121,000. No losses were expected and there were no opening or closing inventories.

Using the units basis of apportioning joint costs, what was the profit or loss on sales of Dolly for March?

A	$(1,500)	C	$50,306
B	$30,000	D	$15,000

ANSWER

The correct answer is D.

Total output	20,000	units (6,000 + 10,000 + 4,000)
Total input	22,000	units
Abnormal loss	2,000	units

Total cost = $363,000

$$\text{Cost per unit} = \frac{\$363,000}{22,000} = \$16.50$$

Cost of 'good' output = 20,000 units × $16.50 = $330,000

$$\text{Amount apportioned to Dolly} = \frac{\text{Units of Dolly}}{\text{Total 'good' units}} \times \$330,000$$

$$= (10,000/20,000) \times \$330,000$$

$$= \$165,000$$

Profit for Dolly = Sales Revenue – apportioned costs

= (10,000 × $18) - $165,000
= $15,000

4 Accounting for by-products

4.1 Introduction

The most common method of accounting for by-products is to deduct the **net realisable value** of the by-product from the cost of the main products.

A by-product has some commercial value and any income generated from it may be treated as follows.

(a)   Income (minus any post-separation further processing or selling costs) from the sale of the by-product may be **added to sales of the main product**, thereby increasing sales turnover for the period.

(b)   The sales of the by-product may be **treated as a separate, incidental source of income** against which are set only post-separation costs (if any) of the by-product. The revenue would be recorded in the income statement as 'other income'.

(c)   The sales income of the by-product may be **deducted from the cost of production** or cost of sales of the main product.

(d)   The **net realisable value of the by-product may be deducted from the cost of production of the main product**. The net realisable value is the final saleable value of the by-product minus any post-separation costs. Any closing inventory valuation of the main product or joint products would therefore be reduced.

The choice of method (a), (b), (c) or (d) will be influenced by the circumstances of production and ease of calculation, as much as by conceptual correctness. The method you are most likely to come across in examinations is method (d). An example will help to clarify the distinction between the different methods.

4.2 Example: Methods of accounting for by-products

During November 20X3, Splatter Co recorded the following results.

Opening inventory	main product P, nil	Cost of production	$120,000
	by-product Z, nil		

Sales of the main product amounted to 90% of output during the period, and 10% of production was held as closing inventory at 30 November.

Sales revenue from the main product during November 20X2 was $150,000.

A by-product Z is produced, and output had a net sales value of $1,000. Of this output, $700 was sold during the month, and $300 was still in inventory at 30 November.

Required

Calculate the profit for November using the four methods of accounting for by-products.

Solution

The four methods of accounting for by-products are shown below.

(a) **Income from by-product added to sales of the main product**

	$	$
Sales of main product ($150,000 + $700)		150,700
Opening inventory	0	
Cost of production	120,000	
	120,000	
Less closing inventory (10%)	12,000	
Cost of sales		108,000
Profit, main product		42,700

The closing inventory of the by-product has no recorded value in the cost accounts.

(b) **By-product income treated as a separate source of income**

	$	$
Sales, main product		150,000
Opening inventory	0	
Cost of production	120,000	
	120,000	
Closing inventory (10%)	12,000	
Cost of sales, main product		108,000
Profit, main product		42,000
Other income		700
Total profit		42,700

The closing inventory of the by-product again has no value in the cost accounts.

(c) **Sales income of the by-product deducted from the cost of production in the period**

	$	$
Sales, main product		150,000
Opening inventory	0	
Cost of production (120,000 − 700)	119,300	
	119,300	
Less closing inventory (10%)	11,930	
Cost of sales		107,370
Profit, main product		42,630

Although the profit is different from the figure in (a) and (b), the by-product closing inventory again has no value.

(d) **Net realisable value of the by-product deducted from the cost of production in the period**

	$	$
Sales, main product		150,000
Opening inventory	0	
Cost of production (120,000 − 1,000)	119,000	
	119,000	
Less closing inventory (10%)	11,900	
Cost of sales		107,100
Profit, main product		42,900

As with the other three methods, closing inventory of the by-product has no value in the books of accounting, but the value of the closing inventory ($300) has been used to reduce the cost of production, and in this respect it has been allowed for in deriving the cost of sales and the profit for the period.

QUESTION

Profits

Randolph manufactures two joint products, J and K, in a common process. A by-product X is also produced. Data for the month of December 20X2 were as follows.

Opening inventories   nil
Costs of processing   direct materials $25,500   direct labour $10,000

Production overheads are absorbed at the rate of 300% of direct labour costs.

		Production Units	Sales Units
Output and sales consisted of:	product J	8,000	7,000
	product K	8,000	6,000
	by-product X	1,000	1,000

The sales value per unit of J, K and X is $4, $6 and $0.50 respectively. The saleable value of the by-product is deducted from process costs before apportioning costs to each joint product. Costs of the common processing are apportioned between product J and product K on the basis of sales value of production.

The individual profits for December 20X2 are:

	Product J $	Product K $		Product J $	Product K $
A	5,250	6,750	C	22,750	29,250
B	6,750	5,250	D	29,250	22,750

ANSWER

The correct answer is A.
The sales value of production was $80,000.

	$	
Product J (8,000 × $4)	32,000	(40%)
Product K (8,000 × $6)	48,000	(60%)
	80,000	

The costs of production were as follows.

	$
Direct materials	25,500
Direct labour	10,000
Overhead (300% of $10,000)	30,000
	65,500
Less sales value of by-product (1,000 × 50c)	500
Net production costs	65,000

The profit statement would appear as follows (nil opening inventories).

		Product J $		Product K $	Total $
Production costs	(40%)	26,000	(60%)	39,000	65,000
Less closing inventory (see working below)	(1,000 units)	3,250	(2,000 units)	9,750	13,000
Cost of sales		22,750		29,250	52,000
Sales	(7,000 units)	28,000	(6,000 units)	36,000	64,000
Profit		5,250		6,750	12,000

Working
Closing inventory = (Production units – sales units) x (production costs/production units)
For J, closing inventory = (8,000 – 7,000) x ($26,000/8,000) = $3,250
For K, closing inventory = (8,000 – 6,000) x ($39,000/8,000) = $9,750

CHAPTER ROUNDUP

↳ **Joint products** are two or more products separated in a process, each of which has a **significant value** compared to the other. A **by-product** is an incidental product from a process which has an **insignificant value** compared to the main product.

↳ The point at which joint and by-products become separately identifiable is known as the **split-off point** or **separation point**. Costs incurred up to this point are called **common costs** or **joint costs**.

↳ The main methods of apportioning joint costs, each of which can produce significantly different results are as follows: physical measurement; and relative sales value apportionment method; sales value at split-off point.

↳ The **relative sales value method** is the most widely used method of apportioning joint costs because (ignoring the effect of further processing costs) it assumes that all products achieve the same profit margin.

↳ The most common method of accounting for by-products is to deduct the **net realisable value** of the by-product from the cost of the main products.

QUICK QUIZ

1   What is the difference between a joint product and a by-product?

2   What is meant by the term 'split-off' point?

3   Name two methods of apportioning common costs to joint products.

4   Describe the four methods of accounting for by-products.

ANSWERS TO QUICK QUIZ

1   A joint product is regarded as an important saleable item whereas a by-product is not.

2   The **split-off point** (or the **separation point**) is the point at which joint products become separately identifiable in a processing operation.

3   Physical measurement and sales value at split-off point.

4   See paragraph 4.1.

Now try ...

Attempt the questions below from the **Exam Question Bank**

Number

Q55 – Q57

13

This chapter looks briefly at some more costing methods. Activity based costing (ABC) is considered to be a modern alternative to absorption costing. You need to concentrate on the ideas behind ABC, target costing, life cycle costing and total quality management as the study guide says that calculations will not be required in your exam.

Alternative costing principles

Study Guide	Intellectual level
B **Cost accounting techniques**	
4 **Alternative cost accounting**	
(a) Explain activity based costing (ABC), target costing, life cycle costing and total quality management (TQM) as alternative cost management techniques	K
(b) Differentiate ABC, target costing and life cycle costing from the traditional costing techniques (Calculations are not required.)	K

1   The reasons for the development of activity based costing

> An alternative to the traditional methods of absorption costing is **activity based costing (ABC).** ABC involves the identification of the factors (cost drivers) which cause the costs of an organisation's major activities. Support overheads are charged to products on the basis of their usage of an activity.

The **absorption costing approach** that we have learned about so far in this chapter was **developed in a time** when most organisations produced only a narrow range of products and **when overhead costs were only a very small fraction of total costs**, direct labour and direct material costs accounting for the largest proportion of the costs. The value of over- or under-absorbed overhead was therefore not too significant.

Nowadays, however, the situation is different. With the advent of advanced manufacturing technology (AMT), **overheads are likely to be far more important.**

(a)   Direct labour may account for as little as 5% of a product's cost.

(b)   The accessibility of information technology now allows for more sophisticated overhead allocation methods than in the past.

In today's business environment it is difficult to justify the use of direct labour or direct material as the basis for allocating overheads. It is against this background that **activity based costing (ABC) has emerged**.

The traditional methods accurately allocate to products the costs of those resources that are used in proportion to the number of units produced of a particular product. Such resources include machine-related costs such as power and lubricants. Many resources are used in non-volume related support activities (which have increased due to AMT), such as setting-up, production scheduling, first item inspection and data processing, however. These support activities assist the efficient manufacture of a wide range of products and are not, in general, affected by changes in production volume. They tend to vary in the long term according to the range and complexity of the products manufactured rather than the volume of output.

The wider the range and the more complex the products, the more support services will be required. Consider, for example, factory X which produces 10,000 units of one product, the Alpha, and factory Y which produces 1,000 units each of ten slightly different versions of the Alpha. Support activity costs in the factory Y are likely to be a lot higher than in factory X but the factories produce an identical number of units. Take setting-up. Factory X will only need to set-up once whereas Factory Y will have to set-up the production run at least ten times for the ten different products. Factory Y will therefore incur more set-up costs.

Traditional costing systems, which assume that all products consume all resources **in proportion to their production volumes**, tend to allocate too great a proportion of overheads to high volume products (which cause relatively little diversity and hence use fewer support services) and too small a proportion of overheads to low volume products (which cause greater diversity and therefore use more support services). ABC attempts to overcome this problem.

The **major ideas behind activity based costing** are as follows.

(a) **Activities cause costs**. Activities include ordering, materials handling, machining, assembly, production scheduling and despatching.

(b) **Producing products creates demand** for the activities.

(c) **Costs are assigned to a product on the basis of the product's consumption of the activities.**

Activity based costing (ABC) involves the identification of the factors which cause the costs of an organisation's major activities. Support overheads are charged to products on the basis of their usage of the factor causing the overheads.

2 Calculating product costs using ABC

An ABC system operates as follows.

| **Step 1** | **Identify** an organisation's **major activities**. |

| **Step 2** | **Identify** the factors which determine the size of the costs of an activity/cause the costs of an activity. These are known as **cost drivers**. |

A **cost driver** is the factor which causes the costs of an activity.

Look at the following examples.

Activity	Cost driver
Ordering	Number of orders
Materials handling	Number of production runs
Production scheduling	Number of production runs
Despatching	Number of despatches

For those costs that vary with production levels in the short term, ABC uses volume-related cost drivers such as labour or machine hours. The cost of oil used as a lubricant on machines would therefore be added to products on the basis of the number of machine hours, since oil would have to be used for each hour the machine ran.

| **Step 3** | **Collect the costs of each activity into** what are known as **cost pools** (equivalent to cost centres under more traditional costing methods). |

| **Step 4** | **Charge support overheads to products on the basis of their usage of the activity. A product's usage of an activity is measured by the number of the activity's cost driver it generates.**

Suppose, for example, that the cost pool for the ordering activity totalled $100,000 and that there were 10,000 orders (the cost driver). Each product would therefore be charged with $10 for each order it required. A batch requiring five orders would therefore be charged with $50. |

Before we move on, try an example for yourself so that you are clear how cost drivers are used to charge overheads to activities. This example only shows activity based costing so you can see how cost drivers are used to allocate costs to products.

2.1 Example: Fred Co

Fred make and sell a number of products. Products A and B are products for which market prices are available at which S can obtain a share of the market as detailed below. Estimated data for the forthcoming period is as follows.

(a) **Product data**

	Product A	Product B	Product C
Production/sales (units)	5,000	10,000	40,000
	$'000	$'000	$'000
Total direct material cost	80	300	2,020
Total direct labour cost	40	100	660

(b) Variable overhead cost is $1,500,000 of which 40% is related to the acquisition, storage and use of direct materials and 60% is related to the control and use of direct labour.

(c) It is current practice in S plc to absorb variable overhead cost into product units using overall company wide percentages on direct material cost and direct labour cost as the absorption bases.

Required

Prepare estimated unit product costs for Product A and Product B where variable overhead is charged to product units using an activity based costing approach where **cost drivers** have been estimated for material and labour related overhead costs as follows.

	Product A	Product B	Product C
Direct material related overheads – **cost driver is material bulk**. The bulk proportions **per unit** are:	4	1	1.5
Direct labour related overheads – **cost driver is number of labour operations** (not directly time related).			
Labour operations per product **unit** are:	6	1	2.0

2.2 Solution

ABC approach

	A	B
	$	$
Direct material cost per unit ($80,000/5,000, $300,000/10,000)	16.00	30.00
Direct labour cost per unit ($40,000/5,000, $100,000/10,000)	8.00	10.00
Variable overhead cost per unit (see below)	71.68	14.17
	95.68	54.17

Workings

(1) **Material-related overheads**

Remember the cost drivers stated in the question. Multiply these by the production/sales for each product. This gives you total cost driver for each product.

		Bulk '000
Number of cost drivers		
Product A	4 × 5,000	20
Product B	1 × 10,000	10
Product C	1.5 × 40,000	60
		90

Then divide overhead by the cost driver

∴ **Overhead per cost driver** = ($1,500,000 × 40%)/90,000
= $600,000 ÷ 90,000
= $6.67

(2)   **Labour-related overheads**

Remember the cost driver is number of labour operations per **unit** so you need to multiply this by production sales to give the total cost drivers for each product.

Number of cost drivers		Labour operations '000
Product A	6 × 5,000	30
Product B	1 × 10,000	10
Product C	2 × 40,000	80
		120

Then divide overhead by the cost driver

∴ **Overhead per cost driver** = ($1,500,000 × 60%)/120,000
$$= \$900,000 \div 120,000$$
$$= \$7.50$$

Variable overhead per unit

	A $	B $
Material related		
$6.67 (per above W1) × 4 or 1	26.68	6.67
Labour related		
$7.50 (per above W2) × 6 or 1	45.00	7.50
	71.68	14.17

Now try another example which compares and contrasts absorption costing and ABC activity based costing

2.3 Example: ABC

Suppose that Cooplan manufactures four products, W, X, Y and Z. Output and cost data for the period just ended are as follows.

	Output Units	Number of production runs in the period	Material cost per unit $	Direct labour hours per unit	Machine hours per unit
W	10	2	20	1	1
X	10	2	80	3	3
Y	100	5	20	1	1
Z	100	5	80	3	3
		14			

Direct labour cost per hour is $5. Overhead costs are as follows.

	$
Short-run variable costs	3,080
Set-up costs	10,920
Production and scheduling costs	9,100
Materials handling costs	7,700
	30,800

Required

Calculate product costs using the following approaches.

(a)   Absorption costing
(b)   ABC

2.4 Solution

Using a conventional absorption costing approach and an absorption rate for overheads based on either direct labour hours or machine hours, the product costs would be as follows.

	W	X	Y	Z	Total
	$	$	$	$	$
Direct material	200	800	2,000	8,000	11,000
Direct labour	50	150	500	1,500	2,200
Overheads *	700	2,100	7,000	21,000	30,800
	950	3,050	9,500	30,500	44,000
Units produced	10	10	100	100	
Cost per unit	$95	$305	$95	$305	

* $30,800 ÷ 440 hours = $70 per direct labour or machine hour

Using activity based costing and assuming that the number of production runs is the cost driver for set-up costs, production and scheduling costs and materials handling costs and that machine hours are the cost driver for short-run variable costs, unit costs would be as follows.

	W	X	Y	Z	Total
	$	$	$	$	$
Direct material	200	800	2,000	8,000	11,000
Direct labour	50	150	500	1,500	2,200
Short-run variable overheads (W1)	70	210	700	2,100	3,080
Set-up costs (W2)	1,560	1,560	3,900	3,900	10,920
Production and scheduling costs (W3)	1,300	1,300	3,250	3,250	9,100
Materials handling costs (W4)	1,100	1,100	2,750	2,750	7,700
	4,280	5,120	13,100	21,500	44,000
Units produced	10	10	100	100	
Cost per unit	$428	$512	$131	$215	

Workings

1	$3,080 ÷ 440 machine hours	=	$7 per machine hour
2	$10,920 ÷ 14 production runs	=	$780 per run
3	$9,100 ÷ 14 production runs	=	$650 per run
4	$7,700 ÷ 14 production runs	=	$550 per run

Summary

Product	Conventional costing Unit cost	ABC Unit cost	Difference
	$	$	$
W	95	428	+333
X	305	512	+207
Y	95	131	+36
Z	305	215	−90

The figures suggest that the traditional volume-based absorption costing system is flawed.

(a)   It under allocates overhead costs to low-volume products (here, W and X with ten units of output) and over allocates overheads to higher-volume products (here Z in particular).

(b)   It under allocates overhead costs to less complex products (here W and Y with just one hour of work needed per unit) and over allocates overheads to more complex products (here X and particularly Z).

EXAM FOCUS POINT

We have used numbers to explain how activity based costing works. The examiner has said, however, that you will not see calculation questions on this area of the syllabus in the exam.

3 ABC versus traditional absorption costing

3.1 Allocation of overheads

Traditional absorption costing allocates overheads to production departments (cost centres) whereas **ABC systems assign overheads to each major activity** (cost pools). With ABC systems, lots of activity-based cost pools are established whereas with traditional absorption costing, overheads tend to be pooled by departments. This can result in many reapportionments of service department costs to ensure that all overheads are allocated to production departments. **ABC** establishes separate cost pools for support activities such as despatching and materials handing. As the costs of these activities are assigned directly to products through cost driver rates, **reapportionment of service department costs is avoided**.

3.2 Absorption of overheads

The principal difference between the two systems is the way in which overheads are absorbed into products. Traditional absorption costing uses usually two absorption bases (labour hours and/or machine hours) to charge overheads to products whereas **ABC uses many cost drivers as absorption bases** (number of orders, number of dispatches and so on). **Absorption rates under ABC should therefore be more closely linked to the causes of overhead costs**.

3.3 Cost drivers and absorption rates

When using ABC, for costs that vary with production levels in the short term, the cost driver will be volume related (labour or machine hours). Overheads that vary with some other activity (and not volume of production) should be traced to products using transaction-based cost drivers such as production runs or number of orders received.

The principal idea of ABC is to focus attention on what causes costs to increase, the cost drivers. Just as there are no rules for what to use as the basis for absorbing costs in traditional absorption costing, there are also difficulties in choosing cost drivers.

(a)   Those **costs that do vary with production volume**, such as power costs, should be **traced to products using production volume-related cost drivers** as appropriate, such as direct labour hours or direct machine hours.

(b)   **Overheads which do not vary with output** but with some other activity should be **traced to products using transaction-based cost drivers**, such as number of production runs and number of orders received.

Focusing attention on what actually causes overheads and tracing overheads to products on the basis of the usage of the cost drivers ensures that a greater proportion of overheads are product related, whereas traditional costing systems allow overheads to be related to products in rather more arbitrary ways. It is this feature of ABC which produces, it is claimed, greater accuracy.

3.4 Further merits of activity based costing

Once the necessary information regarding cost drivers has been obtained, ABC is relatively simple to implement. Here are some other **advantages of ABC**.

(a)   Because of the financial reporting requirement to value inventories at full cost, management accounting has not given sufficient priority to the need to provide meaningful product costs and has simply used absorption costing to produce the full cost. **ABC**, on the other hand, focuses attention on the nature of cost behaviour and **attempts to provide meaningful product costs**.

(b)   ABC uses multiple cost drivers to allocate overhead costs to activities and then to products, and does not simply use a meaningless direct labour hour recovery rate or machine hour recovery rate, that assumes that overhead costs are related to volume of activity only. Only **ABC recognises that many overhead costs arise out of the diversity and complexity of operations**.

(c)   The **complexity of manufacturing has increased**, with wider product ranges, shorter product life cycles, a greater importance being attached to quality and more complex production processes. **ABC recognises this complexity with its multiple cost drivers**.

(d)   In a more competitive environment, companies must be able to assess product profitability realistically. **ABC facilitates a good understanding of what drives overhead costs**.

(e)   In modern manufacturing systems, overhead functions include a lot of non-factory-floor activities such as product design, quality control, production planning, sales order planning and customer service. **ABC is concerned with all overhead costs**, including the costs of these functions, and so it takes management accounting beyond its 'traditional' factory floor boundaries.

3.5 Criticisms of ABC

It has been suggested by critics that **activity based costing has some serious flaws**.

(a)   Some measure of (arbitrary) cost apportionment may still be required at the cost pooling stage for items like rent, rates and building depreciation. If an ABC system has many cost pools the amount of apportionment needed may be greater than ever.

(b)   The ability of a single cost driver to explain fully the cost behaviour of all items in its associated pool is questionable.

(c)   To have a usable cost driver, a cost must be caused by an activity that is measurable in quantitative terms and which can be related to production output. But not all costs can be treated in this way. For example, what drives the cost of the annual external audit?

(d)   ABC is sometimes introduced because it is fashionable, not because it will be used by management to provide meaningful product costs or extra information. If management is not going to use ABC information, a traditional absorption costing system may be simpler to operate.

 QUESTION   Using ABC

(a)   List the features of organisations that would find ABC particularly useful for product costing.

(b)   Briefly explain the reasons why ABC is particularly suitable in a modern business environment and describe any situations where it is not appropriate.

ANSWER

(a)   Here are our suggestions.

(i)   Production overheads are a high proportion of total production costs.
(ii)   The product range is wide and diverse.
(iii)   The amounts of overhead resources used by products varies.
(iv)   Volume is not the primary driver of overhead resource consumption.

(b)   **Reasons for suitability**

(i)   Most modern organisations tend to have a high level of overhead costs, especially relating to support services such as maintenance and data processing. ABC, by the use of carefully chosen cost drivers, traces these overheads to product lines in a more logical and less arbitrary manner than traditional absorption costing.

(ii)   The determination and use of cost drivers helps to measure and improve the efficiency and effectiveness of support departments.

(iii)   Many costs included in general overheads can actually be traced to specific product lines using ABC. This improves product costing and cost management because the costs are made the responsibility of the line manager.

(iv)   ABC forces the organisation to ask such searching questions as 'What causes the demand for the activity?', 'What does the department achieve?', 'Does it add value?' and so on.

(v)   ABC systems may encourage reductions in throughput time and inventory and improvements in quality.

Unsuitable situations

(i) A number of businesses have recently been split into several small autonomous sections. In this situation there may be no need for a sophisticated costing system such as ABC because staff should be aware of cost behaviour.

(ii) ABC can work against modern manufacturing methods such as just-in-time (JIT). JIT seeks to reduce set-up time so that very small batches can be made economically.

(iii) The aim of set-up time reduction is to allow more set-ups, not just to reduce set-up costs. The use of a cost driver based on the number of set-ups will therefore work against JIT principles as it will tend to encourage larger batches.

4 The importance of quality

The modern business environment is remarkably different from the business environment of a decade or so ago. One change has been the **switch in emphasis away from quantity towards quality**. Consumers and **customers** have become **more sophisticated and discerning** in their requirements. They are no longer satisfied with accepting the late delivery of the same old unreliable products from an organisation which does not appear to care for its customers. They want new products, superior on-time delivery performance and an immediate response to their requests. Many organisations are therefore turning to quality to help them to survive the competitive modern business environment. **By developing new products quickly and supplying them on time at a consistently high level of quality such organisations are likely to become the success stories of the new millennium.**

4.1 Costs of quality

When we talk about quality-related costs you should remember that a concern for **good quality saves money**; it is **poor quality that costs money.**

The **cost of quality** is the 'Difference between the actual cost of producing, selling and supporting, products or services and the equivalent costs if there were no failures during production or usage.'

The cost of quality can be analysed into:

Cost of conformance – 'Costs of achieving specified quality standards'

- **Cost of prevention** – 'Costs incurred prior to or during production in order to prevent substandard or defective products or services from being produced'

- **Cost of appraisal** – 'Costs incurred in order to ensure that outputs produced meet required quality standards'

(CIMA Official Terminology)

Cost of non-conformance is 'The cost of failure to deliver the required standard of quality.'

- **Cost of internal failure** – 'Costs arising from inadequate quality which are identified before the transfer of ownership from supplier to purchaser'

- **Cost of external failure** – 'Costs arising from inadequate quality discovered after the transfer of ownership from supplier to purchaser.'

(CIMA Official Terminology)

Quality-related cost	Example
Prevention costs	Quality engineering
	Design/development of quality control/inspection equipment
	Maintenance of quality control/inspection equipment
	Administration of quality control
	Training in quality control
Appraisal costs	Acceptance testing
	Inspection of goods inwards
	Inspection costs of in-house processing
	Performance testing
Internal failure costs	Failure analysis
	Re-inspection costs
	Losses from failure of purchased items
	Losses due to lower selling prices for sub-quality goods
	Costs of reviewing product specifications after failures
External failure costs	Administration of customer complaints section
	Costs of customer service section
	Product liability costs
	Cost of repairing products returned from customers
	Cost of replacing items due to sub-standard products/marketing errors

5 Total quality management

Total quality management (TQM) is the process of applying a zero defect philosophy to the management of all resources and relationships within an organisation as a means of developing and sustaining a culture of continuous improvement which focuses on meeting customer expectations.

Quality combines the following criteria.

(a) How well made a product is, or how well performed if it is a service.
(b) How well it serves its purpose.
(c) How it measures up against its rivals.

Implications of these criteria

(a) That quality is something that **requires care on the part of the provider**.
(b) That quality is largely **subjective** – it is in the eye of the beholder, the **customer**.

The process of the management of quality

(a) Establishing **standards of quality** for a product or service.

(b) Establishing **procedures or production methods** which ought to ensure that these required standards of quality are met in a suitably high proportion of cases.

(c) **Monitoring** actual quality.

(d) Taking **control action** when actual quality falls below standard.

Take the postal service as an example. The postal service might establish a standard that 90% of first class letters will be delivered on the day after they are posted, and 99% will be delivered within two days of posting.

(a) Procedures would have to be established for ensuring that these standards could be met (attending to such matters as frequency of collections, automated letter sorting, frequency of deliveries and number of staff employed).

(b) Actual performance could be monitored, perhaps by taking samples from time to time of letters that are posted and delivered.

(c) If the quality standard is not being achieved, the management of the postal service should take control action (employ more postmen or advertise the use of postcodes again).

Quality management becomes total when it is applied to everything a business does.

Total quality management (TQM) is the process of applying a zero defect philosophy to the management of all resources and relationships within the firm as a means of developing and sustaining a culture of continuous improvement which focuses on meeting customers' expectations.

5.1 Get it right, first time

One of the basic principles of TQM is that the **cost of preventing mistakes is less than the cost of correcting them** once they occur. The aim should therefore be **to get things right first time**.

Every mistake, delay and misunderstanding, directly costs an organisation money through **wasted time and effort**, including time taken in pacifying customers. The **lost potential for future sales because of poor customer service must also be taken into account.**

5.2 Continuous improvement

A second basic principle of TQM is dissatisfaction with the *status quo*: the belief that it is **always possible to improve** and so the aim should be to **'get it more right next time'**.

5.3 Total quality management (TQM) and performance measures

Performance measures for **TQM** must embrace every activity of the organisation.

Because TQM embraces every activity of a business, **performance measures should not be confined to the production process.** Measures should also cover the work of sales, distribution and administration departments, the efforts of external suppliers and the reaction of external customers.

In many cases the measure used will be non-financial ones. They may be divided into three types.

Type of measure	Example
Measuring incoming supplies	Percentage of defective items per delivery Number of returns per supplier
Monitoring work done as it proceeds	Number of rejects per production run Ratio of waste material to used material
Measuring customer satisfaction	Complaints per 10,000 units sold Number of claims under warranty

5.4 The requirements of quality

Mark Lee Inman listed 'eight requirements of quality' in an article for the *ACCA*.

(a) Accept that the only thing that matters is the **customer**.

(b) Recognise the importance of the **customer-supplier relationship**, where customers include internal customers: passing sub-standard material down to another division is not satisfactory.

(c)   Move away from relying on inspecting to a predetermined level of quality and move towards **preventing the cause of the defect in the first place**.

(d)   Each employee or group of **employees must be personally responsible** for defect-free production or service in their domain.

(e)   There must be a move away from 'acceptable' quality levels. **Any level of defects is unacceptable.**

(f)   **All departments** should try obsessively to get things right first time: this applies to misdirected telephone calls and typing errors as much as to production.

(g)   **Quality certification** programmes should be introduced.

(h)   The **cost of poor quality** should be emphasised: good quality generates savings.

QUESTION

Quality

Which of the above 'requirements' has your organisation met? Does your organisation offer a quality product or service? If not, why not?

6 Life cycle costing

Life cycle costing tracks and accumulates costs and revenues attributable to each product over the entire product life cycle.

A **product life cycle** can be divided into four phases.

– Introduction	– Maturity
– Growth	– Decline

6.1 What are life cycle costs?

A product's life cycle costs are incurred **from its design stage through development to market launch, production and sales, and finally to its eventual withdrawal from the market**. The component elements of a product's cost over its life cycle could therefore include the following.

(a)   **Research & development costs**
(b)   The **cost of purchasing any technical data** required
(c)   Retirement and disposal costs
(d)   **Training costs** (including initial operator training and skills updating)
(e)   **Production costs**
(f)   **Distribution costs**
(g)   **Marketing costs**
(h)   **Inventory costs** (holding spare parts, warehousing and so on)
(i)   **Costs**

Life cycle costs can apply to services, customers and projects as well as to physical products.

Traditional cost accumulation systems are based on the financial accounting year and tend to dissect a product's life cycle into a series of 12-month periods. This means that traditional management accounting systems **do not accumulate costs over a product's entire life cycle** and **do not** therefore **assess a product's profitability over its entire life.** Instead they do it on a periodic basis.

Life cycle costing, on the other hand, **tracks and accumulates actual costs and revenues** attributable to each product **over the entire product life cycle.** Hence the total profitability of any given product can be determined.

Life cycle costing is the accumulation of costs over a product's entire life.

6.2 The product life cycle

Every product goes through a life cycle as covered earlier in the text.

(a) **Introduction.** The product is introduced to the market. Potential customers will be unaware of the product or service, and the organisation may have to spend further on advertising to bring the product or service to the attention of the market.

(b) **Growth.** The product gains a bigger market as demand builds up. Sales revenues increase and the product begins to make a profit.

(c) **Maturity.** Eventually, the growth in demand for the product will slow down and it will enter a period of relative maturity. It will continue to be profitable. The product may be modified or improved, as a means of sustaining its demand.

(d) **Decline.** At some stage, the market will have bought enough of the product and it will therefore reach 'saturation point'. Demand will start to fall. Eventually it will become a loss-maker and this is the time when the organisation should decide to stop selling the product or service.

The level of sales and profits earned over a life cycle can be illustrated diagrammatically as follows.

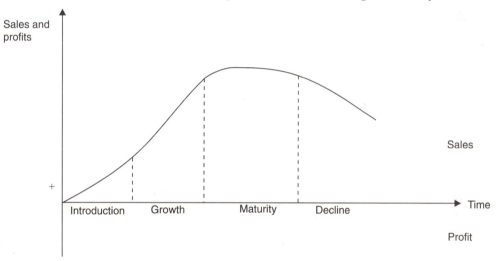

The horizontal axis measures the duration of **the life cycle**, which **can last** from, say, **18 months to several hundred years**. Children's crazes or fad products have very short lives while some products, such as binoculars (invented in the eighteenth century) can last a very long time.

6.3 Problems with traditional cost accumulation systems

Traditional cost accumulation systems do not tend to relate **research and development costs** to the products that caused them. Instead they **write off** these costs on an annual basis **against** the **revenue generated by existing products**. This makes the existing products seem **less profitable** than they really are. If research and development costs are not related to the causal product the true profitability of that product cannot be assessed.

Traditional cost accumulation systems usually **total all non-production costs** and record them as a **period expense**.

6.4 The value of life cycle costing

With life cycle costing, non-production costs are traced to individual products over complete life cycles.

(a) The total of these costs for each individual product can therefore be reported and compared with revenues generated in the future.

(b)   The visibility of such costs is increased.

(c)   **Individual product profitability can be more fully understood** by attributing *all* costs to products.

(d)   As a consequence, **more accurate feedback information** is available on the organisation's success or failure in developing new products. In today's competitive environment, where the ability to produce new and updated versions of products is paramount to the survival of an organisation, this information is vital.

7 Target costing

┌───┐
│ **Target costing** involves setting a target cost by subtracting a desired profit margin from a competitive │
│ market price.   │
└───┘

To compete effectively in today's competitive market, organisations must continually redesign their products with the result that **product life cycles** have become much **shorter.** The **planning, development and design stage** of a product is therefore **critical** to an organisation's cost management process. Considering possible **cost reductions at this stage** of a product's life cycle (rather than during the production process) is now one of the most **important** issues facing management accountants in industry.

Here are some examples of **decisions made at the design stage** which directly **impact on the cost of a product.**

(a)   The number of different components
(b)   Whether the components are standard or not
(c)   The ease of changing over tools

Japanese companies have developed **target costing** as a **response to the problem of controlling and reducing costs over the product life cycle.**

Target costing involves setting a target cost by subtracting a desired profit margin from a competitive market price.

Target cost is an estimate of a product cost which is determined by subtracting a desired profit margin from a competitive market price. This target cost may be less than the planned initial product cost but it is expected to be achieved by the time the product reaches the maturity stage of the product life cycle.

Target costing has its **greatest impact at the design stage** because a large percentage of a product's **life cycle costs are determined by decisions made early in its life cycle.**

The technique requires managers to **change** the way they think about the **relationship between cost, price and profit**.

(a)   **Traditionally** the approach is to **develop a product, determine the production cost** of that product, **set a selling price**, with a **resulting profit** or loss.

(b)   The **target costing approach** is to **develop a product, determine the market selling price and desired profit margin**, with a **resulting cost** which must be achieved.

Do you remember looking at cost plus pricing in Chapter 10? Cost plus pricing is a 'bottom up' approach where you start with full production costs and add a margin to arrive at a selling price. However it does not take account of market conditions.

In contrast, target costing is a 'top down' method and starts with a price that takes account of market conditions and deducts a desired margin to arrive at a target cost.

In 'Product costing/pricing strategy' (*ACCA Students Newsletter*, August 1999), a useful summary of the **steps in the implementation of the target costing process** was provided.

Step 1	Determine a product specification of which an adequate sales volume is estimated.
Step 2	Set a selling price at which the organisation will be able to achieve a desired market share.
Step 3	Estimate the required profit based on return on sales or return on investment.
Step 4	Calculate the target cost = target selling price – target profit.
Step 5	Compile an estimated cost for the product based on the anticipated design specification and current cost levels.
Step 6	Calculate cost gap = estimated cost – target cost.
Step 7	Make efforts to close the gap. This is more likely to be successful if efforts are made to 'design out' costs prior to production, rather than to 'control out' costs during the production phase.
Step 8	Negotiate with the customer before making the decision about whether to go ahead with the project.

When a product is first manufactured, its target cost may well be much lower than its currently-attainable cost, which is determined by current technology and processes. Management can then set **benchmarks for improvement** towards the target costs, by improving technologies and processes. Various techniques can be employed.

(a) Reducing the **number of components**
(b) Using **standard components** wherever possible
(c) **Training** staff in more efficient techniques
(d) Acquiring new, more efficient **technology**
(e) Cutting out **non-value-added activities** (identified using **activity analysis** etc)
(f) Using **different materials**
(g) Using **cheaper staff**

These techniques are known as **value-engineering**.

Even if the product can be produced within the target cost the story does not end there. Target costing can be applied throughout the entire life cycle. **Once the product goes into production target costs will therefore gradually be reduced**. These reductions will be **incorporated into the budgeting process**. This means that **cost savings** must be **actively sought** and made **continuously** over the life of the product.

CHAPTER ROUNDUP

↳ An alternative to the traditional methods of absorption costing is **activity based costing (ABC).** ABC involves the identification of the factors (cost drivers) which cause the costs of an organisation's major activities. Support overheads are charged to products on the basis of their usage of an activity.

↳ When using ABC, for costs that vary with production levels in the short term, the cost driver will be volume related (labour or machine hours). Overheads that vary with some other activity (and not volume of production) should be traced to products using transaction-based cost drivers such as production runs or number of orders received.

↳ **Total quality management (TQM)** is the process of applying a zero defect philosophy to the management of all resources and relationships within an organisation as a means of developing and sustaining a culture of continuous improvement which focuses on meeting customer expectations.

↳ **Life cycle costing** tracks and accumulates costs and revenues attributable to each product over the entire product life cycle.

↳ A **product life cycle** can be divided into four phases.

- Introduction
- Growth

- Maturity
- Decline

↳ **Target costing** involves setting a target cost by subtracting a desired profit margin from a competitive market price.

QUICK QUIZ

1 Life cycle costing is the profiling of cost over a product's production life.

☐ True

☐ False

2 *Fill in the blanks using words from the list (a) to (h).*

Target cost = ... minus ....

Cost gap = ... minus ....

(a) target cost
(b) cost gap
(c) budgeted selling price
(d) production cost
(e) target selling price
(f) estimated cost
(g) estimated selling price
(h) target profit

ANSWERS TO QUICK QUIZ

1   False. It also looks at development costs and so on which are incurred prior to production, and any dismantling costs, which are incurred once production ceases.

2   Target cost = estimated selling price minus target profit
    Cost gap = estimated cost – target cost

Now try ...

Attempt the questions below from the **Exam Question Bank**

Number

Q58 – Q60

part

C

Budgeting

We will be covering two principal forecasting techniques in this chapter, regression analysis and time series analysis. Regression analysis can be applied to costs and revenues while time series analysis is generally applied to revenue.

Forecasting

Study Guide	Intellectual level
C **Budgeting**	
2 **Statistical techniques**	
(a) Explain the advantages and disadvantages of using the high-low method to estimate the fixed and variable element of costing	K
(b) Construct scatter diagrams and lines of best fit	S
(c) Analysis of cost data	
i) Explain the concept of correlation coefficient and coefficient of determination	K
ii) Calculate and interpret correlation coefficient and coefficient of determination	S
iii) Establish a linear function using regression analysis and interpret the results	S
(d) Use linear regression coefficients to make forecasts of costs and revenues	S
(e) Adjust historical and forecast data for price movements	S
(f) Explain the advantages and disadvantages of linear regression analysis	K
(g) Describe the product life cycle and explain its importance in forecasting	K
(h) Explain the principles of time series analysis (cyclical, trend, seasonal variation and random elements)	K
(i) Calculate moving averages	S
(j) Calculation of trend, including the use of regression coefficients	S
(k) Use trend and seasonal variation (additive and multiplicative) to make budget forecasts	S
(l) Explain the advantages and disadvantages of time series analysis	K
(m) Explain the purpose of index numbers.	K
(n) Calculate simple index numbers for one or more variables	S

1 Correlation

1.1 Introduction

Two variables are said to be correlated if a change in the value of one variable is accompanied by a change in the value of another variable. This is what is meant by **correlation**.

Examples of variables which might be correlated are as follows.

- A person's height and weight
- The distance of a journey and the time it takes to make it

1.2 Scattergraphs

One way of showing the correlation between two related variables is on a **scattergraph** or **scatter diagram**, plotting a number of pairs of data on the graph. For example, a scattergraph showing monthly selling costs against the volume of sales for a 12-month period might be as follows.

This scattergraph suggests that there is some correlation between selling costs and sales volume, so that as sales volume rises, selling costs tend to rise as well.

A line of best fit, which is a line drawn by judgement to pass through the middle of the points, thereby having as many points above the line as below it, can then be drawn.

1.3 Degrees of correlation

Two variables might be **perfectly correlated**, **partly correlated** or **uncorrelated**. Correlation can be **positive** or **negative**.

The differing degrees of correlation can be illustrated by scatter diagrams.

1.3.1 Perfect correlation

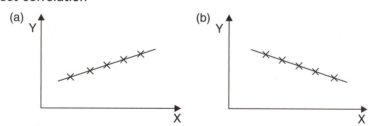

All the pairs of values lie on a straight line. An exact **linear relationship** exists between the two variables.

1.3.2 Partial correlation

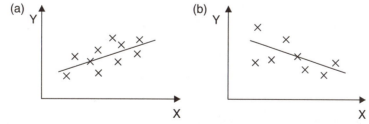

In (a), although there is no exact relationship, low values of X tend to be associated with low values of Y, and high values of X with high values of Y.

In (b) again, there is no exact relationship, but low values of X tend to be associated with high values of Y and vice versa.

1.3.3 No correlation

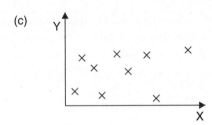

(c)

The values of these two variables are not correlated with each other.

1.3.4 Positive and negative correlation

Correlation, whether perfect or partial, can be **positive** or **negative**.

Positive correlation means that low values of one variable are associated with low values of the other, and high values of one variable are associated with high values of the other.

Negative correlation means that low values of one variable are associated with high values of the other, and high values of one variable with low values of the other.

---

2   The correlation coefficient and the coefficient of determination

2.1 The correlation coefficient

The degree of linear correlation between two variables is measured by the **Pearsonian** (product moment) **correlation coefficient, r**. The nearer r is to +1 or −1, the stronger the relationship.

When we have measured the **degree of correlation** between two variables we can decide, using actual results in the form of pairs of data, whether two variables are perfectly or partially correlated, and if they are partially correlated, whether there is a **high** or **low degree of partial correlation.**

FORMULA TO LEARN

Correlation coefficient, $r = \dfrac{n\sum XY - \sum X \sum Y}{\sqrt{[n\sum X^2 - (\sum X)^2][n\sum Y^2 - (\sum Y)^2]}}$

where X and Y represent pairs of data for two variables X and Y

n = the number of pairs of data used in the analysis

EXAM FOCUS POINT

The formula for the correlation coefficient is given in the exam. Note that this correlation measure measures the **strength** of **linear** relationships.

The correlation coefficient, r must always fall between −1 and +1. If you get a value outside this range you have made a mistake.

- r = **+1**   means that the variables are perfectly positively correlated
- r = **−1**   means that the variables are perfectly negatively correlated
- r = **0**   means that the variables are uncorrelated

2.2 Example: the correlation coefficient formula

The cost of output at a factory is thought to depend on the number of units produced. Data have been collected for the number of units produced each month in the last six months, and the associated costs, as follows.

Month	Output '000s of units X	Cost $'000 Y
1	2	9
2	3	11
3	1	7
4	4	13
5	3	11
6	5	15

Required

Assess whether there is there any correlation between output and cost.

Solution

$$r = \frac{n\sum XY - \sum X \sum Y}{\sqrt{[n\sum X^2 - (\sum X)^2][n\sum Y^2 - (\sum Y)^2]}}$$

We need to find the values for the following.

(a) $\sum XY$ Multiply each value of X by its corresponding Y value, so that there are six values for XY. Add up the six values to get the total.

(b) $\sum X$ Add up the six values of X to get a total. $(\sum X)^2$ will be the square of this total.

(c) $\sum Y$ Add up the six values of Y to get a total. $(\sum Y)^2$ will be the square of this total.

(d) $\sum X^2$ Find the square of each value of X, so that there are six values for X^2. Add up these values to get a total.

(e) $\sum Y^2$ Find the square of each value of Y, so that there are six values for Y^2. Add up these values to get a total.

Workings

X	Y	XY	X^2	Y^2
2	9	18	4	81
3	11	33	9	121
1	7	7	1	49
4	13	52	16	169
3	11	33	9	121
5	15	75	25	225
$\sum X = \underline{\underline{18}}$	$\sum Y = \underline{\underline{66}}$	$\sum XY = \underline{\underline{218}}$	$\sum X^2 = \underline{\underline{64}}$	$\sum Y^2 = \underline{\underline{766}}$

$(\sum X)^2 = 18^2 = 324$ $(\sum Y)^2 = 66^2 = 4,356$

n   =   6

$$r = \frac{(6 \times 218) - (18 \times 66)}{\sqrt{(6 \times 64 - 324) \times (6 \times 766 - 4,356)}}$$

$$= \frac{1,308 - 1,188}{\sqrt{(384 - 324) \times (4,596 - 4,356)}}$$

$$= \frac{120}{\sqrt{60 \times 240}} = \frac{120}{\sqrt{14,400}} = \frac{120}{120} = 1$$

There is **perfect positive correlation** between the volume of output at the factory and costs which means that there is a perfect linear relationship between output and costs.

2.3 Example: the correlation coefficient without the formula

If you are given a question with relatively simple numbers as variables, you may be able to estimate the correlation coefficient without using the formula at all.

The following data is available for the number of materials purchased and the total cost.

Number of units purchased	Total cost
x	y
	$
1	10
2	20
3	30
4	40
5	50

Required

Without using the formula, state the correlation coefficient between the two variables.

Solution

A correlation coefficient of $+1$ means that there is a perfect linear relationship between the two variables. The equation relating the two variables would be of the form $y = a + bx$ (see Section 4 Chapter 4). If you plotted a graph, it would be a straight line.

You can see fairly easily that y is ten times the value of x. So the equation is $y = 10x$. This means that there is perfect positive correlation and the correlation coefficient is $+1$.

Look at the following data.

x	y
0.0	60
0.1	50
0.2	40
0.3	30
0.4	20
0.5	10

Required

Without using the formula, state the correlation coefficient between the two variables.

Solution

You could draw a quick sketch of the graph as follows.

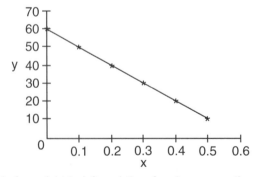

This graph slopes downwards from right to left and therefore has a negative gradient. It is a straight line so we are looking at perfect negative correlation with a correlation coefficient of -1.

Note that the gradient is $-10/0.1 = -100$ and the intercept is 60 (see Section 5, Chapter 4). The equation of the line is therefore $y = -100x + 60$.

2.4 Correlation in a time series

Correlation exists in a time series if there is a relationship between the period of time and the recorded value for that period of time. The correlation coefficient is calculated with time as the X variable although it is convenient to use simplified values for X instead of year numbers.

For example, instead of having a series of years 20X1 to 20X5, we could have values for X from 0 (20X1) to 4 (20X5).

Note that whatever starting value you use for X (be it 0, 1, 2 ... 721, ... 953), the value of r will always be the same.

QUESTION

Correlation

Sales of product A between 20X7 and 20Y1 were as follows.

Year	Units sold ('000s)
20X7	20
20X8	18
20X9	15
20Y0	14
20Y1	11

Required

Determine whether there is a trend in sales. In other words, decide whether there is any correlation between the year and the number of units sold.

ANSWER

Workings

Let 20X7 to 20Y1 be years 0 to 4.

X	Y	XY	X^2	Y^2
0	20	0	0	400
1	18	18	1	324
2	15	30	4	225
3	14	42	9	196
4	11	44	16	121
$\Sigma X = 10$	$\Sigma Y = 78$	$\Sigma XY = 134$	$\Sigma X^2 = 30$	$\Sigma Y^2 = 1{,}266$

$(\Sigma X)^2 = 100 \qquad (\Sigma Y)^2 = 6{,}084$

$n = 5$

$$r = \frac{(5 \times 134) - (10 \times 78)}{\sqrt{(5 \times 30 - 100) \times (5 \times 1{,}266 - 6{,}084)}}$$

$$= \frac{670 - 780}{\sqrt{(150 - 100) \times (6{,}330 - 6{,}084)}} = \frac{-110}{\sqrt{50 \times 246}}$$

$$= \frac{-110}{\sqrt{12{,}300}} = \frac{-110}{110.90537} = -0.992$$

There is **partial negative correlation** between the year of sale and units sold. The value of r is close to – 1, therefore a **high degree of correlation exists**, although it is not quite perfect correlation. This means that there is a **clear downward trend** in sales.

2.5 The coefficient of determination, r²

The **coefficient of determination**, r^2 (alternatively R^2) measures the proportion of the total variation in the value of one variable that can be explained by variations in the value of the other variable. It denotes the strength of the **linear** association between two variables.

Unless the correlation coefficient r is exactly or very nearly +1, –1 or 0, its meaning or significance is a little unclear. For example, if the correlation coefficient for two variables is +0.8, this would tell us that the variables are positively correlated, but the correlation is not perfect. It would not really tell us much else. A more meaningful analysis is available from **the square of the correlation coefficient, r**, which is called the **coefficient of determination**.

The question above entitled 'Correlation' shows that r = –0.992, therefore r^2 = 0.984. This means that over 98% of variations in sales can be explained by the passage of time, leaving 0.016 (less than 2%) of variations to be explained by other factors.

Similarly, if the correlation coefficient between a company's output volume and maintenance costs was 0.9, r^2 would be 0.81, meaning that 81% of variations in maintenance costs could be explained by variations in output volume, leaving only 19% of variations to be explained by other factors (such as the age of the equipment).

Note, however, that if r^2 = 0.81, we would say that 81% of **the variations in y can be explained by variations in x**. We do not necessarily conclude that 81% of variations in y are *caused* by the variations in x. We must beware of reading too much significance into our statistical analysis.

2.6 Correlation and causation

If two variables are well correlated, either positively or negatively, this may be due to **pure chance** or there may be a **reason** for it. The larger the number of pairs of data collected, the less likely it is that the correlation is due to chance, though that possibility should never be ignored entirely.

If there is a reason, it may not be causal. For example, monthly net income is well correlated with monthly credit to a person's bank account, for the logical (rather than causal) reason that for most people the one equals the other.

Even if there is a causal explanation for a correlation, it does not follow that variations in the value of one variable cause variations in the value of the other. For example, sales of ice cream and of sunglasses are well correlated, not because of a direct causal link but because the weather influences both variables.

3 Lines of best fit

3.1 Linear relationships

Correlation enables us to determine the strength of any relationship between two variables but it does not offer us any method of forecasting values for one variable, Y, given values of another variable, X.

If we assume that there is a **linear relationship** between the two variables, however, and we determine the **equation of a straight line (Y = a + bX)** which is a good fit for the available data plotted on a scattergraph, we can use the equation for forecasting: we can substitute values for X into the equation and derive values for Y.

3.1.1 Dependent and independent variables

If you are given two variables, the examiner might not tell you which is x and which is y. You need to be able to work this out for yourself.

y is the dependent variable, depending for its value on the value of x.

x is the independent variable whose value helps to determine the corresponding value of y. Time is usually an independent variable.

For example, the total cost of materials purchases depends on the budgeted number of units of production. The number of production units is the independent variable (x) and the total cost is the dependent variable (y).

3.2 Estimating the equation of the line of best fit

There are a number of techniques for estimating the equation of a line of best fit. We will be looking at **simple linear regression analysis**. This provides a technique for estimating values for a and b in the equation

Y = a + bX

where X and Y are the related variables and
a and b are estimated using pairs of data for X and Y.

4 Least squares method of linear regression analysis

4.1 Introduction

Linear regression analysis (the **least squares method**) is one technique for estimating a line of best fit. Once an equation for a line of best fit has been determined, forecasts can be made.

FORMULA TO LEARN

The least squares method of linear regression analysis involves using the following formulae for a and b in Y = a + bX.

$$b = \frac{n\sum XY - \sum X \sum Y}{n\sum X^2 - (\sum X)^2}$$

$$a = \frac{\sum Y}{n} - b\frac{\sum X}{n}$$

where n is the number of pairs of data

EXAM FOCUS POINT

The formulae will be given in the exam.

The line of best fit that is derived represents the **regression of Y upon X**.

A different line of best fit could be obtained by interchanging X and Y in the formulae. This would then represent the regression of X upon Y (X = a + bY) and it would have a slightly different slope. For examination purposes, always use the regression of Y upon X, where X is the independent variable, and Y is the dependent variable whose value we wish to forecast for given values of X. In a time series, X will represent time.

4.2 Example: the least squares method

(a) Using the data below for variables X (output) and Y (total cost), calculate an equation to determine the expected level of costs, for any given volume of output, using the least squares method.

Time period	1	2	3	4	5
Output ('000 units)	20	16	24	22	18
Total cost ($000)	82	70	90	85	73

(b)   Prepare a budget for total costs if output is 22,000 units.

(c)   Confirm that the degree of correlation between output and costs is high by calculating the correlation coefficient.

Solution

(a)   *Workings*

X	Y	XY	X^2	Y^2
20	82	1,640	400	6,724
16	70	1,120	256	4,900
24	90	2,160	576	8,100
22	85	1,870	484	7,225
18	73	1,314	324	5,329
$\sum X = 100$	$\sum Y = 400$	$\sum XY = 8,104$	$\sum X^2 = 2,040$	$\sum Y^2 = 32,278$

n   =   5 (There are five pairs of data for x and y values)

$$b = \frac{n\sum XY - \sum X \sum Y}{n\sum X^2 - (\sum X)^2} = \frac{(5\times 8,104)-(100\times 400)}{(5\times 2,040)-100^2}$$

$$= \frac{40,520-40,000}{10,200-10,000} = \frac{520}{200} = 2.6$$

$$a = \frac{\sum Y}{n} - b\frac{\sum X}{n} = \frac{400}{5} - 2.6 \times \left(\frac{100}{5}\right) = 28$$

Y   =   28 + 2.6X

where   Y = total cost, in thousands of dollars   X = output, in thousands of units

Note that the fixed costs are $28,000 (when X = 0 costs are $28,000) and the variable cost per unit is $2.60.

(b)   If the output is 22,000 units, we would expect costs to be

28 + 2.6 × 22 = 85.2 = $85,200.

(c) $$r = \frac{520}{\sqrt{200\times\left(5\times 32,278 - 400^2\right)}} = \frac{520}{\sqrt{200\times 1,390}} = \frac{520}{527.3} = +0.99$$

4.3 Regression lines and time series

The same technique can be applied to calculate a **regression line** (a **trend line**) for a time series. This is particularly useful for purposes of forecasting. As with correlation, years can be numbered from 0 upwards.

QUESTION   Trend line

Using the data in the question entitled 'Correlation', calculate the trend line of sales and forecast sales in 20Y2 and 20Y3.

ANSWER

Using workings from the question entitled 'Correlation':

$$b = \frac{(5\times 134)-(10\times 78)}{(5\times 30)-(10)^2} = \frac{670-780}{150-100} = -2.2$$

$$a = \frac{\sum Y}{n} - b\frac{\sum X}{n} = \frac{78}{5} - \frac{(-2.2\times 10)}{5} = 20$$

∴ Y = 20 − 2.2X where X = 0 in 20X7, X = 1 in 20X8 and so on.

Using the trend line, predicted sales in 20Y2 (year 5) would be:

20 – (2.2 × 5) = 9 ie 9,000 units

and predicated sales in 20Y3 (year 6) would be:

20 – (2.2 × 6) = 6.8 ie 6,800 units.

QUESTION

Regression analysis

Regression analysis was used to find the equation Y = 300 – 4.7X, where X is time (in quarters) and Y is sales level in thousands of units. Given that X = 0 represents 20X0 quarter 1 what are the forecast sales levels for 20X5 quarter 4?

ANSWER

X = 0 corresponds to 20X0 quarter 1

Therefore X = 23 corresponds to 20X5 quarter 4

Forecast sales   = 300 – (4.7 × 23)
              = 191.9 = 191,900 units

QUESTION

Forecasting

Over a 36 month period sales have been found to have an underlying regression line of Y = 14.224 + 7.898X where Y is the number of items sold and X represents the month.

What are the forecast number of items to be sold in month 37?

ANSWER

Y   = 14.224 + 7.898X
      = 14.224 + (7.898 × 37)
      = 306.45 = 306 units

5 The reliability of regression analysis forecasts

As with all forecasting techniques, the results from regression analysis will not be wholly reliable. There are a number of factors which affect the reliability of forecasts made using regression analysis.

(a) **It assumes a linear relationship exists between the two variables** (since linear regression analysis produces an equation in the linear format) whereas a non-linear relationship might exist.

(b) It assumes that the value of one variable, Y, can be predicted or estimated from the value of one other variable, X. In reality the value of Y might depend on several other variables, not just X.

(c) When it is used for forecasting, it assumes that what has happened in the past will provide a reliable guide to the future.

(d) When calculating a line of best fit, there will be a range of values for X. In the example in Paragraph 4.2, the line Y = 28 + 2.6X was predicted from data with output values ranging from X = 16 to X = 24. Depending on the degree of correlation between X and Y, we might safely use the estimated line of best fit to predict values for Y in the future, provided that the value of X remains within the range 16 to 24. We would be on less safe ground if we used the formula to predict a value for Y when X = 10, or 30, or any other value outside the range 16 to 24,

because we would have to assume that the trend line applies outside the range of X values used to establish the line in the first place.

    (i)   **Interpolation** means using a line of best fit to predict a value within the two extreme points of the observed range.

    (ii)   **Extrapolation** means using a line of best fit to predict a value outside the two extreme points.

When linear regression analysis is used for forecasting a time series (when the X values represent time) it **assumes that the trend line can be extrapolated into the future**. This might not necessarily be a good assumption to make.

(e)   As with any forecasting process, **the amount of data available is very important**. Even if correlation is high, if we have fewer than about ten pairs of values, we must regard any forecast as being somewhat unreliable. (It is likely to provide more reliable forecasts than the scattergraph method, however, since it uses all of the available data.)

(f)   **The reliability of a forecast will depend on the reliability of the data collected to determine the regression analysis equation**. If the data is not collected accurately or if data used is false, forecasts are unlikely to be acceptable.

A check on the reliability of the estimated line Y= 28 + 2.6X can be made, however, by calculating the coefficient of correlation. From the answer to the example in Paragraph 4.2, we know that r = 0.99. This is a high positive correlation, and r^2 = 0.9801, indicating that 98.01% of the variation in cost can be explained by the variation in volume. This would suggest that a **fairly large degree of reliance** can probably be placed on estimates.

If there is a **perfect linear relationship** between X and Y (r = ±1) then we can predict Y from any given value of X with **great confidence**.

If correlation is high (for example r = 0.9) the actual values will all lie quite close to the regression line and so predictions should not be far out. If correlation is below about 0.7, predictions will only give a very rough guide as to the likely value of Y.

5.1 Advantages of regression analysis

(a)   It gives a definitive line of best fit, taking account of all of the data.

(b)   Linear regression makes efficient use of data and good results can be obtained with relatively small data sets.

(c)   The significance/reliability of the relationship between variables can be statistically tested (but you don't need to know the details of this for FMA.)

(d)   Many processes are linear so are well described by regression analysis. Even many non-linear relationships can be well-approximated by a linear model over a short range.

6   The high-low method

The high-low method is a simple forecasting technique.

6.1 High-low method

(a)   Records of costs in previous periods are reviewed and the costs of the following two periods are selected.

    (i)   The period with the **highest** volume of activity
    (ii)   The period with the **lowest** volume of activity

(b)   The difference between the total cost of these two periods will be the **variable cost** of the difference in activity levels (since the same fixed cost is included in each total cost).

(c)   The variable cost per unit may be calculated from this (difference in total costs ÷ difference in activity levels), and the **fixed cost** may then be determined by substitution.

(d)   This method may be applied to annual sales figures or any other activity as well as costs. **So be prepared to use this outside the context of costs.**

6.2 Example: the high-low method using revenues

The following information concerning sales revenues for a development, Cool Blue, for the last four months have been as follows.

Month	Sales revenues $	Website 'hits'
1	110,000	70,000
2	115,000	80,000
3	111,000	77,000
4	97,000	60,000

Required

Calculate the revenues that should be expected in month five when hits is expected to be 75,000 units. Ignore inflation.

6.3 Solution

(a)

	Hits	Revenue $
High activity	80,000	115,000
Low activity	60,000	97,000
	20,000	18,000

Variable revenue per hit $18,000/20,000 = $0.90

(b)   Substituting in either the high or low volume activity:

		High $		Low $
Total revenue		115,000		97,000
Variable revenue	(80,000 × $0.90)	72,000	(60,000 × $0.90)	54,000
Fixed revenue		43,000		43,000

(c)   Estimated revenues when there are 75,000 hits:

	$
Fixed revenues	43,000
Variable revenues (75,000 × $0.90)	67,500
Total revenues	110,500

6.4 Example: the high-low method with stepped fixed costs

The following data relate to the overhead expenditure of contract cleaners (for industrial cleaning) at two activity levels.

Square metres cleaned	12,750	15,100
Overheads	$73,950	$83,585

When more than 20,000 square metres are industrially cleaned, it is necessary to have another supervisor and so the fixed costs rise to $43,350.

Required

Calculate the estimated overhead expenditure if 22,000 square metres are to be industrially cleaned.

6.5 Solution

	Units		$
High output	15,100	Total cost	83,585
Low output	12,750	Total cost	73,950
	2,350		9,635

$$\text{Variable cost} = \frac{\$9,635}{2,350}$$

$$= \$4.10 \text{ per square metre}$$

Estimated overhead expenditure if 22,000 square metres are to be industrially cleaned:

	$
Fixed costs	43,350
Variable costs (22,000 × $4.10)	90,200
	133,550

QUESTION   Cost model

The Valuation Department of a large firm of surveyors wishes to develop a method of predicting its total costs in a period. The following past costs have been recorded at two activity levels.

	Number of valuations (V)	Total cost (TC)
Period 1	420	82,200
Period 2	515	90,275

The total cost model for a period could be represented as follows.

A   TC = $46,500 + 85V
B   TC = $42,000 + 95V
C   TC = $46,500 – 85V
D   TC = $51,500 – 95V

ANSWER

Although we only have two activity levels in this question we can still apply the high-low method.

	Valuations V	Total cost $
Period 2	515	90,275
Period 1	420	82,200
Change due to variable cost	95	8,075

∴ Variable cost per valuation = $8,075/95 = $85.

Period 2: fixed cost = $90,275 – (515 × $85)
                     = $46,500

Using good MCQ technique, you should have managed to eliminate C and D as incorrect options straightaway. The variable cost must be added to the fixed cost, rather than subtracted from it. Once you had calculated the variable cost as $85 per valuation (as shown above), you should have been able to select option A without going on to calculate the fixed cost (we have shown this calculation above for completeness).

6.6 Example: the high-low method with inflation

You may be asked to use the high-low method when cost inflation is included. You need to deflate (reduce) all of the costs to a base year before the high-low method can be applied.

	Year 1	Year 2	Year 3	Year 4
Sales/production (units)	85,000	93,400	95,800	94,300
Total costs	$337,500	$365,670	$379,080	$382,395
Cost inflation index	100	102	104	106

Required

Establish a linear equation for total costs per annum (at year 1 prices) using the high-low method.

6.7 Solution

Cost data has to be reduced by dividing by the inflation index before the high-low method can be applied.

	Year 1	Year 2	Year 3	Year 4
Cost/inflation index	$337,500	$365,670/1.02	$379,080/1.04	$382,395/1.06
	= $337,500	=$358,500	=$364,500	=$360,750

After adjusting for inflation, the year of highest output (Year 3) is now also the year of the highest cost. Using the high-low method for Year 1 and Year 3:

	Units	Cost $
High	95,800	364,500
Low	85,000	337,500
	10,800	27,000

∴ variable cost per unit = $27,000/10,800
= $2.50

Fixed cost = $337,500 – (85,000 × $2.50)
= $125,000

∴ Total cost (y) = $2.50 x + $125,000 (where x is the number of units)

6.8 Advantages and disadvantages of the high-low method

Advantages

- It is easy to use and understand
- It needs just two activity levels

Disadvantages

- It uses two extreme data points which may not be representative of normal conditions
- Using only two points to determine a formula may mean that the formula is not very accurate

7 The components of time series

- A **time series** is a series of figures or values recorded over time.

- There are four components of a time series: **trend**, **seasonal variations**, **cyclical variations** and **random variations**.

The **time series analysis** forecasting technique is usually used to forecast sales.

A **time series** is a series of figures or values recorded over time.

The following are examples of time series.

(a) Output at a factory each day for the last month
(b) Monthly sales over the last two years
(c) Total annual costs for the last ten years
(d) Retail Prices Index each month for the last ten years
(e) The number of people employed by a company each year for the last 20 years

A graph of a time series is called a **historigram**. (Note the 'ri'; this is not the same as a histogram.) For example, consider the following time series.

Year	Sales $'000
1	20
2	21
3	24
4	23
5	27
6	30
7	28

The historigram is as follows.

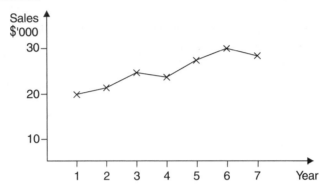

The horizontal axis is always chosen to represent time, and the vertical axis represents the values of the data recorded.

There are several features of a time series which it may be necessary to analyse in order to prepare forecasts.

(a)   A **trend**

(b)   **Seasonal variations** or fluctuations

(c)   **Cycles**, or cyclical variations

(d)   **Non-recurring, random variations**. These may be caused by unforeseen circumstances, such as a change in the government of the country, a war, the collapse of a company, technological change or a fire.

7.1 The trend

TERM

The **trend** is the underlying long-term movement over time in the values of the data recorded.

In the following examples of time series, there are three types of trend.

Year	Output per labour hour Units	Cost per unit $	Number of employees
4	30	1.00	100
5	24	1.08	103
6	26	1.20	96
7	22	1.15	102
8	21	1.18	103
9	17	1.25	98
	(A)	(B)	(C)

(a)   In time series (A) there is a downward trend in the output per labour hour. Output per labour hour did not fall every year, because it went up between years 5 and 6, but the long-term movement is clearly a downward one.

(b)   In time series (B) there is an upward trend in the cost per unit. Although unit costs went down in year 7 from a higher level in year 6, the basic movement over time is one of rising costs.

(c)   In time series (C) there is no clear movement up or down, and the number of employees remained fairly constant around 100. The trend is therefore a static, or level one.

7.2 Seasonal variations

Seasonal variations are short-term fluctuations in recorded values, due to different circumstances which affect results at different times of the year, on different days of the week, at different times of day, or whatever.

Here are two examples of seasonal variations.

(a)   Sales of ice cream will be higher in summer than winter.

(b)   The telephone network may be heavily used at certain times of the day (such as mid-morning and mid-afternoon and much less used at other times (such as in the middle of the night).

QUESTION   Seasonal variations

Can you think of some more examples of seasonal variations?

ANSWER

Here are some suggestions.

(a)   Sales of overcoats will be higher in autumn than in spring.
(b)   Shops might expect higher sales shortly before Christmas, or in their winter and summer sales.
(c)   Sales might be higher on Friday and Saturday than on Monday.

'Seasonal' is a term which may appear to refer to the seasons of the year, but its meaning in time series analysis is somewhat broader, as the examples given above show.

7.3 Example: a trend and seasonal variations

The number of customers served by a company of travel agents over the past four years is shown in the following historigram.

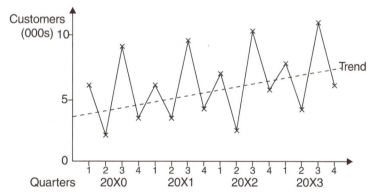

In this example, there would appear to be large seasonal fluctuations in demand, but there is also a basic upward trend.

7.4 Cyclical variations

Cyclical variations are fluctuations which take place over a longer time period than seasonal variations. It may take several years to complete the cycle. For example the sales of fashion items such as flared trousers could be said to be cyclical. The last cycle took approximately 30 years (mid 1960s to mid 1990s) to complete.

QUESTION

Time series components

The following is an extract from a *Financial Times* article.

'It would be wrong to conclude too much from the encouraging 6 per cent growth in BT's inland call volumes in its final quarter. Even so, shareholders should be warmed by signs that its policy of boosting network usage is at long last bearing fruit.

The general economic recovery, of course, goes some way to explain the strong growth in calls. So do enforced price cuts. But the company's belated efforts to market its services also deserve some credit. Over the past year, charge card customers rose two-thirds, residential subscribers to extra services such as call diversion more than doubled, and freephone usage grew 30 per cent. Sunday calls have responded to lower week-end tariffs, though not enough to counterbalance the price cuts. Similarly, discounts targeted at business customers have slowed BT's loss of market share and helped it win back customers from Mercury.

BT realises it has so far exploited only a fraction of this growth opportunity. Britons use their phones much less intensively than their American counterparts. The company therefore plans to step up its marketing campaign in an attempt to create a 'high phone-usage culture'.

Investors, who have heard management promise similar things in the past, may be sceptical whether growth will materialise, given that BT's market share is bound to fall further.'

Required

Explain what the extract tells us about the following.

(a)   The underlying *trend* in telephone usage in the UK and any factors influencing that trend
(b)   *Short-term* (or 'seasonal') variations as they have affected BT's business
(c)   *Cyclical variations* affecting BT's performance

ANSWER

(a)   BT believes that it can accelerate the long-term trend towards higher phone usage in by increased effort in marketing its services. The long-term potential for growth can be seen from the fact that Britons use their phones much less than Americans. Only a fraction of this potential has been tapped so far. Although there is some evidence of this growth in the 6% increase in inland calls in BT's final quarter, it is too early to be sure about whether this increase reflects the underlying trend.

(b)   Types of 'seasonal' variation affecting BT are the fluctuations occurring over a weekly cycle and those occurring over the 24-hour period. The extract refers to changes over the weekly cycle. Calls made on Sundays have grown because of lower prices at the weekend, although this additional volume of business was not enough to outweigh the cut in price. (In other words, there was not a positive effect on revenue: there were more calls, but at lower prices).

(c)   One of the main factors explaining the strong rise in calls in the final quarter is the cyclical variation arising from the general recovery in the economy. (Other factors are price cuts and improved marketing efforts.)

8 Finding the trend

 One method of finding the trend is by the use of **moving averages**. Remember that when finding the moving average of an even number of results, a second moving average has to be calculated so that trend values can relate to specific actual figures.

Look at these monthly sales figures.

Year 6	Sales $'000
August	0.02
September	0.04
October	0.04
November	3.20
December	14.60

It looks as though the business is expanding rapidly – and so it is, in a way. But when you know that the business is a Christmas card manufacturer, then you see immediately that the January sales will no doubt slump right back down again.

It is obvious that the business will do better in the Christmas season than at any other time – that is the seasonal variation with which the statistician has to contend. Using the monthly figures, how can he tell whether or not the business is doing well overall – whether there is a rising sales trend over time other than the short-term rise over Christmas?

One possibility is to compare figures with the equivalent figures of a year ago. However, many things can happen over a period of twelve months to make such a comparison misleading – for example, new products might now be manufactured and prices will probably have changed.

In fact, there are a number of ways of overcoming this problem of distinguishing trend from seasonal variations. One such method is called **moving averages**. This method attempts to **remove seasonal (or cyclical) variations from a time series by a process of averaging so as to leave a set of figures representing the trend**.

8.1 Finding the trend by moving averages

A **moving average** is an average of the results of a fixed number of periods. Since it is an average of several time periods, it is **related to the mid-point of the overall period**.

8.2 Example: moving averages

Year	Sales Units
20X0	390
20X1	380
20X2	460
20X3	450
20X4	470
20X5	440
20X6	500

Task

Take a moving average of the annual sales over a period of three years.

8.3 Solution

(a) Average sales in the three year period 20X0 – 20X2 were

$$\left(\frac{390+380+460}{3}\right) = \frac{1,230}{3} = 410$$

This average relates to the middle year of the period, 20X1.

(b) Similarly, average sales in the three year period 20X1 – 20X3 were

$$\left(\frac{380+460+450}{3}\right) = \frac{1,290}{3} = 430$$

This average relates to the middle year of the period, 20X2.

(c) The average sales can also be found for the periods 20X2 – 20X4, 20X3 – 20X5 and 20X4 – 20X6, to give the following.

Year	Sales	Moving total of 3 years' sales	Moving average of 3 year's sales (÷ 3)
20X0	390		
20X1	380	1,230	410
20X2	460	1,290	430
20X3	450	1,380	460
20X4	470	1,360	453
20X5	440	1,410	470
20X6	500		

Note the following points.

(i) The **moving average series has five figures** relating to the years from 20X1 to 20X5. The **original series had seven figures** for the years from 20X0 to 20X6.

(ii) There is an upward trend in sales, which is more noticeable from the series of moving averages than from the original series of actual sales each year.

EXAM FOCUS POINT

Do not rush headlong into averaging over a certain number of time periods in an exam, but over what period a moving average should be taken. The moving average which is most appropriate will depend on the circumstances and the nature of the time series.

- A moving average which takes an average of the results in many time periods will represent results over a longer term than a moving average of two or three periods.

- On the other hand, with a moving average of results in many time periods, the last figure in the series will be out of date by several periods. In the example above, the most recent average related to 20X5. With a moving average of five years' results, the final figure in the series would relate to 20X4.

- When there is a known cycle over which seasonal variations occur, such as all the days in the week or all the seasons in the year, the most suitable moving average would be one which covers one full cycle.

8.3.1 Moving averages of an even number of results

In the previous example, moving averages were taken of the results in an *odd* number of time periods, and the average then related to the mid-point of the overall period.

If a moving average were taken of results in an even number of time periods, the basic technique would be the same, but the mid-point of the overall period would not relate to a single period. For example, suppose an average were taken of the following four results.

Spring	120	
Summer	90	
Autumn	180	average 115
Winter	70	

The average would relate to the mid-point of the period, between summer and autumn.

The trend line average figures need to relate to a particular time period; otherwise, seasonal variations cannot be calculated. To overcome this difficulty, we **take a moving average of the moving average**. An example will illustrate this technique.

8.4 Example: moving averages over an even number of periods

Calculate a moving average trend line of the following results of Linden Ltd.

Year	Quarter	Volume of sales '000 units
20X5	1	600
	2	840
	3	420
	4	720
20X6	1	640
	2	860
	3	420
	4	740
20X7	1	670
	2	900
	3	430
	4	760

8.5 Solution

A moving average of four will be used, since the volume of sales would appear to depend on the season of the year, and each year has four quarterly results. The moving average of four does not relate to any specific period of time; therefore a second moving average of two will be calculated on the first moving average trend line.

Year	Quarter	Actual volume of sales '000 units (A)	Moving total of 4 quarters' sales '000 units (B)	Moving average of 4 quarters' sales '000 units (B ÷ 4)	Mid-point of 2 moving averages Trend line '000 units (C)
20X5	1	600			
	2	840			
	3	420	2,580	645.0	650.00
	4	720	2,620	655.0	657.50
20X6	1	640	2,640	660.0	660.00
	2	860	2,640	660.0	662.50
	3	420	2,660	665.0	668.75
	4	740	2,690	672.5	677.50
20X7	1	670	2,730	682.5	683.75
	2	900	2,740	685.0	687.50
	3	430	2,760	690.0	
	4	760			

By taking a mid point (a moving average of two) of the original moving averages, we can relate the results to specific quarters (from the third quarter of 20X5 to the second quarter of 20X7).

QUESTION

Trend in sales

What can you say about the trend in sales of Linden Ltd in Paragraph 8.5 above?

ANSWER

The trend in sales is upward.

8.6 Moving averages on graphs

One way of displaying the trend clearly is to show it by plotting the moving average on a graph.

8.7 Example: moving averages on graphs

Actual sales of Slap-It-On suntan lotion for 20X5 and 20X6 were as follows.

	Sales	
	$'000	$'000
	20X5	20X6
January	100	110
February	120	130
March	200	220
April	200	210
May	240	230
June	250	240
July	210	250
August	210	300
September	200	150
October	110	110
November	90	80
December	50	40
	1,980	2,070

Required

Calculate the trend in the suntan lotion sales and display it on a graph. (*Hint.* Calculate an annual moving total.)

8.8 Solution

20X6	Sales	Moving total	Moving average (trend)
	$'000	$'000	$'000
January	110	1,990	165.83
February	130	2,000	166.67
March	220	2,020	168.33
April	210	2,030	169.17
May	230	2,020	168.33
June	240	2,010	167.50
July	250	2,050	170.83
August	300	2,140	178.33
September	150	2,090	174.17
October	110	2,090	174.17
November	80	2,080	173.33
December	40	2,070	172.50

There is one very important point not immediately obvious from the above table, and that is to do with the time periods covered by the moving total and moving average.

(a)   The moving total, as we have seen, is the total for the previous twelve months. The figure of $1,990, for instance, represents total sales from February 20X5 to January 20X6.

(b)   The moving average is the average monthly sales over the previous twelve months. The figure of $165.83, for instance, represents average monthly sales for each month during the period February 20X5 to January 20X6.

When **plotting a moving average on a graph**, it is therefore important to remember that the **points should be located at the mid-point of the period to which they apply**. For example, the figure of $165.83 (moving average at end of January 20X6) relates to the 12 months ending January 20X6 and so it must be plotted in the *middle* of that period (31 July 20X5).

The moving data on suntan lotion sales could be drawn on a graph as follows.

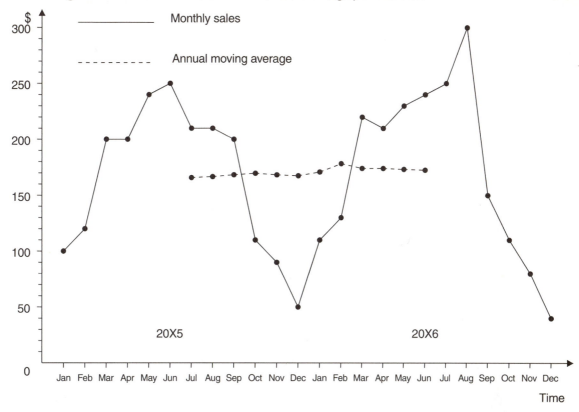

Points to note about this graph are as follows.

(a)   The annual moving average can only be plotted from July 20X5 to May 20X6 as we have no data prior to January 20X5 or after December 20X6.

(b)   The moving average has the effect of smoothing out the seasonal fluctuations in the ordinary sales graph (which is the reason why moving averages are used in the first place).

9   Finding the seasonal variations

Seasonal variations are the difference between actual and trend figures **(additive model).** An average of the seasonal variations for each time period within the cycle must be determined and then adjusted so that the total of the seasonal variations sums to zero.

Once a trend has been established, we can find the **seasonal variations**.

The actual and trend sales for Linden Ltd (as calculated in Paragraph 8.5) are set out below. The **difference between the actual results for any one quarter and the trend figure for that quarter** will be the seasonal variation for that quarter.

9.1 Additive model

Year	Quarter	Actual	Trend	Seasonal variation
20X5	1	600		
	2	840		
	3	420	650.00	–230.00
	4	720	657.50	62.50
20X6	1	640	660.00	–20.00
	2	860	662.50	197.50
	3	420	668.75	–248.75
	4	740	677.50	62.50
20X7	1	670	683.75	–13.75
	2	900	687.50	212.50
	3	430		
	4	760		

The variation between the actual result for any one particular quarter and the trend line average is not the same from year to year, but an **average of these variations can be taken**.

	Q_1	Q_2	Q_3	Q_4
20X5			–230.00	62.50
20X6	–20.00	197.50	–248.75	62.50
20X7	–13.75	212.50		
Total	–33.75	410.00	–478.75	125.00
Average (÷ 2)	–16.875	205.00	–239.375	62.50

Our estimate of the 'seasonal' or quarterly variation is almost complete, but there is one more important step to take. Variations around the basic trend line should cancel each other out, and add up to zero. At the moment, they do not. We therefore **spread the total of the variations** (11.25) **across the four quarters** (11.25 ÷ 4) **so that the final total of the variations sum to zero.**

	Q_1	Q_2	Q_3	Q_4	Total
Estimated quarterly variations	– 16.8750	205.0000	–239.3750	62.5000	11.250
Adjustment to reduce variations to 0	–2.8125	–2.8125	–2.8125	–2.8125	–11.250
Final estimates of quarterly variations	–19.6875	202.1875	–242.1875	59.6875	0
These might be rounded as follows	QI: –20,	QI: 202,	QI:-242,	QI: 60,	Total: 0

QUESTION

Additive model

The results of an additive time series model analysing production are shown below.

	Weekly production '000 units
Week 1	–4
Week 2	+5
Week 3	+9
Week 4	–6

Which of the following statements is/are true in relation to the data shown in the table above?

I   Production is on average 9,000 units above the trend in week 3.
II   Production is on average 4% below the trend in week 1.
III   Production is on average 5% above the trend in week 2.
IV   Production in week 4 is typically 6% below the trend.

A   I only
B   I and II only
C   I and III only
D   II and IV only

ANSWER

A   I   With an additive model, the weekly component represents the average value of actual production minus the trend for that week, so a component of +9 means production is 9,000 units above the trend.

This is the only correct statement.

If you selected option B, C or D, you have confused the additive variation of –4, +5 and –6 (actually –4,000 units, +5,000 units and –6,000 units respectively) with the multiplicative variation of –4%, +5% and –6% respectively. Multiplicative variations are covered later in this chapter.

EXAM FOCUS POINT

The examiner is unlikely to ask you to derive the seasonal variations in a time series, but it is important that you have a good understanding of how to do it.

9.2 A weakness in moving average analysis

The moving average calculations described so far in this chapter are based on an **additive model** which means that we add the values for a number of periods and take the average of those values.

An additive model has the important **drawback** that when there is a **steeply rising or a steeply declining trend, the moving average trend will either get ahead of or fall behind the real trend.**

9.3 Examples

Suppose that we were to take a three-period moving average of the following sales figures.

	Actual sales $'000	Three- year moving total $'000	Moving average $'000
20X1	1,000		
20X2	1,200	3,700	1,233
20X3	1,500	4,800	1,600
20X4	2,100	6,600	2,200
20X5	3,000	9,300	3,100
20X6	4,200	12,900	4,300
20X7	5,700	18,000	6,000
20X8	8,100		

In this example sales are on a steeply rising trend, which means that the moving average value for each year consistently overstates sales because it is partly influenced by the value of sales in the next year. The moving average value for 20X7, for example, is $6,000, which is $300 above actual sales for 20X7. This is because the moving average is partly based on the higher sales value in 20X8. The consequences are as follows.

(a)   The trend sales is not a good representation of actual sales.
(b)   The trend will probably be unsuitable for forecasting.

9.4 Seasonal variations using the multiplicative model

The method of estimating the seasonal variations in the above example was to use the differences between the trend and actual data. This model **assumes that the components of the series are independent** of each other, so that an increasing trend does not affect the seasonal variations and make them increase as well, for example.

The alternative is to use the **multiplicative model** whereby each actual figure is expressed as a proportion of the trend.

It may be easier to understand this model if we state this as an equation. The example below uses the equation to calculate the seasonal variation.

KEY TERM

The **proportional (multiplicative) model** summarises a time series as Y = T × S × R (or Y = T*S*R).

The **trend component** will be the **same whichever model is used** but the values of the **seasonal and random components** will **vary according to the model being applied**. In our examples, we assume that the random component is small and so can be ignored for our purposes. So the multiplicative model will be Y = T × S.

Refer back to our example, Linden Ltd taking the first two years of data only. We can use the equation here to work out the seasonal variations. The trend is calculated in exactly the same way as before. So if Y = T × S then S = Y/T and we can calculate **S = Y/T** for the multiplicative model.

Year	Quarter	Actual (Y)	Trend (T)	Seasonal percentage (Y/T)
20X5	1	600		
	2	840		
	3	420	650.00	0.646
	4	720	657.50	1.095
20X6	1	640	660.00	0.970
	2	860	662.50	1.298
	3	420		
	4	740		

Suppose that seasonal variations for the next four quarters are 0.628, 1.092, 0.980 and 1.309 respectively. The summary of the seasonal variations expressed in proportional terms is therefore as follows.

Year	Q_1 %	Q_2 %	Q_3 %	Q_4 %
20X5			0.646	1.095
20X6	0.970	1.298	0.628	1.092
20X7	0.980	1.309		
Total	1.950	2.607	1.274	2.187
Average	0.975	1.3035	0.637	1.0935

Instead of summing to zero, as **with the additive approach**, the **averages should sum (in this case) to 4.0, 1.0 for each of the four quarters.** They actually sum to 4.009 so 0.00225 has to be deducted from each one.

	Q_1	Q_2	Q_3	Q_4
Average	0.97500	1.30350	0.63700	1.09350
Adjustment	−0.00225	−0.00225	−0.00225	−0.00225
Final estimate	0.97275	1.30125	0.63475	1.09125
Rounded	0.97	1.30	0.64	1.09

Note that the **proportional model is better than the additive model when the trend is increasing or decreasing over time**. In such circumstances, seasonal variations are likely to be increasing or decreasing too. The additive model simply adds absolute and unchanging seasonal variations to the trend figures whereas the proportional model, by multiplying increasing or decreasing trend values by a constant seasonal variation factor, takes account of changing seasonal variations.

10 Deseasonalisation

Deseasonalised data are often used by economic commentators.

Economic statistics, such as unemployment figures, are often in 'seasonally adjusted' or 'deseasonalised' so as to ensure that the overall trend (rising, falling or stationary) is clear. All this means is that **seasonal** variations (derived from previous data) have been **taken out, to leave a figure which might be taken as indicating the trend.**

10.1 Example: deseasonalisation

Actual sales figures for four quarters, together with appropriate seasonal adjustment factors derived from previous data, are as follows.

Quarter	Actual sales $'000	Seasonal adjustments $'000
1	150	+3
2	160	+4
3	164	−2
4	170	−5

Required

Deseasonalise these data.

10.2 Solution

We are reversing the normal process of applying seasonal variations to trend figures, so **we subtract positive seasonal variations (and add negative ones).**

Quarter	Actual sales $'000	Deseasonalised sales $'000
1	150	147
2	160	156
3	164	166
4	170	175

11 Sales forecasting: time series analysis

Forecasting using time series analysis involves calculating a trend line, extrapolating the trend line and adjusting the forecasts by appropriate seasonal variations. The trend line can be extrapolated by eye or by using a common sense 'rule-of-thumb' approach.

The main idea behind time series analysis is the identification of the trend in the data and its separation from seasonal variations. Once that has been done forecasts of future values can be made as follows. Please note that you will not be asked to derive seasonal variations in a time series analysis. The information and inclusion in the following example are for completeness only

(a) **The trend line should be calculated.**

(b) **The trend line should be used to forecast future trend line values.**

(c) **These values should be adjusted by the average seasonal variation applicable to the future period, to determine the forecast for the period.**

Extending a trend line outside the range of known data, in this case forecasting the future from a trend line based on historical data, is known as **extrapolation**.

There are **two principal methods of calculating the forecast trend line.**

11.1 Inspection

The **trend line can be drawn by 'eye'** on a graph in such a way that it appears to lie evenly between the recorded points. **Forecasts can then be read off of an extrapolated trend line.**

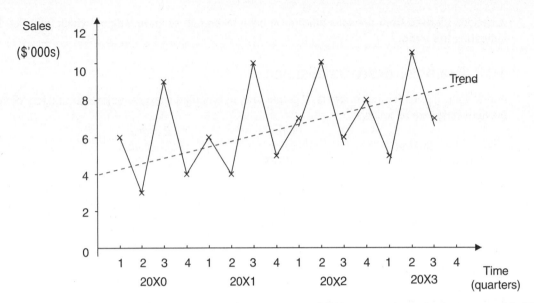

In the diagram above, for example, the trend for sales in 20X3 quarter 4 can be forecast as $9,000 by reading from the 'guessed' trend line. It could then be adjusted by the appropriate seasonal variation to determine the actual forecast.

11.2 Common sense 'rule-of-thumb' approach

This method is simply to **guess what future movements in the trend line might be, based on movements in the past**. It is not a mathematical technique, merely a common sense, rule-of-thumb approach. See if you can produce your own solution to the following problem.

11.3 Example: forecasting by rough approximation

The sales (in $'000) of swimwear by a large department store for each period of three months are as follows.

Quarter	20X4 $'000	20X5 $'000	20X6 $'000	20X7 $'000
First		8	20	40
Second		30	50	62
Third		60	80	92
Fourth	24	20	40	

Required

(a)   Using an additive model, find the centred moving average trend.
(b)   Find the average seasonal variation for each quarter.
(c)   Predict sales for the last quarter of 20X7 and the first quarter of 20X8, stating any assumptions.

11.4 Solution

	Quarter	4 quarter moving total	Centred moving total	Moving average(÷4)
20X4	4			
20X5	1			
	2	122	120	30
	3	118	124	31
	4	130	140	35
20X6	1	150	160	40
	2	170	180	45
	3	190	200	50
	4	210	216	54
20X7	1	222	228	57
	2	234		
	3			

(a)   The centred moving average trend is shown in the right hand column of the table.

(b)   *Seasonal variations*

		Quarter				
		1	2	3	4	Total
Year	20X5		0.00	+29.00	−15.00	
	20X6	−20.00	+5.00	+30.00	−14.00	
	20X7	−17.00				
Total		−37.00	+5.00	+59.00	−29.00	
Average		−18.50	+2.50	+29.50	−14.50	−1
Adjust total variation to nil		+0.25	+0.25	+0.25	+0.25	+1
Average seasonal variation		−18.25	+2.75	+29.75	−14.25	

(c)   We might guess that the trend line is rising steadily, by (57 − 40)/4 = 4.25 per quarter in the period 1st quarter 20X6 to 1st quarter 20X7 (57 being the prediction in 1st quarter 20X7 and 40 the prediction in 1st quarter 20X6).

Since the trend may be levelling off a little, a quarterly increase of +4 in the trend will be assumed.

		Trend	Seasonal variation	Forecast
1st quarter	20X7	57		
4th quarter	20X7 (+ (3 × 4))	69	−14.25	54.75
1st quarter	20X8 (+ (4 × 4))	73	−18.25	54.75

Rounding to the nearest thousand dollars, the forecast sales are $55,000 for each of the two quarters.

QUESTION

Forecast sales

Sales of product X each quarter for the last three years have been as follows (in thousands of units). Trend values, found by a moving averages method, are shown in brackets.

Year	1st quarter	2nd quarter	3rd quarter	4th quarter
1	18	30	20 (18.75)	6 (19.375)
2	20 (20)	33 (20.5)	22 (21)	8 (21.5)
3	22 (22.125)	35 (22.75)	25	10

Average seasonal variations for quarters 1 to 4 are −0.1, +12.4, +1.1 and −13.4 respectively.

Required

Use the trend line and estimates of seasonal variations to forecast sales in each quarter of year 4.

ANSWER

The trend line indicates an increase of about 0.6 per quarter. This can be confirmed by calculating the average quarterly increase in trend line values between the third quarter of year 1 (18.75) and the second quarter of year 3 (22.75). The average rise is

$$\frac{22.75-18.75}{7} = \frac{4}{7} = 0.57, \text{ say } 0.6$$

Taking 0.6 as the quarterly increase in the trend, the forecast of sales for year 4, before seasonal adjustments (the trend line forecast) would be as follows.

Year	Quarter			Trend line
3	*2nd	(actual trend)	22.75, say	22.8
	3rd			23.4
	4th			24.0
4	1st			24.6
	2nd			25.2
	3rd			25.8
	4th			26.4

* last known trend line value.

(Note that you could actually plot the trend line figures on a graph, extrapolate the trend line into the future and read off forecasts from the graph using the extrapolated trend line.)

Seasonal variations should now be incorporated to obtain the final forecast.

	Quarter	Trend line forecast '000 units	Average seasonal variation '000 units	Forecast of actual sales '000 units
Year 4	1st	24.6	−0.1	24.5
	2nd	25.2	+12.4	37.6
	3rd	25.8	+ 1.1	26.9
	4th	26.4	−13.4	13.0

12 Forecasting problems

In summary, time series can be rather simplistic as it assumes past trends will continue indefinitely.

There are a number of changes that also may make it **difficult to forecast** future events.

Type of change	Examples
Political and economic changes	Create uncertainty. For example changes in interest rates, exchange rates or inflation can mean that future sales and costs are difficult to forecast.
Environmental changes	For example the opening of the channel tunnel might have a considerable impact on some companies' markets.
Technological changes	May mean that the past is not a reliable indication of likely future events. For example the availability of faster machinery may make it difficult to use current output levels as the basis for forecasting future production output.
Technological advances	Can also change the nature of production. The advent of advanced manufacturing technology is changing the cost structure of many firms. Direct labour costs are reducing in significance and fixed manufacturing costs are increasing. This causes forecasting difficulties because of the resulting changes in cost behaviour patterns, breakeven points and so on.

BPP
LEARNING MEDIA

Type of change	Examples
Social changes	Alterations in taste and fashion and changes in the social acceptability of different products can cause difficulties in forecasting future sales levels. For example tobacco.

13 Using index numbers

An index is a measure, over time, of the average changes in the value (price or quantity) of a group of items relative to the situation at some period in the past.

- **Composite indices** cover more than one item.

- **Weighting** is used to reflect the importance of each item in the index.

- **Weighted aggregate indices** are found by applying weights and then calculating the index.

- There are two types of weighted aggregate index, the **Laspeyre** (which uses quantities/prices from the base period as the weights) and the **Paasche** (which uses quantities/prices from the current period as weights).

- **Fisher's ideal index** is the geometric mean of the Laspeyre and Paasche indices.

- Index numbers are a very useful way of summarising a large amount of data in a single series of numbers. You should remember, however, that any summary hides some detail and that index numbers should therefore be interpreted with caution.

Index numbers provide a standardised way of comparing the values, over time, of prices, wages, volume of output and so on. They are used extensively in business, government and commerce. No doubt you will be aware of some index numbers – for example, the RPI and the Financial Times All Share Index. This section will explain how to construct indices and will look at associated issues such as their limitations.

An index is a measure, over time, of the average changes in the values (prices or quantities) of a group of items. An index comprises a series of index numbers. Although it is possible to prepare an index for a single item, for example the price of an ounce of gold, such an index would probably be unnecessary. It is only when there is a group of items that a simple list of changes in their values over time becomes rather hard to interpret, and an index provides a useful single measure of comparison.

13.1 Price indices and quantity indices

An index may be a price index or a quantity index.

(a) **A price index measures the change in the money value of a group of items over time**. Perhaps the best known price index in the UK is the Retail Prices Index (RPI) which measures changes in the costs of items of expenditure of the average household.

(b) **A quantity index** (also called a volume index) **measures the change in the non-monetary values of a group of items over time**. An example is a productivity index, which measures changes in the productivity of various departments or groups of workers.

When **one commodity** only is under consideration, we have the following formulae.

(a) **Price index** $= \dfrac{P_n}{P_0} \times 100$

where P_n is the price for the period under consideration and P_0 is the price for the base period.

(b) **Quantity index** $= \dfrac{Q_n}{Q_0} \times 100$

where Q_n is the quantity for the period under consideration and Q_0 is the quantity for the base period.

13.2 Example: single-item indices

If the price of a cup of coffee was 40c in 20X0, 50c in 20X1 and 76c in 20X2, then using 20X0 as a base year the price index numbers for 20X1 and 20X2 would be as follows.

$$20X1 \text{ price index} = \frac{50}{40} \times 100 = 125$$

$$20X2 \text{ price index} = \frac{76}{40} \times 100 = 190$$

If the number of cups of coffee sold in 20X0 was 500,000, in 20X1 700,000 and in 20X2 600,000, then using 20X0 as a base year, the quantity index numbers for 20X1 and 20X2 would be as follows.

$$20X1 \text{ quantity index} = \frac{700,000}{500,000} \times 100 = 140$$

$$20X2 \text{ quantity index} = \frac{600,000}{500,000} \times 100 = 120$$

Given the values of some commodity over time (a time series), there are two ways in which index relatives can be calculated.

In the **fixed base method**, a base year is selected (index 100), and all subsequent changes are measured against this base. Such an approach should only be used if the basic nature of the commodity is unchanged over time.

In the **chain base method**, changes are calculated with respect to the value of the commodity in the period immediately before. This approach can be used for any set of commodity values but must be used if the basic nature of the commodity is changing over time.

13.3 Example: fixed base and chain base methods

The price of commodity was $2.70 in 20X0, $3.11 in 20X1, $3.42 in 20X2 and $3.83 in 20X3. Construct both a chain base index and a fixed base index for the years 20X0 to 20X3 using 20X0 as the base year.

13.4 Solution

Chain base index	20X0	100	
	20X1	115	(3.11/2.70 × 100)
	20X2	110	(3.42/3.11 × 100)
	20X3	112	(3.83/3.42 × 100)

Fixed base index	20X0	100	
	20X1	115	
	20X2	127	(3.42/2.70 × 100)
	20X3	142	(3.83/2.70 × 100)

The chain base relatives show the rate of change in prices from year to year, whereas the fixed base relatives show changes relative to prices in the base year.

13.5 Composite index numbers

Most practical indices cover more than one item and are hence termed **composite index numbers**. The RPI, for example, considers components such as food, alcoholic drink, tobacco and housing. An index of motor car costs might consider components such as finance payments, service costs, repairs, insurance and so on.

Suppose that the cost of living index is calculated from only three commodities: bread, tea and caviar, and that the prices for 20X1 and 20X2 were as follows.

	20X1	20X2
Bread	20c a loaf	40c a loaf
Tea	25c a packet	30c a packet
Caviar	450c a jar	405c a jar

A simple index could be calculated by adding the prices for single items in 20X2 and dividing by the corresponding sum relating to 20X1 (if 20X1 is the base year). In general, if the sum of the prices in the base year is ΣP_0 and the sum of the prices in the new year is ΣP_n, the index is $\frac{\Sigma P_n}{\Sigma P_0} \times 100$. The index, known as a **simple aggregate price index** would therefore be calculated as follows.

	P_0 20X1 $\$$	P_n 20X2 $\$$
Bread	0.20	0.40
Tea	0.25	0.30
Caviar	4.50	4.05
	$\Sigma P_0 = 4.95$	$\Sigma P_n = 4.75$

Year	$\Sigma P_n / \Sigma P_0$	Simple aggregate price index
20X1	$4.95/4.95 = 1.00$	100
20X2	$4.75/4.95 = 0.96$	96

This type of index has a number of disadvantages. It ignores the amounts of bread, tea and caviar consumed (and hence the **importance** of each item), and the units to which the prices refer. If, for example, we had been given the price of a cup of tea rather than a packet of tea, the index would have been different.

To overcome these problems we can use **weighting**. A weighting factor can be thought of as an **indicator of the importance of the component** (such as alcohol in the RPI) with respect to the type of index being calculated.

13.6 Weighted aggregate indices

This method of weighting involves multiplying each component value by its corresponding weight and adding these products to form an aggregate. This is done for both the base period and the period in question. The aggregate for the period under consideration is then divided by the base period aggregate.

The general form of a **weighted aggregate index** is

$\frac{\Sigma wv_n}{\Sigma wv_0}$ where w is the weighting factor

v_0 is the value of the commodity in the base period
v_n is the value of the commodity in the period in question

Price indices are usually weighted by quantities and quantity indices are usually weighted by prices.

QUESTION   Weighted aggregate indexes

What are the formulae for calculating price and quantity weighted aggregate indices if base year weights are used?

ANSWER

Price index: $\dfrac{\Sigma Q_0 P_n}{\Sigma Q_0 P_0} \times 100$

where P_0 represents the prices of items in the base year

P_n represents the prices of items in the new year

Q_0 represents the quantities of the items consumed in the base year

Quantity index: $\dfrac{\Sigma P_0 Q_n}{\Sigma P_0 Q_0} \times 100$

where Q_0 represents the quantities consumed in the base year
$\quad\quad\;\; Q_n$ represents the quantities consumed in the new year
$\quad\quad\;\; P_0$ represents the prices in the base year

13.7 Example: a price index

In the previous example of the cost of living index (Paragraph 9.5), the 20X2 index value could have been calculated as follows, assuming the quantities purchased by each household were as given below.

Item	Quantity Q_0	Price in 20X1 P_0	$P_0 Q_0$	Price in 20X2 P_n	$P_n Q_0$
Bread	6	20	120	40	240
Tea	2	25	50	30	60
Caviar	0.067	450	30	405	27
			200		327

Index in 20X2 $= \dfrac{327}{200} \times 100 = 163.5$

We will now look at an example of a **quantity index**, which measures **changes in quantities** and uses **prices as weights**.

13.8 Example: a quantity index

The Falldown Construction Company uses four items of materials and components in a standard production job.

In 20X0 the quantities of each material or component used per job and their cost were as follows.

	Quantity Units	Price per unit $
Material A	20	2
Material B	5	10
Component C	40	3
Component D	15	6

In 20X2 the quantities of materials and components used per job were as follows.

	Quantity Units
Material A	15
Material B	6
Component C	36
Component D	25

Using 20X0 as a base year, calculate the quantity index value in 20X2 for the amount of materials used in a standard job.

13.9 Solution

	Price P_0	Quantity used in 20X0 Q_0	P_0Q_0 ($)	Quantity used in 20X2 Q_n	P_0Q_n ($)
Material A	$2	20	40	15	30
Material B	$10	5	50	6	60
Component C	$3	40	120	36	108
Component D	$6	15	90	25	150
			300		348

$$\text{Quantity index} = \frac{348}{300} \times 100 = 116$$

This would suggest that the company is using 16% more materials in 20X2 than in 20X0 on a standard job.

13.10 Laspeyre, Paasche and Fisher indices

Laspeyre and Paasche indices are special cases of weighted aggregate indices.

13.11 Laspeyre indices

Laspeyre indices use weights from the base period and are therefore sometimes called base weighted indices.

13.11.1 Laspeyre price index

A **Laspeyre price index** uses **quantities** consumed in the base period as weights. In the notation already used it can be expressed as follows.

$$\textbf{Laspeyre price index} = \frac{\sum P_n Q_o}{\sum P_o Q_o} \times 100$$

13.11.2 Laspeyre quantity index

A **Laspeyre quantity index** uses **prices** from the base period as weights and can be expressed as follows.

$$\textbf{Laspeyre quantity index} = \frac{\sum P_o Q_n}{\sum P_o Q_o} \times 100$$

13.12 Paasche indices

Paasche indices use **current time period weights**. In other words the weights are changed every time period.

13.12.1 Paasche price index

A **Paasche price index** uses **quantities** consumed in the current period as weights and can be expressed as follows.

$$\textbf{Paasche price index} = \frac{\sum P_n Q_n}{\sum P_o Q_n} \times 100$$

13.12.2 Paasche quantity index

A **Paasche quantity index** uses **prices** from the current period as weights and can be expressed as follows.

Paasche quantity index $= \dfrac{\Sigma P_n Q_n}{\Sigma P_n Q_o} \times 100$

13.13 Example: Laspeyre and Paasche price indices

The wholesale price index in Ruritania is made up from the prices of five items. The price of each item, and the average quantities purchased by manufacturing and other companies each week were as follows, in 20X0 and 20X2.

Item	Quantity 20X0 '000 units	Price per unit 20X0 Roubles	Quantity 20X2 '000 units	Price per unit 20X2 Roubles
P	60	3	80	4
Q	30	6	40	5
R	40	5	20	8
S	100	2	150	2
T	20	7	10	10

Required

Calculate the price index in 20X2, if 20X0 is taken as the base year, using the following.

(a)   A Laspeyre index
(b)   A Paasche index

13.14 Solution

Item	Q_o	P_o	Q_n	P_n	Laspeyre P_oQ_o	P_nQ_o	Paasche P_nQ_n	P_oQ_n
P	60	3	80	4	180	240	320	240
Q	30	6	40	5	180	150	200	240
R	40	5	20	8	200	320	160	100
S	100	2	150	2	200	200	300	300
T	20	7	10	10	140	200	100	70
					900	1,110	1,080	950

20X2 index numbers are as follows.

(a)   Laspeyre index $= \quad 100 \times \dfrac{1,110}{900} = 123.3$

(b)   Paasche index $= \quad 100 \times \dfrac{1,080}{950} = 113.7$

The Paasche index for 20X2 reflects the decline in consumption of the relatively expensive items R and T since 20X0. The Laspeyre index for 20X2 fails to reflect this change.

QUESTION

Indexes

A baker has listed the ingredients he used and their prices, in 20X3 and 20X4, as follows.

	Kgs used 20X3 '000s	Price per kg 20X3 $	Kgs used 20X4 '000s	Price per kg 20X4 $
Milk	3	1.20	4	1.50
Eggs	6	0.95	5	0.98
Flour	1	1.40	2	1.30
Sugar	4	1.10	3	1.14

Required

Calculate the following quantity indices for 20X4 (with 20X3 as the base year).

(a)   A Laspeyre index
(b)   A Paasche index

ANSWER

Workings

	Q_o	P_o	Q_n	P_n	Laspeyre P_oQ_o	Laspeyre P_oQ_n	Paasche P_nQ_n	Paasche P_nQ_o
Milk	3	1.20	4	1.50	3.60	4.80	6.00	4.50
Eggs	6	0.95	5	0.98	5.70	4.75	4.90	5.88
Flour	1	1.40	2	1.30	1.40	2.80	2.60	1.30
Sugar	4	1.10	3	1.14	4.40	3.30	3.42	4.56
					15.10	15.65	16.92	16.24

Quantity index numbers for 20X4 are as follows.

(a) **Laspeyre method** $= 100 \times \dfrac{15.65}{15.10} = 103.64$

(b) **Paasche method** $= 100 \times \dfrac{16.92}{16.24} = 104.19$

13.15 Which to use – Paasche or Laspeyre ?

Both patterns of consumption and prices change and a decision therefore has to be made as to whether a Paasche or a Laspeyre index should be used.

The following points should be considered when deciding which type of index to use.

(a) A **Paasche index requires quantities to be ascertained each year**. A Laspeyre index only requires them for the base year. Constructing a Paasche index may therefore be costly.

(b) For the **Paasche index the denominator has to be recalculated each year** because the quantities/prices must be changed to current year consumption/price levels.

For the **Laspeyre index, the denominator is fixed**. The Laspeyre index can therefore be calculated as soon as current prices/quantities are known. The Paasche index, on the other hand, cannot be calculated until the end of a period, when information about current quantities/prices becomes available.

(c) The denominator of a Laspeyre index is fixed and therefore the Laspeyre index numbers for several different years can be **directly compared**. With the Paasche index, on the other hand, comparisons can only be drawn directly between the current year and the base year (although indirect comparisons can be made).

(d) The weights for a Laspeyre index become **out of date**, whereas those for the Paasche index are updated each year.

(e) A **Laspeyre price index** implicitly assumes that, whatever the price changes, the quantities purchased will remain the same. In terms of economic theory, no substitution of cheaper alternative goods and services is allowed to take place. Even if goods become relatively more expensive, it assumes that the same quantities are bought. As a result, the **index tends to overstate inflation**.

(f) The effect of current year weighting when using the Paasche price index means that greater importance is placed on goods that are relatively cheaper now than they were in the base year. As a consequence, the **Paasche price index** tends to **understate inflation**.

In practice, it is common to use a Laspeyre index and revise the weights every few years. (Where appropriate, a new base year may be created when the weights are changed.)

13.16 Fisher's ideal index

Because Laspeyre's index uses base period weights it tends to overstate any change in prices or quantities. When prices increase there is usually a reduction in the quantities consumed. The index numerator is therefore likely to be too large. Likewise, when prices decrease, quantities consumed increase, resulting in an under-weighting of those prices which have decreased and hence an overstatement of change. The Paasche index, on the other hand, tends to understate change.

To overcome these difficulties some statisticians prefer to use **Fisher's ideal index**. This index is found by taking the **geometric mean of the Laspeyre index and the Paasche index**.

Fisher's ideal index = √(Laspeyre × Paasche)

QUESTION
Fisher's index

The Laspeyre index of retail prices for 20X7 (with a base year of 20X1) is 137.2. The corresponding Paasche index is 134.9.

Required

Calculate Fisher's ideal index.

ANSWER

√(137.2 × 134.9) = 136.0

13.17 What items to include

The purpose to which the index is to be put must be carefully considered. Once this has been done, the items selected must be as **representative** as possible, taking into account this purpose. Care must be taken to ensure that the items are **unambiguously defined** and that their values are **readily ascertainable**.

For some indices, the choice of items might be relatively straightforward. For example, the **FT Actuaries All-Share Index**, compiled jointly by the Financial Times, the Institute of Actuaries and the Faculty of Actuaries, is made up of the share prices of approximately 800 companies quoted on The Inventory Exchange. The weights are based on the market capitalisations of the companies (the number of shares in issue multiplied by their market value).

For other indices, the choice of items will be more difficult. The Retail Prices Index is an excellent example of the problem. It would be impossible to include all items of domestic spending and a selective, **representative basket of goods** and services must be found, ranging from spending on mortgages and rents, to cars, public transport, food and drink, electricity, gas, telephone, clothing, leisure activities and so on.

13.18 Collecting the data

Data are required to determine the following.

(a)   The values for each item
(b)   The weight that will be attached to each item

Consider as an example a **cost of living index**. The prices of a particular commodity will vary from place to place, from shop to shop and from type to type. Also the price will vary during the period under consideration. The actual prices used must obviously be some sort of **average**. The way in which the average is to be obtained should be clearly defined at the outset.

When constructing a price index, it is common practice to use the **quantities consumed** as **weights**; similarly, when constructing a quantity index, the **prices** may be used as **weights**. Care must be taken in selecting the basis for the weighting. For example, in a cost of living index, it may be decided to use the consumption of a typical family as the weights, but some difficulty may be encountered in defining a typical family.

13.19 The choice of a base year

The **choice of a base date**, or base year is not significant, except that it should be **representative**. In the construction of a price index, the base year must not be one in which there were abnormally high or low

prices for any items in the basket of goods making up the index. For example, a year in which there is a potato famine would be unsuitable as a base period for the Retail Prices Index.

13.20 The limitations and misinterpretation of index numbers

13.20.1 Limitations

Index numbers are usually only **approximations** of changes in price or quantity over time, and must be interpreted with care.

(a) As we have seen, weightings become **out of date over time**. Unless a Paasche index is used, the weightings will gradually cease to reflect current reality.

(b) **New products or items may appear, and old ones may cease to be significant**. For example, spending has changed in recent years, to include new items such as personal computers and video recorders, whereas the demand for twin tub washing machines has declined. These changes would make the weightings of a price index for such goods out of date.

(c) **The data used to calculate index numbers might be incomplete, out of date, or inaccurate**. For example, the quantity indices of imports and exports are based on records supplied by traders which may be prone to error or even deliberate falsification.

(d) **The base year of an index should be a normal year**, but there is probably no such thing as a perfectly normal year. Some error in the index will be caused by atypical values in the base period.

(e) The '**basket of items**' in an index is often **selective**. For example, the Retail Prices Index (RPI) is constructed from a sample of households and from a basket of less than 400 items.

(f) A **national index** may not be very relevant to an individual town or region. For example, if the national index of wages and salaries rises from 100 to 115, we cannot conclude that the wages and salaries of people in, say, Glasgow, have gone up by 15%.

(g) An index may **exclude important items**: for example, the RPI excludes payments of income tax out of gross wages.

13.20.2 Misinterpretation

You must be careful not to misinterpret index numbers. Several possible mistakes will be explained using the following example of a retail prices index.

	20X0		20X1		20X2
January	340.0	January	360.6	January	436.3
		February	362.5	February	437.1
		March	366.2	March	439.5
		April	370.0	April	442.1

(a) It would be wrong to say that prices rose by 2.6% between March and April 20X2. It is correct to say that prices rose 2.6 points, or

$$\frac{2.6}{439.5} = 0.6\%$$

(b) It would be correct to say that the annual rate of price increases (the rate of inflation) fell between March and April 20X2. It would be a mistake, however, to suppose that a fall in the rate of inflation means that prices are falling, therefore the price index is falling.

The rate of price increases has **slowed down**, but the trend of prices is still **upwards.**

(i) The annual rate of inflation from March 20X1 to March 20X2 is

$$\left(\frac{439.5 - 366.2}{366.2}\right) = 20\%$$

(ii) The annual rate of inflation from April 20X1 to April 20X2 is

$$\left(\frac{442.1 - 370.0}{370.0} \right) = 19.5\%$$

Thus the annual rate of inflation has dropped from 20% to 19.5% between March and April 20X2, even though prices went up in the month between March and April 20X2 by 0.6%. (The price increase between March and April 20X1 was over 1%. This is included in the calculation of the rate of inflation between March 20X1 and March 20X2, but is excluded in the comparison between April 20X1 and April 20X2 where it has been replaced by the lower price increase, 0.6%, between March and April 20X2.)

13.21 The Retail Prices Index (RPI) and Consumer Prices Index (CPI)

The Retail Prices Index measures the change in the cost of living. It is published monthly (on a Tuesday) near the middle of the month by the Office for National Statistics online. Since it measures the monthly change in the cost of living its principal use is as a **measure of inflation**.

The index measures the percentage changes, month by month, in the **average level of prices of 'a representative basket of goods'** purchased by the great majority of households in the United Kingdom. There are over 650 separate representative items that go to make up the RPI. It takes account of practically all wage earners and most small and medium salary earners.

In recent years, the Government has chosen to use the **Consumer Prices Index (CPI)** as the main measure of UK inflation for macroeconomic purposes. Thus the CPI is the basis for the government's inflation target: it is also used to make international comparisons.

The two main differences between the RPI and CPI are the exclusion of spending on many housing costs from the CPI and the inclusion of financial services in the CPI. Also, the CPI is calculated using a wider population and uses different mathematical formulae.

The **Family Expenditure Survey** is a continuing enquiry conducted by the Office for National Statistics into the general characteristics of households, their income and their expenditures. From this information the representative basket of goods is **divided into main groups**. Each group is divided into sections and these sections may be further split into separate items. Each group, section and specific item is weighted according to information from the Family Expenditure Survey to account for its relative importance in the basket.

14 Sales forecasting: the product life cycle

The product life cycle model shows how sales of a product can be expected to vary with the passage of time.

A product will probably go through the stages of introduction, growth, maturity, decline and senility. Different levels of sales and profit can be expected at each stage. Note that the product life cycle is a **model** of what **might** happen, **not a law** prescribing what **will** happen. In other words, not all products go through these stages or even have a life cycle. However, the idea of a life cycle can be useful to experienced marketing staff when forecasting sales and profits.

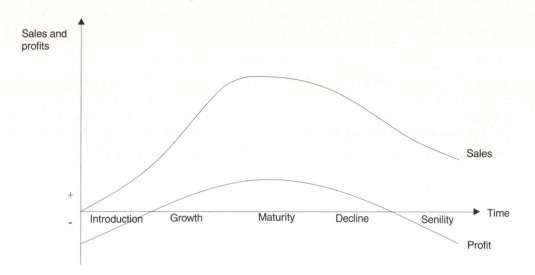

14.1 Introduction

(a)   A new product takes time to find acceptance by would-be purchasers and there is a slow growth in sales. Unit costs are high because of low output and expensive sales promotion.

(b)   The product for the time being is a loss-maker.

14.2 Growth

(a)   If the new product gains market acceptance, sales will eventually rise more sharply and the product will start to make profits.

(b)   As sales and production rise, unit costs fall.

14.3 Maturity

The rate of sales growth slows down and the product reaches a period of maturity which is probably the longest period of a successful product's life. Most products on the market will be at the mature stage of their life. Profits are good.

14.4 Decline

Eventually, sales will begin to decline so that there is over-capacity of production in the industry. Severe competition occurs, profits fall and some producers leave the market. The remaining producers seek means of prolonging the product life by modifying it and searching for new market segments. Many producers are reluctant to leave the market, although some inevitably do because of falling profits.

Remember. It would be very foolish for a forecaster to assume that linear growth in sales will go on forever. Eventually sales will begin to decline.

↳ Two variables are said to be correlated if a change in the value of one variable is accompanied by a change in the value of another variable. This is what is meant by **correlation**.

↳ Two variables might be **perfectly correlated, partly correlated** or **uncorrelated**. Correlation can be **positive** or **negative**

↳ The degree of linear correlation between two variables is measured by the **Pearsonian** (product moment) **correlation coefficient, r**. The nearer r is to $+1$ or -1, the stronger the relationship.

↳ The **coefficient of determination**, r^2 (alternatively R^2) measures the proportion of the total variation in the value of one variable that can be explained by variations in the value of the other variable. It denotes the strength of the **linear** association between two variables.

↳ **Linear regression analysis** (the **least squares method**) is one technique for estimating a line of best fit. Once an equation for a line of best fit has been determined, forecasts can be made.

↳ As with all forecasting techniques, the results from regression analysis will not be wholly reliable. There are a number of factors which affect the reliability of forecasts made using regression analysis.

↳ The high-low method is a simple forecasting technique.

↳ A **time series** is a series of figures or values recorded over time.

↳ There are four components of a time series: **trend, seasonal variations, cyclical variations** and **random variations**.

↳ One method of finding the trend is by the use of **moving averages**. Remember that when finding the moving average of an even number of results, a second moving average has to be calculated so that trend values can relate to specific actual figures.

↳ Seasonal variations are the difference between actual and trend figures **(additive model).** An average of the seasonal variations for each time period within the cycle must be determined and then adjusted so that the total of the seasonal variations sums to zero.

↳ **Deseasonalised data** are often used by economic commentators.

↳ Forecasting using time series analysis involves calculating a trend line, extrapolating the trend line and adjusting the forecasts by appropriate seasonal variations. The trend line can be extrapolated by eye or by using a common sense 'rule-of-thumb' approach.

↳ All forecasts are subject to error, but the likely errors vary from case to case.

↳ An index is a measure, over time, of the average changes in the value (price or quantity) of a group of items relative to the situation at some period in the past.

↳ **Composite indices** cover more than one item.

↳ **Weighting** is used to reflect the importance of each item in the index.

↳ **Weighted aggregate indices** are found by applying weights and then calculating the index.

↳ There are two types of weighted aggregate index, the **Laspeyre** (which uses quantities/prices from the base period as the weights) and the **Paasche** (which uses quantities/prices from the current period as weights).

↳ **Fisher's ideal index** is the geometric mean of the Laspeyre and Paasche indices.

↳ Index numbers are a very useful way of summarising a large amount of data in a single series of numbers. You should remember, however, that any summary hides some detail and that index numbers should therefore be interpreted with caution.

↳ The product life cycle model shows how sales of a product can be expected to vary with the passage of time.

↳ All forecasts are subject to error, but the likely errors vary from case to case.
  (a) The **further into the future** the forecast is for, the **more unreliable** it is likely to be.
  (b) The **less data** available on which to base the forecast, the **less reliable** the forecast.
  (c) The **pattern** of trend and seasonal variations **cannot be guaranteed to continue** in the future.
  (d) There is always the danger of **random variations** upsetting the pattern of trend and seasonal variation.

QUICK QUIZ

1   What is the disadvantage of the scattergraph method?

2   When plotting moving averages on a graph, where should the plotted points be located?

3   Why are average seasonal variations adjusted to sum to zero?

4   What is the weakness of the additive model?

5   What is deseasonalised data?

6   What is extrapolation?

7   What factors affect the accuracy of forecasts?

8   What is the standard calculation for removing the effects of price movements from data?

9   If the relationship between production costs and output is connected by the linear relationship $y = 75x + 47,000$, what is 47,000?

    A   The number of units produced
    B   Total production costs
    C   The production cost if 75 units are produced
    D   The fixed production costs

10   Based on the last 7 periods, the underlying trend of sales is $y = 690.24 - 2.75x$. If the 8th period has a seasonal factor of -25.25, assuming an additive forecasting model, then the forecast for that period, in whole units is

    A   643
    B   646
    C   668
    D   671

11   Which of the following are necessary if forecasts obtained from a time series analysis are to be reliable?

    I   There must be no seasonal variation
    II   The trend must be increasing
    III The model used must fit the past data
    IV   There must be no unforeseen events

    A   I and III only
    B   I and IV only
    C   II and III only
    D   III and IV only

12   What is the general form of a weighted aggregate index?

13   What type of weights do Laspeyre indices use?

14   Why might Fisher's ideal index be used?

1   The disadvantage of the scattergraph method for estimating costs is that the line of best fit is drawn by visual judgement and so is only a subjective approximation of total cost.

2   Points should be plotted at the midpoint of the period to which they apply.

3   Average seasonal variations are adjusted to sum to zero because variations around the basic trend line should cancel each other out and add up to zero.

4   An additive model has the important drawback that when there is a steeply rising or a steeply declining trend, the moving average trend will either get ahead of or fall behind the real trend.

5   Deseasonalised data is data from which the seasonal variations have been removed, leaving a figure which might be taken as indicating the trend.

6   Extrapolation is forecasting the future from a trend line based on historical data.

7   (a)   The further into the future the forecast is for, the more unreliable it is likely to be.

   (b)   The less data available on which to base the forecast, the less reliable the forecast.

   (c)   The pattern of trend and seasonal variations cannot be guaranteed to continue in the future.

   (d)   There is always the danger of random variations upsetting the pattern of trend and seasonal variation.

8   Actual data $\times \dfrac{100}{\text{Index for time period in question}}$

9   D

10   A   If x = 8, y = 690.24 – (2.75 × 8) = 668.24
      Forecast = trend + seasonal component = 668.24 – 25.25 = 642.99 = 643 (to the nearest unit)
      If you selected option B, you calculated the forecast for the seventh period and deducted the seasonal component of the eighth period.
      If you selected option C, you correctly forecast the trend for the eighth period but forgot to deduct the seasonal component.
      If you selected option D, you simply calculated the trend for the seventh period instead of the eighth period.

11   D   I   Provided the seasonal variation remains the same in the future as in the past, it will not make forecasts unreliable.

      II   Provided a multiplicative model is used, the fact that the trend is increasing need not have any adverse effect on the reliability of forecasts.

      III   If the model being used is inappropriate, for example, if an additive model is used when the trend is changing sharply, forecasts will not be very reliable.

      IV   Forecasts are made on the assumption that everything continues as in the past.

      III and IV are therefore necessary and hence the correct answer is D.

12   $\dfrac{\Sigma \, wv_n}{\Sigma \, wv_o}$

13   Weights from the base period

14   The Laspeyre index tends to overstate change, while the Paasche index tends to understate it.

Now try ...

Attempt the questions below from the **Exam Question Bank**

Number

Q61 – Q66

CHAPTER

15

This chapter covers a new topic, **budgeting**.

The chapter begins by explaining the **reasons for operating a budgetary planning and control system**, explains some of the **key terms** associated with budgeting and reminds you of the steps in the preparation of a master budget.

Budgeting

Study Guide

C   Budgeting

1   Nature and purpose of budgeting

(a)   Explain why organisations use budgeting

K

(b)   Describe the planning and control cycle in an organisation

K

2   Statistical techniques

(o)   Explain the role and features of a computer spreadsheet system.

K

(p)   Identify applications for computer spreadsheets and their use in cost and management accounting

S

3   Budget preparation

(f)   Explain and illustrate 'what if' analysis and scenario planning

S

4   Flexible budgets

(a)   Explain the importance of flexible budgets in control

K

(b)   Explain the disadvantages of fixed budgets in control

K

(c)   Identify situations where fixed or flexible budgetary control would be appropriate

S

(d)   Flex a budget to a given level of volume

S

6   Budgetary control and reporting

(d)   Define the concept of responsibility accounting and its significance in control

K

(e)   Explain the concept of controllable and uncontrollable costs

K

(f)   Prepare control reports suitable for presentation to management

S

1   The planning and control cycle

There are seven steps in the planning and control cycle.

Step 1	Identify objectives
Step 2	Identity potential strategies
Step 3	Evaluate strategies
Step 4	Choose alternative courses of action
Step 5	Implement the long-term plan
Step 6	Measure actual results and compare with plan
Step 7	Respond to divergences from plan

The diagram below represents the planning and control cycle. **Planning** involves making choices between alternatives and is primarily a decision-making activity. The **control** process involves measuring and correcting actual performance to ensure that the strategies that are chosen and the plans for implementing them are carried out.

The planning and control cycle

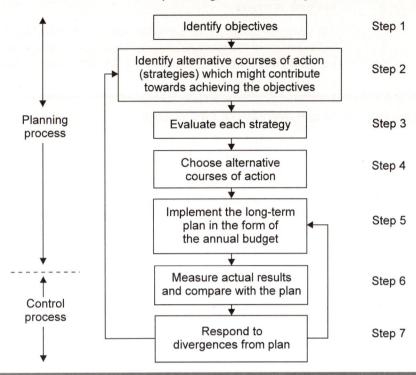

Step 1 Identify objectives

Objectives establish the direction in which the management of the organisation wish it to be heading. Typical objectives include the following.

(a) To maximise profits
(b) To increase market share
(c) To produce a better quality product than anyone else

Objectives answer the question: **'where do we want to be?'**.

Step 2 Identify potential strategies

Once an organisation has decided 'where it wants to be', the next step is to identify a range of possible courses of action or strategies that might enable the organisation to get there.

The organisation must therefore carry out an information-gathering exercise to ensure that it has a full understanding of where it is now. This is known as a 'position audit' or 'strategic analysis' and involves looking both inwards and outwards.

(a) The organisation must gather information from all of its internal parts to find out what resources it possesses: what its manufacturing capacity and capability is, what is the state of its technical know-how, how well it is able to market itself, how much cash it has in the bank, how much it could borrow and so on.

(b) It must also gather information externally so that it can assess its position in the environment. Just as it has assessed its own strengths and weaknesses, it must do likewise for its competitors (threats). Its market must be analysed (and any other markets that it is intending to enter) to identify possible new opportunities. The 'state of the world' must be considered. Is it in recession or is it booming? What is likely to happen in the future? This process is known as SWOT analysis.

Having carried out a strategic analysis, alternative strategies can be identified.

Step 3	**Evaluate strategies**

The strategies must then be evaluated in terms of suitability, feasibility and acceptability in the context of the strategic analysis. Management should select those strategies that have the greatest potential for achieving the organisation's objectives. One strategy may be chosen or several.

Step 4	**Choose alternative courses of action**

The next step in the process is to collect the chosen strategies together and co-ordinate them into a long-term plan, commonly expressed in financial terms.

Typically a long-term financial plan would show the following.

(a)   Projected cash flows
(b)   Projected long-term profits
(c)   Capital expenditure plans
(d)   Forecasts of statement of financial position
(e)   A description of the long-term objectives and strategies in words

Step 5	**Implement the long-term plan**

The long-term plan should then be broken down into smaller parts. It is unlikely that the different parts will fall conveniently into successive time periods. Strategy A may take two and a half years, while Strategy B may take five months, but not start until year three of the plan. It is usual, however, to break down the plan as a whole into equal time periods (usually one year). The resulting short-term plan is called a budget.

Steps 6 and 7	**Measure actual results and compare with plan. Respond to divergences from plan**

At the end of the year actual results should be compared with those expected under the long-term plan. The long-term plan should be reviewed in the light of this comparison and the progress that has been made towards achieving the organisation's objectives should be assessed. Management can also consider the feasibility of achieving the objectives in the light of unforeseen circumstances which have arisen during the year. If the plans are now no longer attainable then alternative strategies must be considered for achieving the organisation's objectives, as indicated by the feedback loop (the arrowed line) linking step 7 to step 2. This aspect of control is carried out by senior management, normally on an annual basis.

The control of day-to-day operations is exercised by lower-level managers. At frequent intervals they must be provided with performance reports which consist of detailed comparisons of actual results and budgeted results. Performance reports provide feedback information by comparing planned and actual outcomes. Such reports should highlight those activities that do not conform to plan, so that managers can devote their scarce time to focusing on these items. Effective control requires that corrective action is taken so that actual outcomes conform to planned outcomes, as indicated by the feedback loop linking steps 5 and 7. Isolating past inefficiencies and the reasons for them will enable managers to take action that will avoid the same inefficiencies being repeated in the future. The system that provides reports that compare actual performance with budget figures is known as responsibility accounting.

QUESTION

Planning cycle

Is your organisation's planning and control cycle similar to the one described here? If it differs, how does it differ? Why does it differ? Try to find out your organisation's objectives and the strategies it is adopting to attain those objectives.

2 Budgetary planning and control systems

A **budget** is a quantified plan of action for a forthcoming accounting period. A **budget** is a plan of what the organisation is aiming to achieve and what is has set as a target whereas a **forecast** is an estimate of what is likely to occur in the future.

The budget is 'a quantitative statement for a defined period of time, which may include planned revenues, expenses, assets, liabilities and cash flows. A budget facilitates planning'.

There is, however, little point in an organisation simply preparing a budget for the sake of preparing a budget. A beautifully laid out budgeted income statement filed in the cost accountant's file and never looked at again is worthless. The organisation should gain from both the actual preparation process and from the budget once it has been prepared.

The **objectives** of a budgetary planning and control system are as follows.

- To ensure the achievement of the organisation's objectives
- To compel planning
- To communicate ideas and plans
- To coordinate activities
- To provide a framework for responsibility accounting
- To establish a system of control
- To motivate employees to improve their performance

Budgets are therefore not prepared in isolation and then filed away but are the fundamental components of what is known as the **budgetary planning and control system**. A budgetary planning and control system is essentially a system for ensuring **communication**, **coordination** and **control** within an organisation. Communication, coordination and control are general objectives: more information is provided by an inspection of the specific objectives of a budgetary planning and control system.

Objective	Comment
Ensure the achievement of the organisation's objectives	Objectives are set for the organisation as a whole, and for individual departments and operations within the organisation. Quantified expressions of these objectives are then drawn up as targets to be achieved within the timescale of the budget plan.
Compel planning	This is probably the most important feature of a budgetary planning and control system. Planning forces management to look ahead, to set out detailed plans for achieving the targets for each department, operation and (ideally) each manager and to anticipate problems. It thus prevents management from relying on ad hoc or uncoordinated planning which may be detrimental to the performance of the organisation. It also helps managers to **foresee potential threats or opportunities**, so that they may **take action now** to avoid or minimise the effect of the threats and to take full advantage of the opportunities.
Communicate ideas and plans	A formal system is necessary to ensure that each person affected by the plans is aware of what he or she is supposed to be doing. Communication might be one-way, with managers giving orders to subordinates, or there might be a two-way dialogue and exchange of ideas.

Objective	Comment
Coordinate activities	The activities of different departments or sub-units of the organisation need to be coordinated to ensure maximum integration of effort towards common goals. This concept of coordination implies, for example, that the purchasing department should base its budget on production requirements and that the production budget should in turn be based on sales expectations. Although straightforward in concept, coordination is remarkably difficult to achieve, and there is often **'sub-optimality'** and conflict between departmental plans in the budget so that the efforts of each department are not fully integrated into a combined plan to achieve the company's best targets.
Provide a framework for responsibility accounting	Budgetary planning and control systems require that managers of **budget centres** are made responsible for the achievement of budget targets for the operations under their personal control.
Establish a system of control	A budget is a **yardstick** against which actual performance is monitored and assessed. Control over actual performance is provided by the comparisons of actual results against the budget plan. Departures from budget can then be investigated and the reasons for the departures can be divided into **controllable** and **uncontrollable** factors.
Motivate employees to improve their performance	The interest and commitment of employees can be retained via a system of feedback of actual results, which lets them know how well or badly they are performing. The identification of controllable reasons for departures from budget with managers responsible provides an incentive for improving future performance.
Provide a framework for authorisation	Once the budget has been agreed by the directors and senior managers it acts as an authorisation for each budget holder to incur the costs included in the budget centre's budget. **As long as the expenditure is included in the formalised budget** the budget holder can carry out day to day operations without needing to seek separate authorisation for each item of expenditure.
Provide a basis for performance evaluation	As well as providing a yardstick for control by comparison, the monitoring of actual results compared with the budget can provide a basis for **evaluating the performance of the budget holder.** As a result of this evaluation the manager might be rewarded, perhaps with a financial bonus or promotion. Alternatively the evaluation process might highlight the need for more investment in staff development and training.

3 Responsibility centres

Responsibility centres can be divided into three types.

- Cost centres
- Profit centres
- Investment centres

Responsibility accounting is a system of accounting that segregates revenue and costs into areas of personal responsibility in order to monitor and assess the performance of each part of an organisation.

A **responsibility centre** is a function or department of an organisation that is headed by a manager who has direct responsibility for its performance.

If a manager is to bear responsibility for the performance of his area of the business he will need information about its performance. In essence, a manager needs to know three things.

Requirements	Examples of information
What are his resources?	Finance, inventories of raw materials, spare machine capacity, labour availability, the balance of expenditure remaining for a certain budget, target date for completion of a job.
At what rate are his resources being consumed?	How fast is his labour force working, how quickly are his raw materials being used up, how quickly are other expenses being incurred, how quickly is available finance being consumed?
How well are the resources being used?	How well are his objectives being met?

Decisions must also be made as to the level of detail that is provided and the frequency with which information is provided. Moreover the cost of providing information must be weighed against the benefit derived from it.

In a traditional system managers are given monthly reports, but there is no logical reason for this except that it ties in with financial reporting cycles and may be administratively convenient. With modern systems, however, there is a danger of **information overload**, since information technology allows the information required to be made available much more frequently.

The task of the management accountant, therefore, is to learn from the managers of responsibility centres what information they need, in what form and at what intervals, and then to design a planning and control system that enables this to be provided.

It is to this end that responsibility centres are usually divided into different categories. Here we shall describe cost centres, profit centres and investment centres.

3.1 Cost centres

A **cost centre** acts as a collecting place for certain costs before they are analysed further.

Cost centres may include the following.

(a)   A **department**
(b)   A **machine** or group of machines
(c)   A **project** (eg the installation of a new computer system)
(d)   A **new product** (allowing development costs to be identified)

To charge actual costs to a cost centre, each cost centre will have a **cost code**. Items of expenditure will be recorded with the appropriate cost code. When costs are eventually analysed, there may well be some apportionment of the costs of one cost centre to other cost centres.

(a)   The costs of those cost centres which receive an apportionment of shared costs should be divided into directly attributable costs (for which the cost centre manager is responsible) and shared costs (for which another cost centre is directly accountable).

(b)   The control system should trace shared costs back to the cost centres from which the costs have been apportioned, so that their managers can be made accountable for the costs incurred.

Information about cost centres might be collected in terms of **total actual costs, total budgeted costs** and **total cost variances** (the differences between actual and budged costs) sub-analysed perhaps into efficiency, usage and expenditure variances. In addition, the information might be analysed in terms of **ratios**, such as the following.

(a)   Cost per unit produced (budget and actual)
(b)   Hours per unit produced (budget and actual)
(c)   Efficiency ratio
(d)   Selling costs per $ of sales (budget and actual)
(e)   Transport costs per tonne/kilometre (budget and actual)

3.2 Profit centres

A **profit centre** is any unit of an organisation (for example, division of a company) to which both revenues and costs are assigned, so that the profitability of the unit may be measured.

Profit centres differ from cost centres in that they **account for both costs and revenues** and the **key performance measure** of a profit centre is therefore **profit**.

For profit centres to have any validity in a planning and control system based on responsibility accounting, **the manager of the profit centre must have some influence over both revenues and costs**, that is, a say in both sales and production policies.

A profit centre manager is likely to be a fairly senior person within an organisation, and a profit centre is likely to cover quite a large area of operations. A profit centre might be an entire division within the organisation, or there might be a separate profit centre for each product, product range, brand or service that the organisation sells. Information requirements will be similarly focused, as appropriate.

In the hierarchy of responsibility centres within an organisation, there are likely to be several cost centres within a profit centre.

3.3 Revenue centres

A **revenue centre** is similar to a cost centre and a profit centre but is accountable for **revenues** only.

For revenue centres to have any validity in a planning and control system based on responsibility accounting, revenue centre managers should normally have control over how revenues are raised.

3.4 Investment centres

An **investment centre** is a profit centre whose performance is measured by its return on capital employed.

This implies that the **investment centre manager has some say in investment policy** in his area of operations as well as being responsible for costs and revenues.

Several profit centres might share the same capital items, for example the same buildings, stores or transport fleet, and so investment centres are likely to include several profit centres, and provide a basis for control at a very senior management level, like that of a subsidiary company within a group.

Control can be exercised by reporting information such as **profit/sales ratios, asset turnover ratios, cost/sales ratios**, and **cost variances**. In addition, the performance of investment centres can be measured by divisional comparisons.

3.5 Traceable and controllable costs

The main problem with measuring controllable performance is in deciding which costs are **controllable** and which costs are **traceable**. The performance of the manager of the division is indicated by the **controllable profit** (and it is on this that he is judged) and the success of the division as a whole is judged on the **traceable profit**.

Consider, for example, depreciation on divisional machinery. Would this be included as a controllable fixed cost or a traceable fixed cost? Because profit centre managers are only responsible for the **costs and revenues** under their control, this means that they do not have control over the investment in non-current assets. The depreciation on divisional machinery would therefore be a **traceable fixed cost** judging the performance of the division, and not of the individual manager.

QUESTION

Cost, profit and investment centres

Find out if your organisation has a system of cost, profit and investment centres. What is the scope of planning and control within each centre?

4 Controllable costs

4.1 Controllable costs and uncontrollable costs

Managers of responsibility centres should only be held accountable for costs over which they have some influence. From a motivation point of view this is important because it can be very demoralising for managers who feel that their performance is being judged on the basis of something over which they have no influence. It is also important from a control point of view in that control reports should ensure that information on costs is reported to the manager who is able to take action to control them.

A **controllable cost** is 'A cost that can be controlled, typically by a cost, profit or investment centre manager'.

(CIMA *Official Terminology*)

Responsibility accounting attempts to associate costs, revenues, assets and liabilities with the managers most capable of controlling them. As a system of accounting, it therefore distinguishes between controllable and uncontrollable costs. Most **variable costs** within a department are thought to be **controllable in the short term** because managers can influence the efficiency with which resources are used, even if they cannot do anything to raise or lower price levels.

A cost which is not controllable by a junior manager or supervisor might be controllable by a senior manager. For example, there may be high direct labour costs in a department caused by excessive overtime working. The supervisor may feel obliged to continue with the overtime in order to meet production schedules, but his senior may be able to reduce costs by deciding to hire extra full-time staff, thereby reducing the requirements for overtime.

A cost which is not controllable by a manager in one department may be controllable by a manager in another department. For example, an increase in material costs may be caused by buying at higher prices than expected (controllable by the purchasing department) or by excessive wastage and spoilage (controllable by the production department) or by a faulty machine producing a high number of rejects (controllable by the maintenance department).

Some costs are **non-controllable**, such as increases in expenditure items due to inflation. Other costs are **controllable, but in the long term rather than the short term**. For example, production costs might be reduced by the introduction of new machinery and technology, but in the short term, management must attempt to do the best they can with the resources and machinery at their disposal.

4.2 The controllability of fixed costs

It is often assumed that all fixed costs are non-controllable in the short run. This is not so.

(a) **Committed fixed costs** are those costs arising from the possession of plant, equipment, buildings and an administration department to **support the long-term needs of the business**. These costs (depreciation, rent, administration salaries) are largely **non-controllable in the short term** because they have been committed by longer-term decisions affecting longer-term needs. When a company decides to cut production drastically, the long-term committed fixed costs will be reduced, but arrangements for settling redundancy terms and the sale of assets cannot be made quickly and in the short term.

(b) **Discretionary fixed costs**, such as advertising, sales promotion, research and development, training costs and consultancy fees are costs which are incurred as a result of a top management decision, but which could be **raised or lowered at fairly short notice** (irrespective of the actual volume of production and sales).

4.3 Controllability and apportioned costs

Managers should only be held accountable for costs over which they have some influence. This may seem quite straightforward in theory, but it is not always so easy in practice to distinguish controllable from uncontrollable costs. **Apportioned overhead costs provide a good example**.

Suppose that a manager of a production department in a manufacturing company is made responsible for the costs of his department. These costs include **directly attributable overhead items** such as the costs of indirect labour employed in the department, the cost of metered power units consumed and indirect materials consumed in the department. However, the department's overhead costs also include an apportionment of costs from other costs centres, such as the following.

(a)   Rent and rates for the building which the department shares with other departments.
(b)   Share of the costs of the maintenance department
(c)   A share of the costs of the central data processing department

Should the production manager be held accountable for any of these apportioned costs?

(a)   Managers should not be held accountable for costs over which they have no control. In this example, apportioned rent and rates costs would not be controllable by the production department manager.

(b)   Managers should be held accountable for costs over which they have some influence. In this example, it is the responsibility of the maintenance department manager to keep maintenance costs within budget and of the DP manager to keep central DP costs within budget. But their costs will be partly variable and partly fixed, and the variable cost element will depend on the volume of demand for their services (the rate of usage of the service). If the production department's staff treat their equipment badly we might expect higher repair costs, and the production department manager should therefore be made accountable for the repair costs that his department makes the maintenance department incur on its behalf.

QUESTION   Committed and discretionary costs

Try to discover some of your organisation's committed fixed costs and discretionary fixed costs.

5 Fixed and flexible budgets

5.1 Fixed budgets

Fixed budgets remain unchanged regardless of the level of activity; **flexible budgets** are designed to flex with the level of activity.

Comparison of a fixed budget with the actual results for a different level of activity is of little use for **control purposes**. Flexible budgets should be used to show what cost and revenues should have been for the actual level of activity.

A fixed budget is a budget which is designed to remain unchanged regardless of the volume of output or sales achieved.

The master budget prepared before the beginning of the budget period is known as the **fixed budget**. The term 'fixed' has the following meaning.

(a)   The budget is **prepared on the basis of an estimated volume of production** and an **estimated volume of sales**, but no plans are made for the event that actual volumes of production and sales may differ from budgeted volumes.

(b)   When actual volumes of production and sales during a control period (month or four weeks or quarter) are achieved, a fixed budget is **not adjusted (in retrospect) to the new levels of activity**.

The major purpose of a fixed budget is at the planning stage, when it seeks to define the broad objectives of the organisation.

5.2 Flexible budgets

A **flexible budget** is a budget which, by recognising different cost behaviour patterns, is designed to change as volumes of output change.

Flexible budgets may be used in one of two ways.

(a) **At the planning stage**. For example, suppose that a company expects to sell 10,000 units of output during the next year. A master budget (the fixed budget) would be prepared on the basis of these expected volumes. However, if the company thinks that output and sales might be as low as 8,000 units or as high as 12,000 units, it may prepare **contingency flexible budgets**, at volumes of, say 8,000, 9,000, 11,000 and 12,000 units. There are a number of advantages of planning with flexible budgets.

   (i)   It is possible to find out well in advance the costs of lay-off pay, idle time and so on if output falls short of budget.

   (ii) Management can decide whether it would be possible to find alternative uses for spare capacity if output falls short of budget (could employees be asked to overhaul their own machines for example, instead of paying for an outside contractor?).

   (iii) An estimate of the costs of overtime, subcontracting work or extra machine hire if sales volume exceeds the fixed budget estimate can be made. From this, it can be established whether there is a limiting factor which would prevent high volumes of output and sales being achieved.

(b) **Retrospectively**. At the end of each month (control period) or year, flexible budgets can be used to compare actual results achieved with what results should have been under the circumstances. Flexible budgets are an essential factor in **budgetary control** and overcome the practical problems involved in monitoring the budgetary control system.

   (i)   Management needs to be informed about how good or bad actual performance has been. To provide a **measure of performance**, there must be a **yardstick** (budget or standard) against which actual performance can be measured.

   (ii) Every business is **dynamic**, and actual volumes of output cannot be expected to conform exactly to the fixed budget. Comparing actual costs directly with the fixed budget costs is meaningless (unless the actual level of activity turns out to be exactly as planned).

   (iii) For **useful control information**, it is necessary to compare **actual results at the actual level of activity achieved against the results that should have been expected at this level of activity**, which are shown by the flexible budget.

QUESTION
Flexible budgets

Why might flexible budgets be particularly useful to the car industry during a recession?

ANSWER

During a recession the car industry often has to put workers on a three- or four-day week due to lack of demand for its products. Budgets therefore have to be reassessed to match the reduced production time available.

6 Preparing flexible budgets

Flexible budgeting uses the principles of marginal costing. In estimating future costs it is often necessary to begin by looking at cost behaviour in the past. For costs which are wholly fixed or wholly variable no problem arises. But you may be presented with a cost which appears to have behaved in the past as a mixed cost (partly fixed and partly variable). The **high-low method** may be used for estimating the level of such a cost in a future period.

6.1 High-low method

(a)   To estimate the fixed and variable elements of semi-variable costs, records of costs in previous periods are reviewed and the **costs of the following two periods** are selected.

      (i)   **The period with the highest volume of output**
      (ii)   **The period with the lowest volume of output**

      (*Note*. The periods with the highest/lowest output may not be the periods with the highest/lowest cost.)

(b)   The **difference** between the total cost of the high output and the total cost of the low output will be the **variable cost of the difference in output levels** (since the same fixed cost is included in each total cost).

(c)   The **variable cost per unit** may be calculated from this (**difference in total costs ÷ difference in output levels**), and the **fixed cost** may then also be determined (**total cost at either output level – variable cost for output level chosen**).

EXAM FOCUS POINT

You may need to use the high-low technique to answer questions on flexible budgets which include semi-variable costs.

6.2 Example: the high-low method

The costs of operating the maintenance department of a television manufacturer for the last four months have been as follows.

Month	Cost	Production volume
	$	Units
1	110,000	7,000
2	115,000	8,000
3	111,000	7,700
4	97,000	6,000

Required

Calculate the costs that should be expected in month five when output is expected to be 7,500 units. Ignore inflation.

6.3 Solution

(a)

	Units		$
High output	8,000	total cost	115,000
Low output	6,000	total cost	97,000
Variable cost of	2,000		18,000
Variable cost per unit	$18,000/2,000 =		$9

(b)   Substituting in either the high or low volume cost:

		High		Low
		$		$
Total cost		115,000		97,000
Variable costs	(8,000 × $9)	72,000	(6,000 × $9)	54,000
Fixed costs		43,000		43,000

(c)   Estimated costs of 7,500 units of output:

	$
Fixed costs	43,000
Variable costs (7,500 × $9)	67,500
Total costs	110,500

QUESTION   High-low

Using the high-low method and the following information, determine the cost of electricity in July if 2,750 units of electricity are consumed.

Month	Cost	Electricity consumed
	$	Units
January	204	2,600
February	212	2,800
March	200	2,500
April	220	3,000
May	184	2,100
June	188	2,200

ANSWER

	Units		$
High units	3,000	total cost =	220
Low units	2,100	total cost =	184
	900		36

Variable cost per unit = $\dfrac{\$36}{900}$ = $0.04

Substituting:

	$
Total cost of 3,000 units	220
Variable costs (3,000 × $0.04)	120
Fixed cost	100

Total cost in July = $(100 + (2,750 × 0.04)) = $210

We can now look at a full example of preparing a flexible budget.

6.4 Example: preparing a flexible budget

(a)   Prepare a budget for 20X6 for the direct labour costs and overhead expenses of a production department at the activity levels of 80%, 90% and 100%, using the information listed below.

      (i)   The direct labour hourly rate is expected to be $3.75.
      (ii)   100% activity represents 60,000 direct labour hours.
      (iii)   Variable costs

Indirect labour	$0.75 per direct labour hour
Consumable supplies	$0.375 per direct labour hour
Canteen and other	
welfare services	6% of direct and indirect labour costs

(iv)   Semi-variable costs are expected to relate to the direct labour hours in the same manner as for the last five years.

Year	Direct labour hours	Semi-Variable Costs $
20X1	64,000	20,800
20X2	59,000	19,800
20X3	53,000	18,600
20X4	49,000	17,800
20X5 (estimate)	40,000	16,000

(v)   *Fixed overhead per labour hour at 100% activity*

	$
Depreciation	0.30
Maintenance	0.20
Insurance	0.10
Rates	0.25
Management salaries	0.40

(vi)   Inflation is to be ignored.

(b)   Calculate the **budget cost allowance (ie expected expenditure)** for 20X6 assuming that 57,000 direct labour hours are worked.

6.5 Solution

(a)

	80% level 48,000 hrs $'000	90% level 54,000 hrs $'000	100% level 60,000 hrs $'000
Direct labour	180.00	202.50	225.0
Other variable costs			
Indirect labour	36.00	40.50	45.0
Consumable supplies	18.00	20.25	22.5
Canteen etc	12.96	14.58	16.2
Total variable costs ($5.145 per hour W1)	246.96	277.83	308.7
Semi-variable costs (W2)	17.60	18.80	20.0
Fixed costs			
Depreciation (60 × $0.3)	18.00	18.00	18.0
Maintenance (60 × $0.2)	12.00	12.00	12.0
Insurance (60 × $0.1)	6.00	6.00	6.0
Rates (60 × $0.25)	15.00	15.00	15.0
Management salaries (60 × $0.4)	24.00	24.00	24.0
Budgeted costs	339.56	371.63	403.7

Working

1 Total variable cost   = direct labour + indirect labour + canteen + consumables

= $4.50 + $0.27 + $0.375 = $5.145

2 Using the high/low method:

	$
Total cost of 64,000 hours	20,800
Total cost of 40,000 hours	16,000
Variable cost of 24,000 hours	4,800

Variable cost per hour ($4,800/24,000)	$0.20

	$
Total cost of 64,000 hours	20,800
Variable cost of 64,000 hours (× $0.20)	12,800
Fixed costs	8,000

Semi-variable costs are calculated as follows.

			$
60,000 hours	(60,000 × $0.20) + $8,000	=	20,000
54,000 hours	(54,000 × $0.20) + $8,000	=	18,800
48,000 hours	(48,000 × $0.20) + $8,000	=	17,600

(b)   The budget cost allowance for 57,000 direct labour hours of work would be as follows.

		$
Variable costs	(57,000 × $5.145)	293,265
Semi-variable costs	($8,000 + (57,000 × $0.20))	19,400
Fixed costs		75,000
		384,665

Note that in each case the fixed costs remain the same when the level of activity changes and **are not flexed**.

6.6 The measure of activity in flexible budgets

The preparation of a flexible budget requires an estimate of the way in which costs (and revenues) vary with the level of activity.

Sales revenue will clearly vary with sales volume, and direct material costs (and often direct labour costs) will vary with production volume. In some instances, however, it may be appropriate to budget for overhead costs as mixed costs (part-fixed, part-variable) which vary with an 'activity' which is neither production nor sales volume. Taking production overheads in a processing department as an illustration, the total overhead costs will be partly fixed and partly variable. The variable portion may vary with the direct labour hours worked in the department, or with the number of machine hours of operation. The better measure of activity, labour hours or machine hours, may only be decided after a close analysis of historical results.

EXAM FOCUS POINT

In an exam **do not fall into the trap of flexing fixed costs**. Do not forget that they remain unchanged regardless of the level of activity. Even if fixed overheads are initially expressed on a 'per unit' basis in a question, remember that once you have calculated the total fixed cost for a given activity level, it will remain unchanged when activity levels alter.

The **measure of activity used to estimate variable costs should satisfy certain criteria**.

Criteria	Detail
Derived from the activity that causes particular costs to vary	
Independent of variable factors other than its own volume	For example, if labour hours are the measure of activity, the level of activity should be measured in labour hours, and not the labour cost of those hours (the latter being prone to the effect of a price change).
Stable	In this respect, a standard unit of output provides a better measure than actual units. For example, if total costs are assumed to vary with direct labour hours, it would be more appropriate to choose 'standard hours produced' as a measure of activity than 'actual hours worked' because the actual hours may have been worked efficiently or inefficiently, and the variations in performance would probably affect the actual costs incurred.

7 Flexible budgets and budgetary control

A prerequisite of flexible budgeting is a knowledge of cost behaviour.

The differences between the components of the fixed budget and the actual results are known as **budget variances**.

Budgetary control is the practice of establishing budgets which identify areas of responsibility for individual managers (for example production managers, purchasing managers and so on) and of regularly comparing actual results against expected results. The differences between actual results and expected results are called **variances** and these are used to provide a guideline for control action by individual managers.

We will be looking at variances in some detail later in the text.

Individual managers are held responsible for **investigating differences** between budgeted and actual results, and are then expected to **take corrective action** or amend the plan in the light of actual events.

The wrong approach to budgetary control is to compare actual results against a fixed budget. Consider the following example.

Tree manufactures a single product, the bough. Budgeted results and actual results for June are shown below.

	Budget	Actual results	Variance
Production and sales of the bough (units)	2,000	3,000	
	$	$	$
Sales revenue (a)	20,000	30,000	10,000 (F)
Direct materials	6,000	8,500	2,500 (A)
Direct labour	4,000	4,500	500 (A)
Maintenance	1,000	1,400	400 (A)
Depreciation	2,000	2,200	200 (A)
Rent and rates	1,500	1,600	100 (A)
Other costs	3,600	5,000	1,400 (A)
Total costs (b)	18,100	23,200	5,100
Profit (a)–(b)	1,900	6,800	4,900 (F)

(a)   In this example, the variances are meaningless for purposes of control. **Costs were higher than budget because the volume of output was also higher**; variable costs would be expected to increase above the budgeted costs. There is no information to show whether control action is needed for any aspect of costs or revenue.

(b)   For control purposes, it is necessary to know the following.

(i)   Were actual costs higher than they should have been to produce and sell 3,000 boughs?
(ii)   Was actual revenue satisfactory from the sale of 3,000 boughs?
(iii)   Has the volume of units made and sold varied from the budget favourably or adversely?

Correct approach to budgetary control

(a)   **Identify fixed and variable costs.**
(b)   **Produce a flexible budget using marginal costing techniques.**

In the previous example of Tree, let us suppose that we have the following information regarding cost behaviour.

(a)   Direct materials and maintenance costs are variable.

(b)   Although basic wages are a fixed cost, direct labour is regarded as variable in order to measure efficiency/productivity.

(c)   Rent and rates and depreciation are fixed costs.

(d)   Other costs consist of fixed costs of $1,600 plus a variable cost of $1 per unit made and sold.

Now that the cost behaviour patterns are known, a budget cost allowance can be calculated for each item of expenditure. This allowance is shown in **a flexible budget** as the **expected expenditure on each item for the relevant level of activity**. The budget cost allowances are calculated as follows.

(a) Variable cost allowances   = original budgets × (3,000 units/2,000 units)
        eg material cost allowance   = $6,000 × $^3/_2$ = $9,000

(b) Fixed cost allowances   = as original budget

(c) Semi-fixed cost allowances   = original budgeted fixed costs
                                     + (3,000 units × variable cost per unit)
        eg other cost allowances   = $1,600 + (3,000 × $1) = $4,600

The budgetary control analysis should be as follows.

	Fixed budget (a)	Flexible budget (b)	Actual results (c)	Budget variance (b)–(c)
Production & sales (units)	2,000	3,000	3,000	
	$	$	$	$
Sales revenue	20,000	30,000	30,000	0
Variable costs				
Direct materials	6,000	9,000	8,500	500 (F)
Direct labour	4,000	6,000	4,500	1,500 (F)
Maintenance	1,000	1,500	1,400	100 (F)
Semi-variable costs				
Other costs	3,600	4,600	5,000	400 (A)
Fixed costs				
Depreciation	2,000	2,000	2,200	200 (A)
Rent and rates	1,500	1,500	1,600	100 (A)
Total costs	18,100	24,600	23,200	1,400 (F)
Profit	1,900	5,400	6,800	1,400 (F)

Note. **(F) denotes a favourable variance and (A) an adverse or unfavourable variance.** Adverse variances are sometimes denoted as (U) for 'unfavourable'.

We can **analyse** the above as follows.

(a) In selling 3,000 units the expected profit should have been, not the fixed budget profit of $1,900, but the flexible budget profit of $5,400. Instead, actual profit was $6,800 ie $1,400 more than we should have expected. One of the reasons for the improvement is that, **given actual output and sales** of 3,000 units, **costs were lower than expected** (and sales revenue exactly as expected).

	$
Direct materials cost variance	500 (F)
Direct labour cost variance	1,500 (F)
Maintenance cost variance	100 (F)
Other costs variance	400 (A)
Fixed cost variances	
Depreciation	200 (A)
Rent and rates	100 (A)
	1,400 (F)

Profit was therefore increased by $1,400 because costs were lower than anticipated.

(b) Another reason for the improvement in profit above the fixed budget profit is the **sales volume**. Tree sold 3,000 boughs instead of 2,000 boughs, with the following result.

	$	$
Sales revenue increased by		10,000
Variable costs increased by:		
direct materials	3,000	
direct labour	2,000	
Maintenance	500	
variable element of other costs	1,000	
Fixed costs are unchanged		6,500
Profit increased by		3,500

Profit was therefore increased by $3,500 because sales volumes increased.

(c) A full variance analysis statement would be as follows.

	$	$
Fixed budget profit		1,900
Variances		
Sales volume	3,500 (F)	
Direct materials cost	500 (F)	
Direct labour cost	1,500 (F)	
Maintenance cost	100 (F)	
Other costs	400 (A)	
Depreciation	200 (A)	
Rent and rates	100 (A)	
		4,900 (F)
Actual profit		6,800

If management believes any variance is significant enough to warrant investigation, they will investigate to see whether any corrective action is necessary or whether the plan needs amending in the light of actual events.

QUESTION

Budgetary control

The budgeted and actual results of Crunch for September were as follows. The company uses a marginal costing system. There were no opening or closing inventories.

	Fixed budget 1,000 units		Actual 700 units	
Sales and production	$	$	$	$
Sales		20,000		14,200
Variable cost of sales				
Direct materials	8,000		5,200	
Direct labour	4,000		3,100	
Variable overhead	2,000		1,500	
		14,000		9,800
Contribution		6,000		4,400
Fixed costs		5,000		5,400
Profit/(loss)		1,000		(1,000)

Required

Prepare a budget that will be useful for management control purposes.

ANSWER

We need to prepare a flexible budget for 700 units.

	Budget 1,000 units $	Per unit $	Flexed budget 700 units $	Actual 700 units $	Variances $
Sales	20,000	(20)	14,000	14,200	200 (F)
Variable costs					
Direct material	8,000	(8)	5,600	5,200	400 (F)
Direct labour	4,000	(4)	2,800	3,100	300 (A)
Variable production overhead	2,000	(2)	1,400	1,500	100 (A)
	14,000	(14)	9,800	9,800	
Contribution	6,000		4,200	4,400	
Fixed costs	5,000	(N/A)	5,000	5,400	400 (A)
Profit/(loss)	1,000		(800)	(1,000)	200 (A)

Note that the differences between actual results (what revenues and costs *were* for 700 units) and the flexed budget (what revenues and costs *should* be for 700 units) have been noted in the right hand column as *variances*. (F) denotes a situation where actual results were better than the flexible budget results whereas (A) denotes a situation where actual results were worse than flexible budget results.

By flexing the budget in the exercise above we removed the effect on sales revenue of the difference between budgeted *sales volume* and actual *sales volume*. But there is still a variance of $200 (F). This means that the actual *selling price* must have been different to the budgeted selling price, resulting in a $200 (F) selling price variance.

7.1 Factors to consider when preparing flexible budgets

The mechanics of flexible budgeting are, in theory, fairly straightforward. In practice, however, there are a number of **points that must be considered before figures are flexed**.

(a)   The **separation of costs into their fixed and variable elements** is not always straightforward.

(b)   Fixed costs may behave in a **step-line** fashion as activity levels increase/decrease.

(c)   Account must be taken of the **assumptions** upon which the original fixed budget was based. Such assumptions might include the constraint posed by limiting factors, the rate of inflation, judgements about future uncertainty, the demand for the organisation's products and so on.

7.2 Fixed and flexible budgets: a summary

7.2.1 Fixed and flexible budgets differences

A fixed budget will not change to take into account variations in production, sales or expenses actually experienced. A flexible budget can do this by adjusting expected total costs for the level of production achieved. The original budget based on a given volume is 'flexed' to the actual volume by analysing budgeted costs over budgeted volume and multiplying by actual units produced.

7.2.2 When fixed and flexible budgets are appropriate

Both sorts of budget are used essentially for cost control, although they also provide management with a yardstick to measure achievement and may thus encourage the attainment of objectives.

Fixed budgets are useful at the **planning stage** as they provide a **common ground** for the preparation of all the many types of budget. At the end of the period, actual results may be compared with the fixed budget and analysed for control. However, this analysis may be distorted by uncorrected errors underlying the estimates on which the fixed budget was constructed.

A **flexible budget** may be needed at the planning stage to **complement the master budget**; output may be budgeted at a number of different possible levels for instance. During the period the flexible budget may then be updated to the actual level of activity and the results compared.

As a result flexible budgets assist management control by providing more dynamic and comparable information. Relying only on a fixed budget would give rise to massive variances; since forecast volume is very unlikely to be matched, the variances will contain large volume differences. Flexible budgets are more likely to pinpoint actual problem areas on which control may be exercised.

EXAM FOCUS POINT

Flexible budgets are a key syllabus area. You should be able to explain why budget variances should be based upon flexed budget figures.

8 Features and functions of spreadsheets

Use of spreadsheets is an essential part of the day-to-day work of an accountant.

8.1 What is a spreadsheet?

A spreadsheet is an electronic piece of paper divided into **rows** and **columns**. The intersection of a row and a column is known as a **cell**.

A spreadsheet is divided into **rows** (horizontal) and **columns** (vertical). The rows are numbered 1, 2, 3 . . . etc and the columns lettered A, B C . . . etc. Each individual area representing the intersection of a row and a column is called a '**cell**'. A cell address consists of its row and column reference. For example, in the spreadsheet below the word '*Jan*' is in cell B2. The cell that the cursor is currently in or over is known as the 'active cell'.

The main examples of spreadsheet packages are Lotus 1 2 3 and Microsoft Excel. We will be referring to **Microsoft Excel**, as this is the most widely-used spreadsheet. A simple Microsoft Excel spreadsheet, containing budgeted sales figures for three geographical areas for the first quarter of the year, is shown below.

	A	B	C	D	E	F
1	BUDGETED SALES FIGURES					
2		Jan	Feb	Mar	Total	
3		$'000	$'000	$'000	$'000	
4	North	2,431	3,001	2,189	7,621	
5	South	6,532	5,826	6,124	18,482	
6	West	895	432	596	1,923	
7	Total	9,858	9,259	8,909	28,026	
8						

8.2 Why use spreadsheets?

Spreadsheets provide a tool for calculating, analysing and manipulating numerical data. Spreadsheets make the calculation and manipulation of data easier and quicker. For example, the spreadsheet above has been set up to calculate the totals **automatically.** If you changed your estimate of sales in February for the North region to $3,296, when you input this figure in cell C4 the totals (in E4 and C7) would change accordingly.

8.2.1 Uses of spreadsheets

Spreadsheets can be used for a wide range of tasks. Some common applications of spreadsheets are:

- Management accounts
- Cash flow analysis and forecasting
- Reconciliations
- Revenue analysis and comparison
- Cost analysis and comparison
- Budgets and forecasts

BPP
LEARNING MEDIA

8.2.2 Cell contents

The contents of any cell can be one of the following.

(a) **Text**. A text cell usually contains **words**. Numbers that do not represent numeric values for calculation purposes (eg a Part Number) may be entered in a way that tells Excel to treat the cell contents as text. To do this, enter an apostrophe before the number eg '451.

(b) **Values**. A value is a **number** that can be used in a calculation.

(c) **Formulae**. A formula **refers to other cells** in the spreadsheet, and performs some sort of computation with them. For example, if cell C1 contains the formula =A1-B1, cell C1 will display the result of the calculation subtracting the contents of cell B1 from the contents of cell A1. In Excel, a formula always begins with an equals sign: = . There are a wide range of formulae and functions available.

8.2.3 Formula bar

The following illustration shows the formula bar. (If the formula bar is not visible, choose **View**, **Formula bar** from Excel's main menu.)

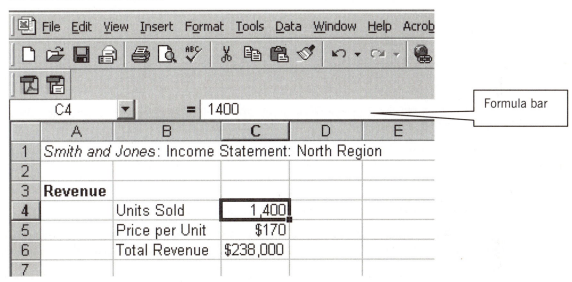

The formula bar allows you to see and edit the contents of the active cell. The bar also shows the cell address of the active cell (C4 in the example above).

EXAM FOCUS POINT

Questions on spreadsheets are likely to focus on the main features of spreadsheets and their issues.

9 Examples of spreadsheet formulae

Formulae in Microsoft Excel follow a specific syntax.

All Excel formulae start with the equals sign =, followed by the elements to be calculated (the operands) and the calculation operators. Each operand can be a value that does not change (a constant value), a cell or range reference, a label, a name, or a worksheet function.

Formulae can be used to perform a variety of calculations. Here are some examples.

(a)   =C4*5. This formula **multiplies** the value in C4 by 5. The result will appear in the cell holding the formula.

(b)   =C4*B10. This **multiplies** the value in C4 by the value in B10.

(c)   =C4/E5. This **divides** the value in C4 by the value in E5. (* means multiply and / means divide by.)

(d)   =C4*B10-D1. This **multiplies** the value in C4 by that in B10 and then subtracts the value in D1 from the result. Note that generally Excel will perform multiplication and division before addition or subtraction. If in any doubt, use brackets (parentheses): =(C4*B10)–D1.

(e)   =C4*117.5%. This **adds** 17.5% to the value in C4. It could be used to calculate a price including 17.5% sales tax.

(f)   =(C4+C5+C6)/3. Note that the **brackets** mean Excel would perform the addition first. Without the brackets, Excel would first divide the value in C6 by 3 and then add the result to the total of the values in C4 and C5.

(g)   = 2^2 gives you 2 **to the power** of 2, in other words 2^2 . Likewise = 2^3 gives you 2 cubed and so on.

(h)   = 4^ (1/2) gives you the **square root** of 4. Likewise 27^(1/3) gives you the cube root of 27 and so on.

Without brackets, Excel calculates a formula from left to right. You can control how calculation is performed by changing the syntax of the formula. For example, the formula =5+2*3 gives a result of 11 because Excel calculates multiplication before addition. Excel would multiply 2 by 3 (resulting in 6) and would then add 5.

You may use parentheses to change the order of operations. For example =(5+2)*3 would result in Excel firstly adding the 5 and 2 together, then multiplying that result by 3 to give 21.

9.1 Displaying the formulae held in your spreadsheet

It is sometimes useful to see all formulae held in your spreadsheet to enable you to see how the spreadsheet works. There are two ways of making Excel **display the formulae** held in a spreadsheet.

(a)   You can 'toggle' between the two types of display by pressing **Ctrl** +` (the latter is the key above the Tab key). Press Ctrl + ` again to get the previous display back.

(b)   You can also click on Tools, then on Options, then on View and tick the box next to 'Formulas'.

In the following paragraphs we provide examples of how spreadsheets and formulae may be used in an accounting context.

9.1.1 Example: formulae

	A	B	C	D	E	F
1	**BUDGETED SALES FIGURES**					
2		Jan	Feb	Mar	Total	
3		$'000	$'000	$'000	$'000	
4	North	2,431	3,001	2,189	7,621	
5	South	6,532	5,826	6,124	18,482	
6	West	895	432	596	1,923	
7	Total	9,858	9,259	8,909	28,026	
8						

(a)   In the spreadsheet shown above, which of the cells have had a number typed in, and which cells display the result of calculations (ie which cells contain a formula)?

(b) What formula would you put in each of the following cells?

(i)   Cell B7
(ii) Cell E6
(iii) Cell E7

(c) If the February sales figure for the South changed from $5,826 to $5,731, what other figures would change as a result? Give cell references.

Solution

(a) Cells into which you would need to enter a value are: B4, B5, B6, C4, C5, C6, D4, D5 and D6. Cells which would perform calculations are B7, C7, D7, E4, E5, E6 and E7.

(b) (i)   =B4+B5+B6 *or better* =SUM(B4:B6)

(ii) =B6+C6+D6 *or better* =SUM(B6:D6)

(iii) =E4+E5+E6 *or better* =SUM(E4:E6) Alternatively, the three monthly totals could be added across the spreadsheet: = SUM (B7: D7)

(c) The figures which would change, besides the amount in cell C5, would be those in cells C7, E5 and E7. (The contents of E7 would change if any of the sales figures changed.)

QUESTION

SUM formulae

The following spreadsheet shows sales of two products, the Ego and the Id, for the period July to September.

	A	B	C	D	E
1	**Sigmund Co**				
2	*Sales analysis - Q3 20X7*				
3		M7	M8	M9	Total
4		$	$	$	$
5	Ego	3,000	4,000	2,000	9,000
6	Id	2,000	1,500	4,000	7,500
7	Total	5,000	5,500	6,000	16,500
8					

Devise a suitable formula for each of the following cells.

(a) Cell B7   (c) Cell E7
(b) Cell E6

ANSWER

(a) =SUM(B5:B6)   (c) =SUM (E5:E6) *or* =SUM(B7:D7)
(b) =SUM(B6:D6)

or (best of all) =IF(SUM(E5:E6) =SUM(B7:D7),SUM(B7:D7),"ERROR")

QUESTION

Formulae

The following spreadsheet shows sales, exclusive of sales tax, in row 6.

	A	B	C	D	E	F	G	H
1	**Taxable supplies Co**							
2	*Sales analysis - Branch C*							
3	*Six months ended 30 June 200X*							
4		Jan	Feb	Mar	Apr	May	Jun	Total
5		$	$	$	$	$	$	$
6	Net sales	2,491.54	5,876.75	3,485.01	5,927.7	6,744.52	3,021.28	27,546.80
7	Sales tax							
8	Total							
9								

Your manager has asked you to insert formulae to calculate sales tax at 17½% in row 7 and also to produce totals.

(a) Devise a suitable formula for cell B7 and cell E8.
(b) How could the spreadsheet be better designed?

ANSWER

(a) For cell B7 =B6*0.175   For cell E8   =SUM(E6:E7)

(b) By using a separate 'variables' holding the sales tax rate and possibly the Sales figures. The formulae could then refer to these cells as shown below.

	A	B	C	D	E	F	G	H
1	**Taxable Supplies Co**							
2	*Sales analysis - Branch C*							
3	*Six months ended 30 June 200X*							
4		Jan	Feb	Mar	Apr	May	Jun	Total
5		$	$	$	$	$	$	$
6	Net sales	=B12	=C12	=D12	=E12	=F12	=G12	=SUM(B6:G6)
7	Sales tax	=B6*B13	=C6*B13	=D6*B13	=E6*B13	=F6*B13	=G6*B13	=SUM(B7:G7)
8	Total	=SUM(B6:B7)	=SUM(C6:C7)	=SUM(D6:D7)	=SUM(E6:E7)	=SUM(F6:F7)	=SUM(G6:G7)	=SUM(H6:H7)
9								
10								
11	*Variables*							
12	Sales	2491.54	5876.75	3485.01	5927.7	6744.52	3021.28	
13	Sales tax rate	0.175						

10 Advantages and disadvantages of spreadsheet software

10.1 Advantages of spreadsheets

- Excel is easy to learn and to use
- Spreadsheets make the calculation and manipulation of data easier and quicker
- They enable the analysis, reporting and sharing of financial information
- They enable 'what-if' analysis to be performed very quickly

10.2 Disadvantages of spreadsheets

- A spreadsheet is only as good as its original design, garbage in = garbage out!

- Formulae are hidden from sight so the underlying logic of a set of calculations may not be obvious

- A spreadsheet presentation may make reports appear infallible

- Research shows that a high proportion of large models contain critical errors

- A database may be more suitable to use with large volumes of data

- Spreadsheets are not good at word processing

- Spreadsheets are not suitable for constructing entire accounting systems

BPP
LEARNING MEDIA

QUESTION

An advantage of a spreadsheet program is that it

A   Can answer 'what if?' questions
B   Checks for incorrect entries
C   Automatically writes formulae
D   Can answer 'when is?' questions

ANSWER

The correct answer is A.

11   Uses of spreadsheet software

Spreadsheets can be used in a variety of accounting contexts. You should practise using spreadsheets, **hands-on experience** is the key to spreadsheet proficiency.

Management accountants will use spreadsheet software in activities such as budgeting, forecasting, reporting performance and variance analysis.

11.1 Budgeting

Spreadsheet packages for budgeting have a number of advantages.

(a)   Spreadsheet packages have a facility to perform **'what if' calculations** at great speed (see Section 11.2). For example, the consequences throughout the organisation of sales growth per month of nil, $^1/_2$%, 1%, $1^1/_2$% and so on can be calculated very quickly.

(b)   Preparing budgets may be complex; budgets may need to go through several drafts. If one or two figures are changed, the **computer will automatically make all the computational changes to the other figures**.

(c)   A spreadsheet model will **ensure that the preparation of the individual budgets is co-ordinated**. Data and information from the production budget, for example, will be automatically fed through to the material usage budget (as material usage will depend on production levels).

These advantages of spreadsheets make them ideal for taking over the **manipulation of numbers**, leaving staff to get involved in the real planning process.

11.2 'What if?' analysis

Once a model has been constructed the consequences of changes in any of the variables may be tested by asking **'what if?' questions, a form of sensitivity analysis**. For example, a spreadsheet may be used to develop a cash budget, such as that shown below.

	A	B	C	D
1		Month 1	Month 2	Month 3
2	Sales	1,000	1,200	1,440
3	Cost of sales	(650)	(780)	(936)
4	Gross profit	350	420	504
5				
6	Receipts:			
7	Current month	600	720	864
8	Previous month	-	400	480
9		-	-	-
10		600	1,120	1,344
11	Payments	(650)	(780)	(936)
12		(50)	340	408
13	Balance b/f	-	(50)	290
14	Balance c/f	(50)	290	698

Typical 'what if?' questions for sensitivity analysis

(a)   What if the cost of sales is 68% of sales revenue, not 65%?

(b)   What if payment from receivables is received 40% in the month of sale, 50% one month in arrears and 10% two months in arrears, instead of 60% in the month of sale and 40% one month in arrears?

(c)   What if sales growth is only 15% per month, instead of 20% per month?

Using the spreadsheet model, the answers to such questions can be obtained simply and quickly, using the editing facility in the program. The information obtained should **provide management with a better understanding of what the cash flow position in the future might be**, and **what factors are critical to ensuring that the cash position remains reasonable**. For example, it might be found that the cost of sales must remain less than 67% of sales value to achieve a satisfactory cash position.

CHAPTER ROUNDUP

↳ There are seven steps in the planning and control cycle.

1 Identify objectives
2 Identify potential strategies
3 Evaluate strategies
4 Choose alternative courses of action
5 Implement the long-term plan
6 Measure actual results and compare with plan
7 Respond to divergences from plan

↳ A **budget** is a quantified plan of action for a forthcoming accounting period. A **budget** is a plan of what the organisation is aiming to achieve and what is has set as a target, whereas a **forecast** is an estimate of what is **likely** to occur in the future.

↳ The **objectives** of a budgetary planning and control system are as follows.

– To ensure the achievement of the organisation's objectives
– To compel planning
– To communicate ideas and plans
– To coordinate activities
– To provide a framework for responsibility accounting
– To establish a system of control
– To motivate employees to improve their performance

↳ Responsibility centres can be divided into three types. Cost centres, profit centres and investment centres.

↳ **Fixed budgets** remain unchanged regardless of the level of activity; **flexible budgets** are designed to flex with the level of activity.

↳ Comparison of a fixed budget with the actual results for a different level of activity is of little use for **control purposes**. Flexible budgets should be used to show what cost and revenues should have been for the actual level of activity.

↳ A prerequisite of flexible budgeting is a knowledge of cost behaviour. The differences between the components of the fixed budget and the actual results are known as budget **variances.**

↳ Use of spreadsheets is an essential part of the day-to-day work of an accountant.

↳ A spreadsheet is an electronic piece of paper divided into rows and columns. The intersection of a row and a column is known as a cell.

↳ Formulae in Microsoft Excel follow a specific syntax.

↳ Spreadsheets can be used in a variety of accounting contexts. You should practise using spreadsheets, **hands-on experience** is the key to spreadsheet proficiency.

QUICK QUIZ

1   Which of the following is not an objective of a system of budgetary planning and control?

    A   To establish a system of control
    B   To coordinate activities
    C   To compel planning
    D   To motivate employees to maintain current performance levels

2   *Choose the appropriate words from those highlighted.*

A **forecast/budget** is an **estimate/guarantee** of what is **likely to occur in the future/has happened in the past.**

A **forecast/budget** is a **quantified plan/unquantified plan/guess** of what the organisation is aiming to **achieve/spend**.

3   Distinguish between a fixed budget and a flexible budget.

4   Flexible budgets are normally prepared on a marginal cost basis. True or false?

5   What are the two main reasons for differences between a fixed budget profit and actual profit?

ANSWERS TO QUICK QUIZ

1   D. The objective is to motivate employees to *improve* their performance.

2   A forecast is an estimate of what is likely to occur in the future.

    A budget is a quantified plan of what the organisation is aiming to achieve.

3   A **fixed budget** is a budget which is designed to remain unchanged regardless of the volume of output or sales achieved.

    A **flexible budget** is a budget which, by recognising different cost behaviour patterns, is designed to change if volumes of output change.

4   True.

5   A fixed budget profit might differ from an actual profit because costs were higher or lower than expected given the actual output and/or sales volumes were different to the level expected.

Now try ...

Attempt the questions below from the **Exam Question Bank**

Number

Q67 – Q70

16

In this chapter we look at how the budget is put together. You need to know the stages in budget preparation and the importance of the principal budget factor. You also need to know how to prepare functional and cash budgets.

The budgetary process

C	Budgeting	
1	**Nature and purpose of budgeting**	
(c)	Explain the administrative procedures used in the budgeting process	K
(d)	Describe the stages in the budgeting process (including sources of relevant data, planning and agreeing draft budgets and purpose of forecasts and how they link to budgeting)	K
3	**Budget preparation**	
(a)	Explain the importance of the principal budget factor in constructing the budget	K
(b)	Prepare sales budgets	S
(c)	Prepare functional budgets (production, raw materials usage and purchases, labour, variable and fixed overheads)	S
(d)	Prepare cash budgets	S
(e)	Prepare master budgets (income statement and statement of financial position)	S

1 Administration of the budget

The **budget manual** is a collection of instructions governing the responsibilities of persons and the procedures, forms and records relating to the preparation and use of budgetary data.

Managers responsible for preparing budgets should ideally be the managers responsible for carrying out the budget.

The **budget committee** is the co-ordinating body in the preparation and administration of budgets.

Having seen why organisations prepare budgets, we will now turn our attention to the administrative procedures that ensure that the budget process works effectively.

1.1 The budget period

The budget period is the time period to which the budget relates.

Except for capital expenditure budgets, the budget period is commonly the accounting year (sub-divided into 12 or 13 control periods).

1.2 Budget documentation: the budget manual

The budget manual is a collection of instructions governing the responsibilities of persons and the procedures, forms and records relating to the preparation and use of budgetary data.

One of the functions of the budget is to improve communication. A budget manual should be produced so that everyone can refer to it for information and guidance about the budgeting process. The budget manual does *not* contain the actual budgets for the forthcoming period; it is more of an **instruction/information manual about the way budgeting operates** in a particular organisation.

A budget manual will usually be prepared by the management accountant.

Content	Detail
Explanation of the objectives of the budgeting process	• The purpose of budgetary planning and control • The objectives of the various stages of the budgeting process • The importance of budgets in the long-term planning and administration of the enterprise
Organisational structures	• An organisation chart • A list of individuals holding budget responsibilities
Outline of the principal budgets	• Relationship between them
Administrative details	• Membership, and terms of reference, of the budget committee • The sequence in which budgets are to be prepared • A timetable
Procedural matters	• Specimen forms and instructions for completing them • Specimen reports • Account codes (or a chart of accounts) • The name of the budget officer to whom enquiries must be sent

1.3 Responsibility for the preparation of budgets

Managers responsible for preparing budgets should ideally be the managers who are responsible for carrying out the budget. For example, the sales manager should draft the sales budget and selling overhead cost centre budget and the purchasing manager should draft the material purchases budget.

1.4 Budget committee

The **co-ordination** and **administration of budgets** is usually the **responsibility of a budget committee** (with the managing director as chairman). The budget committee is **assisted by a budget officer** who is usually an accountant. Every part of the organisation should be represented on the committee, so there should be a **representative from sales**, **production, marketing** and so on. Functions of the budget committee include the following.

(a) Co-ordination of the preparation of budgets, which includes the issue of the budget manual

(b) Issuing of timetables for the preparation of functional budgets

(c) Allocation of responsibilities for the preparation of functional budgets

(d) Provision of information to assist in the preparation of budgets

(e) Communication of final budgets to the appropriate managers

(f) Continuous assessment of the budgeting and planning process, in order to improve the planning and control function

QUESTION
Budgets

(a) Try to obtain a copy of your organisation's budget manual. Is it user friendly? Could it provide more useful information?

(b) Attempt to determine who is on your organisation's budget committee. What role do they play?

2 The budget preparation timetable

The budget preparation process is as follows.

- – Communicating details of the budget policy and budget guidelines.
- – Determining the factor that restricts output
- – Preparation of the sales budget
- – Initial preparation of budgets
- – Negotiation of budgets with superiors
- – Co-ordination and review of budgets
- – Final acceptance of the budgets
- – Budget review

The **principal budget factor** should be identified at the beginning of the budgetary process, and the budget for this is prepared before all the others.

The procedures involved in preparing a budget will differ from organisation to organisation, but the step-by-step approach described here is indicative of the steps followed by many organisations. The preparation of a budget may take weeks or months and the budget committee may meet several times before an organisation's budget is finally agreed.

Step 1	Communicating details of the budget policy and budget guidelines
	The long-term plan is the starting point for the preparation of the annual budget. Managers responsible for preparing the budget must be aware of the way it is affected by the long-term plan so that it becomes part of the process of meeting the organisation's objectives. For example, if the long-term plan calls for a more aggressive pricing policy, the budget must take this into account. Managers should also be provided with important guidelines for wage rate increases, changes in productivity and so on, as well as information about industry demand and output.

Step 2	Determining the factor that restricts output

The principal budget factor (or key budget factor or **limiting budget factor** is the factor that limits an organisation's performance for a given period and is often the starting point in budget preparation.

For example, a company's sales department might estimate that it could sell 1,000 units of product X, which would require 5,000 hours of grade A labour to produce. If there are no units of product X already in inventory, and only 4,000 hours of grade A labour available in the budget period, then the company would be unable to sell 1,000 units of X because of the shortage of labour hours. Grade A labour would be a limiting budget factor, and the company's management must choose one of the following options.

(a) Reduce budgeted sales by 20%.

(b) Try to increase the availability of grade A labour by 1,000 hours (25%) by recruitment or overtime working.

(c) Try to sub-contract the production of 1,000 units to another manufacturer, but still profit on the transaction.

In most organisations the principal budget factor is sales demand: a company is usually restricted from making and selling more of its products because there would be no sales demand for the increased output at a price which would be acceptable/profitable to the company. The principal budget factor may also be machine capacity, distribution and selling resources, the availability of key raw materials or the availability of cash. Once this factor is defined then the rest of the budget can be prepared. For example, if sales are the principal budget factor then the production manager can only prepare his budget after the sales budget is complete.

However in the public sector, the principal budget factor will not be profit related. You need to think about the limiting factor for these organisations in terms of activity, for insurance consultant availability, cash budget or accommodation.

QUESTION

Limiting factors

In the NHS and other public sector organisations, the principal budget factor may not be the same as that faced by private sector organisations.

Required

List three or four limiting factors that would apply to public sector organisations.

ANSWER

Remember that state-run organisations providing services free at the point of consumption often face almost unlimited demand for their services. Therefore resources available usually comprise the limiting factor:

(a)   Cash from government grants and ministries
(b)   Trained staff such as nurses and doctors
(c)   Equipment such as MRI scanners and hospital beds

Step 3	Preparation of the sales budget

For many organisations, the principal budget factor is sales volume. The sales budget is therefore often the primary budget from which the majority of the other budgets are derived.

Before the sales budget can be prepared a sales forecast has to be made.

Sales forecasting is complex and involves the consideration of a number of factors.

(a)   Past sales patterns   (g)   New legislation
(b)   The economic environment   (h)   Distribution
(c)   Results of market research   (i)   Pricing policies and discounts offered
(d)   Anticipated advertising   (j)   Legislation
(e)   Competition   (k)   Environmental factors
(f)   Changing consumer taste

Management can use a number of forecasting methods.

(a)   Sales personnel can be asked to provide estimates.

(b)   Market research can be used (especially if an organisation is considering introducing a new product or service).

(c)   Various mathematical techniques can be used to estimate sales levels.

(d)   Annual contracts, under which major customers set out in advance monthly ranges of possible sales, can be reviewed.

On the basis of the sales forecast and the production capacity of the organisation, a sales budget will be prepared. This may be subdivided, possible subdivisions being by product, by sales area or by management responsibility.

For example, a sales budget might look like this

		North region		South region		Total	
		Units	Value	Units	Value	Units	Value
			$		$		$
January	Product A						
	Product B						
	Total						
February							
March							
April							
May							
June							
July							
August							
September							
October							
November							
December							
Total							
	Product A	6,000	2,400,000	5,000	2,000,000	11,000	4,400,000
	Product B	1,000	560,000	1,200	672,000	2,200	1,232,000

Step 4 **Initial preparation of budgets**

Budget	Detail
Finished goods inventory budget	Decides the planned increase or decrease in finished inventory levels.
Production budget	Stated in units of each product and is calculated as the sales budget in units plus the budgeted increase in finished goods inventories or minus the budgeted decrease in finished goods inventories.
Budgets of resources for production	**Materials usage budget** is stated in quantities and perhaps cost for each type of material used. It should take into account budgeted losses in production. **Machine utilisation budget** shows the operating hours required on each machine or group of machines. **Labour budget or wages budget** will be expressed in hours for each grade of labour and in terms of cost. It should take into account budgeted idle time.
Overhead cost budgets	**Production overheads** **Administration overheads** **Selling and distribution overheads** **Research and development department overheads**
Raw materials inventory budget	Decides the planned increase or decrease of the level of inventories.
Raw materials purchase budget	Can be prepared in quantities and value for each type of material purchased once the raw material usage requirements and the raw materials inventory budget are known.

BPP
LEARNING MEDIA

Budget	Detail
Overhead absorption rate	Can be calculated once the production volumes are planned, and the overhead cost centre budgets prepared.

Step 5

Negotiation of budgets with superiors

Once a manager has prepared his draft budget he should submit it to his superior for approval. The superior should then incorporate this budget with the others for which he or she is responsible and then submit this budget for approval to his or her superior. This process continues until the final budget is presented to the budget committee for approval.

At each stage of the process, the budget would be negotiated between the manager who had prepared the budget and his/her superior until agreed by both parties.

Step 6

Co-ordination of budgets

It is unlikely that the above steps will be problem-free. The budgets must be reviewed in relation to one another. Such a review may indicate that some budgets are out of balance with others and need modifying. The budget officer must identify such inconsistencies and bring them to the attention of the manager concerned. The revision of one budget may lead to the revision of all budgets. During this process the budgeted income statement and budgeted statement of financial position and cash budget should be prepared to ensure that all of the individual parts of the budget combine into an acceptable master budget.

Step 7

Final acceptance of the budget

When all the budgets are in harmony with one another they are summarised into a master budget consisting of a budgeted income statement, budgeted statement of financial position and cash budget.

Step 8

Budget review

The budgeting process does not stop once the budgets have been agreed. Actual results should be compared on a regular basis with the budgeted results. The frequency with which such comparisons are made depends very much on the organisation's circumstances and the sophistication of its control systems but it should occur at least monthly. Management should receive a report detailing the differences and should investigate the reasons for the differences. If the differences are within the control of management, corrective action should be taken to bring the reasons for the difference under control and to ensure that such inefficiencies do not occur in the future.

The differences may have occurred, however, because the budget was unrealistic to begin with or because the actual conditions did not reflect those anticipated (or could have possibly been anticipated). This would therefore invalidate the remainder of the budget.

The budget committee, who should meet periodically to evaluate the organisation's actual performance, may need to reappraise the organisation's future plans in the light of changes to anticipated conditions and to adjust the budget to take account of such changes.

The important point to note is that the budgeting process does not end for the current year once the budget period has begun: budgeting should be seen as a continuous and dynamic process.

QUESTION

A company that manufactures and sells a range of products, with sales potential limited by market share, is considering introducing a system of budgeting.

Required

(a)   List (in order of preparation) the budgets that need to be prepared.

(b)   State which budgets the master budget will comprise.

(c)   Consider how the work outlined in (a) and (b) can be co-ordinated in order for the budgeting process to be successful.

ANSWER

(a)   The sequence of budget preparation will be roughly as follows.

    (i)   Sales budget

       (The market share limits demand and so sales is the principal budget factor. All other activities will depend upon this forecast.)

    (ii)   Finished goods inventory budget (in units)

    (iii)   Production budget (in units)

    (iv)   Production resources budgets (materials, machine hours, labour)

    (v)   Overhead budgets for production, administration, selling and distribution, research and development and so on

    (vi)   Cash budget

(b)   The master budget is the summary of all the budgets. It often includes a summary income statement, statement of financial position and cash budget.

(c)   Procedures for preparing budgets can be contained in a budget manual which shows which budgets must be prepared when and by whom, what each functional budget should contain and detailed directions on how to prepare budgets including, for example, expected price increases, rates of interest, rates of depreciation and so on.

The formulation of budgets can be co-ordinated by a budget committee comprising the senior executives of the departments responsible for carrying out the budgets: sales, production, purchasing, personnel and so on.

The budgeting process may also be assisted by the use of a spreadsheet/computer budgeting package.

3   Functional budgets

Functional (or **departmental**) **budgets** are the budgets for the various functions and departments of an organisation. They therefore include production budgets, marketing budgets, sales budgets, personnel budgets, purchasing budgets and research and development budgets.

We will look at the preparation of a number of types of functional budget in this chapter but the general principles covered can be applied in most situations.

You must work through the examples here and make sure that you understand the principles well.

3.1 Production cost budget

If the principal budget factor was production capacity then the production cost budget would be the first to be prepared.

To assess whether production is the principal budget factor, the **production capacity available** must be determined. This should take into account the following factors.

(a) **Available labour**, including idle time, overtime and standard output rates per hour

(b) **Availability of raw materials** including allowances for losses during production

(c) **Maximum machine hours available**, including expected idle time and expected output rates per machine hour

It is, however, normally sales volume that is the constraint and therefore the production budget is prepared after the sales budget and the finished goods inventory budget.

The **production cost budget** will show the **quantities** and **costs** for **each product** and product group and will tie in with the sales and inventory budgets. This co-ordinating process is likely to show any shortfalls or excesses in capacity at various times over the budget period. If there is likely to be a shortfall then consideration should be given to overtime, subcontracting, machine hire, new sources of raw materials or some other way of increasing output. A significant shortfall means that production capacity is, in fact, the limiting factor.

If capacity exceeds sales volume for a length of time then consideration should be given to product diversification, a reduction in selling price (if demand is price elastic) and so on.

Once the production budget has been finalised, the labour, materials and machine budgets can be drawn up. These budgets will be based on budgeted activity levels, existing inventory positions and projected labour and material costs.

3.2 Example: the preparation of the production budget and direct labour budget

Pearson manufactures two products, P and L, and is preparing its budget for 20X3. Both products are made by the same grade of labour, grade G. The company currently holds 800 units of P and 1,200 units of L in inventory, but 250 of these units of L have just been discovered to have deteriorated in quality, and must therefore be scrapped. Budgeted sales of P are 3,000 units and of L 4,000 units, provided that the company maintains finished goods inventories at a level equal to three months' sales.

Grade G labour was originally expected to produce one unit of P in two hours and one unit of L in three hours, at an hourly rate of $2.50 per hour. In discussions with trade union negotiators, however, it has been agreed that the hourly wage rate should be raised by 50c per hour, provided that the times to produce P and L are reduced by 20%.

Required

Prepare the production budget and direct labour budget for 20X3.

3.3 Solution

The expected time to produce a unit of P will now be 80% of 2 hours = 1.6 hours, and the time for a unit of L will be 2.4 hours. The hourly wage rate will be $3, so that the direct labour cost will be $4.80 for P and $7.20 for L (thus achieving a saving for the company of 20c per unit of P produced and 30c per unit of L).

(a) *Production budget*

		Product P			Product L	
		Units	Units		Units	Units
Budgeted sales			3,000			4,000
Closing inventories	(3/12 × 3,000)	750		(3/12 × 4,000)	1,000	
Opening inventories (minus inventories scrapped)		800			950	
(Decrease)/increase in inventories			(50)			50
Production			2,950			4,050

(b) *Direct labour budget*

	Grade G Hours	Cost $
2,950 units of product P	4,720	14,160
4,050 units of product L	9,720	29,160
Total	14,440	43,320

It is assumed that there will be no idle time among grade G labour which, if it existed, would have to be paid for at the rate of $3 per hour.

3.4 Labour budget

A useful concept in budgeting for labour requirements is the standard hour.

A **standard hour** is the quantity of work achievable at standard performance, expressed in terms of a standard unit of work done in a standard period of time.

Budgeted output of different products or jobs in a period can be converted into standard hours of production, and a labour budget constructed accordingly.

Standard hours are particularly useful when management wants to monitor the production levels of a variety of dissimilar units. For example product A may take five hours to produce and product B, seven hours. If four units of each product are produced, instead of saying that total output is eight units, we could state the production level as
(4 × 5) + (4 × 7) standard hours = 48 standard hours.

3.5 Example: direct labour budget based on standard hours

Canaervon manufactures a single product, the close, with a single grade of labour. Its sales budget and finished goods inventory budget for period 3 are as follows.

Sales	700 units
Opening inventories, finished goods	50 units
Closing inventories, finished goods	70 units

The goods are inspected only when production work is completed, and it is budgeted that 10% of finished work will be scrapped.

The standard direct labour hour content of the close is three hours. The budgeted productivity ratio for direct labour is only 80% (which means that labour is only working at 80% efficiency).

The company employs 18 direct operatives, who are expected to average 144 working hours each in period 3.

Required

(a) Prepare a production budget.
(b) Prepare a direct labour budget.
(c) Comment on the problem that your direct labour budget reveals, and suggest how this problem might be overcome.

3.6 Solution

(a) *Production budget*

	Units
Sales	700
Add closing inventory	70
	770
Less opening inventory	50
Production required of 'good' output	720
Wastage rate	10%

$$\text{Total production required} \quad 720 \times \frac{100^*}{90} = 800 \text{ units}$$

(* Note that the required adjustment is 100/90, not 110/100, since the waste is assumed to be 10% of total production, not 10% of good production.)

(b)   Now we can prepare the direct labour budget.

Standard hours per unit	3
Total standard hours required = 800 units × 3 hours	2,400 hours
Productivity ratio	80%

$$\text{Actual hours required} \quad 2,400 \times \frac{100}{80} = 3,000 \text{ hours}$$

(c)   If we look at the direct labour budget against the information provided, we can identify the problem.

	Hours
Budgeted hours available (18 operatives × 144 hours)	2,592
Actual hours required	3,000
Shortfall in labour hours	408

The (draft) budget indicates that there will not be enough direct labour hours to meet the production requirements. This problem might be overcome in one, or a combination, of the following ways.

(a)   Reduce the closing inventory requirement below 70 units. This would reduce the number of production units required.

(b)   Persuade the workforce to do some overtime working.

(c)   Perhaps recruit more direct labour if long-term prospects are for higher production volumes.

(d)   Discuss with the workforce (or their union representatives) the following possibilities.

(i)   Improve the productivity ratio, and so reduce the number of hours required to produce the output.

(ii)   If possible, reduce the wastage rate below 10%.

3.7 Material purchases budget

QUESTION

Material budget

Taylors manufactures two products, W and S, which use the same raw materials, R and T. One unit of W uses 3 litres of R and 4 kilograms of T. One unit of S uses 5 litres of R and 2 kilograms of T. A litre of R is expected to cost $3 and a kilogram of T $7.

Budgeted sales for 20X2 are 8,000 units of W and 6,000 units of S; finished goods in inventory at 1 January 20X2 are 1,500 units of W and 300 units of S, and the company plans to hold inventories of 600 units of each product at 31 December 20X2.

Inventories of raw material are 6,000 litres of R and 2,800 kilograms of T at 1 January, and the company plans to hold 5,000 litres and 3,500 kilograms respectively at 31 December 20X2.

The warehouse and stores managers have suggested that a provision should be made for damages and deterioration of items held in store, as follows.

Product W :	loss of 50 units
Product S :	loss of 100 units
Material R :	loss of 500 litres
Material T :	loss of 200 kilograms

Required

Prepare a material purchases budget for the year 20X2.

ANSWER

To calculate material purchase requirements, it is first of all necessary to calculate the budgeted production volumes and material usage requirements.

	Product W		Product S	
	Units	Units	Units	Units
Sales		8,000		6,000
Provision for losses		50		100
Closing inventory	600		600	
Opening inventory	1,500		300	
(Decrease)/increase in inventory		(900)		300
Production budget		7,150		6,400

	Material R		Material T	
	Litres	Litres	Kg	Kg
Usage requirements				
To produce 7,150 units of W		21,450		28,600
To produce 6,400 units of S		32,000		12,800
Usage budget		53,450		41,400
Provision for losses		500		200
		53,950		41,600
Closing inventory	5,000		3,500	
Opening inventory	6,000		2,800	
(Decrease)/increase in inventory		(1,000)		700
Material purchases budget		52,950		42,300
Cost per unit		$3 per litre		$7 per kg
Cost of material purchases		$158,850		$296,100
Total purchases cost		$454,950		

EXAM FOCUS POINT

The preparation of a material purchases budget will often require you to manipulate the expression:

opening inventory + purchases − closing inventory = material used in production

A material purchases figure is therefore given by:

closing inventory + material used in production − opening inventory

Likewise a production budget may require manipulation of the expression:

opening inventory + units produced − closing inventory = sales

Now try the following question which draws together budget preparation for functional budgets. Remember the order in which budgets must be prepared using the steps in Section 3.

QUESTION

Functional budget

XYZ company produces three products X, Y and Z. For the coming accounting period budgets are to be prepared based on the following information.

Budgeted sales

Product X	2,000 at $100 each
Product Y	4,000 at $130 each
Product Z	3,000 at $150 each

Budgeted usage of raw material

	RM11	RM22	RM33
Product X	5	2	-
Product Y	3	2	2
Product Z	2	1	3
Cost per unit of material	$5	$3	$4

Finished inventories budget

	Product X	Product Y	Product Z
Opening	500	800	700
Closing	600	1,000	800

Raw materials inventory budget

	RM11	RM22	RM33
Opening	21,000	10,000	16,000
Closing	18,000	9,000	12,000

	Product X	Product Y	Product Z
Expected hours per unit	4	6	8
Expected hourly rate (labour)	$9	$9	$9

Fill in the blanks.

(a) **Sales budget**

	Product X	Product Y	Product Z	Total
Sales quantity	☐	☐	☐	
Sales value	$ ☐	$ ☐	$ ☐	$ ☐

(b) **Production budget**

	Product X Units	Product Y Units	Product Z Units
Budgeted production	☐	☐	☐

(c) **Material usage budget**

	RM11 Units	RM22 Units	RM33 Units
Budgeted material usage	☐	☐	☐

(d) **Material purchases budget**

	RM11	RM22	RM33
Budgeted material purchases	$ ☐	$ ☐	$ ☐

(e) **Labour budget**

Budgeted total wages	$ ☐

ANSWER

(a)

	Sales budget			
	Product X	*Product Y*	*Product Z*	*Total*
Sales quantity	2,000	4,000	3,000	
Sales price	$100	$130	$150	
Sales value	$ 200,000	$ 520,000	$ 450,000	$ 1,170,000

(b)

	Production budget		
	Product X	*Product Y*	*Product Z*
	Units	Units	Units
Sales quantity	2,000	4,000	3,000
Closing inventories	600	1,000	800
	2,600	5,000	3,800
Less opening inventories	500	800	700
Budgeted production	2,100	4,200	3,100

(c)

	Material usage budget			
	Production	*RM11*	*RM22*	*RM33*
	Units	Units	Units	Units
Product X	2,100	10,500	4,200	-
Product Y	4,200	12,600	8,400	8,400
Product Z	3,100	6,200	3,100	9,300
Budgeted material usage		29,300	15,700	17,700

(d)

	Material purchases budget		
	RM11	*RM22*	*RM33*
	Units	Units	Units
Budgeted material usage	29,300	15,700	17,700
Closing inventories	18,000	9,000	12,000
	47,300	24,700	29,700
Less opening inventories	21,000	10,000	16,000
Budgeted material purchases	26,300	14,700	13,700
Standard cost per unit	$5	$3	$4
Budgeted material purchases	$ 131,500	$ 44,100	$ 54,800

(e)

		Labour budget			
Product	*Production*	*Hours required per unit*	*Total hours*	*Rate per hour*	*Cost*
	Units			$	$
X	2,100	4	8,400	9	75,600
Y	4,200	6	25,200	9	226,800
Z	3,100	8	24,800	9	223,200
Budgeted total wages					525,600

3.8 Budgets for departments not involved in manufacturing

Budgets are also prepared for those departments and functions not involved in manufacturing. An organisation may therefore also prepare an administration budget, a marketing budget, a research and development budget and so on. Such budgets do *not* take as their starting point the sales budget (if sales are the principal budget factor) because the level of administration costs, say, is unlikely to vary in proportion to the level of sales. Instead the administration cost budget will be drawn up following meetings between the management accountant and various members of staff ranging from the managing director down to office managers and supervisors.

The example below shows a typical marketing cost budget. Notice that only the selling and agency commission varies directly with the level of sales.

ABC: MARKETING COST BUDGET

	$'000
Description/detail of cost items	
Salaries and wages of marketing staff	X
Advertising expenses	X
Travelling and distribution costs	X
Market research activities	X
Promotional activities and marketing relations	X
Selling and agency commission (2$\frac{1}{2}$% of sales)	X
	X

3.9 Co-ordination of functional budgets

It is vital that the functional budgets are prepared in the correct order (for example, the material usage budget should be prepared after the production budget) and that the **overall process is co-ordinated** to ensure that the budgets are all in balance with each other. There is little point in the material usage budget being based on a budgeted production level of 10,000 units if the budgeted production level specified in the production budget is 15,000 units.

Once prepared, the **functional budgets** must be reviewed to ensure they are consistent with one another.

4 Cash budgets

A **cash budget** is a detailed budget of cash inflows and outflows incorporating both revenue and capital items.

A cash budget is thus a statement in which estimated future cash receipts and payments are tabulated in such a way as to show the forecast cash balance of a business at defined intervals.

4.1 Preparing cash budgets

For example, in December 20X2 an accounts department might wish to estimate the cash position of the business during the three following months, January to March 20X3. A cash budget might be drawn up in the following format.

	Jan $	Feb $	Mar $
Estimated cash receipts			
From accounts payable	14,000	16,500	17,000
From cash sales	3,000	4,000	4,500
Proceeds on disposal of non-current assets		2,200	
Total cash receipts	17,000	22,700	21,500

Estimated cash payments			
To suppliers of goods	8,000	7,800	10,500
To employees (wages)	3,000	3,500	3,500
Purchase of non-current assets		16,000	
Rent and rates			1,000
Other overheads	1,200	1,200	1,200
Repayment of loan	2,500		
	14,700	28,500	16,200
Net surplus/(deficit) for month	2,300	(5,800)	5,300
Opening cash balance	1,200	3,500	(2,300)
Closing cash balance	3,500	(2,300)	3,000

In this example (where the figures are purely for illustration) the accounts department has calculated that the cash balance at the beginning of the budget period, 1 January, will be $1,200. Estimates have been made of the cash which is likely to be received by the business (from cash and credit sales, and from a planned disposal of non-current assets in February). Similar estimates have been made of cash due to be paid out by the business (payments to suppliers and employees, payments for rent, rates and other overheads, payment for a planned purchase of non-current assets in February and a loan repayment due in January).

From these estimates it is a simple step to calculate the excess of cash receipts over cash payments in each month. In some months cash payments may exceed cash receipts and there will be a **deficit** for the month; this occurs during February in the above example because of the large investment in non-current assets in that month.

The last part of the cash budget above shows how the business's estimated cash balance can then be rolled along from month to month. Starting with the opening balance of $1,200 at 1 January a cash surplus of $2,300 is generated in January. This leads to a closing January balance of $3,500 which becomes the opening balance for February. The deficit of $5,800 in February throws the business's cash position into **overdraft** and the overdrawn balance of $2,300 becomes the opening balance for March. Finally, the healthy cash surplus of $5,300 in March leaves the business with a favourable cash position of $3,000 at the end of the budget period.

4.2 The usefulness of cash budgets

The usefulness of cash budgets is that they enable management to make any forward planning decisions that may be needed, such as advising their bank of estimated overdraft requirements or strengthening their credit control procedures to ensure that customers pay more quickly.

The cash budget is one of the most important planning tools that an organisation can use. It shows the **cash effect of all plans made within the budgetary process** and hence its preparation can lead to a **modification of budgets** if it shows that there are insufficient cash resources to finance the planned operations.

It can also give management an indication of **potential problems** that could arise and allows them the opportunity to take action to avoid such problems. A cash budget can show **four positions**. Management will need to take appropriate action depending on the potential position.

4.3 Potential cash positions

Cash position	Appropriate management action
Short-term surplus	• Pay suppliers early to obtain discount • Attempt to increase sales by increasing receivables and inventories • Make short-term investments
Short-term shortfall	• Increase accounts payable • Reduce receivables • Arrange an overdraft
Long-term surplus	• Make long-term investments • Expand • Diversify • Replace/update non-current assets
Long-term shortfall	• Raise long-term finance (such as via issue of share capital) • Consider shutdown/disinvestment opportunities

QUESTION

Cash budget

Tick the boxes to show which of the following should be included in a **cash** budget.

	Include	Do not include
Funds from the receipt of a bank loan		
Revaluation of a non-current asset		
Receipt of dividends from outside the business		
Depreciation of distribution vehicles		
Bad debts written off		
Share dividend paid		

ANSWER

Any item that is a **cash** flow will be included. Non-cash items are excluded from a cash budget.

	Include	Do not include
Funds from the receipt of a bank loan	✓	
Revaluation of a non-current asset		✓
Receipt of dividends from outside the business	✓	
Depreciation of distribution vehicles		✓
Bad debts written off		✓
Share dividend paid	✓	

4.4 Example: cash budgets again

Peter Blair has worked for some years as a sales representative, but has recently been made redundant. He intends to start up in business on his own account, using $15,000 which he currently has invested with a building society. Peter maintains a bank account showing a small credit balance, and he plans to approach his bank for the necessary additional finance. Peter asks you for advice and provides the following additional information.

(a)   Arrangements have been made to purchase non-current assets costing $8,000. These will be paid for at the end of September and are expected to have a five-year life, at the end of which they will possess a nil residual value.

(b)   Inventories costing $5,000 will be acquired on 28 September and subsequent monthly purchases will be at a level sufficient to replace forecast sales for the month.

(c)   Forecast monthly sales are $3,000 for October, $6,000 for November and December, and $10,500 from January 20X4 onwards.

(d)   Selling price is fixed at the cost of inventory plus 50%.

(e)   Two months' credit will be allowed to customers but only one month's credit will be received from suppliers of inventory.

(f)   Running expenses, including rent but excluding depreciation of non-current assets, are estimated at $1,600 per month.

(g)   Blair intends to make monthly cash drawings of $1,000.

Required

Prepare a cash budget for the six months to 31 March 20X4.

Solution

The opening cash balance at 1 October will consist of Peter's initial $15,000 less the $8,000 expended on non-current assets purchased in September. In other words, the opening balance is $7,000. Cash receipts from credit customers arise two months after the relevant sales.

Payments to suppliers are a little more tricky. We are told that cost of sales is $100/150 \times$ sales. Thus for October cost of sales is $100/150 \times \$3,000 = \$2,000$. These goods will be purchased in October but not paid for until November. Similar calculations can be made for later months. The initial inventory of $5,000 is purchased in September and consequently paid for in October.

Depreciation is not a cash flow and so is *not* included in a cash budget.
The cash budget can now be constructed.

CASH BUDGET FOR THE SIX MONTHS ENDING 31 MARCH 20X4

	Oct $	Nov $	Dec $	Jan $	Feb $	Mar $
Payments						
Suppliers	5,000	2,000	4,000	4,000	7,000	7,000
Running expenses	1,600	1,600	1,600	1,600	1,600	1,600
Drawings	1,000	1,000	1,000	1,000	1,000	1,000
	7,600	4,600	6,600	6,600	9,600	9,600
Receipts						
Receivables	–	–	3,000	6,000	6,000	10,500
Surplus/(shortfall)	(7,600)	(4,600)	(3,600)	(600)	(3,600)	900
Opening balance	7,000	(600)	(5,200)	(8,800)	(9,400)	(13,000)
Closing balance	(600)	(5,200)	(8,800)	(9,400)	(13,000)	(12,100)

QUESTION

ABC Co

The following information is available for ABC Co.

	May $	June $
Budgeted sales	30,000	40,000
Gross profit as a percentage of sales	30%	30%
Closing trade payables as a percentage of cost of sales	50	50%
Opening inventory	nil	nil
Closing inventory	nil	nil

How much money should be budgeted for supplier payments in June?

A $10,500
B $14,000
C $24,500
D $30,000

ANSWER

C

	May $	June $
Sales	30,000	40,000
Gross profit (@ 30%)	9,000	12,000
Cost of sales (sales – GP)	21,000	28,000
Closing trade payables (@ 50%)	10,500	14,000

	$
June opening payables	10,500
Increase in amounts owing (COS)	28,000
June closing payables	(14,000)
Amount paid in June	24,500

EXAM FOCUS POINT

Make sure that you read the article written by Beverley Jay on cash budgets, which appeared in the July 2012 edition of Student Accountant.

5 Budgeted income statement and statement of financial position

As well as wishing to forecast its cash position, a business might want to estimate its profitability and its financial position for a coming period. This would involve the preparation of a budgeted income statement and statement of financial position, along with the cash budget which form the master budget.

Just like historical financial statements, **budgeted accounts are based on the accruals concept**. If you keep this point in mind you will often be able to cut through the deliberately confusing detail of examination questions to prepare an answer very quickly.

5.1 Example: preparing a budgeted income statement and statement of financial position

Using the information below, you are required to prepare Peter Blair's budgeted income statement for the six months ending on 31 March 20X4 and a budgeted statement of financial position as at that date.

5.1.1 Example

Peter Blair has worked for some years as a sales representative, but has recently been made redundant. He intends to start up in business on his own account, using $15,000 which he currently has invested with a building society. Peter maintains a bank account showing a small credit balance, and he plans to approach his bank for the necessary additional finance. Peter asks you for advice and provides the following additional information.

 BPP LEARNING MEDIA

(a)   Arrangements have been made to purchase non-current assets costing $8,000. These will be paid for at the end of September 20X3 and are expected to have a five-year life, at the end of which they will possess a nil residual value.

(b)   Inventories costing $5,000 will be acquired on 28 September 20X3 and subsequent monthly purchases will be at a level sufficient to replace forecast sales for the month.

(c)   Forecast monthly sales are $3,000 for October, $6,000 for November and December, and $10,500 from January 20X4 onwards.

(d)   Selling price is fixed at the cost of stock plus 50%.

(e)   Two months' credit will be allowed to customers but only one month's credit will be received from suppliers of inventory.

(f)   Running expenses, including rent but excluding depreciation of non-current assets, are estimated at $1,600 per month.

(g)   Blair intends to make monthly cash drawings of $1,000.

(h)   Peter has prepared a cash budget for his bank manager. This shows a closing bank balance of $12,100 outdrawn at 31 March 20X4.

Required

Prepare a budgeted income statement and statement of financial position for the six months to 31 March 20X4.

5.2 Solution

5.2.1 Notes to help you

Payments to suppliers could be a little tricky. We are told that selling price = cost of sales × 150% = cost of sales × 150/100, and so cost of sales is 100/150 × sales. Thus for March cost of sales is 100/150 × $10,500 = $7,000. These goods will be purchased in March but not paid for until April.

The income statement

The income statement is straightforward. The first figure is sales, which can be computed very easily from the information in the question. It is sufficient to add up the monthly sales figures given there; for the income statement there is no need to worry about any closing receivables. Similarly, cost of sales is calculated directly from the information on gross margin contained in the question.

Depreciation is over five years so the depreciation rate is 20%.

FORECAST TRADING AND INCOME STATEMENT
FOR THE SIX MONTHS ENDING 31 MARCH 20X4

	$	$
Sales (3,000 + (2 × 6,000) + (3 × 10,500))		46,500
Cost of sales ($^2/_3$ × $46,500)		31,000
Gross profit		15,500
Expenses		
Running expenses (6 × $1,600)	9,600	
Depreciation ($8,000 × 20% × 6/12)	800	
		10,400
Net profit		5,100

Items will be shown in the statement of financial position as follows.

(a)   Inventory will comprise the initial purchases of $5,000 (as month-end inventory levels are constant).

(b)   Receivables will comprise sales made in February and March (not paid until April and May respectively).

(c)   Payables will comprise purchases made in March (not paid for until April).

(d)   The bank overdraft is the closing cash figure computed in the cash budget.

FORECAST STATEMENT OF FINANCIAL POSITION AT 31 MARCH 20X4

ASSETS	$	$
Non-current assets $(8,000 – 800 depreciation)		7,200
Current assets		
Inventories	5,000	
Receivables (2 × $10,500)	21,000	
		26,000
		33,200
EQUITY AND LIABILITIES		
Proprietor's interest		
Capital introduced		15,000
Profit for the period	5,100	
Less drawings	6,000	
Deficit retained		(900)
		14,100
Current liabilities		
Bank overdraft	12,100	
Trade payables (March purchases)	7,000	
		19,100
		33,200

Budget questions are often accompanied by a large amount of sometimes confusing detail. This should not blind you to the fact that many figures can be entered very simply from the logic of the trading situation described. For example in the case of Blair you might feel tempted to begin a T-account to compute the closing receivables figure. This kind of working is rarely necessary, since you are told that receivables take two months to pay. Closing receivables will equal total credit sales in the last two months of the period.

Similarly, you may be given a simple statement that a business pays rates at $1,500 a year, followed by a lot of detail to enable you to calculate a prepayment at the beginning and end of the year. If you are preparing a budgeted income statement for the year do not lose sight of the fact that the rates expense can be entered as $1,500 without any calculation at all.

6 The master budget

When all the functional budgets have been prepared, they are summarised and consolidated into a **master budget** which consists of the budgeted income statement, budgeted statement of financial position and cash budget and which provides the overall picture of the planned performance for the budget period

The **master budget** consists of a budgeted income statement, a budgeted statement of financial position and a cash budget.

6.1 Example: a master budget

Plagued Engineering produces two products, Niks and Args. The budget for the forthcoming year to 31 March 20X8 is to be prepared. Expectations for the forthcoming year include the following.

(a)   PLAGUED ENGINEERING
      STATEMENT OF FINANCIAL POSITION AS AT 1 APRIL 20X7

ASSETS	$	$
Non-current assets		
Land and buildings		45,000
Plant and equipment at cost	187,000	
Less accumulated depreciation	75,000	
		112,000
Current assets		
Raw materials	7,650	
Finished goods	23,600	
Receivables	19,500	
Cash	4,300	
		55,050
		212,050
EQUITY AND LIABILITIES		
Capital and assets		
Share capital		150,000
Accumulated profits		55,250
		205,250
Current liabilities		
Payables		6,800
		212,050

(b)   *Finished products*

The sales director has estimated the following.

		Niks	Args
(i)	Demand for the company's products	4,500 units	4,000 units
(ii)	Selling price per unit	$32	$44
(iii)	Closing inventory of finished products at 31 March 20X8	400 units	1,200 units
(iv)	Opening inventory of finished products at 1 April 20X7	900 units	200 units
(v)	Unit cost of this opening inventory	$20	$28
(vi)	Amount of plant capacity required for each unit of product		
	Machining	15 min	24 min
	Assembling	12 min	18 min
(vii)	Raw material content per unit of each product		
	Material A	1.5 kilos	0.5 kilos
	Material B	2.0 kilos	4.0 kilos
(viii)	Direct labour hours required per unit of each product	6 hours	9 hours

Finished goods are valued on a FIFO basis at full production cost.

(c)   *Raw materials*

		Material A	Material B
(i)	Closing inventory requirement in kilos at 31 March 20X8	600	1,000
(ii)	Opening inventory at 1 April 20X7 in kilos	1,100	6,000
(iii)	Budgeted cost of raw materials per kilo	$1.50	$1.00

Actual costs per kilo of opening inventories are as budgeted cost for the coming year.

(d)   *Direct labour*

The standard wage rate of direct labour is $1.60 per hour.

(e)   *Production overhead*

Production overhead is absorbed on the basis of machining hours, with separate absorption rates for each department. The following overheads are anticipated in the production cost centre budgets.

	Machining department	*Assembling department*
	$	$
Supervisors' salaries	10,000	9,150
Power	4,400	2,000
Maintenance and running costs	2,100	2,000
Consumables	3,400	500
General expenses	19,600	5,000
	39,500	18,650

Depreciation is taken at 5% straight line on plant and equipment. A machine costing the company $20,000 is due to be installed on 1 October 20X7 in the machining department, which already has machinery installed to the value of $100,000 (at cost). Land worth $180,000 is to be acquired in December 20X7.

(f)   *Selling and administration expenses*

	$
Sales commissions and salaries	14,300
Travelling and distribution	3,500
Office salaries	10,100
General administration expenses	2,500
	30,400

(g)   There is no opening or closing work in progress and inflation should be ignored.

(h)   Budgeted cash flows are as follows.

	Quarter 1	*Quarter 2*	*Quarter 3*	*Quarter 4*
Receipts from customers	70,000	100,000	100,000	40,000
Payments:				
Materials	7,000	9,000	10,000	5,000
Wages	33,000	20,000	11,000	15,000
Other costs and expenses	10,000	100,000	205,000	5,000

Required

Prepare the following for the year ended 31 March 20X8 for Plagued Engineering Ltd.

(a)   Sales budget
(b)   Production budget (in quantities)
(c)   Plant utilisation budget
(d)   Direct materials usage budget
(e)   Direct labour budget
(f)   Factory overhead budget
(g)   Computation of the factory cost per unit for each product
(h)   Direct materials purchases budget
(i)   Cost of goods sold budget
(j)   Cash budget
(k)   A budgeted income statement account and statement of financial position

6.2 Solution

(a)   *Sales budget*

	Market demand	*Selling price*	*Sales value*
	Units	$	$
Niks	4,500	32.00	144,000
Args	4,000	44.00	176,000
			320,000

(b)   *Production budget*

	Niks Units	*Args* Units
Sales requirement	4,500	4,000
(Decrease)/increase in finished goods inventory	(500)	1,000
Production requirement	4,000	5,000

(c)   *Plant utilisation budget*

Product	Units	*Machining* Hours per unit	Total hours	*Assembling* Hours per unit	Total hours
Niks	4,000	0.25	1,000	0.20	800
Args	5,000	0.40	2,000	0.30	1,500
			3,000		2,300

(d)   *Direct materials usage budget*

	Material A kg	*Material B* kg
Required for production:		
Niks: 4,000 × 1.5 kilos	6,000	–
4,000 × 2.0 kilos	–	8,000
Args: 5,000 × 0.5 kilos	2,500	–
5,000 × 4.0 kilos	–	20,000
Material usage	8,500	28,000
Unit cost	$1.50 per kilo	$1.00 per kilo
Cost of materials used	$12,750	$28,000

(e)   *Direct labour budget*

Product	Production Units	Hours required per unit	Total hours	Rate per hour $	Cost $
Niks	4,000	6	24,000	1.60	38,400
Args	5,000	9	45,000	1.60	72,000
			Total direct wages		110,400

(f)   *Production overhead budget*

	Machining dept $	Assembling dept $
Production overhead allocated and apportioned (excluding depreciation)	39,500	18,650
Depreciation costs		
(i) Existing plant		
(5% of $100,000 in machining)	5,000	
(5% of $87,000 in assembly)		4,350
(ii) Proposed plant		
(5% of 6/12 × $20,000)	500	
Total production overhead	45,000	23,000
Total machine hours (see (c))	3,000 hrs	2,300 hrs
Absorption rate per machine hour	$15	$10

(g)   *Cost of finished goods*

		Niks $		*Args* $
Direct material A	1.5 kg × $1.50	2.25	0.5 kg × $1.50	0.75
B	2.0 kg × $1.00	2.00	4.0 kg × $1.00	4.00
Direct labour	6 hrs × $1.60	9.60	9 hrs × $1.60	14.40
Production overhead				
Machining department	15 mins at $15 per hr	3.75	24 min at $15 per hr	6.00
Assembling department	12 mins at $10 per hr	2.00	18 mins at $10 per hr	3.00
Production cost per unit		19.60		28.15

(h) *Direct material purchases budget*

	A kg	B kg
Closing inventory required	600	1,000
Production requirements	8,500	28,000
	9,100	29,000
Less opening inventory	1,100	6,000
Purchase requirements	8,000	23,000
Cost per unit	$1.50	$1.00
Purchase costs	$12,000	$23,000

(i) *Cost of goods sold budget* (Using FIFO)

	Niks Units		$	Args Units		$
Opening inventories	900	(× 20.00)	18,000	200	(× 28.00)	5,600
Cost of production	4,000	(× 19.60)	78,400	5,000	(× 28.15)	140,750
	4,900		96,400	5,200		146,350
Less closing inventories	400	(× 19.60)	7,840	1,200	(× 28.15)	33,780
Cost of sales	4,500		88,560	4,000		112,570

Notes

(i) The cost of sales of Niks = 900 units at $20 each plus 3,600 units at $19.60 each.

(ii) The cost of sales of Args = 200 units at $28 each plus 3,800 units at $28.15 each.

(j) MASTER BUDGET

Cash budget for year to 31.3.X8

	Quarter 1 $	Quarter 2 $	Quarter 3 $	Quarter 4 $	Total $
Receipts	70,000	100,000	100,000	40,000	310,000
Payments					
Materials	7,000	9,000	10,000	5,000	31,000
Labour	33,000	20,000	11,000	15,000	79,000
Other costs and expenses	10,000	100,000	205,000	5,000	320,000
	50,000	129,000	226,000	25,000	430,000
Receipts less payments	20,000	(29,000)	(126,000)	15,000	
					(120,000)
Opening cash balance b/f	4,300	24,300	(4,700)	(130,700)	4,300
Closing cash balance c/f	24,300	(4,700)	(130,700)	(115,700)	(115,700)

Budgeted income statement for year to 31.3.X8

	Niks $	Args $	Total $
Sales	144,000	176,000	320,000
Less cost of sales	88,560	112,570	201,130
Gross profit	55,440	63,430	118,870
Less selling and administration			30,400
Net profit			88,470

Note. There will be no under-/over-absorbed production overhead in the budgeted income statement.

Budgeted statement of financial position at 31.3.X8

	$	$	$
ASSETS			
Non-current assets			
Land and buildings (W1)			225,000
Plant and equipment at cost (W2)		207,000	
Less accumulated depreciation (W3)		84,850	
			122,150
			347,150

Current assets

Raw materials (W4)	1,900	
Finished goods (W5)	41,620	
Receivables (W6)	29,500	
		73,020
		420,170

EQUITY AND LIABILITIES

Capital and reserves

Share capital	150,000	
Retained profit (W9)	143,720	
		293,720

Current liabilities

Payables (W7)	10,750	
Bank overdraft (W8)	115,700	
		126,450
		420,170

Workings

1

	$
Opening balance at 1.4.X7	45,000
Addition	180,000
Cost at 31.3.X8	225,000

2

	$
Opening balance at 1.4.X7	187,000
Addition	20,000
Cost at 31.3.X8	207,000

3

	$
Opening balance at 1.4.X7	75,000
Addition in period	5,000
((f)(i) and (ii) of solution)	4,350
Accumulated depreciation at 31.3.X8	500
	84,850

4

	A	B	Total
Closing inventory (kgs)	600	1,000	
Cost per kg	× $1.50	× $1.00	
Value of closing inventory	$900	$1,000	$1,900

5

	Niks	Args	Total
Closing inventory (units)	400	1,200	
Cost per unit ((g) of solution)	× $19.60	× $28.15	
	$7,840	$33,780	$41,620

6

	$
Opening balance	19,500
Sales ((a) of solution)	320,000
Receipts (from cash budget)	(310,000)
Closing balance	29,500

7

	$	$
Opening balance at 1.4.X7		6,800
Land	180,000	
Machine	20,000	
Labour	110,400	
Production overhead	39,500	
	18,650	
		58,150
Materials	12,000	
	23,000	
		35,000
Expenses		30,400
		433,950
		440,750
Cash payments (from cash budget)		(430,000)
Closing balance at 31.3.X8		10,750

8   From cash budget $115,750 overdrawn

9

	$
Retained profit b/f	55,250
Profit for year	88,470
Retained profit c/f	143,720

QUESTION

Master budget

Of what does the master budget comprise?

A   The budgeted income statement

B   The budgeted cash flow, budgeted income statement and budgeted statement of financial position

C   The entire set of budgets prepared

D   The budgeted cash flow

ANSWER

B   This is basic knowledge.

CHAPTER ROUNDUP

↳ The **budget manual** is a collection of instructions governing the responsibilities of persons and the procedures, forms and records relating to the preparation and use of budgetary data.

↳ Managers responsible for preparing budgets should ideally be the managers responsible for carrying out the budget.

↳ The **budget committee** is the co-ordinating body in the preparation and administration of budgets.

↳ The **budget preparation process** is as follows.

 – Communicating details of the budget policy and budget guidelines.
 – Determining the factor that restricts output
 – Preparation of the sales budget
 – Initial preparation of budgets
 – Negotiation of budgets with superiors
 – Co-ordination and review of budgets
 – Final acceptance of the budgets
 – Budget review

↳ The **principal budget factor** should be identified at the beginning of the budgetary process, and the budget for this is prepared before all the others.

↳ Once prepared, the **functional budgets** must be reviewed to ensure they are consistent with one another.

↳ The **master budget** consists of a budgeted income statement, a budgeted statement of financial position and a cash budget.

QUICK QUIZ

1 What is meant by the term principal budget factor?

2 What are the eight steps in the preparation of a budget?

3 How can a shortfall in capacity be overcome?

4 The master budget consists of the sales budget and the cash budget. True or false?

5 Which of the following are functional budgets?

 I Purchasing budget
 II Cash budget
 III Sales budget
 IV Marketing cost budget

 A I and II
 B None of the above
 C All of the above
 D I, III and IV

6 When preparing a material purchases budget, what is the quantity to be purchased?

 A Materials required for production – opening inventory of materials – closing inventory of materials

 B Materials required for production – opening inventory of materials + closing inventory of materials

 C Opening inventory of materials – materials required for production – closing inventory of materials

 D Opening inventory of materials + closing inventory of materials – materials required for production

ANSWERS TO QUICK QUIZ

1   A principal budget factor is the factor that limits an organisation's performance for a given period.

2   (a)   Communicating details of the budget policy and budget guidelines
    (b)   Determining the factor that restricts output
    (c)   Preparation of the sales budget
    (d)   Initial preparation of budgets
    (e)   Negotiation of budgets with superiors
    (f)   Co-ordination of budgets
    (g)   Final acceptance of the budgets
    (h)   Budget review

3   Consideration should be given to overtime, subcontracting, machine hire and/or new sources of materials.

4   False. The master budget consists of the budgeted income statement, the budgeted statement of financial position and the cash budget.

5   D   A functional budget is a budget of income and/or expenditure for a particular department or process. A cash budget does not relate to a function.

6   B   It may help you to think in terms of the inputs to a material purchases budget (opening inventory and purchases) and the outputs (closing inventory and the quantity used in production). The inputs should equal the outputs. Any one of the inputs or outputs can then be determined by manipulating opening inventory + purchases = closing inventory + used in production.

Now try ...

Attempt the questions below from the **Exam Question Bank**

Number

Q71 – Q75

17

This chapter looks at how to put budgets into action. Budgets can be motivational but they can also produce undesirable negative reactions. Participative budgeting can help to avoid a negative reaction but there are disadvantages to this approach as well.

Making budgets work

TOPIC LIST	SYLLABUS REFERENCE
1 Behavioural implications of budgeting	C7(a), (b)
2 Participation and performance evaluation	C7(b), (e), (f)
3 The use of budgets as targets	C7(b), (c)
4 The management accountant and motivation	C7(b), (d)

1 Behavioural implications of budgeting

Used correctly a budgetary control system can **motivate** but it can also produce undesirable **negative reactions**.

The purpose of a budgetary control system is to assist management in planning and controlling the resources of their organisation by providing appropriate control information. The information will only be valuable, however, if it is interpreted correctly and used purposefully by managers *and* employees.

The correct use of control information therefore depends not only on the content of the information itself, but also on the behaviour of its recipients. This is because control in business is exercised by people. Their attitude to control information will colour their views on what they should do with it and a number of behavioural problems can arise.

(a) The **managers who set the budget** or standards are **often not the managers** who are then made responsible for achieving budget targets.

(b) The **goals of the organisation as a whole**, as expressed in a budget, **may not coincide with the personal aspirations of individual managers**.

(c) **Control is applied at different stages by different people**. A supervisor might get weekly control reports, and act on them; his superior might get monthly control reports, and decide to take different control action. Different managers can get in each others' way, and resent the interference from others.

1.1 Motivation

Motivation is what makes people behave in the way that they do. It comes from individual attitudes, or group attitudes. Individuals will be motivated by personal desires and interests. These may be in line with the objectives of the organisation, and some people 'live for their jobs'. Other individuals see their job as a chore, and their motivations will be unrelated to the objectives of the organisation they work for.

It is therefore vital that the goals of management and the employees harmonise with the goals of the organisation as a whole. This is known as **goal congruence**. Although obtaining goal congruence is essentially a behavioural problem, **it is possible to design and run a budgetary control system which will go some way towards ensuring that goal congruence is achieved**. Managers and employees must therefore be favourably disposed towards the budgetary control system so that it can operate efficiently.

The management accountant should therefore try to ensure that employees have positive attitudes towards **setting budgets, implementing budgets** (that is, putting the organisation's plans into practice)

and feedback of results (**control information**). If this desirable state of affairs does not exist the organisation is at risk of under-performing as a result of dysfunctional decision-making.

Goal congruence is the state which leads individuals or groups to take actions that are in their self-interest and also in the best interest of the organisation. *CIMA Official Terminology*

Dysfunctional decision making occurs when goal congruence does not exist or is impaired. Managers and others take decisions that promote their self-interest at the expense of the interest of the organisation.

1.1.1 Poor attitudes when setting budgets

If managers are involved in preparing a budget, poor attitudes or hostile behaviour towards the budgetary control system can begin at the **planning stage.**

(a)   Managers may **complain that they are too busy** to spend much time on budgeting.

(b)   They may **build 'slack' into their expenditure estimates**.

(c)   They may argue that **formalising a budget plan on paper is too restricting** and that managers should be allowed flexibility in the decisions they take.

(d)   They may set budgets for their budget centre and **not coordinate** their own plans with those of other budget centres.

(e)   They may **base future plans on past results**, instead of using the opportunity for formalised planning to look at alternative options and new ideas.

On the other hand, **managers may not be involved in the budgeting process**. Organisational goals may not be communicated to them and they might have their budget decided for them by senior management or administrative decision. It is **hard for people to be motivated to achieve targets set by someone else.**

1.1.2 Poor attitudes when putting plans into action

Poor attitudes also arise **when a budget is implemented**.

(a)   Managers might **put in only just enough effort** to achieve budget targets, without trying to beat targets.

(b)   A formal budget might **encourage rigidity and discourage flexibility**.

(c)   **Short-term planning** in a budget **can draw attention away from the longer-term consequences** of decisions.

(d)   There might be **minimal cooperation and communication** between managers.

(e)   Managers will often try to make sure that they **spend up to their full budget allowance, and do not overspend**, so that they will not be accused of having asked for too much spending allowance in the first place.

1.1.3 Poor attitudes and the use of control information

The **attitude of managers towards the accounting control information** they receive **might reduce the information's effectiveness**.

(a)   Management accounting control reports could well be seen as having a relatively **low priority** in the list of management tasks. Managers might take the view that they have more pressing jobs on hand than looking at routine control reports.

(b)   Managers might **resent control information**; they may see it as **part of a system of trying to find fault with their work**. This resentment is likely to be particularly strong when budgets or standards are imposed on managers without allowing them to participate in the budget-setting process.

(c)   If budgets are seen as **pressure devices** to push managers into doing better, control reports will be resented.

(d)   Managers **may not understand the information** in the control reports, because they are unfamiliar with accounting terminology or principles.

(e)   Managers might have a **false sense of what their objectives should be**. A production manager might consider it more important to maintain quality standards regardless of cost. He would then dismiss adverse expenditure variances as inevitable and unavoidable.

(f)   **If there are flaws in the system of recording actual costs**, managers will dismiss control information as unreliable.

(g)   **Control information** might be **received weeks after the end of the** period to which it relates, in which case managers might regard it as out-of-date and no longer useful.

(h)   Managers might be **held responsible for variances outside their control**.

It is therefore obvious that accountants and senior management should try to implement systems that are acceptable to budget holders and which produce positive effects.

1.1.4 Pay as a motivator

Many researchers agree that **pay can be an important motivator**, when there is a formal link between higher pay (or other rewards, such as promotion) and achieving budget targets. Individuals are likely to work harder to achieve budget if they know that they will be rewarded for their successful efforts. There are, however, problems with using pay as an incentive.

(a)   A serious problem that can arise is that **formal reward and performance evaluation systems can encourage dysfunctional behaviour**. Many investigations have noted the tendency of managers to pad their budgets either in anticipation of cuts by superiors or to make the subsequent variances more favourable. And there are numerous examples of managers making decisions in response to performance indices, even though the decisions are contrary to the wider purposes of the organisation.

(b)   The targets must be challenging, but fair, otherwise individuals will become dissatisfied. **Pay can be a demotivator as well as a motivator**!

2   Participation and performance evaluation

There are basically two ways in which a budget can be set: from the **top down (imposed** budget) or from the **bottom up (participatory** budget). Many writers refer to a third style (negotiated). There are three ways of using budgetary information to evaluate managerial performance (**budget constrained style, profit conscious style, non-accounting style**).

2.1 Participation

It has been argued that **participation** in the budgeting process **will improve motivation** and so will improve the quality of budget decisions and the efforts of individuals to achieve their budget targets (although obviously this will depend on the personality of the individual, the nature of the task (narrowly defined or flexible) and the organisational culture).

There are basically two ways in which a budget can be set: from the **top down** (imposed budget) or from the **bottom up** (participatory budget).

2.2 Imposed style of budgeting

An **imposed/top-down budget** is 'A budget allowance which is set without permitting the ultimate budget holder to have the opportunity to participate in the budgeting process'.

(CIMA *Official Terminology*)

In this approach to budgeting, **top management prepare a budget with little or no input from operating personnel** which is then imposed upon the employees who have to work to the budgeted figures.

The times when imposed budgets are effective

(a)   In newly-formed organisations
(b)   In very small businesses
(c)   During periods of economic hardship
(d)   When operational managers lack budgeting skills
(e)   When the organisation's different units require precise coordination

There are, of course, advantages and disadvantages to this style of setting budgets.

(a)   **Advantages**

  (i)   Strategic plans are likely to be incorporated into planned activities.
  (ii)   They enhance the coordination between the plans and objectives of divisions.
  (iii)   They use senior management's awareness of total resource availability.
  (iv)   They decrease the input from inexperienced or uninformed lower-level employees.
  (v)   They decrease the period of time taken to draw up the budgets.

(b)   **Disadvantages**

  (i)   Dissatisfaction, defensiveness and low morale amongst employees. It is hard for people to be motivated to achieve targets set by somebody else.

  (ii)   The feeling of team spirit may disappear.

  (iii)   The acceptance of organisational goals and objectives could be limited.

  (iv)   The feeling of the budget as a punitive device could arise.

  (v)   Managers who are performing operations on a day to day basis are likely to have a better understanding of what is achievable.

  (vi)   Unachievable budgets could result if consideration is not given to local operating and political environments. This applies particularly to overseas divisions.

  (vii)   Lower-level management initiative may be stifled.

2.3 Participative style of budgeting

Participative/bottom-up budgeting is 'A budgeting system in which all budget holders are given the opportunity to participate in setting their own budgets'.   (CIMA *Official Terminology*)

In this approach to budgeting, **budgets are developed by lower-level managers who then submit the budgets to their superiors**. The budgets are based on the lower-level managers' perceptions of what is achievable and the associated necessary resources.

QUESTION   Participative budgets

In what circumstances might participative budgets *not* be effective?

A   In centralised organisations
B   In well-established organisations
C   In very large businesses
D   During periods of economic affluence

ANSWER

The correct answer is A.

An imposed budget is likely to be most effective in a centralised organisation.

As well as in the circumstances in B, C and D, participative budgets are also effective when operational management have strong budgeting skills and when the organisation's different units act autonomously.

Advantages of participative budgets

(a)   They are based on information from employees most familiar with the department.
(b)   Knowledge spread among several levels of management is pulled together.
(c)   Morale and motivation is improved.
(d)   They increase operational managers' commitment to organisational objectives.
(e)   In general they are more realistic.
(f)   Co-ordination between units is improved.
(g)   Specific resource requirements are included.
(h)   Senior managers' overview is mixed with operational level details.
(i)   Individual managers' aspiration levels are more likely to be taken into account.

Disadvantages of participative budgets

(a)   They consume more time.
(b)   Changes implemented by senior management may cause dissatisfaction.
(c)   Budgets may be unachievable if managers are not qualified to participate.
(d)   They may cause managers to introduce budgetary slack and budget bias.
(e)   They can support 'empire building' by subordinates.
(f)   An earlier start to the budgeting process could be required.
(g)   Managers may set 'easy' budgets to ensure that they are achievable.

2.4 Negotiated style of budgeting

A **negotiated budget** is 'A budget in which budget allowances are set largely on the basis of negotiations between budget holders and those to whom they report'.   (CIMA *Official Terminology*)

At the two extremes, budgets can be dictated from above or simply emerge from below but, in practice, different levels of management often agree budgets by a process of negotiation. In the imposed budget approach, operational managers will try to negotiate with senior managers the budget targets which they consider to be unreasonable or unrealistic. Likewise senior management usually review and revise budgets presented to them under a participative approach through a process of negotiation with lower level managers. **Final budgets are therefore most likely to lie between what top management would really like and what junior managers believe is feasible.** The budgeting process is hence a **bargaining process** and it is this bargaining which is of vital importance, **determining whether the budget is an effective management tool or simply a clerical device**.

2.5 Performance evaluation

A very important **source of motivation to perform well** (to achieve budget targets, perhaps, or to eliminate variances) is, not surprisingly, being **kept informed about how actual results are progressing, and how actual results compare with target**. Individuals should not be kept in the dark about their performance.

The information fed back about actual results should have the qualities of good information.

QUESTION   Good information

Cast your mind back to your earlier studies. Which of the following is not a quality of good information?

A   Relevant
B   Complete
C   Timely
D   Cheap

ANSWER

The correct answer is D.

Good information is not necessarily cheap. The cost of providing it should be less than the value of the benefits it provides, however.

Here are the qualities of good information.

(a) Relevance	(f) Completeness
(b) Accuracy	(g) Clarity
(c) Inspires confidence	(h) Appropriately communicated (channel and recipient)
(d) Timely	(i) Manageable volume
(e) Cost of provision less than the value of benefits provided	

2.6 Features of feedback

(a) Reports should be **clear** and **comprehensive**.

(b) The '**exception principle**' should be applied so that **significant variances** are highlighted for investigation.

(c) Reports should identify the **controllable** costs and revenues, which are the items that can be directly influenced by the manager who receives the report. It can be demotivating if managers feel that they are being held responsible for items which are outside their control and which they are unable to influence.

(d) Reports should be **timely**, which means they must be produced in good time to allow the individual to take control action before any adverse results get much worse.

(e) Information should be **accurate** (although only accurate enough for its purpose as there is no need to go into unnecessary detail for pointless accuracy).

(f) Reports should be communicated to the manager who has **responsibility** and **authority** to act on the matter.

Surprisingly research evidence suggests that **all too often accounting performance measures lead to a lack of goal congruence**. Managers seek to improve their performance on the basis of the indicator used, even if this is not in the best interests of the organisation as a whole. For example, a production manager may be encouraged to achieve and maintain high production levels and to reduce costs, particularly if his or her bonus is linked to these factors. Such a manager is likely to be highly motivated. But the need to maintain high production levels could lead to high levels of slow-moving inventory, resulting in an adverse effect on the company's cash flow.

The **impact of an accounting system on managerial performance** depends ultimately on how the information is used. Research by Hopwood has shown that there are three distinct ways of using budgetary information to evaluate managerial performance.

Style of evaluation	Comment
Budget constrained	'The manager's performance is primarily evaluated upon the basis of his ability to continually meet the budget on a short-term basis. This criterion of performance is stressed at the expense of other valued and important criteria and the manager will receive unfavourable feedback from his superior if, for instance, his actual costs exceed the budgeted costs, regardless of other considerations.'
Profit conscious	'The manager's performance is evaluated on the basis of his ability to increase the general effectiveness of his unit's operations in relation to the long-term purposes of the organisation. For instance, at the cost centre level one important aspect of this ability concerns the attention which he devotes to reducing long-run costs. For this purpose, however, the budgetary information has to be used with great care in a rather flexible manner.'

Style of evaluation	Comment
Non-accounting	'The budgetary information plays a relatively unimportant part in the superior's evaluation of the manager's performance.'

A summary of the effects of the three styles of evaluation is as follows.

| | Style of evaluation | | |
	Budget constrained	Profit conscious	Non-accounting
Involvement with costs	HIGH	HIGH	LOW
Job-related tension	HIGH	MEDIUM	MEDIUM
Manipulation of the accounting reports (**bias**)	EXTENSIVE	LITTLE	LITTLE
Relations with the supervisor	POOR	GOOD	GOOD
Relations with colleagues	POOR	GOOD	GOOD

Research has shown no clear preference for one style over another.

2.7 Budgetary slack

Budgetary slack is the difference between the minimum necessary costs and the costs built into the budget or actually incurred.

In the process of preparing budgets, managers might **deliberately overestimate costs and underestimate sales**, so that they will not be blamed in the future for overspending and poor results.

In controlling actual operations, managers must then **ensure that their spending rises to meet their budget**, otherwise they will be 'blamed' for careless budgeting.

A typical situation is for a manager to **pad the budget** and waste money on non-essential expenses so that he uses all his budget allowances. The reason behind his action is the fear that unless the allowance is fully spent it will be reduced in future periods thus making his job more difficult as the future reduced budgets will not be so easy to attain. Because inefficiency and slack are allowed for in budgets, achieving a budget target means only that costs have remained within the accepted levels of inefficient spending.

Conversely, it has been noted that, after a run of mediocre results, some managers **deliberately overstate revenues and understate cost estimates**, no doubt feeling the need to make an immediate favourable impact by promising better performance in the future. They may merely delay problems, however, as the managers may well be censured when they fail to hit these optimistic targets.

3 The use of budgets as targets

In certain situations it is useful to prepare an **expectations budget** and an **aspirations budget**.

Management and the management accountant require strategies and methods for dealing with the **tensions** and **conflict** resulting from the **conflicting purposes** of a budget.

Once decided, budgets become targets. As targets, they can motivate managers to achieve a high level of performance. But **how difficult should targets be**? And how might people react to targets of differing degrees of difficulty in achievement?

(a)   There is likely to be a **demotivating** effect where an **ideal standard** of performance is set, because adverse efficiency variances will always be reported.

(b)   A **low standard of efficiency** is also **demotivating**, because there is no sense of achievement in attaining the required standards, and there will be no impetus for employees to try harder to do better than this.

(c)   A **budgeted level of attainment** could be 'normal': that is, the **same as the level that has been achieved in the past**. Arguably, this level will be **too low**. It might **encourage budgetary slack**.

It has been argued that **each individual has a personal 'aspiration level'**. This is a level of performance in a task with which the individual is familiar, which the individual undertakes for himself to reach. This aspiration level might be quite challenging and if individuals in a work group all have similar aspiration levels it should be possible to incorporate these levels within the official operating standards.

Some care should be taken, however, in applying this.

(a)   If a manager's **tendency to achieve success is stronger than the tendency to avoid failure**, budgets with **targets of intermediate levels of difficulty** are the most **motivating**, and stimulate a manager to better performance levels. Budgets which are either too easy to achieve or too difficult are de-motivating, and managers given such targets achieve relatively low levels of performance.

(b)   A manager's **tendency to avoid failure might be stronger than the tendency to achieve success**. (This is likely in an organisation in which the budget is used as a pressure device on subordinates by senior managers). Managers might then be discouraged from trying to achieve budgets of intermediate difficulty and tend to avoid taking on such tasks, resulting in poor levels of performance, worse than if budget targets were either easy or very difficult to achieve.

It has therefore been suggested that in a situation where budget targets of an intermediate difficulty *are* motivating, such targets ought to be set if the purpose of budgets is to motivate; however, although budgets which are set for **motivational purposes** need to be stated in terms of **aspirations rather than expectations**, budgets for planning and decision purposes need to be stated in terms of the best available estimate of expected actual performance. The **solution** might therefore be to have **two budgets**.

(a)   A **budget for planning and decision making based on reasonable expectations**.

(b)   A second **budget for motivational purposes**, with **more difficult targets of performance** (that is, targets of an intermediate level of difficulty).

These two budgets might be called an **'expectations budget'** and an **'aspirations budget'** respectively.

4 The management accountant and motivation

We have seen that budgets serve many purposes, but in some instances their purposes can conflict and have an effect on management behaviour. Management and the management accountant therefore require strategies and methods for dealing with the resulting tensions and conflict. For example, should targets be adjusted for uncontrollable and unforeseeable environmental influence? But what is then the effect on motivation if employees view performance standards as changeable?

Can performance measures and the related budgetary control system ever **motivate managers** towards achieving the organisation's goals?

(a)   Accounting measures of performance **can't provide a comprehensive assessment** of what a person has achieved for the organisation.

(b)   It is unfair as it is usually **impossible to segregate controllable and uncontrollable components of performance**.

(c)   Accounting **reports tend to concentrate on short-term achievements**, to the exclusion of the long-term effects.

(d)   Many accounting **reports try to serve several different purposes**, and in trying to satisfy several needs actually satisfy none properly.

The management accountant does not have the authority to do much on his or her own to improve hostile or apathetic attitudes to control information. There has to be support, either from senior management or from budget centre managers. However, the management accountant can do quite a lot to improve and then maintain the standard of a budgetary control reporting system.

(a)   **How senior management can offer support**

(i)   Making sure that a **system of responsibility accounting is adopted**. We discussed this in Chapter 15.

(ii) Allowing **managers to have a say in formulating their budgets**.

(iii) Offering **incentives** to managers who meet budget targets.

(iv) **Not regarding budgetary control information as a way of apportioning blame**.

(b) **Budget centre managers should accept their responsibilities**. In-house training courses could be held to encourage a collective, cooperative and positive attitude amongst managers.

(c) **How the management accountant can improve** (or maintain) the **quality of the budgetary control system**

(i) **Develop a working relationship with operational managers**, going out to meet them and discussing the control reports.

(ii) **Explain the meaning of budgets and control reports**.

(iii) **Keep accounting jargon in these reports to a minimum.**

(iv) Make **reports clear and to the point**, for example using the principle of reporting by exception.

(v) Provide control information with a **minimum of delay.**

(vi) **Make control information as useful as possible**, by distinguishing between directly attributable and controllable costs over which a manager should have influence and apportioned or fixed costs which are unavoidable or uncontrollable.

(vii) Make sure that **actual costs are recorded accurately**.

(viii) Ensure that **budgets are up-to-date**, either by having a system of rolling budgets, or else by updating budgets or standards as necessary, and ensuring that standards are 'fair' so that control information is realistic.

IMPORTANT

There are no ideal solutions to the conflicts caused by the operation of a budgetary control system. Management and the management accountant have to develop their own ways of dealing with them, taking into account their organisation, their business and the personalities involved.

QUESTION   Participation in budgets

Discuss the behavioural aspects of participation in the budgeting process and any difficulties you might envisage.

ANSWER

The level of participation in the budgeting process can vary from zero participation to a process of group decision making. There are a number of behavioural aspects of participation to consider.

(a) **Communication**. Managers cannot be expected to achieve targets if they do not know what those targets are. Communication of targets is made easier if managers have participated in the budgetary process from the beginning.

(b) **Motivation**. Managers are likely to be better motivated to achieve a budget if they have been involved in compiling it, rather than having a dictatorial budget imposed on them.

(c) **Realistic targets**. A target must be achievable and accepted as realistic if it is to be a motivating factor. A manager who has been involved in setting targets is more likely to accept them as realistic. In addition, managers who are close to the operation of their departments may be more aware of the costs and potential savings in running it.

(d)   **Goal congruence**. One of the best ways of achieving goal congruence is to involve managers in the preparation of their own budgets, so that their personal goals can be taken into account in setting targets.

Although participative budgeting has many advantages, difficulties might also arise.

(a)   **Pseudo-participation**. Participation may not be genuine, but merely a pretence at involving managers in the preparation of their budgets. Managers may feel that their contribution is being ignored, or that the participation consists of merely obtaining their agreement to a budget which has already been decided. If this is the case then managers are likely to be more demotivated than if there is no participation at all.

(b)   **Coordination**. If participative budgeting is well managed it can improve the coordination of the preparation of the various budgets. There is, however, a danger that too many managers will become involved so that communication becomes difficult and the process become complex.

(c)   **Training**. Some managers may not possess the necessary skill to make an effective contribution to the preparation of their budgets. Additional training may be necessary, with the consequent investment of money and time. It may also be necessary to train managers to understand the purposes and advantages of participation.

(d)   **Slack**. If budgets are used in a punitive fashion for control purposes then managers will be tempted to build in extra expenditure to provide a 'cushion' against overspending. It is easier for them to build in slack in a participative system.

4.1 Profit-sharing schemes

A **profit sharing scheme** is a scheme in which employees receive a certain proportion of their company's year-end profits (the size of their bonus being related to their position in the company and the length of their employment to date).

The advantages of these schemes is that the company will only pay what it can afford out of actual profits and the bonus can also be paid to non-production personnel.

The disadvantages of profit sharing are as follows.

(a)   Employees must **wait until the year end** for a bonus. The company is therefore expecting a long-term commitment to greater efforts and productivity from its workers without the incentive of immediate reward.

(b)   **Factors** affecting profit may be **outside the control** of employees, in spite of their greater efforts.

(c)   **Too many employees** are involved in a single scheme for the scheme to have a great motivating effect on individuals.

4.1.1 Incentive schemes involving shares

It is becoming increasingly common for companies to use their shares, or the right to acquire them, as a form of incentive.

A **share option scheme** is a scheme which gives its members the right to buy shares in the company for which they work at a set date in the future and at a price usually determined when the scheme is set up.

An **employee share ownership plan** is a scheme which acquires shares on behalf of a number of employees, and it must distribute these shares within a certain number of years of acquisition.

Some governments have encouraged companies to set up schemes of this nature in the hope that workers will feel they have a stake in the company which employs them. The **disadvantages** of these schemes are as follows.

(a)   The benefits are not certain, as the market value of shares at a future date cannot realistically be predicted in advance.

(b)   The benefits are not immediate, as a scheme must be in existence for a number of years before members can exercise their rights.

4.1.2 Value added incentive schemes

Value added is an alternative to profit as a business performance measure and it can be used as the basis of an incentive scheme. It is calculated as follows.

Value added = sales – cost of bought-in materials and services

The advantage of value added over profit as the basis for an incentive scheme is that it excludes any bought-in costs, and is affected only by costs incurred internally, such as labour.

A basic value added figure would be agreed as the target for a business, and some of any excess value added earned would be paid out as a bonus. For example, it could be agreed that value added should be, say, treble the payroll costs and a proportion of any excess earned, say one third, would be paid as bonus.

Payroll costs for month	$40,000
Therefore, value added target (× 3)	$120,000
Value added achieved	$150,000
Therefore, excess value added	$30,000
Employee share to be paid as bonus	$10,000

4.1.3 Example: incentive schemes

Swetton Tyres Co manufactures a single product. Its work force consists of 10 employees, who work a 36-hour week exclusive of lunch and tea breaks. The standard time required to make one unit of the product is two hours, but the current efficiency (or productivity) ratio being achieved is 80%. No overtime is worked, and the work force is paid $4 per attendance hour.

Because of agreements with the work force about work procedures, there is some unavoidable idle time due to bottlenecks in production, and about four hours per week per person are lost in this way.

The company can sell all the output it manufactures, and makes a 'cash profit' of $20 per unit sold, deducting currently achievable costs of production but *before* deducting labour costs.

An incentive scheme is proposed whereby the work force would be paid $5 per hour in exchange for agreeing to new work procedures that would reduce idle time per employee per week to two hours and also raise the efficiency ratio to 90%.

Required

Evaluate the incentive scheme from the point of view of profitability.

Solution

The current situation

Hours in attendance	10 × 36	= 360 hours
Hours spent working	10 × 32	= 320 hours

Units produced, at 80% efficiency $\dfrac{320}{2} \times \dfrac{80}{100}$ = 128 units

	$
Cash profits before deducting labour costs (128 × $20)	2,560
Less labour costs ($4 × 360 hours)	1,440
Net profit	1,120

The incentive scheme

Hours spent working	10 × 34	= 340 hours

Units produced, at 90% efficiency $\dfrac{340}{2} \times \dfrac{90}{100} = 153$ units

	$
Cash profits before deducting labour costs (153 × $20)	3,060
Less labour costs ($5 × 360)	1,800
Net profit	1,260

In spite of a 25% increase in labour costs, profits would rise by $140 per week. The company and the workforce would both benefit provided, of course, that management can hold the work force to their promise of work reorganisation and improved productivity.

QUESTION   Labour cost

The following data relate to work at a certain factory.

Normal working day	8 hours
Basic rate of pay per hour	$6
Standard time allowed to produce 1 unit	2 minutes
Premium bonus	75% of time saved at basic rate

What will be the labour cost in a day when 340 units are made?

A $48   B $51   C $63   D $68

ANSWER

Standard time for 340 units (× 2 minutes)	680 minutes
Actual time (8 hours per day)	480 minutes
Time saved	200 minutes

	$
Bonus = 75% × 200 minutes × $6 per hour	15
Basic pay = 8 hours × $6	48
Total labour cost	63

Therefore the correct answer is C.

Using basic MCQ technique you can eliminate option A because this is simply the basic pay without consideration of any bonus. You can also eliminate option D, which is based on the standard time allowance without considering the basic pay for the eight-hour day. Hopefully your were not forced to guess, but had you been you would have had a 50% chance of selecting the correct answer (B or C) instead of a 25% chance because you were able to eliminate two of the options straightaway.

CHAPTER ROUNDUP

↳ Used correctly a budgetary control system can **motivate** but it can also produce **negative** undesirable reactions.

↳ There are basically two ways in which a budget can be set: from the **top down (imposed** budget) or from the **bottom up (participatory** budget). Many writers refer to a third style (negotiated). There are three ways of using budgetary information to evaluate managerial performance (**budget constrained style, profit conscious style, non-accounting style).**

↳ In certain situations it is useful to prepare an **expectations budget** and an **aspirations budget.**

↳ Management and the management accountant require strategies and methods for dealing with the **tensions** and **conflict** resulting from the **conflicting purposes** of a budget.

QUICK QUIZ

1 In what circumstances are imposed budgets effective?

2 *Match the descriptions to the budgeting style.*

Description

(a) Budget allowances are set without the involvement of the budget holder

(b) All budget holders are involved in setting their own budgets

(c) Budget allowances are set on the basis of discussions between budget holders and those to whom they report

Budgeting style

Negotiated budgeting
Participative budgeting
Imposed budgeting

3 *Choose the appropriate words from those highlighted.*

An **expectations/aspirations** budget would be most useful for the purposes of planning and decision making based on reasonable expectations, whereas an **aspirations/expectations** budget is more appropriate for improving motivation by setting targets of an intermediate level of difficulty.

ANSWERS TO QUICK QUIZ

1   (a)   In newly-formed organisations
    (b)   In very small businesses
    (c)   During periods of economic hardship
    (d)   When operational managers lack budgeting skills
    (e)   When the organisation's different units require precise co-ordination

2   (a)   Imposed budgeting
    (b)   Participative budgeting
    (c)   Negotiated budgeting

3   expectations
    aspirations

Now try ...

Attempt the questions below from the **Exam Question Bank**

Number

Q76 – Q78

This chapter looks at the importance of capital investment planning. You need to understand the difference between capital and revenue expenditure and be able to identify relevant and non-relevant costs.

Capital expenditure budgeting

1 Introduction

Capital expenditure often represents a significant investment by a company.

In this chapter we start with a reminder of what distinguishes capital from revenue expenditure. One of the significant differences is that capital expenditure is often for very significant amounts. Therefore expenditure for the wrong reasons or on the wrong assets can have a disastrous effect on an organisation's position.

Therefore the **need for capital expenditure** should be assessed before any firm commitments are made. Separate **capital expenditure budgets** need to be prepared, and expenditure and **non-current assets carefully monitored** for problems or losses.

2 What is capital expenditure?

Capital expenditure results in the acquisition of non-current assets or an improvement in their earning capacity. **Revenue expenditure** is expenditure which is incurred for the purpose of the trade of the business or to maintain the existing earning capacity of non-current assets.

A **non-current asset** is an asset which is acquired and retained in the business with a view to earning profits and not merely turning into cash. It is normally used over more than one accounting period.

Examples of non-current assets

- Motor vehicles (except for a motor trader)
- Plant and machinery
- Fixtures and fittings
- Land and buildings

Non-current assets are to be distinguished from **inventories** which we buy or make in order to sell. Inventories are **current** assets and, as we have already seen, a part of the **working capital** of a business, along with cash and amounts owed to us by customers. For a motor trader, motor vehicles for re-sale are inventories. For an estate agency business, say, company cars are a non-current asset.

2.1 Capital and revenue expenditure

Capital expenditure is expenditure which results in the acquisition of non-current assets, or an improvement in their earning capacity.

So do you recall how capital expenditure is accounted for in the financial statements?

(a)   Capital expenditure is not charged as an expense in the income statement of a business enterprise, although a **depreciation charge** will usually be made to write off the capital expenditure gradually over time. Depreciation charges are expenses in the income statement.

(b)   Capital expenditure on non-current assets results in the appearance of a non-current asset in the **statement of financial position** of the business.

Special methods of accounting for capital expenditure apply in local authorities and in some other public sector organisations. These are not explained further here.

Revenue expenditure is expenditure which is incurred for either of the following reasons.

(a)   For the purpose of the trade of the business. This includes expenditure classified as selling and distribution expenses, administration expenses and finance charges.

(b)   To maintain the existing earning capacity of non-current assets.

Revenue expenditure is charged to the **income statement** of a period, provided that it relates to the trading activity and sales of that particular period.

Suppose that a business purchases a building for $30,000. It then adds an extension to the building at a cost of $10,000. The building needs to have a few broken windows mended, its floors polished and some missing roof tiles replaced. These cleaning and maintenance jobs cost $900. The original purchase ($30,000) and the cost of the extension ($10,000) are capital expenditures, because they are incurred to acquire and then improve a non-current asset. The other costs of $900 are revenue expenditure, because these merely maintain the building and thus the 'earning capacity' of the building.

2.2 Capital income and revenue income

Capital income is the proceeds from the sale of non-trading assets (ie proceeds from the sale of non-current assets, including non-current asset investments). The profits (or losses) from the sale of non-current assets are included in the income statement of a business, for the accounting period in which the sale takes place.

Revenue income is derived from the following sources.

*   The sale of trading assets
*   Interest and dividends received from investments held by the business

2.3 Other capital transactions

The categorisation of capital and revenue items given above does not mention raising additional capital from the owner(s) of the business, or raising and repaying loans. These are transactions which either:

(a)   **Add** to the **cash assets** of the business, thereby creating a corresponding liability (capital or loan), or

(b)   When a loan is repaid, **reduce the liabilities** (loan) and the assets (cash) of the business

None of these transactions would be reported through the income statement.

QUESTION   Capital expenditure

Which of the following are examples of capital expenditure?

A   Purchase of inventories
B   Improvements to the earning capacity of non-current assets
C   Depreciation
D   Settling trade credit balances

ANSWER

B   Capital expenditure is expenditure used to purchase or improve non-current assets.

2.4 Why is the distinction important?

Revenue expenditure results from the purchase of goods and services that will either:

(a)   Be **used fully** in the **accounting period** in which they are purchased, and so be a cost or expense in the income statement, or

(b)   **Result in** a **current asset** as at the end of the accounting period because the goods or services have not yet been consumed or made use of (The current asset would be shown in the statement of financial position and is not yet a cost or expense in the income statement.)

Capital expenditure results in the **purchase** or **improvement of non-current assets**, which are assets that will provide benefits to the business in more than one accounting period, and which are not acquired with a view to being resold in the normal course of trade. The cost of purchased non-current assets is not charged in full to the income statement of the period in which the purchase occurs. Instead, the non-current asset is gradually depreciated over a number of accounting periods.

Since revenue items and capital items are accounted for in different ways, the correct and consistent calculation of profit for any accounting period depends on the correct and consistent classification of items as revenue or capital.

QUESTION
Capital and revenue expenditure

Explain briefly the effect on the final accounts if:

(a)   Capital expenditure is treated as revenue expenditure
(b)   Revenue expenditure is treated as capital expenditure

ANSWER

(a)   If capital expenditure is treated as revenue expenditure, **profits** will be **understated** in the **income statement** and **non-current assets** will be **understated** in the **statement of financial position**.

(b)   If **revenue expenditure** is treated as **capital expenditure**, then the **profits** for the period will be **overstated** in the income statement and **non-current assets** will be **overstated** in the statement of financial position.

2.5 Self constructed assets

Where a business builds its own non-current asset (eg a builder might build his own office), then all the costs involved in building the asset should be included in the recorded cost of the non-current asset. These costs will include raw materials, but also labour costs and related overhead costs. This treatment means that assets which are self-constructed are treated in a similar way as purchased non-current assets.

3   Preparing capital expenditure budgets

Recurring and minor non-current asset purchases may be covered by an annual allowance provided for in the **capital expenditure budget**. Major projects will need to be considered individually and will need to be fully appraised.

The capital expenditure budget is essentially a **non-current assets purchase budget**, and it will form part of the longer term plan of a business enterprise.

Sales, production and related budgets cover, in general, a 12 month period. A detailed capital expenditure budget should be prepared for the budget period but additional budgets should be drawn up for both the medium and long term. This requires an in-depth consideration of the organisation's requirements for land, buildings, plant, machinery, vehicles, fixtures and fittings and so on for the short, medium and long term.

Suitable financing must be arranged as necessary. We looked at sources of finance in earlier chapters. If available funds are limiting the organisation's activities then it will more than likely limit capital expenditure. The capital expenditure budget should take account of this.

Some forms of capital expenditure may be budgeted for by means of a set **annual 'allowance'** for the purchase and replacement of non-current assets. Examples here would be sets of new tools, or relatively minor expenditure such as a few new desks and chairs.

As part of the overall budget coordination process, the capital expenditure budget must be **reviewed in relation to the other budgets**. Proposed expansion of production may well require significant non-current assets expenditure which should be reflected in the budget.

Before major capital expenditure is incurred, we need to be confident that the expenditure is worthwhile. We therefore need to appraise the project on which the expenditure is to be made, to see if it is likely to be of positive value to the business. In the next chapter, we turn to the methods of project appraisal which are available in order to do this.

CHAPTER ROUNDUP

> ↳ **Capital expenditure** often represents a significant investment by a company.
>
> ↳ **Capital expenditure** results in the acquisition of non-current assets or an improvement in their earning capacity. **Revenue expenditure** is expenditure which is incurred for the purpose of the trade of the business or to maintain the existing earning capacity of non-current assets.
>
> ↳ Recurring and minor non-current asset purchases may be covered by an annual allowance provided for in the **capital expenditure budget**. Major projects will need to be considered individually and will need to be fully appraised.

QUICK QUIZ

1   A .... is an asset which is acquired and retained in the business with a view to earning profits and not merely turning into cash.

2   How many periods should non-current asset expenditure benefit a business?

   A   One period
   B   More than one period, otherwise no minimum
   C   At least five periods
   D   At least ten periods

3   Revenue expenditure is expenditure incurred to maintain the existing earning capacity of non-current assets.

   True   ☐

   False ☐

4   What tasks would a capital expenditure budget officer carry out?

5   What types of capital expenditure might be covered by an annual budget allowance?

ANSWERS TO QUICK QUIZ

1   A **non-current asset** is an asset which is acquired and retained in the business with a view to earning profits and not merely turning into cash.

2   B   More than one period is all that is required

3   True

4   Communicating between interested parties; providing budget data; drawing up a timetable; etc.

5   Minor expenditure; and routine replacement of existing items such as books.

Now try ...

Attempt the questions below from the **Exam Question Bank**

Number

Q79 – Q81

In this chapter we continue our studies of capital
expenditure by looking at how to appraise projects to
decide which are worthwhile. You need to understand the
time value of money, the payback period and the internal
rate of return.

Methods of project appraisal

Study Guide		Intellectual level
C	**Budgeting**	
5	**Capital budgeting and discounted cash flows**	
(d)	Explain and illustrate the difference between simple and compound interest, and between nominal and effective interest rates	S
(e)	Explain and illustrate compounding and discounting	S
(f)	Explain the distinction between cash flow and profit and the relevance of cash flow to capital investment appraisal	K
(g)	Identify and evaluate relevant cash flows for individual investment decisions	S
(h)	Explain and illustrate the net present value (NPV) and internal rate of return (IRR) methods of discounted cash flow	S
(i)	Calculate present value using annuity and perpetuity formulae	S
(j)	Calculate NPV, IRR and payback (discounted and non-discounted)	S
(k)	Interpret the results of NPV, IRR and payback calculations of investment viability	S

1 Introduction

A **long-term view** of benefits and costs must be taken when reviewing a capital expenditure project.

We stressed in the last chapter the importance of careful purchasing procedures for capital expenditure. In this chapter we go on to consider how not just capital expenditure but major investment projects in general are **assessed**.

Another other decision that organisations face is how to compare costs and benefits. Some simple approaches (accounting rate of return and payback) take no account of when costs or revenues are incurred or received. However **discounted cash flow approaches** (net present value and payback) take a more sophisticated approach, being based on the principle that a pound received in the future is not worth as much as a pound received today. We shall explain how each of these approaches work, and have a look at their advantages and limitations.

2 Methods of project appraisal

The key methods of project appraisal are:

* The payback period
* Net present value
* Discounted payback period
* Internal rate of return (IRR)

Technical competence 15 requires you to demonstrate you are competent in using management accounting techniques to support planning and decision-making. The knowledge you gain in this chapter will help you demonstrate your competence in this area.

The following sections consider the different methods of project appraisal – the tools you can use when deciding whether or not to make an investment.

IMPORTANT

Relevant and non-relevant costs (see Chapter 18) should be used when applying these methods. If you are not completely clear on them go back and read Section 4 of that chapter.

EXAM FOCUS POINT

In NPV calculations, finance costs are irrelevant as interest is taken into account in the discounting process.

3 The payback period

The **payback period** is the time taken for the initial investment to be recovered in the cash inflows from the project. The payback method is particularly relevant if there are liquidity problems, or if distant forecasts are very uncertain.

The **payback period** method is one which gives greater weight to cash flows generated in earlier years. The payback period is the length of time required before the total cash inflows received from the project is equal to the original cash outlay. In other words, it is the length of time the investment takes to pay itself back.

In the previous example, machine X pays for itself within two years and machine Y in three years. Using the payback method of investment appraisal, machine X is preferable to machine Y.

The payback method has obvious disadvantages. Consider the case of two machines for which the following information is available.

		Machine P	Machine Q
		$	$
Cost		10,000	10,000
Cash inflows year	1	1,000	5,000
	2	2,000	5,000
	3	6,000	1,000
	4	7,000	500
	5	8,000	500
		24,000	12,000

Machine Q pays back at the end of year two and machine P not until early in year four. Using the payback method machine Q is to be preferred, but this ignores the fact that the total profitability of P ($24,000) is double that of Q.

Advantages of payback method	Disadvantages of payback method
It is easy to calculate and understand	Total profitability is ignored.
It is widely used in practice as a first screening method.	The **time value of money is ignored**
Its use will tend to minimise the effects of **risk** and help liquidity, because greater weight is given to earlier cash flows which can probably be predicted more accurately than distant cash flows.	It ignores any cash flows that occur after the project has paid for itself. A project that takes time to get off the ground but earns substantial profits once established might be rejected if the payback method is used, whereas a smaller project, paying back more quickly, may be accepted
It identifies quick cash generators.	The **cut-off period** for deciding what is acceptable is **arbitrary.**

A more scientific method of investment appraisal is the use of **discounted cash flow** (DCF) techniques. Before DCF can be understood it is necessary to know something about the **time value of money**.

QUESTION

Payback period

Project X has the following cash flows.

Year	Cash flow $
0	(105,000)
1	25,000
2	35,000
3	35,000
4	40,000
5	50,000

What is project X's payback period?

A   3 years   C   3.75 years

B   3.25 years   D   4 years

ANSWER

B   (25,000 + 35,000 + 35,000) = 95,000 will be paid back at the end of year 3 leaving 10,000 to be repaid in year 4.

$$\frac{10,000}{40,000} = 0.25 \text{ Therefore payback occurs after 3.25 years.}$$

4   The time value of money

The **time value of money** is an important consideration in decision making.

Money is spent to earn a profit. For example, if an item of machinery costs $6,000 and would earn profits (ignoring depreciation) of $2,000 per year for three years, it would not be worth buying because its total profit ($6,000) would only just cover its cost.

In addition the size of profits or return must be sufficiently large to justify the investment. In the example given in the previous paragraph, if the machinery costing $6,000 made total profits of $6,300 over three years, the return on the investment would be $300, or an average of $100 per year. This would

BPP
LEARNING MEDIA

be a very low return, because it would be much more profitable to invest the $6,000 somewhere else (eg in a bank).

We must therefore recognise that if a capital investment is to be worthwhile, it must earn at least a **minimum profit or return** so that the size of the return will compensate the investor (the business) for the **length of time** which the investor must wait before the profits are made.

When capital expenditure projects are evaluated, it is therefore appropriate to decide whether the investment will make enough profits to allow for the 'time value' of capital tied up. The time value of money reflects people's **time preference** for $100 now over $100 at some time in the future. DCF is an evaluation technique which takes into account the time value of money.

4.1 Discounting and compound interest

If we were to invest $1,000 now in a bank account which pays interest of 10% per annum, with interest calculated once each year at the end of the year, we would expect the following returns.

(a) After one year, the investment would rise in value to:

$1,000 plus 10% = $1,000 (1 + 10%) = $1,000 × (1.10) = $1,100

Interest for the year would be $100. We can say that the rate of **simple interest** is 10%.

(b) If we keep all our money in the bank account, after two years the investment would now be worth:

$1,100 × 1.10 = $1,210.

Interest in year two would be $(1,210 − 1,100) = $110.

Another way of writing this would be to show how the original investment has earned interest over two years as follows.

$1,000 × (1.10) × (1.10) = $1,000 × $(1.10)^2$ = $1,210

(c) Similarly, if we keep the money invested for a further year, the investment would grow to $1,000 × (1.10) × (1.10) × (1.10) = $1,000 × $(1.10)^3$ = $1,331 at the end of the third year. Interest in year three would be $(1,331 − 1,210) = $121.

4.2 Compound interest

This example shows, in a different way to that given earlier in this text, how **compound interest** works. The amount of interest earned each year gets larger because we earn interest on both the original capital and also on the interest now earned in earlier years.

A formula which can be used to show the value of an investment after several years which earns compound interest is:

$S = P(1 + r)^n$

where S = future value of the investment after n years
        P = the amount invested now
        r = the rate of interest, as a proportion. For example, 10% = 0.10, 25% = 0.25, 8% = 0.08
        n = the number of years of the investment

For example, suppose that we invest $2,000 now at 10%. What would the investment be worth after the following number of years?

(a) Five years
(b) Six years

The future value of $1 after n years at 10% interest is given in the following table.

n	$(1 + r)^n$ with r = 0.10
1	1.100
2	1.210
3	1.331
4	1.464
5	1.611
6	1.772
7	1.949

The solution is as follows.

(a) After five years:

S = $2,000 (1.611) = $3,222

(b) After six years:

S = $2,000 (1.772) = $3,544

The principles of compound interest are used in discounted cash flow, except that discounting is compounding in reverse.

4.3 Discounting

With **discounting**, we look at the size of an investment after a certain number of years, and calculate how much we would need to invest now to build up the investment to that size, given a certain rate of interest. This may seem complicated at first, and an example might help to make the point clear. With discounting, we can calculate how much we would need to invest now at an interest rate, of say, 6% to build up the investment to (say) $5,000 after four years.

The compound interest formula shows how we calculate a future sum S from a known current investment P, so that if $S = P (1 + r)^n$, then:

$$P = \frac{S}{(1+r)^n} = S \times \frac{1}{(1+r)^n}$$

This is the basic formula for discounting, which is sometimes written as: $P = S(1 + r)^{-n}$

[$(1 + r)^{-n}$ and $\frac{1}{(1+r)^n}$ mean exactly the same thing.]

To build up an investment to $5,000 after four years at 6% interest, we would need to invest now:

$$P = \$5,000 \times \frac{1}{(1+0.06)^4} = \$5,000 \times 0.792 = \$3,960$$

4.3.1 Further examples of discounting

If you have never done any discounting before, the basic principle and mathematical techniques might take some time to get used to. The following examples might help to make them clearer.

(a) A business person wants to have $13,310 in three years' time, and has decided to put some money aside now which will earn interest of 10% per annum. How much money must he put aside in order to build up the investment to $13,310 as required?

Solution $P = \$13,310 \times \frac{1}{(1.10)^3} = \$10,000$

Proof   After one year the investment would be worth $10,000 × 1.10 = $11,000; after two years it would be $11,000 × 1.10 = $12,100; and after three years it would be $12,100 × 1.10 = $13,310.

(b) Another businessman has two sons who are just 18 years and 17 years old. He wishes to give them $10,000 each on their 20th birthdays and he wants to know how much he must invest now at 8% interest to pay this amount.

The following table is relevant, giving values r = 8% or 0.08. Note that you can read the figures in the 'present value' column from the **Present Value Table** in the Appendix to this Interactive Text: look down the 8% column.

Year n	Future value of $1 $(1 + r)^n$	Present value of $1 $(1 + r)^{-n}$
1	1.080	0.926
2	1.166	0.857
3	1.260	0.794
4	1.360	0.735

The investment must provide $10,000 after two years for the elder son and $10,000 after three years for the younger son.

	After n years n =	Discount factor 8%		Amount provided $	Present value $
Elder son	2	0.857	×	10,000	8,570
Younger son	3	0.794	×	10,000	7,940
Total investment required					16,510

Proof   After two years the investment of $16,510 will be worth $16,510 × 1.166 = $19,251. After paying $10,000 to the elder son, $9,251 will be left after two years. This will earn interest of 8% in year three, to be worth $9,251 × 1.08 = $9,991 at the end of the year. This is almost enough to pay $10,000 to the younger son. The difference ($9) is caused by rounding errors in the table of discount (present value) factors and compound (future value) factors.

(c)   A company is wondering whether to invest $15,000 in a project which will pay $20,000 after two years. It will not invest unless the return from the investment is at least 10% per annum. Is the investment worthwhile? The present value of $1 in two years time at 10% interest is 0.826.

Solution

The return of $20,000 after two years is equivalent to an investment now at 10% of $20,000 × 0.826 = $16,520.

In other words, in order to obtain $20,000 after two years, the company would have to invest $16,520 now at an interest rate of 10%. The project offers the same payment at a cost of only $15,000, so that it must provide a return in excess of 10% and it is therefore worthwhile.

	$
Present value of future profits at 10%	16,520
Cost of investment	15,000
The investment in the project offers the same return, but at a cost lower by	1,520

4.4 Equivalent rates of interest

An **effective annual rate of interest** is the corresponding annual rate when interest is compounded at intervals shorter than a year.

4.4.1 Non-annual compounding

In the previous examples, interest has been calculated **annually**, but this isn't always the case. Interest may be compounded **daily**, **weekly**, **monthly** or **quarterly**.

For example, $10,000 invested for 5 years at an interest rate of 2% per month will have a final value of $10,000 × $(1 + 0.02)^{60}$ = $32,810. Notice that n relates to the number of periods (5 years × 12 months) that r is compounded.

4.4.2 Effective annual rate of interest

The non-annual compounding interest rate can be converted into an effective annual rate of interest. This is also known as the **APR** (annual percentage rate) which lenders such as banks and credit companies are required to disclose.

FORMULA TO LEARN

Effective annual rate of interest: $(1 + R) = (1 + r)^n$

Where   R is the effective annual rate
                r is the period rate
                n is the number of periods in a year

4.4.3 Example: The effective annual rate of interest

Calculate the effective annual rate of interest (to two decimal places) of:

(a)   1.5% per month, compound
(b)   4.5% per quarter, compound
(c)   9% per half year, compound

Solution

(a) $1 + R = (1 + r)^n$
        $1 + R = (1 + 0.015)^{12}$
            $R = 1.1956 - 1$
                $= 0.1956$
                $= 19.56\%$

(b) $1 + R = (1 + 0.045)^4$
            $R = 1.1925 - 1$
                $= 0.1925$
                $= 19.25\%$

(c) $1 + R = (1 + 0.09)^2$
            $R = 1.1881 - 1$
                $= 0.1881$
                $= 18.81\%$

4.5 Nominal rates of interest and the annual percentage rate

A **nominal rate** of interest is an interest rate expressed as a per annum figure although the interest is compounded over a period of less than one year. The corresponding effective rate of interest is the **annual percentage rate (APR)** (sometimes called the compound annual rate, CAR).

Most interest rates are expressed as per annum figures even when the interest is compounded over periods of less than one year. In such cases, the given interest rate is called a **nominal rate**. We can, however, also work out the **effective rate** (**APR** or CAR).

EXAM FOCUS POINT

Students often become seriously confused about the various rates of interest.

*   The **NOMINAL RATE** is the interest rate expressed as a per annum figure, eg 12% pa nominal even though interest may be compounded over periods of less than one year.

*   Adjusted nominal rate = **EQUIVALENT ANNUAL RATE**

*   Equivalent annual rate (the rate per day or per month adjusted to give an annual rate) = **EFFECTIVE ANNUAL RATE**

*   Effective annual rate = **ANNUAL PERCENTAGE RATE (APR)** = **COMPOUND ANNUAL RATE (CAR)**

4.5.1 Example: Nominal and effective rates of interest

A building society may offer investors 10% per annum interest payable half-yearly. If the 10% is a nominal rate of interest, the building society would in fact pay 5% every six months, compounded so that the effective annual rate of interest would be

$[(1.05)^2 - 1] = 0.1025 = 10.25\%$ per annum.

Similarly, if a bank offers depositors a nominal 12% per annum, with interest payable quarterly, the effective rate of interest would be 3% compound every three months, which is

$[(1.03)^4 - 1] = 0.1255 = 12.55\%$ per annum.

QUESTION

Effective rate of interest

A bank adds interest monthly to investors' accounts even though interest rates are expressed in annual terms. The current rate of interest is 12%. Fred deposits $2,000 on 1 July. How much interest will have been earned by 31 December (to the nearest $)?

A $123.00

B $60.00

C $240.00

D $120.00

ANSWER

The nominal rate is 12% pa payable monthly.

$\therefore$ The effective rate $= \dfrac{12\%}{12\,\text{months}} = 1\%$ compound monthly.

$\therefore$ In the six months from July to December, the interest earned $= (\$2,000 \times (1.01)^6) - \$2,000 = \$123.04$.

The correct answer is A.

---

5 Discounted cash flow

Discounted cash flow techniques take account of the time value of money – the fact that $1 received now is worth more because it could be invested to become a greater sum at the end of a year, and even more after the end of two years, and so on. As with payback, discounted cash flow techniques use cash figures before depreciation in the calculations.

Discounted cash flow is a technique of evaluating capital investment projects, using discounting arithmetic to determine whether or not they will provide a satisfactory return.

A typical investment project involves a payment of capital for non-current assets at the start of the project and then there will be returns coming in from the investment over a number of years.

As we noted earlier, DCF can be used in either of two ways: the **net present value method,** or the **internal rate of return** (sometimes called DCF yield, DCF rate of return) method. We will now look at each method in turn.

5.1 The net present value (NPV) method of DCF

> The **net present value method** calculates the present value of all cash flows, and sums them to give the net present value. If this is positive, then the project is acceptable.

The **net present value (NPV) method** of evaluation is as follows.

(a) **Determine the present value of costs**
In other words, decide how much capital must be set aside to pay for the project. Let this be $C.

(b) **Calculate the present value of future cash benefits from the project**
To do this we take the cash benefit in each year and discount it to a present value. This shows how much we would have to invest now to earn the future benefits, if our rate of return were equal to the cost of capital. ('Cost of capital' is explained below.) By adding up the present value of benefits for each future year, we obtain the total present value of benefits from the project. Let this be $B.

(c) **Compare the present value of costs $C with the present value of benefits $B**
The net present value is the difference between them: $(B – C).

(d) **NPV is positive**
The present value of benefits exceeds the present value of costs. This in turn means that the project will earn a return in excess of the cost of capital. Therefore, the project should be accepted.

(e) **NPV is negative**
This means that it would cost us more to invest in the project to obtain the future cash receipts than it would cost us to invest somewhere else, at a rate of interest equal to the cost of capital, to obtain an equal amount of future receipts. The project would earn a return lower than the cost of capital and would not be worth investing in.

5.1.1 Example: The NPV method

Suppose that a company is wondering whether to invest $18,000 in a project which would make extra profits (before depreciation is deducted) of $10,000 in the first year, $8,000 in the second year and $6,000 in the third year. Its cost of capital is 10% (in other words, it would require a return of at least 10% on its investment). You are required to evaluate the project.

Solution

In DCF we make several assumptions. One such assumption is that discounted cash flows (payments or receipts) occur on the last day of each year. For example, although profits are $10,000 during the course of year 1, we assume that the $10,000 is not received until the last day of year 1. Similarly, the profits of $8,000 and $6,000 in years 2 and 3 are assumed to occur on the last day of years 2 and 3 respectively. The cash payment of $18,000 occurs 'now' at the start of year 1. To be consistent, we say that this payment occurs on the last day of the current year which is often referred to as year 0.

The NPV is now calculated with discounting arithmetic. Note that the Present Value Table in the Appendix to this Text gives us the following values.

Year	Present value of $1	
n	$(1 + r)^{-n}$	where r = 0.10
1	0.909	
2	0.826	
3	0.751	

Year	Cash flow $	Present value factor	Present value $
0	(18,000)	1.000	(18,000)
1	10,000	0.909	9,090
2	8,000	0.826	6,608
3	6,000	0.751	4,506
		NPV	2,204

The NPV is positive, which means that the project will earn more than 10%. ($20,204 would have to be invested now at 10% to earn the future cash flows; since the project will earn these returns at a cost of only $18,000 it must earn a return in excess of 10%.)

QUESTION

Present value

A project would involve a capital outlay of $24,000. Profits (before depreciation) each year would be $5,000 for six years. The cost of capital is 12%. Is the project worthwhile?

(Use the Present Value Table in the Appendix.)

ANSWER

Years	Cash flow $	Present value factor	Present value $
0	(24,000)	1.000	(24,000)
1	5,000	0.893	4,465
2	5,000	0.797	3,985
3	5,000	0.712	3,560
4	5,000	0.636	3,180
5	5,000	0.567	2,835
6	5,000	0.507	2,535
		NPV	(3,440)

The NPV is negative and so the project is not worthwhile.

5.1.2 Advantages and disadvantages of NPV

Advantages of NPV	Disadvantages of NPV
Shareholder wealth is **maximised**.	It can be difficult to identify an **appropriate discount rate**.
It takes into account the **time value of money**	For simplicity, cash flows are sometimes all assumed to occur at **year ends**: this assumption may be unrealistic.
It is based on **cash flows** which are less subjective than profit.	Some managers are **unfamiliar** with the concept of NPV
Shareholders will **benefit** if a project with a positive NPV is accepted	

5.2 Discounted payback method

The **discounted payback method** applies discounting to arrive at a payback period after which the NPV becomes positive.

We have seen how discounting cash flows is a way of reflecting the time value of money in investment appraisal. The further into the future a cash flow is expected to be, the more uncertain it tends to be, and the returns or interest paid to the suppliers of capital (ie to investors) in part reflects this uncertainty. The **discounted payback technique** is an adaptation of the payback technique, which we looked at earlier, taking some account of the time value of money. To calculate the discounted payback period, we establish the time at which the net present value of an investment becomes positive.

5.2.1 Example: Discounted payback period

We can calculate the discounted payback period for the example above. Having produced a net present value analysis as in the solution above, we calculate the discounted payback period as follows.

Year	Present value $	Cumulative PV $
0	(18,000)	(18,000)
1	9,090	(8,910)
2	6,608	(2,302)
3	4,506	2,204
	2,204	

Solution

If we assume now that cash flows in year 3 are even, instead of occurring on the last day of the year, the discounted payback period can be estimated as follows.

Discounted payback period
= 2 yrs + 2,302/4,506 yrs
= 2.51 yrs, say 2½ years

This compares with a non-discounted payback period of 2 years for the same project, since the initial outlay of $18,000 is recouped in money terms by year 2. The discounted payback period of 2½ years suggests that if the project must be terminated within that period, it will not have added value to the company.

5.3 Comparison with the basic payback method

Like the basic payback method, the discounted payback method fails to take account of positive cash flows occurring after the end of the payback period.

5.4 The cost of capital

We have mentioned that the appropriate discount rate to use in investment appraisal is the company's **cost of capital**. In practice this is difficult to determine. It is often suggested that the discount rate which a company should use as its cost of capital is one that reflects the return expected by its investors in shares and loan notes, the **opportunity cost of finance**.

Shareholders expect dividends and capital gains; loan notes investors expect interest payments. A company must make enough profits from its own operations (including capital expenditure projects) to pay dividends and interest. The average return is the weighted average of the return required by shareholders and loan note investors. The cost of capital is therefore the **weighted average cost** of all the sources of capital.

5.5 Annuities

Annuities are an annual cash payment or receipt which is the same amount every year for a number of years.

In DCF the term **'annuities'** refers to an annual cash payment which is the same amount every year for a number of years, or else an annual receipt of cash which is the same amount every year for a number of years.

In the question above, the profits are an annuity of $5,000 per annum for six years. The present value of profits is the present value of an annuity of $5,000 per annum for six years at a discount rate of 12%.

When there is an annuity to be discounted, there is a shortcut method of calculation. You may already have seen what it is. Instead of multiplying the cash flow each year by the present value factor for that year, and then adding up all the present values (as shown in the solution above), we can **multiply** the **annuity** by the **sum of the present value factors**.

Thus we could have multiplied $5,000 by the sum of (0.893 + 0.797 + 0.712 + 0.636 + 0.567 + 0.507) = 4.112. We then have $5,000 × 4.112 = $20,560.

This quick calculation is made even quicker by the use of 'annuity' tables. These show the sum of the present value factors each year from year one to year n.

The Annuity Table in the Appendix to this Text shows the following.

Years n	Present value of $1 received per year $\dfrac{[1-(1+r)^{-n}]}{r}$	Notes
1	0.893	PV factor for year 1 only
2	1.690	(0.893 + 0.797)
3	2.402	(add 0.712)
4	3.038	(add 0.636)
5	3.605	(add 0.567)
6	4.112	(add 0.507)

5.5.1 Example: Annuities

A project would involve a capital outlay of $50,000. Profits (before depreciation) would be $12,000 per year. The cost of capital is 10%. Would the project be worthwhile if it lasts:

(a)   Five years
(b)   Seven years

Solution

We can find the discount factors from the Annuity Table in the Appendix.

(a)   If the project lasts five years

Years	Cash flow $	Discount factor 10%	Present value $
0	(50,000)	1.000	(50,000)
1 – 5	12,000 pa	3.791	45,492
		NPV	(4,508)

(b)   If the project lasts seven years

Years	Cash flow $	Discount factor 10%	Present value $
0	(50,000)	1.000	(50,000)
1 – 7	12,000 pa	4.868	58,416
		NPV	8,416

The project is not worthwhile if it last only five years, but it would be worthwhile if it lasted for seven years. The decision to accept or to reject the project must depend on management's view about its duration.

QUESTION   Two projects

(a)   A project costs $39,500. It would earn $10,000 per year for the first three years and then $8,000 per year for the next three. Cost of capital is 10%. Is the project worth undertaking?

(b)   Another project would cost $75,820. If its life is expected to be five years and the cost of capital is 10%, what are the minimum annual savings required to make the project worthwhile?

Use the Annuity Table in the Appendix to derive your answers.

ANSWER

(a)

Present value of $1 per annum, years 1-6	4.355
Less present value of $1 per annum, years 1-3	2.487
Gives present value of $1 per annum, years 4-6	1.868

Year	Cash flow $	Discount factor 10%	Present value $
0	(39,500)	1.000	(39,500)
1 – 3	10,000 pa	2.487	24,870
4 – 6	8,000 pa	1.868	14,944
		NPV	314

The **NPV is positive**, but only just ($314). The project therefore promises a return a little above 10%. If we are confident that the estimates of cost and benefits for the next six years are accurate, the project is worth undertaking. However, if there is some suspicion that earnings may be a little less than the figures shown, it might be prudent to reject it.

(b)   The project will just be worthwhile if the NPV is 0. For the NPV to be 0 the present value of benefits must equal the present value of costs, $75,820.

PV of benefits   = annual savings × present value of $1 per year for 5 years (at 10%)

$75,820   = annual savings × 3.791

$$= \frac{\$75,820}{3.791}$$

Annual savings   = $20,000

This example shows that annuity tables can be used to calculate an annual cash flow from a given investment.

5.5.2 Example: More complex annuity

What is the present value of $2,000 costs incurred each year from years 3 to 6 when the cost of capital is 5%?

Solution

We need to take the annuity factor for years 1 to 6 and deduct the annuity factor for years 1 to 2. This will give us a factor for years 3 to 6 only.

$$\$2,000 \times \begin{bmatrix} \text{PV of \$1 per annum for years 1 - 6 at 5\%} = 5.076 \\ \text{Less PV of \$1 per annum for years 1 - 2 at 5\%} = \underline{1.859} \\ \text{PV of \$1 per annum for years 3 - 6} \qquad = \underline{3.217} \end{bmatrix}$$

PV = $2,000 × 3.217 = $6,434

5.6 Annual cash flows in perpetuity

A perpetuity is an annuity that lasts forever. The present value of a perpetuity of 'a' per annum, commencing in one year, is PV = a/r where r is the cost of capital as a proportion.

It can sometimes be useful to calculate the **cumulative present value of $1 per annum** for every year in perpetuity (that is, **forever**).

When the cost of capital is r, the cumulative PV of $1 per annum in perpetuity is **$1/r**. For example, the PV of $1 per annum in perpetuity at a discount rate of 10% would be $1/0.10 = $10.

Similarly, the PV of $1 per annum in perpetuity at a discount rate of 15% would be $1/0.15 = $6.67 and at a discount rate of 20% it would be $1/0.20 = $5.

5.6.1 Example: More complex perpetuity

An investment will produce an annual return of $1,500 in perpetuity with the first receipt starting in 3 years' time. What is the present value of this perpetuity discounted at 8%?

Solution

Step 1	Calculate the future value of the income one year before the first receipt is due (year 2).
	$1,500/0.08 = $18,750

Step 2	Discount it back to today using a discount factor of 8% over 2 years.
	PV = $18,750 × 0.857
	= $16,068.75

5.7 Calculating a 'breakeven' NPV

You might be asked to calculate how much income would need to be generated for the NPV of a project to be zero. This must be referred to as in **breakeven NPV**.

5.7.1 Example: Breakeven NPV

For the project in the example 5.5.1 above, calculate how much the annual income from the project could reduce before the NPV would reach a 'breakeven' zero level.

Solution

For every $1 reduction in the annual income of $12,000, the NPV will fall by $1 × 4.868 = $4.868.

'Breakeven' fall in income = $8,416 ÷ 4.868 = $1,729

Annual income of $12,000 − $1,729 = $10,271 will result in a 'break-even' NPV of zero.

5.8 Internal rate of return (IRR)

> The **internal rate of return technique** uses a trial and error method to discover the discount rate which produces the NPV of zero. This discount rate will be the return forecast for the project.

The **internal rate of return method** of DCF involves two steps.

* Calculating the rate of return which is expected from a project
* Comparing the rate of return with the cost of capital

If a project earns a **higher rate of return** than the cost of capital, it will be worth undertaking (and its **NPV** would be **positive**). If it earns a **lower rate of return**, it is not worthwhile (and its **NPV** would be **negative**). If a project earns a return which is exactly equal to the cost of capital, its NPV will be 0 and it will only just be worthwhile.

5.8.1 Calculating the internal rate of return

You may find the method of calculating the rate of return to be rather unsatisfactory because it involves some guesswork and approximation. An example will help to illustrate the technique.

Suppose that a project would cost $20,000 and the annual net cash inflows are expected to be as follows. What is the internal rate of return of the project?

Year	Cash flow
	$
1	8,000
2	10,000
3	6,000
4	4,000

The IRR is a rate of interest at which the NPV is 0 and the discounted (present) values of benefits add up to $20,000. We need to find out what interest rate or cost of capital would give an NPV of 0.

We are after two rates of return.

(a) One at which the NPV is a **small positive value**. The actual IRR will be higher than this rate of return.

(b) One at which the NPV is a **small negative value**. The actual IRR will be lower than this rate of return.

The actual IRR will then be found (approximately) by using the two rates in (a) and (b).

In our example, we might begin by trying discount rates of 10%, 15% and 20%.

Year	Cash flow $	Discount factor at 10%	Present value at 10% $	Discount factor at 15%	Present value at 15% $	Discount factor at 20%	Present value at 20% $
0	(20,000)	1.000	(20,000)	1.000	(20,000)	1.000	(20,000)
1	8,000	0.909	7,272	0.870	6,960	0.833	6,664
2	10,000	0.826	8,260	0.756	7,560	0.694	6,940
3	6,000	0.751	4,506	0.658	3,948	0.579	3,474
4	4,000	0.683	2,732	0.572	2,288	0.482	1,928
Net present value			2,770		756		(994)

The IRR is more than 15% but less than 20%. We could try to be more accurate by trying a discount rate of 16%, 17%, 18% or 19%, but in this solution we will use the values for 15% and 20% to estimate the IRR.

To estimate the IRR, we now assume that the NPV falls steadily and at a constant rate between $756 at 15% and $(994) at 20%. This represents a fall of $(756 + 994) = $1,750 in NPV between 15% and 20%. This is an average fall of:

$$\frac{\$1,750}{(20-15)\%} = \$350 \text{ in NPV for each 1\% increase in the discount rate.}$$

Since the IRR is where the NPV is 0, it must be $\dfrac{\$756}{\$350} \times 1\%$ above 15%,

ie about 2.2% above 15% = 17.2%.

5.8.2 A formula for the IRR

A formula for making this calculation (which is known as **interpolation**) is as follows.

$$IRR = A + \left[\frac{a}{a-b} \times (B - A)\right]$$

where A is the discount rate which provides the positive NPV
     a is the amount of the positive NPV
     B is the discount rate which provides the negative NPV
     b is the amount of the negative NPV

In our example, using this formula, the IRR would be calculated as follows.

$$15\% + \left[\frac{756}{756 - 994} \times (20 - 15)\right]\% = 15\% + [\,0.432 \times 5\,]\%$$
$$= 15\% + 2.16\%$$
$$= 17.16\%, \text{ say } 17.2\%$$

5.8.3 Advantages of the IRR method

The following are advantages of using IRR.

(1) It takes into account the **time value of money**, unlike other approaches such as payback.

(2) Results are expressed as a **simple percentage**, and are more easily understood than some other methods.

(3)   It indicates how **sensitive** calculations are to changes in interest rates.

5.8.4 Problems with the IRR method

The following are problems of using IRR.

(a)   Projects with unconventional cash flows can produce **negative** or **multiple IRRs**.

(b)   IRR may be **confused** with return on capital employed (ROCE), since both give answers in percentage terms.

(c)   It may give **conflicting recommendations** with mutually exclusive projects, because the result is given in relative terms (percentages), and not in absolute terms ($s) as with NPV.

(d)   Some **managers** are **unfamiliar** with the IRR method.

(e)   It cannot accommodate **changing interest rates**.

(f)   It assumes that funds can be **re-invested** at a rate equivalent to the IRR, which may be too high.

QUESTION   Machine purchase

LCH Co manufactures product X which it sells for $5 per unit. Variable costs of production are currently $3 per unit, and fixed costs 50c per unit. A new machine is available which would cost $90,000 but which could be used to make product X for a variable cost of only $2.50 per unit. Fixed costs, however, would increase by $7,500 per annum as a direct result of purchasing the machine. The machine would have an expected life of 4 years and a resale value after that time of $10,000. Sales of product X are estimated to be 75,000 units per annum. LCH Co expects to earn at least 12% per annum from its investments. Ignore taxation.

You are required to decide whether LCH Co should purchase the machine.

ANSWER

Savings are 75,000 × ($3 − $2.50) = $37,500 per annum.

Additional costs are $7,500 per annum.

Net cash savings are therefore $30,000 per annum. (Remember, depreciation is not a cash flow and must be ignored as a 'cost'.)

The first step in calculating an NPV is to establish the relevant costs year by year. All future cash flows arising as a direct consequence of the decision should be taken into account. It is assumed that the machine will be sold for $10,000 at the end of year 4.

Year	Cash flow $	PV factor 12%	PV of cash flow $
0	(90,000)	1.000	(90,000)
1	30,000	0.893	26,790
2	30,000	0.797	23,910
3	30,000	0.712	21,360
4	40,000	0.636	25,440
			7,500

The NPV is positive and so the project is expected to earn more than 12% per annum and is therefore acceptable.

QUESTION

Find the IRR of the project given below and state whether the project should be accepted if the company requires a minimum return of 17%.

Time		$
0	Investment	(4,000)
1	Receipts	1,200
2	"	1,410
3	"	1,875
4	"	1,150

ANSWER

The total receipts are $5,635 giving a total profit of $1,635 and average profits of $409. Although the average rate of return (ARR) is not on your syllabus, it gives us a useful starting point for calculating the IRR.

ARR = average profit/average investment × 100%

The average investment is $2,000.

$$\text{Average investment} = \frac{\text{Initial investment - residual value}}{2}$$

$$= \left(\frac{4,000 - 0}{2}\right)$$

$$= \$2,000$$

The ARR is $409 ÷ $2,000 = 20%. We take two thirds of the ARR (approximately 14%) to find an initial estimate of the IRR. The initial estimate of the IRR that we shall try is therefore 14%.

Time	Cash flow	Try 14% Discount factor	PV	Try 16% Discount factor	PV
	$		$		$
0	(4,000)	1.000	(4,000)	1.000	(4,000)
1	1,200	0.877	1,052	0.862	1,034
2	1,410	0.769	1,084	0.743	1,048
3	1,875	0.675	1,266	0.641	1,202
4	1,150	0.592	681	0.552	635
		NPV	83	NPV	(81)

The IRR must be less than 16%, but higher than 14%. The NPVs at these two costs of capital will be used to estimate the IRR.

Using the interpolation formula:

$$IRR = 14\% + \left[\frac{83}{83-81} \times (16\% - 14\%)\right] = 15.01\%$$

The IRR is, in fact, almost exactly 15%. The project should be rejected as the IRR is less than the minimum return demanded.

6 Relevant and non-relevant costs

Relevant costs are future incremental cash flows.

Avoidable costs, differential costs and **opportunity costs** are all relevant costs.

Non-relevant costs include **sunk costs, committed costs** and **notional (imputed) costs**.

Directly attributable fixed costs are relevant costs, general fixed overheads are not.

The costs which should be used for decision making are often referred to as **relevant costs**. Relevant costing is also used in long-term decision making and investment decisions which we will look at in the next chapter.

A **relevant cost** is a future cash flow arising as a direct consequence of a decision.

(a) **Relevant costs are future costs.**

    (i)   A decision is about the future – it cannot change the past. A cost that has been incurred is irrelevant to any decision that is being made 'now'. It is a **sunk cost**.

    (ii)   Costs that have been incurred include not only costs that have already been paid, but also costs that are the subject of legally binding contracts, even if payments due under the contract have not yet been made. These are **committed costs**.

(b) **Relevant costs are cash flows.**

Costs or charges which do not reflect additional cash inflows or spending should be ignored for the purpose of decision making. These include the following.

    (i)   Depreciation, as a fixed overhead incurred.

    (ii)   Notional rent or interest, as a fixed overhead incurred.

    (iii)   All overheads absorbed. Fixed overhead absorption is always irrelevant since it is overheads **to be** incurred which affect decisions.

(c) **Relevant costs are incremental costs.**

A relevant cost is one which arises as a direct consequence of a decision. Only costs which **will differ** under some or all of the available opportunities should be considered. Relevant costs are therefore sometimes referred to as incremental costs. For example, if an employee is expected to have no other work to do during the next week, but will be paid his/her basic wage (of, say, $100 per week) for attending work, the manager might decide to give him/her a job which earns only $40. The net gain is $40 and the $100 is irrelevant to the decision because although it is a future cash flow, **it will be incurred anyway**.

Relevant costs are therefore future, incremental cash flows.

Other terms can be used to describe relevant costs.

Avoidable costs are costs which would not be incurred if the activity to which they relate did not exist.

(a) One of the situations in which it is necessary to identify avoidable costs is in deciding whether or not to discontinue a product. The only costs which would be saved are the **avoidable costs**. These are usually the variable costs and sometimes some specific fixed costs. Costs which would be incurred whether or not the product is discontinued are **unavoidable costs.**

Differential cost is the difference in relevant cost between alternatives.

(b) The term '**differential costs**' is used to compare the differences in cost between **two alternative** courses of action, while '**incremental costs**' is used to state the relevant costs when **two or more**

options are compared. If option A will cost an extra $300 and option B will cost an extra $360, the differential cost is $60.

Opportunity cost is the benefit which has been given up, by choosing one option instead of another.

(c)   Suppose for example that there are three mutually exclusive options, A, B and C. The net profit from each would be $80, $100 and $70 respectively.

Since only one option can be selected option B would be chosen because it offers the biggest benefit.

	$
Profit from option B	100
Less: **opportunity cost** (ie the benefit from the most profitable alternative, A)	**80**
Differential benefit of option B	20

The decision to choose option B would not be taken simply because it offers a profit of $100, but because it offers a differential profit of $20 in excess of the opportunity cost.

Opportunity costs are not recorded in double entry accounts.

6.1 Non-relevant costs

A number of terms are used to describe costs that are **irrelevant for decision making**.

A **sunk cost** is a cost which has already been incurred and hence should not be taken account of in decision making.

(a)   Management decisions can only affect the future. In decision making, managers therefore require information about future costs and revenues which would be affected by the decision under review. A sunk cost has either been charged already as a cost of sales in a previous accounting period or will be charged in a future accounting period. An example of this type of cost is depreciation. If the non-current asset has been purchased, depreciation may be charged for several years but the cost is a sunk cost, about which nothing can now be done.

A **committed cost** is a future cash outflow that will be incurred anyway, whatever decision is taken now about alternative opportunities.

(b)   Committed costs may exist because of contracts already entered into by the organisation, which it cannot get out of.

A **notional cost** is a hypothetical accounting cost to reflect the use of a benefit for which no **actual** cash expense is incurred.

(c)   Examples in cost accounting systems include the following.

(i)   Notional rent, such as that charged to a subsidiary, cost centre or profit centre of an organisation for the use of accommodation which the organisation owns.

(ii)   Notional interest charges on capital employed, sometimes made against a profit centre or cost centre.

(d)   Although **historical costs** are irrelevant for decision making, historical cost data will often provide the best available **basis for predicting** future costs.

BPP
LEARNING MEDIA

6.2 Fixed and variable costs

Unless you are given an indication to the contrary, assume the following.

- **Variable costs will be relevant costs.**
- **Fixed costs are irrelevant to a decision.**

This need not be the case, however, and you should analyse variable and fixed cost data carefully. Do not forget that 'fixed' costs may only be fixed in the short term.

6.2.1 Attributable fixed costs

There might be occasions when a fixed cost is a relevant cost, and you must be aware of the distinction between 'specific' or 'directly attributable' fixed costs, and general fixed overheads.

(a) **Directly attributable fixed costs** are those costs which although fixed within a relevant range of activity level, or regarded as fixed because management has set a budgeted expenditure level.

   (i)   **They increase if certain extra activities are undertaken.**

   (ii) **They decrease/are eliminated entirely if a decision is taken either to reduce the scale of operations or shut down entirely.**

(b) **General fixed overheads** are those fixed overheads which will be **unaffected by decisions to increase or decrease the scale of operations. For example** an apportioned share of fixed costs which would be completely unaffected by the decisions, such as share of head office charges.

Directly attributable fixed costs are relevant to decision making, **general fixed overheads are not**.

7 Some rules for identifying relevant costs

7.1 The relevant cost of using machines

Using machinery will involve some incremental costs, **user costs**. These include repair costs arising from use, hire charges and any fall in resale value of owned assets which results from their use. **Depreciation is *not* a relevant cost**.

7.2 Example: user costs

Sydney Co is considering whether to undertake some contract work for a customer. The machinery required for the contract would be as follows.

(a) A special cutting machine will have to be hired for three months. Hire charges for this machine are $75 per month, with a minimum hire charge of $300.

(b) All other machinery required in the production for the contract has already been purchased by the organisation on hire purchase terms. The monthly hire purchase payments for this machinery are $500. This consists of $450 for capital repayment and $50 as an interest charge. The last hire purchase payment is to be made in two months' time. The cash price of this machinery was $9,000 two years ago. It is being depreciated on a straight line basis at the rate of $200 per month. However, it still has a useful life which will enable it to be operated for another 36 months.

   The machinery is highly specialised and is unlikely to be required for other, more profitable jobs over the period during which the contract work would be carried out. Although there is no immediate market for selling this machine, it is expected that a customer might be found in the future. It is further estimated that the machine would **lose $200 in its eventual sale value** if it is used for the contract work.

Required

Calculate the relevant cost of machinery for the contract.

7.3 Solution

(a)   The cutting machine will incur an incremental cost of $300, the minimum hire charge.

(b)   The historical cost of the other machinery is irrelevant as a past cost; depreciation is irrelevant as a non-cash cost; and future hire purchase repayments are irrelevant because they are committed costs. The only relevant cost is the loss of resale value of the machinery, estimated at $200 through use. This user cost will not arise until the machinery is eventually resold and the $200 should be discounted to allow for the time value of money. However, discounting is ignored here.

(c)   Summary of relevant costs

	$
Incremental hire costs	300
User cost of machinery	200
	500

QUESTION   User cost

A machine which originally cost $12,000 has an estimated life of ten years and is depreciated at the rate of $1,200 a year. It has been unused for some time, as expected orders did not materialise.

A special order has now been received which would require the use of the machine for two months. The current net realisable value of the machine is $8,000. If it is used for the job, its value is expected to fall to $7,500. The net book value of the machine is $8,400.

Routine maintenance of the machine currently costs $40 a month. With use, the cost of maintenance and repairs would increase to $60 a month.

Required

Determine the cost of using the machine for the order.

ANSWER

	$
Loss in net realisable value of the machine through using it on the order $(8,000 – 7,500)	500
Costs in excess of existing routine maintenance costs $(120 – 80)	40
Total marginal user cost	540

CHAPTER ROUNDUP

- ↳ A **long-term view** of benefits and costs must be taken when reviewing a capital expenditure project.

- ↳ The key methods of project appraisal are:

  - The payback period
  - Net present value
  - Discounted payback period
  - Internal rate of return (IRR)

- ↳ The **payback period** is the time taken for the initial investment to be recovered in the cash inflows from the project. The payback method is particularly relevant if there are liquidity problems, or if distant forecasts are very uncertain.

- ↳ The **time value of money** is an important consideration in decision making.

- ↳ An effective annual rate of interest is the corresponding annual rate when interest is compounded at intervals shorter than a year.

- ↳ A **nominal rate** of interest is an interest rate expressed as a per annum figure although the interest is compounded over a period of less than one year. The corresponding effective rate of interest is the **annual percentage rate (APR)**.

- ↳ **Discounted cash flow techniques** take account of the time value of money – the fact that $1 received now is worth more because it could be invested to become a greater sum at the end of a year, and even more after the end of two years, and so on. As with payback, discounted cash flow techniques use cash figures before depreciation in the calculations.

- ↳ The **net present value method** calculates the present value of all cash flows, and sums them to give the net present value. If this is positive, then the project is acceptable.

- ↳ The **discounted payback method** applies discounting to arrive at a payback period after which the NPV becomes positive.

- ↳ **Annuities** are an annual cash payment or receipt which is the same amount every year for a number of years.

- ↳ The **internal rate of return technique** uses a trial and error method to discover the discount rate which produces the NPV of zero. This discount rate will be the return forecast for the project.

- ↳ **Relevant costs** are future incremental cash flows.

- ↳ **Avoidable costs, differential costs** and **opportunity costs** are all relevant costs.

- ↳ Non-relevant costs include **sunk costs, committed costs** and **notional (imputed) costs**.

- ↳ **Directly attributable fixed costs** are relevant costs, general fixed overheads are not.

1 .... is the length of time required before the total of the cash inflows received from a project equals the original cash outlay.

2 Depreciation should be included in DCF calculation.

True ☐   False ☐

3 What is the yardstick for acceptance of projects when using the net present value method?

A   Accept if a profit is made

B   Accept if the present value of future cash flows is positive

C   Accept if payback occurs within an reasonable timeframe

D   Accept if the discount rate that achieves a breakeven return is greater than the company's cost of capital

4 What is the discounted payback period?

5 The .... is the weighted average cost of all sources of capital for an enterprise, used as the discount rate in investment appraisal.

6 What are the two steps involved in assessing whether the internal rate of return of a project is sufficient?

Step 1 –   Step 2 –

7 Which of the following statements is incorrect?

A   Committed costs are relevant costs   C   Incremental costs are relevant costs
B   Future costs are relevant costs   D   Cash flows are relevant costs

8 Define opportunity cost.

9 Which type of cost is described below?

'Costs which would not be incurred if the activity to which they relate did not exist'

A   Differential costs   C   Opportunity costs
B   Sunk costs   D   Avoidable costs

ANSWERS TO QUICK QUIZ

1   **Payback** is the length of time required before the total of the cash inflows received from a project is equal to the original cash outlay.

2   False. Depreciation does not reflect additional cash spent, and so is not a relevant cost.

3   B   Accept the project if the net present value is positive.

4   The time after which the net present value of an investment becomes positive.

5   The **cost of capital** is the weighted average cost of all sources of capital for an enterprise, used as the discount rate in investment appraisal.

6   **Step 1** – Calculate the rate of return expected.

    Step 2 – Compare the rate of return with the cost of capital.

7   A   Committed costs are not relevant costs.

8   Opportunity cost is the benefit which could have been earned, but which has been given up, by choosing one option instead of another.

9   D   Avoidable costs are not incurred if the related activity does not exist.

Now try ...

Attempt the questions below from the **Exam Question Bank**

Number

Q82 – Q89

part

D

Standard costing

20

Standard costing

Just as there are **standards** for most things in our daily lives (cleanliness in hamburger restaurants, educational achievement of nine year olds, number of trains running on time), there are standards for the costs of products and services. Moreover, just as the standards in our daily lives are not always met, the standards for the costs of products and services are not always met. In this chapter we will be looking at standards for **costs**, what they are used for and how they are set.

In the next chapter we will see how **standard costing** forms the basis of a process called **variance analysis**, a vital management control tool.

TOPIC LIST	SYLLABUS REFERENCE
1 What is standard costing?	D1(a), (b)
2 Setting standards	D1(b), (c)

Study Guide   **Intellectual level**

D   Standard costing

1   Standard costing systems

(a)   Explain the purpose and principles of standard costing   K

(b)   Explain and illustrate the difference between standard,   K
      marginal and absorption costing

(c)   Establish the standard cost per unit under absorption and   S
      marginal costing

EXAM FOCUS POINT

Standard costing can be applied under both absorption and marginal costing and is important in calculating variances, which we look at in the next chapter. You may be given the standard cost and required to calculate the variance.

1 What is standard costing?

1.1 Introduction

A **standard cost** is a **predetermined estimated unit cost**, used for inventory valuation and control.

The building blocks of standard costing are standard costs and so before we look at standard costing in any detail you really need to know what a standard cost is.

1.2 Standard cost card

A **standard cost card** shows full details of the standard cost of each product.

The standard cost card of product 1234 is set out below.

STANDARD COST CARD – PRODUCT 1234

	$	$
Direct materials		
Material X – 3 kg at $4 per kg	12	
Material Y – 9 litres at $2 per litre	18	
		30
Direct labour		
Grade A – 6 hours at $1.50 per hour	9	
Grade B – 8 hours at $2 per hour	16	
		25
Standard direct cost		55
Variable production overhead – 14 hours at $0.50 per hour		7
Standard variable cost of production		62
Fixed production overhead – 14 hours at $4.50 per hour		63
Standard full production cost		125
Administration and marketing overhead		15
Standard cost of sale		140
Standard profit		20
Standard sales price		160

Notice how the total standard cost is built up from standards for each cost element: standard quantities of materials at standard prices, standard quantities of labour time at standard rates and so on. It is therefore determined by management's estimates of the following.

- The expected prices of materials, labour and expenses
- Efficiency levels in the use of materials and labour
- Budgeted overhead costs and budgeted volumes of activity

We will see how management arrives at these estimates in Section 2.

But why should management want to prepare standard costs? Obviously to assist with standard costing, but what is the point of standard costing?

1.3 The uses of standard costing

Standard costing has a variety of uses but its two principal ones are as follows.

(a)   To **value inventories** and **cost production** for cost accounting purposes.

(b)   To act as a **control device** by establishing standards (planned costs), highlighting (via **variance analysis** which we will cover in the next chapter) activities that are not conforming to plan and thus **alerting management** to areas which may be out of control and in need of corrective action.

QUESTION   Standard cost card

Bloggs makes one product, the joe. Two types of labour are involved in the preparation of a joe, skilled and semi-skilled. Skilled labour is paid $10 per hour and semi-skilled $5 per hour. Twice as many skilled labour hours as semi-skilled labour hours are needed to produce a joe, four semi-skilled labour hours being needed.

A joe is made up of three different direct materials. Seven kilograms of direct material A, four litres of direct material B and three metres of direct material C are needed. Direct material A costs $1 per kilogram, direct material B $2 per litre and direct material C $3 per metre.

Variable production overheads are incurred at Bloggs Co at the rate of $2.50 per direct labour (skilled) hour.

A system of absorption costing is in operation at Bloggs Co. The basis of absorption is direct labour (skilled) hours. For the forthcoming accounting period, budgeted fixed production overheads are $250,000 and budgeted production of the joe is 5,000 units.

Administration, selling and distribution overheads are added to products at the rate of $10 per unit.

A mark-up of 25% is made on the joe.

Required

Using the above information draw up a standard cost card for the joe.

ANSWER

STANDARD COST CARD – PRODUCT JOE

	$	$
Direct materials		
A – 7 kgs × $1	7	
B – 4 litres × $2	8	
C – 3 m × $3	9	
		24
Direct labour		
Skilled – 8 × $10	80	
Semi-skilled – 4 × $5	20	
		100
Standard direct cost		124
Variable production overhead – 8 × $2.50		20
Standard variable cost of production		144
Fixed production overhead – 8 × $6.25 (W)		50
Standard full production cost		194
Administration, selling and distribution overhead		10
Standard cost of sale		204
Standard profit (25% × 204)		51
Standard sales price		255

Working

$$\text{Overhead absorption rate} = \frac{\$250,000}{5,000 \times 8} = \$6.25 \text{ per skilled labour hour}$$

QUESTION

Marginal costing system

What would a standard cost card for product joe show under a marginal system?

ANSWER

STANDARD COST CARD – PRODUCT JOE

	$
Direct materials	24
Direct labour	100
Standard direct cost	124
Variable production overhead	20
Standard variable production cost	144
Standard sales price	255
Standard contribution	111

Although the use of standard costs to simplify the keeping of cost accounting records should not be overlooked, we will be concentrating on the **control** and **variance analysis** aspect of standard costing.

Standard costing is a control technique which compares standard costs and revenues with actual results to obtain variances which are used to improve performance.

Notice that the above definition highlights the control aspects of standard costing.

1.4 Standard costing as a control technique

Differences between actual and standard costs are called **variances**.

Standard costing therefore involves the following.

- The establishment of predetermined estimates of the costs of products or services
- The collection of actual costs
- The comparison of the actual costs with the predetermined estimates.

The predetermined costs are known as **standard costs** and the difference between standard and actual cost is known as a **variance**. The process by which the total difference between standard and actual results is analysed is known as **variance analysis**.

Although standard costing can be used in a variety of costing situations (batch and mass production, process manufacture, jobbing manufacture (where there is standardisation of parts) and service industries (if a realistic cost unit can be established)), the greatest benefit from its use can be gained if there is a **degree of repetition** in the production process. It is therefore most suited to **mass production** and **repetitive assembly work**.

2 Setting standards

2.1 Introduction

Standard costs may be used in both absorption costing and in marginal costing systems. We shall, however, confine our description to standard costs in absorption costing systems.

As we noted earlier, the standard cost of a product (or service) is made up of a number of different standards, one for each cost element, each of which has to be set by management. We have divided this section into two: the first part looks at setting the monetary part of each standard, whereas the second part looks at setting the resources requirement part of each standard.

2.2 Types of performance standard

Performance standards are used to set efficiency targets. There are four types: ideal, attainable, current and basic.

The setting of standards raises the problem of how demanding the standard should be. Should the standard represent a perfect performance or an easily attainable performance? The type of performance standard used can have behavioural implications. There are four types of standard.

Type of standard	Description
Ideal	These are based on **perfect operating conditions**: no wastage, no spoilage, no inefficiencies, no idle time, no breakdowns. Variances from ideal standards are useful for pinpointing areas where a close examination may result in large savings in order to maximise efficiency and minimise waste. However ideal standards are likely to have an unfavourable motivational impact because reported variances will always be adverse. Employees will often feel that the goals are unattainable and not work so hard.
Attainable	These are based on the hope that a standard amount of work will be carried out efficiently, machines properly operated or materials properly used. **Some allowance is made for wastage and inefficiencies**. If well-set they provide a useful psychological incentive by giving employees a realistic, but challenging target of efficiency. The consent and co-operation of employees involved in improving the standard are required.
Current	These are based on **current working conditions** (current wastage, current inefficiencies). The disadvantage of current standards is that they do not attempt to improve on current levels of efficiency.
Basic	These are **kept unaltered over a long period of time**, and may be out of date. They are used to show changes in efficiency or performance over a long period of time. Basic standards are perhaps the least useful and least common type of standard in use.

Ideal standards, attainable standards and current standards each have their supporters and it is by **no means clear which of them is preferable**.

QUESTION

Performance standards

Which of the following statements is not true?

A   Variances from ideal standards are useful for pinpointing areas where a close examination might result in large cost savings.

B   Basic standards may provide an incentive to greater efficiency even though the standard cannot be achieved.

C   Ideal standards cannot be achieved and so there will always be adverse variances. If the standards are used for budgeting, an allowance will have to be included for these 'inefficiencies'.

D   Current standards or attainable standards are a better basis for budgeting, because they represent the level of productivity which management will wish to plan for.

ANSWER

The correct answer is B.

Statement B is describing ideal standards, not basic standards.

2.3 Direct material prices

Direct material prices will be estimated by the purchasing department from their knowledge of the following.

- Purchase contracts already agreed
- Pricing discussions with regular suppliers
- The forecast movement of prices in the market
- The availability of bulk purchase discounts

Price inflation can cause difficulties in setting realistic standard prices. Suppose that a material costs $10 per kilogram at the moment and during the course of the next twelve months it is expected to go up in price by 20% to $12 per kilogram. What standard price should be selected?

- The current price of $10 per kilogram
- The average expected price for the year, say $11 per kilogram

Either would be possible, but neither would be entirely satisfactory.

(a)   If the **current price** were used in the standard, the reported price variance will become adverse as soon as prices go up, which might be very early in the year. If prices go up gradually rather than in one big jump, it would be difficult to select an appropriate time for revising the standard.

(b)   If an **estimated mid-year price** were used, price variances should be favourable in the first half of the year and adverse in the second half of the year, again assuming that prices go up gradually throughout the year. Management could only really check that in any month, the price variance did not become excessively adverse (or favourable) and that the price variance switched from being favourable to adverse around month six or seven and not sooner.

2.4 Direct labour rates

Direct labour rates per hour will be set by discussion with the personnel department and by reference to the payroll and to any agreements on pay rises with trade union representatives of the employees.

(a)   A separate hourly rate or weekly wage will be set for each different labour grade/type of employee.

(b)   An average hourly rate will be applied for each grade (even though individual rates of pay may vary according to age and experience).

Similar problems when dealing with inflation to those described for material prices can be met when setting labour standards.

2.5 Overhead absorption rates

When standard costs are fully absorbed costs, the **absorption rate** of fixed production overheads will be **predetermined**, usually each year when the budget is prepared, and based in the usual manner on budgeted fixed production overhead expenditure and budgeted production.

For selling and distribution costs, standard costs might be absorbed as a percentage of the standard selling price.

Standard costs under marginal costing will, of course, not include any element of absorbed overheads.

2.6 Standard resource requirements

To estimate the materials required to make each product (**material usage**) and also the labour hours required (**labour efficiency**), **technical specifications** must be prepared for each product by production experts (either in the production department or the work study department).

(a)   The '**standard product specification**' for materials must list the quantities required per unit of each material in the product. These standard input quantities must be made known to the operators in the production department so that control action by management to deal with **excess material wastage** will be understood by them.

(b)   The '**standard operation sheet**' for labour will specify the expected hours required by each grade of labour in each department to make one unit of product. These standard times must be carefully set (for example by work study) and must be understood by the labour force. Where necessary, **standard procedures** or **operating methods** should be stated.

EXAM FOCUS POINT

An exam question may give you actual costs and variances and require you to calculate the standard cost.

CHAPTER ROUNDUP

ↂ A **standard cost** is a **predetermined estimated unit cost**, used for inventory valuation and control.

ↂ A **standard cost card** shows full details of the standard cost of each product.

ↂ Differences between actual and standard cost are called **variances**.

ↂ **Performance standards** are used to set efficiency targets. There are four types: ideal, attainable, current and basic.

QUICK QUIZ

1 A standard cost is ....

2 What are two main uses of standard costing?

3 A control technique which compares standard costs and revenues with actual results to obtain variances which are used to stimulate improved performance is known as:

    A   Standard costing
    B   Variance analysis
    C   Budgetary control
    D   Budgeting

4 Standard costs may only be used in absorption costing.

    True   ☐

    False   ☐

5 Two types of performance standard are

    (a)   ....

    (b)   ....

ANSWERS TO QUICK QUIZ

1   A planned unit cost.

2   (a)   To value inventories and cost production for cost accounting purposes.

     (b)   To act as a control device by establishing standards and highlighting activities that are not conforming to plan and bringing these to the attention of management.

3   A

4   False. They may be used in a marginal costing system as well.

5   (a)   Attainable
     (b)   Ideal

Now try ...

Attempt the questions below from the **Exam Question Bank**

Number

Q90 – Q92

CHAPTER

21

The actual results achieved by an organisation during a reporting period (week, month, quarter, year) will, more than likely, be different from the expected results (the expected results being the standard costs and revenues which we looked at in the previous chapter). Such differences may occur between individual items, such as the cost of labour and the volume of sales, and between the total expected profit/contribution and the total actual profit/contribution.

Management will have spent considerable time and trouble setting standards. Actual results have differed from the standards. The wise manager will consider the differences that have occurred and use the results of these considerations to assist in attempts to attain the standards. The wise manager will use **variance analysis** as a method of **control**.

This chapter examines **variance analysis** and sets out the method of calculating the variances stated below in the Study Guide.

We will then go on to look at the reasons for and significance of cost variances.

Chapter 22 of this **Management Accounting** Interactive Text will build on the basics set down in this chapter by introducing **sales variances** and **operating statements.**

Basic variance analysis

Study Guide	Intellectual level
D **Standard costing**	
2 **Variance calculations and analysis**	
(b) Calculate materials total, price and usage variance	S
(c) Calculate labour total, rate and efficiency variance	S
(d) Calculate variable overhead total, expenditure and efficiency	S
(e) Calculate fixed overhead total, expenditure and, where appropriate, volume, capacity and efficiency variance	S
(f) Interpret the variances	S
(g) Explain factors to consider before investigating variances, explain possible causes of the variances and recommend control action	S
(h) Explain the interrelationships between the variances	K
C **Budgeting**	
6 **Budgetary control and reporting**	
(a) Calculate simple variances between flexed budget, fixed budget and actual sales, costs and profits	S
(b) Discuss the relative significance of variances	K
(c) Explain potential action to eliminate variances	K

EXAM FOCUS POINT

Variance calculation is a very important part of your Management Accounting studies and it is vital that you are able to calculate all of the different types of variance included in the syllabus.

1 Variances

A **variance** is the difference between a planned, budgeted, or standard cost and the actual cost incurred. The same comparisons may be made for revenues. The process by which the **total** difference between standard and actual results is analysed is known as **variance analysis**.

When actual results are better than expected results, we have a **favourable variance** (F). If, on the other hand, actual results are worse than expected results, we have an **adverse variance** (A).

Variances can be divided into three main groups.

- Variable cost variances
- Sales variances
- Fixed production overhead variances.

In the remainder of this chapter we will consider, in detail, variable cost variances and fixed production overhead variances.

2 Direct material cost variances

2.1 Introduction

The direct material total variance can be subdivided into the **direct material price** variance and the **direct material usage** variance.

TERM

The **direct material total variance** is the difference between what the output actually cost and what it should have cost, in terms of material.

The **direct material price variance**. This is the **difference between the standard cost and the actual cost for the actual quantity of material used or purchased.** In other words, it is the difference between what the material did cost and what it should have cost.

The **direct material usage variance**. This is the **difference between the standard quantity of materials that should have been used for the number of units actually produced, and the actual quantity of materials used, valued at the standard cost per unit of material.** In other words, it is the difference between how much material should have been used and how much material was used, valued at standard cost.

2.2 Example: Direct material variances

Product X has a standard direct material cost as follows.

10 kilograms of material Y at $10 per kilogram = $100 per unit of X.

During period 4, 1,000 units of X were manufactured, using 11,700 kilograms of material Y which cost $98,600.

Required

Calculate the following variances.

(a)   The direct material total variance
(b)   The direct material price variance
(c)   The direct material usage variance

Solution

(a)   **The direct material total variance**

This is the difference between what 1,000 units should have cost and what they did cost.

	$
1,000 units should have cost (× $100)	100,000
but did cost	98,600
Direct material total variance	1,400 (F)

The variance is **favourable** because the units cost less than they should have cost.

Now we can break down the direct material total variance into its two constituent parts: the direct material **price** variance and the direct material **usage** variance.

(b)   **The direct material price variance**

This is the difference between what 11,700 kgs should have cost and what 11,700 kgs did cost.

	$
11,700 kgs of Y should have cost (× $10)	117,000
but did cost	98,600
Material Y price variance	18,400 (F)

The variance is **favourable** because the material cost less than it should have.

(c)   **The direct material usage variance**

This is the difference between how many kilograms of Y should have been used to produce 1,000 units of X and how many kilograms were used, valued at the standard cost per kilogram.

1,000 units should have used (× 10 kgs)	10,000 kgs
but did use	11,700 kgs
Usage variance in kgs	1,700 kgs (A)
× standard cost per kilogram	× $10
Usage variance in $	$17,000 (A)

The variance is **adverse** because more material than should have been used was used.

(d)   **Summary**

	$
Price variance	18,400 (F)
Usage variance	17,000 (A)
Total variance	1,400 (F)

2.3 Materials variances and opening and closing inventory

Direct material price variances are usually extracted at the time of the **receipt** of the materials rather than at the time of usage.

Suppose that a company uses raw material P in production, and that this raw material has a standard price of $3 per metre. During one month 6,000 metres are bought for $18,600, and 5,000 metres are used in production. At the end of the month, inventory will have been increased by 1,000 metres. In variance analysis, the problem is to decide the **material price variance**. Should it be calculated on the basis of **materials purchased** (6,000 metres) or on the basis of **materials used** (5,000 metres)?

The answer to this problem depends on how **closing inventories** of the raw materials will be valued.

(a)   If they are valued at **standard cost**, (1,000 units at $3 per unit) the price variance is calculated on material **purchases** in the period.

(b)   If they are valued at **actual cost (**FIFO**)** (1,000 units at $3.10 per unit) the price variance is calculated on materials **used in production** in the period.

A **full standard costing system** is usually in operation and therefore the price variance is usually calculated on **purchases** in the period. The variance on the full 6,000 metres will be written off to the costing profit and loss account, even though only 5,000 metres are included in the cost of production.

There are two main advantages in extracting the material price variance at the time of **receipt**.

(a)   If variances are extracted at the time of receipt they will be **brought to the attention of managers earlier** than if they are extracted as the material is used. If it is necessary to correct any variances then management action can be more timely.

(b)   Since variances are extracted at the time of receipt, **all inventories will be valued at standard price**. This is administratively easier and it means that all issues from inventory can be made at standard price. If inventories are held at actual cost it is necessary to calculate a separate price variance on each batch as it is issued. Since issues are usually made in a number of small batches this can be a time-consuming task, especially with a manual system.

The price variance would be calculated as follows.

	$
6,000 metres of material P purchased should cost (× $3)	18,000
but did cost	18,600
Price variance	600 (A)

444

3 Direct labour cost variances

3.1 Introduction

The direct labour total variance can be subdivided into the **direct labour rate** variance and the **direct labour efficiency** variance.

The **direct labour total variance** is the difference between what the output should have cost and what it did cost, in terms of labour.

The **direct labour rate variance**. This is similar to the direct material price variance. It is the **difference between the standard cost and the actual cost for the actual number of hours paid for.**

In other words, it is the difference between what the labour did cost and what it should have cost.

The **direct labour efficiency variance** is similar to the direct material usage variance. It is the **difference between the hours that should have been worked for the number of units actually produced, and the actual number of hours worked, valued at the standard rate per hour.**

In other words, it is the difference between how many hours should have been worked and how many hours were worked, valued at the standard rate per hour.

The calculation of **direct labour variances** is very similar to the calculation of direct material variances.

3.2 Example: Direct labour variances

The standard direct labour cost of product X is as follows.

> 2 hours of grade Z labour at $5 per hour = $10 per unit of product X.

During period 4, 1,000 units of product X were made, and the direct labour cost of grade Z labour was $8,900 for 2,300 hours of work.

Required

Calculate the following variances.

(a) The direct labour total variance
(b) The direct labour rate variance
(c) The direct labour efficiency (productivity) variance

Solution

(a) **The direct labour total variance**

This is the difference between what 1,000 units should have cost and what they did cost.

	$
1,000 units should have cost (× $10)	10,000
but did cost	8,900
Direct labour total variance	1,100 (F)

The variance is **favourable** because the units cost less than they should have done. Again we can analyse this total variance into its two constituent parts.

(b) **The direct labour rate variance**

This is the difference between what 2,300 hours should have cost and what 2,300 hours did cost.

	$
2,300 hours of work should have cost (× $5 per hr)	11,500
but did cost	8,900
Direct labour rate variance	2,600 (F)

The variance is **favourable** because the labour cost less than it should have cost.

 **445**

(c)   **The direct labour efficiency variance**

	hrs
1,000 units of X should have taken (× 2 hrs)	2,000 hrs
but did take	2,300 hrs
Efficiency variance in hours	300 hrs (A)
× standard rate per hour	× $5
Efficiency variance in $	$1,500 (A)

The variance is **adverse** because more hours were worked than should have been worked.

(d)   **Summary**

	$
Rate variance	2,600 (F)
Efficiency variance	1,500 (A)
Total variance	1,100 (F)

4   Variable production overhead variances

The variable production overhead total variance can be subdivided into the variable production overhead **expenditure** variance and the variable production overhead **efficiency** variance (**based on actual hours**).

4.1 Example: Variable production overhead variances

Suppose that the variable production overhead cost of product X is as follows.

    2 hours at $1.50 = $3 per unit

During period 6, 1,000 units of product X were made. The labour force worked 2,020 hours, of which 60 hours were recorded as idle time. The variable overhead cost was $3,075.

Calculate the following variances.

(a)   The variable overhead total variance
(b)   The variable production overhead expenditure variance
(c)   The variable production overhead efficiency variance

Since this example relates to variable production costs, the total variance is based on actual units of production. (If the overhead had been a variable selling cost, the variance would be based on sales volumes.)

	$
1,000 units of product X should cost (× $3)	3,000
but did cost	3,075
Variable production overhead total variance	75 (A)

In many variance reporting systems, the variance analysis goes no further, and expenditure and efficiency variances are not calculated. However, the adverse variance of $75 may be explained as the sum of two factors.

(a)   The hourly rate of spending on variable production overheads was higher than it should have been, that is, there is an expenditure variance.

(b)   The labour force worked inefficiently, and took longer to make the output than it should have done. This means that spending on variable production overhead was higher than it should have been, in other words there is an efficiency (productivity) variance. The variable production overhead efficiency variance is exactly the same, in hours, as the direct labour efficiency variance, and occurs for the same reasons.

It is usually assumed that **variable overheads are incurred during active working hours**, but are not incurred during idle time (for example the machines are not running, therefore power is not being consumed, and no indirect materials are being used). This means in our example that although the labour force was paid for 2,020 hours, they were actively working for only 1,960 of those hours and so variable production overhead spending occurred during 1,960 hours.

The **variable production overhead expenditure variance** is the difference between the amount of variable production overhead that should have been incurred in the actual hours actively worked, and the actual amount of variable production overhead incurred.

(a)

	$
1,960 hours of variable production overhead should cost (× $1.50)	2,940
but did cost	3,075
Variable production overhead expenditure variance	135 (A)

The **variable production overhead efficiency variance**. If you already know the direct labour efficiency variance, the variable production overhead efficiency variance is exactly the same in hours, but priced at the variable production overhead rate per hour.

(b) In our example, the efficiency variance would be as follows.

1,000 units of product X should take (× 2hrs)	2,000 hrs
but did take (active hours)	1,960 hrs
Variable production overhead efficiency variance in hours	40 hrs (F)
× standard rate per hour	× $1.50
Variable production overhead efficiency variance in $	$60 (F)

(c) **Summary**

	$
Variable production overhead expenditure variance	135 (A)
Variable production overhead efficiency variance	60 (F)
Variable production overhead total variance	75 (A)

5 Fixed production overhead variances

EXAM FOCUS POINT

At the ACCA Teachers' Conference in 2009, the examiner highlighted fixed production overhead variances (particularly the capacity variance) as being an area where students perform poorly. Make sure you study this section carefully and attempt all the questions to ensure you will not be one of these students!

5.1 Introduction

The fixed production overhead total variance can be subdivided into an **expenditure** variance and a **volume** variance. The fixed production overhead volume variance can be further subdivided into an efficiency and capacity variance.

You may have noticed that the method of calculating cost variances for variable cost items is essentially the same for labour, materials and variable overheads. Fixed production overhead variances are very different. In an **absorption costing system**, they are an attempt to explain the **under– or over-absorption of fixed production overheads** in production costs. We looked at under/over absorption of fixed overheads in Chapter 8.

The fixed production overhead total variance (ie the under– or over-absorbed fixed production overhead) may be broken down into two parts as usual.

- An **expenditure** variance
- A **volume** variance. This in turn may be split into two parts
  - **A volume efficiency variance**
  - **A volume capacity variance**

You will find it easier to calculate and understand **fixed overhead variances**, if you keep in mind the whole time that you are trying to 'explain' (put a name and value to) any under– or over-absorbed overhead.

EXAM FOCUS POINT

You will need to be able to distinguish between marginal and absorption costing. The variances introduced above and discussed below relate to an absorption costing system. Marginal costing is dealt with in Chapter 22. In the marginal costing system the only fixed overhead variance is an expenditure variance.

5.2 Under/over absorption

Remember that the **absorption rate** is calculated as follows.

$$\text{Overhead absorption rate} = \frac{\text{Budgeted fixed overhead}}{\text{Budgeted activity level}}$$

Remember that the budgeted fixed overhead is the **planned** or **expected** fixed overhead and the budgeted activity level is the **planned** or **expected** activity level.

If either of the following are incorrect, then we will have an under– or over-absorption of overhead.

- The numerator (number on top) = Budgeted fixed overhead
- The denominator (number on bottom) = Budgeted activity level

5.3 The fixed overhead expenditure variance

The fixed overhead expenditure variance occurs if the numerator is incorrect. It measures the under– or over-absorbed overhead caused by the **actual total overhead** being different from the budgeted total overhead.

Therefore, fixed overhead expenditure variance = **Budgeted (planned) expenditure – Actual Expenditure.**

5.4 The fixed overhead volume variance

As we have already stated, the fixed overhead volume variance is made up of the following sub-variances.

- Fixed overhead efficiency variance
- Fixed overhead capacity variance

These variances arise if the denominator (ie the budgeted activity level) is incorrect.

The fixed overhead efficiency and capacity variances measure the under– or over-absorbed overhead caused by the **actual activity level** being different from the budgeted activity level used in calculating the absorption rate.

There are two reasons why the **actual activity** level may be different from the **budgeted activity level** used in calculating the absorption rate.

(a)   The workforce may have worked more or less efficiently than the standard set. This deviation is measured by the **fixed overhead efficiency variance.**

(b)   The hours worked by the workforce could have been different to the budgeted hours (regardless of the level of efficiency of the workforce) because of overtime and strikes etc. This deviation from the standard is measured by the **fixed overhead capacity variance.**

5.5 How to calculate the variances

In order to clarify the overhead variances which we have encountered in this section, consider the following definitions which are expressed in terms of how each overhead variance should be calculated.

Fixed overhead total variance is the difference between fixed overhead incurred and fixed overhead absorbed. In other words, it is the under– or over-absorbed fixed overhead.

Fixed overhead expenditure variance is the difference between the budgeted fixed overhead expenditure and actual fixed overhead expenditure.

Fixed overhead volume variance is the difference between actual and budgeted (planned) volume multiplied by the standard absorption rate per *unit*.

Fixed overhead volume efficiency variance is the difference between the number of hours that actual production should have taken, and the number of hours actually taken (that is, worked) multiplied by the standard absorption rate per *hour*.

Fixed overhead volume capacity variance is the difference between budgeted (planned) hours of work and the actual hours worked, multiplied by the standard absorption rate per *hour*.

You should now be ready to work through an example to demonstrate all of the fixed overhead variances.

5.6 Example: Fixed overhead variances

Suppose that a company plans to produce 1,000 units of product E during August 20X3. The expected time to produce a unit of E is five hours, and the budgeted fixed overhead is $20,000. The standard fixed overhead cost per unit of product E will therefore be as follows.

        5 hours at $4 per hour = $20 per unit

Actual fixed overhead expenditure in August 20X3 turns out to be $20,450. The labour force manages to produce 1,100 units of product E in 5,400 hours of work.

Task

Calculate the following variances.

(a)   The fixed overhead total variance
(b)   The fixed overhead expenditure variance
(c)   The fixed overhead volume variance
(d)   The fixed overhead volume efficiency variance
(e)   The fixed overhead volume capacity variance

Solution

All of the variances help to assess the under– or over-absorption of fixed overheads, some in greater detail than others.

(a)   **Fixed overhead total variance**

	$
Fixed overhead incurred	20,450
Fixed overhead absorbed (1,100 units × $20 per unit)	22,000
Fixed overhead total variance	1,550 (F)
(= under-/over-absorbed overhead)	

The variance is favourable because more overheads were absorbed than budgeted.

(b) **Fixed overhead expenditure variance**

	$
Budgeted fixed overhead expenditure	20,000
Actual fixed overhead expenditure	20,450
Fixed overhead expenditure variance	450 (A)

The variance is adverse because actual expenditure was greater than budgeted expenditure.

(c) **Fixed overhead volume variance**

The production volume achieved was greater than expected. The fixed overhead volume variance measures the difference at the standard rate.

	$
Actual production at standard rate (1,100 × $20 per unit)	22,000
Budgeted production at standard rate (1,000 × $20 per unit)	20,000
Fixed overhead volume variance	2,000 (F)

The variance is **favourable** because output was greater than expected.

(i) The labour force may have worked efficiently, and produced output at a faster rate than expected. Since overheads are absorbed at the rate of $20 per unit, more will be absorbed if units are produced more quickly. This **efficiency variance** is exactly the same in hours as the direct labour efficiency variance, but is valued in $ at the standard absorption rate for fixed overhead.

(ii) The labour force may have worked longer hours than budgeted, and therefore produced more output, so there may be a **capacity variance**.

(d) **Fixed overhead volume efficiency variance**

The volume efficiency variance is calculated in the same way as the labour efficiency variance.

1,100 units of product E should take (× 5 hrs)	5,500 hrs
but did take	5,400 hrs
Fixed overhead volume efficiency variance in hours	100 hrs (F)
× standard fixed overhead absorption rate per hour	× $4
Fixed overhead volume efficiency variance in $	$400 (F)

The labour force has produced 5,500 standard hours of work in 5,400 actual hours and so output is 100 standard hours (or 20 units of product E) higher than budgeted for this reason and the variance is **favourable**.

(e) **Fixed overhead volume capacity variance**

The volume capacity variance is the difference between the budgeted hours of work and the actual active hours of work (excluding any idle time).

Budgeted hours of work	5,000 hrs
Actual hours of work	5,400 hrs
Fixed overhead volume capacity variance	400 hrs (F)
× standard fixed overhead absorption rate per hour	× $4
Fixed overhead volume capacity variance in $	$1,600 (F)

Since the labour force worked 400 hours longer than planned, we should expect output to be 400 standard hours (or 80 units of product E) higher than budgeted and hence the variance is **favourable**.

The variances may be summarised as follows.

	$
Expenditure variance	450 (A)
Efficiency variance	400 (F)
Capacity variance	1,600 (F)
Over-absorbed overhead (total variance)	$1,550 (F)

EXAM FOCUS POINT

In general, a favourable cost variance will arise if actual results are less than expected results. Be aware, however, of the **fixed overhead volume variance** and the **fixed overhead volume capacity variance** which give rise to favourable and adverse variances in the following situations.

- A favourable fixed overhead volume variance occurs when actual production is **greater than** budgeted (planned) production

- An adverse fixed overhead volume variance occurs when actual production is **less than budgeted** (planned) production

- A favourable fixed overhead volume capacity variance occurs when actual hours of work are **greater than** budgeted (planned) hours of work

- An adverse fixed overhead volume capacity variance occurs when actual hours of work are **less than** budgeted (planned) hours of work

You may remember a similar graph appearing in Chapter 8. This one shows over-absorption of overheads.

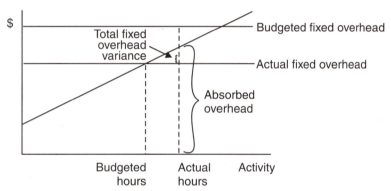

Do not worry if you find fixed production overhead variances more difficult to grasp than the other variances we have covered. Most students do. Read over this section again and then try the following practice questions.

QUESTION   Capacity variance

A manufacturing company operates a standard absorption costing system. Last month 25,000 production hours were budgeted and the budgeted fixed production overhead cost was $125,000. Last month the actual hours worked were 24,000 and the standard hours for actual production were 27,000.

What was the fixed production overhead capacity variance for last month?

A $5,000 Adverse
B $5,000 Favourable
C $10,000 Adverse
D $10,000 Favourable

ANSWER

The correct answer is A.

Standard fixed overhead absorption rate per hour = $125,000/25,000 = $5 per hour

Fixed overhead volume capacity variance

Budgeted hours of work	25,000 hrs
Actual hours of work	24,000 hrs
Fixed overhead volume capacity variance	1,000 hrs (A)
× standard fixed overhead absorption rate per hour	× $5
Fixed overhead volume capacity variance in $	$ 5,000 (A)

Refer to the exam focus point above for the rules on how to identify an adverse fixed overhead volume capacity variance. Remember that the capacity variance represents part of the over/under absorption of overheads. As the company worked less hours than budgeted (and the standard fixed overhead absorption rate is calculated using budgeted hours) this will result in an under-absorption of overheads.

The following information relates to the questions shown below

Barbados has prepared the following standard cost information for one unit of Product Zeta.

Direct materials	4kg @ $10/kg	$40.00
Direct labour	2 hours @ $4/hour	$8.00
Fixed overheads	3 hours @ $2.50	$7.50

The fixed overheads are based on a budgeted expenditure of $75,000 and budgeted activity of 30,000 hours.

Actual results for the period were recorded as follows.

Production	9,000 units
Materials – 33,600 kg	$336,000
Labour – 16,500 hours	$68,500
Fixed overheads	$70,000

QUESTION

Material variances

The direct material price and usage variances are:

	Material price	Material usage
	$	$
A	–	24,000 (F)
B	–	24,000 (A)
C	24,000 (F)	–
D	24,000 (A)	–

ANSWER

Material price variance

	$
33,600 kg should have cost (× $10/kg)	336,000
and did cost	336,000
	–

Material usage variance

9,000 units should have used (× 4kg)	36,000 kg
but did use	33,600 kg
	2,400 kg (F)
× standard cost per kg	× $10
	24,000 (F)

The correct answer is therefore A.

QUESTION

The direct labour rate and efficiency variances are:

	Labour rate	Labour efficiency
	$	$
A	6,000 (F)	2,500 (A)
B	6,000 (A)	2,500 (F)
C	2,500 (A)	6,000 (F)
D	2,500 (F)	6,000 (A)

ANSWER

Direct labour rate variance

	$
16,500 hrs should have cost (× $4)	66,000
but did cost	68,500
	2,500 (A)

Direct labour efficiency variance

9,000 units should have taken (× 2 hrs)	18,000 hrs
but did take	16,500 hrs
	1,500 (F)
× standard rate per hour (× $4)	× $4
	6,000 (F)

The correct answer is therefore C.

QUESTION

The total fixed production overhead variance is:

A $5,000 (A)
B $5,000 (F)
C $2,500 (A)
D $2,500 (F)

ANSWER

	$
Fixed production overhead absorbed ($7.50 × 9,000)	67,500
Fixed production overhead incurred	70,000
	2,500 (A)

The correct answer is therefore C.

6 Flexed budgets and variances

Total variances are the difference between flexed budget figures and actual figures.

You may remember from Chapter 15 that a flexed budget is a budget that is prepared at the actual activity level that was achieved in the period. It shows what the costs should have been at that activity level. We can compare these costs to the actual costs to obtain variances. These variances are the total variances, for example, the total materials variance, rather than the material price variance or usage variance.

XYZ Co prepared a cost budget for one of its products, product X, based on production of 3,000 units of the product.

Number of units produced	3,000
	$
Direct materials	300,000
Direct labour	30,000
Variable overheads	9,000

In reality, only 1,000 units were produced and the actual costs were $98,600 for materials, $8,900 for labour and $3,075 for variable overheads.

We can flex the budget to see what the costs for 1,000 units should have been.

Number of units produced	3,000	1,000
	Budget	*Flexed budget*
	$	$
Direct materials	300,000	100,000*
Direct labour	30,000	10,000**
Variable overheads	9,000	3,000***

* $300,000/3,000 = $100 per unit	$100 × 1,000 units	= $100,000
** $30,000/3,000 = $10 per unit	$10 × 1,000 units	= $10,000
*** $9,000/3,000 = $3 per unit	$3 × 1,000 units	= $3,000

We can now compare the flexed budget which shows what the costs should have been, with the actual costs.

Number of units produced	*1,000*	*1,000*	*Difference*
	Flexed budget	*Actual*	*Total variance*
	$	$	$
Direct materials	100,000	98,600	1,400 (F)
Direct labour	10,000	8,900	1,100 (F)
Variable overheads	3,000	3,075	75 (A)

If you look back at sections 2, 3 and 4 you will see that the total variances that we calculated are the same as the ones we have calculated here using the flexed budget.

7 The reasons for cost variances

One of the competences in your PER is about demonstrating that you are competent in using relevant management accounting planning and control techniques to support management. One of the skills you might need in order to fulfil this objective is to compare actual figures with budget and identify and explain any differences. This section can be used to help you to develop that skill in the workplace.

There are many possible reasons for cost variances arising, as you will see from the following list of possible causes.

7.1 General causes of variances

There are four general causes of variances,

(a) **Inappropriate standard**. Incorrect or out of date standards could have been used which will not reflect current conditions. For example, a material price standard may have been wrong if an old price was used or the wrong type of material was priced.

(b) **Inaccurate recording of actual costs**. For example, if time sheets are filled in incorrectly this may lead to variances.

(c) **Random events**. Examples include unusual adverse weather conditions or a flu epidemic. These may cause additional unforeseen costs.

(d)   **Operating inefficiency.** If the variance is not caused by inappropriate standards, inaccurate recording or random events, then it must be due to operating efficiency. The operating efficiency may be due to controllable or uncontrollable factors.

	Variance	Favourable	Adverse
(a)	Material price	Unforeseen discounts received More care taken in purchasing Change in material standard	Price increase Careless purchasing Change in material standard
(b)	Material usage	Material used of higher quality than standard More effective use made of material Errors in allocating material to jobs	Defective material Excessive waste Theft Stricter quality control Errors in allocating material to jobs
(c)	Labour rate	Use of apprentices or other workers at a rate of pay lower than standard	Wage rate increase Use of higher grade labour
(d)	Labour efficiency	Output produced more quickly than expected because of work motivation, better quality of equipment or materials, or better methods. Errors in allocating time to jobs	Lost time in excess of standard allowed Output lower than standard set because of deliberate restriction, lack of training, or sub-standard material used Errors in allocating time to jobs
(e)	Overhead expenditure	Savings in costs incurred More economical use of services	Increase in cost of services used Excessive use of services Change in type of services used
(f)	Overhead volume efficiency	Labour force working more efficiently (favourable labour efficiency variance)	Labour force working less efficiently (adverse labour efficiency variance)
(g)	Overhead volume capacity	Labour force working overtime	Machine breakdown, strikes, labour shortages

8 The significance of cost variances

8.1 Introduction

Materiality, controllability, the type of standard being used, the interdependence of variances and the cost of an investigation should be taken into account when deciding whether to investigate reported variances.

Once variances have been calculated, management have to decide whether or not to investigate their causes. It would be extremely time consuming and expensive to investigate every variance therefore managers have to decide which variances are worthy of investigation.

There are a number of factors which can be taken into account when deciding whether or not a variance should be investigated.

(a)   **Materiality.** A standard cost is really only an **average** expected cost and is not a rigid specification. Small variations either side of this average are therefore bound to occur. The problem is to decide whether a variation from standard should be considered **significant** and worthy of investigation. **Tolerance limits** can be set and only variances which exceed such limits would require investigating.

(b) **Controllability**. Some types of variance may not be controllable even once their cause is discovered. For example, if there is a general worldwide increase in the price of a raw material there is nothing that can be done internally to control the effect of this. If a central decision is made to award all employees a 10% increase in salary, staff costs in division A will increase by this amount and the variance is not controllable by division A's manager. Uncontrollable variances call for a change in the plan, not an investigation into the past.

(c) **The type of standard being used**.

    (i) The efficiency variance reported in any control period, whether for materials or labour, will depend on the **efficiency level** set. If, for example, an **ideal standard** is used, variances will always be **adverse**.

    (ii) A similar problem arises if **average price levels** are used as standards. If inflation exists, favourable price variances are likely to be reported at the beginning of a period, to be offset by adverse price variances later in the period as inflation pushes prices up.

(d) **Interdependence between variances** . Quite possibly, individual variances should not be looked at in isolation. One variance might be inter-related with another, and much of it might have occurred only because the other, inter-related, variance occurred too. We will investigate this issue further in a moment.

(e) **Costs of investigation.** The costs of an investigation should be weighed against the benefits of correcting the cause of a variance.

8.2 Interdependence between variances

When two variances are interdependent (interrelated) one will usually be adverse and the other one favourable.

8.3 Interdependence – materials price and usage variances

It may be decided to purchase cheaper materials for a job in order to obtain a favourable **price variance**. This may lead to higher materials wastage than expected and therefore, **adverse usage variances occur**. If the cheaper materials are more difficult to handle, there might be some **adverse labour efficiency variance** too.

If a decision is made to purchase more expensive materials, which perhaps have a longer service life, the price variance will be adverse but the usage variance might be favourable.

8.4 Interdependence – labour rate and efficiency variances

If employees in a workforce are paid higher rates for experience and skill, using a highly skilled team should incur an **adverse rate variance** at the same time as a **favourable efficiency variance**. In contrast, a **favourable rate variance** might indicate a high proportion of inexperienced workers in the workforce, which could result in an **adverse labour efficiency variance** and possibly an **adverse materials usage variance** (due to high rates of rejects).

CHAPTER ROUNDUP

↳ A **variance** is the difference between a planned, budgeted, or standard cost and the actual cost incurred. The same comparisons can be made for revenues. The process by which the **total** difference between standard and actual results is analysed is known as the **variance analysis**.

↳ The direct material total variance can be subdivided into the **direct material price** variance and the **direct material usage** variance.

↳ Direct material price variances are usually extracted at the time of **receipt** of the materials, rather than at the time of usage.

↳ The direct labour total variance can be subdivided into the **direct labour rate** variance and the **direct labour efficiency** variance.

↳ The variable production overhead total variance can be subdivided into the variable production overhead **expenditure** variance and the variable production overhead **efficiency** variance **(based on active hours).**

↳ The fixed production overhead total variance can be subdivided into an **expenditure** variance and a **volume** variance. The fixed production overhead volume variance can be further subdivided into an **efficiency** and a **capacity** variance.

↳ Total variances are the difference between flexed budget figures and actual figures.

↳ Materiality, controllability, the type of standard being used, the interdependence of variances and the cost of an investigation should be taken into account when deciding whether to investigate reported variances.

QUICK QUIZ

1   Subdivide the following variances.

(a)   Direct materials cost variance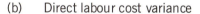

(b)   Direct labour cost variance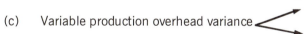

(c)   Variable production overhead variance

2   What are the two main advantages in calculating the material price variance at the time of receipt of materials?

3   Adverse material usage variances might occur for the following reasons.

I   Defective material
II   Excessive waste
III   Theft
IV   Unforeseen discounts received

A   I
B   I and II
C   I, II and III
D   I, II, III and IV

4   List the factors which should be taken into account when deciding whether or not a variance should be investigated.

ANSWERS TO QUICK QUIZ

1   (a)   Price / Usage

     (b)   Rate / Efficiency

     (c)   Expenditure / Efficiency

2   (a)   The earlier variances are extracted, the sooner they will be brought to the attention of managers.

     (b)   All inventories will be valued at standard price which requires less administration effort.

3   C

4
- Materiality
- Controllability
- Type of standard being used
- Interdependence between variances
- Costs of investigation

Now try ...

Attempt the questions below from the **Exam Question Bank**

Number

Q93 – Q96

Further variance analysis

The objective of cost variance analysis, which we looked at in the previous chapter, is to assist management in the **control of costs**. Costs are, however, only one factor which contribute to the achievement of planned profit. **Sales** are another important factor and sales variances can be calculated to aid management's control of their business. We will therefore begin this chapter by examining **sales variances**.

Having discussed the variances you need to know about, we will be looking in Section 2 at the **ways in which variances should be presented to management** to aid their control of the organisation.

We then consider in Section 3 how **marginal cost variances** differ from absorption cost variances and how marginal costing information should be presented.

Finally we will consider **how actual data can be derived from standard cost details and variances**.

TOPIC LIST	
1 Sales variances	D2 (a)
2 Operating statements	D3 (a), (b)
3 Variances in a standard marginal costing system	D3 (b)
4 Deriving actual data from standard cost details and variances	D2 (i)
5 Control action	C6 (c)

Study Guide

		Intellectual level
D	**Standard costing**	
2	**Variance calculations and analysis**	
(a)	Calculate sales price and volume variance	S
(i)	Calculate actual or standard figures where the variances are given	K
D	**Standard costing**	
3	**Reconciliation of budgeted and actual profit**	
(a)	Reconcile budgeted profit with actual profit under standard absorption costing	S
(b)	Reconcile budgeted profit or contribution with actual profit or contribution under standard marginal costing	S

EXAM FOCUS POINT

Variance analysis is traditionally a very popular exam topic. Make sure that you are able to prepare operating statements and explain why calculated variances have occurred. You will not be expected to prepare a whole operating statement in the exam, but you may be tested on your understanding of these statements.

1 Sales variances

1.1 Selling price variance

The **selling price variance** is a measure of the effect on expected profit of a different selling price to standard selling price. It is calculated as the difference between what the sales revenue should have been for the actual quantity sold, and what it was.

1.2 Example: Selling price variance

Suppose that the standard selling price of product X is $15. Actual sales in 20X3 were 2,000 units at $15.30 per unit. The selling price variance is calculated as follows.

	$
Sales revenue from 2,000 units should have been (× $15)	30,000
but was (× $15.30)	30,600
Selling price variance	600 (F)

The variance calculated is **favourable** because the price was higher than expected.

1.3 Sales volume profit variance

The **sales volume profit variance** is the difference between the actual units sold and the budgeted (planned) quantity, valued at the standard profit per unit. In other words, it measures the increase or decrease in standard profit as a result of the sales volume being higher or lower than budgeted (planned).

460

1.4 Example: Sales volume profit variance

Suppose that a company budgets to sell 8,000 units of product J for $12 per unit. The standard full cost per unit is $7. Actual sales were 7,700 units, at $12.50 per unit.

The **sales volume profit variance** is calculated as follows.

Budgeted sales volume	8,000 units
Actual sales volume	7,700 units
Sales volume variance in units	300 units (A)
× standard profit per unit ($(12–7))	× $5
Sales volume variance	$1,500 (A)

The variance calculated above is **adverse** because actual sales were less than budgeted (planned).

QUESTION
Selling price variance

Jasper Co has the following budget and actual figures for 20X4.

	Budget	Actual
Sales units	600	620
Selling price per unit	$30	$29

Standard full cost of production = $28 per unit.

Required

Calculate the selling price variance and the sales volume profit variance.

ANSWER

Sales revenue for 620 units should have been (× $30)	18,600
but was (× $29)	17,980
Selling price variance	620 (A)

Budgeted sales volume	600 units
Actual sales volume	620 units
Sales volume variance in units	20 units (F)
× standard profit per unit ($(30 – 28))	× $2
Sales volume profit variance	$40 (F)

1.5 The significance of sales variances

The possible **interdependence** between sales price and sales volume variances should be obvious to you. A reduction in the sales price might stimulate bigger sales demand, so that an adverse sales price variance might be counterbalanced by a favourable sales volume variance. Similarly, a price rise would give a favourable price variance, but possibly at the cost of a fall in demand and an adverse sales volume variance.

It is therefore important in analysing an unfavourable sales variance that the overall consequence should be considered, that is, has there been a counterbalancing favourable variance as a direct result of the unfavourable one?

2 Operating statements

2.1 Introduction

Operating statements show how the combination of variances reconcile budgeted profit and actual profit.

So far, we have considered how variances are calculated without considering how they combine to reconcile the difference between budgeted profit and actual profit during a period. This reconciliation is usually presented as a report to senior management at the end of each control period. The report is called an **operating statement** or **statement of variances**.

An operating statement is a regular report for management of actual costs and revenues, usually showing variances from budget.

An extensive example will now be introduced, both to revise the variance calculations already described, and also to show how to combine them into an operating statement.

2.2 Example: Variances and operating statements

Sydney manufactures one product, and the entire product is sold as soon as it is produced. There are no opening or closing inventories and work in progress is negligible. The company operates a standard costing system and analysis of variances is made every month. The standard cost card for the product, a boomerang, is as follows.

STANDARD COST CARD – BOOMERANG

		$
Direct materials	0.5 kilos at $4 per kilo	2.00
Direct wages	2 hours at $2.00 per hour	4.00
Variable overheads	2 hours at $0.30 per hour	0.60
Fixed overhead	2 hours at $3.70 per hour	7.40
Standard cost		14.00
Standard profit		6.00
Standing selling price		20.00

Selling and administration expenses are not included in the standard cost, and are deducted from profit as a period charge.

Budgeted (planned) output for the month of June 20X7 was 5,100 units. Actual results for June 20X7 were as follows.

Production of 4,850 units was sold for $95,600.
Materials consumed in production amounted to 2,300 kgs at a total cost of $9,800.
Labour hours paid for amounted to 8,500 hours at a cost of $16,800.
Actual operating hours amounted to 8,000 hours.
Variable overheads amounted to $2,600.
Fixed overheads amounted to $42,300.
Selling and administration expenses amounted to $18,000.

Required

Calculate all variances and prepare an operating statement for the month ended 30 June 20X7.

Solution

(a)		$
2,300 kg of material should cost (× $4)		9,200
but did cost		9,800
Material price variance		600 (A)

(b) 4,850 boomerangs should use (× 0.5 kgs)   2,425 kg
      but did use   2,300 kg
      Material usage variance in kgs   125 kg (F)
      × standard cost per kg   × \$4
      Material usage variance in \$ \$ 500 (F)

(c)   \$
      8,500 hours of labour should cost (× \$2)   17,000
      but did cost   16,800
      Labour rate variance   200 (F)

(d) 4,850 boomerangs should take (× 2 hrs)   9,700 hrs
      but did take (active hours)   8,000 hrs
      Labour efficiency variance in hours   1,700 hrs (F)
      × standard cost per hour   × \$2
      Labour efficiency variance in \$ \$3,400 (F)

(e) **Idle time variance** 500 hours (A) × \$2   \$1,000 (A)

(f)   \$
      8,000 hours incurring variable o/hd expenditure should cost (× \$0.30)   2,400
      but did cost   2,600
      Variable overhead expenditure variance   200 (A)

(g) **Variable overhead efficiency variance** in hours is the same as the
      labour efficiency variance:
      1,700 hours (F) × \$0.30 per hour   \$ 510 (F)

(h)   \$
      Budgeted fixed overhead (5,100 units × 2 hrs × \$3.70)   37,740
      Actual fixed overhead   42,300
      Fixed overhead expenditure variance   4,560 (A)

(i)   \$
      4,850 boomerangs should take (× 2 hrs)   9,700 hrs
      but did take (active hours)   8,000 hrs
      Fixed overhead volume efficiency variance in hrs   1,700 hrs (F)
      × standard fixed overhead absorption rate per hour   × \$3.70
      Fixed overhead volume efficiency variance in \$ 6,290 (F)

(j)   \$
      Budgeted hours of work (5,100 × 2 hrs)   10,200 hrs
      Actual hours of work   8,000 hrs
      Fixed overhead volume capacity variance in hrs   2,200 hrs (A)
      × standard fixed overhead absorption rate per hour   × \$3.70
      Fixed overhead volume capacity variance in \$ 8,140 (A)

(k)   \$
      Revenue from 4,850 boomerangs should be (× \$20)   97,000
      but was   95,600
      Selling price variance   1,400 (A)

(l) Budgeted sales volume   5,100 units
      Actual sales volume   4,850 units
      Sales volume profit variance in units   250 units
      × standard profit per unit   × \$6 (A)
      Sales volume profit variance in \$ \$1,500 (A)

There are several ways in which an operating statement may be presented. Perhaps the most common format is one which **reconciles budgeted profit to actual profit**. In this example, sales and administration costs will be introduced at the end of the statement, so that we shall begin with 'budgeted profit before sales and administration costs'.

Sales variances are reported first, and the total of the budgeted profit and the two sales variances results in a figure for 'actual sales minus the standard cost of sales'. The cost variances are then reported, and an actual profit (before sales and administration costs) calculated. Sales and administration costs are then deducted to reach the actual profit for June 20X7.

SYDNEY – OPERATING STATEMENT JUNE 20X7

	$	$
Budgeted (planned) profit before sales and administration costs		30,600
Sales variances: price	1,400 (A)	
volume	1,500 (A)	
		2,900 (A)
Actual sales minus the standard cost of sales		27,700

	(F)	(A)	
Cost variances	$	$	
Material price		600	
Material usage	500		
Labour rate	200		
Labour efficiency	3,400		
Labour idle time		1,000	
Variable overhead expenditure		200	
Variable overhead efficiency	510		
Fixed overhead expenditure		4,560	
Fixed overhead volume efficiency	6,290		
Fixed overhead volume capacity		8,140	
	10,900	14,500	3,600 (A)
Actual profit before sales and administration costs			24,100
Sales and administration costs			18,000
Actual profit, June 20X7			6,100

	$	$
Check		
Sales		95,600
Materials	9,800	
Labour	16,800	
Variable overhead	2,600	
Fixed overhead	42,300	
Sales and administration	18,000	
		89,500
Actual profit		6,100

3 Variances in a standard marginal costing system

3.1 Introduction

There are two main differences between the variances calculated in an absorption costing system and the variances calculated in a marginal costing system.

- In the marginal costing system **the only fixed overhead variance is an expenditure variance**.
- The sales volume variance is **valued at standard contribution margin**, not standard profit margin.

In all of the examples we have worked through so far, a system of standard absorption costing has been in operation. If an organisation uses **standard marginal costing** instead of standard absorption costing, there will be two differences in the way the variances are calculated.

(a)   In marginal costing, fixed costs are not absorbed into product costs and so there are no fixed cost variances to explain any under or over absorption of overheads. There will, therefore, be **no fixed overhead volume variance**. There will be a fixed overhead expenditure variance which is calculated in exactly the same way as for absorption costing systems.

(b)   The **sales volume variance** will be valued at **standard contribution margin** (sales price per unit minus variable costs of sale per unit), **not** standard **profit** margin.

3.2 Preparing a marginal costing operating statement

Returning once again to the example of Sydney, the variances in a system of standard marginal costing would be as follows.

(a)   There is **no fixed overhead volume variance** (and therefore no fixed overhead volume efficiency and volume capacity variances).

(b)   The standard contribution per unit of boomerang is $(20 - 6.60) = \$13.40$, therefore the **sales volume contribution variance** of 250 units (A) is valued at ($\times$ $13.40) = $3,350 (A).

The other variances are unchanged. However, this operating statement differs from an absorption costing operating statement in the following ways.

(a)   It begins with the budgeted **contribution** ($30,600 + budgeted fixed production costs $37,740 = $68,340).

(b)   The subtotal before the analysis of cost variances is actual sales ($95,600) less the standard **variable** cost of sales ($4,850 $\times$ $6.60) = $63,590.

(c)   **Actual contribution** is highlighted in the statement.

(d)   Budgeted (planned) fixed production overhead is adjusted by the fixed overhead expenditure variance to show the **actual** fixed production overhead expenditure.

Therefore a marginal costing operating statement might look like this.

SYDNEY – OPERATING STATEMENT JUNE 20X7

	$	$	$
Budgeted (planned) contribution			68,340
Sales variances: volume		3,350 (A)	
price		1,400 (A)	
			4,750 (A)
Actual sales minus the standard variable cost of sales			63,590
	(F)	(A)	
Variable cost variances			
Material price		600	
Material usage	500		
Labour rate	200		
Labour efficiency	3,400		
Labour idle time		1,000	
Variable overhead expenditure		200	
Variable overhead efficiency	510		
	4,610	1,800	
			2,810 (F)
Actual contribution			66,400
Budgeted (planned) fixed production overhead		37,740	
Expenditure variance		4,560 (A)	
Actual fixed production overhead			42,300
Actual profit before sales and administration costs			24,100
Sales and administration costs			18,000
Actual profit			6,100

Notice that the actual profit is the same as the profit calculated by standard absorption costing because there were no changes in inventory levels. Absorption costing and marginal costing do not always produce an identical profit figure.

QUESTION

Variances

Piglet, a manufacturing firm, operates a standard marginal costing system. It makes a single product, PIG, using a single raw material LET.

Standard costs relating to PIG have been calculated as follows.

Standard cost schedule – PIG

	Per unit $
Direct material, LET, 100 kg at $5 per kg	500
Direct labour, 10 hours at $8 per hour	80
Variable production overhead, 10 hours at $2 per hour	20
	600

The standard selling price of a PIG is $900 and Piglet Co produce 1,020 units a month.

During December 20X0, 1,000 units of PIG were produced. Relevant details of this production are as follows.

Direct material LET

90,000 kgs costing $720,000 were bought and used.

Direct labour

8,200 hours were worked during the month and total wages were $63,000.

Variable production overhead

The actual cost for the month was $25,000.

Inventories of the direct material LET are valued at the standard price of $5 per kg.

Each PIG was sold for $975.

Required

Calculate the following for the month of December 20X0.

(a)   Variable production cost variance
(b)   Direct labour cost variance, analysed into rate and efficiency variances
(c)   Direct material cost variance, analysed into price and usage variances
(d)   Variable production overhead variance, analysed into expenditure and efficiency variances
(e)   Selling price variance
(f)   Sales volume contribution variance

ANSWER

(a)   This is simply a 'total' variance.

	$
1,000 units should have cost (× $600)	600,000
but did cost (see working)	808,000
Variable production cost variance	208,000 (A)

(b)   **Direct labour cost variances**

	$
8,200 hours should cost (× $8)	65,600
but did cost	63,000
Direct labour rate variance	2,600 (F)

1,000 units should take (× 10 hours)	10,000 hrs
but did take	8,200 hrs
Direct labour efficiency variance in hrs	1,800 hrs (F)
× standard rate per hour	× $8
Direct labour efficiency variance in $	$14,400 (F)

Summary	$
Rate	2,600 (F)
Efficiency	14,400 (F)
Total	17,000 (F)

(c)   **Direct material cost variances**

	$
90,000 kg should cost (× $5)	450,000
but did cost	720,000
Direct material price variance	270,000 (A)

1,000 units should use (× 100 kg)	100,000 kg
but did use	90,000 kg
Direct material usage variance in kgs	10,000 kg (F)
× standard cost per kg	× $5
Direct material usage variance in $	$50,000 (F)

Summary	$
Price	270,000 (A)
Usage	50,000 (F)
Total	220,000 (A)

(d)   **Variable production overhead variances**

	$
8,200 hours incurring o/hd should cost (× $2)	16,400
but did cost	25,000
Variable production overhead expenditure variance	8,600 (A)

Efficiency variance in hrs (from (b))	1,800 hrs (F)
× standard rate per hour	× $2
Variable production overhead efficiency variance	$3,600 (F)

Summary

	$
Expenditure	8,600 (A)
Efficiency	3,600 (F)
Total	5,000 (A)

(e) **Selling price variance**

	$
Revenue from 1,000 units should have been (× $900)	900,000
but was (× $975)	975,000
Selling price variance	75,000 (F)

(f) **Sales volume contribution variance**

Budgeted sales	1,020 units
Actual sales	1,000 units
Sales volume variance in units	20 units (A)
× standard contribution margin ($(900 – 600))	× $300
Sales volume contribution variance in $	$6,000 (A)

Workings

	$
Direct material	720,000
Total wages	63,000
Variable production overhead	25,000
	808,000

QUESTION

Reconciling contributions

A company uses standard marginal costing. Last month the standard contribution on actual sales was $10,000 and the following variances arose.

	$
Total variable costs variance	2,000 (A)
Sales price variance	500 (F)
Sales volume contribution variance	1,000 (A)

What was the actual contribution for last month?

A $7,000
B $7,500
C $8,000
D $8,500

ANSWER

The correct answer is D.

	$
Standard contribution on actual sales	10,000
Add: favourable sales price variance	500
Less: adverse total variable costs variance	(2,000)
Actual contribution	8,500

QUESTION

Calculating actual contribution from variances

A company uses standard marginal costing. Last month, when all sales were at the standard selling price, the standard contribution from actual sales was $50,000 and the following variances arose:

	$
Total variable costs variance	3,500 (A)
Total fixed costs variance	1,000 (F)
Sales volume contribution variance	2,000 (F)

What was the actual contribution for last month?

A $46,500
B $47,500
C $48,500
D $49,500

ANSWER

The correct answer is A.

	$
Standard contribution on actual sales	50,000
Less: Adverse total variable costs variance	(3,500)
Actual contribution	46,500

---

4 Deriving actual data from standard cost details and variances

Variances can be used to derive actual data from standard cost details.

Rather than being given actual data and asked to calculate the variances, you may be given the variances and required to calculate the actual data on which they were based. See if you can do these two questions.

QUESTION

Rate of pay

XYZ uses standard costing. The following data relates to labour grade II.

Actual hours worked	10,400 hours
Standard allowance for actual production	8,320 hours
Standard rate per hour	$5
Rate variance (adverse)	$416

What was the actual rate of pay per hour?

A $4.95
B $4.96
C $5.04
D $5.05

ANSWER

The correct answer is C.

$$\text{Rate variance per hour worked} = \frac{\$416}{10,400} = \$0.04 \text{ (A)}$$

Actual rate per hour = $(5.00 + 0.04) = $5.04.

You should have been able to eliminate options A and B because they are both below the standard rate per hour. If the rate variance is adverse then the actual rate must be above standard. Option D is incorrect because it results from basing the calculations on standard hours rather than actual hours.

QUESTION

Quantity of material

The standard material content of one unit of product A is 10kg of material X which should cost $10 per kilogram. In June 20X4, 5,750 units of product A were produced and there was an adverse material usage variance of $1,500.

Required

Calculate the quantity of material X used in June 20X4.

ANSWER

Let the quantity of material X used = Y

5,750 units should have used (× 10kg)	57,500 kg
but did use	Y kg
Usage variance in kg	(Y – 57,500) kg
× standard price per kg	× $10
Usage variance in $	$1,500 (A)

$$\therefore \quad 10(Y - 57,500) = 1,500$$
$$Y - 57,500 = 150$$
$$\therefore \quad Y = 57,650 \text{ kg}$$

---

5 Control action

> A variance should only be investigated if the expected value of benefits from investigation and any control action exceed the costs of investigation.
>
> If the cause of a variance is controllable, action can be taken to bring the system back under control in future. If the variance is uncontrollable, but not simply due to chance, it will be necessary to review forecasts of expected results, and perhaps to revise the budget.

If a variance is assessed as significant then control action may be necessary.

Since a variance compares historical actual costs with standard costs, it is a statement of what has gone wrong (or right) in the past. By taking control action, managers can do nothing about the past, but they can use their analysis of past results to identify where the 'system' is out of control. If the **cause of the variance is controllable, action can be taken to bring the system back under control in future. If the variance is uncontrollable, on the other hand, but *not* simply due to chance, it will be necessary to revise forecasts of expected results, and perhaps to revise the budget.**

It may be possible for control action to restore actual results back on course to achieve the original budget. For example, if there is an adverse labour efficiency variance in month 1 of 1,100 hours, control action by the production department might succeed in increasing efficiency above standard by 100 hours per month for the next 11 months.

It is also possible that control action might succeed in restoring better order to a situation, but the improvements might not be sufficient to enable the company to achieve its original budget. For example if for three months there has been an adverse labour efficiency in a production department, so that the cost per unit of output was $8 instead of a standard cost of $5. Control action might succeed in improving efficiency, so that unit costs are reduced to $7, $6 or even $5, but the earlier excess spending means that the profit in the master budget will not be achieved.

Depending on the situation and the control action taken, the action may take immediate effect, or it may take several weeks or months to implement. The effect of control action might be short-lived, lasting for only one control period; but it is more likely to be implemented with the aim of long-term improvement.

5.1 Possible control action

The **control action which may be taken will depend on the reason why the variance occurred**. Some reasons for variances are outlined in the paragraphs below.

5.2 Measurement errors

In practice it may be extremely difficult to establish that 1,000 units of product A used 32,000 kg of raw material X. Scales may be misread, the pilfering or wastage of materials may go unrecorded, items may be wrongly classified (as material X3, say, when material X8 was used in reality), or employees may make adjustments to records to make their own performance look better.

An investigation may show that **control action is required to improve the accuracy of the recording system** so that measurement errors do not occur.

5.3 Out of date standards

Price standards are likely to become out of date when changes to the costs of material, power, labour and so on occur, or in **periods of high inflation**. In such circumstances an **investigation of variances is likely to highlight a general change in market prices** rather than efficiencies or inefficiencies in acquiring resources.

Standards may also be out of date where operations are subject to **technological development** or if **learning curve effects** have not been taken into account. Investigation of this type of variance will provide information about the inaccuracy of the standard and **highlight the need to frequently review and update standards.**

5.4 Efficient or inefficient operations

Spoilage and better quality material/more highly skilled labour than standard are all likely to affect the efficiency of operations and hence cause variances. **Investigation** of variances in this category should **highlight the cause of the inefficiency or efficiency and will lead to control action to eliminate the inefficiency being repeated** or action to **compound the benefits of the efficiency**. For example, stricter supervision may be required to reduce wastage levels.

5.5 Random or chance fluctuations

A standard is an **average** figure. It represents the midpoint of a range of possible values and therefore actual results are likely to deviate unpredictably within the predictable range.

As long as the variance falls within this range, it will be classified as a random or chance fluctuation and **control action will not be necessary**.

QUESTION

Report on variances

As the management accountant of the ABC Production Co you have prepared the following variance report for the general manager.

VARIANCE REPORT: SEPTEMBER 20X5

	Variance (Adverse) $	Variance (Favourable) $	Total variance $
Material			(2,000)
Usage	5,500		
Price		3,500	
Labour			(1,500)
Utilisation	3,000		
Rate		1,500	
Overhead			(500)
Price		4,500	
Efficiency	2,000		
Capacity	3,000		

Actual costs for September 20X5 were as follows.

	$
Materials	$100,000
Labour	$80,000
Overheads	$75,000
Total	$255,000

The general manager tells you that he is quite satisfied with this result because the total adverse variance of $4,000 is only 1.57% of total costs.

Required

Write a brief report to the General Manager giving *your own* interpretation of the month's results.

ANSWER

REPORT ON RESULTS FOR SEPTEMBER 20X5

1   TERMS OF REFERENCE

This report provides a management accounting interpretation of the company's results for September 20X5. The report was prepared by A N Employee, Management Accountant and submitted to A Boss, General Manager, on XX October 20X5.

2   METHOD

Using the management accounting department's variance report for September 20X5 and actual cost data for the month, the company's results were analysed.

3   FINDINGS

Total variance

The total variance may only be 1.57% of total costs but this total disguises a number of significant adverse and favourable variances which need investigating.

Materials variances

The fact that there is a favourable price variance and an adverse usage variance could indicate interdependence. The purchasing department may have bought cheap materials but these cheaper materials may have been more difficult to work with so that more material was required per unit produced. The possibility of such an interdependence should be investigated. Whether or not there is an interdependence, both variances do require investigation since they represent 5.5% (usage) and 3.5% (price) of the actual material cost for the month.

Labour variances

Again there could be an interdependence between the adverse utilisation variance and the favourable rate variance, less skilled (and lower paid) employees perhaps having worked less efficiently than standard. Discussions with factory management should reveal whether this is so. Both variances do need investigation since they again represent a high percentage (compared with 1.57%) of the actual labour cost for the month (3.75% for the utilisation variance and 1.875% for the rate variance).

Overhead variances

An investigation into the fixed and variable components of the overhead would facilitate control information. The cause of the favourable price variance, which represents 6% of the total overhead costs for the month, should be encouraged.

The adverse overhead variances in total represent 6.67% of actual overhead cost during the month and must therefore be investigated. The capacity variance signifies that actual hours of work were less than budgeted hours of work. The company is obviously working below its planned capacity level. Efforts should therefore be made to increase production so as to eradicate this variance.

4   CONCLUSION

It is not the total of the monthly variances which should be considered but the individual variances, as a number of them represent significant deviations from planned results. Investigations into their causes should be performed and control action taken to ensure that either performance is back under control in future if the cause of the variance can be controlled, or the forecasts of expected results are revised if the variance is uncontrollable.

QUESTION

Control problems

Jot down ideas for answering the following questions.

(a)   Explain the problems concerning control of operations that a manufacturing company can be expected to experience in using a standard costing system during periods of rapid inflation.

(b)   Suggest a method by which the company could try to overcome the problems to which you have referred in answer to (a) above, indicating the shortcoming of the method.

ANSWER

(a)   (i)   Inflation should be budgeted for in standard prices. But how can the rate of inflation and the timing of inflationary increases be accurately estimated? Who decides how much inflationary 'allowance' should be added to the standards?

(ii)   How can actual expenditure be judged against a realistic 'standard' price level. Ideally, there would be an external price index (for example, one published by the government's Office for National Statistics) but even external price indices are not reliable guides to the prices an organisation ought to be paying.

(iii)   The existence of inflation tends to eliminate the practical value of price variances as a pointer to controlling spending.

(iv)   Inflation affects operations more directly. Usually costs go up before an organisation can put up the prices of its own products to customers. Inflation therefore tends to put pressure on a company's cash flows.

(v)   To provide useful and accurately-valued variances the standard costs ought to be revised frequently. This would be an administrative burden on the organisation.

(vi)   If the organisation uses standard costs for pricing or inventory valuation, frequent revisions of the standard would be necessary to keep prices ahead of costs or inventories sensibly valued.

(b)   To overcome the problems, we could suggest the following.

(i)   Frequent revision of the standard costs. *Problem* – the administrative burden.

(ii)   Incorporating estimates of the rate of inflation and the timing of inflation into standard costs. *Problem* – accurate forecasting.

CHAPTER ROUNDUP

↳ The **selling price variance** is a measure of the effect on expected profit of a different selling price to standard selling price. It is calculated as the difference between what the sales revenue should have been for the actual quantity sold and what it was.

↳ The **sales volume profit variance** is the difference between the actual units sold and the budgeted (planned) quantity, valued at the standard profit per unit. In other words, it measures the increase or decrease in standard profit as a result of the sales volume being higher or lower than budgeted (planned).

↳ **Operating statements** show how the combination of variances reconcile budgeted profit and actual profit.

↳ There are two main differences between the variances calculated in an absorption costing system and the variances calculated in a marginal costing system.

　– In a marginal costing system **the only fixed overhead variance is an expenditure variance.**
　– The sales volume variance is **valued at standard contribution margin**, not standard profit margin.

↳ Variances can be used to derive actual data from standard cost details.

↳ A variance should only be investigated if the expected value of benefits from investigation and any control action exceed the costs of investigation. If the cause of a variance is controllable, action can be taken to bring the system back under control in future. If the variance is uncontrollable, but not simply due to chance, it will be necessary to review forecasts of expected results, and perhaps to revise the budget.

QUICK QUIZ

1　What is the sales volume profit variance?

2　A regular report for management of actual cost, and revenue, and usually comparing actual results with budgeted (planned) results (and showing variances) is known as

　A　Bank statement
　B　Variance statement
　C　Budget statement
　D　Operating statement

3　If an organisation uses standard marginal costing instead of standard absorption costing, which two variances are calculated differently?

ANSWERS TO QUICK QUIZ

1   It is a measure of the increase or decrease in standard profit as a result of the sales volume being higher or lower than budgeted (planned).

2   D

3   (a)   In marginal costing there is no fixed overhead volume variance (because fixed costs are not absorbed into product costs).

    (b)   In marginal costing, the sales volume variance will be valued at standard contribution margin and not standard profit margin.

Now try ...

Attempt the questions below from the **Exam Question Bank**

Number

Q97 – Q100

part

E

Performance measurement

CHAPTER

23

We looked briefly at objectives and goals in Chapter 1. Here we return to goals and objectives in the context of performance measurement. You need to understand how mission statements link to key performance indicators. This chapter also explains the concepts of economy, efficiency and effectiveness.

Performance measurement

Study Guide	Intellectual level
E **Performance measurement**	
1 **Performance measurement overview**	
(a) Discuss the purpose of mission statements and their role in performance measurement	K
(b) Discuss the purpose of strategic and operational and tactical objectives and their role in performance measurement	K
(c) Discuss the impact of economic and market conditions on performance measurement	K
(d) Explain the impact of government regulation on performance measurement	K
2 **Performance measurement - application**	
(a) Discuss and calculate measures of financial performance (profitability, liquidity, activity and gearing) and non-financial measures	S
(b)(iii) Discuss critical success factors and key performance indicators and their link to objectives and mission statements	K
(b)(iv) Establish critical success factors and key performance indicators in a specific situation	S
(c)(i) Explain the concepts of economy, efficiency and effectiveness	K
(c)(ii) Describe performance indicators for economy, efficiency and effectiveness	K
(c)(iii) Establish performance indicators for economy, efficiency and effectiveness in a specific situation	S

Technical competence 16 requires you to demonstrate you are competent in measuring and evaluating financial performance. The knowledge you gain in this chapter will help you demonstrate your competence in this area.

1 Performance measurement and the planning and control system

The higher direction of an organisation requires a clear vision, in general terms, of what the organisation should be doing in the longer term and how it should go about doing it. This may be encapsulated in a **mission statement**.

Performance measurement aims to establish how well something or somebody is doing in relation to a planned activity. The 'thing' may be one of the following.

(a) A machine
(b) A factory
(c) An organisation as a whole

The 'body' may be one of the following

(a) An individual employee
(b) A manager
(c) A group of people

Performance measurement is a **vital part** of the **control process.** The essence of control is that **actual performance is compared with a standard or target that was established earlier. For machines, processes**, departments and individuals such targets are laid down by the budgetary process and published in the budget itself. At a higher level, when we are trying to control the whole organisation, a slightly more complex process is required.

To begin with, the normal budgetary control process has benefit at this level. The forecast income statement and statement of financial position, which are the final product of the budget process, obviously represent overall targets for the organisation. However, these targets are not sufficient for the proper control of a large organisation: they only provide guidance for a very short period and only in terms of decisions that have already been taken. Even if a new process is scheduled to come into operation during the next year, that is the result of decisions long past. The budgetary process offers little guidance for the longer-term progress of the organisation.

We must now take a brief look at the world of strategic management. It is in this arena that the wider direction of the organisation is determined. Strategic managers must look several years into the future and decide what they want the organisation to do and where they want it to go. An important part of this process is the design and refinement of the organisational **mission statement**. This should encapsulate the **vision** of top management: what it is they are trying to achieve and, in general terms, how they wish to achieve it.

1.1 Elements of mission

Purpose. Why does the company exist?

(a) To create wealth for shareholders?
(b) To satisfy the needs of **all stakeholders** (including employees, society at large, for example)?

Strategy. Mission provides the commercial logic for the organisation, and so defines two things

(a) The **products or services** it offers and therefore its competitive position.
(b) The **competences** by which it hopes to prosper, and its way of competing.

Strategic scope. An organisation's strategic scope is defined by the **boundaries** its managers set for it. These boundaries may be set in terms of geography, market, business method, product or any other parameter that **defines the nature of the organisation**.

Policies and standards of behaviour. The mission needs to be converted into everyday performance. For example, a firm whose mission covers excellent customer service must deal with simple matters such as politeness to customers, speed at which phone calls are answered and so forth.

Values and culture. Values are the basic, perhaps unstated, beliefs of the people who work in the organisation.

The values of the business as a **collective entity** are in tune with the **personal values** of the individuals working for it. In conflicts of ethics, clashes between organisational and personal values are hard to resolve if someone's principles disagree with what the organisation wants.

For there to be a strong, motivating sense of mission, the four elements above must be mutually reinforcing.

1.2 The importance of mission

Although hard to quantify (and hence, from an accounting viewpoint, of dubious value) mission is taken seriously by many firms.

(a) Values and feelings are integral elements of **consumers' buying decisions**, as evidenced by advertising, branding and market research. Customers not only ask 'What do you sell?' but 'What do you stand for?'

(b) A respect for quantifiable information is part of the professional culture and training of the accountant; other people have different values and priorities.

(c) Studies into organisational behaviour suggest that employees are **motivated** by more than money. A sense of mission and values can help to motivate employees.

(d) Many firms take mission seriously in strategic management.

1.3 Mission statements

Mission statements are formal statements of an organisation's mission. They might be reproduced in a number of places (eg at the front of an organisation's annual report, on publicity material, in the chairman's office, in communal work areas and so on). There is no standard format, but they should possess certain characteristics.

(a)   **Brevity** – easy to understand and remember
(b)   **Flexibility** – to accommodate change
(c)   **Distinctiveness** – to make the firm stand out

1.4 Mission and planning

Although the mission statement might be seen as a set of abstract principles, it can play an important **role in the planning process**.

(a)   **Plans should outline the fulfilment of the organisation's mission**. To take the example of a religious organisation (the best example of a 'missionary organisation'), the mission of spreading the gospel might be embodied in plans to send individuals as missionaries to various parts of the world, plans for fund-raising activities, or even targets for the numbers of new converts.

(b)   **Evaluation and screening**. Mission also acts as a yardstick by which plans are judged.

    (I)   The mission of an ethical investment trust would preclude investing in tobacco firms.
    (ii)   Mission helps to ensure consistency in decisions.

(c)   **Implementation**. Mission also affects the implementation of a planned strategy, in the culture and business practices of the firm.

2 Goals and objectives

A hierarchy of SMART goals and objectives cascades downwards from the mission statement, eventually providing the targets for the periodic budget process.

From the vision and mission, **goals** are derived.

(a)   **Operational goals** can be expressed as objectives. Here is an example.
        Operational goal: 'Cut costs'. The objective: 'Reduce budget by 5%'

(b)   **Non-operational goals** A university's goal might be to 'seek truth'.
        Not all goals can be measured.

In practice most organisations set themselves **quantified objectives** in order to enact the corporate mission. Many objectives are:

(a)   **S**pecific
(b)   **M**easurable
(c)   **A**ttainable
(d)   **R**esults-orientated
(e)   **T**ime-bounded

There should be **goal congruence**. The goals set for different parts of the organisation should be consistent with each other.

2.1 Primary and secondary objectives

Some objectives are more important than others. In the hierarchy of objectives, there is a **primary corporate objective** and other **secondary objectives** which should combine to ensure the achievement of the overall corporate objective.

For example, if a company sets itself an objective of growth in profits, as its primary aim, it will then have to develop strategies by which this primary objective can be achieved. An objective must then be set for each individual strategy. Secondary objectives might then be concerned with sales growth, continual technological innovation, customer service, product quality, efficient resource management or reducing the company's reliance on debt capital.

2.2 Long-term objectives and short-term objectives

Objectives may be long-term and short-term. A company that is suffering from a recession in its core industries and making losses in the short term might continue to have a long term primary objective of achieving a growth in profits, but in the short term its primary objective might be survival.

2.3 Strategic, tactical and operational objectives

Objectives can also be classified as **strategic, tactical** or **operational.** We looked at strategic, tactical and operational information in Chapter 1. Strategic objectives would include matters such as required levels of company profitability. Tactical objectives would concern the **efficient and effective use of** an organisation's **resources**, for example, target productivity. Operational objectives would include guidelines for ensuring that **specific tasks are carried out**. For example, the manager of a sales territory may specify weekly sales targets for each sales representative.

3 Commercial goals and objectives

Objectives are normally **quantified** statements of what the organisation actually intends to achieve over a period of time.

Uses of objectives

(a) Objectives **orientate the activities** of the organisation towards the fulfilment of the organisation's mission, in theory if not always in practice.

(b) The mission of a **business**, whether stated or not, must include **profitability**.

(c) Objectives can also be used as standards **for measuring the performance** of the organisation and departments in it.

3.1 Corporate and unit objectives

Corporate objectives concern the firm as **a whole**, for example:

(a)	Profitability	(g)	Customer satisfaction
(b)	Market share	(h)	Quality
(c)	Growth	(i)	Industrial relations
(d)	Cash flow	(j)	Added value
(e)	Return on capital employed	(k)	Earnings per share
(f)	Risk		

Similar objectives can be developed for each **strategic business unit (SBU).** (An SBU is a part of the company that for all intents and purposes has its own distinct products, markets and assets.)

Unit objectives are specific to individual units of an organisation.

(a) **Commercial**

(i) Increase the number of customers by x% (an objective of a sales department)

(ii) Reduce the number of rejects by 50% (an objective of a production department)

(iii) Produce monthly reports more quickly, within 5 working days of the end of each month (an objective of the management accounting department)

(b)   **Public sector**

   (i)   Introduce x% more places at nursery schools (an objective of a borough education department)

   (ii)   Respond more quickly to calls (an objective of a local police station, fire department or hospital ambulance service)

(c)   **General**

   (i)   Resources (eg cheaper raw materials, lower borrowing costs, 'top-quality college graduates')

   (ii)   Market (eg market share, market standing)

   (iii) Employee development (eg training, promotion, safety)

   (iv)   Innovation in products or processes

   (v)   Productivity (the amount of output from resource inputs)

   (vi)   Technology

3.2 Primary and secondary objectives

Some objectives are more important than others. There is a **primary corporate objective** (restricted by certain constraints on corporate activity) and other **secondary objectives** which are strategic objectives which should combine to ensure the achievement of the primary corporate objective.

(a)   For example, if a company sets itself an objective of growth in profits, as its primary objective, it will then have to develop strategies by which this primary objective can be achieved.

(b)   Secondary objectives might then be concerned with sales growth, continual technological innovation, customer service, product quality, efficient resource management (eg labour productivity) or reducing the company's reliance on debt capital.

3.3 Trade-off between objectives

When there are several key objectives, some might be achieved only **at the expense of others**. For example, a company's objective of achieving good profits and profit growth might have adverse consequences for the cash flow of the business, or the quality of the firm's products.

There will be a **trade-off** between objectives when strategies are formulated, and a choice will have to be made. For example, there might be a choice between the following two options.

Option A   15% sales growth, 10% profit growth, a $2 million negative cash flow and reduced product quality and customer satisfaction.

Option B   8% sales growth, 5% profit growth, a $500,000 surplus cash flow, and maintenance of high product quality/customer satisfaction.

If the firm chose option B in preference to option A, it would be trading off sales growth and profit growth for better cash flow, product quality and customer satisfaction. The long-term effect of reduced quality has not been considered.

3.4 Critical success factors

As long ago as 1955 *Lewis* made a study of *GEC's* management reporting system and found that it produced reports on the following factors.

(a)	Profitability	(e)	Personnel development
(b)	Market share	(f)	Employee attitudes
(c)	Productivity	(g)	Public responsibility
(d)	Product leadership	(h)	Balance between short-range and long-range goals

These are examples of 'critical success factors'.

A **critical success factor** is a performance requirement that is fundamental to competitive success.

There are usually **fewer than ten** of these factors that any one executive should monitor. Furthermore, they are very time dependent so they should be **re-examined** as often as necessary to keep abreast of the current business climate.

Critical success factors can be set and used by **identifying objectives and goals, determining which factors are critical for accomplishing each objective** and then determining a small number of performance measures for each factor. For example, if next day delivery were an objective, an employee attitude survey that revealed indifference (or over-defensiveness) towards customer complaints about late deliveries would be an indication of failure.

A critical success factor is 'An element of the organisational activity which is central to its future success. Critical success factors (CSFs) may change over time, and may include items such as product, quality, employee attitudes, manufacturing flexibility and brand awareness'.   (*CIMA Official Terminology*)

Johnson, Scholes and Whittington define CSFs as: 'those components of strategy where the organisation must excel to outperform competition. These are underpinned by competences which ensure this success.'

The importance of this definition is that it links to the idea of performance. If an organisation has identified the components of its strategy where it needs to outperform the competition, is also needs some way of being able to measure its performance in those areas.

These key performance measures – key performance indicators (KPIs) – are a key part of the control system for reviewing how successfully a strategy has been implemented and how well an organisation is performing.

However, note that the definitions of CSFs highlights that, in order to be successful, organisations have to perform well across a range of key processes. Therefore CSFs and KPIs should focus on key operational processes, and should not focus only on financial performance.

3.5 The problem of short-termism

Short-termism is when there is a bias towards short-term rather than long-term performance. It is often due to the fact that managers' performance is measured on short-term results.

Short-termism is when there is a bias towards short-term rather than long-term performance.

Organisations often have to make a trade-off between short-term and long-term objectives. Decisions which involve the **sacrifice of longer-term objectives** include the following.

(a)   Postponing or abandoning capital expenditure projects, which would eventually contribute to growth and profits, in order to protect short term cash flow and profits.

(b)   Cutting R&D expenditure to save operating costs, and so reducing the prospects for future product development.

(c)   Reducing quality control, to save operating costs (but also adversely affecting reputation and goodwill).

(d)   Reducing the level of customer service, to save operating costs (but sacrificing goodwill).

(e)   Cutting training costs or recruitment (so the company might be faced with skills shortages).

Managers may also **manipulate** results, especially if rewards are linked to performance. This can be achieved by changing the timing of capital purchases, building up inventories and speeding up or delaying payments and receipts.

3.6 Methods to encourage a long-term view

Steps that could be taken to encourage managers to take a long-term view, so that the 'ideal' decisions are taken, include the following.

(a) **Making short-term targets realistic**. If budget targets are unrealistically tough, a manager will be forced to make trade-offs between the short and long term.

(b) **Providing sufficient management information** to allow managers to see what trade-offs they are making. Managers must be kept aware of long-term aims as well as shorter-term (budget) targets.

(c) **Evaluating managers' performance** in terms of contribution to long-term as well as short-term objectives.

(d) **Link managers' rewards to share price**. This may encourage goal congruence.

(e) **Set quality based targets** as well as financial targets. Multiple targets can be used.

3.7 The link between mission statements and key performance indicators

Mission statement	• The business's rationale for existing
↓	
Strategic objectives	• Quantified embodiments of mission (timescales, profitability)
↓	
Critical success factors	• Elements which are central to future success
↓	
Key performance indicators	• Measures used to assess performance

CASE STUDY

RCH, an international hotel group with a very strong brand image has recently taken over TDM, an educational institution based in Western Europe. RCH has a very good reputation for improving the profitability of its business units and prides itself on its customer focus. The CEO of RCH was recently quoted as saying 'Our success is built on happy customers: we give them what they want'. RCH continually conducts market and customer research and uses the results of these researches to inform both its operational and longer term strategies.

TDM is well-established and has always traded profitably. It offers a variety of courses including degrees both at Bachelor and Masters levels and courses aimed at professional qualifications. TDM has always concentrated on the quality of its courses and learning materials. TDM has never seen the need for market and customer research as it has always achieved its sales targets. Its students consistently achieve passes on a par with the national average. TDM has always had the largest market share in its sector even though new entrants continually enter the market. TDM has a good reputation and has not felt the need to invest significantly in marketing activities. In recent years, TDM has experienced an increasing rate of employee turnover.

RCH has developed a sophisticated set of Critical Success Factors which is integrated into its real-time information system. RCH's rationale for the take-over of TDM was the belief that it could export its customer focus and control system, based on Critical Success Factors, to TDM. RCH believed that this would transform TDM's performance and increase the wealth of RCH's shareholders.

(i)   Four critical success factors which be appropriate for TDM are:

- **Customer satisfaction** with courses and learning materials
- **Employee satisfaction**
- The **quality** of its teaching and materials
- **Reputation** and brand image

(ii)   KPIs for each of the CSFs could be:

Customer satisfaction

Student satisfaction rating – at the end of a course, or at the end of a module within a course, students could be asked to complete a questionnaire rating their satisfaction with various aspects of the course (for example, the knowledge levels of the staff, the quality of the supporting materials, and the approachability / availability of staff to ask them questions).

If students are happy with the level of tuition they receive, they are more likely to book on subsequent courses with TDM than if they are dissatisfied with the courses. Similarly, they may share their experiences with their peers, in turn influencing their decision about where to book courses. Consequently, TDM needs to ensure that student satisfaction levels are maintained as high as possible, and it is important that TDM knows how its students (its customers) feel about the services it offers.

Client retention – A number of the students attending the courses aimed at professional qualifications are likely to have been funded by their employers. If employers continue to send their students to TDM rather than one of its rivals in the market, this suggests they are happy with the level of tuition and service their students are receiving. The pass rates that students achieve are likely to be a significant influence on client satisfaction in this respect.

Employee satisfaction

Staff turnover – The quality of TDM's teaching staff is crucial in maintaining customer satisfaction, so it is important for TDM to retain its best staff. TDM has been experiencing an increasing rate of employee turnover, and this could be indicative of dissatisfaction amongst the staff. The management at TDM should be keen to prevent this upward trend in staff turnover from increasing, making this an important measure to look at.

Staff absenteeism – High levels of absence are likely to also indicate dissatisfaction among the staff. If absenteeism is rising, in conjunction with employee turnover, then there is a danger that the quality of service provided to students will suffer. For example, if an experienced lecturer phones in 'sick' at short notice, their classes may have to be taken by an inexperienced lecturer who is not such an expert in a subject, meaning the students could receive lower quality tuition.

Quality of teaching and materials

Market share – TDM currently has the largest market share in its sector, despite carrying out relatively little marketing activity, and despite new entrants continually entering the market. It will important to monitor TDM's market share, because the share of the market TDM can capture will have a direct impact on its revenues and consequently on the wealth of RCH's shareholders. Customers will only continue to use TDM if they feel it is providing courses and materials which are high quality, and also which offer value for money. If market share starts to fall, it may be an indication TDM is not delivering this value for money to its customers.

Accreditations – TDM's courses will be accredited by academic and professional bodies. TDM has always concentrated on the quality of its courses and learning materials, so external accreditations will provide an independent corroboration of this quality. The quality of course tuition and learning materials, in turn, is likely to feed back into the level of customer satisfaction with TDM's courses.

Reputation and brand image

Brand reputation – TDM has never seen the need for market and customer research, and has always had a good reputation. However, given the continuing entrance of new competitors into the market, TDM needs to ensure that its brand reputation is maintained. This is important if TDM is to ensure potential customers will choose to come on its courses rather than going to one of its competitors.

Pass rates – TDM's students consistently achieve passes on a par with the national average. However, if some of TDM's rivals regularly achieve passes rates above the national average the competitors will be

able to use this as a marketing message to try to win business away from TDM – particularly in respect of the professional qualifications business. If students, or their employers, think that selecting one tuition provider in preference to another can affect their chances of passing their exam, they are likely to select the tuition provider with the highest pass rate.

4 Performance measures

> Performance measure can be divided into two groups.
>
> – **Financial performance measures**
> – **Non-financial performance measures**
>
> Financial performance measures include **profit, revenue, costs, share price** and **cash flow.**
>
> Non-financial performance measures include **product quality, reliability** and **customer satisfaction**.
>
> Performance measures can be **quantitative** or **qualitative.**
>
> **Non-financial indicators (NFIs)** are useful in a modern business environment.

4.1 Deciding what measures to use

When an organisation is content that it has set appropriate objectives it then becomes possible to consider how progress towards the achievement of these objectives is to be measured. This is what is meant by performance measurement. Just as different objectives are appropriate to each business, so different performance measures may be appropriate for any given objective. The choice of performance measures will vary from organisation to organisation.

Factors to consider	Detail
Measurement needs resources	This means people, equipment and time to collect and analyse information. The **costs and benefits** of providing resources to produce a performance indicator must be carefully weighed up.
Performance must be measured in relation to something	If not, measurement is meaningless. Overall performance should be measured against the **objectives** of the organisation. If the organisation has no clear objectives, the first step in performance measurement is to set them. The second is to identify the factors that are critical to the success of those objectives. These are the **critical success factors** discussed earlier.
Measures must be relevant	This means finding out what the organisation does and how it does it so that measures reflect what actually occurs.
Measurement needs responses	Managers will only respond to measures that they find **useful**. The management accountant therefore needs to adopt a modern marketing philosophy to the provision of performance measures: satisfy customer wants, not pile 'em high and sell 'em cheap.

4.2 Monitoring performance measures

Once suitable performance measures have been selected they must be **monitored on a regular basis** to ensure that they are providing useful information. There is little point in an organisation devoting considerable resources to measuring market share if an increase in market share is not one of the organisation's objectives.

4.3 A range of performance measures

Performance measures may be divided into two groups.

(a)   Financial performance measures
(b)   Non-financial performance measures.

4.4 Financial performance measures

Financial performance is fundamental to businesses.

Measure	Example
Profit	**Profit** is the most common measure of all. Return on investment is also frequently used. 'ICI increased pre-tax profits to $233m'.
Revenue	'the US businesses contributed $113.9m of total group turnover of $409m'.
Costs	'The US dollar's fall benefited pre-tax profits by about $50m while savings from the cost-cutting programme instituted in 1991 were running at around $100m a quarter'.
Share price	'The group's shares rose 31c to 1,278c despite the market's fall'.
Cash flow	'Cash flow was also continuing to improve, with cash and marketable securities totalling $8.4bn on March 31, up from $8bn at December 31'.

Note that the monetary amounts stated are **only given meaning in relation to something else**. Financial results should be compared against a **yard-stick** such as the following.

(a)   Budgeted **sales**, **costs** and **profits**

(b)   **Standards** in a standard costing system

(c)   The **trend** over time (last year/this year, say)

(d)   The results of **other parts of the business**

(e)   The results of **other businesses**

(f)   The **economy** in general

(g)   **Future potential** (for example the performance of a new business may be judged in terms of nearness to breaking even).

4.5 Non-financial performance measures

The use of non-financial performance measures has increased in recent years.

A key reason why non-financial performance measures are used is that they are considered to be **leading indicators** of financial performance. For example if customer satisfaction is low this could imply a future fall in profits due to decreased sales demand. The non-financial measure of poor customer satisfaction has given an indication that the financial measure of future sales may change.

You can appreciate the benefits of non-financial performance indicators when you contrast them with financial performance measures and the effect both might have on management.

(a)   **Non-financial performance measures** can provide managers with incentives to improve long-term financial performance. Focusing on customer satisfaction encourages repeat business which is good for long term profitability.

(b)   **Financial performance measures** used alone may provide managers with shorter term incentives which could be detrimental to the business in the long term. For example price increases applied in the short term to meet financial targets could damage customer relations in the long term if quality has not improved.

4.6 Quantitative and qualitative performance measures

Quantitative information is capable of being expressed in numbers. Qualitative information is not numeric. Qualitative information can sometimes be converted into numeric through tools such as ranking scales. For example 1 = Good, 2 = Average, 3 = Poor.

BPP
LEARNING MEDIA

(a)   An example of a **quantitative** performance measure is 'You have been late for work **twice** this week and it's only Tuesday!'.

(b)   An example of a **qualitative** performance measure is 'My bed is **very** comfortable'.

The first measure is likely to find its way into a **staff appraisal report**. The second would feature in a bed manufacturer's **customer satisfaction survey**. Both are indicators of whether their subjects are doing as good a job as they are required to do.

Qualitative measures are by nature **subjective** and **judgmental** but they can still be useful. They are especially valuable when they are derived from several **different sources**, as the likelihood of an unreliable judgement is reduced.

Consider the statement.

'Seven out of ten customers think our beds are very comfortable.'

This is a **quantitative measure** of customer satisfaction (7 out of 10), as well as a **qualitative measure** of the perceived performance of the beds (very comfortable).

4.6.1 Non-financial indicators

Changes in cost structures, the competitive environment and the manufacturing environment have led to an **increased use of NFIs.**

In recent years there have been significant changes in organisations. Changes in the cost structures, manufacturing and increased competition have meant that organisations need to look at new measures of performance.

These changes have led to a shift from treating financial figures as the foundation of performance measurement to treating them as one of a range of measures.

Changes in cost structures

Modern technology requires massive investment and product life cycles have got shorter. A greater proportion of costs are sunk and a large proportion of costs are planned, engineered or designed into a product/service before production/delivery. **At the time the product/service is produced/delivered, it is therefore too late to control costs.**

Changes in competitive environment

Financial measures do not convey the full picture of a company's performance, especially in a **modern business environment**.

'In today's worldwide competitive environment companies are competing in terms of product quality, delivery, reliability, after-sales service and customer satisfaction. None of these variables is directly measured by the traditional responsibility accounting system, despite the fact that they represent the major goals of world-class manufacturing companies.'

Changes in manufacturing environment

New manufacturing techniques and technologies focus on minimising throughput times, inventory levels and set-up times. But managers can reduce the costs for which they are responsible by increasing inventory levels through maximising output. If a performance measurement system **focuses principally on costs**, managers may **concentrate on cost reduction and ignore other important strategic manufacturing goals**.

Organisations are increasingly using quantitative and qualitative **non-financial indicators (NFIs)**. Here are some examples.

(a)	Quality rating	(e)	Rework
(b)	Number of customer complaints	(f)	Delivery to time
(c)	Number of warranty claims	(g)	Non-productive hours
(d)	Lead times	(h)	System (machine) down time

Unlike traditional variance reports, measures such as these can be **provided quickly** for managers, per shift or on a daily or even hourly basis as required. They are likely to be **easy to calculate**, and **easier** for non-financial managers **to understand** and therefore to use effectively.

Anything can be compared if it is meaningful to do so. The measures should be **tailored to the** circumstances. For example, the number of coffee breaks per 20 pages of text might indicate to you how hard you are studying!

Non-financial indicators typically combine elements from the table below.

Errors/failure	Time	Quantity	People
Defects	Second	Range of products	Employees
Equipment failures	Minute	Parts/components	Employee skills
Warranty claims	Hour	Units produced	Customers
Complaints	Shift	Units sold	Competitors
Returns	Cycle	Services performed	Suppliers
Stockouts	Day	kg/litres/metres	
Lateness/waiting	Month	m^2/m^3	
Misinformation	Year	Documents	
Miscalculation		Deliveries	
Absenteeism		Enquiries	

Traditional measures derived from these lists like 'kg (of material) per unit produced' or 'units produced per hour' are very common. What may at first seem a fairly **unlikely combination** may also be very revealing. For example, 'miscalculations per 1,000 invoices' would show how accurately the invoicing clerk was working.

QUESTION

Non-financial indicators

Using the above chart make up five non-financial indicators and explain how each might be useful.

ANSWER

Here are five suggested indicators, showing you how to use the chart.

(a) Services performed late v total services performed
(b) Total units sold v total units sold by competitors (indicating market share)
(c) Warranty claims per month
(d) Documents processed per employee
(e) Equipment failures per 1,000 units produced

There are, of course, many other possibilities.

EXAM FOCUS POINT

If you are asked about suitable performance measures in an exam, think about NFIs. Remember that anything can be compared if it is meaningful to do so.

BPP LEARNING MEDIA

4.6.2 Ratios

Ratios are a useful performance measurement technique.

(a)   It is **easier to look at changes over time** by comparing ratios in one time period with the corresponding ratios for periods in the past.

(b)   Ratios are often **easier to understand than absolute measures** of physical quantities or money values. For example, it is easier to understand that 'productivity in March was 94%' than 'there was an adverse labour efficiency variance in March of $3,600'.

(c)   Ratios **relate one item to another, and so help to put performance into context**. For example the profit/sales ratio sets profit in the context of how much has been earned per $1 of sales, and so shows how wide or narrow profit margins are.

(d)   Ratios can be used as **targets,** for example for productivity. Managers will then take decisions which will enable them to achieve their targets.

(e)   Ratios provide a way of **summarising** an organisation's results, and **comparing** them with similar organisations.

4.6.3 Percentages

A percentage expresses one number as a proportion of another and **gives meaning to absolute numbers**. Market share, capacity levels, wastage and staff turnover are often expressed using percentages.

4.7 Economy, efficiency and effectiveness

Economy, efficiency and effectiveness are all generally desirable features of organisational performance.

(a)   **Economy** lies in operating at minimum cost. However, an over-parsimonious approach will reduce **effectiveness.**

(b)   **Effectiveness** is achieving established objectives. There are usually several ways to achieve objectives, some more costly than others.

(c)   **Efficiency** consists of attaining desired results at minimum cost. It therefore combines **effectiveness** with **economy**.

You should be aware that some people use the word *efficiency* in a more restricted sense than that explained above, to mean the same thing as **productivity**; that is, the ratio of output to input. This is actually a specifically engineering use, as in *the efficiency of a motor*. The point of using the word in this way is to emphasise that it is possible to be very productive in doing the wrong thing: no amount of *efficiency* (in this sense) will make a company profitable if it brings the wrong products to market. You can recognise this use of *efficiency* because it becomes necessary to combine it with *effectiveness* in order to discuss good practice. Thus, if you come across an exam question that asks you how a company can improve its 'efficiency and effectiveness', *efficiency* is being used in the more restricted way. This usage is very common in the public sector, where people are frequently unsure of what their organisation's purpose is and precisely what it is supposed to be doing.

EXAM FOCUS POINT

When you use the ratios in this section in many cases you will use a profit figure and/or a capital employed figure. Unless you are told otherwise, use earning before interest and tax (EBIT) as profit, and shareholder funds plus long-term liabilities for capital employed. Please note that EBIT is the same as PBIT or profit before interest and tax.

The assessment of economy, efficiency and effectiveness should be a part of the normal management process of any organisation, public or private.

(a)   Management should carry out **performance reviews** as a regular feature of their control responsibilities.

(b)   Independent assessments of management performance can be carried out by 'outsiders', perhaps an internal audit department, as value for money audits (VFM audits).

4.7.1 Studying and measuring the three Es

Economy, efficiency and effectiveness can be studied and measured with reference to the following.

(a)   **Inputs**

    (i)   Money

    (ii)   Resources – the labour, materials, time and so on consumed, and their cost

    For example, a value-for-money (VFM) audit into state secondary education would look at the efficiency and economy of the use of resources for education (the use of schoolteachers, school buildings, equipment, cash) and whether the resources are being used for their purpose: what is the pupil/teacher ratio and are trained teachers being fully used to teach the subjects they have been trained for?

(b)   **Outputs**, in other words the **results of an activity**, measurable as the services actually produced, and the quality of the services.

    In the case of a VFM audit of secondary education, outputs would be measured as the number of pupils taught and the number of subjects taught per pupil; how many examination papers are taken and what is the pass rate; what proportion of students go on to further education at a university or college.

(c)   **Impacts**, which are the **effect that the outputs** of an activity or programme have in **terms of achieving policy objectives.**

Policy objectives might be to provide a minimum level of education to all children up to the age of 16, and to make education relevant for the children's future jobs and careers. This might be measured by the ratio of jobs vacant to unemployed school leavers. A VFM audit could assess to what extent this objective is being achieved.

As another example from education, suppose that there is a programme to build a new school in an area. The inputs would be the costs of building the school, and the resources used up; the outputs would be the school building itself; and the impacts would be the effect that the new school has on education in the area it serves.

4.7.2 Examples of indicators

To assess **overall performance** of a public service (ie those areas/issues generally considered to be important), indicators can be usefully divided into three groups.

(a)   **Financial indicators to measure efficiency**

    (i)   Cost per unit of activity (eg cost per arrest/bed-night in a hospital/pupil)

    (ii)   Variance analysis

    (iii)   Comparisons with benchmark information

    (iv)   Cost component as a proportion of total costs (eg administration costs as a proportion of total costs)

    (v)   Costs recovered as a proportion of costs incurred (eg payment received from householders requesting collection of bulky/unusual items of refuse)

(b)   **Non-financial (quantifiable) indicators to measure effectiveness**

    (i)   Quality of service/output measures (eg exam results, crime rates)

    (ii)   Utilisation of resources (eg hospital bed occupancy ratios, average class sizes)

    (iii)   Flexibility/speed of response (eg hospital waiting lists)

(c) **Qualitative indicators to measure effectiveness**

   (i)   Workplace morale

   (ii) Staff attitude to dealing with the public (eg can they provide the correct information in a helpful and professional manner)

   (iii) Public confidence in the service being provided (eg will a pupil be well educated, a patient properly cared for)

4.8 Comparing state controlled entities with the private sector

(a) **Difference in objectives**

State controlled bodies are all, ultimately, **responsible to government** for their activities, and their purposes are defined in the laws that establish them. They have a range aims and objectives but rarely will they set out to trade at a profit. Nevertheless, their managers will be expected to exercise **good stewardship** and **prevent waste of resources**. Objectives will usually be defined in terms of the **provision of a service** that is deemed to be beneficial to society.

(b) **Difference in income**

An important feature of **public sector bodies** is that they have little control over their income. This is because they depend upon government for the funds they need to operate. The funds they receive will be influenced by a large number of factors, including current public opinion, government aspirations, the skill of their leaders in negotiation, the current state of the public finances overall and the current economic climate.

4.9 Performance measurement in the public sector

Performance measurement in the public sector has traditionally been perceived as presenting **special difficulties.**

4.9.1 Problem 1

With public sector services, there has **rarely been any market competition** and **no profit motive**. In the private sector, these two factors help to guide the process of fixing proper prices and managing resources economically, efficiently and effectively. Since most public sector organisations cannot be judged by their success against competition nor by profitability, other methods of assessing performance have to be used.

4.9.2 Problem 2

Different stakeholders hold different expectations of public sector organisations. For example, parents, employers, the community at large and central government might require different things from the education sector. And even within groups of stakeholders, such as parents, there might be a mix of requirements. Priorities of all the groups might change over time. Schools have to reconcile the possibly conflicting demands made on them but to make explicit statements of objectives might show that they are favouring one group of stakeholder at the expense of another.

4.9.3 Problem 3

Given the role of government in public sector organisations, long-term organisational objectives are sometimes sacrificed for short-term political gains.

4.9.4 Problem 4

In the public sector, **performance measures are difficult to define**. Measures of output quantity and output quality themselves provide insufficient evidence of, for example, a local authority's success in serving the community.

4.9.5 Ways in which these problems could be managed/overcome

(a) Set up systems for regional benchmarking (making allowances for known regional differences).

(b) Change the way in which such organisations are controlled to restrict political interference.

(c) Carry out cost-benefit-analyses in an attempt to place a financial value on services being provided.

(d) Use independent agencies (of experts) to make objective decisions based upon their experience and information provided.

5 Measuring profitability and productivity

> **Profitability** can be measured by **return on investment (ROI)/return on capital employed (ROCE), profit margin, gross profit margin or cost/sales ratios**.

5.1 Profitability

5.1.1 Return on investment (ROI)

Return on investment (ROI) (also called **return on capital employed (ROCE)**) is calculated as (profit/capital employed) × 100% and shows how much profit has been made in relation to the amount of resources invested.

Profits alone do not show whether the return is sufficient, in view of the value of assets committed. Thus if company A and company B have the following results, company B would have the better performance.

	A	B
	$	$
Profit	5,000	5,000
Sales	100,000	100,000
Capital employed	50,000	25,000
ROI	10%	20%

The profit of each company is the same but company B only invested $25,000 to achieve that profit whereas company A invested $50,000.

ROI may be calculated in a number of ways, but management accountants prefer to exclude from profits all revenues and expenditures not related to the core operation of the business (such as interest payable and income from trade investments). **Profit before interest and tax** is therefore often used.

Similarly **all assets of a non-operational nature** (for example trade investments and intangible assets such as goodwill) **should be excluded** from capital employed.

Profits should be related to average capital employed. In practice many companies calculate the ratio **using year-end assets**. This can be misleading. If a new investment is undertaken near to year end and financed, for example, by an issue of shares, the capital employed will rise by the finance raised but profits will only have a month or two of the new investment's contribution.

What does the ROI tell us? What should we be looking for? There are **two principal comparisons** that can be made.

(a) The change in ROI from one year to the next
(b) The ROI being earned by other entities

EXAM FOCUS POINT

In an exam you may not be given the capital employed figure and you may be given several different profit figures.

Capital employed = non-current assets + investments + current assets − current liabilities

Profit = operating profit before tax

ROCE can also be calculated as: Operating profit/(Ordinary shareholders funds + non-current liabilities)

QUESTION

ROCE

	$
Turnover	3,527,508
Gross profit	2,469,265
Operating profit	1,814,578
Non-current assets	2,291,000
Cash at bank	2,309,791
Short-term borrowings	474,670
Trade receivables	221,222
Trade payables	232,346

Calculate the return on capital employed.

ANSWER

Capital employed = non-current assets + investments + current assets − current liabilities
= $2,291,000 + $2,309,791 +$ 221,222 − $474,670 − $232,346
= $4,114,997

ROCE = 1,814,578/4,114,997 × 100%
= 44.10%

5.1.2 Profit margin

The **profit margin (profit to sales ratio)** is calculated as (profit ÷ revenue) × 100%.

The profit margin provides a simple measure of performance for management. Investigation of unsatisfactory profit margins enables control action to be taken, either by reducing excessive costs or by raising selling prices.

5.2 Example: the profit to sales ratio

A company compares its year 2 results with year 1 results as follows.

	Year 2 $	Year 1 $
Sales	160,000	120,000
Cost of sales		
Direct materials	40,000	20,000
Direct labour	40,000	30,000
Production overhead	22,000	20,000
Marketing overhead	42,000	35,000
	144,000	105,000
Profit	16,000	15,000
Profit to sales ratio	10%	12½%

Ratio analysis on the above information shows that there is a decline in profitability in spite of the $1,000 increase in profit, because the profit margin is less in year 2 than year 1.

5.2.1 Gross profit margin

The profit to sales ratio above was based on a profit figure which included non-production overheads. The **pure trading activities of a business can be analysed** using the gross profit margin, which is calculated as (gross profit ÷ turnover) × 100%.

For the company in Paragraph 5.2 the gross profit margin would be

((16,000 + 42,000)/160,000) × 100% = 36.25% in year 2 and ((15,000 + 35,000)/120,000) × 100% = 41.67% in year 1.

5.2.2 Cost/sales ratios

There are three principal ratios for analysing income statement information.

(a)   Production cost of sales ÷ sales
(b)   Distribution and marketing costs ÷ sales
(c)   Administrative costs ÷ sales

When particular areas of weakness are found subsidiary ratios are used to examine them in greater depth. For example, for production costs the following ratios might be used.

(a)   Material costs ÷ sales value of production
(b)   Works labour costs ÷ sales value of production
(c)   Production overheads ÷ sales value of production

5.3 Example: cost/sales ratios

Look back to the example above. A more detailed analysis would show that higher direct materials are the probable cause of the decline in profitability.

	Year 2	Year 1
Material costs/sales	25%	16.7%

Other cost/sales ratios have remained the same or improved.

5.4 Productivity

This is the quantity of the product or service produced **(output) in relation to** the resources put in **(input)**. For example so many units produced per hour, or per employee, or per tonne of material. It measures **how efficiently resources are being used**.

QUESTION   Performance measures

An invoicing assistant works in a department with three colleagues. She is paid $8,000 per annum. The department typically handles 10,000 invoices per week.

One morning she spends half an hour on the phone to her grandfather, who lives in Australia, at the company's expense. The cost of the call proves to be $32.

Required

From this scenario identify as many different performance measures as possible, explaining what each is intended to measure. Make any further assumptions you wish.

ANSWER

Invoices per employee per week: 2,500 (activity)

Staff cost per invoice: $0.06 (cost/profitability)

Invoices per hour: 2,500/(7 × 5) = 71.4 (productivity)

Cost of idle time: $32 + $2.20 (half-hourly rate) = $34.20 (cost/profitability)

You may have thought of other measures and probably have slight rounding differences.

IMPORTANT

Where a ratio includes capital employed, you should use shareholders funds plus long-term liabilities unless you are told otherwise.

6 Performance measures based on the statement of financial position

Asset turnover is a measure of how well the assets of a business are being used to generate sales. It is calculated as (sales ÷ capital employed).

The **current ratio** is the 'standard' test of liquidity and is the ratio of current assets to current liabilities. The **quick ratio**, or **acid test ratio**, is the ratio of current assets less inventories to current liabilities.

6.1 Asset turnover

Asset turnover is a measure of how well the assets of a business are being used to generate sales. It is calculated as (sales ÷ capital employed).

For example, suppose two companies each have capital employed of $100,000 and Company A makes sales of $400,000 per annum whereas Company B makes sales of only $200,000 per annum. Company A is making a higher turnover from the same amount of assets, in other words twice as much asset turnover as Company B, and this will help A to make a higher return on capital employed than B. Asset turnover is **expressed as 'x times' so that assets generate x times their value in annual turnover**. Here, Company A's asset turnover is 4 times and B's is 2 times.

6.1.1 Interrelationship between profit margin, asset turnover and ROI

Profit margin and asset turnover together explain the ROI. The relationship between the three ratios is as follows.

Profit margin × asset turnover = ROI

$$\frac{\text{Profit}}{\text{Sales}} \times \frac{\text{Sales}}{\text{Capital employed}} = \frac{\text{Profit}}{\text{Capital employed}}$$

6.2 Liquidity ratios: current ratio and quick ratio

The **current ratio** is the 'standard' test of liquidity and is the ratio of current assets to current liabilities.

$$\text{Current ratio} = \frac{\text{current assets}}{\text{current liabilities}}$$

The idea behind the current ratio is that a company should have enough current assets that give a promise of 'cash to come' to meet its future commitments to pay off its current liabilities. Obviously, a ratio in excess of 1 should be expected. Otherwise, there would be the prospect that the company might be unable to pay its debts on time. In practice, a ratio comfortably in excess of 1 should be expected, but what is 'comfortable' varies between different types of businesses.

Companies are not able to convert all their current assets into cash very quickly. In particular, some manufacturing companies might hold large quantities of raw material inventories, which must be used in production to create finished goods inventories. Finished goods inventories might be warehoused for a long time, or sold on lengthy credit. In such businesses, **where inventory turnover is slow, most inventories are not very 'liquid' assets**, because the cash cycle is so long. For these reasons, we **calculate an additional liquidity ratio**, known as the quick ratio or acid test ratio.

The **quick ratio**, or **acid test ratio**, is the ratio of current assets less inventories to current liabilities.

$$\text{Quick ratio} = \frac{\text{current assets less inventories}}{\text{current liabilities}}$$

This ratio should ideally be at least 1 for companies with a slow inventory turnover. For companies with a fast inventory turnover, a quick ratio can be comfortably less than 1 without suggesting that the company is in cash flow trouble.

Both the current ratio and the quick ratio offer an indication of the company's liquidity position, but the absolute figures should not be interpreted too literally. It is often said that an acceptable current ratio is 1.5 and an acceptable quick ratio is 0.8, but these should only be used as a guide. Different businesses operate in very different ways. A supermarket, for example, might have a current ratio of 0.40 and a quick ratio of 0.16. due to low receivables (people do not buy groceries on credit), low cash (good cash management), medium inventories (high inventories but quick turnover, particularly in view of perishability) and very high payables (many supermarkets buy their supplies of groceries on credit).

What is important is the trend of these ratios, which will show whether liquidity is improving or deteriorating. If a supermarket has traded for the last 10 years (very successfully) with current ratios of 0.40 and quick ratios of 0.16 then it ought to be able to continue in business with those levels of liquidity. If in the following year the current ratio were to fall to 0.38 and the quick ratio to 0.09, further investigation would be needed. It is the relative position that is far more important than the absolute figures.

A current ratio and a quick ratio can get bigger than they need to be however. A company that has large volumes of inventories and receivables might be over-investing in working capital, and so tying up more funds in the business than it needs to. This would suggest poor management of (receivables) or inventories by the company.

QUESTION

Liquidity ratio

The following details have been extracted from the accounts of PQR plc. The company's year ends on 31 March.

	Year 2 $m	Year 3 $m	Year 4 $m
Revenue	100	103	108
Gross profit	33.0	34.0	35.6
Net profit	15	15	15
Non-current assets	64	72	68
Inventory	4	4	4
Receivables	8	11	15
Payables	5	6	6
Cash at bank	5	-	-
Bank overdraft	-	6	5

Required

(a)   Calculate the following for each of the three years.

   (i)   Gross profit percentage
   (ii)   Net profit percentage
   (iii)   Quick ratio (acid test)

(b)   Comment briefly on the ratios you have calculated

ANSWER

(a)

		Year 2	Year 3	Year 4
(i)	Gross profit %	(33/100) × 100% = 33%	(34/103) × 100% = 33%	(35.6/108) × 100% = 33%
(ii)	Net profit %	(15/100) × 100% = 15%	(15/103) × 100% = 14.56%	(15/108) × 100% = 13.9%
(iii)	Quick ratio	(8 + 5)/5 = 2.6	11/(6 + 6) = 0.9	15/(6 + 5) = 1.4

(b)   Revenue has risen only slightly over the three years with the gross profit margin remaining high at 33%. This suggests that selling prices and costs have been increased only in line with inflation.

Net profit margin has fallen. While the fall is not great it indicates that expenditure on overheads has increased. The fall should be investigated and an attempt made to ensure that the trend does not continue.

The quick ratio fell sharply in Year 3, although it has since recovered. The more worrying aspect of the changes to working capital is that there is less cash (a bank overdraft) and more receivables. It is worth enquiring whether this is due to poor credit control or extending credit in an effort to boost or maintain sales.

It appears from the above that the company is showing a healthy profit, but needs to pay attention to working capital. It should be emphasised, however, that it is difficult to draw conclusions without knowing the sector in which PQR operates or any details about the performance of its competitors.

EXAM FOCUS POINT

In the December 2011 examiner's report, the examiner commented that only 23% of students selected the correct answer for a question on current ratio and acid test ratio. The question asked about the effect on the ratios if more inventory was purchased. The examiner said that the best way to answer these types of question is to substitute in some simple numbers to test out the effects of the transaction.

6.3 Example: effect on current and quick ratio

At the beginning of the month, a company has current assets of $1.6m including inventory of $0.6m and current liabilities of $1.1m. What would be the effect on the value of the current and quick ratios if the company had sold some inventory on credit back to the supplier?

6.4 Solution

The question gives us some numbers that we can use and we can substitute in some simple numbers for the ones that are missing.

Current ratio at the beginning of the month:

$$\frac{\text{Current assets}}{\text{Current liabilities}} = \frac{1.6}{1.1} = 1.45$$

Current ratio at the end of the month:

Let's say the inventory sold on credit was $0.5m. The current assets (inventory) would reduce by $0.5m and the current assets (receivables) would increase by $0.5m.

$$\frac{\text{Current assets}}{\text{Current liabilities}} = \frac{1.6 - 0.5 + 0.5}{1.1} = 1.45$$

Therefore there would be no change in the current ratio.

Quick ratio at the beginning of the month:

$$\frac{\text{Current assets less inventories}}{\text{Current liabilities}} = \frac{1.6 - 0.6}{1.1} = 0.91$$

Quick ratio at the end of the month:

Again we say that the inventory sold on credit was $0.5m. The reduction in inventory means that total current assets become $1.6 - $0.5 = $1.1. The total inventory becomes $0.6 - $0.5 = $0.1 The receivables would increase by $0.5m and so the current assets would increase by $0.5m.

$$\frac{\text{Current assets less inventories}}{\text{Current liabilities}} = \frac{1.1 - 0.1 + 0.5}{1.1} = 1.36$$

Therefore the quick ratio has increased.

6.5 Efficiency ratios: control of receivables, payables and inventory

A rough measure of the average length of time it takes for a company's receivables to pay what they owe is the **accounts receivable collection period**. The **accounts payable payment period** is a rough measure of the average length of time it takes a company to pay what it owes.

The **inventory turnover period** indicates the average number of days that items of **inventory** are held for.

Inventory turnover is a measure of how vigorously a business is trading.

The **working capital period** (or **average age of working capital**) identifies how long it takes to convert the purchase of inventories into cash from sales.

6.5.1 Accounts receivable collection period

The estimated average **accounts receivable collection period** is a rough measure of the average length of time it takes for a company's receivables to pay what they owe and is calculated as (trade receivables/sales) × 365 days or (trade receivables/ sales) × 12 months.

The **estimate of receivables days is only approximate** because the statement of financial position value of receivables might be abnormally high or low compared with the organisation's 'normal' level.

A supermarket should have a very low accounts receivable collection period since sales should not be on credit. Sales of most organisations, however, are usually made on 'normal credit terms' of payment within 30 days. A period significantly in excess of this might be representative of poor management of funds of a business. However, some companies must allow generous credit terms to win customers. Exporting companies in particular may have to carry large amounts of receivables, and so their average collection period might be well in excess of 30 days.

The **trend of the collection period over time is probably the best guide**. If the period is increasing year on year, this is indicative of a poorly managed credit control function (and potentially therefore a poorly managed company).

6.5.2 Inventory turnover period

Inventory turnover period is a calculation of the number of days inventory is held for and is calculated as (inventory ÷ cost of sales) × 365 days or (inventory ÷ cost of sales) × 12 months.

As with the average debt collection period, this is only an approximate estimated figure, but one which should be reliable enough for comparing changes year on year.

Presumably if we add together the inventory days and the receivable days, this should give us an indication of how soon inventory is convertible into cash. Both ratios therefore give us a further indication of the company's liquidity.

6.5.3 Inventory turnover

'Cost of sales ÷ inventory' is termed **inventory turnover**, and is a measure of how vigorously a business is trading.

A **lengthening inventory turnover period** from one year to the next indicates either a **slowdown in trading** or a **build-up in inventory levels**, perhaps suggesting that the investment in inventories is becoming excessive.

When you are interpreting inventory turnover data you should consider the type of organisation and the systems it operates.

(a) Obviously there should be a marked difference between the inventory turnover of a retail organisation such as a supermarket, and a manufacturing group.

(b) In an organisation which operates a just in time system you would expect to see very high inventory turnover, but you may also notice other effects such as low storage costs and higher prices paid for supplies.

6.5.4 Accounts payable payment period

Accounts payable payment period or **days** provides a rough measure of the average length of time it takes a company to pay what it owes. It is ideally calculated by the formula (payables/purchases) × 365 days or (payables/purchases) × 12 months. Cost of sales can be used as an approximation for purchases.

This ratio **often helps to assess a company's liquidity**. An increase is often a sign of lack of long-term finance or poor management of current assets, resulting in the use of extended credit from suppliers, increased bank overdraft and so on.

6.5.5 Working capital period

Working capital control is concerned with minimising funds tied up in net current assets while ensuring that sufficient inventory, cash and credit facilities are in place to enable trading to take place. Calculation of the ratio provides some insight into working capital control.

The **working capital period** (or **average age of working capital**) identifies how long it takes to convert the purchase of inventories into cash from sales and is calculated as (working capital/cost of sales) × 365 days. The ratio can also be calculated as (working capital/ operating costs) × 365 days.

Care needs to be taken when determining the ideal ratio. Reduce it too low and there may be insufficient inventory and other current assets to sustain the volume of trade, but taking too much credit from suppliers may jeopardise relationships and/or cause suppliers to increase prices.

A ratio in excess of a target indicates that working capital levels are probably too high and that management action is needed to reduce them. This may involve stringent control of receivables, a reduction in inventory levels and/or a more efficient use of available credit facilities. A receivables days ratio, inventory turnover period and payables turnover period can be calculated to determine where the problem lies.

The ratio has two principal limitations.

(a) It is based on the working capital level on one particular day, which may not be representative of working capital levels throughout the entire period.

(b) Working capital includes a figure for inventory which may be a very subjective valuation.

QUESTION   Liquidity and working capital

Calculate liquidity and working capital ratios from the accounts of the DOG Group, a manufacturer of products for the construction industry. Discuss your results.

	Year 8 $m	Year 7 $m
Revenue	2,065.0	1,788.7
Cost of sales	1,478.6	1,304.0
Gross profit	586.4	484.7

EXTRACT FROM THE STATEMENT OF FINANCIAL POSITION
Current assets

Inventories	119.0	109.0
Receivables (note 1)	400.9	347.4
Short-term investments	4.2	18.8
Cash at bank and in hand	48.2	48.0
	572.3	523.2

Payables: amounts falling due within one year

Loans and overdrafts	49.1	35.3
Corporation taxes	62.0	46.7
Dividend	19.2	14.3
Payables (note 2)	370.7	324.0
	501.0	420.3

Notes		$m	$m
1	Trade receivables	329.8	285.4
2	Trade payables	236.2	210.8

ANSWER

	Year 8	Year 7
Current ratio	(572.3/501.0) = 1.14	(523.2/420.3) = 1.24
Quick ratio	(453.3/501.0) = 0.90	(414.2/420.3) = 0.99
Accounts receivable payment period	(329.8/2,065.0) × 365 = 58 days	(285.4/1,788.7) × 365 = 58 days
Inventory turnover period	(119.0/1,478.6) × 365 = 29 days	(109.0/1,304.0) × 365 = 31 days
Accounts payable payment period	(236.2/1,478.6) × 365 = 58 days	(210.8/1,304.0) × 365 = 59 days

DOG is a manufacturing group serving the construction industry, and so would be expected to have a comparatively lengthy accounts receivables' turnover period, because of the relatively poor cash flow in the construction industry. It is clear that management compensates for this by ensuring that they do not pay for raw materials and so on before they have sold their inventories of finished goods (hence the similarity of receivables and payables turnover periods).

DOG's current ratio is a little lower than average but its quick ratio is better than average and very little less than the current ratio. This suggests that inventory levels are strictly controlled, which is reinforced by the low inventory turnover period. It would seem that working capital is tightly managed, to avoid the poor liquidity which could be caused by a high accounts receivables payment period and comparatively high payables period.

6.6 Debt and gearing/leverage ratios

Debt ratios are concerned with how much the company **owes in relation to its size** and whether it is getting into heavier debt or improving its situation.

(a) When a company is heavily in debt, and seems to be getting even more heavily into debt, banks and other would-be lenders are very soon likely to refuse further borrowing and the company might well find itself in trouble.

(b) When a company is earning only a modest profit before interest and tax, and has a heavy debt burden, there will be very little profit left over for shareholders after the interest charges have been paid.

Leverage is an alternative term for gearing and the words have the same meaning.

6.6.1 Capital gearing or leverage

Capital gearing is concerned with the amount of debt in a company's **long-term** capital structure. **Gearing ratios** provide a long-term measure of liquidity.

$$\text{Gearing ratio} = \frac{\text{Prior charge capital (long-term debt)}}{\text{Prior charge capital} + \text{shareholders equity}}$$

Prior charge capital is long-term loans and preference shares (if any). It does not include loans repayable within one year and bank overdraft, unless overdraft finance is a permanent part of the business's capital.

6.6.2 Interest cover

The **interest cover** ratio shows whether a company is earning enough profits before interest and tax to pay its interest costs comfortably, or whether its interest costs are high in relation to the size of its profits, so that a fall in profit before interest and tax (PBIT) would then have a significant effect on profits available for ordinary shareholders.

$$\text{Interest cover} = \frac{\text{PBIT}}{\text{Interest charges}}$$

An interest cover of 2 times or less would be low, and it should really exceed 3 times before the company's interest costs can be considered to be within acceptable limits. Note it is usual to exclude preference dividends from 'interest' charges.

6.7 Limitations of income statement and statement of financial position measures

(a) **On their own, they do not provide information to enable managers to gauge performance or make control decisions.** Yardsticks are needed for comparison purposes.

(b) The measures used **must be carefully defined**. For example, should 'return' equal profit before interest and taxation, profit after taxation, or profit before interest, taxation and investment income?

(c) Measures compared over a period of time at historical cost will not be properly comparable where **inflation** in prices has occurred during the period, unless an adjustment is made to the measures to make allowance for price level differences.

(d) The measures of **different companies** cannot be properly compared where each company uses a **different method to do the following**.

    (i)   Value closing inventories (for example FIFO, LIFO, or marginal/absorbed cost)
    (ii)   Apportion overheads in absorption costing
    (iii)   Value non-current assets (for example at net book value, replacement cost and so on)
    (iv)   Estimate the life of assets in order to calculate depreciation
    (v)   Account for research and development costs
    (vi)   Account for goodwill

(e) Remember that measures calculated using **historical costs** may not be a guide to the future.

QUESTION

Ratio calculations

You are given summarised results of an electrical engineering business as follows.

INCOME STATEMENT FOR YEAR ENDED 31 DECEMBER YEAR 1

	$'000
Revenue	60,000
Cost of sales	42,000
Gross profit	18,000
Operating expenses	15,500
Profit	2,500

STATEMENT OF FINANCIAL POSITION AT 31 DECEMBER YEAR 1

	$'000	$'000
Non-current assets		12,500
Current assets		
Inventory	14,000	
Receivables	16,000	
Cash	500	
		43,000
EQUITY AND LIABILITIES		
Capital and reserves		19,000
Current liabilities (payables only)		24,000
		43,000

Required

Calculate the following ratios, clearly showing the figures used in the calculations.

(a)   Current ratio
(b)   Quick/acid test ratio
(c)   Inventory turnover in days
(d)   Accounts receivable collection period in days
(e)   Accounts payable payment period in days
(f)   Gross profit percentage
(g)   Net profit percentage
(h)   ROCE
(i)   Asset turnover

ANSWER

(a)   Current ratio   = (Current assets/current liabilities)   = (30,500/24,000) = 1.27

(b)   Acid test ratio   = (Current assets – inventory/current liabilities)
  = (16,500/24,000) = 0.6875

(c)   Inventory turnover   = (Inventory/cost of sales) × 365 days   = (14,000/42,000) × 365 = 122 days

(d)   Accounts receivable collection period
  = (Receivables/sales) × 365 days   = (16,000/60,000) × 365 = 97 days

(e)   Accounts payable   = (Payables/cost of sales) × 365 days   = (24,000/42,000) × 365 = 209 days

(f)   Gross profit %   = (Gross profit/sales) × 100%   = (18,000/60,000) × 100% = 30%

(g)   Net profit %   = (Net profit/sales) × 100%   = (2,500/60,000)× 100% = 4.2%

(h)   ROCE   = (Profit/capital employed) × 100%   = (2,500/19,000) × 100% = 13.16%

(i)   Asset turnover   = (Sales/capital employed)   = (60,000/19,000) = 3.2 times

QUESTION

Limitations of ratios

Comment on any limitations of the ratios used in the last question and of comparisons made using such ratios.

ANSWER

Limitations of the ratios and inter-company comparisons

There are a number of limitations of which management should be aware before drawing any firm conclusions from a comparison of these ratios.

(a) The ratios are merely averages, based on year-end statement of financial position data, which may not be representative.

(b) These ratios could be affected by any new investment towards the end of the financial year. Such investment would increase the value of the assets or capital employed, but the profits from the investment would not yet have accumulated in the income statement. Generally, newer assets tend to depress the asset turnover and hence the ROCE in the short term. It is possible that this is the cause of our company's lower asset turnover and ROCE.

(c) Although the trade association probably makes some attempt to standardise the data, different member companies may be using different accounting policies, for example in calculating depreciation and valuing inventory.

(d) Our company's analyst may have used a different formula for calculating one or more of the ratios. For example, as noted above, there are a variety of ways of calculating capital employed. It is likely, however, that the trade association would provide information on the basis of calculation of the ratios.

(e) The member companies will have some activities in common, hence their membership of the trade association. Some may, however, have a diversified range of activities, which will distort the ratios and make direct comparison difficult.

6.8 Internal and external analysis

External analysis of companies' performance using **financial accounts** is relatively straightforward since the **range of possible measures** tends to be **limited** by the scarcity of the information available. We have covered most of these measures in this section and the previous one.

The **analysis of a company's internal management accounts** uses more or less the same measures as a starting point. The level of analysis and detail found in internal accounts tends to be much greater than in published financial accounts, however, and so more extensive analysis is possible.

In the October 2000 edition of the *ACCA Technician Bulletin,* the author of the article 'Internal Financial Analysis' illustrated how the performance of two sales regions could be analysed using **conventional ratios** and other **performance measures specific to the situation**.

(a) Initially, using observations based upon absolute figures (sales, level of receivables, bad debts written off)

(b) Then using the conventional receivables days ratio

(c) Finally, using other relationships that might give further insights (bad debts per $1,000 of sales, cost per employee, debts collected per employee)

7 External considerations

External conditions can affect performance.

So far we have looked in detail at some important aspects of performance measurement, but they have all been concerned with information pertaining to the internal processes of the organisation. This approach is necessary, but the analysis is not complete. The organisation is not sealed off from its environment: it is subject to the conditions present in that environment and its performance is influenced by them. We must always be aware when measuring performance of the influence of external conditions and changes in them.

For a commercial business, success is subject to general economic and market conditions.

(a)   **Market conditions**. A business operates in a competitive environment and suppliers, customers and competitors all influence one another's operations. The entry of a new and dynamic competitor, for example is certain to have an effect on budgeted sales.

(b)   **General economic conditions** influence businesses most obviously by raising or lowering overall demand and supply. The role of government is very important here since government economic policy affects demand in particular quite rapidly. Changes in interest rates are determined largely by government policy and have a direct effect on credit sales.

For non-profit organisations that do not trade, economic conditions and government policy are still important. Charities depending on donations will be subject to general feelings of prosperity or otherwise, while public bodies may have their available funds controlled directly or indirectly by government.

The general conclusion from these and similar considerations is that appropriate attention should be paid to general and specific external conditions when measuring performance. We have already seen some aspects of this when we considered the proper use of variances. Sales variances in particular are often traceable to external conditions. However, it is important that external conditions are not over-emphasised and used as an excuse. Judgement is needed here, both on the part of those responsible for interpreting the bald facts of numerical analysis, and on that of those to whom reports are submitted.

Finally, note that the effect of external conditions is not always adverse! Managers may be as quick to claim the credit for high performance caused by good conditions as they are to blame poor conditions for their own failings.

7.1 Government influence

The government does not have a direct interest in private sector organisations (except for those in which it actually holds shares). However, the government does often have a strong indirect interest in business' affairs.

(a)   **Taxation**
The government raises taxes on sales and profits and on shareholders' dividends. It also expects businesses to act as tax collectors for income tax and sales tax.

(b)   **Encouraging new investments**
The government might provide **funds** towards the cost of some investment projects. It might also encourage private investment by offering **tax incentives.**

(c)   **Encouraging a wider spread of share ownership**
In the UK, the government has made some attempts to encourage more private individuals to become company shareholders, by means of **attractive privatisation issues** (such as in the electricity, gas and telecommunications industries) and tax incentives, such as ISAs (Individual Savings Accounts) to encourage individuals to invest in shares.

(d)   **Legislation**
The government also influences businesses through legislation, including the Companies Acts, legislation on employment, health and safety regulations, legislation on consumer protection and consumer rights and environmental legislation.

(e) **Economic policy**

A government's economic policy will affect business activity. For example, **exchange rate policy** will have implications for the revenues of exporting firms and for the purchase costs of importing firms. Policies on **economic growth, inflation, employment, interest rates** and so on are all relevant to business activities.

7.2 Problems of comparing state regulated entities with private sector organisations

Private sector organisations are largely free from state control. This makes it more difficult to compare the performance of a state regulated entity with a private sector organisation.

The performance of state controlled entities can be either constrained or enhanced by government regulation. For example, state hospitals are obliged to provide universal care whereas private hospitals are permitted to 'cherry pick' their patients. Public sector colleges may be subsidised by the state whereas private sector colleges may not. This makes performance measurement comparisons between the public and private sector much more difficult.

CHAPTER ROUNDUP

⤷ The higher direction of an organisation requires a clear vision, in general terms, of what the organisation should be doing in the longer term and how it should go about doing it. This may be encapsulated in a **mission statement**.

⤷ A hierarchy of SMART goals and objectives cascades downwards from the mission statement, eventually providing the targets for the periodic budget process.

⤷ **Short-termism** is when there is a bias towards short-term rather than long-term performance. It is often due to the fact that managers' performance is measured on short-term results.

⤷ Performance measure can be divided into two groups.

– **Financial performance measures**
– **Non-financial performance measures**

⤷ Financial performance measures include **profit**, **revenue**, **costs**, **share price** and **cash flow**.

⤷ Non-financial performance measures include **product quality**, **reliability** and **customer satisfaction**.

⤷ Performance measures can be **quantitative** or **qualitative.**

⤷ **Non-financial indicators (NFIs)** are useful in a modern business environment.

⤷ Changes in cost structures, the competitive environment and the manufacturing environment have led to an **increased use of NFIs**.

⤷ **Profitability** can be measured by **return on investment (ROI)/return on capital employed (ROCE), profit margin, gross profit margin** or **cost/sales ratios.**

⤷ **Asset turnover** is a measure of how well the assets of a business are being used to generate sales. It is calculated as (sales ÷ capital employed).

⤷ The **current ratio** is the 'standard' test of liquidity and is the ratio of current assets to current liabilities. The **quick ratio**, or **acid test ratio**, is the ratio of current assets less inventories to current liabilities.

⤷ A rough measure of the average length of time it takes for a company's receivables to pay what they owe is the **accounts receivables collection period**. The **accounts payable payment period** is a rough measure of the average length of time it takes a company to pay what it owes.

⤷ The **inventory turnover period** indicates the average number of days that items of **inventory** are held for.

⤷ **Inventory turnover** is a measure of how vigorously a business is trading.

⤷ The **working capital period** (or **average age of working capital**) identifies how long it takes to convert the purchase of inventories into cash from sales.

⤷ **External conditions** can affect performance.

QUICK QUIZ

1   List five possible financial performance measures.

2   Costs are down by 15% is an example of a qualitative performance measure. True or false?

3   How is ROI calculated?

4   When should a current ratio in excess of 1 be expected?

5   Should the quick ratio for a company with fast inventory turnover be greater than 1?

6   ROCE is $\dfrac{\text{Profit before interest and tax}}{\text{Capital employed}} \times 100\%$

    True   ☐

    False ☐

7   The debt ratio is a company's long-term debt divided by its net assets.

    True   ☐

    False ☐

ANSWERS TO QUICK QUIZ

1   Profit, revenue, costs, share price and cash flow. Of course there are others.

2   False. It is quantitative.

3   (Profit ÷ capital employed) × 100%

4   A current ratio in excess of 1 should always be expected.

5   No, it may be less than 1.

6   **True**. Profit before interest and tax or PBIT is the figure used in the Question *Ratio calculations* in the chapter.

7   **False**. Refer to Section 6 if you are unclear what the ratio is made up of.

Now try ...

Attempt the questions below from the **Exam Question Bank**

Number

Q101 – Q104

24

This chapter continues with performance measurement and includes measuring performance in service industries and not-for-profit organisations.

Applications of performance measurement

Study Guide		Intellectual level
E	**Performance measurement**	
4	**Monitoring performance and reporting**	
(c)	Discuss the measurement of performance in service industry situations	K
(d)	Discuss the measurement of performance in non-profit seeking and public sector organisations	K
(e)	Discuss measures that may be used to assess managerial performance and the practical problems involved	K
(f)	Discuss the role of benchmarking in performance measurement	K
(g)	Produce reports highlighting key areas for management attention and recommendations for improvement	S
2	**Performance measurement - application**	
Perspectives of the balanced scorecard		
(b)(i)	Discuss the advantages and limitations of the balanced scorecard	K
(b)(ii)	Describe performance indicators for financial success, customer satisfaction, process efficiency and growth	K
Economy, efficiency and effectiveness		
(c)(iv)	Discuss the meaning of each of the efficiency, capacity and activity ratios	K
(c)(v)	Calculate the efficiency, capacity and activity ratios in a specific situation	S
Unit costs		
(d)(i)	Describe performance measures which would be suitable in contract and process costing environments	K
Resource utilisation		
(e)(i)	Describe measures of performance utilisation in service and manufacturing environments	K
(e)(ii)	Establish measures of resource utilisation in a specific situation	S
Profitability		
(f)(i)	Calculate return on investment and residual income	S
(f)(ii)	Explain the advantages and limitations of return on investment and residual income	K
Quality of service		
(g)(i)	Distinguish performance measurement issues in service and manufacturing industries	K
(g)(ii)	Describe performance measures appropriate for service industries	K

1 Performance measures for manufacturing businesses

In a customer-focused organisation, basic **measures for sales** can be supplemented by a host of others including customer rejects/returns: total sales.

Performance measures for **materials** and **labour** include **variances.**

Performance can be measured using the **standard hour.**

Efficiency, **activity** and **capacity ratios** provide useful information.

1.1 Performance measures for sales

Traditionally sales performance is measured in terms of price and volume variances, and a sales mix variance. Other possible measures include revenue targets and target market share. They may be analysed in detail: by country, by region, by individual products, by salesperson and so on.

In a customer-focused organisation the basic information 'Turnover is up by 14%' can be supplemented by a host of other indicators.

(a) **Customer rejects/returns: total sales**. This ratio helps to monitor customer satisfaction, providing a check on the efficiency of quality control procedures.

(b) **Deliveries late: deliveries on schedule**. This ratio can be applied both to sales made to customers and to receipts from suppliers. When applied to customers it provides an indication of the efficiency of production and production scheduling.

(c) **Flexibility measures** indicate how well able a company is to respond to customers' requirements. Measures could be devised to measure how quickly and efficiently **new products** are launched, and how well procedures meet **customer needs**.

(d) **Number of people served and speed of service**, in a shop or a bank for example. If it takes too long to reach the point of sale, future sales are liable to be lost.

(e) **Customer satisfaction questionnaires,** for input to the organisation's management information system.

1.2 Performance measures for materials

Traditional measures are **standard costs,** and price and usage **variances**. Many traditional systems also analyse **wastage**.

Measures used in **modern manufacturing environments** include the number of **rejects** in materials supplied, and the **timing and reliability of deliveries** of materials.

1.3 Performance measures for labour

Labour costs are traditionally measured in terms of **standard performance** (ideal, attainable and so on) and rate and efficiency **variances**.

Qualitative measures of labour performance concentrate on matters such as **ability to communicate, interpersonal relationships** with colleagues, **customers' impressions** and **levels of skills** attained.

Managers can expect to be judged to some extent by the performance of their staff. High profitability or tight cost control are not the only indicators of managerial performance!

1.4 Performance measures for overheads

Standards for variable overheads and efficiency variances are traditional measures. Various time based measure are also available.

(a) **Machine down time: total machine hours**. This ratio provides a measure of machine usage and efficiency.

(b)   **Value added time: production cycle time.** Value added time is the direct production time during which the product is being made. The production cycle time includes non-value-added times such as set-up time, downtime, idle time and so on. The 'perfect' ratio is 100%, but in practice this optimum will not be achieved. A high ratio means non-value-added activities are being kept to a minimum.

1.5 Measures of performance using the standard hour

Sam manufactures plates, mugs and eggcups. Production during the first two quarters of 20X5 was as follows.

	Quarter 1	Quarter 2
Plates	1,000	800
Mugs	1,200	1,500
Eggcups	800	900

The fact that 3,000 products were produced in quarter 1 and 3,200 in quarter 2 does not tell us anything about Sam's performance over the two periods because plates, mugs and eggcups are so different. The fact that the production mix has changed is not revealed by considering the total number of units produced. The problem of how to **measure output when a number of dissimilar products are manufactured** can be overcome, however, by the **use of the standard hour**.

The standard hour (or standard minute) is the **quantity of work achievable at standard performance, expressed in terms of a standard unit of work done in a standard period of time.**

The standard time allowed to produce one unit of each of Sam's products is as follows.

	Standard time
Plate	½ hour
Mug	⅓ hour
Eggcup	¼ hour

By measuring the standard hours of output in each quarter, a more useful output measure is obtained.

		Quarter 1		Quarter 2	
Product	Standard hours per unit	Production	Standard hours	Production	Standard hours
Plate	½	1,000	500	800	400
Mug	⅓	1,200	400	1,500	500
Eggcup	¼	800	200	900	225
			1,100		1,125

The output level in the two quarters was therefore very similar.

1.6 Efficiency, activity and capacity ratios

Standard hours are useful in computing levels of **efficiency, activity and capacity**. Any management accounting reports involving budgets and variance analysis should incorporate control ratios. The three main control ratios are the efficiency, capacity and activity ratios.

(a)   The **capacity ratio compares actual hours worked and budgeted hours**, and measures the **extent to which planned utilisation has been achieved.**

(b)   The **activity** or **production volume ratio compares the number of standard hours equivalent to the actual work produced and budgeted hours.**

(c)   **The efficiency ratio** measures the **efficiency of the labour force** by **comparing equivalent standard hours for work produced and actual hours worked.**

1.7 Example: ratios and standard hours

Given the following information about Sam for quarter 1 of 20X5, calculate a capacity ratio, an activity ratio and an efficiency ratio and explain their meaning.

Budgeted hours   1,100 standard hours
Standard hours produced   1,125 standard hours
Actual hours worked   1,200

1.8 Solution

$$\text{Capacity ratio} = \frac{\text{Actual hours worked}}{\text{Budgeted hours}} \times 100\% = \frac{1,200}{1,100} \times 100\% = 109\%$$

$$\text{Activity ratio} = \frac{\text{Standard hours produced}}{\text{Budgeted hours}} \times 100\% = \frac{1,125}{1,100} \times 100\% = 102\%$$

The overall activity or production volume for the quarter was 2% greater than forecast. This was achieved by a 9% increase in capacity.

$$\text{Efficiency ratio} = \frac{\text{Standard hours produced}}{\text{Actual hours worked}} \times 100\% = \frac{1,125}{1,200} \times 100\% = 94\%$$

The labour force worked 6% below standard levels of efficiency.

2   Performance measures for manufacturing environments

In a **jobbing** environment each job undertaken is unique. Products are made to the specific requirements of individual customers. This has a number of implications for performance measurement.

(a)   Detailed planning should be undertaken and performance targets set. As so many variables are involved this is a complicated process, and the likelihood of targets not being achieved is significant.

(b)   **Suppliers may be different for each job**, making it **harder to set standards** for quality, speed of delivery and so on.

(c)   **Customer satisfaction** measures are particularly **important** in this environment (payment might depend contractually upon customer satisfaction). Feedback on performance should be obtained from the customer during the job.

(d)   Because each job will be different the organisation will have to be extremely **flexible**. Measures of success in adapting to new requirements will provide a key indicator. Measures of **employee skills** will be equally important.

(e)   It is likely that the job will need to be completed within a certain **time** and therefore an ongoing check must be kept of performance in relation to the **deadline**.

A **contract** or **project** is simply a large job that takes a considerable length of time. The same considerations apply regarding performance measurement as in a jobbing environment. The following are also relevant.

(a)   The size and consequences of **overspending** may be huge.

(b)   The longer timescale means that progress must be measured even more carefully, since there is more likelihood of slippage if **deadlines** seem a long way off.

In a **batch** production environment, products are more **standardised**, although some costs and activities may be unique to a specific batch. Standardisation of products means that materials requirements and labour and machinery capabilities are also more standardised. **Performance standards** can be set for materials quality and usage, labour efficiency, suppliers and so on.

The high degree of standardisation in a **process costing** environment means that it is **ideal for setting performance standards**. However, costs, materials usage/wastage, labour inefficiencies, machine breakdowns and so on cannot be traced to a specific item. These features can only be measured on an average per unit basis. A measure like 'cost per unit' in a processing environment reflects **average performance over a period** of time. It may therefore be more difficult to improve upon existing performance standards as **inefficiencies may not be easily identifiable.**

A number of performance indicators can be used to assess operations. They are particularly relevant to the internal business and customer perspectives of the balanced scorecard.

- Quality
- Number of customer complaints and warranty claims
- Lead times
- Rework
- Delivery to time
- Non-productive hours
- System (machine) down time

These indicators can also be expressed in the form of ratios or percentages for comparative purposes. Like physical measures, they can be produced quickly and trends can be identified and acted upon rapidly. Examples of useful ratios might be as follows.

(a) **Machine down time: total machine hours**. This ratio could be used to monitor machine availability and can provide a measure of machine usage and efficiency.

(b) **Component rejects: component purchases**. This ratio could be used to control the quality of components purchased from an external supplier. This measure can be used to monitor the performance of new suppliers.

(c) **Deliveries late: deliveries on schedule**. This ratio could be applied to sales made to customers as well as to receipts from suppliers.

(d) **Customer rejects/returns: total sales**. This ratio helps to monitor customer satisfaction, providing a check on the efficiency of quality control procedures.

(e) **Value added time: production cycle time**. Value added time is the direct production time during which the product is being made and value is therefore being added.

2.1 Performance measurement for manufacturing

Performance measurement in manufacturing is increasingly using non-financial measures. Malcolm Smith identifies four over-arching measures for manufacturing environments.

- **Cost**: cost behaviour
- **Quality**: factors inhibiting performance
- **Time**: bottlenecks, inertia
- **Innovation**: new product flexibility

2.1.1 Cost

Possible non-financial or part-financial indicators are as follows.

Area	Measure
Quantity of raw material inputs	Actual v target number
Equipment productivity	Actual v standard units
Maintenance efforts	No. of production units lost through maintenance No. of production units lost through failure No. of failures prior to schedule
Overtime costs	Overtime hours/total hours
Product complexity	No. of component parts
Quantity of output	Actual v target completion
Product obsolescence	% shrinkage
Employees	% staff turnover
Employee productivity	direct labour hours per unit
Customer focus	% service calls; % claims

2.1.2 Quality

Integrating quality into a performance measurement system suggests attention to the following items.

Area	Measure
Quality of purchased components	Zero defects
Equipment failure	Downtime/total time
Maintenance effort	Breakdown maintenance/total maintenance
Waste	% defects; % scrap; % rework
Quality of output	% yield
Safety	Serious industrial injury rate
Reliability	% warranty claims
Quality commitment	% dependence on post-inspection % conformance to quality standards
Employee morale	% absenteeism
Leadership impact	% cancelled meetings
Customer awareness	% repeat orders; number of complaints

2.1.3 Time

A truly just-in-time system is an ideal to which many manufacturing firms are striving. Time-based competition is also important for new product development, deliveries etc. The management accounting focus might be on throughput, bottlenecks, customer feedback and distribution.

Area	Measure
Equipment failure	Time between failures
Maintenance effort	Time spent on repeat work
Throughput	Processing time/total time per unit
Production flexibility	Set-up time
Availability	% stockouts
Labour effectiveness	Standard hours achieved / total hours worked
Customer impact	No. of overdue deliveries Mean delivery delay

2.1.4 Innovation

Performance indicators for innovation can support the 'innovation and learning' perspective on the balanced scorecard. Some possible suggestions are outlined below.

Area	Measure
The ability to introduce new products	% product obsolescence Number of new products launched Number of patents secured Time to launch new products
Flexibility to accommodate change	Number of new processes implemented Number of new process modifications

Area	Measure
Reputation for innovation	Media recognition for leadership Expert assessment of competence Demonstrable competitive advantage

3 Performance measures for services

Performance measures covering the following **six 'dimensions'** have been suggested for service organisations.

- Competitive performance
- Financial performance
- Quality of service
- Flexibility
- Resource utilisation
- Innovation

3.1 Service businesses

A service business does not produce a physical product. Instead it provides a service, for example a haircut, or insurance.

(a) A service is **intangible**. The actual benefit being bought can not be touched.

(b) The production and consumption of a service are **simultaneous**, and therefore it cannot be inspected for quality in advance.

(c) Services are **perishable**, that is, they cannot be stored. For example a hairdresser cannot do haircuts in advance and keep them stocked away in case of heavy demand.

(d) A service is **heterogeneous**. The service received will vary each time. Services are more reliant on people. People are not robots, so how the service is delivered will not be identical each time.

QUESTION

Service measures

Consider how the factors intangibility, simultaneity, perishability and heterogeneity apply to the various services that you use: public transport, your bank account, meals in restaurants, the postal service, your annual holiday and so on.

3.2 'Dimensions' of performance measurement

Performance measurement in service businesses is made more difficult because of the four factors listed above. However, performance measurement is possible, the key being to ensure what you are measuring has been clearly enough defined. A range of performance measures covering **six 'dimensions'** are used.

3.2.1 Competitive performance

Competitive performance focuses on factors such as sales growth, market share and ability to obtain new business.

3.2.2 Financial performance

Like any other business, a service business needs to plan, and its short-term plans can be drawn up in the form of a **budget**.

(a) There might be a **budgeted expenditure limit** for individual activities within the business.

(b)   **Standard performance measures** (such as standard cost per unit of activity or standard quantity of 'output' per unit of resource used up (ie productivity)) can be established as targets.

QUESTION
Productivity measure

A secretary working in a bank is paid $12,000 per annum and produces 4,500 letters a year. Devise a cost per unit of activity and a standard measure of productivity.

ANSWER

$$\frac{\$12,000}{4,500} = \$2.66 \text{ per letter}$$

$$\frac{4,500}{(365-52-52)} = 17.24 \text{ letters per working day, ignoring holidays.}$$

Other answers are possible.

3.2.3 Quality of service

Service quality is measured principally by **qualitative measures**, although some quantitative measures are used by some businesses. An equipment hire company used a 'successful hire indicator'. This was expressed as a percentage. All hires has to be classified as successful or unsuccessful (based on equipment performance) when equipment was returned.

The following table shows the measures used to assess 4 quality factors and the means of obtaining the information by British Airports Authority (BAA), a transport facility service provider.

Service quality factors	Measures	Mechanisms
Access	Walking distances Ease of finding way around	Customer survey and internal operational data
Cleanliness/tidiness	Cleanliness of environment and equipment	Customer survey and management inspection
Comfort	Crowdedness of airport	Customer survey and management inspection
Friendliness	Staff attitude and helpfulness	Customer survey and management inspection

QUESTION
Measuring service quality

What do you conclude are the two main means of measuring service quality at BAA?

ANSWER

Customer surveys and management inspection

3.2.4 Flexibility

Flexibility has three aspects.

Aspect	Detail
Speed of delivery	This is vital in some service industries. Measures include factors such as waiting time in queues. In other types of service it may be more a question of timeliness. Does the auditor turn up to do the annual audit during the appointed week? Is the audit done within the time anticipated by the partner or does it drag on for weeks? These aspects are all easily measurable in terms of 'days late'. Depending upon the circumstances 'days late' may also reflect on inability to cope with fluctuations in demand.
Ability to respond to customers' specifications	This will depend on the type of service. A professional service such as legal advice must be tailored exactly to the customer's needs. Performance is partly a matter of customer perception. Customer attitude surveys may be appropriate. Performance also depends on the diversity of skills possessed by the service organisation. This can be measured in terms of the mix of staff skills and the amount of time spent on training.
Coping with demand	This is measurable in quantitative terms. For example train companies can measure the extent of overcrowding. Customer queuing time can be measured for banks and retailers. Professional services can measure levels of overtime worked.

3.2.5 Resource utilisation measures

Resource utilisation is usually measured in terms of **productivity**. The ease with which this may be measured varies according to the service being delivered. The main input resource of a firm of accountants, for example, is the **time** of staff. The main output of an accountancy firm is **chargeable hours**. Productivity will therefore be measured as the ratio of chargeable hours to total hours.

Here are some resource utilisation ratios.

Business	Input	Output
Accountancy firms	Man hours available	Chargeable hours
Commonwealth Hotels	Rooms available	Rooms occupied
Railway companies	Train miles available	Passenger miles
Barclays Bank	Number of staff	Number of accounts

3.2.6 Innovation

Companies do not have to innovate to be successful, but it helps! Others will try to steal their market, and so others' innovations must at least be matched. In a modern environment in which product quality, product differentiation and continuous improvement are the order of the day, a company that can find innovative ways of satisfying customers' needs has an important **competitive advantage**

The **innovating process can be measured** in terms of **how much it costs to develop a new service, how effective the process is** (that is, how innovative is the organisation, if at all?), and **how quickly it can develop new services**. In more concrete terms this might translate into the following.

(a) The **amount of spending on research and development**, and whether these costs are recovered from new service sales (and how quickly).

(b) The **proportion of new services to total services** provided.

(c) The **time between identification of the customer need for a new service and making it available**.

QUESTION

Competitiveness and resource utilisation

A service business has collected some figures relating to its year just ended.

	Budget	Actual
Customer enquiries		
New customers	6,000	9,000
Existing customers	4,000	3,000
Business won		
New customers	2,000	4,000
Existing customers	1,500	1,500
Types of services performed		
Service A	875	780
Service B	1,575	1,850
Service C	1,050	2,870
Employees		
Service A	5	4
Service B	10	10
Service C	5	8

Required

Calculate figures that illustrate competitiveness and resource utilisation.

ANSWER

Competitiveness can only be measured from these figures by looking at how successful the organisation is at converting enquiries into firm orders.

Percentage of enquiries converted into firm orders

	Budget	Actual
New customers (W1)	33%	44%
Existing customers (W1)	37.5%	50%

Resource utilisation can be measured by looking at average services performed per employee.

	Budget	Actual	Rise
Service A (W2)	175	195	+11.4%
Service B (W2)	157.5	185	+17.5%
Service C (W2)	175	358.75	+105.0%

Workings

1   For example 2,000/6,000 = 33%
2   For example 875/5 = 175

What comments would you make about the results of these calculations? How well is the business doing?

3.2.7 Setting a standard, budget or target

A standard, budget or target can be set for a service department in a number of ways.

(a)   There might be a budgeted expenditure limit for the department.

(b)   **Standard performance measures** might be established as targets for efficiency. Standard performance measures are possible where the department carries out routine activities for much of its work.

(c)   Targets or standards might be set for the **quality of the service**.

     (i)   To provide training to employees up to a quantifiable standard
     (ii)   To respond to requests for help within a specified number of minutes, hours or days
     (iii)   To respond to materials requisitions within a specified period of time

(d)   To perform a **targeted quantity of work** with a budgeted number of staff.

(e)   **To meet schedules for completing certain work**.

     (i)   Scheduled dates for completion of each stage in a product development project in the R&D department

     (ii)   Scheduled dates for the DP department to complete each stage of a new computer project

(f)   **To make a profit**. A service department might be designated as a profit centre. It would charge other departments for the services it provides at a 'commercial' transfer price rate, and it would be expected to earn a 'profit' on the work it does.

3.2.8 Standards for cost or efficiency

Two methods of setting a standard measure of performance in a service department are:

- Standard cost per unit of activity
- Standard quantity of 'output' per unit of resource used up

With both methods, there has to be a measurable quantity or volume of activity in the department. Both types of standard can be employed within a control system, and they are not mutually exclusive.

Examples of standard measures of performance in service departments might be as follows.

(a)   In the accounts receivable section of an accounts department, for example, the volume of activity could be measured by:

     (i)   Number or value of invoices issued
     (ii)   Number or value of payments received
     (iii)   The number or value of bad debts

     A budget for the section could then establish a standard cost per invoice issued, or a standard cost per £1 received or receivable, or a standard % of bad debts. In addition, there could be standards for the number or value of invoices issued per man/day.

(b)   In a sales department, activity could be measured by the number and value of orders taken, the number of customer visits, or the number of miles travelled by sales representatives. There could be a standard cost per customer visit, a standard cost per £1 of sales, and so on. Alternatively, standards could be set for the amount of work done per unit of resource consumed, and in a sales department, such standards include:

     (i)   Standard number of customer visits per salesperson per day
     (ii)   Standard number and value of sales per customer visit
     (iii)   Standard number of miles travelled per £1 of sales

(c)   In a transport department, activity could be measured in tonne/miles (tonnes of goods delivered and miles travelled) and standards could be established for:

     (i)   Cost per tonne/mile
     (ii)   Drivers' hours per tonne/mile
     (iii)   Miles per gallon consumed

3.2.9 Measuring and evaluating performance

Once a target, budget or standard has been set, we have a basis for evaluating performance, by comparing actual results against the target.

3.2.10 Selecting measures of performance

Key item(s) of performance to be measured should be identified. Examples include return, growth, productivity, market share, and cost control.

(a)   Return can be measured as ROI, RI, profit and so on.

(b)   Growth can be measured by sales growth, profit growth, investment spending, capacity fill and so on.

(c)   Productivity measures can be applied to machinery as well as labour.

(d)   Market position and status, or quality of product/service, could be measured by market research, or through customer responses and complaints.

(e)   Cost control involves identifying the nature of the costs that ought to be controlled and comparing actual spending with budget.

This can be applied to the finance function.

(a)   **Define the boundaries** of the finance function. Does it include data processing, for example, or inventory control or treasury management?

(b)   **Define formal objectives** for the function as a whole, and then for each main section, for supervisory and managerial staff and for the operation of systems (for example payroll).

(c)   Ascertain what **activities** each section does (or should do) to achieve its objectives.

(d)   **Identify appropriate measures**, on the basis of the objectives and activities identified. The 'pyramid' approach should be used, with successively more detailed information for successively junior levels of staff.

(e)   Select suitable **bases of comparison**. Possibilities are time, budgets, standards or targets, intra-group comparison, or intra-organisational comparison, if verifiably comparable data is available.

Dimension	Type	Example
Competitive performance	Competitor focused	Market share Prices Product features
	Customer focused	Customer retention Customer numbers
Financial performance	Profitability	Profit Working capital cycle
	Liquidity	Bad debts
Quality of service	Reliability	Punctuality Dependability of service and staff
	Responsiveness	Response times Number of phone lines Delivery speed (for goods ordered online or by phone)
	Courtesy	Politeness Respect to customers
	Competence	Staff skill Expertise Knowledge Diligence
	Availability	Product availability Product range
	Accessibility	Ease of finding site
Flexibility	Delivery speed	Customer waiting time Time from customer enquiry to job completion
	Volume	Spare capacity to deal with peak times
	Specification	Number of product lines Range of staff

Dimension	Type	Example
Resource utilisation	Human resources	Labour hours worked
		Skill levels of work performed by staff grade
	Premises	% of area used for value-adding services, or customer-facing services
Innovation	Cost	Development cost per new product line / service
	Speed	Time taken from:
		– concept to prototype launch
		– concept to offered to customers

4 Performance measures for non-profit-seeking organisations

Performance of **NPMOs** can be measured as follows.

- In terms of inputs and outputs
- By judgement
- By comparison

4.1 Non-profit-seeking organisations (NPMOs)

NPMOs include private sector organisations such as charities and churches and much of the public sector. Commercial organisations generally have market competition and the profit motive to guide the process of managing resources economically, efficiently and effectively. However, NPMOs **cannot** by definition **be judged by profitability** nor do they generally have to be successful against competition, so other methods of assessing performance have to be used.

A major problem with many NPMOs, particularly government bodies, is that it is **difficult to define their objectives**.

QUESTION   Objectives

One of the objectives of a local government body could be 'to provide adequate street lighting throughout the area'.

(a)   How could the 'adequacy' of street lighting be measured?

(b)   Assume that other objectives are:

    (i)   to improve road safety in the area; and

    (ii)   to reduce crime.

    How much does 'adequate' street lighting contribute to each of these aims?

(c)   What is an excessive amount of money to pay for adequately lit streets, improved road safety and reduced crime? How much is too little?

ANSWER

Mull over these questions and discuss them in class or with colleagues if possible. It is possible to suggest answers, perhaps even in quantitative terms, but the point is that there are no *easy* answers, and no right or wrong answers.

4.2 How can performance be measured?

Performance is often judged in terms of inputs and outputs. This ties in with the **'value for money'** criteria often used to assess NPMOs.

(a) **Economy** (spending money frugally)

(b) **Efficiency** (getting out as much as possible for what goes in)

(c) **Effectiveness** (getting done, by means of (a) and (b), what was supposed to be done)

Effectiveness is the relationship between an organisation's outputs and its objectives, **efficiency** is the relationship between inputs and outputs, and **economy** means controlling expenditure.

(a) **Multiple objectives**

They tend to have multiple objectives, so that even if they can all be clearly identified it is impossible to say which is the overriding objective.

(b) **Measuring outputs**

Outputs can seldom be measured in a way that is generally agreed to be meaningful. (For example, are good exam results alone an adequate measure of the quality of teaching?) Data collection can be problematic. For example, unreported crimes are not included in data used to measure the performance of a police force.

(c) **Lack of profit measure**

If an organisation is not expected to make a profit, or if it has no sales, indicators such as ROI and RI are meaningless.

(d) **Nature of service provided**

Many not-for-profit organisations provide services for which it is difficult to define a cost unit. For example, what is the cost unit for a local fire service? This problem does exist for commercial service providers but problems of performance measurement are made simple because profit can be used.

(e) **Financial constraints**

Although every organisation operates under financial constraints, these are more pronounced in not-for-profit organisations. For instance, a commercial organisation's borrowing power is effectively limited by managerial prudence and the willingness of lenders to lend, but a local authority's ability to raise finance (whether by borrowing or via local taxes) is subject to strict control by central government.

(f) **Political, social and legal considerations**

(i) Unlike commercial organisations, public sector organisations are subject to strong political influences. Local authorities, for example, have to carry out central government's policies as well as their own (possibly conflicting) policies.

(ii) The public may have higher expectations of public sector organisations than commercial organisations. A decision to close a local hospital in an effort to save costs, for example, is likely to be less acceptable to the public than the closure of a factory for the same reason.

(iii) The performance indicators of public sector organisations are subject to far more onerous legal requirements than those of private sector organisations.

(iv) Whereas profit-seeking organisations are unlikely in the long term to continue services making a negative contribution, not-for-profit organisations may be required to offer a range of services, even if some are uneconomic.

4.3 Solutions

4.3.1 Inputs

Performance can be judged in terms of **inputs**. This is very common in everyday life. If somebody tells you that their suit cost $750, you would generally conclude that it was an extremely well-designed and

good quality suit, even if you did not think so when you first saw it. The drawback is that you might also conclude that the person wearing the suit had been cheated or was a fool, or you may happen to be of the opinion that no piece of clothing is worth $750. So it is with the inputs and outputs of a not-for-profit organisations.

4.3.2 Judgement

A second possibility is to accept that performance measurement must to some extent be subjective. Judgements can be made by **experts** in that particular not-for-profit activity or by the **persons who fund the activity**.

4.3.3 Comparisons

We have said that most not-for-profit organisations do not face competition but this does not mean that all are unique. Bodies like local governments, health services and so on can judge their performance **against each other** and **against the historical results of their predecessors**. And since they are not competing with each other, there is less of a problem with confidentiality and so **benchmarking** is easier.

In practice, **benchmarking** usually encompasses:

- Regularly comparing aspects of performance (functions or processes) with best practitioners
- Identifying gaps in performance
- Seeking fresh approaches to bring about improvements in performance
- Following through with implementing improvements
- Following up by monitoring progress and reviewing the benefits

4.3.4 Quantitative measures

Unit cost measurements like 'cost per patient day' or 'cost of borrowing one library book' can fairly easily be established to allow organisations to assess whether they are doing better or worse than their counterparts.

Efficiency measurement of inputs and outputs is illustrated in three different situations as follows.

(a) **Where input is fixed**

$$\frac{\text{Actual output}}{\text{Maximum output obtainable for a given input}}$$

25/30 miles per gallon = 83.3% efficiency

(b) **Where output is fixed**

$$\frac{\text{Minimum input needed for a given output}}{\text{Actual input}}$$

55/60 hours to erect scaffolding = 91.7% efficiency

(c) **Where input and output are both variable**

Actual output ÷ actual input
compared with
standard output ÷ standard input

$9,030/7,000 meals = $1.29 per meal

$9,600/7,500 meals = $1.28 per meal
Efficiency = 99.2%

As a further illustration, suppose that at a cost of $40,000 and 4,000 hours (inputs) in an average year two policemen travel 8,000 miles and are instrumental in 200 arrests (outputs). A large number of possibly meaningful measures can be derived from these few figures, as the table below shows.

	$40,000	4,000 hours	8,000 miles	200 arrests
Cost $40,000		$40,000/4,000 = $10 per hour	$40,000/8,000 = $5 per mile	$40,000/200 = $200 per arrest
Time 4,000 hours	4,000/$40,000 = 6 minutes patrolling per $1 spent		4,000/8,000 = ½ hour to patrol 1 mile	4,000/200 = 20 hours per arrest
Miles 8,000	8,000/$40,000 = 0.2 of a mile per $1	8,000/4,000 = 2 miles patrolled per hour		8,000/200 = 40 miles per arrest
Arrests 200	200/$40,000 = 1 arrest per $200	200/4,000 = 1 arrest every 20 hours	200/8,000 = 1 arrest every 40 miles	

These measures **do not necessarily identify cause and effect** (do teachers or equipment produce better exam results?) **or personal responsibility and accountability**. Actual performance needs to be compared as follows.

(a) With standards, if there are any	(d) With targets
(b) With similar external activities	(e) With indices
(c) With similar internal activities	(f) Over time, as trends

Not-for-profit organisations are forced to use a wide range of indicators and can be considered early users of a balanced scorecard approach (covered in Section 8 of this chapter.) 4.3.4.1 Performance measurement in the public sector

In public sector organisations, an increasing volume of information on performance and 'value for money' is produced for internal and external use. The ways in which performance can be measured depends very much upon which organisation is involved.

(a) The first question which would need to be asked is 'what are the **aims** and **objectives** of the organisation?' For example, the objective of Companies House is to maintain and make available records of company reports.

(b) The next question to ask is 'How can we tell if the organisation is **meeting** the objectives?' Quantified information - ie information in the form of numbers - will be useful, and this will consist mainly of output and performance measures and indicators. For these, targets can be set. Any individual organisational unit should have no more than a handful of key targets.

Individual targets are likely to fall under the headings:

(a) **Financial performance targets**
(b) **Volume of output targets**
(c) **Quality of service targets**
(d) **Efficiency targets**

4.4 Performance measurement in central government

Over recent years, much of the work of central government has been reorganised into semi-autonomous **executive agencies**, which we mentioned earlier in the chapter.

The following are examples of targets related to **financial performance** in executive agencies.

(a) **Full cost recovery** (National School of Government, Central Office of Information and others), plus unit cost targets

(b) **Commercial revenue** to offset costs (Met Office)

(c) **Non-Exchequer income** as a **percentage** of **total income** (National Engineering Laboratory)

Targets related to **output** can be difficult to set. In many cases the output of executive agencies is not tangible. For example, Historic Royal Palaces not only deals with visitors, whose numbers can be counted, but is also responsible for maintaining the fabric of royal palaces - an output which is more

difficult to measure. In such cases, performance will be best measured by appraising the **progress** of the **project** as a whole.

Example of **quality** targets set for executive agencies include the following.

(a) **Timeliness**

    (i)   Time to handle applications

    (ii)   Car driving tests to be reduced to 6 weeks nationally (Driving Standards Agency)

(b) **Quality of product**

    (i)   Number of print orders delivered without fault (HMSO)

    (ii)   95% business complaints handled within 5 days

    (iii)   85% overall customer satisfaction rating

Efficiency improvements may come through reducing the cost of inputs without reducing the quality of outputs. Alternatively, areas of activity affecting total costs may be reduced. Targets related to **efficiency** include the following.

(a) **Percentage reduction** in **price paid** for purchases of stationery and paper

(b) Reduction in the ratio of **cost of support services** to **total cost**

(c) 8.7% **efficiency increase** in the use of **accommodation**

4.5 Performance measurement in local government

The performance measures chosen by local authorities usually consist of **comparative statistics** and **unit costs**.

The following list illustrates the types of comparative statistics that could be used.

PERFORMANCE MEASURES IN LOCAL GOVERNMENT	
For the authority's total expenditure and for each function	Net cost per 1,000 population Manpower per 1,000 population
Primary education, secondary education	Pupil/teacher ratio Cost per pupil
School meals	Revenue/cost ratio Pupils receiving free meals as a proportion of school roll
Home helps	Contract hours per 1,000 population over 65
Police	Population per police officer Serious offences per 1,000 population
Fire	Proportion of area at high risk
Public transport	Passenger journeys per week per 1,000 population
Highways	Maintenance cost per kilometre

5   Management performance measures

Possible **management performance measures** include the following.

- – Subjective measures
- – Judgement of outsiders
- – Upward appraisal
- – Accounting measures

BPP
LEARNING MEDIA

We have not so far **distinguished between measures of performance of individual managers** and **measures of performance of what it is they manage**

The distinction is very important. A manager may improve performance of a poorly performing division, but the division could still rank as one of the poorest performing divisions within the organisation. If the manager is assessed purely on the division's results then he will not appear to be a good performer.

The problem is deciding which performance measures should be used to measure management performance and which should be used to measure the performance of the business.

It is difficult to devise performance measures that relate specifically to a manager to judge his or her performance **as a manager**. It is possible to calculate statistics to assess the manager as an **employee** (days absent, professional qualifications obtained, personality and so on), but this does not measure managerial performance.

It is necessary to consider a manager in relation to his or her **area of responsibility**. If we want to know how good a manager is at marketing, the marketing performance of his or her division is the **starting point**. Then we must consider to what extent the manager is able to **influence** the performance, and the performance **trend.**

It is unreasonable to assess managers' performance in relation to matters that are beyond their control. Management performance measures should therefore **only include those items that are directly controllable by the manager in question.**

5.1 Possible management performance measures

Measures	Detail
Subjective measures	An example is ranking performance on a scale of 1 to 5. This approach is imprecise but does measure managerial performance rather than divisional performance. The process must be perceived by managers to be fair. The judgement should be made by somebody impartial, but close enough to the work of each manager to appreciate the efforts he has made and the difficulties he faces.
Judgement of outsiders	An organisation might, for example, set up a bonus scheme for directors under which they would receive a bonus if the share price outperforms the FT-SE 100 index for more than three years. This is fair in that the share price reflects many aspects of performance, but it is questionable whether they can all be influenced by the directors concerned.
Upward appraisal	This involves staff giving their opinions on the performance of their managers. To be effective this requires healthy working relationships.
Accounting measures	These can be used, but must be tailored according to what or whom is being judged.

6 Responsibility centre performance measures

6.1 Typical performance measures

In order to ensure that junior managers in an organisation make decisions that are in the best interests of the organisation as a whole, senior managers generally introduce the following systems of performance measures.

Responsibility centre	Manager responsible for?	Financial performance measures
Cost centre	Costs	Variances
Revenue centre	Revenues only	Revenues
Profit centre	Costs and revenues	Controllable profit
Investment centre	Costs, revenues and assets	Return on Investment and Residual Income

We looked at variances in Part D of this Interactive Text, and we are now going to turn our attention to the following performance measures.

(a) Controllable profit
(b) Return on Investment (ROI)
(c) Residual Income (RI)

6.2 Traditional performance measures – cost centres

As we have already seen, variance analysis is often used as a way of measuring the performance of cost centres. Despite giving detailed explanations of why the variances have occurred, variance analysis as a performance indicator does have a number of disadvantages.

(a) It is concerned with controlling costs and inefficiencies in the short term only and may lead to conflict with an organisation's longer-term objectives.

(b) The variances are only as good as the standards on which they are based.

(c) It is not always obvious which managers are responsible for which variances. For example, are direct materials price variances the responsibility of the production manager or the purchasing manager, or both?

6.3 Traditional performance measures – profit centres

Profit centres often use controllable profit statements as a way of measuring the performance of both individual managers and their divisions. A proforma controllable profit statement is shown below.

6.4 Example: controllable profit statement

	Car sales $	Petrol $	Total $
Sales	315,000	25,000	340,000
Variable costs			
Plates, tax, MOT	(105,000)		(105,000)
Car valeting cost	(50,000)		(50,000)
Fuel	–	(15,000)	(15,000)
Contribution	160,000	10,000	170,000
Traceable fixed costs			
Fixed cleaning costs for showroom	(6,000)		(6,000)
Wages	(40,000)	(5,000)	(45,000)
Traceable profit	114,000	5,000	119,000
Common costs			
Building maintenance			(12,000)
Management salaries			(35,000)
Budgeted profit			72,000

The main problem with controllable profit statements is in deciding which costs are **controllable** and which costs are **traceable**. The performance of the manager of the division is indicated by the **controllable profit** (and it is on this that he is judged) and the success of the division as a whole is judged on the **traceable profit**.

Consider, for example, depreciation on divisional machinery. Would this be included as a controllable fixed cost or a traceable fixed cost? Because profit centre managers are only responsible for the **costs**

and revenues under their control, this means that they do not have control over the investment in non-current assets. The depreciation on divisional machinery would therefore be a **traceable fixed cost** judging the performance of the division, and not of the individual manager.

6.5 Traditional performance measures – investment centres

Managers of investment centres have responsibility for costs, revenues and capital investment. Divisional performance is commonly measured using the following.

(a) **Return on Investment** (ROI)
(b) **Residual Income** (RI)

Return on Investment (ROI) is calculated as follows.

$$ROI = \frac{\text{Controllable (traceable) profit}}{\text{Controllable (traceable) investment}} \times 100\%$$

Residual Income (RI) is calculated as follows.

RI = Controllable (traceable) profit – imputed interest charge on controllable (traceable) investment

6.6 Example: calculation of ROI and RI

Division M is a division of MR plc. The following data relate to Division M.

Net assets	$20m
Annual profit	$5m
Cost of capital	15% per annum

MR plc is considering two proposals.

Proposal 1

Invest a further $2m in non-current assets to earn an annual profit of $0.40m.

Proposal 2

Dispose of non-current assets at their net book value of $5.5m. This would lead to profits falling by $1m per annum. Proceeds from the disposal of these non-current assets would not be credited to Division M (but to the Holding Company of MR plc instead).

Required

(a) Calculate the current Return on Investment and Residual Income for Division M.

(b) Consider each of the two proposals and show how the Return on Investment and Residual Income would change if these proposals were adopted.

6.7 Solution

(a) **Current Return on Investment**

$$\text{Return on Investment} = \frac{\text{Traceable profit}}{\text{Traceable investment}} \times 100\%$$

$$= \frac{\$5m}{\$20m} \times 100\%$$

$$= 25\%$$

Residual Income = Traceable profit – imputed interest charge on traceable investment
= $5m – (15% × $20m)
= $5m – $3m
= $2m

The Return on Investment (25%) exceeds the cost of capital (15%) and the residual income is positive (+$2m) and therefore Division M is performing well.

(b) Let us now look at the situations that would arise if proposals 1 and 2 were to be adopted.

Proposal 1

New traceable profit	= $5m + $0.4m
	= $5.4m
∴ New traceable investment	= $20m + $2m
	= $22m
∴ **New Return on Investment**	= $\dfrac{£5.4m}{£22m} \times 100\%$
	= 24.5%
∴ **New Residual Income**	= $5.4m − (15% × $22m)
	= $5.4m − $3.3m
	= $2.1m

Proposal 2

New traceable profit	= $5m − $1m
	= $4m
New traceable investment	= $20m − $5.5m
	= $14.5m
∴ **New Return on Investment**	= $\dfrac{\$4m}{\$14.5m} \times 100\%$
	= 27.6%
∴ **New Residual Income**	= $4m − (15% × $14.5m)
	= $4m − $2.18m
	= $1.82m

Summary

	Current	Proposal 1	Proposal 2
Return on Investment (%)	25	24.5	27.6
Residual Income ($m)	2	2.1	1.82

Based on ROI alone, proposal 2 would appear the best showing a **relative** increase in return when proposal 1 shows a decrease.

However the RI suggests the opposite is true and proposal 1 is best. This is because RI focuses purely on the **absolute** result.

When considering proposal 2, divisional managers should also consider the asset rate of return.

$$\text{Asset rate of return} = \frac{\text{Change in profit}}{\text{Change in investment}}$$

$$= \frac{\$1m}{\$5.5m} \times 100\%$$

$$= 18.2\%$$

Since MR plc's current rate of return is 25%, any asset which has a rate of return less than this should be disposed of. It is important to remember, therefore, that whichever proposal is accepted, it should lead to goal congruence.

6.8 Advantages of Return on Investment and Residual Income

Return on Investment is a relative measure, whereas **Residual Income** is an absolute measure. Consequently, Residual Income, as an absolute measure of performance is used to select proposals based on the absolute increase in profits, rather than the relative increases.

This can be demonstrated in the example above where the ROI increases to 29% with proposal 2, but the reality is that Residual Income only increases by an absolute value of $0.2m. Residual Income therefore allows you to select a proposal that will maximise your wealth (in absolute terms).

Residual Income can also be related to the net present value (NPV) of a project, and supports the NPV approach. Therefore, organisations that maximise Residual Income will not necessarily, but are likely to maximise NPV in the long run (and hence shareholder wealth).

6.9 Disadvantages of Return on Investment and Residual Income

These performance measures have a number of common disadvantages.

(a)   It can be difficult to identify controllable (traceable) profits.

(b)   When organisations value assets at net book value, ROI and RI generally **increase** as assets get older. Consequently, management may hold on to out-of-date plant and machinery.

(c)   Both ROI and RI involve a cost of capital figure which must be estimated. The cost of capital is difficult to calculate and is not known with certainty.

(d)   Both ROI and RI measure divisional performance based on a single value. Most organisations these days are of such a complex nature that a single figure is unlikely to be adequate for an investment decision.

(e)   As a general rule, most investment projects with positive NPVs have correspondingly low ROI and RI figures in early years. This can lead to the project being rejected in the first few years of a new investment, because the payoffs are long term.

7 Non-financial objectives

> **Non-financial objectives** include the welfare of employees and society in general and the fulfilment of responsibilities towards customers and suppliers.

A company may have important **non-financial objectives**, which will limit the achievement of financial objectives. Examples of non-financial objectives are as follows.

(a)   **The welfare of employees**

A company might try to provide **good wages and salaries**, comfortable and safe working conditions, good training and career development, and good pensions. If redundancies are necessary, many companies will provide generous redundancy payments, or spend money trying to find alternative employment for redundant staff.

(b)   **The welfare of management**

Managers will often take decisions to improve their **own circumstances**, even though their decisions will incur expenditure and so reduce profits. High salaries, company cars and other perks are all examples of managers promoting their own interests.

(c)   **The provision of a service**

The major objectives of some companies will include fulfilment of a responsibility to **provide a service** to the public. Examples are the privatised British Telecom and British Gas. Providing a service is of course a key responsibility of government departments and local authorities.

(d)   **The fulfilment of responsibilities towards customers**

Responsibilities towards **customers** include providing in good time a product or service of a **quality** that customers expect, and dealing **honestly and fairly** with customers. **Reliable supply arrangements,** also **after-sales service arrangements,** are important.

(e)   **The fulfilment of responsibilities towards suppliers**

Responsibilities towards **suppliers** are expressed mainly in terms of **trading relationships**. A company's size could give it considerable power as a buyer. The company should not use its power unscrupulously. Suppliers might rely on getting prompt payment, in accordance with the agreed terms of trade.

(f)   **The welfare of society as a whole**

The management of some companies is aware of the role that their company has to play in exercising **corporate social responsibility**. This includes **compliance with applicable laws and regulations** but is wider than that. Companies may be aware of their responsibility to minimise pollution and other harmful 'externalities' (such as excessive traffic) which their activities generate. In delivering 'green' environmental policies, a company may improve its corporate image as well as reducing harmful externality effects. Companies also may consider their **'positive' responsibilities**, for example to make a contribution to the community by local sponsorship.

Other non-financial objectives are growth, diversification and leadership in research and development.

7.1 Financial and non-financial objectives

Non-financial objectives do not negate financial objectives, but they do suggest that the simple theory of company finance, that the objective of a firm is to maximise the wealth of ordinary shareholders, is too simplistic. Financial objectives may have to be compromised in order to satisfy non-financial objectives.

8 The balanced scorecard

The **balanced scorecard** measures performance in four different perspectives: customer satisfaction, financial success, process efficiency and growth.

So far in our discussion we have focussed on performance measurement and control from a financial point of view. Another approach, originally developed by Kaplan and Norton, is the use of what is called a 'balanced scorecard' consisting of a **variety of indicators both financial and non-financial.** This approach has developed over the years and is used by a wide range of companies. Consequently, different terminology may be used by different companies.

The **balanced scorecard approach** is 'An approach to the provision of information to management to assist strategic policy formulation and achievement. It emphasises the need to provide the user with a set of information which addresses all relevant areas of performance in an objective and unbiased fashion. The information provided may include both financial and non-financial elements, and cover areas such as profitability, customer satisfaction, internal efficiency and innovation.'

(CIMA *Official Terminology*)

The balanced scorecard focuses on **four different perspectives**, as follows.

Perspective	Question	Explanation
Customer satisfaction	What do existing and new customers value from us?	Gives rise to targets that matter to customers: cost, quality, delivery, inspection, handling and so on.
Process efficiency	What processes must we excel at to achieve our financial and customer objectives?	Aims to improve internal processes, decision making and resource utilisation.
Growth	Can we continue to improve and create future value?	Considers the business's capacity to maintain its competitive position through the acquisition of new skills and the development of new products.
Financial success	How do we create value for our shareholders?	Covers traditional measures such as growth, profitability and shareholder value but set through talking to the shareholder or shareholders direct.

The scorecard is 'balanced' in the sense that managers are required to think in terms of all four perspectives, to prevent improvements being made in one area at the expense of another.

The types of measure (**key performance indicators**) which may be monitored under each of the four perspectives include the following in the example on the next page. The list is not exhaustive but it will give you an idea of the possible scope of a balanced scorecard approach. The measures selected, particularly within the process efficiency perspective, will vary considerably with the type of organisation and its objectives.

Two examples of how a balanced scorecard might appear are given below. One refers to a restaurant which is a profit-making business. The other refers to a charity. Use these examples to think about how a balanced scorecard may appear in your own workplace.

Balanced Scorecard for a restaurant

Financial Success

GOALS	MEASURES (KPI)
To grow and open new restaurants	New restaurants opened
Profitable	Net profit margins

Customer Satisfaction

GOALS	MEASURES (KPI)
Great service	Excellent results on customer survey
Repeat business	Customers booking to come again
Innovative food	New menus on a regular basis

Process Efficiency

GOALS	MEASURES (KPI)
Timely food delivery	Time from order to delivery
Efficient staff	Processing of food order, few mistakes
Low food wastage	Amount of food discarded

Growth

GOALS	MEASURES (KPI)
Trained staff	Employees with relevant training and qualifications
New menu choices	Number of new dishes introduced

Balanced Scorecard for a charity

Financial Success

GOALS	MEASURES (KPI)
Income from charitable donations	Donations received
	Lower costs and/or increased income from all sources
Improved margins	

Customer Satisfaction

GOALS	MEASURES (KPI)
Continued donor support	Pledges given and direct debits set up
Donor involvement in initiatives	Fundraising and charity dinners

Process Efficiency

GOALS	MEASURES (KPI)
Reduce overheads	Lower overheads measured by monitoring and accounts
Claim back tax on gift aid	Improved reclaim times for gift aided donation

Growth

GOALS	MEASURES (KPI)
More projects supported	Number of projects given support
More fundraisers	Number of fundraisers recruited
More money pledged	Amount of donations promised

EXAM FOCUS POINT

Key performance indicators should be:

- specific as to profitability
- measurable and distinct
- relevant measuring achievement of a **critical success factor**

Each organisation has to decide which performance measure to use under each heading.

The following **important features** of this approach have been identified.

(a) It looks at both **internal and external matters** concerning the organisation.
(b) It is **related to the key elements of a company's strategy**.
(c) **Financial and non-financial measures** are linked together.

The balanced scorecard approach may be particularly useful for performance measurement in organisations which are unable to use simple profit as a performance measure. For example the **public sector** has long been forced to use a **wide range of performance indicators**, which can be formalised with a balanced scorecard approach.

QUESTION   Balanced scorecard

For each of the following performance indicators, identify one balanced scorecard perspective being measured.

(a) Labour cost per unit manufactured
(b) Asset turnover
(c) Training expenditure as a percentage of sales turnover
(d) Return on capital employed
(e) Percentage of on-time deliveries
(f) Percentage of turnover generated by new products
(g) Percentage of quality control rejects

ANSWER

(a) Process efficiency (the improvement of internal processes)
(b) Process efficiency (the intensity of asset usage)
(c) Growth or possibly process efficiency
(d) Financial success
(e) Customer satisfaction, or possibly process efficiency
(f) Growth
(g) Process efficiency, or possibly customer satisfaction

8.1 Advantages and disadvantages

As with all techniques, problems can arise when it is applied.

Advantages	Explanation
All four perspectives considered by managers	Managers need to look at both **internal** and **external** matters affecting the organisation. They also need to link together **financial** and **non-financial** measures. Therefore they can see how factors in one area affect all other areas.

Advantages	Explanation
Consistency between objectives, control systems and staff	It can be difficult to incorporate objectives into control systems such as budgets. So targets set by a budget, say, may conflict with objectives. Moreover, staff may put their own interpretation on objectives against the actual intention of the original objective. The balanced scorecard should improve communication between different levels of the organisation. The balanced scorecard strives to keep all of these factors in balance.

Disadvantages	Explanation
Conflicting measures	Some measures in the scorecard such as research funding and cost reduction may naturally conflict. It is often difficult to determine the balance which will achieve the best results.
Selecting measures	Not only do appropriate measures have to be devised but the number of measures used must be agreed. Care must be taken that the impact of the results is not lost in a sea of information.
Expertise	Measurement is only useful if it initiates appropriate action. Non-financial managers may have difficulty with the usual profit measures. With more measures to consider this problem will be compounded.
Interpretation	Even a financially-trained manager may have difficulty in putting the figures into an overall perspective.

9 Benchmarking

Benchmarking is an attempt to identify best practices and by comparison of operations to achieve improved performance.

Benchmarking is another type of comparison exercise through which an organisation attempts to improve performance.

The idea is to seek the best available performance against which the organisation can monitor its own performance.

CIMA's *Official Terminology* defines benchmarking as 'The establishment, through data gathering, of targets and comparators, through whose use relative levels of performance (and particularly areas of underperformance) can be identified. By the adoption of identified best practices it is hoped that performance will improve.'

CIMA lists four types of benchmarking.

Type	Description
Internal benchmarking	A method of comparing one operating unit or function with another within the same industry
Functional benchmarking	Internal functions are compared with those of the best external practitioners of those functions, regardless of the industry they are in (also known as **operational** or **generic** benchmarking)
Competitive benchmarking	Information is gathered about direct competitors, through techniques such as reverse engineering*
Strategic benchmarking	A type of competitive benchmarking aimed at strategic action and organisational change

* **Reverse engineering**: buying a competitor's product and dismantling it, in order to understand its content and configuration

From this list you can see that a benchmarking exercise **does not necessarily have to involve the comparison of operations with those of a competitor**. Indeed, it might be difficult to persuade a direct competitor to part with any information which is useful for comparison purposes. Functional benchmarking, for example, does not always involve direct competitors. For instance a railway company may be identified as the 'best' in terms of on-board catering, and an airline company that operates on different routes could seek opportunities to improve by sharing information and comparing their own catering operations with those of the railway company.

A 1994 survey of *The Times* Top 1,000 companies (half of which were in manufacturing) revealed that the business functions most subjected to benchmarking in the companies using the technique were **customer services, manufacturing, human resources and information services.**

9.1 Obtaining information

Financial information about competitors is **easier** to acquire than non-financial information. Information about **products** can be obtained from **reverse engineering**, **product literature**, **media comment** and **trade associations**. Information about **processes** (how an organisation deals with customers or suppliers) is more **difficult** to find.

Such information can be obtained from **group companies** or possibly **non-competing organisations in the same industry**.

9.2 Why use benchmarking?

9.2.1 For setting standards

Benchmarking allows **attainable standards** to be established following the examination of both **external and internal information**. If these standards are **regularly reviewed** in the light of information gained through benchmarking exercises, they can become part of a programme of **continuous improvement** by becoming increasingly demanding.

9.2.2 Other reasons

Anna Green, in her article *The Borrowers* in the October 1996 edition of Pass magazine, explains the **benefits** of benchmarking.

(a)   Its flexibility means that it can be used in both the public and private sector and by people at different levels of responsibility.

(b)   Cross comparisons (as opposed to comparisons with similar organisations) are more likely to expose radically different ways of doing things.

(c)   It is an effective method of implementing change, people being involved in identifying and seeking out different ways of doing things in their own areas.

(d)   It identifies the processes to improve.

(e)   It helps with cost reduction.

(f)   It improves the effectiveness of operations.

(g)   It delivers services to a defined standard.

(h)   It provides a focus on planning.

'Most importantly benchmarking establishes a desire to achieve continuous improvement and helps develop a culture in which it is easier to admit mistakes and make changes.'

CASE STUDY

Japan's top car maker, Toyota, was once considered to be a benchmark for other firms in terms of efficiency and minimising unnecessary costs. Last month they began trying to reduce costs even more (aiming for a fifth) by using more shared components within the cars. However, Volkswagen already

uses shared components in several of its Audi and Volkswagen brands and is now considered to be the benchmark instead of Toyota.

Guardian.co.uk 9 May 2012

Benchmarking works, it is claimed, for the following reasons.

(a)   The comparisons are carried out by the managers who have to live with any changes implemented as a result of the exercise.

(b)   Benchmarking focuses on improvement in key areas and sets targets which are challenging but 'achievable'. What is *really* achievable can be discovered by examining what others have achieved: managers are thus able to accept that they are not being asked to perform miracles.

Benchmarking has other advantages: it can provide **early warning of competitive disadvantage** and should lead to a greater incidence of **teamworking** and **cross-functional learning.**

QUESTION

Benchmarking

We've looked at the advantages of benchmarking. Can you think of any disadvantages?

ANSWER

-   Difficulties in deciding which activities to benchmark
-   Identifying the 'best in class' for each activity
-   Persuading other organisations to share information
-   Successful practices in one organisation may not transfer successfully to another
-   The danger of drawing incorrect conclusions from inappropriate comparisons

CHAPTER ROUNDUP

↳ In a customer-focused organisation, basic **measures for sales** can be supplemented by a host of others including customer rejects/returns: total sales.

↳ Performance measures for **materials** and **labour** include **variances.**

↳ Performance can be measured using the **standard hour.**

↳ **Efficiency**, **activity** and **capacity ratios** provide useful information.

↳ Performance measures covering the following **six 'dimensions'** have been suggested for service organisations.

 – Competitive performance
 – Financial performance
 – Quality of service
 – Flexibility
 – Resource utilisation
 – Innovation

↳ Performance of **NPMOs** can be measured as follows.

 – In terms of inputs and outputs
 – By judgement
 – By comparison

↳ Possible **management performance measures** include the following.

 – Subjective measures
 – Judgement of outsiders
 – Upward appraisal
 – Accounting measures

↳ **Non-financial objectives** include the welfare of employees and society in general and the fulfilment of responsibilities towards customers and suppliers.

↳ The **balanced scorecard** measures performance in four different perspectives: customer satisfaction, financial success, process efficiency and growth.

↳ Benchmarking is an attempt to identify best practices and by comparison of operations to achieve improved performance

QUICK QUIZ

1   What does the performance measure 'deliveries late: deliveries on schedule' indicate?

2   Suggest a measure for assessing machine usage and efficiency.

3   How is the efficiency ratio calculated?

4   What are the three aspects of flexibility?

5   What does 'economy' mean in terms of measuring the performance of an NPMO?

6   In the context of a balanced scorecard approach to performance measurement, to which of the four perspectives does each measure relate?

	Performance measure	Perspective
(a)	Time taken to develop new products	....
(b)	Percentage of on-time deliveries	....
(c)	Average set-up time	....
(d)	Return on capital employed	....

7   To which perspective of the balanced scorecard could the measure 'training day per employee' be most appropriately applied?

A   Customer
B   Internal
C   Growth
D   Financial

ANSWERS TO QUICK QUIZ

1   The efficiency of production and production scheduling.

2   Machine down time: total machine hours

3   (Standard hours produced ÷ actual hours worked) × 100%

4   Speed of delivery, ability to respond to customers' specifications and coping with demand.

5   Spending money frugally

6   (a)   Growth
    (b)   Customer
    (c)   Internal
    (d)   Financial

7   C

Now try ...

Attempt the questions below from the **Exam Question Bank**

Number

Q105 – Q109

This is a relatively short and simple chapter to end your studies of Management Accounting on! We look at a topic very important to accountants – cost reduction. The syllabus requires you to be able to evaluate cost reduction methods.

Cost management

1 Cost control and cost reduction

> **Cost reduction** is a planned and positive approach to reducing expenditure.

Cost reduction should not be confused with cost control.

Cost control is concerned with regulating the costs of operating a business and keeping costs within acceptable limits.

The limits will usually be the standard cost or target cost limits set out in the formal operational plan or budget. If actual costs differ from planned costs by a significant amount, cost control action will be necessary.

You might like to think of cost control as an exercise in good housekeeping; the wasteful use of valuable resources is avoided and efficiency and cost consciousness are encouraged.

Cost reduction, in contrast, **starts with an assumption that current cost levels**, or planned cost levels, **are too high**, even though cost control might be good and efficiency levels high.

Cost reduction is a planned and positive approach to reducing expenditure.

Cost control action ought to lead to a reduction in excessive spending. A **cost reduction programme**, on the other hand, **aims to reduce expected cost levels** to below current budgeted or standard levels by changing methods of working.

Cost control aims to reduce costs to budget or standard level, cost reduction aims to reduce costs to below budget or standard level, as budgets and standards do not necessarily reflect the cost and conditions which minimise costs.

2 Planning for cost reduction

> Cost reduction measures ought to be planned programmes to reduce costs rather than crash programmes to cut spending levels.

There are two basic **approaches to cost reduction**.

(a) **Crash programmes to cut spending levels**

If an organisation is having problems with its profitability or cash flow, the management might decide **on an immediate programme to reduce spending**. Some current projects might be abandoned, capital expenditures deferred, employees made redundant or new recruitment stopped. The absence of careful planning might make such crash programmes look like panic measures. Poorly-planned crash programmes to reduce costs could result in reductions in operational efficiency. For example, decisions by a company to reduce the size of its legal department or its internal audit section might cut staff costs in the short term but increase costs in the longer term.

(b)   **Planned programmes to reduce costs**

Many companies tend to introduce crash programmes for cost reduction in times of crisis and ignore the problem completely in times of prosperity. A far better approach is to have **continual assessments** of the organisation's products, production methods, services, internal administration systems and so on.

Cost reduction exercises should therefore be **planned** campaigns to cut expenditure; they should **preferably be continuous** and long-term, so that short-term cost reductions are not soon reversed and 'forgotten'.

Difficulties introducing cost reduction programmes

(a)   There may be **resistance from employees** to the pressure to reduce costs. They may feel threatened by the change. The purpose and scope of the campaign should be fully explained to employees to reduce uncertainty and (hopefully) resistance.

(b)   The programme may be limited to a small area of the business with the result that **costs are reduced in one cost centre, only to reappear as an extra cost in another cost centre**.

(c)   Cost reduction campaigns are **often introduced as a rushed, desperate measure** instead of a carefully organised, well thought-out exercise.

Cost reduction does not happen of its own accord. **Managers must make positive decisions to reduce costs.**

(a)   A planned programme of cost reduction must begin with the assumption that some costs can be significantly reduced. The benefits of cost savings must be worthwhile, and should exceed the costs of achieving them.

(b)   Areas for potential cost reduction should be investigated, and unnecessary costs identified.

(c)   Cost reduction measures should be proposed, agreed, implemented and then monitored.

QUESTION

Cost reduction

Before looking for ways in which costs can be reduced it is useful to consider the reasons why unnecessary costs occur. Can you think of any examples?

ANSWER

Here are some thoughts. You may well have come up with different ideas.

(a)   Lack of information, for example about new materials, products or processes

(b)   Lack of ideas

(c)   Genuine but incorrect beliefs, for example the belief that quantities are too small to justify mass production techniques

(d)   Changed circumstances, for example a failure to take advantage of better processes that are now available

3   The scope of cost reduction campaigns

The scope of a cost reduction **campaign should embrace the activities of the entire company.** In a manufacturing company this would span purchasing and distribution levels within the organisation from the shop floor upwards. Non-manufacturing industries and public sector organisations should equally look at **all areas** of their activities.

A cost reduction campaign should have a **long-term aim as well as short-term objectives.**

(a)   In the short term only variable costs, for the most part, are susceptible to cost reduction efforts. Many fixed costs (for example rent) are not easily changed.

(b)   Some fixed costs are avoidable in the short term (for example advertising or sales promotion expenditure). These are called *discretionary fixed costs*.

(c)   In the long term most costs can be either reduced or avoided. This includes fixed cost as well as variable cost expenditure items.

4   Methods of cost reduction: improving efficiency

One way of reducing costs is to improve the efficiency of materials usage, the productivity of labour or the efficiency of machinery or other equipment.

One way of reducing costs is to improve the efficiency of material usage, the productivity of labour, or the efficiency of machinery or other equipment. There are several ways in which this might be done.

Improved materials usage might be achieved by reducing levels of wastage, where wastage is currently high.

QUESTION   Reducing wastage

How can wastage be reduced?

ANSWER

Here are some suggestions.

(a)   Changing the specifications for cutting solid materials.

(b)   Introducing new equipment that reduces wastage in processing or handling materials.

(c)   Identifying poor quality output at an earlier stage in the operational processes.

(d)   Using better quality materials. Even though more expensive, better quality materials might save costs because they are less likely to tear or might last longer.

Improving labour productivity

(a)   Giving pay incentives for better productivity.

(b)   Changing work methods to eliminate unnecessary procedures and make better use of labour time.

(c)   Improving the methods for achieving co-operation between groups or departments.

(d)   Setting more challenging standards of efficiency. Standards should be tight but achievable. If efficiency standards are too lax, it is likely that the work force will put in the minimum effort needed to achieve the required standard. Given the right motivation among the work force, more challenging standards will encourage greater effort.

(e)   Introducing standards where they did not exist before.

Improving the efficiency of equipment usage

(a)   Making better use of equipment resources. For example, if an office PC is only in use for 50% of its available time, it might be possible to put another application on to it, and so improve office productivity.

(b)   Achieving a better balance between preventive maintenance and machine 'down-time' for repairs.

QUESTION
Improving efficiency

A machine may be maintained at one of three levels, 1, 2 and 3. The monthly costs of the maintenance work, and the monthly hours of production lost, are as follows.

Level	Maintenance cost $	Hours lost (cost $350/hour)
1	4,000	14
2	5,200	10
3	6,700	6

Required

Determine which level of maintenance should be chosen.

ANSWER

Level	Maintenance cost $	Cost of hours lost $	Total cost $
1	4,000	4,900	8,900
2	5,200	3,500	8,700
3	6,700	2,100	8,800

Level 2 should be chosen, to give the lowest total monthly cost.

Once improved standards of efficiency have been set, as a means of reducing costs, it is important that cost *control* should be applied by management.

5 Methods of cost reduction: material costs

Materials costs can be reduced by attacking the costs of wastage. Other ways of reducing materials costs are as follows.

(a) A company could **obtain lower prices for purchases** of materials and components. Bulk purchase discounts might be obtainable. Alternatively, a more cost-conscious approach to buying, with a system of putting all major purchase contracts out to tender, might help to reduce prices.

(b) A company could **improve stores control and cut stores costs**. You should be aware of the **concept of the economic ordering quantity**, which is the size of order that will minimise the combined costs of ordering items for inventory and stockholding costs. Stockholding costs might be reduced by dealing with problems of obsolescence, deterioration of items in store or theft.

(c) It might be possible to **use alternative materials**. Cheaper substitute materials might be available.

QUESTION
Material cost reduction

Standardisation of parts and components might offer enormous cost reduction potential for some manufacturing industries. Can you think why this might be the case?

ANSWER

(a) If a manufacturer has fewer types of components to manufacture, he will be able to increase the length of production runs, and so reduce production costs. Non-standard parts tend to be produced in small runs, and unit costs will be higher as a consequence.

(b) Standardisation helps to cut purchasing cost for the following reasons.

(i) There are fewer items to buy and inventory. The company can purchase in bulk, and so perhaps obtain bulk purchase discounts.

(ii) It may be possible to buy standard parts from more than one supplier, and so purchasing will be more competitive.

6 Methods of cost reduction: labour costs

Work study is a means of raising the productivity of an operating unit by the reorganisation of work. There are two main parts to work study: **method study** and **work measurement**.

Organisation and methods (O & M) is a term for techniques, including method study and work measurement, that are used in examining clerical, administrative and management procedures in order to make improvements.

Methods of reducing labour costs	Detail
Improving efficiency or productivity	
Changing the methods of work	A work study or O & M programme (see below) might be set up to look for cost savings from improved work methods.
Replacing people with machinery	The substitution of labour by automatic equipment can reduce costs substantially.

6.1 Work study

Work study is a means of raising the production efficiency (productivity) of an operating unit by the reorganisation of work. There are two main parts to work study: method study and work measurement.

Method study is the systematic recording and critical examination of existing and proposed ways of doing work in order to develop and apply easier and more effective methods, and reduce costs.

Work measurement involves establishing the time for a qualified worker to carry out a specified job at a specified level of performance

Main objectives of a work study

(a) The analysis, design and improvement of work systems, work places and work methods

(b) The establishment of **standards** enable an organisation to determine labour and equipment requirements, assess performance, plan operations, cost operations and products and calculate realistic wage levels.

(c) The development and application of job evaluation schemes based on job descriptions

(d) The specification of plant facilities, layout and space utilisation

(e) The assessment of the most profitable alternative combinations of personnel, materials and equipment

(f) The development of procedures for the planning and control of work and material usage

(g) The development of procedures for presenting information to management about work performance

The use of work study has grown rapidly over the past decade. Why?

(a) Tangible results are produced quickly
(b) No large capital outlay is required
(c) It is, in its basic form, simple and readily grasped in outline, by all
(d) The facts it produces can be used to increase efficiency throughout the organisation
(e) There is no work to which it cannot be applied

The obvious application of work study is in production where it was first developed, but the technique is now applied in such industries as building and construction, agriculture, transport, hospitals, national and local government and service industries.

Direct observation methods of work study involve observing jobs in practice, but **synthetic methods** are used to estimate the work of work study content of jobs without having to observe them. An example of a synthetic method is a 'tick sheet' that a customer service person ticks after each customer is served.

6.2 Organisation and methods (O & M)

Organisation and methods (O&M) is a term for techniques, including method study and work measurement, that are used to examine clerical, administrative and management procedures in order to make improvements.

O & M is **primarily concerned with office work** and looks in particular at areas such as the following.

(a) Organisation
(b) Duties
(c) Staffing
(d) Office layout
(e) Methods of procedure and documentation and the design of forms
(f) Office mechanisation

Work study and O & M are perhaps associated in your mind with establishing standard times for work, but remember that the real aim is to decide the **most efficient methods** of getting work done, as well as establishing standard times for work done by this method. More efficient methods and tighter standards will improve efficiency and productivity, and so reduce costs.

QUESTION
O&M

Do you think a work study or O&M programme would discover any ways in which the work methods you use could be improved so as to reduce costs?

7 Other aspects of cost reduction

7.1 Finance costs

Finance costs might offer some scope for savings.

(a) There might be a finance cost in taking credit from suppliers, in the form of an **opportunity cost of failing to take advantage of discounts for early payment** that suppliers might be offering.

(b) Similarly, a company should give some thought to the credit terms it offers to customers. Finance tied up in working capital involves a cost. (This might be the interest charges on a bank overdraft, the cost of borrowing long-term finance, or the opportunity cost of the capital tied up.) Costs might be reduced by **reassessing policies for offering early payment discounts** to credit customers.

(c) A company might wish to reassess its sources of finance. **Is it borrowing at the lowest obtainable rates**?

(d) Savings might be achievable from **improved foreign exchange dealings**, for companies involved in buying and selling abroad.

7.2 Rationalisation

Where organisations grow, especially by means of mergers and takeovers, there is a tendency for work to be duplicated in different parts of the organisation. Two or three factories, for example, might make the same product, when it would be more economical to concentrate all production in one factory. The **elimination of unnecessary duplication and the concentration of resources** is a form of rationalisation. The end result of such rationalisation is therefore to reduce costs through greater efficiency.

7.3 Expense items

Expense items, other than materials and labour, may be a significant part of total costs, and these too should be controlled. Examples are as follows.

(a)   **Capital expenditure proposals should be carefully evaluated.**

(b)   Management should **continually question** the need for any cost item.

(c)   Consultancy organisations may be used to advise companies how to reduce specialised expense items such as information technology (IT).

7.4 Control over spending decisions

Cost reduction might be achieved if improved control over spending decisions is achieved. Often, costly spending decisions are taken by managers without proper consideration of the long-term cost.

Authority for different types of spending is usually given to management at various levels in the hierarchy, depending on the nature of the cost. Consider the following example.

Nature of cost	Authorised by	Based on a cost of	Ten year cost
Purchase of equipment for $200,000: ten year life	Board	$200,000	$200,000
Hire of office manager; salary $20,000	Director	$20,000	$200,000
Hire of two secretaries; wages $200 per week each	Office Manager	$200/week each	$200,000
Wage deal, 100 employees getting an extra $400 a year	?	$40,000	$400,000

In the example the hire of two secretaries is as costly as the purchase of the equipment, yet the level of control is lower. It would make more sense for the hire of the secretaries to require the higher level of authorisation. The hire of labour is in many ways a more permanent investment than buying equipment. Machinery can be sold, but it is much more difficult to reduce staffing levels.

QUESTION
Spending decisions

Find out who makes the spending decisions in your organisation. Are office managers able to commit your organisation to potentially high levels of spending over the long-term, as in the example above?

---

8   Value analysis

Value analysis is a planned, scientific approach to cost reduction, which reviews the material composition of a product and the product's design so that modifications and improvements can be made which do not reduce the value of the product to the customer or user.

Value engineering is the application of similar techniques to new products.

Value analysis considers four aspects of value: **cost value, exchange value, use value** and **esteem value**.

An approach to cost reduction, which embraces many of the techniques already mentioned, is value analysis (VA) and value engineering.

Value analysis is a planned, scientific approach to cost reduction, which reviews the material composition of a product and the product's design so that modifications and improvements can be made which do not reduce the value of the product to the customer or the user.

The **value of the product must therefore be kept the same or else improved, at a reduced cost.** The administration of a value analysis exercise should perhaps be the responsibility of a cost reduction committee.

Value engineering is the application of value analysis techniques to new products, so that new products are designed and developed to a given value at minimum cost.

8.1 What is different about value analysis?

Two features of value analysis distinguish it from other approaches to cost reduction.

(a)   It encourages innovation and a more radical outlook for ways of reducing costs.

(b)   It recognises the various types of value which a product or service provides, analyses this value, and then seeks ways of improving or maintaining aspects of this value at a lower cost. Other techniques often ignores this value aspect.

Not every exercise in value analysis results in suggestions for radically different ways of making a product or service. But value analysis can result in radical ideas for change, because ideas for cost reduction are not constrained by the existing product design.

Conventional cost reduction techniques try to achieve the lowest production costs for a specific product design whereas value analysis recognises that the real goal should be the least-cost method of making a product that achieves its desired function, not the least-cost method of accomplishing a product design to a mandatory and detailed specification.

8.2 Value

Four aspects of 'value' should be considered.

Cost value is the cost of producing and selling an item.

Exchange value is the market value of the product or service.

Use value is what the article does, the purposes it fulfils.

Esteem value is the prestige the customer attaches to the product.

(a)   Value analysis seeks to reduce unit costs, and so cost value is the one aspect of value to be reduced.

(b)   Value analysis attempts to provide the same (or a better) use value at the lowest cost. Use value therefore involves considerations of the performance and reliability of the product or service.

(c)   Value analysis attempts to maintain or enhance the esteem value of a product at the lowest cost.

QUESTION   Value analysis

Classify the following features of a product, using the types of value set out above.

(a)   The product can be sold for $27.50.
(b)   The product is available in six colours to suit customers' tastes.
(c)   The product will last for at least ten years.

ANSWER

(a)   Exchange value
(b)   Esteem value
(c)   Use value

Value analysis involves the **systematic investigation of every source of cost and technique** of production with the aim of cutting all unnecessary costs. An unnecessary cost is an additional cost incurred without adding use, exchange or esteem value to a product.

There might be a **conflict between reducing costs and maintaining the aesthetic value** (esteem value) of a product. Whereas a value analysis exercise should not result in a sacrifice of the product's function in order to cut costs, it might result in a product that is not as pleasing aesthetically. Where cost cutting and aesthetics are incompatible, there should **be a clear direction from senior management** about which is more important.

9 The scope of value analysis

Value analysis concentrates on product design, components, material costs and production methods.

Any commercial organisation should be continually seeking lower costs, better products and higher profits. These can be achieved in any of the following ways.

(a) Cost elimination or cost prevention
(b) Cost reduction
(c) Improving product quality and so selling greater quantities at the same price as before
(d) Improving product quality and so being able to increase the sales price

Value analysis can achieve all four of these objectives.

QUESTION   Benefits of VA

What are the other possible benefits of a VA programme?

ANSWER

(a) Improved product performance and product reliability
(b) Improved product quality
(c) An increased product life, in terms of both the marketable life of the product (for the company) and the usable life of each product unit (for the customer)
(d) Possibly, shorter delivery 'lead times' to customers because of a shorter production cycle
(e) The increased use of standardisation (standard parts and components) which contributes to lower costs for the customer
(f) A more economic use of scarce resources
(g) Encouraging employees to show innovation and creative ideas

Three areas of special importance are as follows.

Area	Method
Product design	At the **design stage** value analysis is called **value engineering**. The designer should be cost conscious and avoid unnecessary complications. **Simple product design** can avoid production and quality control problems, thereby resulting in lower costs.
Components and material costs	The purchasing department should beware of lapsing into habit with routine buying decisions. Buyers ought to be **fully aware** of technology changes, and significant changes in material prices that new technology creates. The purchasing department has a crucial role to play in reducing costs and improving value by obtaining the desired quality materials at the lowest possible price.
Production methods	These ought to be reviewed continually, on a product-by-product basis, especially with changing technology.

10 Carrying out a value analysis

The steps in a value analysis study are as follows.

- – Select a product or service for investigation.
- – Obtain and record information about it.
- – Evaluate the product.
- – Consider alternatives.
- – Select the least-cost alternative.
- – Make a recommendation.
- – If accepted, implement the recommendation.
- – After a period, evaluate the outcome and measure the cost savings.

Typical considerations in value analysis

(a) **Can a cheaper substitute material be found** which is as good, if not better, than the material currently used?

(b) **Can unnecessary weight or embellishments be removed** without reducing the product's desirability?

(c) **Is it possible to use standardised components** thereby reducing the variety of units used and produced? Variety reduction through standardisation facilitates longer production runs at lower unit costs.

(d) **Is it possible to reduce the number of components,** for example could a product be assembled safely with a smaller number of screws?

The origins of value analysis were in the engineering industry, but its principles and applications spread much wider. **Value analysis can be applied to services, or aspects of office work, or to management information systems** (for example the value of information, reports and so on).

10.1 The steps in value analysis

A value analysis study should be carried out by a team of experts, preferably with **varying backgrounds**, which blends experience, skill and imagination. A team will typically consist of three to seven members who collectively possess the necessary skills to examine the product, service or operation.

Value analysis should be an **inter-disciplinary exercise**, and ought to involve a management accountant but also managers concerned with method study and work measurement, estimating, engineering, planning, production, purchasing and marketing. Other experts might be called on to contribute to the team's work.

Steps in value analysis

Step 1	**Selecting a product or service for study**. The product selected should be one which accounts for a high proportion of the organisation's costs, since the **greatest cost savings should be obtainable from high cost areas**. The choice should also take into account the expected future life of the product and the stage of its 'life cycle' that it has reached. A product reaching the end of its marketable life is unlikely to offer scope for substantial savings, unless cost reduction measures would also extend the product's life.
Step 2	**Obtaining and recording information**. The questions to be asked include: What is the product or service supposed to do? Does it succeed? What are the costs of the product or service? Are there alternative ways of making or providing it? What do these alternatives cost?
Step 3	**Analysing the information and evaluating the product**. Each aspect of the product or service. Any cost reductions should be achieved without the loss of use or esteem value. (Or at least, cost savings must exceed any loss in value suffered.) The type of questions

to be asked and answered in the analysis stage are as follows.

- (a) Are all the parts necessary?
- (b) Can the parts be obtained or made at a lower cost?
- (c) Can standardised parts be used?
- (d) Are all the features of the product or service necessary?
- (e) Can any of the features be incorporated at a lower cost?
- (f) Does the value provided by each feature justify its cost?
- (g) Can the product be made or the service performed at a lower cost?

Step 4   **Considering alternatives**. From the analysis, a variety of options can be devised. This is the **'new ideas' stage** of the study, and alternative options would mix ideas for eliminating unnecessary parts or features, combining several features into one, standardising certain components or features, or introducing new methods of operation or new sources of supply (for example external purchase of components instead of in-house manufacture). New advances in technology might be considered, and a creative approach should underlie this phase of the exercise.

Step 5   **Selection of the least cost alternative**. The evaluation of each alternative should be recorded, and costs (and other aspects of value) compared.

Step 6   **Recommendation**. The **preferred alternative** should then be recommended to the decision makers for approval. The VA team itself will not have the authority to decide whether or not a cost reduction proposal should be implemented.

Step 7   **Implementation and follow-up**. Once a value analysis proposal is approved and accepted, its **implementation must be properly planned and co-ordinated**. The VA team should review the implementation and, where appropriate, improve the new product or method in the light of practical experience.

To be successful, **value analysis programmes must have the full backing of senior management**. Management must therefore do the following.

- (a) Give the VA programme their visible **support**, for example acting as a member of a VA steering group, attending VA training sessions and so on.

- (b) **Establish goals** for the programme to achieve.

- (c) **Select the personnel** for the value analysis team and establish a VA 'organisation' within the company.

- (d) Give the VA programme a **sufficient budget** to carry out its work properly.

- (e) Insist on a **continuing audit** of the achievements of the VA programme.

- (f) Give **rewards** to individuals and groups for outstanding achievements.

CHAPTER ROUNDUP

↳ **Cost reduction** is a planned and positive approach to reducing expenditure.

↳ Cost reduction measures ought to be planned programmes to reduce costs rather than crash programmes to cut spending levels.

↳ One way of reducing costs is to improve the efficiency of materials usage, the productivity of labour or the efficiency of machinery or other equipment.

↳ **Work study** is a means of raising the productivity of an operating unit by the reorganisation of work. There are two main parts to work study: **method study** and **work measurement**.

↳ **Organisation and methods (O & M)** is a term for techniques, including method study and work measurement, that are used in examining clerical, administrative and management procedures in order to make improvements.

↳ **Value analysis** is a planned, scientific approach to cost reduction, which reviews the material composition of a product and the product's design so that modifications and improvements can be made which do not reduce the value of the product to the customer or user.

↳ **Value engineering** is the application of similar techniques to new products.

↳ **Value analysis** considers four aspects of value: **cost value, exchange value, use value** and **esteem value**.

↳ Value analysis concentrates on product design, components, material costs and production methods.

↳ The steps in a value analysis study are as follows.

   – Select a product or service for investigation.
   – Obtain and record information about it.
   – Evaluate the product.
   – Consider alternatives.
   – Select the least-cost alternative.
   – Make a recommendation.
   – If accepted, implement the recommendation.
   – After a period, evaluate the outcome and measure the cost savings.

QUICK QUIZ

1   What are the main difficulties of introducing cost reduction programmes?

2   Suggest five ways in which labour productivity might be improved.

3   What is method study?

4   In which areas of office work might an O & M study be applied?

5   Define the four aspects of value to be considered in a value analysis exercise.

6   *Choose the correct words from those highlighted*

    Value **engineering/analysis** is cost avoidance or cost prevention before production whereas value **engineering/analysis** is cost reduction during production.

1   The major difficulties with introducing cost reduction programmes are as follows.

(a)   There may be resistance from employees to the pressure to reduce costs, usually because the nature and purpose of the campaign has not been properly explained to them, and because they feel threatened by the change.

(b)   The programme may be limited to a small area of the business with the result that costs are reduced in one cost centre, only to reappear as an extra cost in another cost centre.

(c)   Cost reduction campaigns are often introduced as a rushed, desperate measure instead of a carefully organised, well thought-out exercise.

2   Labour productivity might be improved by the following methods.

(a)   Giving pay incentives for better productivity.

(b)   Changing work methods to eliminate unnecessary procedures and make better use of labour time.

(c)   Improving the methods for achieving co-operation between groups or departments.

(d)   Setting more challenging standards of efficiency to aim for. Given the right motivation among the work force, more challenging standards will encourage greater effort.

(e)   Introducing standards where they did not exist before.

3   Method study is the systematic recording and critical examination of existing and proposed ways of doing work in order to develop and apply easier and more effective methods, and reduce costs.

4   (a)   Organisation
(b)   Duties
(c)   Staffing
(d)   Office layout
(e)   Methods of procedure and documentation and the design of forms
(f)   Office mechanisation

5   (a)   *Cost value* is the cost of producing and selling an item.
(b)   *Exchange value* is the market value of the product or service.
(c)   *Use value* is what the article does, the purposes it fulfils.
(d)   *Esteem value* is the prestige the customer attaches to the product.

6   **Value engineering, value analysis**

Now try ...

Attempt the questions below from the **Exam Question Bank**

Number

Q110 – Q112

Exam question and answer bank

1 Accounting for management

1   Which of the following statements is false?

    A   Management accounts detail the performance of an organisation over a defined period and the state of affairs at the end of that period

    B   There is no legal requirement to prepare management accounts

    C   Limited liability companies must prepare financial accounts

    D   The format of management accounts is entirely at management discretion   **(2 marks)**

2   Diane carries out routine processing of invoices in the purchasing department of L Co. Joanne is Diane's supervisor. Lesley is trying to decide how many staff will be needed if some proposed new technology is implemented. Tracey is considering the new work that L Co will be able to offer and the new markets it could enter, once the new technology is well established.

    Which member of L Co carries out tactical activities?

    A   Diane
    B   Joanne
    C   Lesley
    D   Tracey   **(2 marks)**

3   Which of the following statements is false?

    A   Financial accounting information can be used for internal reporting purposes

    B   Routine information can be used to make decisions regarding both the long term and the short term

    C   Management accounting provides information relevant to decision making, planning, control and evaluation of performances

    D   Cost accounting can only be used to provide inventory valuations for internal reporting   **(2 marks)**

4   Which of the following is not part of the planning stage in the decision-making process?

    A   Deciding on the optimal way in which an objective might be achieved

    B   Identifying ways which might contribute to the achievement of specified objectives

    C   Obtaining data about actual results

    D   Identifying goals or objectives   **(2 marks)**

2 Sources of data

5   A company which makes rechargeable batteries selects some of the batteries for examination. The procedure used chooses two random numbers, say n and m. Starting at the nth battery, every battery at an interval of m is then chosen for examination.

    This type of sampling is known as:

    A   Stratified
    B   Systematic
    C   Random
    D   Multistage   **(2 marks)**

6   Which of the following statements about stratification is/are true?

    I   The sample selected will be representative of the population

    II   The structure of the sample will reflect that of the population if the same proportion of individuals is chosen from each stratum

    III   It requires prior knowledge of each item in the population

A	I and III only	C	II and III only	
B	I, II and III	D	III only	**(2 marks)**

7   Which of the following is an example of discrete data from a primary source?

A   A report in a newspaper giving retail sales for the month
B   An eye witness account of the number of customers
C   A website showing the average height for children aged 7
D   A colleague's measurement of the distance from the office to the head office   **(2 marks)**

8   Which of the following is a disadvantage of quota sampling?

A   It is expensive
B   It is administratively complicated
C   A sampling frame is necessary
D   It can result in certain biases   **(2 marks)**

9   A survey of heights of lampposts is carried out to find out if there is any variation across the country.

What sort of data is being collected in such a survey?

A	Quantitative	Discrete	
B	Qualitative	Discrete	
C	Quantitative	Continuous	
D	Qualitative	Continuous	**(2 marks)**

3   Cost classification

10   Which of the following items might be a suitable cost unit within the accounts payable department of a company?

(i)   Postage cost   (iii)   Supplier account
(ii)   Invoice processed

A	Item (i) only	C	Item (iii) only	
B	Item (ii) only	D	Items (ii) and (iii) only	**(2 marks)**

11   Which of the following are direct expenses?

(i)   The cost of special designs, drawing or layouts
(ii)   The hire of tools or equipment for a particular job
(iii)   Salesman's wages
(iv)   Rent, rates and insurance of a factory

A	(i) and (ii)	C	(i) and (iv)	
B	(i) and (iii)	D	(iii) and (iv)	**(2 marks)**

12   Which of the following would be appropriate cost units for a passenger coach company?

		Appropriate	Not appropriate
(a)	Passenger/kilometre		
(b)	Vehicle per kilometre		
(c)	Fixed cost per kilometre		

(2 marks)

13   A cost which contains both fixed and variable elements, and so is partly affected by changes in the level of activity, is called

A	A direct cost	C	An unavoidable cost	
B	A semi-variable cost	D	A prime cost	

(2 marks)

14   A company employs three drivers to deliver goods to its customers. The salaries paid to these drivers are:

A   A part of prime cost
B   A direct production expense
C   A production overhead
D   A selling and distribution overhead   **(2 marks)**

4   Cost behaviour

15   Variable costs are conventionally deemed to

A   be constant per unit of output
B   vary per unit of output as production volume changes
C   be constant in total when production volume changes
D   vary in total from period to period when production is constant   **(2 marks)**

16   The following is a graph of total cost against level of activity.

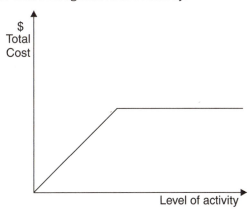

To which one of the following costs does the graph correspond?

A   Photocopier rental costs, where a fixed rental is payable up to a certain number of copies each period. If the number of copies exceeds this amount, a constant charge per copy is made for all subsequent copies during that period.

B   Vehicle hire costs, where a constant rate is charged per mile travelled, up to a maximum monthly payment regardless of the miles travelled.

C   Supervisor salary costs, where one supervisor is needed for every five employees added to the staff.

D   The cost of direct materials, where the unit rate per kg purchased reduces when the level of purchases reaches a certain amount.   **(2 marks)**

17   Identify which type of cost is being described in (a)-(d) below.

VARIABLE COST	FIXED COST	STEPPED FIXED COST	SEMI-VARIABLE COST

(a)   This type of cost stays the same, no matter how many units you produce

(b)   This type of cost increases as you produce more units. The sum of these costs are also known as the marginal cost of a unit

(c)   This type of cost is fixed but only within certain levels of activity

(d)   This type of cost contains both fixed and variable elements

(2 marks)

18   At the beginning of the year, Bob Co enters into a rental agreement with a landlord who is entitled, under the terms of the agreement, to change the rent (either upwards or downwards) according to economic conditions. Bob Co cannot cancel the agreement during the first six months.

For the first six months of the agreement, Bob Co could classify the rent as a

A   Fixed cost   C   Semi-variable cost
B   Avoidable cost   D   Uncontrollable cost   **(2 marks)**

19   Brady Co is a painting and decorating company. The following information is available for two periods:

	Period 1	Period 2
Square metres decorated	10,000	14,000
Total cost	$44,000	$56,000

When more than 12,000 square metres are decorated, the fixed costs increase by $6,000.

The total cost for period 3 if 15,500 square metres are decorated is $ ⬚   **(2 marks)**

5 Presenting information

20   The costs of materials for product B are made up as follows.

Material P: $1,000

Material Q: $600

Material R: $1,025

Material S: $375

If the material proportions were displayed on a pie chart, how many degrees would material Q represent?

A   72 degrees   C   144 degrees
B   120 degrees   D   204 degrees   **(2 marks)**

21   The following table shows the typical salary of part qualified accountants in five different regions of Flatland

Area	Salary
	$
Southeast	21,500
Midlands	20,800
Northeast	18,200
Northwest	17,500
Southwest	16,700

The best diagram to draw to highlight the differences between areas is

A   A pie diagram   C   A percentage component bar chart
B   A line graph   D   A simple bar chart   **(2 marks)**

22   You have just calculated for the last two six-monthly periods, the running costs of a factory, broken down into five categories. You are using a computer package which can produce radar charts, pie-charts, time series graphs and scatter diagrams, amongst others. The graphics to illustrate best the relative sizes of the cost categories in this situation will be

A   Line graphs   C   Radar charts
B   Pie charts   D   Scatter diagrams   **(2 marks)**

6 Material costs

23 The following data relates to an item of raw material

Unit cost of raw material	$20
Usage per week	250 units
Cost of ordering material, per order	$400
Annual cost of holding inventory, as a % of cost	10%
Number of weeks in a year	48

What is the economic order quantity, to the nearest unit?

A	316 units	C	1,549 units	
B	693 units	D	2,191 units	**(2 marks)**

24 The following data relates to the material control account of Duckboard Co, a manufacturing company, for the month of October.

	$
Opening inventory	18,500
Closing inventory	16,100
Deliveries from suppliers	142,000
Returns to suppliers	2,300
Cost of indirect materials issued	25,200

How would the issue of direct materials have been recorded in the cost accounts?

			$	$
A	*Debit*	Material control account	119,200	
	Credit	Work in progress control account		119,200
B	*Debit*	Work in progress control account	119,200	
	Credit	Material control account		119,200
C	*Debit*	Material control account	116,900	
	Credit	Work in progress control account		116,900
D	*Debit*	Work in progress control account	116,900	
	Credit	Material control account		116,900

(2 marks)

25 Bovver Co manufactures one product (the Tate). The following information relates to the Tate:

EOQ	6,000 units
Average usage	150 units per day
Minimum usage	90 units per day
Maximum usage	195 units per day
Lead time	25 – 30 days

The maximum inventory level is [   ] units. **(2 marks)**

Questions 26 and 27 are based on the following data

Date		Units	Unit Price $	Value $
1 Jan	Balance b/f	100	5.00	500.00
3 Mar	Issue	40		
4 June	Receipt	50	5.50	275.00
6 June	Receipt	50	6.00	300.00
9 Sept	Issue	70		

26 If the first-in, first-out method of pricing had been used the value of the issue on 9 September would have been:

A	$350	B	$355	C	$395	D	$420	

(2 marks)

27   If the last-in, first-out method of pricing had been used the value of the issue on 9 September would have been:

A $350   B $395   C $410   D $420

(2 marks)

28   Harry P Co uses 62,500 units of material HP at an even rate during the year. Each order placed with the supplier of the units is for 5,000 units, which is the EOQ. The company holds buffer inventory of 1,250 units. The annual cost of holding one unit in inventory is $5.

What is the total annual cost of holding inventory of the unit?

A $12,500   B $15,625   C $18,750   D $25,000

(2 marks)

7   Accounting for labour

29   Gross wages incurred in department 1 in June were $54,000. The wages analysis shows the following summary breakdown of the gross pay. Overtime was worked to catch up on a backlog after several employees were off sick.

	Paid to direct labour $	Paid to indirect labour $
Ordinary time	25,185	11,900
Overtime: basic pay	5,440	3,500
premium	1,360	875
Shift allowance	2,700	1,360
Sick pay	1,380	300
	36,065	17,935

What is the direct wages cost for department 1 in June?

A $25,185   C $34,685
B $30,625   D $36,065   **(2 marks)**

30   The wages control account for A Co for February is shown below.

WAGES CONTROL ACCOUNT

	$		$
Bank	128,400	Work in progress control	79,400
Balance c/d	12,000	Production overhead control	61,000
	140,400		140,400
		Balance b/d	12,000

Which of the following statements about wages for February is *not* correct?

A   Wages paid during February amounted to $128,400
B   Wages for February were prepaid by $12,000
C   Direct wages cost incurred during February amounted to $79,400
D   Indirect wages cost incurred during February amounted to $61,000   **(2 marks)**

The following information relates to questions 31 and 32.

Slocombe Co budgeted to produce 10,000 units of its product (the Brahms) in the budgeted time of 50,000 hours. During the period the company produced 12,500 units in a total time of 68,750 hours.

31   The capacity ratio for the period was [   ] %   (work to one decimal place).

(2 marks)

32   The production volume ratio for the period was [   ] %   (work to one decimal place).

(2 marks)

33   A company had 500 workers at the beginning of a period. During the period, 70 workers left the company for various reasons and 46 new workers were employed.

What is the labour turnover rate for the period (to the nearest %)?

The labour turnover rate for the period is ☐ %

(2 marks)

34   An employee is paid on a piecework basis. The basis of the piecework scheme is as follows:

1 to 100 units   – $0.25 per unit

101 to 200 units – $0.35 per unit

201 to 299 units – $0.45 per unit

with only the additional units qualifying for the higher rates. Rejected units do not qualify for payment.

During a particular day the employee produced 250 units of which 31 were rejected as faulty.

What did the employee earn for their day's work?

A $68.55
B $82.50
C $98.55
D $112.50   **(2 marks)**

8   Accounting for overheads

Questions 35 and 36 are based on the following data

A company absorbs overheads based on labour hours. Data for the latest period are as follows.

Budgeted labour hours	8,500
Budgeted overheads	$148,750
Actual labour hours	7,928
Actual overheads	$146,200

35   Based on the data given above, what is the labour hour overhead absorption rate?

A $17.20 per hour   C $18.44 per hour
B $17.50 per hour   D $18.76 per hour   **(2 marks)**

36   Based on the data given above, what is the amount of under-/over-absorbed overhead?

A $2,550 under-absorbed overhead   C $7,460 over-absorbed overhead
B $2,550 over-absorbed overhead   D $7,460 under-absorbed overhead   **(2 marks)**

37   The budgeted production overheads and other budget data of Eiffel Co are as follows.

Budget	Production dept X
Overhead cost	$36,000
Direct materials cost	$32,000
Direct labour cost	$40,000
Machine hours	10,000
Direct labour hours	18,000

What would be the absorption rate for Department X using the various bases of apportionment?

(a)   % of direct material cost =   ☐

(b)   % of direct labour cost =   ☐

(c)   % of total direct cost =   ☐

(d)   Rate per machine hour =   ☐

(e)   Rate per direct labour hour = [   ]   **(2 marks)**

38   Factory overheads can be absorbed by which of the following methods?

(i)   Direct labour hours
(ii)   Machine hours
(iii)   As a % of prime cost
(iv) $x per unit

A   (i), (ii), (iii) or (iv)
B   (i) or (ii) only
C   (i), (ii) or (iii) only
D   (ii), (iii) or (iv) only   **(2 marks)**

39   Which of the following would be the most appropriate basis for apportioning machinery insurance costs to cost centres within a factory?

A   The number of machines in each cost centre
B   The floor area occupied by the machinery in each cost centre
C   The value of the machinery in each cost centre
D   The operating hours of the machinery in each cost centre   **(2 marks)**

40   A factory consists of two production cost centres (A and B) and two service cost centres (C and D). The total allocated and apportioned overhead for each is as follows:

A	B	C	D
$95,000	$82,000	$46,000	$30,000

It has been estimated that each service cost centre does work for the other cost centres in the following proportions:

	A	B	C	D
Percentage of service cost centre X to	40	40	–	20
Percentage of service cost centre Y to	30	60	10	–

After the reapportionment of service cost centre costs has been carried out using a method that fully recognises the reciprocal service arrangements in the factory, what is the total overhead for production cost centre A?

A $122,400
B $124,716
C $126,000
D $127,000

9   Absorption and marginal costing

41   The overhead absorption rate for product Y is $2.50 per direct labour hour. Each unit of Y requires 3 direct labour hours. Inventory of product Y at the beginning of the month was 200 units and at the end of the month was 250 units. What is the difference in the profits reported for the month using absorption costing compared with marginal costing?

A   The absorption costing profit would be $375 less
B   The absorption costing profit would be $125 greater
C   The absorption costing profit would be $375 greater
D   The absorption costing profit would be $1,875 greater   **(2 marks)**

42   B Co makes a product which has a variable production cost of $21 per unit and a sales price of $39 per unit. At the beginning of 20X5, there was no opening inventory and sales during the year were 50,000 units. Fixed costs (production, administration, sales and distribution) totalled $328,000. Production was 70,000 units.

The value of closing inventory is $ [   ].   **(2 marks)**

43   Davy Crockett Co makes hats, mainly for fancy dress costumes. The company expected to produce 25,000 hats during the year which would be expected to incur $125,000 in fixed costs.

The total cost of each hat is $30 (including fixed costs) and the company can sell them for $40 each. Sales during the year were 15,000 hats from a production volume of 20,000. Actual fixed costs were $80,000 and there was no opening inventory.

What is the marginal costing net profit for the year? $[   ]   **(2 marks)**

44   HMF Co produces a single product. The budgeted fixed production overheads for the period are $500,000. The budgeted output for the period is 2,500 units. Opening inventory at the start of the period consisted of 900 units and closing inventory at the end of the period consisted of 300 units. Using marginal costing principles the profit was $800,000. If absorption costing principles were applied, what would the profit for the period be?

A $925,000
B $675,000
C $920,000
D $680,000

(2 marks)

45   A company producing a single product reported the following profits.

Basis	Profit
Marginal costing	$100,000
Absorption costing	$110,000

Fixed overheads per unit for the period were $5.

Which of the following statements are true?

(i)   Closing inventory levels are 2,000 units higher than opening inventory
(ii)   Opening inventory levels are 2,000 units higher than closing inventory
(iii)   It is impossible to say whether inventory levels have changed
(iv)   More units were produced than sold during the period

A   (iv) only
B   (ii) and (iv)
C   (iii) only
D   (i) and (iv)   **(2 marks)**

10 Job, batch and service costing

46   In which of the following situation(s) will job costing normally be used?

[   ]   Production is continuous

[   ]   Production of the product can be completed in a single accounting period

[   ]   Production relates to a single special order   **(2 marks)**

47   Consider the following features and identify whether they relate to job costing, contract costing, service costing or none of these costing methods.

J =   Job costing
C =   Contract costing
S =   Service costing
N =   None of these costing methods

(i)   Production is carried out in accordance with the wishes of the customer   [   ]

(ii)   Work is usually of a relatively long duration   [   ]

(iii)   Work is usually undertaken on the contractor's premises   [   ]

(iv)   Costs are averaged over the units produced in the period   [   ]

BPP
LEARNING MEDIA

(v)   It establishes the costs of services rendered

(2 marks)

48   Ali Pali Co is a small jobbing company. Budgeted direct labour hours for the current year were 45,000 hours and budgeted direct wages costs were $180,000.

Job number 34679, a rush job for which overtime had to be worked by skilled employees, had the following production costs.

		$	$
Direct materials			2,000
Direct wages			
Normal rate (400 hrs)		2,000	
Overtime premium		500	
			2,500
Production overhead			4,000
			8,500

Production overhead is based on a direct labour hour rate

If production overhead had been based on a percentage of direct wages costs instead, the production cost of job number 34679 would have been:

A	$5,500	C	$10,250
B	$9,000	D	$10,750

(2 marks)

49   Which of the following is a feature of job costing?

A   Production is carried out in accordance with the wishes of the customer
B   Associated with continuous production of large volumes of low-cost items
C   Establishes the cost of services rendered
D   Use of equivalent units

(2 marks)

11 Process costing

50   A chemical is manufactured in two processes, X and Y. Data for process Y for last month are as follows.

Material transferred from process X	2,000 litres @ $4 per litre
Conversion costs incurred	$12,240
Output transferred to finished goods	1,600 litres

No losses occur in the process.

Closing work in progress is fully complete for material, but is only 50 per cent processed.

What is the value of the closing work in progress (to the nearest $)?

A	$1,360	C	$2,960
B	$2,160	D	$4,320

(2 marks)

51   20,000 litres of liquid were put into a process at the beginning of the month at a cost of $4,400. The output of finished product was 17,000 litres. The normal level of waste in this process is 20% and the waste which is identified at the end of the process can be sold at $0.50 per litre.

What is the abnormal gain or loss and what is the cost per unit?

A   Abnormal gain $1,000, cost per unit $0.15
B   Abnormal loss $1,000, cost per unit $0.15
C   Abnormal loss $1,000, cost per unit $0.28
D   Abnormal gain $1,000, cost per unit $0.28

(2 marks)

52 A food manufacturing process has a normal wastage of 10% of input. In a period, 3,000 kg of material was input and there was an abnormal loss of 75 kg. No inventories are held at the beginning or end of the process.

The quantity of good production achieved was [ ] kg. **(2 marks)**

53 A company makes a product, which passes through a single process.

Details of the process for the last period are as follows.

Materials	5,000 kg at 50c per kg
Labour	$700
Production overheads	200% of labour

Normal losses are 10% of input in the process, and without further processing any losses can be sold as scrap for 20c per kg.

The output for the period was 4,200 kg from the process.

There was no work in progress at the beginning or end of the period.

The value of the abnormal loss for the period is $ [ ] **(2 marks)**

54 In a process account, abnormal losses are valued

A   At good production cost less scrap value
B   At their scrap value
C   The same as good production
D   Nil   **(2 marks)**

12 Process costing, joint products and by-products

55 SH Co manufactures three joint products and one by-product from a single process.

Data for May are as follows.

Opening and closing inventories	Nil
Raw materials input	$90,000
Conversion costs	$70,000

Output

		Units	Sales price $ per unit
Joint product	J	2,500	36
	K	3,500	40
	L	2,000	35
By-product M		4,000	1

By-product sales revenue is credited to the process account. Joint costs are apportioned on a physical units basis.

What were the full production costs of product K in May?

A $45,500   C $68,250
B $46,667   D $70,000   **(2 marks)**

56 Samakand Preparations Co operates a continuous process producing three products and one by-product. Output from the process for one month was as follows.

	Selling price per unit $	Output Units
Joint product		
A	38	20,000
B	54	40,000
C	40	35,000
By-product		
D	4	20,000

Total output costs were $4,040,000.

The saleable value of the by-product is deducted from process costs before apportioning costs to each joint product. Using the sales revenue basis for allocating joint costs, the unit valuation for joint product B was (to 2 decimal places):

A $49.50   C $50.00
B $45.00   D $100.00   (2 marks)

57   Robbie Co manufactures three products in a common process. Details of production and sales for a period are as follows:

Product	Production (units)	Sales (units)	Selling price per unit $
Gary	20,000	18,000	50
Howard	15,000	10,000	40
Jason	10,000	6,000	90

Common costs for the period are $1,500,000.

Using the sales value method, what is the cost allocated to product Howard during the period, assuming that no other costs are incurred in production?

Cost for product Howard is $ ☐   (2 marks)

13 Alternative costing principles

58   Which one of the following ideas is NOT usually associated with a TQM environment?

A   Continuous improvement
B   Right first time
C   Reduced customer service
D   Zero defects   (2 marks)

59   Which of the following statements about activity based costing is/are correct?

1   Short-term variable overhead costs should be traced to products using volume-related cost drivers, such as machine hours or direct labour hours

2   Long-term variable production overheads are driven partly by the complexity and diversity of production work, as well as by the volume of output

3   Transactions undertaken by support department personnel are the appropriate cost drivers for long-term variable costs

4   Overheads should be charged to products on the basis of their usage of an activity. A product's usage of an activity is measured by the number of the activity's cost driver it generates

A   All of the above

B   1 only

C   2 only

D   1, 3 and 4 only   (2 marks)

60   Setting controls for the process of manufacture or service delivery is known as:

A   Inspection
B   Quality control
C   Quality circles
D   Internal failure costs   (2 marks)

14 Forecasting

61 In a time series analysis, the multiplicative model is used to forecast sales and the following seasonal variations apply. Remember, instead of summing to zero, as with the additive approach, the averages should sum (in this case) to 4.0, 1.0 for each of the four quarters.

Quarter	1	2	3	4
Seasonal variation	0.45	1.22	1.31	?

The seasonal variation for quarter 4 is

A   0.02
B   1.02
C   1.98
D   2.98   **(2 marks)**

62 A company's weekly costs ($C) were plotted against production level (P) for the last 50 weeks and a regression line calculated to be C = 1,000 + 250P. Which statement about the breakdown of weekly costs is true?

A   Fixed costs are $1,000. Variable costs per unit are $5.
B   Fixed costs are $250. Variable costs per unit are $4.
C   Fixed costs are $250. Variable costs per unit are $1,000.
D   Fixed costs are $1,000. Variable costs per unit are $250.   **(2 marks)**

63 The value of the correlation coefficient between x and y is 0.9. Which of the following is correct?

A   There is a weak relationship between x and y

B   x is 90% of y

C   If the values of x and y were plotted on a graph, the line relating them would have a slope of 0.9

D   There is a very strong relationship between x and y   **(2 marks)**

64 The correlation coefficient between A and B is 0.4 and the correlation coefficient between C and D is –0.7.

Which of the following statements is correct:

A   There is a stronger relationship between A and B than between C and D
B   There is a stronger relationship between C and D than between A and B
C   The relationship between A and B and between C and D is the same
D   There is insufficient information to determine which relationship is stronger   **(2 marks)**

65 Four years ago material X cost $5 per kg and the price index most appropriate to the cost of material X stood at 150.

The same index now stands at 430.

What is the best estimate of the current cost of material X per kg?

A $1.74 ($5 × 150 ÷ 430)
B $9.33 ($5 × (430 – 150) ÷ 150
C $14.33 ($5 × 430 ÷ 150)
D $21.50 ($5 × 430 ÷ 100)   **(2 marks)**

66 If $\Sigma X = 100$, $\Sigma Y = 400$, $\Sigma X^2 = 2,040$, $\Sigma Y^2 = 32,278$, $\Sigma XY = 8,104$ and n = 5, which of the following values for a and b are correct in the formula Y = a + bX?

	a	b
A	28	-2.6
B	28	+2.6
C	-28	-2.6
D	-28	+2.6

(2 marks)

15 Budgeting

67   Which of the following may be considered to be objectives of budgeting?

(i)   Coordination
(ii)   Communication
(iii)   Expansion
(iv)   Resource allocation

A   All of them   C   (ii) and (iii) only
B   (i), (ii) and (iv) only   D   (i) and (iii) only   **(2 marks)**

68   The following observations have been made of total overhead cost.

Output level (units)	5,000	10,000
Total overhead cost ($)	14,000	27,000

The variable element of total overhead cost is known to increase by $1 per unit at output levels above 7,000 units.

What is the variable element of total overhead cost at an output level of 5,000 units?

A $2.00 per unit ($27,000 – $14,000 – 3,000 units × $1) ÷ (10,000 units – 5,000 units)

B $2.60 per unit ($27,000 – $14,000) ÷ (10,000 units – 5,000 units)

C $3.20 per unit ($27,000 – $14,000 + 3,000 units × $1) ÷ (10,000 units – 5,000 units)

D $3.60 per unit ($27,000 – $14,000) ÷ (10,000 units – 5,000 units) + $1   **(2 marks)**

69   A manufacturing company always carries finished goods inventory equal to 20% of the next month's budgeted sales.

Sales for the current month are 2,000 units and are budgeted to be 20% higher next month.

How many units will be produced in the current month?

A   2,080
B   1,920 (400 + 2000 – 480)
C   2,000 (no adjustment)
D   2400 (2000 + 400)   **(2 marks)**

70   Which type of centre would have its performance measured by its return on capital employed?

A   Cost centre
B   Revenue centre
C   Investment centre
D   Capital centre   **(2 marks)**

16 The budgetary process

71   What does the statement 'sales is the principal budget factor' mean?

A   The level of sales will determine the level of cash at the end of the period
B   The level of sales will determine the level of profit at the end of the period
C   The company's activities are limited by the level of sales it can achieve
D   Sales is the largest item in the budget   **(2 marks)**

72   Which of the following is unlikely to be contained with a budget manual?

A   Organisational structures
B   Objectives of the budgetary process
C   Selling overhead budget
D   Administrative details of budget preparation   **(2 marks)**

73   Which of the following is not a functional budget?

    A   Production budget
    B   Distribution cost budget
    C   Selling cost budget
    D   Cash budget   **(2 marks)**

74   PQ Co plans to sell 24,000 units of product R next year. Opening inventory of R is expected to be 2,000 units and PQ Co plans to increase inventory by 25 per cent by the end of the year. How many units of product R should be produced next year?

    A   23,500 units
    B   24,000 units
    C   24,500 units
    D   30,000 units   **(2 marks)**

75   Which one of these costs would *not* be included in the cash budget of a travel company?

    ☐   Depreciation of computer terminals
    ☐   Commission paid to travel agents
    ☐   Capital cost of a new computer
    ☐   Advertising expenses   **(2 marks)**

17 Making budgets work

76   Which of the following statements about participative budgeting is/are false?

    (i)   Morale and motivation are improved
    (ii)   They may cause managers to introduce budgetary slack
    (iii)   They are quicker to produce than non-participative budgets

    A   (i) and (ii) only
    B   (ii) and (iii) only
    C   (iii) only
    D   (i) , (ii) and (iii)   **(2 marks)**

77   *Choose the appropriate words from those highlighted.*

    The correct approach to budgetary control is to compare **actual/budgeted** results with a budget that has been flexed to the **actual/budgeted** level of activity.   **(2 marks)**

78   What is goal congruence (in terms of organisational control systems)?

    A   When the goals of management and employees harmonise with the goals of the organisation as a whole
    B   When the goals of management harmonise with the goals of employees
    C   When the work-related goals of management harmonise with their personal goals
    D   When an organisation's goals harmonise with those of its customers   **(2 marks)**

18 Capital expenditure budgeting

79   Which of the following are examples of revenue expenditure?

    (i)   Purchasing inventory
    (ii)   Maintenance of production equipment
    (iii)   Purchasing a factory building
    (iv)   Paying employee salaries

    A   (i), (ii) and (iii) only
    B   (i), (ii) and (iv) only
    C   (i), (iii) and (iv) only
    D   (ii), (iii) and (iv) only   **(2 marks)**

80   Build Co is a company that constructs office buildings and has decided that it will build its new
      head office. Which of the following costs should be included in the recorded cost of the new
      building?

      (i)   Raw materials
      (ii)   Labour costs
      (iii)   Related overhead costs
      (iv)   Legal costs that will be incurred to purchase the land

      A   All of them
      B   (i), (ii) and (iii) only
      C   (i), (iii) and (iv) only
      D   (ii), (iii) and (iv) only   (2 marks)

81   Raven Co is considering a new investment and is following the steps of the decision making and
      control cycle. Which step of the cycle follows immediately after detailed evaluation?

      A   Project monitoring
      B   Post-completion audit
      C   Implementation
      D   Authorisation   (2 marks)

19 Methods of project appraisal

82   Which method of investment appraisal leads to the selection of projects that maximise
      shareholder wealth?

      A   Discounted payback
      B   Wealth rate of return
      C   Net present value
      D   Internal rate of return   (2 marks)

83   The following information relates to a two-year project.

Initial investment	$1million
Cash inflow Year 1	$750,000
Cash inflow Year 2	$500,000
Cost of capital Year 1	10%
Cost of capital Year 2	15%

      What is the net present value of the project (to the nearest $500)?

      A   ($12,000)
      B   ($55,000)
      C $77,000
      D $116,500   (2 marks)

84   HMF Co is evaluating a project which requires investments of $5,000 now and $2,000 at the
      end of Year 1. The cash inflow will be $7,000 at the end of Year 2 and $6,000 at the end of
      Year 3. Calculate the NPV to the nearest $. The cost of capital is 16%.

      NPV $....................   (2 marks)

85   Which of the following statements are true?

      (i)   An investment with a positive NPV is viable
      (ii)   IRR is technically superior to NPV
      (iii)   Both IRR and NPV give the same accept or reject decision, regardless of the pattern of the
               cash flows

      A   (i) and (ii) only
      B   (i) and (iii) only
      C   (i) only
      D   (i), (ii) and (iii)   (2 marks)

86   A company is considering investing $320,000 in a project which will generate the following cash inflows.

Year	Cash flow
1	$73,400
2	$282,000
3	$37,900

The net present value of the project's cash flows, at a cost of capital of 17% is (to the nearest $)
$.............. **(2 marks)**

87   A Co has three options for machine B. One of these options involves modifying the machine now at a cost of $7,200, which will mean that the company does not have to hire an alternative machine at a cost of $19,800. This modification would mean that machine B would have to be disposed of in one year's time at a cost of $4,000. Ignoring the time value of money, calculate the relevant cost of this option.

$.............. **(2 marks)**

88   How much will an investor have after five years if she invests $5,000 at 12% simple interest per annum?

$.............. **(2 marks)**

89   If the interest rate is 8%, what would you pay for a perpetuity of $1,500 starting in one year's time? (to the nearest $)

$.............. **(2 marks)**

20 Standard costing

90   JC Co operates a bottling plant. The liquid content of a filled bottle of product T is 2 litres. During the filling process there is a 30% loss of liquid input due to spillage and evaporation. The standard price of the liquid is $1.20 per litre. The standard cost of the liquid per bottle of product T, to the nearest cent, is

A	$2.40	C	$3.12
B	$2.86	D	$3.43	**(2 marks)**

91   Standard costing provides which of the following? Tick all that apply.

(a)   Targets and measures of performance

(b)   Information for budgeting

(c)   Simplification of inventory control systems

(d)   Actual future costs   **(2 marks)**

92   What is an attainable standard?

A   A standard which includes no allowance for losses, waste and inefficiencies. It represents the level of performance which is attainable under perfect operating conditions

B   A standard which includes some allowance for losses, waste and inefficiencies. It represents the level of performance which is attainable under efficient operating conditions

C   A standard which is based on currently attainable operating conditions

D   A standard which is kept unchanged, to show the trend in costs   **(2 marks)**

21 Basic variance analysis

93 The standard cost information for SC's single product shows the standard direct material content to be 4 litres at $3 per litre.

Actual results for May were:

Production   1,270 units
Material used   5,000 litres at a cost of $16,000

All of the materials were purchased and used during the period. The direct material price and usage variances for May are:

	Material price	*Material usage*
A	$1,000 (F)	$240 (F)
B	$1,000 (A)	$240 (F)
C	$1,000 (F)	$240 (A)
D	$1,000 (A)	$256 (F)

(2 marks)

94 In a period 4,920 units were made with a standard labour allowance of 6.5 hours per unit at $5 per hour. Actual wages were $6 per hour and there was a favourable efficiency variance of $36,000.
Calculate the number of labour hours actually worked.   ....

(2 marks)

95 Which of the following would help to explain a favourable direct material price variance?

		Would help to explain variance	*Would not help to explain variance*
(a)	The standard price per unit of direct material was unrealistically high	☐	☐
(b)	Output quantity was greater than budgeted and it was possible to obtain bulk purchase discounts	☐	☐
(c)	The material purchased was of a higher quality than standard	☐	☐

(2 marks)

96 Extracts from H Co's records for June are as follows.

	Budget	*Actual*
Production	3,936 units	3,840 units
Direct labour cost	$15,744	$17,280

What is the total direct labour cost variance?

A $1,536 (F)
B $1,536 (A)
C $1,920 (F)
D $1,920 (A)

(2 marks)

22 Further variance analysis

97 W Co uses a standard absorption costing system. The following data relates to one of its products.

	$ per unit	$ per unit
Selling price		27.00
Variable costs	12.00	
Fixed costs	9.00	
		21.00
Profit		6.00

Budgeted sales for control period 7 were 2,400 units, but actual sales were 2,550 units. The revenue earned from these sales was $67,320.

Profit reconciliation statements are drawn up using absorption costing principles. What sales variances would be included in such a statement for period 7?

	Price	Volume
A	$1,530 (F)	$900 (F)
B	$1,530 (A)	$900 (F)
C	$1,530 (F)	$900 (A)
D	$1,530 (A)	$900 (A)

(2 marks)

98 A standard marginal costing system:

(i) calculates fixed overhead variances using the budgeted absorption rate per unit
(ii) calculates sales volume variances using the standard contribution per unit
(iii) values finished goods stock at the standard variable cost of production

Which of the above statements is/are correct?

A	(i), (ii) and (iii)	C	(ii) and (iii) only
B	(i) and (ii) only	D	(i) and (iii) only

(2 marks)

99 Diddly Co earned a profit of $305,000 in the last month. Variances were as follows.

Labour:	Rate	15,250 (F)
	Efficiency	10,750 (A)
Material:	Usage	8,675 (A)
	Price	9,825 (F)
Variable overheads	Efficiency	6,275 (A)
	Expenditure	2,850 (F)
Fixed overheads:	Expenditure	7,000 (F)
Sales:	Price	25,000 (A)
	Volume	32,000 (F)

What was Diddly Co's budgeted profit for last month?

A	$321,225	C	$371,925
B	$288,775	D	$254,300

(2 marks)

100 The B Co uses a standard absorption costing system and produces one product, the Blob. The following information is available for September.

Standard cost per Blob $31
Budgeted sales (units)   7,100
Actual sales (units)   6,600
Sales price variance $1,250 (A)
Sales volume variance $4,500 (A)

Calculate the sales revenue for September

A $256,750
B $252,250
C $262,750
D $265,250   **(2 marks)**

23 Performance measurement

101   The following information relates to P Limited at 31 December 20X0.

	$
Inventories	1,550
Short term payables	2,100
Receivables	1,300
Cash at bank	1,250

Which of the following is the quick ratio for P Limited to two decimal places?

A   1.95
B   1.21
C   0.62
D   0.74   **(2 marks)**

102   Which of the following is a non-financial performance measure?

A   Share price
B   Delivery time
C   Cash flow
D   Revenue   **(2 marks)**

103   The following information relates to P Limited at 31 December 20X4.

	$
Revenue	3,000
Gross profit	990
Net profit	450
Non-current assets	1,920

Calculate the net profit percentage.

A   15%
B   33%
C   66%
D   85%   **(2 marks)**

104   The following information relates to P Limited at 31 December 20X7.

	$
Revenue	3,000
Gross profit	990
Net profit	450
Inventory	125
Trade receivables	260
Cash	1,920

Calculate the accounts receivable payment period. (All sales are on credit.)

A   32 days
B   49 days
C   95 days
D   211 days   **(2 marks)**

24 Application of performance measures

105 *Match the definition to the term.*

Terms		*Definition*	
(a)	Economy	(1)	Ensuring outputs succeed in achieving objectives
(b)	Efficiency	(2)	Getting out as much as possible for what goes in
(c)	Effectiveness	(3)	Spending money frugally

A   a =1, b =2, c = 3
B   c =1, b = 2, a = 3
C   b = 1, c = 2, a = 3
D   a = 1, c = 2, b = 3   **(2 marks)**

106 Which of the following is a feature of the Residual Income performance measure?

A   It is a relative measure
B   It measures divisional performance based on multiple values
C   It generally decreases as assets get older
D   It helps you to select a proposal that will maximise wealth in absolute terms   **(2 marks)**

107 Which of the following is **not** a perspective associated with the balanced scorecard?

A   Customer satisfaction
B   Financial success
C   Reliability
D   Growth   **(2 marks)**

108 In the last year a division's controllable return on investment was 25% and its controllable profit was $80,000. The cost of finance appropriate to the division was 18% per annum.

What was the division's controllable residual income in the last year?

A	$5,600	$80,000 × (0.25 − 0.18)
B	$22,400	$80,000 − ($80,000 ÷ 0.25 × 0.18)
C	$74,400	$80,000 − ($80,000 × (0.25 − 0.18)
D	$76,400	$80,000 − ($80,000 × 0.25 × 0.18) **(2 marks)**

109 The following information is available for the month of June.

Budgeted hours	2,850 standard hours
Standard hours produced	3,150 standard hours
Actual hours worked	3,000

The following information is available for the month of July.

Budgeted hours	2,750 standard hours
Standard hours produced	2,800 standard hours
Actual hours worked	3,000

Calculate the percentage change in the activity ratio from June to July. Work to the nearest whole percent.

A   92%
B   8%
C   9%
D   109%   **(2 marks)**

25 Cost management

110 *Match the statements to either cost control or cost reduction.*

Terms		*Statement*	
(a)	Cost control	(1)	Often carried out on an ad hoc basis
(b)	Cost reduction	(2)	Directed towards reducing expected costs below current or standard levels
		(3)	The regulation of the costs of operating a business
		(4)	Concerned with keeping costs within acceptable Limits

(2 marks)

111 *Match the definition to the term.*

Terms		*Definition*	
(a)	Cost value	(1)	The market value of the product or service
(b)	Exchange value	(2)	The cost of producing and selling an item
(c)	Use value	(3)	The prestige the customer attaches to the product
(d)	Esteem value	(4)	What the article does, the purpose it fulfils

(2 marks)

112 (1) Work measurement is the systematic recording and critical examination of existing and proposed ways of doing work in order to develop and apply easier and more effective methods, and reduce costs

(2) Work study is a means of raising the production efficiency (productivity) of an operating units by the reorganisation of work

Which statements are true?

A   Both are true
B   Both are false
C   (1) is true and (2) is false
D   (1) is false and (2) is true

(2 marks)

1   Accounting for management

1   A   **Financial accounts** (not management accounts) detail the performance of an organisation over a defined period and the state of affairs at the end of that period. **Management accounts** are used to aid management record, plan and control the organisation's activities and to help the decision-making process.

2   C   Diane and Joanne work at operational level as they are concerned with routine activities. Lesley is at an intermediate level and is managing resources. She is therefore part of tactical management. Tracey is concerned with direction setting for the business and is therefore part of strategic management.

3   D   Cost accounting can also be used to provide inventory valuations for external reporting.

4   C   Obtaining data about actual results is part of the control process.

2   Sources of data

5   B   **Systematic sampling** is a sampling method which works by selecting every n^{th} item (or m^{th} in this case) after a random start.

6   B   The sample selected will be representative since it guarantees that every important category will have elements in the final sample. So I is true. The structure of the sample will reflect that of the population if the same proportion of individuals is chosen from each stratum. So II is true. The main disadvantage of stratification is that it requires prior knowledge of each item in the population. So III is true.

7   B   An eye witness's account is primary data and the number of customers is discrete data. A report in a newspaper is secondary data. A website is secondary data and height is continuous data. Distance is continuous data.

8   D   Quota sampling is cheap and administratively easy so A and B are false. No sampling frame is necessary because the interviewer questions every person they meet up to the quota, so C is false. The method can result in certain biases. For example, an interviewer in a shopping centre may fill their quota by only meeting people who can go shopping during the week.

9   C   The heights of lampposts is an example of quantitative data as they can be measured. Since the lampposts can take on any height, the data is continuous. You should have been able to eliminate options B and D immediately since qualitative data are data that cannot be measured but which reflect some quality of what is being observed.

3   Cost classification

10   D   It would be appropriate to use the cost per invoice processed and the cost per supplier account for control purposes. Therefore items (ii) and (iii) are suitable cost units and the correct answer is D.

Postage cost, item (i), is an expense of the department, therefore option A is not a suitable cost unit.

If you selected option B or option C you were probably rushing ahead and not taking care to read all the options. Items (ii) and (iii) *are* suitable cost units, but neither of them are the *only* suitable suggestions.

11   A   Special designs, and the hire of tools etc for a particular job can be traced to a specific cost unit. Therefore they are direct expenses and the correct answer is A.

Item (iii) is a selling and distribution overhead and item (iv) describes production overheads.

			Appropriate	Not appropriate
12	(a)	Vehicle cost per passenger - kilometre	✓	
	(b)	Fuel cost for each vehicle per kilometre	✓	
	(c)	Fixed cost per kilometre		✓

13 B A direct cost is one that can be directly related to a unit of output; an unavoidable cost is one that would be incurred whether or not a certain activity took place.

14 D The deliveries occur after a sale is made, therefore drivers' wages are a selling and distribution overhead. Options A, B and C are all a part of production cost, incurred before an item is sold.

4 Cost behaviour

15 A Variable costs are conventionally deemed to increase or decrease in direct proportion to changes in output. Therefore the correct answer is A. Descriptions B and D imply a changing unit rate, which does not comply with this convention. Description C relates to a fixed cost.

16 B The cost depicted begins as a linear variable cost, increasing at a constant rate in line with activity. At a certain point the cost becomes fixed regardless of the level of activity. The vehicle hire costs follow this pattern.

Graphs for the other options would look like this.

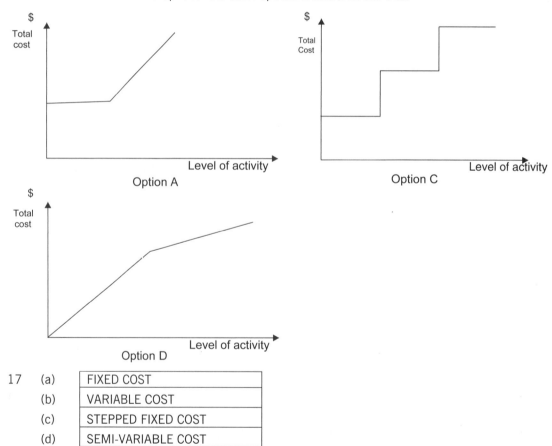

17	(a)	FIXED COST
	(b)	VARIABLE COST
	(c)	STEPPED FIXED COST
	(d)	SEMI-VARIABLE COST

18 D Bob cannot control the rent within the six-month period as he is unable to get out of the agreement during this time, therefore the rent is an **uncontrollable** cost.

Rent is not a fixed cost as the landlord may change it during the period.

Bob has agreed to pay the rent therefore he cannot avoid it (that is, rent is not an unavoidable cost).

A semi-variable cost comprises a fixed and a variable element, which is not the case with Bob Co's rent.

19   The total cost for period 3 if 15,500 square metres are decorated is $58,250

The first step is to eliminate the extra fixed costs from period 2 total costs so that we are comparing 'like with like'.

Total costs with no extra fixed costs = $56,000 - $6,000 = $50,000

We can now use the high-low method in the usual way to calculate variable cost per unit.

	Square metres		$
High output	14,000	Total cost	50,000
Low output	10,000	Total cost	44,000
	4,000		6,000

Variable cost per square metre = $6,000/4,000 = $1.50

Using the high level to calculate fixed costs:

	$	
Total costs	56,000	(includes the step up in fixed costs)
Total variable costs	21,000	(14,000 square metres x $1.50 per sq m)
Total fixed costs	35,000	

Total cost for 15,500 square metres:

	$	
Total variable costs	23,250	(15,500 square metres x $1.50)
Total fixed costs	35,000	(see above)
Total costs	58,250	

5   Presenting information

20   A

Material	Cost $	Percentage %	Degrees
P	1,000	33.3	120
Q	600	20	72*
R	1,025	34.2	123
S	375	12.5	45
	3,000	100	360

*600/3,000 × 360° = 72°

21   D   The best diagram to draw to highlight the differences between areas is a simple bar chart. A simple bar chart is a chart consisting of one or more bars, in which the length of each bar indicates the magnitude of the corresponding data items. This is the best diagram to draw to highlight the differences of typical salaries in different areas.

22   B   Pie charts illustrate the way in which one or more totals are broken down into their components.

6   Material costs

23   D $EOQ = \sqrt{\dfrac{2 \times \$400 \times (250 \times 48)}{\$20 \times 10\%}} = 2,191$

Therefore the correct answer is D.

If you selected option A you used **weekly** usage in the calculations instead of the annual usage.

If you selected option B you did not take ten per cent of the material cost as the annual inventory holding cost.

If you selected option C you omitted the 2.

24 D The easiest way to solve this question is to draw up a stores ledger control account.

STORES LEDGER CONTROL ACCOUNT

	$		$
Opening inventory b/f	18,500	Payables (returns)	2,300
Payables/cash (deliveries)	142,000	Overhead account (indirect materials)	25,200
		WIP (balancing figure)	116,900
		Closing inventory c/f	16,100
	160,500		160,500

If you selected option C you determined the correct value of the direct materials issued but you **reversed the entries**.

If you selected options A or B you placed the figure for returns on the **wrong side of your account**, and in option A you **reversed the entries** for the issue of direct materials from stores.

25 The maximum inventory level is 9,600 units.

Reorder level = maximum usage x maximum lead time
= 195 x 30 = 5,850 units

Maximum inventory level = reorder level + reorder quantity − (minimum usage x minimum lead time)
= 5,850 + 6,000 − (90 x 25)
= 9,600 units

26 B Using FIFO, the issue on 9 September would consist of the remaining 60 units from the opening balance (40 units were issued on 3 March) plus 10 units from the batch received on 4 June.

	$
60 units × $5	300
10 units × $5.50	55
	355

If you selected **option A** you used the opening inventory rate of $5 for all the units issued: you didn't notice that 40 of these units had already been issued on 3 March.

If you selected **option C** you ignored the opening inventory and based your calculations only on the receipts during the year.

Option D is incorrect because it values all the issues at the latest price paid, $6 per unit.

27 C Using LIFO, the issue on 9 September would consist of the 50 units received on 6 June, plus 20 of the units received on 4 June.

	$
50 units × $6	300
20 units × $5.50	110
	410

Option A is incorrect because it is based on the opening inventory rate of $5 per unit – this is certainly not the latest batch received.

Option B is a FIFO calculation based on the receipts on 4 and 6 June.

Option D is incorrect because it values all the issues at the latest price paid, $6 per unit. However there were only 50 units in this batch. The price for the remaining 20 units issued is the $5.50 per unit paid for the next latest batch received.

28   C   [Buffer inventory + (EOQ/2)] × annual holding cost per component

= [1,250 + (5,000/2)] × \$5

= \$18,750

7   Accounting for labour

29   B   The only direct costs are the wages paid to direct workers for ordinary time, plus the basic pay for overtime.

\$25,185 + \$5,440 = \$30,625.

If you selected option A you forgot to include the basic pay for overtime of direct workers, which is always classified as a direct labour cost.

If you selected option C you have included overtime premium and shift allowances, which are usually treated as indirect costs. However, if overtime and shiftwork are incurred specifically for a particular cost unit, then they are classified as direct costs of that cost unit. There is no mention of such a situation here.

Option D includes sick pay, which is classified as an indirect labour cost.

30   B   The credit balance on the wages control account indicates that the amount of wages incurred and analysed between direct wages and indirect wages was **higher** than the wages paid through the bank. Therefore there was a \$12,000 balance of **wages owing** at the end of February and statement B is not correct. Therefore the correct option is B.

Statement A is correct. \$128,400 of wages was paid from the bank account.

Statement C is correct. \$79,400 of direct wages was transferred to the work in progress control account.

Statement D is correct. \$61,000 of indirect wages was transferred to the production overhead control account.

31   The capacity ratio for the period was $\boxed{137.5}$ %

$$\text{Labour capacity ratio} = \frac{\text{Actual hours worked}}{\text{Hours budgeted}} \times 100\% = (68,750/50,000) \times 100\% = 137.5\%$$

32   The production volume ratio for the period was $\boxed{125}$ %

$$\text{Production volume ratio} = \frac{\text{Output measured in expected or standard hours}}{\text{Hours budgeted}}$$

$$= \left(\frac{12,500 \times 5 \text{ hours}}{50,000}\right) \times 100\%$$

$$= 125\%$$

[Expected hours per unit = budgeted hours (50,000 units) / budgeted output (10,000)]

33   The labour turnover rate for the period is $\boxed{9}$%.

$$\text{Labour turnover rate} = \frac{\text{Replacements}}{\text{Average number of employees in period}} \times 100\%$$

Average number of employees = (500 + [500 − 70 + 46])/2 = 488

Labour turnover rate = (46/488) × 100% = 9%

34 **A** Number of units qualifying for payment   = 250 – 31
                                                       = 219

Piecework payment to be made:

	$
First 100 units @ $0.25	25.00
Next 100 units @ $0.35	35.00
Last 19 units @ $0.45	8.55
	68.55

Option B is not correct because it includes payment for the 31 rejected units. If you selected **option C** you calculated the correct number of units qualifying for payment, but you evaluated all of them at the higher rate of $0.45 per unit. **Option D** is incorrect because it includes the 31 rejected units, and evaluates them all at the higher rate of $0.45 per unit.

8 Accounting for overheads

35 **B** Overhead absorption rate $= \dfrac{\text{budgeted overheads}}{\text{budgeted labour hours}} = \dfrac{\$148,750}{8,500} = \$17.50$ per hr

If you selected option A you divided the actual overheads by the budgeted labour hours. Option C is based on the actual overheads and actual labour hours. If you selected option D you divided the budgeted overheads by the actual hours.

36 **D**

	$
Overhead absorbed $= \$17.50 \times 7,928 =$	138,740
Overhead incurred $=$	146,200
Under-absorbed overhead $=$	7,460

If you selected options A or B you calculated the difference between the budgeted and actual overheads and interpreted it as an under or over absorption. If you selected option C you performed the calculations correctly but misinterpreted the result as an over absorption.

37 (a) % of direct material cost =   112.5%

(b) % of direct labour cost =   90%

(c) % of total direct cost =   50%

(d) Rate per machine hour = $3.60

(e) Rate per direct labour hour = $2

Workings

(a) % of direct materials cost $\dfrac{\$36,000}{\$32,000} \times 100\% = 112.5\%$

(b) % of direct labour cost $\dfrac{\$36,000}{\$40,000} \times 100\% = 90\%$

(c) % of total direct cost $\dfrac{\$36,000}{\$72,000} \times 100\% = 50\%$

(d) Rate per machine hour $\dfrac{\$36,000}{10,000\,\text{hrs}} = \$3.60$ per machine hour

(e)   Rate per direct labour hour $\dfrac{\$36,000}{18,000\,hrs}$ = $2 per direct labour hour

38 A   All of the overhead absorption methods are suitable, depending on the circumstances.

Method (i), direct labour hours, is suitable in a labour-intensive environment. **Method (ii)**, machine hours, is suitable in a machine-intensive environment. **Method (iii)**, a percentage of prime cost, can be used if it is difficult to obtain the necessary information to use a time-based method. **Method (iv)**, a rate per unit, is suitable if all cost units are identical.

39 C   The insurance cost is likely to be linked to the cost of replacing the machines, therefore the most appropriate basis for apportionment is the value of machinery.

Options A, **B and D** would all be possible apportionment bases in the absence of better information, but option C is preferable.

40 D $127,000

	Production centre A $	Production centre B $	C $	D $
Overhead costs	95,000	82,000	46,000	30,000
First C apportionment	18,400	18,400	(46,000)	9,200
			0	39,200
First D apportionment	11,760	23,520	3,920	(39,200)
			3,920	0
Second C apportionment	1,568	1,568	(3,920)	784
			0	784
Second D apportionment	235	471	78	(784)
			78	0
Third C apportionment	31	31	(78)	16
			0	16
Third D apportionment (approx)	6	10	0	(16)
	127,000	126,000	0	0

9   Absorption and marginal costing

41 C   Difference in profit   = change in inventory level × fixed overhead per unit
                               = (200 – 250) × ($2.50 × 3)
                               = $375

The absorption costing profit will be greater because inventories have increased.

If you selected option A you calculated the correct profit difference but the absorption costing profit would be greater because fixed overheads are carried forward in the increasing inventory levels.

If you selected option B you multiplied the inventory difference by the direct labour-hour rate instead of by the total overhead cost per unit, which takes three hours.

If you selected option D you based the profit difference on the closing inventory only (250 units × $2.50 × 3).

42   The contribution per unit is $39-$21 = $18

Closing inventory volume   = 70,000 units – 50,000 units

                             = 20,000 units

Value of closing inventory   = 20,000 units × $18

                             = $360,000

43

	$	$
Sales (at $40 per unit)		600,000
Opening inventory	–	
Variable production cost ($25 × 20,000) (W1)	500,000	
Less closing inventory ($25 × 5,000)	125,000	
Variable cost of sales		375,000
Contribution		225,000
Less fixed costs		80,000
Profit		145,000

W1 Variable production cost per unit = Total cost per unit – fixed cost per unit
= $30 – ($125,000/25,000 units) = $25 per unit

44   D

	Units
Opening inventory	900
Closing inventory	300
Decrease	600 × ($500,000/2,500) = $120,000 lower

Profit under absorption costing = $800,000 - $120,000 = $680,000

45   D   2,000 more units of product have been produced than sold, resulting in the same increase in inventory levels.

Closing inventories will not include any fixed overheads where marginal costing is used as they are written off in the period incurred.

However where absorption costing is used, $5 of additional fixed cost will be included per unit of increase in inventory over the period, accounting for the profit being $10,000 higher under this method for the period.

10 Job, batch and service costing

46   ☑ Production of the product can be completed in a single accounting period

☑ Production relates to a single special order

Job costing is appropriate where each cost unit is **separately identifiable** and is of relatively **short duration**.

47   (i)   Production is carried out in accordance with the wishes of the customer | J |

(ii)   Work is usually of a relatively long duration | C |

(iii)   Work is usually undertaken on the contractor's premises | N |

(iv)   Costs are averaged over the units produced in the period | S |

(v)   It establishes the costs of services rendered | S |

48   D

Hours for job 34679	= 400 hours
Production overhead cost	$4,000
∴ Overhead absorption rate ($4,000 ÷ 400)	$10 per direct labour hour
Budgeted direct labour hours	45,000
∴ Total budgeted production overheads	$450,000
Budgeted direct wages cost	$180,000
∴ Absorption rate as % of wages cost	= $450,000/$180,000 × 100%
	= 250%

Cost of job 34679

	$
Direct materials	2,000
Direct labour, including overtime premium *	2,500
Overhead (250% × $2,500)	6,250
Total production cost	10,750

* The overtime premium is a direct labour cost because the overtime was worked specifically for this job.

If you selected option A you got your calculation of the overhead absorption rate 'upside down' and derived a percentage rate of 40 per cent in error. If you selected option B you did not include the overtime premium and the corresponding overhead. If you selected option C you did not include the overtime premium in the direct labour costs.

49   A   Job costing is a costing method applied where work is undertaken to customers' special requirements. Option B describes process costing, C describes service costing and D describes process costing.

11 Process costing

50   C   **Step 1. Determine output and closing WIP**

			Equivalent units of production				
Input Units	Output	Total Units	Process X Units	%	Conversion costs Units	%
2,000	Finished units	1,600	1,600	100	1,600	100
	Closing inventory (bal)	400	400	100	200	50
2,000		2,000	2,000		1,800	

Step 2. Calculate cost per unit of output and WIP

Input	Cost $	Equivalent units	Cost per equivalent unit $
Process X material	8,000	2,000	4.00
Conversion costs	12,240	1,800	6.80
			10.80

Step 3. Calculate total cost of closing WIP

Using the unit rates from answer (a) step 2:

	Cost element	Number of equivalent units	Cost per equivalent unit $	Total $
Work in progress	Process X material	400	4.00	1,600
	Conversion costs	200	6.80	1,360
				2,960

If you selected option A you only included the conversion costs in your calculation. If you selected option B you did not account for the fact that closing WIP was fully complete for materials and multiplied total cost per equivalent unit by 200. Option D does not allow for the fact that the work in progress (WIP) is incomplete when calculating the total cost of WIP.

51   A   Abnormal gain 1,000 litres and cost per unit $0.15

PROCESS ACCOUNT

	Litres	$		Litres	$
Materials	20,000	4,400	Normal waste (4,000 × $0.50)	4,000	2,000
			Finished goods	17,000	2,550
Abnormal gain	1,000	150			
	21,000	4,550		21,000	4,550

Workings

Normal loss = 20% × 20,000 litres = 4,000 litres

Expected output = 20,000 – 4,000 = 16,000 litres

$$\text{Cost per unit} = \frac{\text{Process costs - scrap proceeds of normal loss}}{\text{Expected output}}$$

$$= \frac{\$4,400 - (4,000 \times \$0.50)}{16,000 \text{ litres}}$$

$$= \frac{\$4,400 - \$2,000}{16,000 \text{ litres}}$$

$$= \frac{\$2,400}{16,000 \text{ litres}}$$

$$= \$0.15$$

52   The quantity of good production achieved was $\boxed{2,625}$ kg.

Good production   = input – normal loss – abnormal loss
                                = 3,000 – (10% × 3,000) – 75
                                = 3,000 – 300 – 75
                                = 2,635 kg

53   The value of the abnormal loss for the period is $ $\boxed{300}$

	kg
Input	5,000
Normal loss (10% × 5,000 kg)	(500)
Abnormal loss	(300)
Output	4,200

$$\text{Cost per kg} = \frac{\text{Input costs - scrap value of normal loss}}{\text{Expected output}}$$

$$= \frac{\$4,600^{*} - \$100}{5,000 - 500}$$

$$= \frac{\$4,500}{4,500} = \$1.00$$

Value of abnormal loss = 300 × $1.00 = $300

	$
*Materials (5,000 kg × 0.5)	2,500
Labour	700
Production overhead	1,400
	4,600

54   C   Abnormal losses have the same value as good production.

12 Process costing, joint products and by-products

55   C   Net process costs

	$
Raw materials	90,000
Conversion costs	70,000
Less by-product revenue	(4,000)
Net process costs	156,000

BPP LEARNING MEDIA

Apportionment of net process costs

		Units		Apportioned costs
			$	$
Product	J	2,500	$156,000 × (2,500/8,000)	48,750
	K	3,500	$156,000 × (3,500/8,000)	68,250
	L	2,000	$156,000 × (2,000/8,000)	39,000
		8,000		156,000

If you selected option A or B you apportioned a share of the process costs to the by-product, and with option B or D you did not deduct the by-product revenue from the process costs.

56 A *Workings*

	Sales revenue	
Joint product	$	
A	760,000	($38 × 20,000)
B	2,160,000	($54 × 40,000)
C	1,400,000	($40 × 35,000)
Total sales revenues	4,320,000	

Joint costs to be allocated = Total output costs – sales revenue from by-product D

= $4,040,000 – $80,000 ($4 × 20,000)
= $3,960,000

$$\text{Costs allocated to joint product B} = \frac{\$2,160,000}{\$4,320,000} \times \$3,960,000$$

$$= \$1,980,000$$

$$\text{Unit valuation (joint product B)} = \frac{\$1,980,000}{40,000}$$

$$= \$49.50 \text{ (to 2 decimal places)}$$

If you selected option B, you forgot to deduct the sales revenue (from by-product D) from the joint costs to be allocated.

If you selected option C, you excluded by-product D from your calculations completely.

If you selected option D, you divided the total sales revenue (instead of the joint costs to be allocated) by the number of units of joint product D.

57   The correct answer is $360,000.

Remember to allocate costs according to **sales value of production** rather than sales value of units sold.

Sales value of production:	$
Gary (20,000 units x $50)	1,000,000
Howard (15,000 x $40)	600,000
Jason (10,000 x $90)	900,000
	2,500,000

Common costs allocated to Howard = ($600,000/$2,500,000) × $1,500,000
= $360,000

13 Alternative costing principles

58 C Reduced customer service. The TQM philosophy includes accepting that the only thing that matters is the customer.

59 D **1:** Short-term variable overhead costs vary with the volume of activity, and should be allocated to products accordingly.

2: This statement is not completely correct. Many overhead costs, traditionally regarded as fixed costs, vary in the long run with the volume of certain activities, although they do not vary immediately. The activities they vary with are principally related to the complexity and diversity of production, not to sheer volume of output. For example, set-up costs vary in the long run with the number of production runs scheduled, not the number of units produced.

3: For example, the number of credit investigations undertaken within the credit review department of a bank would be the cost driver of the department's costs.

4: Following on from 3 above, a mortgage might require three credit investigations and hence the mortgage should bear the proportion of the departments' costs reflected by three credit investigations.

60   B   Quality control. Note that inspection is concerned with looking at products made or supplies delivered to establish whether they are up to specification.

14 Forecasting

61   B   As this is a multiplicative model, the seasonal variations should sum (in this case) to 4 (an average of 1) as there are four quarters.

Let x = seasonal variation for quarter 4.

$$0.45 + 1.22 + 1.31 + x = 4$$
$$2.98 + x = 4$$
$$x = 4 - 2.98$$
$$= 1.02$$

If you selected option A you subtracted the sum of the seasonal variations from 3 instead of 4.

If you selected option D, you forgot to subtract the sum of the seasonal variations for quarters 1-3 from 4.

62   D   If C = 1,000 + 250P, then fixed costs are $1,000 and variable costs are $250 per unit.

63   D   The correlation coefficient of 0.9 is very close to 1 and so there is a very strong relationship between x and y.

64   B   It does not matter what the **sign** of the correlation coefficient is – the **size** of the correlation coefficient between C and D (0.7) is larger than that between A and B (0.4) therefore the relationship between C and D is stronger than between A and B.

65   C   The calculation in C applies the relative increase in the price index to the specific material X.

66   B   The least squares method of linear regression analysis involves using the following formulae for a and b in Y = a + bX.

$$b = \frac{n\sum XY - \sum X \sum Y}{n\sum X^2 - (\sum X)^2}$$

$$= \frac{(5 \times 8,104) - (100 \times 400)}{(5 \times 2,040) - 100^2}$$

$$= \frac{40,520 - 40,000}{10,200 - 10,000}$$

$$= \frac{520}{200}$$

$$= 2.6$$

At this stage, you can eliminate options A and C.

$$a = \overline{Y} - b\overline{X}$$
$$= \frac{400}{5} - 2.6 \times (\frac{100}{5})$$
$$= 28$$

15 Budgeting

67 B Coordination (i) is an objective of budgeting. Budgets help to ensure that the activities of all parts of the organisation are coordinated towards a single plan. Communication (ii) is an objective of budgeting. The budgetary planning process communicates targets to the managers responsible for achieving them, and it should also provide a mechanism for junior managers to communicate to more senior staff their estimates of what may be achievable in their part of the business. Expansion (iii) is not in itself an objective of budgeting. Although a budget may be set within a framework of expansion plans, it is perfectly possible for an organisation to plan for a reduction in activity. Resource allocation (iv) is an objective of budgeting. Most organisations face a situation of limited resources and an objective of the budgeting process is to ensure that these resources are allocated among budget centres in the most efficient way

68 A The calculation in A uses the high-low method but adjusts for the additional variable element over 7,000 units (by subtracting the affected 3,000 units of $1 each).

If you selected B then you did not take into account the increase in the variable element for above 7,000 units.

If you selected C then you added instead of subtracted 3,000 units to adjust for the increase in the variable element.

If you selected D you performed an unadjusted high-low calculation initially and added the increase in variable element per unit at the end.

69 A The correct calculation is as follows:

	Units	Comment
Sales	2,000	Current month sales
Less opening inventory	(400)	20% of sales (2,000) in the current month
Add closing inventory	480	20% of budgeted sales (2,400 × 20% = 480)
	2,080	

70 C The correct answer is: Investment centre.

16 The budgetary process

71 C The **principal budget factor** is the factor which limits the activities of an organisation.

Although cash and profit are affected by the level of sales (options A and B), sales is not the only factor which determines the level of cash and profit.

72 C This is a detail budget.

73 D A functional budget is a budget prepared for a particular function or department. A cash budget is the cash result of the planning decisions included in all the functional budgets. It is not a functional budget itself. Therefore the correct answer is D.

The production budget (option A), the distribution cost budget (option B) and the selling cost budget (option C) are all prepared for specific functions, therefore they are functional budgets.

74   C   Units
         Required for sales   24,000
         Required to increase inventory (2,000 × 0.25)   500
                                                                              24,500

         If you selected option A you subtracted the change in inventory from the budgeted sales.
         However, if inventories are to be increased then extra units must be made for inventory.

         Option B is the budgeted sales volume, which would only be equal to budgeted production
         if there were no planned changes to inventory volume.

         If you selected option D you increased the sales volume by 25 per cent, instead of
         adjusting inventory by this percentage.

75   ☑   Depreciation of computer terminals

         Depreciation is not a cash flow, so it would not be included in a cash budget.

17 Making budgets work

76   C   (i) and (ii) are true but (iii) is false because participative budgets consume more time
         than non-participative budgets.

77   The correct approach to budgetary control is to compare **actual** results with a budget that has
         been flexed to the **actual** level of activity

78   A   When the goals of management and employees harmonise with the goals of the
         organisation as a whole

18 Capital expenditure budgeting

79   B   Purchasing a building would be classed as capital expenditure. Expenditure on
         maintaining the earning capacity of non-current assets is classed as revenue
         expenditure.

80   A   All the costs can be included in the recorded cost of a self-constructed non-current
         asset.

81   D   Authorisation follows detailed evaluation in the decision making and control cycle.

19 Methods of project appraisal

82   C   The main benefit of using net present value is that it maximises shareholder wealth.

83   C   Discounting at 10% for one year = $1/1.10$ and for two years = $1/1.10 \times 1/1.10$ but if the
         interest changes in year 2 to 15% then the discount rate is $1/1.10 \times 1/1.15$.

Year	Cash flow	PV factor	PV
0	($1,000,000)	1	($1,000,000)
1	$750,000	$1/1.10 = 0.909$	$681,750
2	$500,000	$1/1.0 \times 1/1.15 = 0.909 \times 0.870$	$395,415
		NPV =	$77,165

Alternatively:

NPV   = -$1,000,000 + $750,000/1.10 + $500,000/(1.10 × 1.15)
      = $77,000 (to the nearest $500)

84       $2,323

Net present value

Year	Cash flow	Discount factor	Present value
	$		$
0	(5,000)	1.000	(5,000)
1	(2,000)	0.862	(1,724)
2	7,000	0.743	5,201
3	6,000	0.641	3,846
Net present value			2,323

85   C   It is true that an investment with a positive NPV is financially viable. The IRR is not superior to the NPV. NPV and IRR only give the same accept or reject decision when the cash flows are conventional.

86   ($27,451)

Year	Cash flow	DCF	PV
	$		$
0	(320,000)	1	(320,000)
1	73,400	0.855	62,757
2	282,000	0.731	206,142
3	37,900	0.624	23,650
		NPV	(27,451)

87   Modification = $7,200, hire costs avoided = $(19,800) and disposal costs = $4,000 and so the relevant cost is a saving of $8,600.

88     $8,000. Interest = $5,000 × 12% × 5 years = $3,000.

Total value of investment = 5,000 + 3,000 = 8,000.

89     $18,750. $1,500/0.08 = $18,750

20 Standard costing

90   D   Required liquid input = 2 litres × $\frac{100}{70}$ = 2.86 litres

Standard cost of liquid input = 2.86 × $1.20 = $3.43 (to the nearest cent)

If you selected option A you made no allowance for spillage and evaporation. Option B is the figure for the quantity of material input, not its cost. If you selected option C you simply added an extra 30 per cent to the finished volume. However, the wastage is 30 per cent of the liquid **input**, not 30 per cent of output.

91   (a)   Targets and measures of performance   ✓

    (b)   Information for budgeting   ✓

    (c)   Simplification of inventory control systems   ✓

    (d)   Actual future costs

Standard costing provides targets for achievement, and yardsticks against which actual performance can be monitored (**item (a)**). It also provides the unit cost information for evaluating the volume figures contained in a budget (**item (b)**). Inventory control systems are simplified with standard costing. Once the variances have been eliminated, all inventory units are evaluated at standard price (**item (c)**).

Item (d) is incorrect because standard costs are an estimate of what will happen in the future, and a unit cost target that the organisation is aiming to achieve.

92　　B　　An attainable standard assumes efficient levels of operation, but includes **allowances** for normal loss, waste and machine downtime.

Option A describes an **ideal standard**
Option C describes a **current standard**
Option D describes a **basic standard**

21 Basic variance analysis

93　　B

	$
Material price variance	
5,000 litres did cost	16,000
But should have cost (× $3)	15,000
	1,000 (A)
Material usage variance	
1,270 units did use	5,000 litres
But should have used (× 4 litres)	5,080 litres
Usage variance in litres	80 (F)
× standard cost per litre	$3
	240 (F)

If you selected options A or C you calculated the money values of the variances correctly but misinterpreted their direction.

If you selected option D you valued the usage variance in litres at the actual cost per litre instead of the standard cost per litre.

94　　The number of labour hours actually worked was　24,780

4,920 units should have taken (× 6.5 hrs)	31,980
but did take	x

The variance in hours is therefore (31,980 − x) hrs × standard rate ($5)

$$
\begin{aligned}
\text{Labour efficiency variance} &= 159,900 - 5x \\
\text{or } 36,000 &= 159,900 - 5x \\
5x &= 159,900 - 36,000 \\
x &= \frac{123,900}{5} \\
&= 24,780
\end{aligned}
$$

95

		Would help to explain variance	Would not help to explain variance
(a)	The standard price per unit of direct material was unrealistically high	✓	
(b)	Output quantity was greater than budgeted and it was possible to obtain bulk purchase discounts	✓	
(c)	The material purchased was of a higher quality than standard		✓

Statement (a) is consistent with a favourable material price variance. If the standard is high then actual prices are likely to be below the standard.

Statement (b) is consistent with a favourable material price variance. Bulk purchase discounts would not have been allowed at the same level in the standard, because purchases were greater than expected.

Statement (c) is not consistent with a favourable material price variance. Higher quality material is likely to cost more than standard, resulting in an adverse material price variance.

96　D　Standard labour cost per unit = $15,744/3,936 units = $4 per unit

	$
Standard direct labour cost for 3,840 units (× $4)	15,360
Actual direct labour cost	17,280
	1,920 (A)

22 Further variance analysis

97　B

	$
Revenue from 2,550 units should have been (× $27)	68,850
but was	67,320
Sales price variance	1,530 (A)

Actual sales	2,550 units
Budgeted sales	2,400 units
Variance in units	150 units (F)
× standard profit per unit ($(27 – 12))	× $6
Sales volume variance in $	$900 (F)

If you selected option A, C or D, you calculated the monetary values of the variances correctly, but misinterpreted their direction.

98　C　Statement (i) is not correct. Fixed overhead is not absorbed into production costs in a marginal costing system.

Statement (ii) is correct. Sales volume variances are calculated using the standard contribution per unit (and not the standard profit per unit which is used in standard absorption costing systems).

Statement (iii) is correct. As stated above, fixed overhead is not absorbed into production costs in a marginal costing system.

99　B　Remember you are working in **reverse** (you have been given actual profit), so all **adverse** variances have to be **added back** to actual profit and **favourable** variances **deducted** to arrive at budgeted profit.

		Fav. $	Adv. $	$
Actual profit				305,000
Variances:				
Labour:	Rate	(15,250)		
	Efficiency		10,750	
Material:	Price	(9,825)		
	Usage		8,675	
Variable overheads:	Efficiency		6,275	
	Expenditure	(2,850)		
Fixed overheads:	Expenditure	(7,000)		
Sales:	Price		25,000	
	Volume	(32,000)		
		(66,925)	50,700	
Net favourable variance				(16,225)
Budgeted profit				288,775

100　C　**Sales volume variance**

Should have sold	7,100 units
But did sell	6,600 units
	500 units (A)
x unit profit margin	× $p
	4,500 (A)

So unit profit margin = 4,500/500 = $9

Sales price variance

Selling price = cost + profit margin = $31+$9 = $40

	$
Sales revenue from 6,600 units should have been(x $40)	264,000
But was	?
	1,250(A)

Sales revenue   = $264,000 - $1,250
                  = $262,750

23 Performance measurement

101   B   ($1,300 + $1,250) ÷ $2,100 = 1.21

If you selected A you calculated the current ratio and included inventory in your calculation.

C is receivables divided by payables.

D is inventory divided by payables.

102   B   A, C and D are all financial performance measures.

103   A   15%

Net profit percentage = 450/3,000 × 100% = 15%

104   A   32 days. Accounts receivable payment period = trade receivables/revenue × 365 days = 260/3,000 × 365 days

                = 32 days

24 Application of performance measures

105   B   (a) (3)
                (b) (2)
                (c) (1)

106   D   Residual income is an **absolute** measure (compared to Return on Investment which is a relative measure) which allows you to select a proposal that will maximise your wealth in absolute terms.

It measures divisional performance divisional performance based on a **single value** and as assets get older it generally **increases**. This is because the number subtracted from traceable profits decreases as the book value decreases.

107   C   The fourth perspective not listed is process efficiency.

108   B   Residual Income (RI) = traceable profit – imputed interest charge on traceable investment

You are given the return on investment and know that:

ROI = traceable profit/traceable investment

Therefore to arrive at the traceable investment you can re-arrange the formula above to:

Traceable investment = traceable profit/ROI = $80,000/25% = $80,000/0.25 = $320,000.

Substituting $320,000 back into the first formula together with other information in the question gives an RI of $22,400.

RI = $80,000 – ($320,000 × 0.18) = ($80,000 – $57,600) = $22,400

109 B   June

Activity ratio = (Output measured in std hrs/Budgeted hours) × 100%
= (3,150/2,850) × 100%
= 111% (to the nearest whole percent)

July

Activity ratio = (Output measured in std hrs/Budgeted hours) × 100%
= (2,800/2,750) × 100%
= 102% (to the nearest whole percent)

Difference between June and July activity ratio	= 111 – 102
	= 9
9 as a percentage of June's activity ratio of 111	= 9/111 × 100%
	= 8%

25 Cost measurement

110   Cost reduction (1) and (2)
          Cost control (3) and (4)

111 (b)   Exchange value   (1)   The market value of the product or service
     (a)   Cost value   (2)   The cost of producing and selling an item
     (d)   Esteem value   (3)   The prestige the customer attaches to the product
     (c)   Use value   (4)   What the article does, the purpose it fulfils

112 D   The first statement describes method study, not work measurement so (1) is false. (2) is
          true.

FORMULA SHEET GIVEN IN THE EXAM

Regression analysis

$$y = a + bx$$

$$a = \frac{\sum Y}{n} - b\frac{\sum X}{n}$$

$$b = \frac{n\sum XY - \sum X\sum Y}{n\sum X^2 - (\sum X)^2}$$

$$r = \frac{n\sum XY - \sum X\sum Y}{\sqrt{[n\sum X^2 - (\sum X)^2][n\sum Y^2 - (\sum Y)^2]}}$$

Economic order quantity

$$\sqrt{\frac{2C_0 D}{C_h}}$$

Economic batch quantity

$$\sqrt{\frac{2C_0 D}{C_h(1 - \frac{D}{R})}}$$

PRESENT VALUE TABLE

Present value of £1 ie $(1+r)^{-n}$

where r = interest rate,

n = number of periods until payment

Periods (n)					Discount rates (r)					
	1%	2%	3%	4%	5%	6%	7%	8%	9%	10%
1	0.990	0.980	0.971	0.962	0.952	0.943	0.935	0.926	0.917	0.909
2	0.980	0.961	0.943	0.925	0.907	0.890	0.873	0.857	0.842	0.826
3	0.971	0.942	0.915	0.889	0.864	0.840	0.816	0.794	0.772	0.751
4	0.961	0.924	0.888	0.855	0.823	0.792	0.763	0.735	0.708	0.683
5	0.951	0.906	0.863	0.822	0.784	0.747	0.713	0.681	0.650	0.621
6	0.942	0.888	0.837	0.790	0.746	0.705	0.666	0.630	0.596	0.564
7	0.933	0.871	0.813	0.760	0.711	0.665	0.623	0.583	0.547	0.513
8	0.923	0.853	0.789	0.731	0.677	0.627	0.582	0.540	0.502	0.467
9	0.914	0.837	0.766	0.703	0.645	0.592	0.544	0.500	0.460	0.424
10	0.905	0.820	0.744	0.676	0.614	0.558	0.508	0.463	0.422	0.386
11	0.896	0.804	0.722	0.650	0.585	0.527	0.475	0.429	0.388	0.350
12	0.887	0.788	0.701	0.625	0.557	0.497	0.444	0.397	0.356	0.319
13	0.879	0.773	0.681	0.601	0.530	0.469	0.415	0.368	0.326	0.290
14	0.870	0.758	0.661	0.577	0.505	0.442	0.388	0.340	0.299	0.263
15	0.861	0.743	0.642	0.555	0.481	0.417	0.362	0.315	0.275	0.239

(n)	11%	12%	13%	14%	15%	16%	17%	18%	19%	20%
1	0.901	0.893	0.885	0.877	0.870	0.862	0.855	0.847	0.840	0.833
2	0.812	0.797	0.783	0.769	0.756	0.743	0.731	0.718	0.706	0.694
3	0.731	0.712	0.693	0.675	0.658	0.641	0.624	0.609	0.593	0.579
4	0.659	0.636	0.613	0.592	0.572	0.552	0.534	0.516	0.499	0.482
5	0.593	0.567	0.543	0.519	0.497	0.476	0.456	0.437	0.419	0.402
6	0.535	0.507	0.480	0.456	0.432	0.410	0.390	0.370	0.352	0.335
7	0.482	0.452	0.425	0.400	0.376	0.354	0.333	0.314	0.296	0.279
8	0.434	0.404	0.376	0.351	0.327	0.305	0.285	0.266	0.249	0.233
9	0.391	0.361	0.333	0.308	0.284	0.263	0.243	0.225	0.209	0.194
10	0.352	0.322	0.295	0.270	0.247	0.227	0.208	0.191	0.176	0.162
11	0.317	0.287	0.261	0.237	0.215	0.195	0.178	0.162	0.148	0.135
12	0.286	0.257	0.231	0.208	0.187	0.168	0.152	0.137	0.124	0.112
13	0.258	0.229	0.204	0.182	0.163	0.145	0.130	0.116	0.104	0.093
14	0.232	0.205	0.181	0.160	0.141	0.125	0.111	0.099	0.088	0.078
15	0.209	0.183	0.160	0.140	0.123	0.108	0.095	0.084	0.074	0.065

ANNUITY TABLE

Present value of an annuity of 1 ie $\dfrac{1-(1+r)^{-n}}{r}$.

where r = interest rate,

n = number of periods

Periods (n)	\ 1%	2%	3%	4%	Discount rates (r) \ 5%	6%	7%	8%	9%	10%
1	0.990	0.980	0.971	0.962	0.952	0.943	0.935	0.926	0.917	0.909
2	1.970	1.942	1.913	1.886	1.859	1.833	1.808	1.783	1.759	1.736
3	2.941	2.884	2.829	2.775	2.723	2.673	2.624	2.577	2.531	2.487
4	3.902	3.808	3.717	3.630	3.546	3.465	3.387	3.312	3.240	3.170
5	4.853	4.713	4.580	4.452	4.329	4.212	4.100	3.993	3.890	3.791
6	5.795	5.601	5.417	5.242	5.076	4.917	4.767	4.623	4.486	4.355
7	6.728	6.472	6.230	6.002	5.786	5.582	5.389	5.206	5.033	4.868
8	7.652	7.325	7.020	6.733	6.463	6.210	5.971	5.747	5.535	5.335
9	8.566	8.162	7.786	7.435	7.108	6.802	6.515	6.247	5.995	5.759
10	9.471	8.983	8.530	8.111	7.722	7.360	7.024	6.710	6.418	6.145
11	10.368	9.787	9.253	8.760	8.306	7.887	7.499	7.139	6.805	6.495
12	11.255	10.575	9.954	9.385	8.863	8.384	7.943	7.536	7.161	6.814
13	12.134	11.348	10.635	9.986	9.394	8.853	8.358	7.904	7.487	7.103
14	13.004	12.106	11.296	10.563	9.899	9.295	8.745	8.244	7.786	7.367
15	13.865	12.849	11.938	11.118	10.380	9.712	9.108	8.559	8.061	7.606

(n)	11%	12%	13%	14%	15%	16%	17%	18%	19%	20%
1	0.901	0.893	0.885	0.877	0.870	0.862	0.855	0.847	0.840	0.833
2	1.713	1.690	1.668	1.647	1.626	1.605	1.585	1.566	1.547	1.528
3	2.444	2.402	2.361	2.322	2.283	2.246	2.210	2.174	2.140	2.106
4	3.102	3.037	2.974	2.914	2.855	2.798	2.743	2.690	2.639	2.589
5	3.696	3.605	3.517	3.433	3.352	3.274	3.199	3.127	3.058	2.991
6	4.231	4.111	3.998	3.889	3.784	3.685	3.589	3.498	3.410	3.326
7	4.712	4.564	4.423	4.288	4.160	4.039	3.922	3.812	3.706	3.605
8	5.146	4.968	4.799	4.639	4.487	4.344	4.207	4.078	3.954	3.837
9	5.537	5.328	5.132	4.946	4.772	4.607	4.451	4.303	4.163	4.031
10	5.889	5.650	5.426	5.216	5.019	4.833	4.659	4.494	4.339	4.192
11	6.207	5.938	5.687	5.453	5.234	5.029	4.836	4.656	4.486	4.327
12	6.492	6.194	5.918	5.660	5.421	5.197	4.988	4.793	4.611	4.439
13	6.750	6.424	6.122	5.842	5.583	5.342	5.118	4.910	4.715	4.533
14	6.982	6.628	6.302	6.002	5.724	5.468	5.229	5.008	4.802	4.611
15	7.191	6.811	6.462	6.142	5.847	5.575	5.324	5.092	4.876	4.675

Index

BPP
LEARNING MEDIA

Review form

Name: _____   Address: _____

_____

_____

How have you used this Interactive Text?
(Tick one box only)

☐ Distance learning (book only)

☐ On a course: college _____

☐ As a tutor

☐ With 'correspondence' package

☐ Other _____

Why did you decide to purchase this Interactive Text? *(Tick one box only)*

☐ Have used BPP Texts in the past

☐ Recommendation by friend/colleague

☐ Recommendation by a lecturer at college

☐ Saw advertising

☐ Other _____

Which BPP products have you used?

☑ Text   ☐ Kit   ☐ i-Pass   ☐ Passcards

During the past six months do you recall seeing/receiving any of the following?
(Tick as many boxes as are relevant)

☐ Our advertisement in *ACCA Student Accountant*

☐ Our advertisement in *Teach Accounting*

☐ Other advertisement _____

☐ Our brochure with a letter through the post

☐ ACCA E-Gain email

☐ BPP email

☐ Our website www.bpp.com

Which (if any) aspects of our advertising do you find useful?
(Tick as many boxes as are relevant)

☐ Prices and publication dates of new editions

☐ Information on Interactive Text content

☐ Facility to order books off-the-page

☐ None of the above

Your ratings, comments and suggestions would be appreciated on the following areas

	Very useful	Useful	Not useful
Introductory section (How to use this Interactive Text)	☐	☐	☐
Key terms	☐	☐	☐
Examples	☐	☐	☐
Questions and answers	☐	☐	☐
Fast forwards	☐	☐	☐
Quick quizzes	☐	☐	☐
Exam alerts	☐	☐	☐
Exam Question Bank	☐	☐	☐
Exam Answer Bank	☐	☐	☐
Index	☐	☐	☐
Structure and presentation	☐	☐	☐
Icons	☐	☐	☐

	Excellent	Good	Adequate	Poor
Overall opinion of this Interactive Text	☐	☐	☐	☐

Do you intend to continue using BPP products?   ☐ Yes   ☐ No

Please note any further comments and suggestions/errors on the reverse of this page. The BPP author of this edition can be emailed at heatherfreer@bpp.com

Please return this form to: Ian Blackmore, FIA Range Manager, BPP Learning Media, FREEPOST, London, W12 8BR

Review form (continued)

Please note any further comments and suggestions/errors below